RESEARCH METHODS IN THE
SOCIAL SCIE

RESEARCH METHODS
IN THE
SOCIAL SCIENCES

Editors

BRIDGET SOMEKH AND CATHY LEWIN

⑤ SAGE Publications
London ● Thousand Oaks ● New Delhi

SAGE Publications Ltd
1 Oliver's Yard
55 City Road
London EC1Y 1SP

SAGE Publications Inc.
2455 Teller Road
Thousand Oaks, California 91320

SAGE Publications India Pvt Ltd
B-42, Panchsheel Enclave
Post Box 4109
New Delhi 110 017

British Library Cataloguing in Publication data

A catalogue record for this book is available from the British Library

ISBN 0-7619-4401-X
ISBN 0-7619-4402-8 (pbk)

Library of Congress Control Number: 2004106249

Production by Deer Park Productions, Tavistock, Devon
Typeset by TW Typesetting, Plymouth, Devon
Printed in Great Britain by TJ International Ltd, Trecerus Industrial Estate, Padstow, Cornwall

CONTENTS

CONTENTS

ACKNOWLEDGEMENTS

We would like to thank all the contributors who have made the production of this book so fascinating and enjoyable. Their scholarship and dedicated commitment to 'getting it right' are the keys to the book's quality, and we greatly appreciate their good nature over many months in the face of our editorial demands and draconian word limits. We would also like to thank Erica Burman and Julienne Meyer for their help in consolidating the interdisciplinarity of the book.

When I began teaching in higher education some thirty years ago I was assigned to a course entitled Social Research Methods. Such courses constituted a core component of a first degree in Sociology. Methods courses, as they were known, were, together with courses on social theory, part of the core curriculum of a sociology degree. The reason I had been assigned to teach on this course related to my recent experience as a graduate student where I had been conducting fieldwork for over a year. It was argued I would be able to use my first hand experience of designing projects and collecting data alongside discussing some of the problems I had encountered in doing research when teaching undergraduate students. It is interesting to note that the course focussed predominantly on the collection of data and this reflected the books that were available at that time. Many of the volumes were not easily accessible to an undergraduate audience and in any case concentrated predominantly upon research techniques; essentially quantitative and survey based approaches to social investigation. In short, courses in research methods seemed, at least to me, to bear little resemblance to the research experience.

It was therefore my job to make the world of social research more accessible to a student body by drawing on illustrative material and by making sure that we did not just discuss methods in isolation from other aspects of social investigation. In particular, it was important to examine how projects were designed and how the driving force behind any investigation is not the methods or techniques that the researcher chooses to use but rather the questions that he or she poses in the investigation. It was also important to think about theories that influence the way in which themes and questions were handled during an investigation. Furthermore, some space needed to be devoted not only to ways in which data were collected but also on approaches to data analysis. Accordingly, the course brought together illustrative material from the process of doing research, coupled with the textbook approach, which focused on some methods

of investigation. It is this issue that has often been hotly debated over the years in relation to the teaching of research methods. It is, after all, at the very heart of social science research, as this volume clearly illustrates. Yet there are many different interpretations about the ways in which students can be introduced to the conduct of social investigation. Among the questions that might be asked are:

- How does research begin?
- How are problems formulated?
- How is the research problem influenced by the theories that are used?
- What form does the research design take?
- What kinds of methods of social investigation can be used to assess the research problem?
- What are the techniques of social science research that can be used?
- What approaches can be taken to analysing data?
- In what ways do quantitative and qualitative research complement each other?
- What processes occur during the course of research that impact on the researcher and the research findings?
- In what ways can research be communicated, disseminated and published?

These are some of the core issues in social investigation that have to be handled in any course. It is therefore, important that any volumes that are produced are capable of assisting the teacher and the student in acquiring a first rate education on ways to do research.

In the late 1970s and early 1980s social science witnessed a range of 'new' approaches to research methodology that influenced the way courses were taught. No longer was there a heavy reliance on the reference book about methods of social investigation, nor for that matter, was the material that was available just based on American work. Instead, groups of researchers came together to reflect critically on their research experience and with this came a new genre of writing and working, where the focus of attention was on the process of research rather than mere techniques. Styles of writing were very different. First they were often first person accounts; secondly, they were accounts that provided detailed illustrative material that rarely dealt with techniques of social investigation; thirdly, they focused mainly on approaches to collecting data and in turn experiences in the field; fourthly, they tended to be accounts that were about qualitative rather than quantitative research. While these approaches helped to re-dress the balance of material available to teach social research it still did not get to grips with the resources required to provide a rounded experience for those who wanted to understand how social science research was designed, conducted, analysed, reported and widely disseminated. Nor for that matter, could the way in which theory influenced research be found in any one volume. In this respect, those who have engaged in research and writing about social research methodology have often taken particular perspectives on social investigation and as a consequence, we have continued to search for ways to introduce the beginning student to the experience of becoming a working social scientist who is engaged in empirical research.

At this point a reader might ask why these comments have been focussed entirely on undergraduate education? The answer is quite simple. It was very rare in the UK to find systematic courses devoted to social research outside highly specialized Masters degrees before the 1990s. This was a feature of UK higher education which was very different from the approaches in other countries. In American PhD programmes, for example, taught courses in research methods have long been a compulsory element, but this had not been my experience when teaching in UK universities. It was only when the Economic and Social Research Council (ESRC) established their Training Guidelines that systematic training courses were provided for all postgraduate students in the UK in receipt of support from the ESRC. This has influenced the way in which social science departments have thought about graduate education. As a consequence, it is now very rare to find graduate students in the social sciences, whether or not they are supported by the ESRC, being registered for graduate studies without receiving a systematic training in social research. This has not gone unnoticed among publishers and we have witnessed a wide range of outlets for material on social research methodology. Indeed, it is very en-couraging to find numerous book series, edited collections and individual specialist volumes devoted to social research. As a result the beginning researcher now has the opportunity to understand the complex sets of relationships involved in the conduct of social investigation. No longer is the student left alone to conduct studies using their 'favourite' methods; instead they are exposed to a sophisticated analysis, which draws together different elements of the research process. In this respect, this book is to be welcomed, as it draws together within one volume a wide range of resource material. Indeed the editors indicate that this volume is to be viewed as a collection of resources as there is no specific order in which the chapters should be read. It is for the reader to decide which range of material he or she requires to extend and develop their education as a social researcher and to use it in their work

The advantage of this volume is that it brings together material that relates to the process of social research, its design, its sponsorship, its funding, the role of the researcher and the ethical issues with which the researcher must engage. It also addresses the major theories that are adopted and examines different styles of social research from those of a fundamental kind through to more applied and policy focussed work. Research Methods in the Social Sciences is a comprehensive volume that addresses some of the key challenges for university teachers and researchers in the 21st century. The volume demonstrates that considerable advances have taken place in the last thirty years. No longer is it enough to write about research technique but instead it is important to engage with other aspects of the research process. The topics that are covered in the nine sections of this volume illustrate what it means to be a reflective researcher engaged in self-critical analysis whilst drawing on key advances in the social sciences. The team that has been assembled to produce the material constitute some of the leading researchers in the social sciences in Britain, Australia and North America. They have assembled a volume that covers qualitative and quantitative investigation, as well as methodological issues that focus on different theories, which have a direct impact on research practice. They also examine issues that relate to reading and interpreting research in the light of contemporary debates within the research community.

This volume offers an excellent resource for undergraduate and postgraduate study as well as for the young social researcher setting out on a research career. It is apparent from the various chapters that 'doing research' is no longer based on the face to face interview but may well be more likely to involve professional researchers engaged in telephone interviewing. Case studies and life histories are used alongside surveys. Written evidence is just part of the material that is used by the social scientist alongside visual evidence provided by photographs, films, and videos. Overall, this volume brings together a complex set of writing that illustrates major advances in social science research that will provide an excellent training for those who are charting out a new career in the social sciences at the beginning of the 21st Century. We can have great confidence that drawing on the material in this volume will provide an excellent beginning. We can also be confident that many of these researchers will make substantial contributions to the study of research methodology themselves. In this respect the picture is ever-evolving as we engage in further writing on and about social research. Whatever form our writing takes, I think it is well to heed the advice of C. Wright Mills who suggested that research methodology needed to be based on the work of those involved in doing social research. This volume certainly lives up to that requirement as all those that have engaged in the writing are working social scientists who have played a major role in advancing our knowledge of research methods and social science research – long may it continue to develop and flourish as a field of investigation.

Robert G Burgess
Vice Chancellor
University of Leicester
June 2004

INTRODUCTION

This book is intended as a resource and – we hope – indispensable companion to welcome you into the community of social science researchers. It is written by active researchers, many of international reputation, who share the common characteristic of being fascinated by the process of research. They do research, day to day, as a central or integral part of their work and many also teach research methods to graduate students working for higher degrees.

The writers are drawn from across the social science disciplines and come from many countries: the USA, Great Britain, Australia, Austria, Canada, Denmark, Germany, Mexico, the Netherlands, New Zealand and Sweden. The origin of the book lies in the International Centres for Research in Education (ICARE), an alliance of Manchester Metropolitan University and the University of East Anglia in the UK, Deakin University in Australia and the University of Illinois at Urbana-Champaign in the USA. The range of work carried out by researchers at these four universities provided the knowledge and expertise for a large number of chapters, and their extensive international academic networks have made it easy to draw in other experts. As a result, the book offers the opportunity of learning about a wide range of social science research methodology and methods from authors who are among the best in the world in their field.

The coverage of the book is very wide, spanning all the key theories and ideas which underpin research methodology in the social sciences and a very large number of methods of data collection and analysis. Part I provides an introduction to the key characteristics of social science research, including both a general overview and six discipline-specific glosses upon it. In Parts II to V and Part VIII, each chapter provides a scholarly introduction to key concepts and issues, 'stories from the field' illustrating the process of carrying out research, and an annotated bibliography of around twelve texts. This pattern is somewhat modified in Parts VI and VII on quantitative and statistical methods, where Chapters 25, 26 and 27 present the key concepts and theoretical explanations and Chapters 28–32 consist of five 'stories from the field' as illustrative examples. Readers are invited to read the chapters – in any order they wish – to gain an overview of all the possible approaches to research as a preliminary to designing their own research study. Thereafter, the idea is to select specific theories and methods and use the annotated bibliographies in the relevant chapters as the starting point for more extended, in-depth reading.

The Key Concepts section of each chapter provides an overview of the main themes that have shaped thinking in that area of methodology or method over the last twenty or thirty years as well as the issues and ideas which are currently at the forefront of academic debate. The Stories from the Field sections that follow provide a narrative account of carrying out a research study using this specific methodology or method. They are accounts 'from the inside' revealing the complexity and fascination of carrying out research and dispelling any notion that there is one right way to be followed. In most cases they reveal how and why decisions about the research design were taken, describe the experience of carrying out the work, including some of the problematic issues that arose and how they were addressed, and reflect on the way in which knowledge and understanding developed. Alternatively, in a few cases they provide a vivid description of the research issues and outcomes in a form of reporting appropriate to the methodology concerned. The annotated bibliographies are limited to not more than twelve articles, books or websites, each with a personal note from the author explaining why it has been selected, so that the choice of what to read first should be much easier than is usual when faced with reading lists.

An important feature of this book is that it resists any simple notion that research can be carried out to recipes. While acknowledging that researchers tend to work within recognizable paradigms (perhaps most easily understood as 'clubs' of researchers who share common assumptions about what counts as quality in research), the book rejects the idea that these paradigms can be easily categorized into 'types' that remain static and impose a particular approach to research design. It is premised on the notion that differing understandings of the nature of knowledge and truth (epistemology), values (axiology) and being (ontology) are the key determinants of methodology, providing the overarching framework within which appropriate theoretical frameworks and research methods are selected as the first step in research design. For this reason, the implications for research design of the particular methodology or method are discussed in a subsection of the key concepts section of each chapter and no typology of research design is given in Part I.

The international and interdisciplinary character of the book is embedded in the collaborative approach taken to writing each chapter. Every chapter is co-authored in some form: in Part I on *Research Communities in the Social Sciences* by six specialists from different disciplines; in Parts II–V and VIII by partnerships, or occasionally threesomes, which often span two different countries and/or two different disciplines. The authors of Chapters 25, 26 and 27 in Part VI collaborated closely with the authors of the Stories from the Field in Part VII, and although Chapters 28–32 are presented as separate chapters this is for ease of citation only. The first drafts of the Key Concepts and Stories from the Field sections were written by different authors who then exchanged their drafts and reviewed each others' work. Each chapter was then revised to take on board these comments and draw the two halves together through fairly extensive editing and, where appropriate, the inclusion of cross-references. The cultural differences between different social science disciplines and the differing assumptions that underpin research in different countries made this process challenging for many of the partnerships. In many cases the collaboration has led to intense debate and considerable learning.

- Part I: *Research Communities in the Social Sciences* provides an overview of the key factors that distinguish social science research from research in the natural sciences, the arts and the humanities.
- Part II: *Listening, Exploring the Case and Theorizing* contains six chapters on research which focus on making meaning from the study of people and their contexts.
- Part III: *Researching for Impact* contains six chapters

which look at research that sets out to make a difference and influence both policy and practice.

- Part IV: *Observing, Querying, Interpreting* has two chapters which raise issues about the nature of knowledge and three which focus on the process of interpretation and illuminative enquiry, grounded in empirical data.
- Part V: *Reading and Representing Socio-Cultural Meanings* contains five chapters whose starting point is the culturally embedded nature of human experience. The first of these discusses narrative as a means of developing socio-cultural understanding of individuals, the next two explore ways in which visual images can be generated as data and analysed, and the final two chapters present socio-psychological theories which can be used as the basis for developing understanding of human activity.
- Part VI: *Sampling, Classifying and Quantifying* opens with two chapters that trace the links between positivism and contemporary social science methods. This is followed by three chapters that provide an introduction to quantitative methods and statistics.
- Part VII: *Quantitative Methods in Action* contains six chapters, the first five providing Stories from the Field that illustrate quantitative and statistical methods in action, the sixth focusing on ways of combining quantitative and qualitative methods.
- Part VIII: *Researching in Postmodern Contexts* contains six chapters which consider how social science research has developed new methods in response to the wave of contemporary challenges about the nature of knowledge, truth and being. These reflect the complex and unpredictable nature of human experience in today's world as a result of processes such as globalization and raise particularly interesting issues for social science researchers.
- Part IX: *Participating in the Research Community* covers a wide range of issues that are important for the working practices and careers of social science researchers. It is divided into four sections on 'ensuring the impact of research', 'designing and carrying out a research project', 'carrying out sponsored research' and 'building a research career'.

This book is dedicated to Robert, John, Jack and Poppy

PART I

RESEARCH COMMUNITIES IN THE SOCIAL SCIENCES

Bridget Somekh
Education and Social Research Institute, Manchester Metropolitan University, UK
Erica Burman
Research Institute of Health and Social Change, Manchester Metropolitan University, UK
Sara Delamont
Department of Sociology, Cardiff University, UK
Julienne Meyer
St Bartholomew's School of Nursing and Midwifery, City University, UK
Malcolm Payne
St Christopher's Hospice, London, UK
Richard Thorpe
Leeds University Business School, UK

The authors would like to thank Fazal Rizvi, Professor in Educational Policy Studies at the University of Illinois, USA, and an Adjunct Professor at Deakin University, Australia, for providing additional material to strengthen the international perspectives in this chapter.

Key features of research in the social sciences

Bridget Somekh

Research in the social sciences draws on various long-established traditions. Its origins might, for example, be said to lie with the Greek philosophers, Plato and Aristotle, who developed ways of conceptualizing and categorizing knowledge, truth and human experience during the fourth century BC. Fundamentally, social science research is concerned with people and their life contexts, and with philosophical questions relating to the nature of knowledge and truth (epistemology), values (axiology) and being (ontology) which underpin human judgements and activities.

Empirical social science research – that is research which involves the collection of data about people and their social contexts by a range of methods – draws heavily upon the traditions and practices of disciplines such as anthropology, sociology, psychology, history and creative arts. Anthropology contributes a tradition of participant observation and interviews, field note-taking and heuristic interpretation of culture. For example, from Geertz we learn the importance of reading the cultural meanings in details of behaviour such as winks, and writing about research using 'thick description' to give readers the experience of 'being there' (Geertz, 1973). From sociology, we learn how social relations are formed and reproduced. Psychology provides us with an understanding of human behaviour. History contributes a tradition of document analysis (the weighing of evidence in the light of the likely biases of the informant) and accords importance to contemporary records, including personal testimony in letters and note books. The creative arts contribute a tradition of aesthetics (discernment and judgement of worth) and accord importance to creativity and imagination in interpretation. The notion of the social scientist creating knowledge by bringing vision to the interpretation of facts was central to the work of Mills (1959) and more recently researchers such as Eisner (1991) have emphasized the importance of the social scientist as connoisseur.

As a recognized and codified practice, however, social science research has its origins in the emergence of the nation-state with its political demands for the classification and analysis of individuals and populations. Anthropology, for example, emerged in the service of colonialism. The very term social science indicates its emergence in relation to, sometimes in opposition to, natural science. Early twentieth-century social scientists struggled to extricate themselves from the accusations made by logical positivism that research which lacked the solid foundation of measurement was no better than fancy and invention. They sought to develop methods which conformed to the methodology of the natural sciences, and researchers such as George Homans ('general theory') and Kurt Lewin ('force field theory') focused on seeking generalizable laws governing the behaviour of human groups. Today the historical shaping of social science research in a struggle to be 'other' than, but equivalent to, natural science research lingers in the imagination of the public, politicians and policy-makers. There remains a political dimension to being a social science researcher, pursuing knowledge and understanding of individuals, social groups and organizations, in a world where status is not accorded equally to different research methodologies. There has also been a considerable amount of debate about the uses of social scientific knowledge, and how it could be and should be applied to both control and modify people's behaviour. The questions about ethical limits to the application of social scientific knowledge have been widely debated.

This political dimension has led researchers to develop elaborate methodological fortresses in which particular understandings of knowledge, truth, values and being give firm foundations for research design and provide defensive bulwarks against external criticism (including criticism from other academics). Often called 'paradigms', following Thomas Kuhn's (1970) influential work, these ways of seeing the world provide security in what Foucault (1972: 131) called a 'regime of truth' or set of values and beliefs expressed in a discourse that maps out what can – and cannot – be said. Specific aspects of the paradigm are, of course, continuously under debate, rather in the manner of small building work to improve the

defensibility of a fortress. While paradigms provide important frameworks of ideas for thinking about research methodology, their development has had the unfortunate effect of polarizing social science researchers. There is a tendency for oppositional groups to belittle the work of the others, often by means of attaching grossly simplified (and therefore meaningless) epithets to their work such as 'positivist' (for quantitative and statistical methods) and 'subjective' (for interpretive methods).

In recent years, there have also been attempts to think about social sciences not only in their local and national frames, but also in global ones. It has been argued, for example, that disciplines of the social science emerged to serve nation-building projects, and that globalization has raised new questions about the nature of identity, culture and social relations as well as power configurations. Following both large-scale movement of people across the globe and the recognition of global interrelations, the issues of difference have come to occupy a central place within the social sciences, not only in anthropology and sociology but also in other disciplinary and policy fields. The issues of postcoloniality in a globalizing world raise a whole range of questions that can no longer be ignored. Thus, for example, theorists have begun to speak of a global rather than a national sociology (Cohen and Kennedy, 2000). This has affected the nature and scope of research methodologies and methods. It may have even pushed social scientists towards more interdisciplinary work, something that was long resisted by them.

In this book, the full spectrum of research methods of social science are presented rather than drawing on any particular paradigm. While it is recognized that some methodological frameworks are incompatible with others, the overarching premise of the book is to indicate how a wide range of researchers choose a methodology and methods which are appropriate to both the area of enquiry and their own way of seeing the world. Readers are invited to explore the ideas in these chapters, seeking to learn with an open mind, and revisit and challenge previously held assumptions. Ideal researchers are perhaps, in the words of one of the founders of scientific method:

Mindes, that have not suffered themselves to fixe, but have kept themselves open and prepared to receive continual Amendment, which is exceeding Rare. (Francis Bacon, 1597, 'On Custome and Education').

Social science research differs from research in the natural sciences as a result of its focus on people – individuals and groups – and their behaviour within cultures and organizations that vary widely socially and historically. There is an unpredictability in the behaviour of human beings. Medical research is able to use probability theories to develop therapeutic drugs because bodily systems function relatively autonomously from the mind (though even this idea is undergoing change). Social science research cannot develop similarly powerful solutions to social problems since the mind enables individuals and groups to take decisions that vary with widely different motives. Human experience is characterized by complexity, and social science researchers need to resist the temptation to impose unwarranted order through the application of 'one size fits all' theories.

Specialist branches of the social sciences, such as psychology and sociology, provide a bedrock of concepts and theories for the study of people, available to those working in more applied fields such as education, health sciences, social work and business administration. For example, in anthropology Benedict (1935: 161–201) explores the way in which individuals are shaped by their society, while at the same time reconstructing and shaping society itself. In cultural psychology, Wertsch (1998) builds on the work of Vygotsky to explore the ways human activity is 'mediated' by cultural tools and artefacts so that human agency is constantly enabled or constrained by cultural and current contexts. In the history and philosophy of science, Haraway (1992: 10–13) analyses how primatology has been studied and interpreted by 'the interacting dualisms, sex/gender and nature/culture' and how the underlying assumption in both biology and anthropology that 'sex and the west are axiomatic' led to a construction of western primatology as 'simian orientalism', in which primates are cast by scientists as eastern-exotic/'primitive' alter egos.

In the last quarter of the twentieth century social science research methods diversified considerably, thanks largely to the influence of feminist theories that challenged many assumptions – such as the personal/political dichotomy – on the grounds that they derived from masculine hegemonies. Feminist research 'puts social construction of gender at the center of one's inquiry' (Lather, 1991: 71), reconstructing the process of research at all levels from the chosen focus of study to relationships with participants, methods of data collection, choice of analytical

concepts and approaches to reporting. An important feature of this work has been the rediscovery of women social scientists from earlier generations and reinstatement of their work (Delamont, 2003: 78–95).

Quality in social science research rests upon the persuasive power of its outcomes and therefore, fundamentally, upon how it uses language to construct and represent meaning. Recently, postmodernism and deconstruction have challenged the whole idea that social science research should generate coherent meaning, accusing researchers of imposing an unwarranted order on data in order to present an – often formulaic – 'grand narrative'. Haraway (1991: 187) makes explicit the dilemmas that face social science researchers as a result of the new epistemologies arising from feminism and deconstruction, arguing that we need '*simultaneously* [. . .] a critical practice for recognizing our own "semiotic technologies" for making meanings, *and* a no-nonsense commitment to faithful accounts of a "real" world.'

As a result of its focus on people, ethical issues are centrally important in social science research. Knowledge confers power, so in collecting data researchers need to be guided by principles of respect for persons and obtaining informed consent. The publication of outcomes confronts social science researchers with the need to consider the possible impact of their reports on the people who have been part of it. Standard procedures such as 'anonymizing' participants and organizations raise further ethical questions since people's ideas can be seen as their intellectual property and in some cases it would certainly be unethical to quote them without also accrediting the source.

Springing from moral and ethical principles, social science researchers vary considerably in terms of the kinds of relationship they establish with participants, as indicated by the terms they use to describe them. Some adopt the stance of an outsider carrying out research on 'subjects'; some adopt the stance of a participant carrying out research in close contact with 'informants'; some adopt the stance of a partner, carrying out research with 'co-researchers'; some adopt the stance of facilitators, inviting 'practitioner-researchers' to carry out their own research rather than having research done for them by an 'outsider'. These decisions all imply different ways of distributing power within the relationship, but whatever stance is adopted power differentials are never entirely within the researcher's control and can never be excised. This in turn has an impact on the quality and reliability of the data that can be collected. Social science researchers typically emphasize the need to establish a relationship of trust with the participants as the necessary condition for carrying out high-quality research. However, since relationships are organic rather than static, trust is a slippery concept. Human beings (can) never reveal all that is in their minds and with this realization has come an increasing emphasis on the negotiation of the research contract, whether implicit or explicit.

Most people reading this book will be simultaneously embarking on their own research project, whether for a higher degree or as part of a research team in the workplace. So it is important to emphasize that all research involves a set of activities that take place over time and have to be planned in advance. Researchers require a whole host of life skills such as: personal time management; enlisting others to work with you; organizational skills to assemble data and arrange it for easy retrieval; fascination with detail during the phase of immersion in data; curiosity and creativity to notice the meaning and patterns that emerge from it; synthesizing ideas and constructing and testing out theories; reflexive self-awareness to explore your own impact on the material you are analysing; critical reasoning to evaluate your interpretations in relation to those of others; and presenting reports both in writing and orally which have sufficient persuasive power to command attention.

Social science research is an art as well as a science, and the skills and knowledge needed to be a researcher can only be acquired through experience over time. There are always judgements to be made and decisions to be taken about how best to go about research. Fundamental to the achievement of high quality is the preparedness and ability of social science researchers to critique their work and reflect on how it could have been done differently, and whether that might have changed the outcomes and, if so, how. Reflexivity, not recipes, is the hallmark of the good social science researcher.

Principles of research in six social science disciplines

The rest of Part I, divided into six subsections, introduces the culture, values and politics that frame and influence research practice and underpinning methodologies within each of six disciplines of the social sciences. They are intended to illustrate the processes of history and tradition by which research in each discipline is shaped. There are, of course, a large number of social science disciplines and it has not been possible to include all here. We have included first the two major underpinning disciplines, Psychology and Sociology, from which we believe that all other social sciences draw models and theories. These are followed by four disciplines, Education, Health, Social Policy, and Management and Business, which have been particularly strongly influenced by political fashions and ideologies in many countries during the last half century, and which are illustrative of the constraining and shaping processes of the sociology of knowledge. They have been chosen because of their fundamental importance in influencing social organization in a civil society. In choosing these six disciplines we have been influenced by the need to provide support and guidance for researchers working in fields in which the interrelationship between theory and practice is critically important, and where there is often a need for researchers to become involved in researching the process of innovation and development. Many other social science disciplines, for example Anthropology and Economics, could make a stronger claim than some of these for their significance and impact in the social sciences as a whole, and we have ensured that many chapters of the book draw upon them for inspiration.

Psychology
Erica Burman

The origins of the modern psychology of western societies lie in the political demands of the nation-state ranging from how the introduction of compulsory primary-level schooling led to the 'need' to distinguish educational levels, to assessing the mental and physical 'abilities' of soldiers recruited for imperial wars. Hence notwithstanding its concern with the seemingly private or personal worlds of individual minds, family relationships and (usually small) group activity, psychology is far from being separate from broader social interests. The current popularity of psychology merely continues a long-standing strategy to shape appropriate forms of citizenship through interventions at the level of the individual.

Contemporary psychology has many subdisciplinary divisions: for example, developmental, social, cognitive, educational, clinical – and more recently forensic, health and community psychology. Some are now accorded distinct professional status while others are considered more 'academic' specialisms. Most have been subject to shifting sets of methodological and theoretical paradigms: behaviourist, cognitive, humanist, deconstructionist. They all elaborate their own model of their subject as well as corresponding procedures for the investigation of its qualities.

Yet the early psychologists were both theoretical and applied in their concerns, and took an integrated approach to their investigations. Their methods combined observation, experimentation and interpretation. Notwithstanding the current focus of mainstream psychology on experimental techniques and statistical analyses, early key psychological studies were based on case studies with small sample sizes that were frequently accompanied by wide-ranging political, philosophical and social commentary and speculation.

Hence while psychology may have emerged to fulfil a political need for a science of the individual, its apparently specialist knowledge belies the ways it is imbued by its own cultural conditions. Its influence extends far beyond psychological 'laboratories' or elite academic settings. Psychological theories profoundly inflect a whole range of practices dealing with the assessment and evaluation of our lives: in schools, in work, in hospitals, in prisons – and even (or especially?) in our kitchens and bedrooms. Foucault (1981) aptly described psychoanalysis as a secular confessional and we increasingly look to psychological and psychotherapeutic ideas for advice. This 'psy complex' (Rose, 1985; Ingleby, 1985) invites us to construct a sense of interiority, or self-hood, through subscription to some – now secularized – authority. In this sense Foucault's analyses are particularly relevant as psychology plays a key role in forms of self-regulation or 'governmentality' by which liberal democracies define and limit 'normality', alongside informing how we experience ourselves as freely choosing the norms we live with and by (Rose, 1985, 1990).

The history of psychology is not a pretty one. Cyril Burt was the first person in Britain to be officially employed as a 'psychologist' – by London County Council in 1913. Other early psychologists were explicit advocates of eugenics (Richards, 1997), and their legacies remain in the statistical tests they invented. Burt's impact remains on the tripartite structure of the schooling system, as well as founding and editing the *British Journal of Statistical Psychology*. This is alongside having fabricated results (and research personnel!) to support his claims of the

heritability of intelligence (Kamin, 1977). Despite repudiating his 'data', the discipline of psychology has continued to benefit from his achievement in inscribing its place within social policy. In this, claims to 'science' were part of a legitimation strategy to build a credible arena of theory and practice.

Thus far from being 'scientific', in the usually accepted sense of being value-free or neutral, psychological research has from its inception been imbued with distinct policy (and personal) agendas. Psychology is the reflexive discipline par excellence – since it is about people studying people. Addressing this has made psychology rather a self-preoccupied discipline, endlessly exploring the methodological artefacts of its own (sometimes rather bizarre) interventions. Much psychological literature discusses conceptual devices that have been elaborated to try to describe and then screen out researcher effects: documenting how research participants (or 'subjects') are sensitive to particular contextual conditions (such as primacy, recency or halo 'effects' and other demand and volunteer 'characteristics'). These analyses remain relevant within quantitative psychology, particularly experimental or survey design.

From the late 1970s the turn to qualitative and interpretive approaches ushered in more participative and humanist psychological research, positioning those who are studied as active constructors and expert interpreters of their own psychologies. Feminist critiques imported an attention to the ways social structural differences – such as gender – enter into research relationships and to more subtle ways that gendered representations and assumptions structure theoretical and methodological paradigms. Rather than being something to be screened out in the pursuit of accurate measurement, subjectivity – whether of the researcher or the researched – emerges as vital to include and address in generating rigorous and relevant analyses.

Hence psychology poses starkly a key conundrum posed by power/knowledge relations within the social sciences. Is method theory? If it is not – or not only – this, what theory has psychology generated that is not merely recycled common sense dressed up in jargon or poached from other disciplines? Rose (1985) persuasively argued that the emerging discipline of psychology gained its distinctive role through the generation of methods that masquerade as theory. That is, psychological expertise resides only in controlling and applying (i.e. the administration of) technologies of assessment: testing, measurement and classification. Linked to this interest in power/knowledge relations, Pyschology has, in recent years, also witnessed a 'pyschoanalytical turn', including an emphasis on clinical methods, designed to unearth fundamental assumptions in identity formations, underlining the importance of reflexivity.

Thus psychology's complicity within strategies of social regulation makes it a prime arena for the study of both oppression and resistance. Contemporary critical, constructionist and feminist researchers focus on psychological practices as a way of studying ideology in action. Here discursive and other critical interpretive frameworks work both to engage with psychological methods and theories, and to maintain some critical distance from them.

Sociology

Sara Delamont

Sociology began in the nineteenth century, as thinkers in the industrializing countries puzzled over the social upheavals caused by the Industrial Revolution, the rapid growth of cities and the accompanying social changes. Three internal disputes characterized sociology then, and continue to divide it today: about epistemologies and theories; about empirical topics and methods; and about intellectual politics. Those unfamiliar with the discipline can find a more nuanced version of this summary in Delamont (2003).

One dispute is between those who prioritize thinking (theorizing) over empirical research. A second is between those who wish to harness sociology to political causes and those who wish it to be a non-political academic discipline. The third, within the empiricists, is between those who want research to emulate the natural sciences (loosely called positivists) and those who argue that because sociology investigates humans, who are reflexive beings, the methods must take account of that (interpretivists). Positivists use both quantitative and qualitative methods, while interpretivists use only qualitative ones. These perennial debates were central to the most famous sociology department of them all: Chicago in the Golden Age (1893–1933) and in the Second Silver Age (1945–65) (Fine, 1995).

The leading figures in the development of sociology have been German, French and American. Many world leaders in sociology, such as Ulrich Beck and Anthony Giddens, are primarily desk-bound. Theorizing has higher status than empirical work. In the Anglophone world, theorists from continental Europe

are often revered for their ideas (Foucault for example) but the agenda setters for empirical research (qualitative and quantitative) are mainly American. Advances in multidimensional scaling, in telephone interviewing, in autoethnography and in visual methods are led from the USA.

The second and third disputes are fundamental to empirical sociology, and are complicated by controversies over gender, race and sexuality. James Davis (1994: 188), for example, is a positivist who wants American sociology to eschew all political issues, and writes furiously that the discipline's 'weak immune system' has allowed it to be contaminated by 'humanistic sociology', 'critical theory', 'grounded theory', 'ethnomethodology', 'postmodernism', 'ethnic studies' and 'feminist methodology'. His objects of hatred are a mixture of interpretivist perspectives and explicitly politically engaged stances such as anti-racism and anti-sexism. Until 1968 sociology was predominantly quantitative and positivist and used functional theories. There were qualitative researchers, but they were relatively unfashionable. Then, when the USA and other capitalist countries went through political upheavals, sociology diversified. In the USA the anti-war movement, Black Power and the rise of Women's and Gay Liberation disrupted social sciences. In Europe the events of 1968, with working-class and student protest, had a similar effect. The overthrow of positivist, functionalist sociology was predicted by Alvin Gouldner (1971) in *The Coming Crisis of Western Sociology*. After 1968 four perspectives became fashionable: neo-Marxism (non-functionalist but often using positivist methods), conflict theories, ideas grounded in the sociology of knowledge, and interactionist approaches (symbolic interactionism, phenomenology and ethnomethodology) (Giddens, 1973).

The lasting challenges to the orthodoxy of 1968 came with the poststructuralism and postmodernism of Lyotard (1984) and Foucault (1979) and radical ideas from the black, gay and women's movements, namely critical race theory, queer theory and feminism. Sociology in the nineteenth century was male dominated, but since the 1890s there have been female scholars in the discipline, especially in empirical research. There have been, and are, women positivists and interpretivists, women opposed to politically engaged sociology and those who espouse it.

It is easy to be misled by the high-profile authors such as Denzin (2003) who are relentlessly innovative and passionate about the cultural turn and post-post-

postmodernism and thus think the whole discipline is suffused with radical ideas, and by much postcolonial sociology that seeks to study social relations in its broader global and historical context. In fact much of the research done in the USA remains very conventional and is not at methodological frontiers. Most sociologists in the world, and especially in America, are positivists in practice, who conduct traditional surveys by interview and questionnaire, analyse the data by SPSS, and present the results in journals and reports to sponsors written to a conventional hypothetical-deductive format and deploying essentially functionalist theories.

In research methods the biggest changes since 1968 are due to more sophisticated computing and the increased acceptability of qualitative methods. Analysis is more elaborate (Hardy and Bryman, 2004). Computing advances have revolutionized quantitative research: techniques that once took weeks now take seconds. The increased use of elaborate statistics makes much research hard to understand for a non-specialist. In qualitative research software to handle text (CAQDAS) has transformed analysis (Fielding, 2001). The rise of qualitative methods, evident from the number of journals and books devoted to them, has been spectacular. However, the core concerns of serious scholars have not changed over a century.

Researchers need to pick sensible research questions, design their investigations carefully, collect data honestly, analyse them imaginatively, write them up accessibly and generalize from them cautiously, all the time engaging in ruthless self-scrutiny to avoid bias, selective blindness and negligence, and to be their own toughest critics. Few sociologists live up to that ideal: but we should all strive to.

Educational research

Bridget Somekh

Educational research draws extensively on the disciplines of sociology, psychology and philosophy. In this sense, education is not a discrete discipline, although it has been one of the focal sites for the development of social science theory. Key figures include Dewey (1944), who conceived of education as a child-centred process that underpinned democracy, and Greene (1988) who saw education as a means of personal growth.

Educational research is concerned not only with the activities of teachers and students in schools, but all life-long learning from cradle to grave. Governments fund education for the benefit of individuals and society as a whole. There are differences of opinion about the purposes of education, based on ideological factors. Some see education as primarily for the benefit of the individual and others see it as the means of producing the human resources necessary to maintain the economy. Research has to work within and around these different conceptions of education. Inevitably, therefore, educational research has a political dimension.

Key organizing concepts for education are those of curriculum and pedagogy. These terms are not always used with the same meanings. For example, curriculum can be taken to mean the specified learning set out in policy documents or the actual learning which results from students' experiences in the classroom (the 'traditional curriculum of teachers': Stenhouse, 1975; 'folk pedagogies': Bruner, 1996). Learning theories are also contested. For example, Piaget suggests that learning is dependent upon the child's development through fairly well-recognized stages, whereas Vygotsky suggests that the key factor in the development of mind is the process of interaction between the child and adults or peers (Bruner, 1997). Recently, Lave and others have emphasized the importance of 'situating' learning in directly supportive contexts (e.g. Lave and Wenger, 1991).

Many educational researchers focus their attention on the processes whereby the power relations in society privilege some students at the expense of others. Bourdieu's (1977) theory of 'cultural capital' provides a framework for understanding how factors such as social class and parental education reproduce both social privilege and exclusion. Bowles and Gintis (1976) exemplified the operation of these theories in practice. Gilligan (1982) showed how social systems, including schooling and theory development, systematically discriminated against girls.

Educational research is increasingly politicized as a result of governments believing that there is a direct link between educational achievement and a strong economy. This has led to considerable interest in comparative league tables between countries based on standardized tests administered to students. The initial superiority of countries such as Singapore and Taiwan in key areas of numeracy and literacy led in the UK to government mandates for teachers to adopt pedagogic practices such as 'whole-class teaching'. This has been coupled with increasing pressure from governments to fund only research perceived to be 'relevant' (directly relating to the implementation and subsequent improvement of policies). Based on a model from medical research, educational researchers have been exhorted (and pressured through funding mechanisms) to adopt an 'evidence-based' approach. The need for bureaucrats to justify spending on education has led to increasing demands for 'hard data' generated by pseudo-positivist methods that purport to establish cause and effect between educational practice and improved test scores.

'School effectiveness' research uses quantitative methods to identify and track those features of schooling that correlate with high student outcomes. 'School improvement' research, which is frequently closely linked with development work, is generally more subtle than 'effectiveness' research, using a wider range of data and placing more emphasis on trends and changes over time. For example, there is a strong tradition of school ethnographies that have shown how theories of curriculum can be diverted in practice, for example through the influence of the 'hidden curriculum' embodied unintentionally in the (sub)cultures of schooling. Lightfoot's study (1983) exemplifies how this approach can illuminate educational practice.

A key problem in educational research relates to how policies for action might emerge from empirical investigations, and even more crucially how these might transform practice. Action research by teachers is recognized as a powerful strategy for bringing about improvements in teaching and learning and professional development (Elliott, 1991). This has been acknowledged and extended by policy-makers to include the larger notion of 'user involvement' of stakeholders in the implementation of research and – where possible – with its design. Recently in the UK the government has directly funded teachers to carry out research, generally within tightly prescribed limits regarding the subject of study (related to policy implementation), the methods of data collection and the form of reporting. 'Systematic reviews' of research literature have been funded by government to identify evidence of good practice and teachers have been encouraged to read this and other research and implement its findings.

Education research is often seen as *educational* in its processes as well as its effects. For example, researchers who acknowledge the educative nature of carrying out research are likely to adopt more participatory methods and may place less emphasis on seeking objective data and more on feeding back preliminary findings to enable practitioners to learn from research knowledge as it is generated. Constructing research as 'educative' has ethical implications and has effects in terms of the quality of outcomes, for example through its ability to fine-tune findings to the field of study and increase their impact on practice, perhaps with less emphasis on producing generalizable findings.

Health research
Julienne Meyer

Health research is concerned with the health of individuals, the care they receive and the services that are delivered to them. The activity of health research is informed by a number of different disciplines, for example medicine, nursing, allied health, social work, health economics, health management, medical sociology, health psychology, health and social care policy. However, historically health research has been dominated by the single discipline of medicine, which has tended to draw on positivist notions of science. In the past, medicine has held considerable power in shaping the research agenda and its prestige continues to influence the practice and governance of research today. This can be seen in the disproportionate funding still spent on medical research, its dominant presence in funding bodies and research committees and the tendency, until more recently, for systems and paperwork (e.g. ethical approval) to primarily meet the needs of large-scale quantitative medical research (e.g. randomized control trials), as opposed to more in-depth, smaller-scale qualitative studies. Researchers should be mindful of this historical legacy when applying for funding for health research, seeking ethical approval for their studies, dealing with gatekeepers to access research participants and seeking to publish their findings in more traditional academic journals.

More recently, medicine's authority over health research has been challenged. This is partly because the idea of health itself is a highly contested one, especially so in cross-cultural contexts. There is now more emphasis on involving actual and potential users of health services in research in order to make research more responsive to and appropriate for the needs of the population. This culture of being inclusive is being driven directly by government strategy, which is also encouraging use of a wider range of methods, a richer mix of multidisciplinary perspectives and better quality control mechanisms for research and its implementation. These changes are part of a wider societal shift towards replacing or reforming established research institutions, disciplines, practices and policies. Gibbons et al. (1994), focusing on research and development in science and technology, argue the need for a new mode of research that emphasizes reflexivity, transdisciplinarity and heterogeneity. They suggest that research should not be set within a particular disciplinary framework (e.g. medicine), but should be undertaken in the context of its application (e.g. health and social care settings) and involve the close interaction of many actors throughout the process of knowledge production (e.g. different academic disciplines, multidisciplinary practitioners and users of health services).

However, these developments need to be set in the context of the simultaneous emergence of evidence-based healthcare internationally. Evidence-based practice is concerned with the implementation of the best available external clinical evidence from systematic research. International networks now exist to support the development of evidence-based medicine in the form of the Cochrane Collaboration, which has centres in the UK and continental Europe, North and South America, Africa, Asia and Australasia. To ensure better coordination from the centre, structures have been put in place to systematically review the quality of research findings and to disseminate good practice across a variety of health and social care disciplines. Researchers are expected to produce the evidence for best practice and practitioners are required to implement it. This linear approach to research and development has been challenged (Trinder and Reynolds, 2000).

Historically the evidence-based movement was seen to be associated with positivist notions of science and criticized for placing undue emphasis on randomized controlled trials as a gold standard against which to compare other evidence in systematic reviews of the literature (Hicks and Hennessey, 1997). It was argued that this approach ignored the contributions of other forms of research and failed to address the fact that scientific research appears to have had little impact on practice (Walshe et al., 1995). More recently, the evidence-based practice movement has responded to this by trying to eliminate bias through further refinements of the review process to produce a somewhat false sense of certainty. However, research is inherently a political process and, while debates continue as to whether the evidence-based movement has been guilty of focusing

too heavily on scientific evidence to guide practice, qualitative research has slowly been incorporated into the mainstream. This can be seen as part of a general trend in many applied social science disciplines leading increasingly to a focus on practitioner-centred research (Meyer, 1993). In healthcare, these approaches are gaining ground especially within nursing (Rolfe, 1998) and it is argued that they fit well with the espoused values of new modes of research and practice development (Meyer, 2003).

Hence, an interesting paradox has emerged in the early twenty-first century. As political forces encourage health researchers to become more inclusive and use a wider range of methods, the same forces have imposed structures (e.g. research governance and evidence-based practice) to make health research less flexible and under more government control. For instance, practitioners wishing to research their own practice are constrained from doing so by bureaucratic systems of ethical approval. While these systems are designed to protect patients and NHS staff participating in research, they involve considerable time and effort and can be off-putting to those who wish to undertake small-scale work. The focus on tightening up governance systems thus runs counter to the encouraged use of more creative research (Normand et al., 2003).

Social policy research
Malcolm Payne

Social policy, in the British tradition, studies both the political and social debate within which policy is formed and local and interpersonal effects of policy implementation. In the USA, the focus of public policy studies is more directly on government policy-formation, and work concerned with welfare policy is treated in many countries as an aspect of the academic study of social work. Comparative work on the effect of international trends in different systems of provision has also had an impact on the limited assumptions of much nationally based research. The international trends themselves have been a product of the impact of global institutions such as the OECD, UNICEF and UNESCO, increasingly promoting neo-liberal thinking, often imposing policy choices on nation-states.

This wide range of research topics relies on many of the well-established techniques of social science research such as attitude and opinion surveys or observational and interview studies. However, social policy has a particular focus on analysis of official data and documents, and on placing official and informal policies on how social resources are distributed in a broad historical, philosophical and social context.

For example, Martin's (1984) analysis of scandals in long-stay hospitals in the 1960s used detailed documentary and historical analysis to explore how scandals emerged and official investigations led to political action. Reith's (1998) study of the official reports on 28 community care scandals in the 1990s points to how the policy effects of the scandals studied by Martin led to the discharge of many long-stay patients into the community in the 1980s, and thus to failings in community services in the 1990s. She analyses the failings exposed in mental health inquiries to show how social work practice during the 1990s changed, and draws lessons for future practice.

Social policy studies are often actively engaged in the political process, through the influence of 'think-tanks' and government initiatives. Social policy researchers carry out studies of how policy is implemented, the impact of policy changes and the evaluation of possible alternative patterns of service. For example, Townsend participated in a controversial government committee on health inequalities (Townsend and Davidson, 1988), which showed that poorer people were more likely to be unhealthy and to receive poorer services. In a later local social survey, Townsend et al. (1988) were able to show how people with ill-health were clustered in particular deprived communities.

Any major service development is likely to be the product of research or to be evaluated. For example, the care management element of the community care system implemented in the UK in the 1990s was strongly influenced by a service innovation in Kent importing American ideas evaluated by a university research unit (Davies and Challis, 1986). The project followed the establishment of teams, training of staff, introduction of service systems, economic and practical outcomes and effectiveness. After legislation introduced a new system, the government funded research to evaluate its success, which lay in achieving the government's economic objectives to restrict costs rather than professional objectives to improve services (Lewis and Glennerster, 1996). This included the collection of national statistics and case studies of different kinds of local authority. Both these studies interviewed participants in both informal and structured ways and analysed service data. Research studies by social work professionals, mainly using semi-

structured interviews, have highlighted the loss of expertise and routinization of social work practice that has resulted (Gorman and Postle, 2003). Public authorities and charities audit and evaluate their everyday services and innovations, requiring consumer surveys and more complex measures to achieve public participation.

Such research has usually focused on a specific area of service or social problem, such as housing, health or poverty. However, social policy has also been concerned with generalizing about the process by which policy is formed. Levin (1997) identifies the three main processes to be researched as the formulation of policy, its adaptation in political and social processes and its implementation. Research may focus on powerful stakeholders, participants (such as politicians or service users), interests (such as the conflict between provider and consumer interests) and processes, such as participants' actions and decisions, and the outcomes of these.

Some examples illustrate the range of methods. Hall's (1976) study of the Seebohm reorganization of the social services and Nesbitt's (1995) account of the social security reforms of the 1980s used interviews with influential policy-makers, as well as documentary sources. Policy process analysis (Hill, 1997) looks at how services are managed and organized to implement policies. Sometimes, this is done by observational studies of organizations, such as Lipsky's (1980) work on street-level bureaucracy, in which he shows that discretion exercised by workers at quite low levels of organizations can redirect policy initiatives. Much of this work has links with management and public administration studies. Pithouse's (1998) ethnographic study of how workers managed childcare work in a local social services office involved both observation and interviews with professionals to show how they interpreted and managed complex work implementing official policy.

Research in Management and Business Studies

Richard Thorpe

Social science as applied to management and industrial organization began from the 'scientific' approach adopted by managers such as F.W. Taylor, Gantt and Gilbreth (Lupton, 1966). Taylor (1947) maintained that the functions managers should perform were planning, organizing, coordinating and controlling. He stressed the systematic study of work, focusing on such aspects as poor tools, organization and management. The research methods of this early period were based on natural science principles and adopted experimental designs. After 1945 business schools sought greater academic respectability and disciplines such as finance, marketing, operations research and organizational behaviour strengthened greatly. During the 1960s a view developed that the key to effective management was the ability to take decisions, particularly under conditions of uncertainty (Cyert and March, 1963). As a consequence quantitative methods of analysis and model building still dominate the curricula of many business schools, especially in the USA and France.

However, in a parallel development, some researchers moved their attention to the psychological and sociological aspects of work. With this shift in focus came new and different methods, such as the study of groups and relationships at work using participant observers (Roethlisberger and Dickson, 1939). These studies demonstrated the importance of informal leaders and showed that satisfaction came from the quality of supervision and the social relationships formed as well as from monetary reward. Early contingency theorists, as they became known, undertook careful diagnosis of key variables on a case-by-case basis, focusing on a range of organizational issues, including the type of technology within a firm's organizational structure (Woodward, 1959) and the impact of market volatility on management systems (Burns and Stalker, 1961). Adopting a 'best fit' approach the methods used in these investigations were both quantitative and qualitative. There was a gradual recognition that positivistic methods, with an emphasis on objectivity, were not always the most appropriate. As globalization increased, the focus shifted further to the ways in which management is practised from international and cross-cultural perspectives (Hofstede, 1980). It continues to be the case that different countries value different methodological approaches to research: these too are culturally bound.

During the last two decades 'classical' theory (namely Taylor) and 'decisions' theory (namely Cyert and March) have come under attack. Both are 'normative' theories which have implications for the questions that are worth researching and the methods to be employed. However, in both there is some confusion between what management is and what it ought to be. This has led to critiques which suggest that approaches to management research should

adapt to meet the challenges of the future (Porter and McKibbin, 1988). There is also more or less universal recognition that managers need to be concerned with the application of theories in the workplace as opposed to simply the ideas themselves. The 1990s saw the emergence of a postmodern debate in management which queried beliefs in 'one world' with 'one truth', and began to develop a radical relativism that conceived of a world where no consensus exists and 'no rigorous evaluative criteria remain' (Holbrook and Hirschmann, 1982). Key assumptions concerning new forms of capitalism have also been a major strand in critical management studies.

Forms of research

The main classifications of research that have emerged from the management tradition described above are pure, applied and action research.

Pure research, which is sometimes referred to as domain driven, is intended to lead to theoretical development: there may, or may not, be any practical implications of this. Results are disseminated through academic media. Applied research is intended to lead to the solution of specific problems and usually involves working with clients who identify the problems. In these studies it is important to try to explain what is happening. Phillips and Pugh (1987) stress that genuine research must include consideration of 'why' questions as well as 'what' questions.

Action research studies start from the view that research should lead to change, and therefore that change should be incorporated into the research process itself. Classical action research starts from the idea that if you want to understand something well you should try changing it, and this is most frequently adopted in organization development (French and Bell, 1978). The collaborative features of action research mean that participants are likely to learn a lot from the process itself, and their interest may be on what happens next rather than on any formal account of research findings. Within the action research tradition, Gibbons et al. (1994) introduced an important debate on the nature of knowledge and approaches to knowledge generation in management. Mode 1 knowledge generation occurs within the context of existing institutions and academic disciplines. In contrast, mode 2 is transdisciplinary and created in context by those who combine their tacit/practitioner understandings with those of academics. The key aspect of mode 2 knowledge

11

production is that it occurs as a result of the interaction that takes place between theory and practice. Management also requires both thought and action. Not only do most managers feel that research should lead to practical consequences, they are also quite capable of taking action themselves in the light of research results.

References

Benedict, R. (1935) *Patterns of Culture*. London: Routledge & Kegan Paul.

Bourdieu, P. (1977) *Outline of a Theory of Practice*. Cambridge and New York: Cambridge University Press.

Bowles, S. and Gintis, H. (1976) *Schooling in Capitalist America*. New York: Basic Books.

Bruner, J. (1996) *The Culture of Education*. Cambridge, MA and London: Harvard University Press.

Bruner, J. (1997) 'Celebrating divergence: Piaget and Vygotsky', *Human Development*, 40: 63–73.

Burns, T. and Stalker, G. (1961) *The Management of Innovation*. London: Tavistock Press.

Cohen, R. and Kennedy, P. (2000) *Global Sociology*. New York: New York University Press.

Cyert, R.M. and March, J.G. (1963) *A Behavioural Theory of the Firm*. Englewood Cliffs, NJ: Prentice Hall.

Davies, B. and Challis, D. (1986) *Matching Resources to Needs in Community Care*. Aldershot: Gower.

Davis, J. (1994) 'What's wrong with sociology?', *Sociological Forum*, 9: 179–97.

Delamont, S. (2003) *Feminist Sociology*. London and Thousand Oaks, CA: Sage.

Denzin, N.K. (2003) *Performance Ethnography*. London: Sage.

Department of Health (2001a) *Governance Arrangements for NHS Research Ethics Committees*. London: Department of Health.

Dewey, J. (1944) *Democracy and Education*. New York: Free Press.

Eisner, E.W. (1991) *The Enlightened Eye*. New York: Macmillan.

Elliott, J. (1991) *Action Research for Educational Change*. Buckingham, UK and Bristol, PA: Open University Press.

Fielding, N. (2001) 'Computer applications in qualitative research', in P. Atkinson, A. Coffey, S. Delamont, J. Lofland and L. Lofland (eds), *Handbook of Ethnography*. London: Sage, pp. 453–67.

Fine, G.A. (ed.) (1995) *A Second Chicago School?* Chicago: University of Chicago Press.

Foucault, M. (1972) *Power/Knowledge: Selected Interviews and Other Writings 1972–77*. Bury St Edmunds, UK: Harvester Press.

Foucault, M. (1979) *Discipline and Punish*. New York: Vintage.

Foucault, M. (1981) *History of Sexuality 1: An Introduction*. London: Penguin.

French, W.L. and Bell, C.H. (1978) *Organizational Development*. Englewood Cliffs, NJ: Prentice-Hall.

Geertz, C. (1973) *The Interpretation of Cultures*. London: Fontana/New York: Basic Books.

Gibbons, M., Limoges, C., Nowotny, H., Schwartzman, S., Scott, P. and Trow, M. (1994) *The New Production of Knowledge: The Dynamics of Science and Research in Contemporary Societies*. London: Sage.

Giddens, A. (1973) *The Class Structure of the Advanced Societies*. London: Heinemann.

Gilligan, C. (1982) *In a Different Voice: Psychological Theory and Women's Development*. Cambridge, MA and London: Harvard University Press.

Gorman, H. and Postle, K. (2003) *Transforming Community Care: A Distorted Vision?* Birmingham: Venture.

Gouldner, A. (1971) *The Coming Crisis of Western Sociology*. London: Heinemann.

Greene, M. (1988) *The Dialectic of Freedom*. New York: Teachers College Press.

Hall, P. (1976) *Reforming the Welfare*. London: Heinemann.

Haraway, D. (1991) *Simians, Cyborgs, and Women*. London: Free Association.

Haraway, D. (1992) *Primate Visions*. London and New York: Verso.

Hardy, M. and Bryman, A. (eds) (2004) *Handbook of Analysis*. London: Sage.

Harre, R. and Secord, P. (1972) *The Explanation of Social Behaviour*. Oxford: Basil Blackwell.

Hicks, C. and Hennessy, D. (1997) 'Mixed messages in nursing research: their contribution to the persisting hiatus between evidence and practice', *Journal of Advanced Nursing*, 25: 595–601.

Hill, M. (1997) *The Policy Process in the Modern State*, 2nd edn. Harlow: Prentice Hall.

Hofstede, G. (1980) *Cultures Consequences*. Beverly Hills, CA: Sage.

Holbrook, M.B. and Hirschmann, E.C. (1982) 'The experiential aspects of consumption', *Journal of Consumer Research*, 9: 132–40.

Ingleby, D. (1985) 'Professionals as socializers: the "psy complex"', *Research in Law, Deviance and Social Control*, 7: 79–109.

Kamin, L. (1977) *The Science and Politics of I.Q.* London: Penguin.

Kuhn, T.S. (1970) *The Structure of Scientific Revolutions*, 2nd edn, enlarged. Chicago and London: University of Chicago Press.

Lather, P. (1991) *Getting Smart: Feminist Research and Pedagogy with/in the Postmodern*. New York and London: Routledge.

Lave, J. and E. Wenger (1991) *Situated Learning: Legitimate Peripheral Participation*. Cambridge, New York and Melbourne: Cambridge University Press.

Levin, P. (1997) *Making Social Policy: The Mechanisms of Government and Politics, and How to Investigate Them*. Buckingham: Open University Press.

Lewis, J. and Glennerster, H. (1996) *Implementing the New Community Care*. Buckingham: Open University Press.

Lightfoot, S.L. (1983) *The Good High School*. New York: Basic Books.

Lipsky, M. (1980) *Street-Level Bureaucracy: Dilemmas of the Individual in Public Services*. New York: Russell Sage Foundation.

Lupton, T. (1966) *Management and the Social Sciences*. Administrative Staff College, Abingdon, Oxfordshire, UK.

Lyotard, J.-F. (1984) *The Postmodern Condition*. Minneapolis, MN: University of Minnesota Press.

Martin, J.P. (1984) *Hospitals in Trouble*. Oxford: Blackwell.

Meyer, J. (1993) 'New paradigm research in practice: the trials and tribulations of action research', *Journal of Advanced Nursing*, 18(7): 1066–72.

Meyer, J. (2003) 'Questioning design and method: exploring the value of action research in relation to R&D in primary care', *Primary Health Care Research and Development*, 4: 99–108.

Mills, C.W. (1959) *The Sociological Imagination*. London and New York: Oxford University Press.

Nesbitt, S. (1995) *British Pensions Policy Making in the 1980s: The Rise and Fall of a Policy*. Aldershot: Avebury.

Normand, C., Meyer, J. and Bentley, J. (2003) 'Research ethics and complex studies', *Nursing Times Research*, 8(1): 17–23.

Phillips, E.M. and Pugh, D.S. (1987) *How to Get a PhD: A Handbook for Students and Their Supervisors*. Buckingham: Open University Press.

Pithouse, A. (1998) *Social Work: The Social Organisation of an Invisible Trade*, 2nd edn. Aldershot: Ashgate.

Porter, L.W. and McKibbin, L.E. (1988) *Management Education and Development: Drift or Thrust into the 21st Century?* New York: McGraw-Hill.

Reith, M. (1998) *Community Care Tragedies: A Practice Guide to Mental Health Inquiries*. Birmingham: Venture.

Richards, G. (1997) *'Race', Racism and Psychology*. London: Routledge.

Roethlisberger, F.J. and Dickson, W.J. (1939) *Management and the Worker*. Cambridge, MA: Harvard University Press.

Rolfe, G. (1998) *Expanding Nursing Knowledge*. Oxford: Butterworth-Heinemann.

Rose, N. (1985) *The Psychological Complex*. London: Routledge & Kegan Paul.

Rose, N. (1990) *Inventing Ourselves*. London: Routledge.

Stenhouse, L. (1975) *An Introduction to Curriculum Research and Development*. London: Heinemann.

Taylor, F.W. (1947) *Scientific Management*, London: Harper & Row.

Townsend, P. and Davidson, N. (eds) (1988) *Inequalities in Health: The Black Report: The Health Divide*. London: Penguin.

Townsend, P., Phillimore, P. and Beattie, A. (1988) *Health and Deprivation: Inequality and the North*. London: Routledge.

Trinder, L. and Reynolds, S. (2000) *Evidence-Based Practice: A Critical Appraisal*. Oxford: Blackwell Science.

Walshe, K., Ham, C. and Appleby, J. (1995) 'Given in evidence', *Health Service Journal*, 29(June): 28–9.

Wertsch, J.V. (1998) *Mind as Action*. New York and Oxford: Oxford University Press.

Woodward, J. (1959) *Management and Technology*. London: HMSO.

PART II

INTRODUCTION TO PART II: LISTENING, EXPLORING THE CASE AND THEORIZING

Introduction

This part of the book, the first after the general introduction, presents two methodological approaches – ethnography and case study – which provide a basic foundation for qualitative research in the social sciences, along with two of the most common ways of collecting data within these approaches – research diaries (or field notes) and interviewing. These are followed by a succinct explanation of grounded theory, probably the most influential approach developed in the twentieth century to the analysis of qualitative data. The final chapter on ethical issues in generating public knowledge is of central importance to all the others – and indeed to the whole of this book.

Research is about the generation of public knowledge through systematic – and often private – processes. We have deliberately started the book by looking at methodologies and methods which focus on the personal, and on the person of the researcher as a 'research instrument' (Peshkin, 1988). Ethical issues are central to the researcher's practice whatever the methodology adopted, so this chapter needed to come near the beginning. In this book quantitative and qualitative methodologies are drawn together as reciprocal ways of researching human behaviour and social interaction, and both require sensitivity in dealing with research participants/informants. However, ethical issues can become particularly complex when research adopts methodologies and methods, such as those presented here, which involve the researcher's self in making meaning from the analysis of human behaviour and self-presentation. This was

another reason for locating the chapter on ethical issues here.

None of the chapters is, of course, discrete. The methodologies and methods presented in Part II have implications for others which follow in Parts III–VIII, and vice versa. For example, a core concept in both ethnography and case study is culture which is also dealt with in considerable depth in Part V on Reading and Representing Socio-Cultural Meanings. The difference is perhaps that chapters here draw more heavily on anthropology and sociology whereas those in Part V focus on socio-cultural interaction and representation which have been strongly influenced by the socio-cultural psychology of Vygotsky and the semiotics of Saussure.

Many issues are raised in the chapters in Part II which will be further explored and clarified later in the book. In particular, Torrance's focus on 'the social construction of meaning' (Stark and Torrance, in this volume), Altrichter's observations about 'the fuzzy borderline between description and interpretation' (Altrichter and Holly, in this volume) and Corbin's emphasis on taking account of 'multiple realities' (Corbin and Holt, in this volume) invite cross-references to the chapters in Part IV on Observing, Querying, Interpreting. The methodologies and methods introduced here, and variations of the grounded theory approach to analysis, also provide the starting point for the more politically oriented approaches presented in Part III on Researching for Impact. Essentially Parts II, III and IV are all concerned with understanding the meaning for individuals of their lives and experiences and to varying extents in giving them a 'voice'.

References

Peshkin, A. (1988) 'In search of subjectivity – one's own', *Educational Researcher*, October: 17–21

CHAPTER

1

ETHNOGRAPHY

Juliet Goldbart
Department of Psychology and Speech Pathology, Manchester Metropolitan University, UK
David Hustler
Education and Social Research Institute, Manchester Metropolitan University, UK

Key concepts

David Hustler

The word *ethnography* literally means 'writing about people', and it is the interest in what some would regard as distinctive about people that has led to a boom in all sorts of ethnographic varieties over the last 40 years. The distinctive features revolve around the notions of people as *meaning*-makers, around an emphasis on understanding how people *interpret* their worlds, and the need to understand the particular cultural worlds in which people live and which they both construct and utilize.

Certain key ideas follow from this: that social behaviour cannot be reduced to predictable 'variables' along the lines of the natural sciences (Blumer, 1967); that people actively collaborate in the *construction* and maintenance of the cultural meanings which inform their actions; and that researchers therefore need to find ways of engaging with those meanings and the processes through which they are constructed. It also follows that ethnographic work tends by its very ambitions and nature to focus on a limited range of cases, often only one case or social setting. A central purpose behind ethnography therefore is to get involved in this or that social world, to find out how its participants see that world, and to be able as researchers to describe how its culture ticks. The particular 'culture' could be a hospital ward (Roth, 1963), a school (Woods, 1979), or any society (or grouping within society). We can see here the strong links with *anthropological* traditions. For some researchers, it can only be 'proper' ethnography if the researcher is a *participant observer* in the *everyday lives* of whichever society or *group* s/he is studying. You will, however, find the term ethnography linked to a wide

range of studies, not all of which make extensive or even any use of participant observation in the strong sense of the term. However, whether the researcher spends years living with this or that group or is attempting via interviews to access and understand interpretations, it is clear that the researcher as a 'human instrument' brings to bear (unavoidably) his or her own interpretations and cultural orientations into the picture.

What links many of these approaches then is a *reaction to positivism* and associated purely quantitative approaches to the study of social life. The key link is with the emergence of *'interpretative' theoretical ideas* of one form or another. Ethnographic studies have been informed by symbolic interactionism, phenomenology, ethnomethodology, critical theory, feminism and some postmodernist strands. There is a large variety of texts about ethnography or with sections on ethnography, some of them suggesting that ethnography is a specific method and others making more of ethnography as a school of thought. There have also been many attempts to operate with an ethnographic orientation as an insider-researcher, action researcher or practitioner researcher and this has of course led to considerable debate about these distinctive researcher identities and ambitions within ethnographic work. Our own 'story from the field' which follows was driven by a strong problem resolution and services improvement interest. Given this variety, it is not surprising that in the *Handbook of Ethnography* (Atkinson et al., 2001) the editors see their central goal as 'mapping ethnographic diversity'. There certainly is diversity and there is no real substitute for reading three or four different ethnographies, rooted in differing theoretical branches, if you wish to get an initial feeling for the range and variety of ethnographic work.

It is in the detailed descriptions and analyses of what people say and do (primarily, but not necessarily exclusively, using qualitative data) that ethnographers have revelled. In early ethnographic work especially we find exhortations that ethnography stands or falls on the provision of 'rich' details of cultural scenes, on what some have called 'thick description' (Geertz, 1988), through which the reader can develop a strong sense of the particular realities involved (we come close again here to the notion of ethnography as sharing with anthropology an inescapable parallel with travellers' journeys, and a subscription to validity claims through persuasive illumination). An extensive literature has built up here concerning how we might value the knowledge claims made in ethnographic work. Lincoln and Guba (1985, 1989) talk of 'trans-ferability' (and other writers have opted for terms such as 'plausibility' or 'verisimilitude') regarding those criteria which are rooted in convincing the reader through drawing her or him into the world of the participants and sensing the believability of that world. Other knowledge value criteria are more to do with credibility deriving from matters to do with the nature of the reported research process (e.g. how long in the field, mix of data sources, account of the decision-making research process, adequate attention to reflexivity issues, the checking out of interpretations with participants, etc.). In some texts on ethnography you will also find references to how researchers need to avoid going into the field with specific hypotheses, how these and theory more generally emerge over time through *interrelated processes of data-gathering and analysis*. Much ethnographic work emphasizes the role of *theory generation*, of the discovery of theory, and this too can be viewed as a reaction to the positivist focus on the testing of theory and on verification and refutation. There are strong links here with the work on and debates around the so-called discovery of grounded theory (Glaser and Strauss, 1967).

Ethnographic research in health has often had a specific focus on improving aspects of service delivery or organization: exploring, for example, how cultural beliefs and practices might impact on concepts of health, illness and treatment, how health professionals' ethnocentricity might affect the perceptions of clients or other health workers, and what factors affect the acceptability of certain health interventions (e.g. Savage, 2000). In contrast, much of the UK work in the early days of the emergence of ethnographic approaches to schools and classrooms spoke of the need to *explore* the world of the classroom, to *document the perspectives* of teachers and pupils, to *generate rich case studies*. This is in principle not so different from the early ambitions of work done within the Chicago school, particularly the urban ethnographies tied to occupational sociology. Several of these early ethnographic studies were informed also by a concern to 'tell the story', or let the voices be heard, of less fortunate or marginal members, or less visible members, within society. Occasionally the goal of accessing the less visible social worlds has almost seemed an end in itself, bringing with it accompanying accusations of being motivated by little more than curiosity about the bizarre or the exotic. In common with critiques of the social psychologically oriented symbolic interactionism linked to Mead (Blumer, 1966), much early ethnographic work also led to some criticism for the neglect of the influence of broader political and economic structures. This led to approaches which attempted to link a 'bottom-up' interest in participants' meanings with broader structural and political dimensions. Out of this much of the work of the 'critical ethnographers' was born, with a particular interest in linking 'micro' and 'macro' approaches (Anderson, 1989; Shacklock and Smyth, 1998).

Hardly surprisingly, many of the early ethnographic studies and exhortations are regarded as methodologically somewhat naive and perhaps even romantic in their attempts to capture the 'natural' worlds of their 'subjects'. Many of the more recent theoretical persuasions informing ethnographic work, including feminist approaches, have struggled with the 'role' of the ethnographic researcher, the researcher's 'self' (Behar, 1996) and the researcher as author (Lather, 1996). Issues here concern how to, for example, disrupt the power of the researcher and author, and how to enable participants' voices to be heard in ways which are not too strongly filtered through the researcher's lens (Fine and Weiss, 1998). Central here (and this is where we move beyond a straightforward 'naturalism') are ideas associated with 'reflexivity', with the recognition that we are part of the social worlds we are studying and that the researchers' own interpretive processes and authorial position need to be taken account of. As our contribution to 'stories from the field' illustrates, the issues to do with 'outsider' status are multidimensional, and re-emerge again and again at differing moments in the research process. These concerns for how we can approach the understanding of and reporting of differing cultures within or outside our 'own' society (as an 'outsider') have been struggled with for a long time (e.g. from a phenomenological angle, the work of Schutz in 'The stranger', 1964).

It may be helpful to avoid imagining that there is some solution or resolution to being 'the human instrument'; rather, take careful note of how others, and you yourself, go about doing ethnographic work. Part of this must of course involve attention to the ethics and the politics of ethnographic research. Once we accept the notion of a 'human instrument', it becomes clear how complex and multifaceted the task is. Much has been written about 'entering the field', about negotiating entry and gaining access. A lot has also been written about the role of 'key informants' and on how the researcher may be perceived in relation to the internal hierarchies and micro-politics of the group or organization under study. Not so much has been written about emotional ups and downs, about leaving the field or about what participants may have gained or lost through the ethnographers' work (though here it is worth looking at the commentary by Sparkes, 1998). Coffey (1999) reminds us how personal the ethnographic research process can be and points to some of those neglected dimensions such as the role of the emotions and the sexual status of the researcher. Likewise, it may not be especially useful to attempt to define the precise boundaries of what is and what is not ethnography. However, it can be seen that it is essential to have some understanding of the epistemological bases of ethnographic work and to build up some acquaintance with a range of ethnographic studies. Reading ethnographies is almost always more interesting than reading about them anyway ... and reading most ethnographies since the late 1970s will serve to illustrate what Geertz (1988) described as the 'blurred genres' operating, setting the stage for the continuing troubles and dilemmas regarding how to represent the experience of others (and how to legitimize our attempts).

Implications for research design

We do seem to have moved beyond the notion that just because ethnographic work is inherently unpredictable, there is no point to thinking about research design and you should just get stuck in. Much ethnographic work is concerned with developing theoretical ideas rather than testing out existing hypotheses, but it is silly to imagine that you should (or could) 'enter the field' with a blank mind.

Initial questions could be fairly specific such as an interest in just what teachers and pupils view as appropriate or inappropriate behaviour in the playground, or somewhat more general, such as what makes a 'good' patient from the point of view of nurses. Whether or not this interest stemmed from a personal experience or something in the literature, the initial question can be pursued and perhaps sharpened initially through both further reading and also documenting some of your own thoughts/feelings/assumptions in the territory. It is here that you are already beginning to address 'reflexivity' issues and starting on what many would regard as an essential tool in any ethnographic work, some form of research diary or journal.

Any ethnographer needs to be open to research problem reformulation. Just what is practically possible can often shape ethnographic work, as can 'early days in the field' as you begin to sample particular settings involving particular participants at particular times. It is important to recognize that you *are* always 'sampling', to document how you are sampling and as the ethnography develops to plan your sampling more explicitly. This planning can be shaped by an interest in checking out a particular idea, for example that views on appropriate playground behaviour may change somewhat at different times of day, or your developing interest in how nurses share experiences and stories about 'difficult' patients. We can see in these examples, both a sharpening of focus and a shifting of focus. It should be apparent that ethnography is a constant process of decision-making, that openness to smaller or very major changes in research design is crucial, and that data-gathering and data-analysis are interrelated and ongoing throughout most ethnographic research.

Having read a number of ethnographies, you will be aware of the wide range of formats and styles: those which try to separate out quite sharply the 'description or narrative' from the 'analysis'; those which interpenetrate the researchers' and other participants' accounts; those which structure the text around a form of 'natural history' of the research; or those which organize the text by major analytical themes, and so on. It is a conventional wisdom, for ethnography perhaps more than any other methodology, to allocate yourself considerable time after leaving the field for writing up, for gaining some distance from the material and revisiting it. However, you do need to attend to your own commitments, as the research develops, in terms of audience and participants' possible participation, and that means thinking through the resources your research is building up for final text production and the voices to be heard.

Stories from the Field – ethnographic interviews: an outsider looking in

Juliet Goldbart

This *story from the field* is an account of research, using ethnographic interviewing, to explore the appropriacy of Western approaches to early intervention to families in urban India, conducted in collaboration with colleagues from the Indian Institute for Cerebral Palsy (IICP) in Kolkata. Early intervention is the provision of therapy, support and other services to infants and young children with developmental disabilities or chronic medical conditions with or through their family members. The driving force behind this project, and much of the research I do, is a desire to improve the services offered to families with a child with a severe disability.

It is not uncommon in ethnography for researchers to be outsiders to the community or culture being described. In this project, however, I was doubly an outsider. I had just three weeks' lecturing experience in India when the project started. I worked closely with Swapna Mukherjee, an experienced teacher of children with disabilities in Kolkata, and without her and other Indian colleagues, it would have been impossible for me to participate in the project, let alone make any sense of the findings, as the issues we were exploring were essentially cultural. As a British born and educated psychologist with 15 years' experience of lecturing to speech and language therapy students, and a school governor, I am an insider in UK health and education systems. I also have children, though neither of them has major special educational needs requiring long-term specialist management. Thus I have little experience of having to fight for services for my children as is the reality for many parents of children with severe impairments both in the UK (e.g. Paradice and Adewusi, 2002) and in countries of the South (e.g. McConkey et al., 2000). Consequently, I felt that there were several problematic issues around my involvement, which I will discuss later.

In this project, the ethnographic work was carried out to inform a wider study evaluating a service for families of children with cerebral palsy on the outskirts of Kolkata. Services for families with children with severe disabilities are not widely available in India. Those services that have developed, particularly in urban settings, have tended to adopt Western models of service delivery (Peshawaria and Menon, 1991). It seemed to us that this was predicated on many assumptions about Indian life and culture which needed to be explored before Western models could be assumed to be appropriate. Following the work of O'Toole (1989), who examined similar issues in Guyana, we wanted to look at:

- parents' expectations for developmental milestones such as sitting and walking;
- parents' beliefs concerning the amenability to teaching of key developmental skills and parents' roles in this teaching;
- whether parents have sufficient time available to carry out teaching or therapy with their children.

In Western approaches to early intervention, play is seen as a highly important context for developing cognition and communication (e.g. Brodin, 1999). Evidence on perceptions of play in India was inconsistent, perhaps because of the great diversity of family life in India. This led to a fourth topic:

- what toys the family have and how parents spend their time with their child with disabilities.

We adapted O'Toole's work into a series of open-ended questions which could be presented as a questionnaire or as an interview. The preferred language of the majority of our participants was Bengali. The questions, therefore, were translated from English into Bengali by Swapna. In order to check that the terms used were as close as possible to the original, the questions were then independently back-translated into English and the resulting version was discussed and amended until we were all satisfied that the original meanings were being conveyed accurately by the translation. We were particularly concerned about the way that the term 'toys' was translated. From research we had read, we knew that we needed a word that did not convey only commercially produced toys. Our informants suggested that the Bengali word 'khalna', meaning 'plaything', would allow parents to include reference to household equipment, like pans and spoons, or natural objects, such as sticks and stones, as well as purchased items such as dolls, toy animals and cars.

There were other issues that I struggled with. One was my concern over my unwanted status as 'Western expert' and the power imbalance that this introduced into my interactions with my Indian co-researchers. This was reinforced by my role as higher degree supervisor for two of my IICP colleagues. Being used to a relatively non-hierarchical university department where first names were used by staff and students alike, I had to work to remember to use titles when talking to and about others, but failure to do this would have been seen as rude. I struggled quite successfully against being called Ma'am by 'junior' colleagues, but it was two years before anyone told me that my nickname among the Institute's drivers was 'Bullet Memsahib' – coined, apparently, because 'Juliet' is difficult to pronounce in Bengali and I walked faster than any woman they had ever met!

In order to work successfully in a culture not my own and through a language I knew little of, my IICP colleagues and I had to move to a point where we felt more like co-workers. I think that we did this by recognizing and valuing each others' areas of expertise, both within and outside the project. The parents who were to be the participants helped greatly by being willing to extend their friendship and their confidence in Swapna to me.

My second concern was around the assumptions I knew I was at risk of making in setting up the research, both my own and those I inherited from Western research literature. These related to areas like the role of women, attitudes towards disability and links between housing and economic status. This made ethnographic interviewing a particularly valuable research method as it allows interviewees to explain their answers from their own perspectives.

My third concern was the risk of making cultural misapprehensions in interpreting the findings. To address this we fed back the findings to two groups of around ten participants and asked for their views (see below).

The study generated a great array of findings. They are available in three papers – Goldbart and Mukherjee (1999a, 1999b, 2000), so I will only give a few examples here. First, parents' norms for some developmental milestones were closely aligned to those from Western sources. This was particularly true for 'sitting unsupported' and 'walking unaided' which could be seen as having a basis in physical develop-

ment. However, there were important differences in some milestones which are significant in early intervention programmes. For example, 'talking' was expected by participants far earlier than Western norms. Parents in the feedback group suggested that traditionally, in India, the strings of intonated babble that babies produce from around eight months were viewed as words. So, particularly for older parents, babies' babble is the start of talking, a perspective that would fit with contemporary views on the linguistic nature of babbling (Holowka and Petitto, 2002).

Explanations for the earlier expectations for dressing without help are more obvious. In Kolkata, where the temperature rarely drops below 18C, children typically wear underpants, a slip-on dress or pull-on shorts and tee-shirt with sandals. It is hardly surprising that they can dress independently earlier than children who have to wrestle with buttons and zips, tights or long trousers. Unlike talking and dressing, parents expected independent toileting later than Western norms. Toilet facilities for families in the study varied hugely; from homes with several bathrooms, each with a plumbed-in toilet, to homes with no running water where children were held over an open sewer to defecate. Our parent discussants felt that learning to use an Indian-style toilet and washing oneself with a jug of water was more difficult than coping with a Western-style toilet and wiping oneself with toilet paper. So, though successful toilet training was very important to them, parents expected it to be a gradual process. Intervention programmes designed for India would have to take these issues into account.

The 56 participating parents, predominantly but not exclusively mothers, were asked who in the household carried out a range of domestic tasks, such as cooking, cleaning, shopping and childcare. Their responses demonstrated that mothers, some of whom were in full-time employment, carried a heavy responsibility for domestic tasks. Female relatives, particularly in joint or extended families, and in the more affluent families, paid servants, helped, particularly in cooking and cleaning. However, fathers and other male relatives hardly participated in household tasks, with the notable exception of shopping, for which they were largely responsible. Precise data on how this compares to Western households is not available but there would seem to be limits on what can be expected of mothers in terms of participation in home-based teaching and therapy programmes, particularly where the mother is a wage earner without domestic help.

All respondents identified at least two playthings. Their nature varied greatly, from a rattle made from a discarded shampoo bottle filled with stone chippings to computer games, though the most commonly cited were bats and balls, toy vehicles and dolls. The majority of parents spontaneously identified *playing* as something they did with their child. Together, these findings made us confident that play-based intervention would be feasible for many families.

To guard against the results of the study being misinterpreted through my Western eyes, key issues were discussed with volunteer groups of parents. Their reflections were invaluable. For example, I suggested naively that being part of a joint family was advantageous for project parents as there were more people with whom to share domestic responsibilities. This idea was refuted by simple maths – there are also more people to cook and clean for in joint families! Furthermore, mothers, particularly mothers of a child with a disability, may have a low status in the complex social network of a joint family, needing permission from parents-in-law to attend an intervention project. From this, the IICP staff decided to hold 'family days' where relatives would be invited to see the project, with the hope that this would enhance their approval of mothers' participation.

My positive spin on family roles – 'well at least your husbands do the shopping' – was met with wry smiles and a swift response that this was a ploy to control what was cooked and served in the house. However, there was some disagreement amongst the parents on what they felt men's role should be in the family. About a third felt strongly that their partners worked long hours and did not participate in household activities by mutual consent. Their overtime paid for domestic help or the labour-saving devices, like washing machines, that made their lives as mothers of children with severe disabilities far easier.

Through ethnographic interviewing we gained a rich insight into the lives and beliefs of the parents participating in the project. They gave us information which should enhance the service offered to them and many other families with a child with disability in India. While many aspects of Western early intervention seem to be appropriate to this part of India, there were some significant issues of cultural divergence which would need to be addressed for intervention approaches to be congruent with the lives of the families for which they were intended.

Annotated bibliography

Atkinson, P., Coffey, A., Delamont, S., Lofland, J. and Lofland, L. (eds) (2001) *Handbook of Ethnography*. London: Sage.

An extensive book pursuing a variety of current issues and dilemmas to do with representation and epistemology regarding ethnography. It is the sort of text you go hunting in, rather than attempting to read it through. This handbook conveys, deliberately so, the variety of ethnographic forms and substantive interests.

Besio, K. (2003) 'Steppin' in it: postcoloniality in northern Pakistan', *Area*, 35(1): 24–33.

Participation in the essential but gendered chore of dung collecting provides Besio with a context for a partial defence of postcolonial ethnography. By conceptualizing her research as located within a *contact zone*, Besio explores the conflicts faced by researchers, particularly feminist researchers, in postcolonial settings. A challenging, witty paper.

Fine, M. and Weis, L. (1998) 'Writing the "wrongs" of fieldwork: confronting our own research/writing dilemmas in urban ethnographies', in G. Shacklock and J. Smyth (eds), *Being Reflexive in Critical Educational and Social Research*. London: Falmer Press, pp. 13–35.

A very powerful account of the troubles and dilemmas of fieldwork in the authors' attempts to write for, with and about poor and working-class informants in the USA.

Hammer, C.S. (1998) 'Toward a "thick description" of families: using ethnography to overcome the obstacles to providing family-centered early intervention services', *American Journal of Speech–Language Pathology*, 7: 5–22.

Hammer argues that we need far richer information on families if we are going to offer intervention which is congruent with their daily lives, and provides examples of how to achieve this.

Hammersley, M. and Atkinson, P. (1995) *Ethnography: Principles in Practice*, 2nd edn. London: Routledge.

One of the best known and widely used basic texts on ethnography. It is a well-structured text working through matters such as research design, access, analysis, writing, etc., with lots of examples from the ethnographic literature.

Lancy, D. (1996) *Playing on the Mother-Ground*. New York: Guilford Press.

This is a fascinating and vivid account of childhood in rural Liberia, illustrating the more anthropological 'wing' of ethnography. Lancy describes his use of participant observation and other methods to document how Kpelle children learn to be successful adult members of their society.

Pollard, A. and Filer, A. (1999) *The Social World of Pupil Career*. London and New York: Cassell.

This is one of a series of books which report on a longitudinal study of children's experience of schooling. It is very readable and illustrates one approach to the conduct and reporting of ethnographic work over a considerable period of time.

Sinclair, S. (1997) *Making Doctors*. New York: Berg.

An ethnography on the induction and training of doctors. It provides interesting new insights into the medical fraternity and ties back to the work of Howard Becker and Erving Goffman.

Woods, P. (1986) *Inside Schools: Ethnography in Educational Research*. London: Routledge & Kegan Paul.

This is a very readable and sensible textbook on how to go about doing ethnography in schools. The theoretical perspective is that of symbolic interactionism and it contains lots of examples (many from the author's own studies).

Further references

Anderson, G.L. (1989) 'Critical theory in education: origins, current status and new directions', *Review of Educational Research*, 59: 240–70.

Behar, R. (1996) *The Vulnerable Observer: Anthropology that Breaks Your Heart*. Boston, MA: Beacon Press.

Blumer, H. (1966) 'Sociological implications of the thought of George Herbert Mead', *American Journal of Sociology*, 71: 535–44.

Blumer, H. (1967) 'Sociological analysis and the variable', in J.G. Manis and B.N. Meltzer (eds), *Symbolic Interaction: A Reader in Social Psychology*. Boston, MA: Allyn & Bacon.

Brodin, J. (1999) 'Play in children with severe multiple disabilities: play with toys – a review', *International Journal of Disability, Development and Education*, 46: 25–34.

Coffey, A. (1999) *The Ethnographic Self; Fieldwork and the Representation of Identity*. London: Sage.

Geertz, C. (1988) *Works and Lives: The Anthropologist as Author*. Stanford, CA: Stanford University Press.

Glaser, B. and Strauss, A. (1967) *The Discovery of Grounded Theory*. Chicago: Aldine.

Goldbart, J. and Mukherjee, S. (1999a) 'The appropriateness of western models of parent involvement in Calcutta. Part 1: Parents' views on teaching and child development', *Child: Care, Health and Development*, 25: 335–47.

Goldbart, J. and Mukherjee, S. (1999b) 'The appropriateness of western models of parent involvement in Calcutta. Part 2: Implications of family roles and responsibilities', *Child: Care, Health and Development*, 25: 348–58.

Goldbart, J. and Mukherjee, S. (2000) 'Play and toys in West Bengal: self-reports of parents of children with cerebral palsy', *International Journal of Disability, Development and Education,* 47: 337–53.

Holowka, S. and Petitto, L.A. (2002) 'Left hemisphere cerebral specialization for babies while babbling', *Science*, 297: 1515.

Lather, P. (1996) 'Troubling clarity: the politics of accessible language', *Harvard Educational Review*, 66(3): 7525–45.

Lincoln, Y.S. and Guba, E.G. (1985) *Naturalistic Inquiry*. Newbury Park, CA: Sage.

Lincoln, Y.S. and Guba, E.G. (1989) 'Ethics: the failure of positivist science', *Review of Higher Education*, 12(3): 221–40.

McConkey, R., Mariga, L., Braadland, N. and Mphole, P. (2000) 'Parents as trainers about disability in low income countries', *International Journal of Disability, Development and Education*, 47: 310–17.

O'Toole, B. (1989) 'The relevance of parental involvement programmes in developing countries', *Child: Care, Health and Development*, 15: 329–42.

Paradice, R. and Adewusi, A. (2002) ' "It's a continuous fight isn't it?": parents' views of educational provision for children with speech and language difficulties', *Child Language Teaching and Therapy*, 18: 257–88.

Peshawaria, R. and Menon, D. (1991) 'Working with the families of children with mental handicap in India: various models', *Counselling Psychology Quarterly*, 4: 345–50.

Roth, J. (1963) *Timetables*. New York: Bobbs-Merrill.

Savage, J. (2000) 'Ethnography and healthcare', *British Medical Journal*, 321: 1400–2.

Schutz, A. (1964) 'The stranger: an essay in social psychology', in A. Brodersen (ed.), *Studies in Social Theory*. The Hague: Martinus Nijhoff, pp. 91–105.

Shacklock, G. and Smyth, J. (eds) (1998) *Being Reflexive in Critical Educational and Social Research*. London: Falmer Press.

Sparkes, A. (1998) 'Reciprocity in critical research? Some unsettling thoughts', in G. Shacklock and J. Smyth (eds), *Being Reflexive in Critical Educational and Social Research*. London: Falmer Press, pp. 67–82.

Woods, P. (1979) *The Divided School*. London: Routledge & Kegan Paul.

CHAPTER

2

RESEARCH DIARIES

Herbert Altrichter
Department of Education and Psychology, Johannes Kepler University, Linz, Austria
Mary Louise Holly
Faculty Professional Development Centre, Kent State University, Kent, Ohio, USA

Key concepts

Herbert Altrichter

History

Whether they are called diaries, log books, journals, field notes or lab books, some version of this type of 'external memory' has been used by researchers in many disciplines for recording their daily observations in the field: for example, in ethnographical research (see Malinowski, 1967) or in zoological field research (see DeVore, 1970). This lead has been taken up by qualitative social research (see Whyte, 1955) that made intensive use of research diaries as a means to record data from participant observation and from conversations with key informants.

Inspired by sociological field research, qualitative educational research has developed using similar methods. An early example is Philip Jackson's (1968) *Life in Classrooms*. In this book the author tried to 'move up close to the phenomena of the teacher's world' (1968: 159). Interestingly, he argued that 'in addition to participant observers it might be wise to foster the growth of observant participators in our schools' (1968: 175). A step in this direction is taken by another landmark book, *The Complexities of an Urban Classroom* (Smith and Geoffrey, 1968), written collaboratively by a participant observer and an observant teacher. In Britain, Armstrong (1980) worked with a diary as the basis for detailed description and analysis of a primary classroom in his book *Closely Observed Children* 'about intellectual growth and intellectual achievement; about understanding the understanding of children'.

There is, however, another source diary writing may tap into. 'From the very beginning of European culture, texts have been written with the aim of

increasing self-understanding, becoming aware of self-delusions, and articulating and reducing pain' (Werder, 1986: 4). Diaries in which the self and its surrounding conditions were investigated have ranged from Saint Augustine's *Confessions* to the scores of anonymous diaries by which everyday people reflect on their lives. At first sight, such diaries appear as introspective texts or as 'literature', but only rarely as research. Yet, introspective diaries can lead to important insights. As Elias Canetti (1981) points out, conversation with oneself in a diary can be a 'dialogue with a cruel partner.'

Elements

Research diaries include a range of items:

- *data* obtained by observation, interviews and informal conversations;
- additional *'found items'*, such as photographs, letters and so on;
- *contextual information* about the ways these data were collected;
- *reflections* on research methods;
- *ideas and plans for subsequent research steps.*

Obviously, research diaries include items of different type and quality, and they include both 'data' and pieces of reflection, interpretation and analysis. This heterogeneity may make some researchers feel uneasy; however, it is also the source from which its major and *specific qualities* may be developed:

- Diaries invite 'miscellaneous entries' which otherwise may get lost: short memos or occasional observations can be recorded, and linked with interpretative ideas and reflections about research issues. Because of this *continuity*, a diary may become the researcher's companion documenting the development of perceptions and insights across various stages of the research.

- By including both data and interpretation, commentaries and reflection, diaries enable *ongoing analysis* throughout data collection and can be used to push forward the research (see Glaser and Strauss, 1967); preliminary results of analysis can indicate which additional data are necessary to fill in the gaps in a theoretical framework and to evaluate intermediate results.

Recommendations for different kinds of diary entries

Memos are produced when trying to recall experiences over specific periods of time (e.g. during a classroom lesson, a court session, etc.). The memo often provides the only possibility of collecting data on quickly flowing practical activities. In order to give memo writing sufficient detail and accuracy, Bogdan and Biklen (1982) suggest the following procedures:

- The *earlier* a memo is written after an event the better.
- Before writing down from memory, *do not talk about the events* as this may modify your recollection.
- The *chronology* of events is generally the best way to arrange written records. However, as it is important to make entries as 'complete' as possible, anything you remember later can be added to the end.
- Sometimes it is possible to *jot down catchwords and phrases* during the course of the activity you want to record. Later on, when writing the diary, these catchwords and phrases will prove useful as aide-memoires.
- Memory can improve with time and leisure for recall. Reserve time after an activity to record it. The time necessary is often underestimated. In general, plan an hour for writing a memo on an hour-long activity.
- Memos are written primarily to describe and document events after they have taken place. Since descriptions are frequently interspersed with interpretations, it is useful to distinguish between *descriptive sequences* and *interpretative sequences*.

Descriptive sequences within memos and other records contain accounts of activities, descriptions of events, reconstructions of dialogues, gestures, intonation and facial expressions, portraits of individuals, e.g. their appearance, their style of talking and acting, description of a place, facilities, etc. When acting as a participant researcher, your behaviour is an important part of these descriptions. Detail is more important than the summary, the particular is more important than the general, and the account of an activity is more important than its evaluation. Whenever possible, provide exact quotations or paraphrase (marked as such). Record words and phrases that are typical of a person, group or institution as exactly as possible.

Interpretative sequences (feelings, speculations, ideas, hunches, explanations of events, reflections on assumptions and prejudices, development of theories, etc.) are appropriate entries in research diaries. Interpretations occur both when writing down experiences and later when reflecting upon them.

In daily life, writing is often reread, mistakes discovered and many things become clearer. Data analysis is a kind of rereading of existing data with the intention of reorganizing, interpreting and evaluating them with respect to your research interest. On rereading, it is often easier to judge which things are important than it is at the time of writing. You may discover new relationships between ideas and insights to follow up. Questions emerge and it is easy to see what needs to be done and how thoughts expressed in the text can be usefully restructured. We distinguish three types of 'interpretative sequences': theoretical notes, methodological notes and planning notes.

Research entails making connections between data and understanding them. In reflecting on data, various ideas come to mind. In *theoretical notes* you try to capture these ideas and save them from oblivion. They put forward explanations relevant to the research question being investigated. Relationships between events are noted for further research. Writing theoretical notes is useful for:

- clarifying a concept or an idea;
- making connections between various accounts and other bits of information;
- identifying surprising or puzzling situations worth following up;
- connecting your experience to the concepts of an existing theory;
- formulating a new hypothesis;

- realizing hitherto unconscious assumptions and formulating their theoretical implications.

Methodological notes contain the researcher's observations and reflections on research strategy, methods and activities as the research unfolds. Thereby, issues of methodological critique and ideas for alternative methods and procedures are noted which may help to develop the quality of the research project and the competence of the researcher. Theoretical notes can be an integral part of the diary entry or added in the preliminary analysis. They might address questions such as these:

- Under what circumstances did I use particular research methods? What biases might be associated with them?
- What role did I play in the situation under investigation?
- What comments arise from my experience of specific research methods and strategies?
- What decisions did I make about the future course of my research, and why?
- What conflicts and ethical dilemmas did I encounter and how did I deal with them?

In research strategies which combine research with practical action, such as practitioner research, action research or organizational development, a third type of 'interpretative sequences' becomes important: *planning notes*. When writing or rereading diary entries, new ideas emerge for the improvement of practical action, for example about:

- alternative courses of practical action;
- what was forgotten and how to address it next time;
- what has to be thought through more carefully;
- additional information that seems essential.

Planning notes enable more systematic use of the stream of ideas. The diary thus becomes a 'memory bank'. It reminds us of plans to put into practice at some later date. It facilitates shaping a plan by recording the context of the original aspirations enabling us to keep its purposes clear in the course of development.

Suggestions for writing research diaries

Writing a diary is a personal matter. Depending on the research, every diary writer develops a style and idiosyncrasies that make diary writing valuable as a research tool. Some suggestions are offered below for your consideration. (For further recommendations see Altrichter et al., 1993: 12.)

1 *Write regularly.* For example, entries might be written after each lesson in which a particular teaching strategy has been implemented, or after each meeting with a social group to be studied. Some people reserve times for writing to prevent it from being drowned in the whirlpool of daily necessities.

2 People unaccustomed to diary writing often experience a *difficult period before diary writing becomes personally satisfying*. We found diary writing easier if we collaborated with a research partner with whom we could read and discuss extracts.

3 Collaboration does not take away from the *private nature of a diary*. The decision to make parts of it available to other people remains with the author. The privacy of the diary makes it easier to disregard considerations of style and punctuation. Self-censorship disturbs the free flow of thoughts; editing can come later if the results are to be published.

4 *Structure and space* can make orientation and data analysis easier. Paragraphs, headings, numbers, underlining, various fonts, etc. may be used to *structure the text*.

5 In the factual account, include information for understanding the situation and for reconstructing it later: 'Observations, feelings, reactions, interpretations, reflections, ideas, and explanations' (Kemmis and McTaggart, 1982: 40). When using electronic means, text can easily be added to notes, and later copied and moved without disturbing the original text; artefacts can be scanned into the diary at the researcher's discretion.

6 *Include relevant items*: jotted notes, photographs, copies of documents, pupils' work, etc. If research activities and the data obtained by them (for example, an interview or lesson transcript) cannot be recorded, directly cross-reference them in the diary.

7 Because research diaries contain various kinds of records, this wide-ranging approach corresponds to our everyday form of tackling problems, and it also brings challenges. One is coping with the fuzzy borderline between *description and interpretation*. The 'ladder of inference' described by Argyris et al. (1985: 56) may be helpful in this respect.

8 Occasionally it is helpful to do a *provisional analysis of the diary entries* (Altrichter et al., 1993: 119). This shows whether descriptions and interpretations are in useful balance, which of the initial research questions can be answered from existing data, and which additional data are necessary. It also helps in planning the next research steps. Last but not least, it reduces the danger of being flooded by 'data overload' during an investigation.

Ethical issues relating to keeping a diary

Like all data, a diary constitutes a record. Diaries are usually private and contain intimate accounts and reflections. Other persons' diaries cannot be made public (i.e. used in written or spoken accounts of the research) without clearance from their authors.

When diaries contain interview data or observation notes made by someone else, it is usually best to clear the data immediately with the person concerned. This can be done by providing the person with a photocopy of the relevant passage. Diaries are also frequently used in covert social research. For the ethical issues which arise thereby see Piper and Simons in this volume.

Implications for research design

In any type of research where a person or a group is trying to make sense of experience, and where the eye of the beholder is a variable in the research, research diaries are called for. Clifford Geertz (1983) noted that researchers can be viewed as 'spectators'. The forms used to document the subjects of the researcher's gaze in these cases shape what can be seen and what is available for later scrutiny. While no one would dispute the challenges involved in understanding other's lives, it may be even more difficult for researchers to become spectators of their own observations and interpretations.

Diaries are nearly always used in concert with other forms of documentation and data collection, most notably interviews, more formal observations and artefacts. When diaries are used as data, they too are subjected to procedures of qualitative analysis as part of a comprehensive process of data analysis.

Diaries can be particularly useful for making detours, for taking side roads that offer possible insights into phenomena that were not obvious or predictable when the research journey began. They are useful for keeping track of one's thinking during the data collection and analysis phases of research, and can help the researcher not only to document the action as it happens, but to capture interpretations at points along the way. What might have seemed a diversion may become an important discovery in the light of new information.

In projects where the primary methods of research are quantitative, diaries may be employed as log books where notations provide a sense of continuity to various activities. Multi-person projects may commission a person to keep a project diary in which project decisions, the ways they were arrived at, the arguments used for them and the alternatives that were discussed are documented.

Stories from the Field
Mary Louise Holly

If, as Foucault (1972) observed, everything is already interpretation, the research diary can make more interpretation visible, enabling the researcher to be a spectator of the 'facts' and of the reconstructive process which brings them into being, and, from that, to generate new understandings. To illustrate different types of research diaries and issues related to their use, we draw from the diaries of recognized scholars and from teachers trying to understand and improve their practice.

Whose eyes can see what?

Several important issues attend the researcher's points of view.

What are the assumptions and perspectives of the researcher?

What, by virtue of the researcher's tools and the perspectives (philosophical assumptions, past experience, biography, motivation, biology) is the researcher able to see? Where are the blind spots, those derived from the research (explicit unknowns) and researcher (explicit and implicit), and how might these influence the inquiry and results? Sartre's 'intellectual' comes forth here: 'the mind that watches itself'. What is the researcher's warrant for the 'story'? A look into Bronislaw Malinowski's diary (1967) enables the reader to place his work into a context that says as much about Malinowski and what he was able to see as it does about those he observed.

Tuesday, 4.17: Overall mood: strong nervous excitement and intellectual intensity on the surface combined with inability to concentrate, superirritability and supersensitivess of mental epidermis and feeling permanently being exposed in an uncomf. position to the eyes of a crowded thoroughfare: an incapacity to achieve inner privacy. I am on a war footing with my boys ... and the Vakuta people irritate me with their insolence and cheekiness although they are fairly helpful to my work ...

As researchers write freely they can begin to see biases and distortions in their own thinking; unconscious processes are made conscious through language. Many a writer, like Florida Scott-Maxwell (1968: 8), has discovered this.

[My notebook is] my dear companion, or my undoing. I put down my sweeping opinions, prejudices, limitations, and just here the book fails me for it makes no comment. It is even my wailing wall, and when I play that grim, comforting game of noting how wrong everyone else is, my book is silent, and I listen to the stillness, and I learn.

What do mental and biological factors like emotion, motivation and memory contribute to documenting and reconstructing experience in the diary?

As is apparent in these examples, the researcher is subject to the same emotions and mental operations as are casual observers. While this may seem a liability, it is also an asset. The research diary provides structure for the writer to capture and make sense of experiences using different brain systems than those that recorded them. Learning involves emotion – whether it is Scott-Maxwell's wailing wall or Malinowski's irritation with the customs of his subjects – that calls forth particular ways of interpreting experience. 'Our hopes, fears, and desires influence how we think, perceive, and remember' (LeDoux, 2002: 24). Emotion is a call to further investigation as it indicates an area where unconscious interpretation is more obviously at work.

Einstein's observation that one cannot solve a problem by thinking at the same level at which it was created holds for a research question: one needs to 'solve' the 'problem' or gain perspective on it from a different level. Keeping a research diary is both an aid to memory and a process for *generating new perspectives and making connections* – for learning from critical

reflection, bringing together emotional and cognitive systems of the brain (LeDoux, 1996: 2002), enabling different levels of analysis, synthesis, interpretation and portrayal.

Craig Carson, a kindergarten teacher, uses the research diary as a workspace in which to record and process daily experiences in his classroom. He uses a disturbing incident with a parent as motivation to push his inquiry into new realms. In his diary he draws together bits of information that become data as he reassembles them in the light of his questions. As he describes the problem that the incident uncovers, he begins to identify and bring together salient pieces of the puzzle.

I was ambushed ... in a conference ... Near the end of our time she asks 'do you think there is something strange about Melody?' What a shot! There has been a feeling I could never grasp but always disturbing that, yes, something is strange about Melody ... She does not seem to be a whole child but I could never lead myself past vague generalities ... Now I'm committed to figuring this puzzle out ... Melody is spotless jumpers, fancy blouses, patent leather shoes, socks with no holes, and freshly curled blond hair ... Melody shares, cares for her friends, isn't bossy and never gets in trouble or causes anyone else to have difficulty. The children regret that she has only two sides since that limits the number of people who can sit by her ... [Craig continues for several pages] I think I know what it is ... I spend so much time working with kids who are 5 and act 3 that I failed to realize that here was a five-year-old who acted nine ... Mom has dedicated her last 5–6 years completely to her children and she wants them to be perfect ... [Melody's] never played outside in the rain, stomped in every mud puddle, climbed a tree or had the satisfaction of kicking her little brother ... (Holly, 1989: 64–5).

Craig was one of seven classroom teachers who took part in a study that used diaries as a way to study teaching and professional development (Holly, 1997). In the beginning of the study, the diaries were one of three main data collection sources (with seminar transcriptions and classroom observations). It soon became apparent that the diary was more than a data-gathering device, and that collegial discussion, observations and diaries were, together, a powerful method for learning from practice.

'Journal' was distinguished from 'diary' when teachers began to use them for learning. Different types of writing were distinguished. Diary writing was often stream of consciousness writing, which, as veteran teacher Kate Martin observed, was a bit dangerous if taken out of context: 'Sometimes I write just to let off steam, and as you read this you may get the wrong impression.'

Interpretation and description: Inseparable?

Writing enables the researcher to gain distance from an experience, to reconstruct and re-evaluate it from alternative points of view. What is my logic here? What isn't here? What is more obviously interpretation and what would other observers see as factual accounting? The issue is less interpretation than consciousness of interpretation.

A scholar can become conscious of interpretation *during* the process of describing phenomena but more easily *after* interpretation has been rendered: 'How do I know what I think until I see what I say?' As one describes what one observes, one is interpreting it; one brings the observation into being (MacLure, 2003). We know more than we know we know, and what we know may have little obvious correlation to what we think we know and how we think we know it. That is, much of our knowing is unconscious; we often have meagre data of a conscious nature; and we, unlike other species, can often quite successfully replace absent stimuli with theorizing and imagination (Gregory, 1999).

Take a scholar in the arts, naturalist poet Mary Oliver, for example, who, for over thirty years, has kept small 'notebooks' which inform her poetry.

> What I write down is extremely exact in terms of phrasing and cadence ... The words do not take me to the reason I made the entry, but back to the felt experience, whatever it was. This is important. I can, then, think forward again to the idea – that is, the significance of the event – rather than back upon it. It is the instant I try to catch in the notebooks, not the comment, not the thought (Oliver, 1995: 46).

Art may be closer to 'reality' as people know it than so-called objective (stripped of obvious interpretation) accounts. The research diary, as Leonardo da Vinci's 'sketchbook' illustrates, can be a space where ideas are generated.

Commitment and attachment: a distinction worth noting?

The researcher, committed to clear vision and disciplined interpretation, is also, by virtue of being human, vulnerable to what Daniel Schacter (2001) describes as the 'seven sins of memory', three of which – bias, distortion and misattribution – can cause problems in the research setting. These sins are not something that the researcher can prevent but they can be identified and taken into account by using the research diary to identify attachments that obviously distort vision.

The boxed example (see next page), from another teacher's journal, illustrates how Jerry Jenson documents a conversation with a child on one side of his diary, struggles with conscious interpretation and attachment to his own point of view in the middle, and later responds to an outside researcher's questions. This is an example of a data-gathering tool, the diary, and the questions of the researcher becoming obvious interventions into the teacher's reflections (Holly, 1989: 24).

Stories and narratives

The distinction between story and narrative, as described by Clandinin and Connelly (1998: 155), is useful to consider in relation to research diaries: '... people by nature lead storied lives and tell stories of those lives, whereas narrative researchers describe such lives, collect and tell stories of them, and write narratives of experience.' The earlier diary excerpt from Craig Carson, according to this argument, would be story, the researcher studying and portraying it, a narrative. Craig writing about his diary reflections would also be narrative as he tries to make sense of it as an observer.

If the researcher's diary is a 'dialogue with a cruel partner' it is also the site of discovery and creativity, where the terrain becomes an evolving, heuristic map the researcher draws in conversation with the 'facts'.

	Actual conversation	Interpretation	Researcher questions
Adam:	Mr Jensen, would you tell me how to spell igloo?	Perhaps I'm too structured – rigid. I am concerned that Adam doesn't participate in a lot of the classroom activities as I feel he should. It comes down to responsibility.	How so?
Me:	Sure Adam. (I write it for him on the board) What assignment are you working on?		
Adam:	Assignment?	I am responsible for what Adam does in his second year of schooling and so far he has been uncooperative. *I need a sense of direction with him and we haven't found a common ground so far.*	I am responsible?
Me:	Yes. (looking toward the board) Spelling? Phonics? Language? Reading? Which assignment?		
Adam:	Oh, I'm done with all those things.		What would that look like? Direction? A common ground?
Me:	Are you writing a story then?		
Adam:	Well, yes, and no, well, yes I guess I am. Well, I'm going to.		
Me:	So you've finished up and you are going to write a story?		
Adam:	Well, no not exactly. I haven't finished my reading yet.		

Annotated bibliography

Altrichter, H., Posch, P. and Somekh, B. (1993) *Teachers Investigate Their Work. An Introduction to the Methods of Action Research*. London: Routledge.

The book is written for practitioners who want to research their own practice and contains practical exercises for developing research competence. It also includes a chapter on 'research diaries' that it considers one of the most important research methods and a 'companion of the researcher's development' which gives form and continuity to the research process.

Armstrong, M. (1980) *Closely Observed Children: The Diary of a Primary Classroom*. London: Writers & Readers in association with Chameleon.

This classic study takes you into the classroom of Stephen Rowland and 32 nine-year-old students, as meticulously documented and described by Michael Armstrong who studied intellectual development focusing on children's 'moments of intellectual absorption'.

Burgess, R.G. (ed.) (1982) *Field Research: A Sourcebook and Field Manual*. London: George Allen & Unwin.

The sections on 'Recording field data: "Keeping field notes" ' by R. Burgess, 'The art of note-taking' by B. Webb and 'The diary of an anthropologist' by B. Malinowski contain valuable insights and suggestions from the researchers.

Burgess, R.G. (1984) *In the Field: An Introduction to Field Research*. London: George Allen & Unwin.

Of particular note is a chapter on 'Methods of field research 3: using personal documents' in which the section on 'Diaries and diary interviews' contains excerpts from diary entries and commentary, as well as diary interviews and commentary.

Denzin, N. and Lincoln, Y. (eds) (1998) *Collecting and Interpreting Qualitative Materials*. Thousand Oaks, CA: Sage.

Of special interest are chapters by N. Denzin: 'The art and politics of interpretation', L. Richardson: 'Writing: a method of inquiry' and J. Clandinin and M. Connelly: 'Personal experience methods'.

Holly, M.L. (1989) *Writing to Grow: Keeping a Personal Professional Journal*. Portsmouth, NH: Heinemann.

This book, based on a study of seven elementary school teachers who kept journals to capture everyday experiences and life in their classrooms, offers an introduction to journal writing as a method for reflective practice, case studies and action research.

Holly, M.L., Arhar, J. and Kasten, W. (2004) *Action Research for Teachers: Travelling the Yellow Brick Road*, 2nd edn. Upper Saddle River, NJ: Prentice-Hall.

Research journals are incorporated into this text. As the process of action research unfolds, readers can develop their own journals as they complete the exercises at the end of each section. Of special interest are case studies, journal examples and chapters on writing as a research process and on narrative writing.

Malinowski, B. (1967) *A Diary in the Strict Sense of the Term*. London: Kegan Paul & Harcourt.

This book contains inside perspectives with the details of daily life and motivations in the life of the anthropologist during his research.

Whyte, W.F. (1955) *Street Corner Society*. Chicago: University of Chicago Press.

In the appendix, this classic study's author takes the reader into the research process 'On the evolution of "street corner society"' starting with the personal background of the researcher and how the study evolved from 'Finding Cornerville' through to 'Reflections on field research'.

Further references

Argyris, C., Putnam, R. and McLain Smith, D. (1985) *Action Science. Concepts, Methods, and Skills for Research and Intervention*. San Francisco: Jossey-Bass.

Bogdan, R. and Biklen, S. (1982) *Qualitative Research for Education: An Introduction to Theory and Methods*. Boston: Allyn & Bacon.

Canetti, E. (1981) *Das Gewissen der Worte*. Frankfurt am Main: Fischer.

Clandinin, J. and Connelly, M. (1998) 'Personal experience methods', pp. 423–7 in N. Denzin and Y. Lincoln (eds), *Collecting and Interpreting Qualitative Materials*. Thousand Oaks, CA: Sage.

DeVore, I. (1970) *Selections from Field Notes. 1959 March–August*. Washington, DC: Curriculum Development Associates.

Foucault, M. (1972) *The Archaeology of Knowledge*. London: Tavistock.

Geertz, C. (1983) *Local Knowledge: Further Essays in Interpretive Anthropology*. New York: Basic Books.

Glaser, B. and Strauss, A. (1967) *Discovery of Grounded Theory: Strategies for Qualitative Research*. Berlin: Aldine de Gruyter.

Gregory, R. (1999) *The Searching Brain*. In Rita Carter, Mapping the Mind. London: University of California Press.

Holly, M.L. (1997) *Keeping a Professional Journal*, 2nd edn. Geelong, Victoria: Deakin University Press.

Jackson, P.W. (1968) *Life in Classrooms*. New York: Holt, Rinehart & Winston.

Kemmis, S. and McTaggart, R. (1982) *The Action Research Planner*, 2nd edn. Geelong, Victoria: Deakin University Press.

Ledoux, J. (1996) *The Emotional Brain: The Mysterious Underpinnings of Emotional Life*. New York: Simon & Schuster.

Ledoux, J. (2002) *Synaptic Self*. New York: Penguin.

Oliver, M. (1995) *Blue Pastures*. New York: Harcourt Brace.

Maclure, M. (2003) *Discourse in Educational and Social Research*. Buckingham: Open University Press.

Schacter, D. (2001) *The Seven Sins of Memory: How the Mind Forgets and Remembers*. Boston: Houghton Mifflin.

Scott-Maxwell, F. (1968) *The Measure of My Days*. New York: Alfred A. Knopf.

Smith, L.M. and Geoffrey, W. (1968) *The Complexities of an Urban Classroom*. New York: Holt, Rinehart & Winston.

Werder, L. v.: (1986) . . . *triffst Du nur das Zauberwort. Eine Einführung in die Schreib- und Poesietherapie*. Munich and Weinheim: Psychologie Verlags Union.

3

CASE STUDY

Sheila Stark

Education and Social Research Institute, Manchester Metropolitan University, UK
Harry Torrance
Education and Social Research Institute, Manchester Metropolitan University, UK

Key concepts

Harry Torrance

Case study is not easily summarized as a single, coherent form of research. Rather it is an 'approach' to research which has been fed by many different theoretical tributaries, some, deriving from social science, stressing social interaction and the social construction of meaning *in situ*; others, deriving from medical or even criminological models, giving far more emphasis to the 'objective' observer, studying 'the case'. What is common to all approaches is the emphasis on study-in-depth; but what is not agreed is the extent to which the researcher can produce a definitive account of 'the case', from the outside, so to speak, rather than a series of possible readings of 'the case', from the inside. In this chapter we shall be discussing the claims and problems of case study from the point of view of a broadly sociological perspective rather than a medical perspective. Thus while case study can involve studying the pathologies of individual patients, pupils, etc. we focus much more on the social construction of the case, the site of the social/educational encounter and the nature of the case as realized in social action. Our discussion of cases assumes a policy focus – a 'case' of curriculum development, a 'case' of innovative training, and so on – combined with a physical location, i.e. teaching or training carried out in a particular site. Where we include reference to the study of individuals in our definition, we do so from the position of asking what does 'the case' look like for this teacher or this student, i.e. from this participant's point of view?

Thus case study seeks to engage with and report the complexity of social activity in order to represent the meanings that individual social actors bring to those settings and manufacture in them. Case study assumes that 'social reality' is created through social interaction, albeit situated in particular contexts and histories, and seeks to identify and describe before trying to analyse and theorize. It assumes that things may not be as they seem and privileges in-depth inquiry over coverage: understanding 'the case' rather than generalizing to a population at large. As such case study is aligned with and derives much of its rationale and methods from ethnography and its constituent theoretical discourses – symbolic interactionism, phenomenology and ethnomethodology (cf Atkinson et al., 2001). It is very much within the 'social constructivist' perspective of social science.

The strength of case study is that it can take an example of an activity – 'an instance in action' (Walker, 1974) – and use multiple methods and data sources to explore it and interrogate it. Thus it can achieve a 'rich description' (Geertz, 1973) of a phenomenon in order to represent it from the participants' perspective. Case studies can be produced of new institutions (currently, for example, 'Charter Schools' in the USA), new social programmes (e.g. new welfare-to-work or urban education programmes) or new policies (using testing to drive the reform of schooling), which aspire to tell-it-like-it-is from the participants' point of view, as well as hold policy to account in terms of the complex realities of implementation and the unintended consequences of policy in action. Case study thus is particular, descriptive, inductive and ultimately heuristic – it seeks to 'illuminate' the readers' understanding of an issue (Parlett and Hamilton, 1972).

The weakness of case study is that it is not possible to generalize statistically from one or a small number of cases to the population as a whole, even though many case study reports imply that their findings are generalizable; we are asked to give them credence precisely because they are not idiosyncratic accounts, but because they illuminate more general issues. Clearly this is a matter for judgement and the quality of the evidence presented. Some have argued that good case studies appeal to the capacity of the reader for 'naturalistic generalization' (Stake, 1994, 1995). It is argued that readers recognize aspects of their own experience in the case and intuitively generalize from the case, rather than the sample (of one) being statistically representative of the population as a whole. We find this argument convincing, but others may not.

The other major epistemological issue to be addressed by case study is where to draw the boundaries – what to include and what to exclude and, thus, what is the claim to knowledge that is being made – what is it a case of? Too often the boundaries of a case have been assumed to be coterminous with the physical location of the school or the factory or whatever the focus of interest was. But of course schooling involves parents and, perhaps, local employers; manufacturing involves suppliers, customers, etc. Drawing boundaries around a phenomenon under study is not so easy. Also, institutions have histories and memories manifested through the understandings and actions of individuals. Likewise policies impinge on practice, teachers do not just 'choose' what to teach and how to teach it. Similarly our understandings of what schools or other institutions are for are generated in particular social and historical circumstances, as are our understandings of the nature of professionalism and the proper role for nurses, doctors, teachers, etc. So case studies need to pay attention to the social and historical context of action, as well as the action itself (Ragin and Becker, 1992).

Thus drawing the boundaries of a case is not straightforward and involves crucial decisions. These are informed in different ways by different disciplinary assumptions and are currently practised differently in different professional contexts.

The anthropological/sociological tradition emphasizes long-term participant observation of, usually, a single setting and is exemplified in the 'Chicago School' of sociology, for example Whyte's study of a Chicago street gang (*Street Corner Society*, 1956) or Becker et al.'s study of medical training (*Boys in White*, 1961). UK education examples would include Hargreaves (1967: a case study of a secondary modern

school), Lacey (1970: a case study of a grammar school) and Ball (1981: a case study of a comprehensive school). The emphasis in the fieldwork is very much on coming to know the 'insider' perspective by observing participants going about their 'ordinary' business in their 'natural' setting – that is to say by long-term immersion in 'the field'. Some interviewing and informal conversations will also be used to help interpret the observations. The underpinning idea is that of accessing the participants' perspective – the meaning that action has for them – but reporting is oriented towards theoretical explanations of the action and contributing to social theory.

The applied research and evaluation tradition arose later, in the late 1960s in the USA and the early 1970s in the UK, largely as a reaction to quasi-experimental curriculum evaluation designs which revealed too little useful information, especially about how innovations were implemented in action (Parlett and Hamilton, 1972). While the basic orientation and methods of ethnography were borrowed – that is interview and observation – the balance between them had to be radically altered because evaluative case studies had to be completed in weeks rather than months (or years), and because the researchers had a substantive interest in the particular professional dilemmas and problems of participants. Thus interviewing became widely used to gather data rather than observation, and the validity of the findings were based on comparing and contrasting across multiple cases and respondent validation of draft reports, rather than just the researcher's long-term observations and interpretations. Key features of such an approach are intensive, interview-based, 'condensed fieldwork' (Walker, 1974) and 'multi-site case study' (Stenhouse, 1982). Respondent validation, initially a methodological tool, also developed into a defining ethical and political aspiration of the approach, whereby representing the participants' perspectives was elevated to reporting the participants' views in their own (interview-derived) words. Ultimately this returns us to crucial epistemological issues about who defines what 'the case' is a case of – the researcher or the researched? Key theoretical articulations of the approach can be found in Lincoln and Guba (1985), Stake (1995) and House and Howe (1999), while further engagement with the issue of whether or not researchers can ever really represent 'the other' can be found in Stronach and MacLure (1997). UK examples of such work include MacDonald and Walker (1976) and Simons (1987). The underpinning idea is to identify and describe the impact of a programme or innovation-in-action, with the report being oriented towards improving decision-making and practice, not social theory, responding rather:

> to program activities than to intents . . . to audience requirements for information, and [to] . . . different value perspectives . . . (Stake, 1983: 292).

Currently both of these approaches to case study can be found in practice and discussed in the literature, though often the divergence and genealogy of different approaches is either largely ignored (Bassey, 1999) or treated as irrelevant for present investigative purposes (Schostak, 2002). Certainly there is no point in inventing typologies of case study just for the sake of them, yet how case studies are accomplished and, even more important for novice researchers, how they are judged still largely depends on the 'tradition' in which they are conducted. Moving beyond origins, current practice can probably be said to include ethnographic case studies (as above), policy ethnographics (related to ethnographic case studies, as above, but treating policy as the case, e.g. Gewirtz et al., 1995), evaluative case studies (as above), educational or professional case studies (as above but with more of an emphasis on professional improvement rather than evaluative decision-making) and action research case studies (related to evaluative case studies, as above, but with the emphasis on planned development *in situ*; cf. Brown and Jones, 2001; Carr and Kemmis, 1986; Elliott, 1991).

Implications for research design

Decisions have to be taken about which case or cases to select for study, how and where boundaries are to be drawn, how much time can be spent in each fieldwork site and what methods of investigation to employ. A key issue concerns depth versus coverage, and within the logic of a case study approach, the recommended choice is always depth. However, where resources allow it is always helpful to compare and contrast across cases if possible and investigate the range of possible experience within a programme, for example studying a 'good' apparently successful example of a new social programme, and a 'bad' apparently unsuccessful example. How have such intuitive judgements come to be made by key informants? Are there substantive differences between the cases? If so, why? If only one case study is being

conducted an element of comparison can also be brought in by reference to other studies reported in the literature (e.g. Ball, 1981; built on the earlier work of Hargreaves, 1967, and Lacey, 1970). Another way to address the breadth versus depth issue is to visit a range of potential fieldwork sites and conduct interviews with key personnel, then engage in 'progressive focusing' (Parlett and Hamilton, 1972) whereby the particular sites selected for detailed study emerge from an initial 'trawl' and analysis of key issues.

The most commonly employed research methods are interviews, documentary analysis and observation, with the balance between them being largely determined by the resources available and the disciplinary and professional tradition in which the case study is being conducted (see above). It can be particularly helpful to ask respondents to identify and reflect on a 'critical incident' in their work or situation – a key example for them of what are the important issues in the case. An important criticism is that reliance on such methods, and especially on interviewing alone, can result in an overly empiricist analysis – locked into the 'here-and-now' of participants' perceptions. This can be addressed by attention to relevant literature and by the methods employed, as long as they are used self-consciously to look beyond the immediate. Thus interviews offer an insight into respondents' memories and explanations of why things have come to be what they are, as well as descriptions of current problems and aspirations. Documents can be examined for immediate content, changing content over time and the values that such changing content manifests. Observations can offer an insight into the sedimented, enduring *verities* of doctor-patient relationships or police procedure or schooling – rows of desks, percentage of teacher talk as against pupil talk, etc. – which are often at variance with new policies and/or the espoused preferences of participants. Additionally, data can be derived from well beyond the physical location of the case, and the case becomes not just one example of a policy *in situ*, in action, but the policy itself. Thus a vertical 'core' can be taken through 'the system' from central policy-maker, to local authority interpretation of policy, to local implementation and mediation, asking questions at each level of the system of where this policy has come from as well as where it is going ('antecedents, transactions and outcomes': Stake, 1967).

Stories from the Field

Sheila Stark

This example draws upon data collected during a two-year national study undertaken for the English National Board for Nursing, Midwifery and Health Visiting (ENB) (Stark et al., 2000). The study evaluated the effectiveness of multi-professional teamworking in a range of mental health settings, examining both educational preparation and clinical practice. The research team (comprising six members) used a mixed methodological approach, incorporating data collected via five aspects. In order to advise the ENB of the implications of the mental health context for educational provision for multi-professional teamwork, the research team needed to gain deep insights and understandings in different work and team situations. Case study was a major feature of the methodology because it afforded both depth and breadth to assess such knowledge. It served to illuminate a number of conflicts and contradictions in the policy, the educational and practice arenas of mental health nursing and, further, illustrated how the resulting 'turbulence' gave rise to disjunctions and tensions in and between discourses, theories and practices. We used case studies in two different ways. First, we selected eight case study sites that were geographically diverse in order to provide a level of national representation. Second, we developed 'nested' case studies within these case study sites for educational purposes. The use of the latter was not predetermined, at the outset, as part of the research design, but developed as a consequence of responding flexibly to how best to use the data. Part of our remit was to advise the ENB of the implications of our findings for educational provision and to link this with the notion of evidence-based practice. Developing and illustrating how case studies could be used as educational tools, therefore, facilitated the achievement of this aim.

The case study sites

In order to represent regional and national diversity in mental health contexts eight regional case study sites were selected. Selection was based on detailed criteria that we developed, simplified here as:

- representation of the eight National Health Service (NHS) regions;
- geographical/demographical factors within these regions;
- higher education provision for pre- and post-registration nursing;
- mental health service provision (including representation of primary, secondary and tertiary levels);
- access to service user groups.

The team, however, found making the final selection of sites tricky for the following reasons:

- we each prioritized the variables within the selection criteria differently, depending on our research interests;
- the number of potentially 'interesting' sites outweighed our resources (in particular time);
- the response from potential participants who we approached for information/documents to inform our decision[1] was sluggish and sometimes non-existent.

Ultimately, our selection was based on the following:

1   Which sites provided us with documents needed for analysis?
2   Given the response to (1) did we still have the desired geographical/demographical mix and professional criteria? If so . . .
3   . . . we then had the luxury of selecting sites based on (i) what was our research interest/s? and (ii) more pragmatically, did we have family/friends who lived in the area (who might be able to put us up for a night!)?

Timetable

The case studies were undertaken over a nine-month period. All six team members undertook at least one case study with the full-time research assistant working across all eight in order to: (i) ensure one team member had a general overview of all sites; (ii) bring a level of internal consistency to the data collection; and (iii) enable cross-checking between team members where joint visits were undertaken. Visits to each site ranged from one day to a week at any one time, and revisits until an average of 12 days were completed in each site (the range was 10–15 days). In total 101 days were spent gathering data in the field. The number of days allocated was constrained by the amount of external funding received. (Case study research often involves a compromise in relation to time spent in the field, since negotiating access then writing up field notes, transcribing tapes and subsequently analysing this data can result in several additional days' work. A ratio of around one day in the field to three days in the office is not uncommon. Advice to novice researchers is often to stay in the field until a 'saturation point' is reached and few new findings are being collected. In reality, however, other constraining factors, e.g. time, money, gatekeepers' consent, etc., may affect the decision.)

Within each site we visited at least one educational institution, a range of different practice settings, and a range of service user groups and voluntary agencies. During a 'typical' day in the field the researcher generally visited 2–3 locations and undertook several observations and interviews. The team met every two weeks to discuss the fieldwork and to maximize opportunities for progressive focusing of the data collection. It also enabled theorizing to be a continuous feature of the inquiry.

Ethical issues

We sought ethical clearance in all the regions. We found that organizations and groups approached this task differently, some being strict about ethical committees approving our protocol, while others were more relaxed, especially where patients were not involved.[2] All 'gatekeepers' appreciated the abstract we had developed outlining the research, together with consent letters that were constructed to empower the *participants* (as opposed to placing the emphasis on protecting the researchers).We protected the anonymity of the case study regions, even to the funding body. Pseudonyms were given to participants.[3]

Data collection methods

The case studies combined *on-site documentary analysis* (operational policies, clinical protocols, service specifications, audit outcomes and so on) with *individual interviews* of key players, *group interviews*, *observations* and *critical incident analysis*.

The results from a preliminary aspect (a large-scale national survey) were used to decide who to interview, what areas needed to be observed and which documents would be helpful to collect while in the field. (Researchers using case study without the aid of survey data to help focus their fieldwork are advised to do preliminary work before entering the field, especially where time is limited. This may involve a preliminary literature/document review, informal conversations with people linked with the area and so

on. Sitting in/walking around a communal area on site to get a 'feel' for the place can be an extremely fruitful exercise for this type of preliminary assessment.)

We visited educationalists, service professionals and service users in order that our data could be *triangulated*. The group interviews incorporated features of *focus group interviewing*, that is to say the latter parts of the interview encouraged participants, as a group, to envisage ways forward for the role, organization, as well as relevant policy and practice contexts. The group interviewer role combined aspects of *ethnographic interviewing and facilitation* (Wilson, 1997). The *critical incident deconstruction* encouraged participants to be reflective about practical incidents in order to deepen their understanding of significant issues. Several *observational sessions*, in different care settings and educational environments, provided us with rich descriptive data of the general milieu in which teamworking was positioned.

Interview and observation schedules were developed in order to ensure comparable data was collected from each site. However, an initial analysis of the data, together with the survey findings, led us to believe that there was no significant regional difference in the respondents' responses. As a result, as well as pursuing common areas of inquiry we also decided to include more specific areas for closer scrutiny. Each team member focused on particular features that were interesting and accessible in each site. For example, one of us had excellent access to interesting service user groups while another was more interested in the post-registration provision; another looked at pre-registration and others selected different care settings for investigation. This approach resulted in a shift in our research design and the development of 'nested' case studies, as outlined in the introduction and expanded upon below.

Data analysis

Data was descriptive in the form of *transcribed taped interviews* and *extensive field notes*. Team members analysed their own data, or worked jointly where joint visits had occurred. *Analytic memos* were used to share interpretations amongst team members. Many of our insights involved the *deconstruction* of multi-professional relationships, practitioner 'baggage', group pressure and individual influence.

Once the team accepted the evidence that regional difference between sites was not significant, a methodological decision was made that the case study boundaries were permeable and thus what we wrote in the report showed no allegiance to case boundaries. A version of grounded theory (Glaser and Strauss, 1967) was used enabling us to theorize from our interpretations that emerged from the data. As a result, the final report contained the following chapters: (1) Service users experience; (2) Policy; (3) Practice; and (4) Education. Within these chapters up to eight significant themes were discussed using data (in the form of extensive quotes) from all the case study sites. Treated cumulatively, confidence in the robustness of recurring patterns increased thus enabling us to make tentative cross-site generalizations without exaggerating these claims.[4] Contextual variations, however, within each setting were not overlooked when significant.

As previously mentioned, in addition to the themed chapters, *six specific case studies* using the data collected from the geographical areas were written up (i.e. case studies 'nested' within case studies sites). These case studies, using rich and thickly described instances, were offered to the reader as 'surrogate experiences' (Stake, 1988). Further, we use these cases in an educational way (see below).

'Nested' case studies

Case studies can be a way to offer learners (and others) a research-based 'working theory' with which to analyse situations: a theory of, for and about practice. To this end, we developed a series of case studies that were used as learning tools. The case studies did not 'represent' each site, but neither was their selection arbitrary. They were written in the first person and provided personal accounts, or 'readings', of our experience and interpretation of individual and group working patterns and relationships. For example, the case study entitled 'Being or Doing' represented the users' views of their care; 'A Victorian Façade' illustrated the complexities of multi-professional teamworking in acute care; 'The (dys)functional Team' also illustrated teamworking, but emphasized the power of stereotypes and professional rivalry.

What we felt was often missing in the use of case studies for educational purposes was the learners' ability to *read* the situation. We believed this involved learning to give a *layered reading*. (In the ENB report we highlighted this layered approach by working through an example (see Stark et al., 2000).) The purpose of each case study was stated at the beginning. The case study itself was followed by a series of 'learning points' that aimed to engage the learner in a critical identification of the complexities and dilemmas of policy and practical contexts. In doing so they would build their own evidence-base located in the 'everyday' context and not built on the 'ideal' (optimal). From here, it was a short step to developing and applying theory from their previous layers of observation and analysis that helped to explain team discourses and practices.

Summary

Our use of case studies in this national evaluation did not offer *definitive judgements* on the role of the mental health nurse (MHN) within multi-professional teams and the educational provision for these roles. We offered formative and timely feedback to the ENB, as well as a contextualized summative judgement on the current situation, and in doing so contributed to the development of evidence-based professional knowledge. In this respect our case study approach was firmly within the 'applied research and evaluation' tradition.

Further, since we believed teamworking needed to be understood in contextual terms, we used nested case studies to help learners to understand the conflictual pressures of professional performance in contemporary conditions of continuous change. Such an understanding might help learners and managers avoid the sorts of 'ideal versus real' schisms that can lead to cynicism as individuals fail to achieve the utopian dream.

1. At the time, there was a plethora of research being carried out in mental health practice areas. We met much resistance from some individuals who questioned why they should get involved in 'yet another piece of research'. Promising to provide feedback to participants (and then actively doing so) was generally all they desired, since they felt their voice often fell into 'a black hole', so what was the point of giving their time?
2. Since this evaluation took place there have been tighter controls introduced in relation to research in the health profession in the UK. For example, in 2001 the Department of Health published the *Research Governance Framework for Health and Social Care* (DoH, 2001); a proliferation in the number of Local Research Ethics Committees and Multi-centre Research Ethics Committees has taken place and a review of other ethical legislation and

regulation is ongoing (see, for example, *http://www.doh.gov.uk/research/rd3/nhsrandd/researchgovernance/ethics/ethics.htm*).

3. In our more recent experience of using case studies we are finding that participants are often choosing *not* to be anonymized. An issue arises, however, when not everyone associated with the case study agrees to this.

4. In order to strengthen the robustness of our generalizations we developed a hybrid instrument (a report-and-respond survey) giving interim feedback to participants based on the case study data (reporting) and designed to provoke further comment (responding) (see Stark et al., 2000).

Annotated bibliography

Atkinson, P., Coffey, A., Delamont, S., Lofland, J. and Lofland, L. (eds) (2001) *Handbook of Ethnography*. London: Sage (especially editorial introduction and Part 1: 'Mapping ethnographic diversity').

This is an excellent collection of articles summarizing the theoretical foundations and current state of practice of ethnography.

Brown, T. and Jones, L. (2001) *Action Research and Postmodernism*. Buckingham: Open University Press.

A very well-informed review grounded in empirical data and a series of excellent examples of the extent to which case study researchers, especially those conducting action research, can or should impose their own meanings and interpretations on the actions of others.

House, E. and Howe, K. (1999) *Values in Evaluation and Social Research*. Thousand Oaks, CA: Sage.

A review and summary of case study approaches within the 'applied research and evaluation' tradition, particularly focusing on the design of qualitative evaluations of social programmes, the need to seek out and represent the view of 'stakeholders', and the need to recognize the role of values and value judgements in social research.

Murphy, R. and Torrance, H. (eds) (1987) *Evaluating Education: Issues and Methods*. London: Paul Chapman Publishing.

A 'course reader' for the Open University which contains a number of key methodological papers including Parlett, M R and Hamilton, D. (1972) 'Evaluation as Illumination: a new approach to the study of innovatory programs'; Stenhouse, L. (1980) 'The study of samples and the study of cases'; and Stenhouse, L. (1982) 'The conduct, analysis and reporting of case study in educational research and evaluation'.

Ragin, C. and Becker, H. (eds) (1992) *What Is a Case?* Cambridge: Cambridge University Press.

Collection of papers exploring and representing the 'anthropological/sociological' participant observation tradition in case study.

Schostak, J. (2002) *Understanding, Designing and Conducting Qualitative Research in Education*. Buckingham: Open University Press.

A theoretically very well-informed guide to designing and conducting qualitative research, especially through case study approaches; includes a great deal of experienced, practical advice and how to 'frame the project'.

Stake, R. (1995) *The Art of Case Study Research*. Thousand Oaks, CA: Sage.

Excellent treatment of different approaches to case study but particularly focusing on the role and sensitivity of the researcher in teasing out the nuances of a case.

Walker R. (1974) 'The Conduct of Educational Case Studies: Ethics, Theory and Procedures', reprinted in M. Hammersley (ed.) (1993) *Controversies in Classroom Research*, 2nd edn. Buckingham: Open University Press.

The first full articulation of the 'applied research and evaluation' approach emphasizing the changing circumstances of research activity and purpose and the need for 'condensed fieldwork'.

Yin, R. (1994) *Case Study Research: Design and Methods*, 2nd edn. Thousand Oaks, CA: Sage.
A rather 'technical' how-to-do-it book which perhaps glosses over some of the more problematic philosophical issues in the nature of qualitative knowledge production but nevertheless contains a good deal of helpful advice.

Further references

Ball, S.J. (1981) *Beachside Comprehensive*. Cambridge: Cambridge University Press.

Bassey, M. (1999) *Case Study in Educational Settings*. Buckingham: Open University Press.

Becker, H., Geer, B., Hughes, E. and Strauss, A. (1961) *Boys in White*. New Brunswick, NJ: Transaction Books.

Carr, W. and Kemmis, S. (1986) *Becoming Critical*. London: Falmer Press.

Department of Health (2001) *Research Governance Framework for Health and Social Care*. London: Department of Health Publications.

Elliott, J. (1991) *Action Research for Educational Change*. Buckingham: Open University Press.

Geertz, C. (1973) *The Interpretation of Culture*. New York: Basic Books.

Gewirtz, S., Ball, S. and Bowe, R. (1995) *Markets Choice and Equity in Education*. Buckingham: Open University Press.

Glaser, B.G. and Strauss, A.L. (1967) *The Discovery of Grounded Theory. Strategies for Qualitative Research*. New York: Aldine.

Hargreaves, D.H. (1967) *Social Relations in a Secondary School*. London: Routledge.

Lacey, C. (1970) *Hightown Grammar*. Manchester: Manchester University Press.

Lincoln, Y.S. and Guba, E. (1985) *Naturalistic Inquiry*. Thousand Oaks, CA: Sage.

MacDonald, B. and Walker, R. (1976) *Changing the Curriculum*. London: Open Books.

Parlett, M.R. and Hamilton, D. (1972) 'Evaluation and illumination', reprinted in R. Murphy and H. Torrance (eds) (1988) *Evaluating Education: Issues and Methods*. London: Paul Chapman Publishing, pp. 57–73.

Simons, H. (1987) *Getting to Know Schools in a Democracy*. London: Falmer Press.

Stake, R.E. (1967) 'The Countenance of Educational Evaluation', *Teachers College Record*, 68: 7.

Stake, R.E. (1983) 'Program evaluation, particularly responsive evaluation', in G. Madaus, M. Scriven and D.L. Stufflebeam (eds), *Evaluation Models: Viewpoints on Educational and Human Services Evaluation*. Boston: Kluwer.

Stake, R.E. (1988) 'Seeking sweet water – case study methods in educational research', in R. Jaeger (ed.), *Complementary Methods for Research in Education*. Washington, DC: American Educational Research Association, pp. 253–300.

Stake, R.E. (1994) 'Case studies', in N.K. Denzin and Y.S. Lincoln (eds), *Handbook of Qualitative Research*. Newbury Park, CA: Sage, pp. 236–47.

Stark, S., Stronach, I., Warne, T., Skidmore, D., Cotton, A. and Montgomery, M. (2000) *Teamworking in Mental Health: Zones of Comfort and Challenge. ENB Research Report Series, 'Researching Professional Education'*. London: ENB.

Stenhouse L. (1982) 'The conduct, analysis and reporting of case study in educational research and evaluation', reprinted in R. Murphy and H. Torrance (eds) (1987) *Evaluating Education: Issues and Methods*. London: Paul Chapman Publishing, pp. 74–80.

Stronach, I. and MacLure, M. (1997) *Educational Research Undone: The Postmodern Embrace*. Buckingham: Open University Press.

Whyte, W.F. (1956) *Street Corner Society*, 1st edn. Chicago: University of Chicago Press (3rd edn, 1981).

Wilson, V. (1997) 'Focus groups: a useful method for educational research?', *British Educational Research Journal*, 23(2): 209–24.

INTERVIEWING AND FOCUS GROUPS

Rosaline S. Barbour
School of Nursing and Midwifery, University of Dundee, UK
John Schostak
Education and Social Research Institute, Manchester Metropolitan University, UK

Key concepts

Everyone thinks they know something about interviewing – and quite rightly too! The media images are everywhere. There are the crime series which show the rough, tough, police officer interrogating the suspect to find the 'truth'. There is the image of the psychiatrist during a clinical interview delving into the mind of the client to uncover repressed realities. There is the job selection committee interviewing a candidate who puts on a performance to present the best image possible. Then there is the reporter interviewing a politician trying to dig out a clear, unambiguous statement. And, as a final image, there is the street survey where 'random' passers-by are interviewed for their views about some topic of the day, product or service.

Implicit in our images of interviews are a number of key concepts that fundamentally impact on their utility as methods to be employed by researchers:

- the 'messiness' of encounters with others;
- the 'performances' of those engaged in communication;
- the level of 'commitment' to being engaged in communication;
- 'truth';
- 'reality';
- 'suspicion';
- the hidden agendas at play;
- the tactics and strategies employed to 'unearth' information;

This list is not exhaustive. However, it is indicative of the problem: what status can we give to the words of the other?

Unfortunately, it does not stop there. Take the example of the investigative reporter interviewing an informant who is in fear of losing a job, or indeed of being injured or killed if found out, but who feels it is right to tell others what it means to live and work within a given organization. Knowledge is power. But those who leak 'knowledge' that others wish to remain silenced are in positions of great vulnerability. In a group situation certain voices may also be muted. And when the statements are printed, they are taken out of the lived context and placed into another – the public domain, the domain where words are twisted, given alternative meanings, 'interpreted' in the light of other evidence. Investigations and pressure may be brought to bear to find the 'informant' – will the cloak be lifted? Think too of the pressures that may bear upon a focus group member whose views are clearly out of step with the majority in the group – there is the temptation to conceal those views, or, for some, there may be the temptation to play the radical outsider and give wildly exaggerated opinions.

What about focus groups? They've attained unprecedented popularity with researchers. Politicians and marketing consultants love them, and with New Labour in the UK endlessly using them to gauge public opinion, they have become a household term. We all discuss and debate in a variety of groups and, to some extent, we all possess some of the skills required to moderate or participate in focus group discussions, whether we chair committee meetings, run or take part in workshops or attend dinner parties. There can be a downside to the over-enthusiastic use of any method (Krueger, 1993), and this is particularly the case with focus groups convened in order to inform policy decisions, which may as a result be based on little more than a whim arising from views expressed in hastily convened brainstorming sessions. However, their increasing use by researchers is well justified as they can access group norms and provide insights into the formation of views which cannot be so readily achieved via individual interviews. Additionally they often give facilitators the chance to observe how individuals within groups react to the views of others and seek to defend their own views.

Taking such thoughts as these into account, the key concepts can be refined as:

1 *Power* – the power structures that are the context to the exchange taking place between interviewer and interviewee or within the focus group.
2 *Social position* – the relative positions of the actors involved in the interview or focus group process in the context of the social arrangements that embed them (the legal, economic, religious, community, organizational, cultural, gender, ethnic and so on structures).
3 *Value* – the value that the 'information' has as a commodity for sale (in the media, as blackmail, as 'leverage' in some dispute, as a 'juicy quote' to enliven a dissertation or publication); the value of the interview as evocative of 'truth', of 'reality', of the 'conditions of everyday life', the value of the interviewee's words as 'testimony' of a way of life.
4 *Trust* – given all the vulnerabilities, the desire to make a good impression, the desire to conceal shady dimensions, trust is a delicate gift, easily broken. To what extent is it the guarantor of accuracy, the underwriter of 'truth', 'honesty', 'reality', 'objectivity'?
5 *Meaning* – the meaning heard by one individual may not be the same as that intended by the speaker. Interviews and focus groups provide an opportunity to check the meanings intended. However, it can be argued that there are unconscious or latent meanings that, although not intended, may provide a 'truth' or reveal an alternative 'reality' that underpins apparent actions. The words employed to represent experiences, realities, points of view, expressions of self are all open to alternative meanings.
6 *Interpretation* – if there are multiple meanings, then interpretation is critical. However, what rules, what approaches, what frameworks can be employed to underpin the process of making and selecting appropriate, 'correct', 'significant' interpretations?
7 *Uncertainty* – with multiple meanings and multiple interpretations a stable resting place may be difficult, even impossible, to find.

These concepts – and others – *problematize* interviewing and focus group discussions as natural ways of 'getting' the data. So what strategies are available to ensure that data are useful and evoke real, 'true', trustworthy and accurate representations of 'experience', events seen, values espoused and beliefs held?

The evocation of the real

The sense of the 'real' is at the heart of the interview and is the focus for political contention. There are three kinds of strategy for getting at the 'real' in interviews. These I call: imposition, grounded and emergence.

Impositional strategies begin with a list of themes, issues, problems, questions to be covered. These may be drawn from a review of the literature, the imagination or an 'expert group'. Once identified they are generally tested with small groups to reduce ambiguity and to identify questions that produce the most useful spread of information, as a way of standardizing the questions that can be applied across a large sample. The aim of this 'closed interview' format is to generate the conditions for generalization across populations. Some flexibility may be built in by including some 'open ended' questions thus generating semi-structured interviews. These enable the interviewer to capture unexpected issues and information. However, such a method as a quasi-natural science approach can be criticized for not adopting strategies appropriate to the specific nature of social contexts and processes (Pawson and Tilley, 1997; Schostak, 2002). Finally, such impositional strategies reinforce the power of the interviewer over that of the interviewee and create the suspicion that the other is 'hiding something' that must be found out. What does the interviewer really want? What is it that the interviewee is keeping secret? What is it that the interviewer is really going to do with the data collected? In whose interests will it be used? There is, as Bourdieu has pointed out, an implicit violence here, a symbolic violence.

Through a range of interviews, Bourdieu and his team wanted to evoke French working-class experience (Bourdieu, 1993). How should the interviews be conducted to meet this aim? The aim was to provide a stage for the *voices* of those who live in the slum suburbs providing testimony of the inequalities, the injustices, the tensions, the anxieties of everyday life in a country that is one of the richest in the world. Bourdieu (1993: 1389–447) provided a rationale for his approach. It is through an ever vigilant self-reflexivity in the very process of interviewing itself that the researcher guards against the multiple complex influences of all the social pressures and traps (1993: 1391). How does one reduce the symbolic violence that the researcher may bring to bear upon the interviewee? That is, there is the presumed power, social status and knowledge of the researcher that may be used to manipulate the interview. There is the agenda of concerns that the interviewer may impose upon the interview which may prevent the interviewees raising the concerns of their own lives. The interviewer should adopt the pose of the listener in a way that parallels the language and manners of the interviewee and does not impose or objectivize the person who is invited to speak.

Clearly, the interview is much more than just a tool, like a drill to screw deeper into the discursive structures that frame the worlds of 'subjects'. It is as much a way of seeing, or rather a condition for seeing anything at all. Kvale (1996) regards the 'InterView' as a way of bringing together the multiple views of people. I regard the inter-view (Schostak, in press) as the space between views, not the views themselves but the negative condition under which people may express their views to each other and to themselves. It is the very condition for critical reflective dialogue to emerge and be maintained and for a provisional consensus 'for all practical purposes' to be framed without it falling into sterile, totalitarian monologue (see Schostak, 2002). This kind of dialogic approach to the interview and the focus group has implications for research design.

Between one-to-one interviews and the groups of everyday life sits the focus group. Rather than convening groups of strangers – advised by most marketing research texts – it is generally better to get as close as possible to the real-life situations where people discuss, formulate and modify their views and make sense of their experiences as in peer groups or professional teams. However, there are problems, such as obvious and hidden 'pecking orders', the histories they have with each other, their possible animosities and the considerable potential for confusion about the purpose of the meeting.

Once convened, focus groups can – and do – take on a life of their own. Although capitalizing on the privileged 'fly on the wall' status, the researcher cannot abdicate responsibility for the impact which taking part in a focus group discussion may have on continuing relationships within the group. Some of the banter observed during sessions is, of course, part and parcel of social interaction and the usual way in which group members act towards each other (and may or may not be inherently interesting to the researcher – depending on the topic of the research). However, in bringing even a pre-existing group together for research purposes, we may ask people to cross boundaries which they do not normally do in the contexts in which they usually meet. This raises the particular challenge of ensuring confidentiality which is crucially important to address 'up front' at the start and not assume this work has already been done.

Focus groups are not simply cheap and dirty surveys. Treating them as such ignores fundamental differences in sampling. Focus group studies generally employ either convenience or purposive sampling, neither of which produces a representative sample. Treating focus group data as if they can simply be aggregated and 'multiplied up' is to overlook the importance of group dynamics. Focus groups are not an effective way of measuring attitudes or, even, of eliciting people's 'real views'. This is because they are, fundamentally, a social process through which participants co-produce an account of themselves and their ideas which is specific to that time and place. This is why focus groups tend to veer towards consensus. Sim cautions:

> It is difficult, and probably misguided, to attempt to infer an attitudinal consensus from focus group data. An apparent conformity of view is an emergent property of the group interaction, not a reflection of individual participants' opinions. (1998: 350)

Implications for research design

So what is research design? The phrase 'research design' sounds powerful, clean, scientific, solid. A bit scary. Really, at times, it can feel like a mess. Employing laboratory-designed methods for research that focuses upon the complex, dynamic, plastic worlds of everyday social and personal life is rather like taking a pile driver to do lace work. Yet, there are ways of thinking through design that evoke rather than impose on the realities of people's experiences. We've already started thinking about some of the decisions to be made and practicalities involved in using focus groups. This kind of approach evolves often unexpectedly as the research unfolds. That means there is no recipe about how to put the ingredients together that will be appropriate to all possible cases. However, the design will take into account such issues as:

- access to people;
- the range of perspectives/discursive communities;
- the problem profile;
- ethics of data collection, processing and use;
- making the record;
- representation of the experience of the research process and the experiences of the subjects of the research;
- analytic processing;
- writing up.

The question is, how to put these together in a way that makes sense within the specific circumstances of a given research enterprise. In particular, if it is to be emergent and/or grounded and/or dialogic the kinds of questions that are likely to focus the research are:

- Who talks to who, when, where and why?
- Who avoids talking to who, when, where and why?
- Who talks about who, when, where and why?
- What do they talk about, when, where and why?
- What do they keep quiet about, when, where and why?
- And, in each case, under what circumstances and to who?

From these kinds of questions a *key list of people* can be identified where each person acts in relation to some other individual and/or group (cf, Schostak, 1983, 1985, 2002).

This emphasis upon relationships between actors directed in some way towards each other (whether in friendship, hate, fear or indeed indifference) creates the conditions for the triangulation (or cross-checking of views, facts and so on) and also for establishing the degree of generalization across groups, contexts, discourse communities, and over time. This can be used to advantage in snowball sampling, where the researcher may not be aware, at the outset, of all the relevant players involved. However, to gain access to

people in this way requires the building of trust (is the interviewing going to reveal hidden views that could damage friendships, careers and even threaten lives?). Such sensitivities are especially important when selecting focus group participants (see the section on Stories from the Field). Hence, a fundamental concern is the development of an ethical framework to govern access to people and places and govern the ways in which what is seen and heard is going to be represented and used. Such a framework generally focuses upon negotiating the principles under which anonymity, confidentiality and rights of access are to be constructed. The danger is that such principles are developed routinely, rather like an audit, or indeed quasi-bureaucratically as in the various ethics committees that govern research in health contexts. To reduce symbolic violence the principles should be individually negotiated with each interviewee before each interview (see Enquiry Learning Unit website).

Designing focus group studies

Despite their apparent accessibility focus groups present a number of challenges to the researcher:

- the logistics of accessing participants and convening groups;
- the potential and limitations of 'piggybacking' on existing meetings;
- the heightened influence of gatekeepers;
- group dynamics – individuals who play to an audience and those who may be intimidated and reluctant to contribute;
- striking a balance between encouraging spontaneity and adhering to the research agenda;
- the difficulty of ensuring confidentiality.

Groups and communities are fluid entities and gaining permission to attend a forthcoming meeting of a group is not necessarily the same thing as securing agreement from everyone who actually attends the next session. Representation is an equally tricky concept, as anyone who has attempted to secure participation from user and carer representatives will know from their own experience. Many people who agree to become involved in discussions – whether these are committee meetings, public debates or focus groups – may very well have their own agenda, which may or may not reflect the concerns of others in similar circumstances. Gatekeepers assume great importance in setting up focus groups and time spent briefing such individuals on the purpose of our work is time well spent – otherwise they may inadvertently select people out as well as select them in (Kitzinger and Barbour, 1999).

Stories from the Field

Rosaline S. Barbour

This section refers specifically to the use of focus groups as an important form of interviewing in research. Focus groups rely on the researcher as the principal data generating tool. We do not stand back from our group members and merely 'collect' their responses; we actively engage with them, often thinking on our feet as we invite them to explore with us the limitations they might place around their responses and how they would contextualize their views. This is why focus group topic guides tend to be very short and sparse, leaving room for the researcher to pick up on such leads as these arise. Even as data are generated, focus group moderators engage in preliminary analysis by beginning to theorize and inviting participants to theorize about similarities and differences revealed through discussions. As with developing interview schedules, however, there is considerable skill in utilizing such 'off the cuff' probes without slipping into asking leading questions (Barbour et al., 2000). Pilot work can pay enormous dividends by developing a few questions and probes that stimulate discussion about the key research topics. Stimulus materials (newspaper clippings, excerpts from TV soaps, etc.) can be valuable in focusing discussion on the research agenda. However, this can backfire on the unwary researcher by conjuring up even more compelling associations so side-tracking discussion. It is, therefore, important to test out beforehand any materials you may be thinking of using.

Focus groups are especially attractive: not only can they be extremely enjoyable to run, they are often regarded as the easy option. However, setting them up is bedevilled by many logistical problems. Achieving diversity is difficult enough in interview studies without the added complication of having to find mutually convenient times for several individuals. Using pre-existing meeting slots is a particularly attractive solution. It is important to allow plenty of time for recruitment (and even to explore the possibility of using a short questionnaire/pro-forma to collect some basic demographic data while simulta-

neously inviting people to take part in focus group sessions). In a study exploring decision-making with regard to redeeming prescriptions we (Barbour and colleagues) used a combination of leaflets, posters and even a market stall. However, it was difficult in an area of high unemployment to find many individuals who were not exempt from prescription charges. We spent many hours sifting through our responses and trying to match people according to payment category, age and availability. To the problem of everyone not turning up on the day, add the possibility of more people coming along – even perhaps bringing friends. This did happen to us as a result of word of mouth and growing awareness of the study. It is well nigh impossible to predict turnout as, like voting behaviour at general elections, it can be influenced by factors such as the weather. Fortunately we had chosen to work in pairs, with one moderating the group and the other taking notes on the sequence of talk (Kitzinger and Barbour, 1999), and were able to run two groups. It is also a good idea to book two rooms, where possible, affording the opportunity to run two parallel groups rather than turning people away.

Many qualitative methods texts offer valuable advice about sampling, generally failing to acknowledge, however, the extent to which researchers may not have as much control as they like to think. Rewarding though it is to draw a matrix which reflects our ideal group composition, it is not always possible to find enough willing individuals in particular localities who are available at the times at which we plan to hold our focus groups. Some may be reluctant to discuss their experiences in a public forum, or there may be particular sensitivities involved in bringing together certain individuals or groups. Pragmatically, we may combine focus groups with an interview for individuals who cannot attend focus group sessions or whose views are so extreme they are deemed likely to inhibit discussion during focus groups. This was the approach used in a study of professionals' views and experiences of living wills (Thompson et al., 2003), which sought the views of known advocates of living wills as well as those of staff members who might seldom have come across this issue.

Ideally, our groups and their membership would correspond to the carefully thought-out diagrams produced in our offices. Since the focus group – rather than the individual participant – is our unit of analysis, it makes sense to attempt to convene groups so that all the participants share some important characteristic (i.e. that they are homogeneous rather than heterogeneous). For this reason many focus group researchers do not bother to take note of individual speakers in focus group sessions, arguing that it is sufficient to know that the discussion arose, for example, in the young women's group rather than the elderly men's one. However, I would argue that this approach severely limits the analytic potential of the data. Say all of the participants are young women, this is not their only defining characteristic: perhaps they are of varying ethnicity, sexual orientation and social class and they may live in different localities. While not desirable – or, indeed, possible – to carry out detailed comparisons for presentation in a final report, such observed differences may provide valuable hunches, usefully informing further sampling. I recently collaborated with four general practitioners (GPs/family physicians) on a study of GPs' views and experiences of sickness certification. Anticipating the importance of the practice setting both on patient demands and GPs' responses, we convened focus groups with GPs working in different localities: affluent and deprived, rural, urban and suburban. However, discussions suggested there might be specific issues for GP registrars (still undergoing training), locums (moving constantly between practices) and GP principals (who carry management responsibility and have a long-term commitment to this particular practice and patients). This was not something we expected at the outset. We then carried out a second phase of sampling to convene one group comprising exclusively of GP registrars, one of locums and one of GP principals. The original formulation of 'grounded theory' (Glaser and Strauss, 1968) exhorted us to return to the field to test out emergent hypotheses. In the current funding climate, this is generally a luxury which we – or at least our funders – cannot afford. However, focus groups are well placed to allow us to exercise a degree of flexibility which ultimately enables us to maximize the comparative – and hence, analytic – potential of our datasets.

Finally, focus group researchers are not in the business of determining whether or not participants' stories are 'true'. In the course of running a series of workshops on the topic of people's experiences of calling GPs out of hours, I showed a video of a focus group session to delegates who included one healthcare professional who had apparently been involved in the very incident one of my filmed respondents was describing. (This goes to show that the research community – even in a UK-wide context – is surprisingly small.) This healthcare professional mounted a vigorous attack on focus groups as a method, since this filmed individual had, as far as she was concerned, presented an account which was, quite simply, 'not true', thus casting doubt, in her eyes, on the whole research venture. I tried to explain that all accounts are partial and partisan and are used rhetorically at the same time as they purport to be accurate representations of what has taken place. As a researcher, I stressed, I was not so much interested in establishing the 'truth' of the matter, but was intrigued by the reasons this individual had for presenting the story in this way: what point was she trying to make? We would be well advised to remember that focus group transcripts are 'texts'. Rather than take these at face value and risk romanticizing the accounts of our respondents, we should, as Paul Atkinson (1997) advises, ensure that we subject these to the same critical scrutiny as we do other texts, bearing in mind that they are socially constructed. Thus, while we may be concerned with evoking the 'real', rigour is paramount.

Annotated bibliography

Arksey, H. and Knight, P. (1999) *Interviewing for Social Scientists*. London, Thousand Oaks, CA and New Delhi: Sage.

This provides a readable introduction to all the key concepts.

Barbour, R.S. and Kitzinger, J. (eds) (1999) *Developing Focus Group Research: Politics, Theory and Practice*. London: Sage.

This edited collection brings together experienced focus group researchers, from a range of disciplines who take a critical look at the potential and limitations of the method and make suggestions as to how it can be further developed.

Bloor, M., Frankland, J., Thomas, M. and Robson, K. (2001) *Focus Groups in Social Research*. London: Sage.

This is an extremely valuable guide to designing focus group research, convening and conducting focus groups and analysing focus group data. It has a very useful chapter on virtual focus groups.

Bourdieu, P. (1993) *La Misère du Monde*. Éditions du Seuil. It was published in English as *The Weight of the World: Social Suffering in Contemporary Society*, trans. P.P. Ferguson. Oxford: Polity, 1999.

The book is a collection of interviews, powerfully representing the lives of the poor. The methodological appendix by Bourdieu is especially worth reading for its approach and the issues it raises concerning symbolic violence.

Crabtree, B.F., Yanoshik, M.K., Miller, W.I. and O'Connor, P.J. (1993) 'Selecting individual or group interviews', in D.L. Morgan (ed.), *Successful Focus Groups: Advancing the State of the Art*. London: Sage, pp. 137–49.

This chapter is helpful with regard to deciding when it is appropriate to use interviews and when focus groups are more appropriate.

Gubrium, J.F. and Holstein, J.A. (2003) *Postmodern Interviewing*. London, Thousand Oaks, CA and New Delhi: Sage.

The book contains a useful set of reprints from their *Handbook of Interview Research* (Sage: 2001). **It provides insights into the ways in which postmodern researchers have employed the process of interviewing.**

Kvale, S. (1996) *InterViews. An Introduction to Qualitative Research Interviewing*. London, Thousand Oaks, CA and New Delhi: Sage.

The book provides a good introduction to the processes of interviewing without being too textbookish.

Murphy, B., Cockburn, J. and Murphy, M. (1992) 'Focus groups in health research', *Health Promotion Journal of Australia*, 2(2): 37–40.

This provides many useful hints on running focus groups.

Puwar, N. (1997) 'Reflections on interviewing women MPs', *Sociological Research Online*, 2(1): < http://www.socresonline.org.uk/socresonline/2/1/4.html >.

This online article is particularly useful as a discussion of the issue of interviewing the powerful.

Roberts, B. (2002) *Biographical Research*. Buckingham and Philadelphia: Open University Press.

Although not strictly a book on interviewing, it provides key insights into a powerful dimension of the interview as a key process in the construction of biographies and autobiographies.

Rubin, H.J. and Rubin, I.S. (1995) *Qualitative Interviewing: The Art of Hearing Data*. Thousand Oaks, CA: Sage.

The task of hearing is not easy. Too often people hear only what they want to hear. Worth a read.

Sim, J. (1998) 'Collecting and analyzing qualitative data: issues raised by the focus group', *Journal of Advanced Nursing*, 28(2): 345–52.

This contains a very thoughtful discussion.

Further references

Atkinson, P. (1997) 'Narrative turn or blind alley?', *Qualitative Health Research*, 7: 325–44.

Barbour, R.S., Featherstone, V.A. and members of WoReN (2000) 'Acquiring qualitative skills for primary care research: review and reflections on a three-stage workshop. Part 1: Using interviews to generate data', *Family Practice*, 17(1): 76–82.

Enquiry Learning Unit: < http://enquirylearning.net/ >.

Glaser, B.G. and Strauss, A.L. (1968) *The Discovery of Grounded Theory*. London: Weidenfeld & Nicholson.

Hussey, S., Hoddinott, P., Wilson, P., Dowell, J. and Barbour, R.S. (2004) 'The sickness certification system in the United Kingdom: a qualitative study of views of general practitioners in Scotland', *British Medical Journal*, 328: 88–91.

Johnson, A. (1996) ' "It's good to talk": the focus group and the sociological imagination', *Sociological Review*, 44(3): 517–38.

Kitzinger, J. and Barbour, R.S. (1999) 'Introduction: the challenge and promise of focus groups', in R.S. Barbour and J. Kitzinger (eds), *Developing Focus Group Research: Politics, Theory and Practice*. London: Sage, pp. 1–20.

Kitzinger, J. and Farquhar, C. (1999) 'The analytic potential of "sensitive moments" in focus group discussions', in R.S. Barbour and J. Kitzinger (eds), *Developing Focus Group Research: Politics, Theory and Practice*. London: Sage, pp. 156–72.

Krueger, R.A. (1993) 'Quality control in focus group research', in D.L. Morgan (ed.), *Successful Focus Groups: Advancing the State of the Art*. London: Sage, pp. 65–83.

Pawson, R. and Tilley, N. (1997) *Realistic Evaluation*. London and Thousand Oaks, CA: Sage.

Phillips, T.P., Schostak, J.F. and Tyler, J. (2000) *Practice and Assessment in Nursing and Midwifery: Doing It for Real*, Research Reports Series No. 16. London: English Nursing Board.

Schostak, J.F. (1983) 'Making and breaking lies in a pastoral care context', *Research in Education*, 30: 71–93.

Schostak, J.F. (1985) 'Creating the narrative case record', *Curriculum Perspectives*, 5(1): 7–13.

Schostak, J.F. (2002) *Understanding, Designing and Conducting Qualitative Research in Education. Framing the Project*. Buckingham and Philadelphia: Open University Press.

Schostak, J.F. (in press) *Interviewing and Representation in Qualitative Research Projects*. Buckingham and Philadelphia: Open University Press.

Thompson, T., Barbour, R.S. and Schwartz, L. (2003) 'Adherence to advance directives in critical care decision-making: a vignette study', *British Medical Journal*, 327: 1011–14.

GROUNDED THEORY

Juliet Corbin D.N.Sc
International Institute for Qualitative Methodology, University of Alberta, Canada
Nicholas L. Holt
Faculty of Physical Education and Recreation, University of Alberta, Canada

Key concepts

Juliet Corbin

Grounded theory is a theory generating research methodology. The end product of the research endeavour is not a set of findings or a few themes. Rather it is an integrated theoretical formulation that gives understanding about how persons or organizations or communities experience and respond to events that occur. Before going further, it is important to define what is meant by theory. In simple language, a theory is a set of concepts that are integrated through a series of relational statements (Hage, 1972). Since the purpose of the research is to generate theory, the user of grounded theory method does not enter the field guided by a predefined theoretical formulation, though a researcher may have an underlying general perspective or belief system, such as feminism or symbolic interactionism. These perspectives often influence the questions that are raised and the take on analysis. Any theory that results from such a process represents participants' responses and interpretation of events (which when retold by participants' become reconstructions of actual events). As data the reconstructions are filtered once more through the eyes of the researcher who then constructs a theoretical formulation. The formulation may then be brought back to participants for validation of interpretations. Thus one might say that the theory is not only a reconstruction of events, but also a co-construction between researcher and participants (Charmaz, 2000). In a postmodern world, where everything is subject to scrutiny and remains debatable as to what actually transpired, one often hears criticisms of methodologies that lead to theory development. Are they valid ways of generating knowl-

edge? What can be said of grounded theory is that it is theory development based on actual data gathered through qualitative research. Despite the fact that events are processed and interpreted through the eyes of both participant and researcher, thus a construction, the grounding of theory in data tends to make it more reflective of practical situations than speculatively derived theory (Glaser and Strauss, 1967). Why do we need theory? In disciplines such as education it is difficult to imagine building a practice that is not based on theoretical knowledge, imperfect though it may be. Where else would insight and understanding into situations come from? Best of all, theory by its very nature can always be modified and extended to fit the situation.

In this chapter we are presenting the constructionist view of theory development; however, this is not the position of some grounded theorists. Glaser (1992), for example, holds that theory emerges from data. The notion of emergence implies that a theory is inherently embedded in the data and it is the task of the analyst to discover what that theory is. The distinction between a constructionist and an emergent view is somewhat subtle but important because the emergent viewpoint implies 'one reality' or one 'truth' embedded in data, whereas the constructionist viewpoint acknowledges 'multiple realities' or multiple ways of interpreting a specific set of data. Also, if one accepts that theory is constructed or even co-constructed out of data, there is no reason why an analyst can't use a variety of analytic tools such as asking questions and using diagrams to facilitate that construction (Strauss and Corbin, 1998). The use of analytic tools is not 'forcing data' as Glaser implies (Glaser, 1992). Analytic tools are designed to clarify thinking, provide alternative ways of thinking about data and facilitate the teasing out of relevant concepts from data. You need them to stay on course because of the strong tendency of human bias.

Grounded theory has been labelled by Denzin and Lincoln (1994) as post-positivistic. Perhaps at one time such labelling was accurate but the method has evolved beyond that. It acknowledges that there is 'no one truth' or one theory in the data and that theory is a construction from data. Grounded theory is a method in flux and a method that has different meanings to different people. What is important is that when Glaser and Strauss first published *The Discovery of Grounded Theory* (1967) the ideas it promoted were revolutionary. The book was an argument against the usual 'armchair' theorizing and positivistic approaches to doing research which were so popular at the time. Instead, it urged researchers to go out into the field and to ground their theories in actual data. Though the original book provided some guidelines for how one might develop theory from data, there was no detailed methodology. That is, the early book itself did not define grounded theory as a research method. Rather grounded theory as a method evolved over time as a result of that text.

Since concepts form the foundation of theory, the first step in developing a grounded theory is 'concept identification'. In grounded theory, the discovery of concepts begins with the first interviews or observations. The importance of alternating data collection with analysis cannot be overemphasized. Concepts are identified from distinct events/incidents in the data, which may be actions and interactions, or meanings given to events or emotions that are expressed about certain events. This early coding is sometimes referred to as 'open coding' as the text is opened up and broken apart for intensive scrutiny. As concepts evolve during analysis they are used as a basis for subsequent data collection. In other words, it is not research participants per se that are sampled but events that give greater understanding and definition to the evolving concepts. One interview or observation may yield any number of incidents or events that are coded as a particular concept or some aspect of it. In grounded theory, concepts are derived from multiple sources of qualitative data. They include narrative interviews, observations, documents, biographies, videos, photographs and any combination of these. Gathering data on the same topic through a variety of means is a way of validating research findings through triangulation.

Concepts do not wave red flags and denote their significance to the researcher. Events or experiences

significant to participants could pass unnoticed by researchers. Identification of relevant concepts involves an interaction with the data (Strauss and Corbin, 1998) in which the analysis makes comparisons and asks questions, thereby heightening sensitivity to the words of participants. Field notes or interview passages are examined, line by line or paragraph by paragraph, asking questions such as what is going on here? What is this data all about? (This detailed line-by-line analysis is often referred to as microanalysis.) As questions are answered, events are given names that stand for and explain what is going on. The analyst then moves to the next bit of data and compares it to the first. Is what is being expressed in the data conceptually the same or is it different? If it pertains to the same idea previously expressed it is given the same name and the details that surround it are used to fill in more information about that concept's properties and dimensions. If it pertains to something different, it is given another conceptual name and that concept is explored for further detail. Other questions include who and what is involved, when, where, how it is expressed, what meanings are given and so on. The idea is to identify as many properties and dimensions of a concept as possible. Properties and dimensions not only define a concept they give it specificity and differentiate it from other concepts.

During theory development data reduction occurs, so that a data set is represented by a manageable number of relevant categories – themselves concepts, but more abstract ones. The analyst groups concepts into categories by making comparisons and asking questions – the same strategies as used to identify concepts, looking for commonalities between concepts, that is something in the data that indicates how these concepts might come together. The process of weaving the data back together around groups of concepts is known as 'axial coding'. Though a distinction is often made between open and axial coding, during analysis open and axial coding occur almost simultaneously for it is impossible for an analyst to pick out a concept from data without recognizing its possible connections to other bits of data and concepts. Once a researcher has grouped concepts into categories the data gathered earlier about each concept become part of the properties and dimensions of what are now subcategories of a larger category. At this point one may have six or seven major categories containing many subcategories. The data are then reduced further by synthesizing them under an even more abstract concept, the core category. Constructing the core category from the identified concepts is termed selective coding – because one must choose from among many possibilities the construct that is most representative. The core category explains what is going on in this research in a larger sense. It is an integrative concept but detailed in the sense that it is explained through all of the information contained under the individual categories and their properties and dimensions. Of course, researchers conceptualize differently and put different emphasis on the data depending upon their professional backgrounds and underlying ideologies. The important thing is not what conceptual names are applied to data but that other researchers and critics are able to follow the analytic logic that led to the choice of concepts.

No discussion of grounded theory would be complete without mentioning theoretical sampling, category saturation and memos. Theoretical sampling refers to data gathering directed by emerging concepts: the researcher follows the trail of concepts looking for sites, persons or events that enable further comparisons of data, thereby extending knowledge about the properties, dimensions and relationships between concepts. Saturation denotes the point in the research process when no new concepts or further properties or dimensions of existing concepts emerge from data. Although some additional properties and dimensions may continue to be found, as a general rule, when the researcher reaches a point when the data seem repetitive, one might say that saturation has occurred. Some researchers continue data collection until they discover the 'negative case'. If one thinks in terms of concepts and dimensional ranges rather than cases, the negative example represents an extreme point on a dimensional range of a concept. It does not necessarily contradict the theory but adds to its breadth by expanding its possibilities. For example, in studying control, if an example emerges where little or no control seems to be exerted this does not invalidate the notion of control but only leads one to ask, why or how come in this instance it is absent. This constant questioning of incoming findings is how theory is modified and extended.

Memo writing is an especially important component of theory development because it enables the researcher to keep track of ever-evolving concepts and more and more complex ideas. Memos are written records of an analyst's thoughts, interpretations and directions to self. Without memos a researcher would have no way of keeping track of the developing theory. Memos evolve in complexity, length and content over time. Whether the researcher is using a very sophisticated computer program or writing memos the old-fashioned way by hand, being able to retrieve conceptual ideas and formulations is essential to reaching final integration and having a dense and logical theory. Memo writing begins with the first analytic sessions and continues through the writing phase.

Developing a grounded theory is a lengthy and time-consuming process and a researcher must be willing to live with ambiguity until the analytic story begins to fall into place, which can be considerably late in the research process. The ambiguity, hard work involved and time necessary to construct theory are definitely limitations of the method. One of the method's strengths, however, is its ability to identify salient practice problems and the structural and personal conditions that lead to those problems. Perhaps the most valuable aspect of grounded theory methodology is its ability to generate basic concepts, thereby providing the stepping stones necessary to develop and update a disciplinary body of knowledge.

Implications for research design

Developing a grounded theory is not for everyone. From the onset one has to be very clear that developing theory, not a listing of themes or a description of a phenomenon, is the goal of the research. That said here is some practical advice for those who wish to embark upon such an endeavour. Start by finding colleagues or academic advisers who are knowledgeable about and sympathetic to the approach. Next, determine the question. The question driving a grounded theory is purposefully open and broad allowing the researcher to discover relevant variables in the data. An example of such a question is, 'How does having a chronic illness affect the experience of pregnancy?' Notice that this question does not specify any variables but allows significant variables to be discovered in the research process. Also, there is no need for a theoretical framework. Though a researcher brings a perspective to the research, such as feminism or symbolic interactionism, these perspectives guide the question and influence interpretations. They don't drive the research. Remember, theory is supposed to be constructed from data and not imposed on the data. Meeting the requirements of Human

Subjects and Research Committees calls for specific information about data collection procedures. This sometimes presents a problem for grounded theorists but not an insurmountable one. My advice is to write a proposal that is as honest as one can be at the time. Provide an overestimate of the number of subjects one might need and give a list of topics for possible observations and/or questions, but make the lists conceptual and broad leaving room for flexing the design later. Though the ideal in a grounded theory study is to follow each data collection session with a period of analysis, this it is not always possible for very practical reasons. One takes participants when one can get them and makes do with the time and money that one has. However, it is easier to collect more data on a concept while in the field than to go back later in order to fill in gaping holes in one's evolving theory. There is another benefit to keeping up with analysis. It allows the researcher to bring interpretations back to participants in order to obtain their reactions. Participant feedback not only contributes to the co-construction of the theory but also enables the researcher to make changes or modifications to theory as needed. Also important is to keep a journal of one's own experiences, feelings and difficulties while doing the research. It helps to put one's interpretations into context. Writing up a grounded theory is perhaps more difficult than writing up conventional research because there are no specific guidelines. What is important is capturing the essence of participants' stories while at the same time presenting those stories within a logical framework that gives insight and understanding into possible meanings. Remember to follow each analytic session with memos and diagrams because these become the inspiration and actual material upon which to base the writing.

Stories from the Field

Nicholas L. Holt

Introduction

The purpose of this story is to discuss three challenges I (Holt) experienced while building a grounded theory for my PhD thesis. The study examined talent development in elite adolescent soccer players. The issues chosen for analysis relate to theoretical sampling, concerns about forcing the data and falling into an analytic rut. The nature of these challenges and the judgements made to 'solve' them will be addressed.

Overview of analytic approach

Strauss and Corbin (1998) suggested that grounded theorists are not so much interested in individual actors but are more concerned with discovering patterns of action/interaction with changes in conditions, either internal or external to the process itself. Since I wanted to investigate the experiences of elite adolescent soccer players as they attempted to become professionals, the provision within grounded theory to focus on processes of change and interactions between individuals within structural organizations made it appealing. I chose Strauss and Corbin's version of grounded theory because it fitted with my philosophical approach and seemed to offer a series of guidelines that could be adapted to the logistical demands of my particular study.

The system of data management I employed was based on a progression from description, through conceptual ordering, to theorizing (Strauss and Corbin, 1998). Microanalysis and open coding were used to break the data down into discrete categories based on their properties and dimensions. Conceptual ordering, which is the finishing point for some qualitative studies, was the precursor for theorizing. Theorizing involved the formulation of ideas into a logical, systematic and explanatory scheme, at the heart of which was the interplay of making inductions (i.e. deriving concepts) and deductions (i.e. hypothesizing relationships between concepts). Axial and selective coding were used during this stage to put the data back together in a coherent manner.

Challenge 1: Theoretical sampling

One of the more predicable challenges I faced in conducting this study involved recruiting an appropriate sample. Although sampling traditionally tends to become more focused as research advances (Strauss and Corbin, 1998), I identified a specific group of participants at the start of the project. I wanted to interview adolescent soccer players who were competing at professional and/or international levels. I also wanted to speak to the coaches of these players. It was important that all the participants were operating in the most elite environments available to provide maximum insight into the developmental processes experienced in elite soccer.

As I was based in Canada, I recruited members of the Canadian under 20 and under 17 international teams, formally interviewing 20 players (average

age = 16.8 years), informally interviewing their coaches and observing behaviours during training camps. However, I was acutely aware that soccer was not a major sport in Canada, and that for my theory to be taken seriously I would need to go to a major soccer playing nation. Therefore, to increase the potential of developing a useful theory, I also sampled 14 young players (average age = 16.2 years) employed by professional soccer clubs in England and six professional youth-level coaches. Overall then, data collection consisted of three fieldwork trips – Montreal, Toronto and England – all completed during the summer of 2000.

In grounded theory the researcher engages in data analysis as soon as the first data are collected. However, each fieldwork trip involved intensive data collection with two or three interviews per day, so it was difficult to fully analyse data immediately. As such, I engaged in more extensive data analysis between fieldwork trips, but the interplay between data analysis and data collection (whereby analysis leads to new questions to ask in the field) was limited at best. Once all the fieldwork had been completed, I started to compare the Canadian and English data. I discovered that new questions arose as I became more involved in the complexities of data analysis. I realized that I needed to go *back into the field* but I could not afford another set of fieldwork trips. To solve this problem during the final stages of data analysis and theory development, six informal confirmatory interviews were conducted with older players (average age = 25.2 years) who possessed professional playing experience in both England and Canada. These 'second-round' interviews helped add to the depth and variability of the data collected and facilitated increased interaction between data collection and data analysis. These players were able to provide alternative examples by reflecting on their own experiences as youth soccer players, and they commented on my evolving theoretical interpretations.

Challenge 2: Forcing the data

It was important to separate the two data sets in order to analyse them for the purpose of cultural comparison. All Canadian data were analysed first using the techniques of microanalysis and open coding. Once the Canadian data had been accounted for, and a variety of descriptive concepts and categories developed, the English data were similarly (descriptively) analysed. As this point every effort was made to allow

concepts unique to a particular data set to emerge inductively from the data.

I was aware of the potential danger of forcing the English data into the pre-established concepts and categories and emerging conceptual framework created from the Canadian data. I was also aware that Glaser (1992) criticized the Straussian approach for forcing the data to produce 'full conceptual description' rather than theory grounded in the data. I felt this could be a potential flaw of my study. Constant comparison was a particularly important technique to avoid forcing the data because it facilitated the comparison of concepts *within* a particular data set as well as *between* the respective data sets. It was important to ensure that raw data extracts included in a concept within a particular data set invoked the same attributes and dimensions. It was also important to ensure that concepts were used consistently to describe the data across the data sets. Accordingly, if data did not fit with an existing concept, a new concept was created. As the study progressed 21 concepts were created, represented by nine subcategories and four main categories. Engaging in the constant comparative process enabled me to tease out subtleties in the data, ensure that concepts were located in the appropriate subcategory/category and identify differences between Canadian and English experiences.

Challenge 3: Falling into an analytic rut

One problem I did not anticipate occurred when I found myself falling into an analytic rut. Following the conceptual ordering of the data, the final theorizing step was undertaken. Theorizing is based on developing explanations between the data whereby concepts are connected (using statements of relationship) to form an explanatory theoretical framework. This moves the findings beyond conceptual ordering to theory. I found it very difficult to suddenly switch into a 'theory' mode from the 'descriptive' mode I had been working in. It seemed that I had focused too much on following the order of description – conceptualization – theory building, rather than approaching every step of the process with the intention of developing theory. This extract from my memos revealed the problem:

Although I've got a range of concepts, subcategories, and categories they don't seem to be coming together. I might be concentrating too much on describing what I think is going on, but the more I 'interpret' the further away from the data I get. I thought that by going through all the steps in the process, the theory would come together. Maybe I got some of the description wrong (maybe I missed a step?). Go back and check.

Following the recording of this memo I engaged in a circular process of going back to the raw data and juggling certain concepts and subcategories, hoping that the connections between the data would be revealed. And thus the analytic rut deepened because I was still thinking descriptively (that is, I was concerned with ensuring that the appropriate raw data had been coded into the appropriate concept). I somehow expected the theory to come together of its own volition as long as I got the description right. In fact, I realized that I was working and thinking too much at the descriptive level, rather than looking at the bigger picture and attempting to make theoretical connections. I reflected that perhaps because I was a neophyte grounded theorist a more descriptive account would be 'safer' (and easier to get past my committee!). But of course, theory cannot be developed by description alone. Fortunately, my supervisor (Juliet Corbin) encouraged me to use a range of analytic tools to move beyond this analytic rut.

Inherent within the grounded theory coding procedures are certain techniques that enable the analyst to make theoretical interpretations and form statements of relationship between concepts. I fully embraced these techniques in an attempt to break out of my analytic rut. The data were ordered to form a storyline that explained what was apparently going on. Diagrams were used to visually examine relationships between categories. I reviewed and assessed my memos and notes intermittently and compared them with the emerging theory. The emerging theory was also compared with previous talent development research to illuminate plausible connections. Finally, using the comparative techniques of 'flip-flop' and 'systematic comparison of two or more phenomena' (Strauss and Corbin, 1998: 94–5), I compared adolescent soccer players' careers to the career of a lawyer I knew.

The techniques helped change my mode of thinking which subsequently enabled me to move out of my analytic rut and helped me to develop a better understanding of factors that underpinned the pursuit of a soccer career. For example, by comparing soccer players to lawyers I considered that a lawyer learns his/her trade during adulthood, whereas a soccer player learns during childhood and adolescence. I went on to consider: 'Do lawyers dream about the law during childhood? What factors motivate them to study late nights? When will they be rewarded for their many years of training?' I then compared these thoughts to the demands facing adolescent soccer players. In doing so I was able to attain creative analytic insights at a more theoretical level as I sought to link categories together as opposed to simply describing concepts. Such 'far out' comparisons mirror the classic work of sociologist E.C. Hughes, who made comparisons between 'professionals' like psychiatrists and prostitutes (cf. Strauss and Corbin, 1998).

Conclusions

In the example presented here I learned the importance of theoretical sampling and maintaining close contact with participants throughout the study. The 'second round' participants were useful in helping confirm or refute some of my interpretations as I attempted to build theory. My concerns about forcing the English data into the Canadian findings were allayed by relying on the appropriate use of the constant comparative method. Finally, I was able to break out of an analytic rut by embracing a range of analytic tools that helped change my mode of thinking from the descriptive to the more conceptual and theoretical.

I learned that even though theorizing was the final step in developing grounded theory, theorizing can and maybe should occur along every step of the research process. I had spent a lot of time working on identifying and categorizing a list of unique concepts and categories rather than seeking relationships between the data. With hindsight, I reflected that I could have engaged in theorizing rather than descriptive analysis as soon as the first data were collected. I realized that good research is reflexive and good researchers adapt to the demands of the situation. Talking through problems with colleagues and working where there is an atmosphere of support certainly help, but it is clear that research constantly requires judgements. Although some problems can be anticipated and planned for, others can only come to light in the process of doing research. It seems that the lesson is to anticipate as many problems as possible while remaining flexible, reflexive and responsive to difficult decisions as they arise.

Annotated bibliography

Charmaz, K. (1990) 'Discovering chronic illness: using grounded theory', *Social Science Medicine*, 30: 1161–72.

This article demonstrates the range of insights and understandings that a researcher can gain on a subject, here chronic illness, using the grounded theory approach. It is also an excellent example of how to write up one's grounded theory findings using a blend of theoretical formulations and words of participants.

Charmaz, K. (2000) 'Grounded theory: objectivist and constructivist methods', in N. Denzin and Y. S. Lincoln (eds), *Handbook of Qualitative Research*. Thousand Oaks, CA: pp. 509–35.

This chapter presents a constructionist view of grounded theory while at the same time retaining the method's essential features. It is an important chapter because it shows how other authors conceptualize and think about grounded theory.

Clarke, A. (2004, in press) *Situational Analyses: Grounded Theory After the Postmodern Turn*. Thousand Oaks, CA: Sage.

This book takes grounded theory methodology beyond constructionism. It addresses differences and complexities of social life articulated from a postmodern perspective. The book provides another option for thinking about grounded theory and brings it into the postmodern era while retaining the theory building foundation.

Creswell, J.W. and Brown, N.L. (1992) 'How chairpersons enhance faculty research: a grounded theory study', *Review of Higher Education*, 16(1): 41–62.

This is an example of a theory generated using grounded theory methodology. Again it is useful to study the article in terms of how findings are presented in an article format.

Glaser, B. (1992) *Basics of Grounded Theory Analysis*. Mill Valley, CA: Sociology Press.

An alternative approach to grounded theory written in response to Strauss and Corbin's (1990) book.

Holt, N.L. and Dunn, J.G.H. (2004, in press) 'Toward a grounded theory of the psychosocial competencies and environmental conditions associated with becoming a professional soccer player', *Journal of Applied Sport Psychology*, 4.

This article summarizes the thesis referred to in the Stories from the Field section above. It gives a detailed description of the theory that emerged and an account of how certain techniques associated with grounded theory were used to produce it.

Patton, M.Q. (2002) *Qualitative Research and Evaluation Methods*, 3rd edn. Thousand Oaks, CA: Sage.

This is my favourite general book about qualitative research. It's well written, complete and charming. It doesn't detail how to do analysis but it does take the reader through the entire research process.

Strauss, A. and Corbin, J. (1998) *Basics of Qualitative Research*, 2nd edn. Thousand Oaks, CA: Sage (1st edn, 1990).

This book now in its second edition is a bestseller. It provides a set of procedures and techniques that can be used to analyse qualitative data whether the aim is description or theory development. The procedures and techniques presented in this book are meant as a guide and not as a set of directives and should be used flexibly.

Further references

Denzin, N.K and Lincoln, Y.S (1994) 'Introduction', in N.K. Denzin and Y.S. Lincoln (eds), *Handbook of Qualitative Research*. Thousand Oaks, CA: Sage, pp. 1–17.
Hage, J. (1972) Techniques and Problems of Theory Construction in Sociology. New York: John Wiley & Sons.
Glaser, B. and Strauss, A. (1967) *The Discovery of Grounded Theory*. Chicago: Aldine.

6

ETHICAL RESPONSIBILITY IN SOCIAL RESEARCH

Heather Piper
Education and Social Research Institute, Manchester Metropolitan University, UK
Helen Simons
School of Education, University of Southampton, UK

Key concepts

Helen Simons

Ethical principles are abstract and it is not always obvious how they should be applied in given situations ... Some of the most intractable ethical problems arise from conflicts among principles and the necessity of trading one against the other. The balancing of such principles in concrete situations is the ultimate ethical act. (House, 1993: 168)

Introduction

Ethics in research is a situated practice as the quotation above implies. Ethical decisions are the result of a weighing up of a myriad of factors in the specific complex social and political situations in which we conduct research. Frequently sets of principles are drawn up to guide our actions in the field as well as protect the rights of participants in research. In some disciplines research proposals have to pass through ethical committees which judge not only whether the research is sensitive to human 'subjects' but in many cases also whether the methodology is sound and appropriate for the research in question. This chapter outlines different ways of conceiving how to act ethically in social research and highlights the moral dilemmas we may encounter. It first outlines the traditional key concepts associated with conducting ethical social science research such as informed consent, confidentiality and anonymity and publication access. Secondly, it briefly examines the increasing trend in publication of ethical principles and guidelines by professional organizations and the institutionalization of ethical committees. Thirdly, the concept of situated ethics is elaborated. Finally the

role of the researcher is examined as ethical guidelines more often than not pay more attention to the rights of participants than the ethical rights *of* and/or danger *for* the researcher. Ethical practice is often defined as 'doing no harm'. In this chapter we take the view that we should also aspire to do 'good', in other words to conduct research that benefits participants in positive ways.

Informed consent

With some exceptions, those who argue that certain participant observation studies could never be conducted if informed consent was the norm, most writers of social science ethics adhere to a concept of informed consent. This means that those interviewed or observed should give their permission in full knowledge of the purpose of the research and the consequences for them of taking part. Frequently, a written informed consent form has to be signed by the intending participant. However achieving informed consent is not a straightforward process. First, there is often a tension between 'fully' informing and gaining access, as outlining all the potential consequences may limit access. Secondly it may not always be possible to foresee the consequences in advance. A more appropriate concept is 'rolling informed consent', that is the renegotiation of informed consent once the research is underway and a more realistic assessment of the risks to participants can be made. Thirdly, informed consent is needed from each person interviewed and/or observed, not simply the major gatekeeper in an institution or project. Fourthly, there is the difficulty of gaining informed consent from groups where there may be peer pressure to participate, or from individuals, for example those with learning difficulties, or children, in contexts where the adult has authority and/or responsibility for their behaviour or assessment.

Confidentiality and anonymity

The second common assumption in ethical social science practice is confidentiality in the process of conducting the research and the anonymization of individuals in reporting. These are often linked as though the second, that is to say using pseudonyms in reporting, justifies the reporting of information obtained in confidence. However, the two concepts require separate consideration. Confidentiality is a principle that allows people not only to talk in confidence, but also to refuse to allow publication of any material that they think might harm them in any way. Anonymization is a procedure to offer some protection of privacy and confidentiality. Though helpful in the attempt not to identify people, anonymization cannot guarantee that harm may not occur. How people will react to research reports cannot be foreseen in advance. The context, unless massively disguised, often reveals clues to identity even when names and places are changed. Moreover, not all people in a research study can be anonymized and the number to whom this applies is often more than we frequently envisage. In such situations, a sound ethical principle is to seek clearance from the individuals concerned for use of the data in a specific context or report.

There are some situations, in bereavement counselling for instance, where the argument has been made that in order to help individuals cope with the grieving process, it is important to keep the person who has died 'alive', so to speak, visibly and through discussion using their real names and faces. To anonymize in this context is tantamount to a double death. A second reason for not anonymizing is to encourage the development of ethical reflexivity between the participants and the researcher, through a process of honest, open deliberation of the issues and possible consequences so that the outcome is morally and ethically defensible to all. Finally, anonymization may be inappropriate in those forms of action and participatory research where participants, individually or jointly, research their own practice or policy context. In such contexts naming is important to acknowledge an individual's contribution to generating knowledge.

Prepublication access

The principle of giving participants the opportunity to read a research report before it goes public appears on first sight to adhere to the principle of respect for persons. However, much depends upon the intent. If it is merely to warn participants of critical elements so they will not be shocked when a report goes public, this offers more protection to the researcher than to participants. If it offers an opportunity for the participants to comment upon and possibly add to the report, this demonstrates greater respect for potential difference of interpretation and the right to a fair voice.

Ethical guidelines

Many social researchers draw up ethical principles and procedures reflecting the above concerns and based upon traditional research ethics of duties, rights and analysis of harm and benefit. Others embody in such statements democratic values of justice, fairness and respect for privacy of persons and public knowledge. For example, Simons (1989) and, in relation to children, Alderson and Morrow (2003).

Increasingly professional associations have also written guidelines to facilitate ethical practice. Some aspire to set standards to judge the quality of the research. Others are couched in terms of codes and rules. Yet others prefer statements of principle which offer guidance for ethical decision-making and a basis from which possible codes and rules might be developed. Such guidelines traditionally embody a normative ethics – concerned with how people ought to behave (Newman and Brown, 1996).

Ethical guidelines vary on a number of other dimensions, such as the extent to which they do or do not make a distinction between ethical-moral and scientific-methodological issues and the quasi-legal language in which they are sometimes written. Often there is a lack of clarity between ethical and legal issues. For example, treating participants 'fairly and equally' is written into the Human Rights Act and is now a legal imperative. It still remains an ethical issue, however, how 'treating fairly' is interpreted.

Ethical committees

Ethical committees have long been established in the field of medicine and increasingly they are being set up in the social sciences and other professional fields. They exist to ensure that researchers have considered the ethical issues that are likely to arise and have developed protocols to protect participants from harm. In many cases such committees also act as the guardians of what is to count as research methodology. Some have claimed (Furedi, 2002) that ethical committees are in practice acting as gatekeepers of methodology and we are focused on preventing litigation than ensuring ethical practice. As a consequence they may inhibit freedom to research, especially topics that may be sensitive. Where this happens, their function has become part of the culture of managerialism, and is not necessarily to do with ethics at all.

Situated ethics

Principles provide a shared frame of reference and are useful to guide ethical decision-making. However, they are abstract statements of intent and cannot be followed simply as rules. Ethical practice depends on how the principles are interpreted and enacted in the precise socio-political context of the research. For examples of such concrete ethical decisions in practice see Simons and Usher (2000) and Lee-Treweek and Linkogle (2000).

The application of general principles and codes of practice nearly always stems from a rational, reasoning approach to the consideration of individuals' rights, duties and obligations of different groups. With the growth of feminist research, postmodern thinking, participatory and democratic practices, a different concept of ethics is being invoked – the ethics of care (Gilligan, 1982; Noddings, 1984). This is more concerned with relationships, people's lives and context than universal laws and principles. This approach has much in common with the ethical discourse of social justice (House, 1993) and the redistribution of power in research and evaluation relationships (MacDonald, 1976). It also has affinities with forms of participatory research which encourage participants to develop their own ethical practice in the groups and contexts in which they work and an ethics which takes into account the specific cultural differences between people.

Situated ethics, in summary, acknowledges the uniqueness and complexity of each situation and any ethical decision needs to take cognisance of the precise way in which many of the above factors are played out in the specific socio-political context. To what should the researcher appeal?

Some have suggested the ultimate recourse is to one's own conscience. However, to be justifiable as an ethical practice, this would need to be accompanied by a disciplined self-reflexive approach to one's own behaviour. Others have recommended

broadening the reference point. Soltis (1990) suggests that an issue/situation be considered from three different perspectives: of the person (the researcher in this case), the profession and the public, noting the different dilemmas that occur for each. Newman and Brown (1996) offer a framework for ethical decision-making that includes intuition, rules and codes, principles and theory, personal values and beliefs and action, listing a few questions to ask of oneself in regard to each. This may appear overly rationalistic. However given the uncertainty, complexity and finely tuned professional judgement we have to make in the 'ethical moment' (Usher, 2000), it draws our attention to a range of issues we may need to integrate into our consciousness to inform ethical decision-making in research.

Ethics for the researcher

Ethical principles and guidelines tend to focus on protecting participants from harm or in some cases on empowering them. Rarely is so much ethical attention paid to the researcher. However, this is changing as awareness grows about the risks and ethical danger a researcher may face studying certain contexts. Lee-Treweek and Linkogle (2000) make a strong case for redressing the predominant focus of ethics by considering the ethical dangers that can confront a social researcher in field situations. They provide a framework for considering ethical issues by drawing distinctions between risk and emotional, physical and ethical danger. It is only the ethics that concern us here, that is to say the risks associated with making judgements in the field, though there may be links with emotional – and even physical – danger in facing ethical dilemmas. Making wrong judgements about what to study or how to study social life has consequences for how one's research is seen by others. Ethical danger is perhaps at its most critical, say Lee-Treweek and Linkogle (2000: 5–6), when studying unfamiliar cultures, where there is the risk of unconsciously breaching cultural norms through the lens of one's own, and when studying extremist groups. It is sometimes for this reason, or in order to study groups for which one might not gain research access, that covert participant observation is employed (Bulmer, 1982). In some forms of research, however, such as naturalistic or phenomenological inquiry, deceptive research practices are inherently unacceptable (Lincoln, 1990).

Implications for research design

While it is rarely possible to anticipate all the ethical dilemmas you may encounter in doing research, there are a number of steps you can take in your research design to indicate that you are thinking ethically:

- Consider at the outset what ethical issues might arise (numerous questions and frameworks exist in the literature to facilitate such thinking), and think through, in one or two instances, how these would be addressed.
- Be conscious of what kind of ethics you personally aspire to and what values you hold in relation to the research topic.
- Think through the ethical implications of any methodology you choose – for example, does it respect participants' rights? Does it balance this with the responsibility for generating public knowledge? Does it provide scope for participants' ethical development if this is part of your purpose? Does it honour those who are less enfranchised? Does it respect cultural, gender and age differences?
- Draw up a brief set of ethical procedures to guide data collection and dissemination. This is especially important if you have to submit your research proposal to an ethical committee. It will not be possible to encapsulate all the ethical dilemmas that may arise, but it will demonstrate that you have thought about the issues and have some reference points for acting ethically in the field. Indicate that you are working within the ethical guidelines (where they exist) of your department, profession or university.
- Pilot any potential methodological tools to ensure that questions are unobtrusive (though do not equate this with non-challenging) and culture, gender and age sensitive.
- In your ethical procedures indicate how you will maintain respect for persons while making research knowledge public. Include a consideration of issues such as non-coercion (do you require an opt-out clause?), potential benefit to participants (what might they gain from this research? What might they lose?) and potential harm (what might be the consequences and for whom?).
- Think through how and in what form you might report in-depth experiences of individuals and what rights you will give them in this process.

- Become familiar with any legislation that exists in relation to your topic and act within it.
- Decide what position you will adopt on informed consent, confidentiality and anonymity, control over data and access before publication. Decisions on these issues will to some extent be determined by the choice you make as to whether you prefer to be guided by an ethical tradition that favours universal laws and principles, one that is more relational and situation specific or one that is democratic in intent and/or participatory in process and outcome.

Stories from the Field

Heather Piper

The story told here – of a project commissioned by the Royal Society for the Protection of Animals (RSPCA) – was chosen not only for the ethical issues it raised at the time but also after the research process was completed (Piper et al., 2001). In particular, this choice of project illustrates how it is not always possible or necessarily desirable to have a pre-prepared blueprint for ethical research practice. The example is one of situated ethics and ethical reflexivity – two concepts raised in the previous section – where ethical issues are considered to be a collaborative venture, to be resolved in a particular context at a particular time.

This research project attempted to identify why children harm animals in response to concern that such violence was apparently on the increase. The steering group comprised mainly colleagues from within the university (including teacher and social work educators) plus an RSPCA officer. During the planning stages many potential ethical problems were raised. Of particular concern was the proper response to young people stating they had harmed an animal because they had been, or were being, abused. This expectation stemmed from an assumption among some in the RSPCA and elsewhere, which resulted from research in America that supports this claim (Ressler et al., 1988). There was disagreement in the steering group about what the researchers should do if faced with such an admission. Most thought that children claiming they were being abused should be dealt with by following child protection procedures, that is reporting the claim to the relevant professional responsible, but one member differed and was quite adamant that all such information should be treated as confidential. This led to lengthy discussions where many previously hidden ethical differences emerged. These included differing views on confidentiality if children divulged harming behaviour, safety issues, privileging children over animals and vice versa, and the differing professional socialization of teachers, social workers and RSPCA officers.

The issue was not resolved in one meeting. I consulted with members of the university ethics committee in an attempt to learn from the experiences of others. Searching the literature indicated that many others were similarly confused about this issue. The matter was finally resolved by preparing a briefing paper for wider circulation, identifying literature that indicated the reporting of abuse as a legal imperative, not just a moral or ethical one. This allowed a way forward, even though not everyone was happy. We agreed that all interviews would begin with the statement 'I can promise confidentiality on anything you may tell me except on anything that leads me to be concerned for your own or another's safety, in which case I must do whatever is necessary to ensure that you or the person being harmed is protected.' This example perhaps serves to demonstrate not only the difficulty in getting people with opposing views to agree, but also how once a resolution has been found, ethical issues generally become enshrined in law and therefore are no longer the subject of discussion (see Masson, 2000).

As it transpired, during the period of the research no child or young person made any claim that they had been harmed themselves. Thus in a sense the lengthy preparation for this eventuality had been unnecessary, although the issue clearly needed airing. Perhaps significantly the main concerns of the RSPCA officer differed in certain respects from those of other contributors. She was more concerned with the researcher becoming aware of animal abuse but not reporting it to *her*. For her, this was a legal *and* moral imperative. Again a lengthy exchange took place. The RSPCA representative was finally persuaded that it would be impossible to conduct research that asked children for examples of their harming behaviour towards animals, only to immediately report them for telling us. We would be acting in bad faith, would risk disrepute, and children, schools and families would understandably be angry and likely to accuse us of coercion. We ensured that all information that was passed to the RSPCA either verbally or in report format was totally anonymized

so it would be impossible to identify not only an individual but also a group or school, in terms of who had said what.

Again, although a way forward was identified, not everyone was content. Indeed, the particular solution we reached perhaps suggests that some of us privilege people over animals in unquestioning ways. This was not an approach exemplified by many of the young people we contacted, 'We need to learn how to look after animals at school . . . teach how they are just like people'. As an aside it is perhaps worth adding that I had underestimated my responses to hearing the stories of children harming animals. I had rather naively thought that I would be quite hardened to this, whereas I knew from previous experience that I would not be hardened to hearing children describe their own abuse. In the event it was difficult not to be affected by hearing young people describe in the first person how they fastened cats to railway lines and then watched them die, and tied fireworks to cats' tails and then set them alight. Such accounts did not lead me to want to report the young people to the RSPCA, but in a few extreme cases it became apparent that the young people were disturbed in various ways. Fortunately these accounts took place with other professionals present (often their teachers) who were in a position to know what help was already available; otherwise I might have felt compelled to pass on my worries even if not the detail. On reading interview transcripts some colleagues have questioned whether the children were speaking the truth or saying some of these things for effect. This is impossible to know for sure, as it is always impossible to know whether what one is told in the research process is truthful, but there was little doubt in my mind or the minds of other adults present that we were hearing accounts of events that had occurred as described. Yet the young people would often be shocked by each others' accounts, and demonstrated an 'ethical' code of conduct of their own that differed from the majority view: 'I'd kill anyone who harmed my dog'.

Another issue considered early on was whether young people could give consent to their own involvement in the research process or whether their parents or carers would need to give permission on their behalf. Again, this is an issue where there is considerable disagreement, many feeling that it should be parents who give permission. Whereas the United Nations Convention on the Rights of the Child agreed in 1995 that children should make their own such decisions, it was only in 2000 in the UK that the Human Rights Act which incorporates this view actually came into force. In this particular research project schools did not feel the need to gain specific informed consent from parents. In most other research I have conducted, the majority of schools have asked me to write a letter which they then distribute to various classes or particular young people and I only see those children and young people who have brought back a signed letter of parental consent. Unusually, this did not happen. Schools distributed questionnaires during PSHE (Personal, Social and Health Education) lessons and these were completed during the lesson. This would often then be followed up in another PSHE lesson with a group interview, usually led by the teacher, which was recorded and then passed to me for transcription and analysis. In some instances I, or another researcher, would carry out the group interview, but a teacher would usually (although not always) be present. The teachers involved clearly thought this was an interesting and appropriate topic for them to use in this way and many volunteered to be involved in any future similar work.

Again, there is always the possibility that children and young people are unlikely to give accurate accounts of their violent behaviour if their teacher (or indeed the researcher) is present, regardless of conditional promises of confidentiality – but most children and young people found their own way around this difficulty. The majority of harming stories were all told in the third person: 'I saw someone throw a bag of gerbils from the top of the flats.' Either we were to believe that the majority of our sample had witnessed harming while not taking part themselves, or else we were left with the more likely scenario that sometimes they were describing their own behaviour. However, in terms of any ethical responsibility, such information could only be dealt with as a third-person account.

Ethical dilemmas continued to emerge throughout the research process and did not end with the practical aspects of the research. At meetings with others from the RSPCA (and conversations since the project ended) we became aware that a joint initiative with the National Society for the Prevention of Cruelty to Children (NSPCC) was being planned. These initiatives (which were likely to attract considerable publicity and funding) were premised on the assumption that all violence is linked and that if a child harms an animal they will either have been abused or will have witnessed severe violence within their home environment. However, the findings of the research project were not compatible with these assumptions. Instead, it became apparent that *many* children (depending on the definition of harming applied) harmed animals, not just the few known to the RSPCA and other services. There were occasions where the transmission of this message from the research was inhibited by a variety of means. For example, during the research process, groups of adults (trainee teachers, social workers and others) had admitted to harming animals as children and, given the potential significance of this, we had hoped to explore this further. We wished to distribute a questionnaire at a joint NSPCA and RSPCA conference where children harming animals was to be discussed, but the conference organizers prevented this at the last moment. As the event was partially televised and we were taken by surprise, we were ill equipped to argue for the public's right to know. The research received a great deal of media coverage that has led to frequent invitations from the media to appear on various radio or TV programmes. But the story journalists (and others) wanted to hear was not the more nuanced one we wished to present (supported by our research) but rather the sensational one that argues that damaged children become damaged adults and in some instances mass murderers. As a result, many invitations to appear on such programmes were withdrawn at the negotiation stage. It has also been much more difficult than usual to get the results published in academic journals. This is an example of the ethical and professional danger indicated by Lee-Treweek and Linkogle (2000). The papers, which argue against a simplistic application of dubious causal explanations, have been rejected by (mainly) American journals, and it is only relatively recently that a couple have finally made it into print (Piper, 2003a; Piper, 2003b).

Annotated bibliography

Many books on qualitative research also include chapters on ethics which cover and extend many of the issues discussed in this chapter. Only books focusing entirely on ethics are included in this Annotated Bibliography.

Alderson, P. and Morrow, V. (2003) *Ethics, Social Research and Consulting with Young People*. London: Barnados.

An extensive discussion of ethics in research with children and young people, raising a series of questions and dilemmas for the researcher in relation to traditional ethics, recent legislation and ethical practice.

Burgess, R.G. (ed.) (1989) *The Ethics of Educational Research*. Lewes: Falmer Press.

Explores ethical dimensions in different forms of educational research such as case study, action research and quantitative research, and in different contexts. Several chapters suggest specific principles and procedures to guide ethical decision-making in practice.

Lee-Treweek, G. and Linkogle, S. (eds) (2000) *Danger in the Field: Risks and Ethics in Social Research*. London and New York: Routledge.

Focuses through case examples on how researchers have faced danger in the field. Only one section refers to actual ethical danger (the others being physical, emotional and professional). Important for drawing our attention to the need to consider ethics for the researcher as well as for participants.

Mauthner, M., Birch, M., Jessop, J. and Miller, T. (eds) (2002) *Ethics in Qualitative Research*. London: Sage.

Examines the theories and intentions of ethics in the 'lived experiences' of the research process by a group of feminist researchers conducting qualitative research largely in family and household studies.

Newman, D.L. and Brown, R.D. (1996) *Applied Ethics for Program Evaluation*. London and Thousand Oaks, CA: Sage.

A thorough exploration of ethics and morality, ethics and methodology, differences between standards, codes, rules, principles and theories, in the evaluation of social programmes.

Oliver, P. (2003) *The Student's Guide to Research Ethics*. Maidenhead: Open University Press.

Explores ethical issues the research student may encounter at each stage of the research process from design to publication and dissemination.

Punch, M. (1986) *The Politics and Ethics of Fieldwork*. London: Sage.

Focuses on participant observational studies in sociology and anthropology, exploring the ethical dilemmas and hidden moral agendas the fieldworker encounters in close relationships in the field.

Simons, H. and Usher, R. (2000) *Situated Ethics in Educational Research*. London: Routledge/Falmer.

Makes the case for ethics as a situated practice in different research traditions and contexts – feminist, postmodern, evaluation, participatory, image based. Each chapter is case-based exploring the particular ethical issues that arose in unique socio-political settings including those of race, postcolonial, and healthcare.

Further references

Bulmer, M. (ed.) (1982) *Social Research Ethics*. London: Macmillan.
Furedi, F. (2002) 'Don't rock the research boat', *Times Higher Educational Supplement*, 11 January: 20.
Gilligan, C. (1982) *In a Different Voice*. Cambridge, MA: Harvard University Press.
House, E.R. (1993) *Professional Evaluation: Social Impact and Political Consequences*. Newbury Park, CA: Sage.
Lincoln, Y.S. (1990) 'Toward a categorical imperative for qualitative research', in E.W. Eisner and A. Peshkin (eds), *Qualitative Inquiry in Education: The Continuing Debate*. New York: Teachers College, Columbia University, pp. 277–95.

MacDonald, B. (1976) 'Evaluation of and the control of education', in D. Tawney (ed.), *Curriculum Evaluation Today: Trends and Implications*. London: Macmillan.

Masson, J. (2000) 'Researching Children's Perspectives: legal issues', in A. Lewis and G. Lindsay (eds), *Researching Children's Perspectives*. Buckingham and Philadelphia, PA: Open University Press, pp. 34–44.

Noddings, N. (1984) *Caring: A Feminine Approach to Ethics and Moral Education*. Berkeley, CA: University of California Press.

Piper, H. (2003a) 'Children and young people harming animals: intervention through PSHE?', *Research Papers in Education*, 18(2): 197–213.

Piper, H. (2003b) 'The linkage of animal abuse with interpersonal violence: a sheep in wolf's clothing?', *Journal of Social Work*, 3(2): 161–77.

Piper, H., Johnson, M., Myers, S. and Pritchard, J. (2001) *Why Do People Harm Animals? Attitudes of Children and Young People*. Manchester: Manchester Metropolitan University; Horsham, West Sussex: RSPCA.

Ressler, R.K., Burgess, A.W. and Douglas, J.E. (1988) *Sexual Homicide: Patterns and motives*. Lanham, MD: Lexington Books.

Simons, H. (1989) 'Ethics of case study in educational research and evaluation', in R.G. Burgess (ed.), *The Ethics of Educational Research*. Lewes: Falmer Press, pp. 114–40.

Soltis, J.F. (1990) 'The ethics of qualitative research', in E.W. Eisner and A. Peshkin, (eds), *Qualitative Inquiry in Education: The Continuing Debate*. New York: Teachers College, Columbia University, pp. 247–57.

Usher, R. (2000) 'Deconstructive happening, ethical moment', in H. Simons and R. Usher (eds), *Situated Ethics in Educational Research*. London: Routledge/Falmer, pp. 162–85.

PART III

RESEARCHING FOR IMPACT

Introduction

All the chapters in this section foreground issues of power. The three chapters on feminist, critical race theory and queer theory/lesbian and gay perspectives focus on difference and raise issues in relation to power and knowledge. The voices of marginalized groups (their standpoints) are celebrated and the authority of the traditional constructors of knowledge is questioned. These chapters share with the chapter on action research, which follows, a concern with resisting oppression and promoting social justice. Practitioners at the centre of action research often need to negotiate their role carefully in relation to others involved including those perceived to be in positions of greater power such as managers/administrators and 'expert researchers'. At the same time they need to be confident that the outcomes of such research, while contributing to improving practices in their own setting, will be of value to others and treated respectfully.

The final two chapters in Part III, on policy analysis and sponsored evaluation (often called programme evaluation), engage with power issues at a different level. Their focus is on the analysis and evaluation of policies and initiatives of governments which frame social practices and issue directives, and which are increasingly influenced by processes of globalization and by the copycat phenomenon that Blackmore calls 'travelling policies'. In sponsored evaluations, which by definition are undertaken on behalf of a sponsoring body such as a government department or an international body, power issues

enter the terrain of the research itself, inherent in the relationship between the independent evaluator and the commissioning sponsor with a vested interest in the outcome. Evaluation research also places the evaluators in a position of power vis-à-vis the team responsible for implementing the programme or initiative, so that evaluators need to take considerable care to set up procedures that enable them to operate ethically while still remaining independent so that they can act effectively in the interests of the public whose taxes have funded the initiative.

The chapters in this section all deal with approaches to research that are designed to make an impact, whether on personal practice, national policy or society as a whole. In this sense none of them conforms to the traditional model of research as an objective, impartial set of procedures aimed at uncovering facts and 'the truth.' In reality, none of the chapters in this book supports an approach based on such a naive epistemology; nevertheless the chapters in Part III challenge these notions more directly and more fundamentally. Whereas some of the approaches put forward in chapters in Part VIII are more radical in their epistemological and ontological assumptions, they tend to be less engaged with research participants and hence more detached from the field of study than the chapters in Part III. The exception is sponsored evaluation which often adopts a more traditional model of relationships with programme participants and sponsors; here too however, researchers often undertake evaluation work because it offers the opportunity of making an impact through influencing policy development.

CHAPTER

7

FEMINIST METHODOLOGIES

Diane Burns
Sheffield City Council, UK
Melanie Walker
School of Education, University of Sheffield, UK

Key concepts

Melanie Walker

Feminist research has had a significant impact over the last three decades. It has contributed to the development of many key methodological ideas, for example standpoint, positionality and reflexivity, while also foregrounding critical enquiries into gender, gender relations and society. Feminism and feminist research has been at the forefront of challenging the silencing of women's voices in society and research and in challenging a narrow, gendered kind of science, which cast women in passive and subordinate roles and excluded them from scientific practices by virtue of them being 'emotional' and hence incapable of 'reason'. Crucially, feminist research aspires to be for women as much as it is about women.

Feminist research is thus always more than a matter of method, and raises philosophical issues of ontology (one's world view and how this shapes what can be known about the world and indeed what it means to be a full human being) and epistemology (what counts as knowledge and ways of knowing). Reinharz (1992: 243–4) advances ten claims for feminist research, including that: feminism is a perspective, not a research method; feminist research involves an ongoing criticism of non-feminist scholarship; feminist research is guided by feminist theory; and feminist research aims to create social change. Weiner (1994) offers three principles as a guide: feminist research involves a critique of unexamined assumptions about women and dominant forms of knowing and doing; it involves a commitment to improve life chances for girls and women; and it is concerned with developing equitable professional and personal practices. It is thus critical, political and praxis-oriented.

Approaches to feminist research involve understanding feminist theories, or *feminisms*, as there are different theoretical understandings of the causes of gendered oppressions and gender inequalities and therefore different proposed analyses and solutions. *Feminist theories* seek to explain, challenge and hence change the existing patterns of relations between the sexes. The social construction of gender and gendered consciousness – how we understand ourselves to be women and men, girls and boys – is at the centre of feminist inquiry. Research might therefore be described as feminist when femaleness and maleness and the differences and dominations between and within them are made a central feature of research questions, conceptualization and analysis. What feminist methodologies have in common is a shared commitment to drawing attention to the deep and irreducible connections between knowledge and power (privilege), and to making problematic gender in society and social institutions in order to develop theories that advance practices of gender justice. Aspiring feminist researchers need to read in the area of feminist theories both to generate an appropriate conceptual framework to guide their choice of research questions and methods and as a means to reflect on and even challenge their own taken-for-granted assumptions about gender relations (see Acker, 1994; Ahmed et al., 2000; Delamont, 2003; Nicholson, 1997; Weedon, 1987, 1999; Weiner, 1994).

Feminist methodologies have also been shaped by developments in *feminist epistemology* and there is some overlap with the historical emergence of diverse feminist theories. The challenge has been to traditional epistemologies founded on the search for certainty and a refusal of the personal and the political (see Griffiths, 1995: chapter 4). Sandra Harding

(1987) has identified three epistemological positions: feminist empiricism, feminist standpoint and feminist postmodernism. These epistemological positions shape ways of seeing the world and hence our views of knowledge. In the 1960s and 1970s *feminist empiricism* was characterized by a critique of male-centred and hence partial knowledge about social reality. Research was criticized for reflecting masculine cultural values and presenting male experiences as universal, as Dale Spender (1982: 24) declaimed in relation to higher education curricula:

> Women have been kept 'off the record' in most, if not all, branches of knowledge by the simple process of men naming the world as it appears to them. They have taken themselves as the starting point, defined themselves as central, and then proceeded to describe the rest of the world in relation to themselves.

The response to such exclusion and distortion was to add women into research to eliminate sexist bias from the research process in order to produce value-free (objective) knowledge (see, for example, Eichler, 1988). The point was to begin including girls' and women's experiences and their *voices*. The notion of voice is then central to feminist methodologies.

However, the idea of 'non-sexist' research failed to problematize the role the researcher, her experiences and her consciousness plays in theorizing, explanation and the production of social knowledge. Regarding her second stage of *feminist standpoint*, Harding criticized the goal of objectivity in traditional research as masculinist; the pursuit of this goal has obscured the partiality (and privileged positioning) of those constructing the knowledge. Harding claimed that women have a broader perspective on social reality because of their understanding of their own gendered oppression (their standpoint), and that the subjectivity of the researcher is crucial in the research design and must be taken into account in her interpretation. What then follows is the argument that there can be no certain grounds for belief.

This then leads to the key concept of *positionality*, that is the implication of the researcher in the production of knowledge and a breaking down of the masculinist separation of the private [world of the researcher] through the public [activity of research]. Lennon and Whitford (1994: 2) summarize: 'It is not simply due to bad practice that masculine subjects have allowed their subjectivity to imprint on their product. Such imprinting is inevitable. Knowledge bears the mark of its producer.' Stanley and Wise (1993) argue that knowledge produced from an acknowledged standpoint is less distorted, more visible and hence revisable than knowledge which erases its partiality. Others like Mies (1983) argue that when the standpoint is that of the excluded and marginalized, the researcher has a kind of 'double vision' which incorporates both her own view and that of the dominant so that her account is more complete and less partial. Harding argues that feminist standpoint generates the best feminist research and scholarship because of three methodological features:

1 a focus on women's experiences, new empirical and theoretical resources;
2 new purpose for social science research, to be transformative for women;
3 new subject matter of inquiry: locating the researcher in the same critical plane as the research (from Harding, 1987: 9).

An early example of these three precepts in action is Ann Oakley's research (1981: 41) into the experiences of mothers. She argued that conventions about the uninvolved interviewer did not stand up to scrutiny in researching women's lives. Women's voices are heard in research, when 'the relationship of interviewer and interviewee is non-hierarchical and when the interviewer is prepared to invest his or her own personal identity in the relationship'. This in turn demands a critical *reflexivity* regarding the assumptions we bring to our research and how we conduct our research. This is not uncontested in feminist research. Daphne Patai (1994), for example, deplores the obsession with self-reflexivity, while Acker (1994) raises questions about how the researcher can move beyond her own experience, and how if she 'bonds' with her subjects can she retain the capacity to do critical research. Attempts to collaborate with participants and develop responsive interpretations might simply lead to new forms of duplicity (see Stacey, 1991). A recent example of research which addresses reflexivity in a productive and intellectually rigorous way are Jean Barr's (1999) reflexive research stories.

Some researchers have interpreted standpoint epistemology to mean that research on women can only be done by women, in other words they 'essentialize' women. However, a focus on women's experiences as the subject matter of research has revealed the diversity of these experiences and the diversity of women, as the Combahee River collective had begun to point out as early as 1977 in 'A Black Feminist Statement' (in Nicholson, 1997: 63–70). They raised an early concern with 'racism in the white women's movement' (1997: 69). This leads us to Harding's third stage of *feminist postmodernism* and the concept of 'difference'. At issue here is that the same tools (of positionality, voice and experience) which had enabled women to critique male-centred knowledge were tools also to question the right of white, middle-class women to speak for all women. Black feminists in particular began to question who can know and whose experiences are informing the knowledge produced from a perspective of differences among women themselves (see hooks, 1984; Collins, 1990). Thus while the oppression of women was acknowledged as universal, ethnic and race differences mean that this oppression is differently inflected for different women, and in some circumstances women themselves might be positioned in an oppressive relationship to other women and even to some men. Here the privileged position of white women in apartheid South Africa comes to mind as one example. All knowledge, including women's knowledge, is then partial and situated. To this was added a postcolonial literature challenging western models of feminist thought, and new scholarship that took up lesbian lives and the experiences of disabled women (see Olesen, 2000). The diversity as well as the commonality of women's experiences is then also the proper subject for inquiry. In feminist research it is now more usual to address the complexity of the interplay between gender and other axes of *difference*.

Any homogeneity among women, and hence arguably the political project centred on women's emancipation, is called into question by *postmodernism* which argues that there are many versions of social reality, all of which are equally valid. This might also be described as a feminist relativist epistemology. There can be no stable category of 'woman'. The deconstructive project of postmodernism seems at odds with the reconstructive project (or 'grand narrative') of feminism and the desire to carry out empirical research which attempts to offer constructive (and potentially emancipatory) solutions to problems of gender injustices. Arguably feminist researchers need to find ways to engage with difference and complexity while not losing sight of the bigger issues around women's (and some men's) oppression. As the 1997 United Nations Development Programme *Human Development Report* pointed out, there is no country that treats women as well as it treats its men.

Implications for research design

There are no methods which are specific to feminist research. In the early stages of feminist research quantitative methods were criticized as being contrary to the epistemological basis of feminism (see, for example, Reinharz, 1992). Now, however, feminists make use of quantitative (see Jayaratne and Stewart, 1995; Kelly et al., 1995; Oakley, 2000) and qualitative data, and adopt methodologies like ethnography, action research, life histories and autobiographies as appropriate to the research questions being posed. They might use surveys, interviews, questionnaires, observation, photography and so on. The design implications are ones of principle. Methodological issues that will shape research design include complexity, gendered experiences, the ethical and research relationship with the researched, positionality, and the production and dissemination of research knowledge (see Olesen, 2000: 217). Given debates about 'situated knowledge' and 'the crisis of representation' in social science research, we should not assume that experience 'speaks' for itself. Griffiths (1995) offers four precepts for feminist research. While she argues that the knowledge generated is grounded in experiences and subjectivities, it is also inflected by acknowledged power relations and subject to theorizing which, she says, is indispensable. Finally, the knowledge produced is revisable. To this we might add the visibility of the research process so that we make explicit the logic of our methodology and interpretation and acknowledge also the possible silences in our research. Moreover, we should not assume that matching the race and gender (or other forms of difference) of researcher and researched is necessarily appropriate (although it may be), or that this 'insiderliness' provides full access to women's knowledge. In doing feminist research we confront further ethical and analytical difficulties around how we represent and write women's voices to produce what Skeggs (1997) calls 'responsible knowledge'.

Reinharz (1992: 243–4) offers ten claims, some mentioned earlier, for feminist research to be borne in mind in designing a study. On the other hand, Acker (1994) warns against a checklist to be built into the research design and focuses rather on the importance of the researcher bringing a feminist framework to the analysis and the research product. She offers an example from her own research which highlights the difficulty of undertaking feminist research in certain contexts, and how research data which did not start out with a specific feminist focus generated feminist research when it was analysed later using a gendered lens. In the end, one of the best ways to get a feel for research design in feminist research is to read feminist studies, for example Beverley Skeggs' (1997) exemplary study and Kenway et al.'s (1998) fascinating account of gender reform in Australian schools (and see Olesen, 2000, for extensive references to feminist studies in education and health).

Stories from the Field

Diane Burns

Introduction

This story from the field draws upon an ethnographic, action-based study of a self-help, lobbying organization that works toward improving the lives of lone parents in the UK. During the research the organization provided information, training courses and childcare, and campaigned and lobbied on behalf of its membership. In 1995 I was elected to become a member of the National Co-ordinating Committee and in 1996 the organization became the focus of my doctoral research. My volunteer involvement and my research plans were a reflection of my interests and commitments to engage in action aiming to achieve social change. I examined organizational identities, action and the experiences of women involved in the organization. I sought to develop a methodology where it would be possible for us to reflect on organizational practices and issues and bring our thinking and analysis about this back into our work. I also sought to carry out the research in a way that attended to women's concerns and power issues within both the research process and organizational dynamics.

I was researching the organization from the 'inside'. This meant I was both privy to and a participant in the kinds of conversations, discussions and tensions someone researching from a position 'outside' the organization would not be. However, this closeness also meant that I was subject to the power dynamics that figured within the organization.

Ethical considerations, therefore, were not merely guided by research guidelines but also by organizational practices concerning who speaks and what sort of things are spoken and written about. Nearing the end of my study it became necessary to create a distance between the organization and my research to prevent my analysis from being shaped by processes through which stories and narratives of the organization were usually produced. For ethical reasons, in this chapter, I have not illustrated the specifics of these dilemmas much further – opting instead to frame the issues involved within wider debates around feminist methodologies.

Feminist methodologies

As Walker points out (this chapter), feminism and feminist methodology are not monolithic but numerous, a contested terrain and a source of continual debate among feminist scholars. DeVault (1996) writes that feminist scholars also share commitments for a:

- methodology that shifts the focus of practice from men's concerns in order to reveal the locations and perspectives of all women;
- science that minimizes harm and control in the research process;
- methodology which will support research of value to women, leading to social change or action beneficial to women.

In seeking a methodology that reveals the locations and perspectives of all women, I analysed a range of data, including research diaries, collated documents and interviews with 15 people involved in the organization. For this chapter I am going to outline the dilemmas within this methodology – particularly when conducting interviews and analysing the transcribed audio recordings.

Issues of accountability in research relations

Each participant was interviewed separately, loosely following a set of open-ended questions about their past and present involvement in the organization. The participants were aware of their rights and the purpose of the research and that they would be given access to the transcribed interview and have the opportunity to make changes to their transcript. I was also committed to making the interviews as confidential as possible but was aware of the strong possibility that members of the organization might recognize someone's identity from a snippet of transcript. Issues around confidentiality were complicated further by the conversations that took place between participants who chose to talk to each other about their experiences of taking part and the content of their interviews.

The interviewing took place between 1996 and 1999. I was aware that we were engaging in more critical discussions as time went by. I think this was due to the growing familiarity and developing relationships with participants and in our growing awareness of each other's shared and different locations within, and perspectives about, the organization. Our discussions also included negotiations about participant's rights, and the obligations directing my practice as a researcher rather than a manager no doubt figured in permitting a more critical talk about the organization during the interviews. Certainly some participants had decided to participate in an interview because they already had views and perspectives to articulate and felt it important that I, and ultimately the research, chronicled these.

Many feminist scholars and researchers have written about the power differentials between researcher and the researched and many have worked to challenge and reshape research practices. I also was concerned about power differentials and to name and discuss these with participants and at least attempt to remedy them. For example, alongside the backdrop of the researcher–participant relationships, we were also aware of reflecting on whom we were speaking 'as' and 'to' when we speak (for example paid and unpaid workers, white woman and black woman, and so on). This was important as the positions we occupied influenced our dialogue and action. Participants could speak in a critical way about issues and events as 'a friend' that they might not chose to share with me as a manager, for example. In this case, I am bound by the informal 'contract' agreed with each participant – involving confidentiality and a commitment to privilege their 'voice'. However, this particular 'voice' of a participant may not be articulated outside of the interview. An ethical tension ensues where a focus on all women's concerns produced a set of diverse and alternative accounts about the organization, one often contrary to the other, which had an overall effect of disrupting the monolithic and coherent accounts about/produced by 'the organization'. Therefore, my understanding of a 'feminist informed' approach to interviewing, one which was concerned with asymmetrical power relations, attending to the accounts and views of the women involved and incorporating these into the research process, along with my intention to maintain confidentiality as best I could, were being shaped by both the research and organizational relations. In this way the process involved in setting up and participating in interviews created a new didactic space and provided the potential for occupying different discursive subject positions (see Garvey, 1992: 326) from those which figured within the dynamics of the organization.

Presenting and analysing women's 'voices'

In the next stage of the research I was faced with the tough question of what I was going to do with the women's accounts – how to analyse them? I am sure the participants had many different concerns when constructing these accounts and were speaking to many different audiences (potential and imagined) when articulating them. My aim was for analysis that paid due attention to the 'voices' of women, their experiences and perspectives but did so without presenting any one 'voice' as if it was more valid than another. But I also did not want to gloss over or leave unattended the organizational issues that different women were identifying within these accounts.

The way I approached addressing this dilemma was to develop a discursive analytical framework that blended aspects and practices of:

- narrative analysis which permits a focus on the stories people tell and draws attention to how the story functions, why they are being told in that way at that particular moment (see Riessman, 1993);
- discourse analysis which, following the work of Foucault, aimed to understand how power and ideology operate through systems of discourse. I took the approach that discourses produce different speaking positions that we occupy, and constitute the experiences of the organization and our identities, so that we interpret the organization as discursively negotiated, constructed and reconstructed;
- poetic ethnography which is concerned with writing that breaks with the idea that there is a connection between lived experience and the written word – this is about showing not telling experience (see Denzin, 1997).

I identified narratives within the interview transcripts which told a variety of stories about the history of the organization, women's roles in this work and how they experienced this part of their lives. I then broke up the narratives and explicated the discourses that figured within these stories. I paid attention to the ways in which these discourses functioned within the texts, their reflections in different organizational identities and the power relations they produce and reproduce. This allowed a critical reflection of the ways in which language is implicated in structuring organizational dynamics and power relations. I then shaped the broken transcripts into poems. I did this by discarding my own utterances to leave only the participant's words and I then reshaped these words into poems. In effect the poems offered a different way to *write experience* while creating a space within the thesis for the reinsertion of voice at the moment of speaking.

My commitment to incorporate women's voices into the research process and my attempt not to privilege one account over another raised wider concerns about who can speak about the organization and what it is legitimate to say (and to whom). The analytical approach allows a range of voices and a variety of stories to be present within the thesis. Moreover, within the institutional framework of the academy, issues exist about the permissible and forbidden forms of an authorial 'voice' within a PhD thesis, and the multi-vocal (re)presentation went some way to disrupt and offer alternatives to constructing a singular coherent and seamless account.

However, I found the multi-vocal (re)presentation I developed to also be problematic. Accounts of/ produced by an organization are usually coherent ones and often become the formal or dominant version. Individual participants have access to these accounts, and have no doubt contributed to their production, but they also have 'other' or alternative accounts that reflect different perspectives, other storied experiences of the organization. The research presented these various stories side by side, following the goal for a methodology that revealed the locations and perspectives of all participants. However, one effect of treating all stories as being valid is that a

rather messier picture than official accounts construct is produced. Furthermore, this approach leaves readers (whether internally or externally located to the organization) open to judge, if they wish, which of the narratives are recounting experiences and events as 'more or less' interesting or as 'more or less' accurate and so on, therefore raising concerns about the *validity* of some voices. The approach to take seriously the different concerns and voices of women may be one that feminist scholars (and other researchers) appreciate – but in my research it had the effect of drawing critical attention to the processes through which accounts are produced. My efforts to analyse the process could therefore undermine the accounts of women's experiences, accounts that ultimately challenge the dominant discourses which circulate in political arenas and welfare practices.

A final note

Engaging in action was an important part of my practice and I volunteered to be involved in the organization because I wanted to make a contribution to both the organization's work and its development. The research is one of the contributions I made and the analysis of the thesis was both for the organization and in pursuit of my own ends in being awarded a doctoral degree. However, my involvement brought me into close relations with the organization and the people participating in the research. This closeness meant that my research engaged with the internal world of an organization, but the multi-vocal representations of that internal world ran counter to and invoked anxieties, as my work also disrupted the coherent stories of the organization and drew attention to the organizational processes involved in their production.

Annotated bibliography

Barr, J. (1999) *Liberating Knowledge: Research, Feminisms and Adult Education.* Leicester: NIACE.
Jean Barr revisits three earlier research projects and explores how different understandings of feminism might have generated alternative research stories. Through this she skilfully weaves elements of her own autobiography and development.

Berge, B.-M. with Ve, H. (2000) *Action Research for Gender Equity.* Buckingham: Open University Press.
The research draws on feminist poststructural theories and shows how action research can be a method for feminist change and gender equity in schools. It provides empirical accounts of nine teachers and their pupils in Sweden.

Bloom, L.R. (2001) *Under the Sign of Hope: Feminist Methodology and Narrative Interpretation*. New York: SUNY Press.

Bloom shows how feminist poststructuralism can be a useful lens for doing research (see also Kenway et al., 1998). She interrogates her methodology as she conducts her research by consistently being reflective of her actions, narrative methodology and the relationships involved in her research.

Griffiths, M. (1995) *Feminisms and the Self. The Web of Identity*. London: Routledge.

While the book concentrates on a critique and a construction of feminist philosophy it offers useful chapters on epistemology, methodology and autobiography.

Harding, S. (1987) *Feminism and Methodology*. Buckingham: Open University Press.

Germinal text distinguishing between method, methodology and epistemology.

Middleton, S. (1993) *Educating Feminists. Life History and Pedagogy*. New York: Teachers College Press.

This is of interest to those planning to use life history methods, offering chapters which include a personal life history of Middleton's own development of a feminist pedagogy and a compelling case study which considers the politics of life history research.

Oakley, A. (2000) *Experiments in Knowing. Gender and Method in the Social Sciences*. Cambridge: Polity Press.

Oakley's book explores the divisions between quantitative and qualitative methods. She argues for a relevant understanding of qualitative and experimental methods and rehearses the considerable problems, in her view, of a retreat into qualitative methods as offering a more democratic way of knowing.

Olesen, V. (2000) 'Feminisms and qualitative research at and into the millenium', in N. Denzin and Y.S. Lincoln (eds), *The Handbook of Qualitative Research*, 2nd edn. London: Sage, pp. 215–56.

Provides numerous useful references to substantive and methodological feminist studies, together with an account of the key methodological issues and questions facing contemporary feminist research.

Personal Narratives Group (eds) (1989) *Interpreting Women's Lives*. Bloomington, IN: Indiana University Press.

This collection offers a rich insight into the ways in which women's voices and life stories can inform scholarly research. It includes anthropologists, historians, literary scholars and a social scientist among the chapter authors.

Reinharz, S. (1992) *Feminist Methods in Social Research*. New York and Oxford: Oxford University Press.

Examines the full range of feminist research methods and the relationship between feminism and methodology.

Weiler, K. and Middleton, S. (eds) (1999) *Telling Women's Lives*. Buckingham: Open University Press.

A useful collection exploring the history of women in education in which the contributors reflect on methodological issues in the process of history writing (for example the nature of historical evidence) and consider the impact of recent theoretical debates on their own scholarship.

Further references

Acker, S. (1994) *Gendered Education*. Buckingham: Open University Press.

Ahmed, S., Kilby, J., Lury, C., McNeil, M. and Skeggs, B. (eds) (2000) *Transformations. Thinking Through Feminism*. London: Routledge.

Collins, P. (1990) *Black Feminist Thought: Knowledge, Consciousness and the Politics of Empowerment*. New York: Routledge, Chapman & Hall.

Delamont, S. (2003) *Feminist Sociology*. London: Sage.

Denzin, N. (1997) *Interpretive Ethnography: Ethnographic Practices for the 21st Century*. Thousand Oaks, CA: Sage.

DeVault, M.L. (1996) 'Talking back to sociology: distinctive contributions of feminist methodology', *Annual Review of Sociology*, 22: 29–50.

Eichler, M. (1988) *Nonsexist Research Methods: A Practical Guide*. London: Allen & Unwin.

Garvey, N. (1992) 'Technologies and effects of heterosexual coercion', *Feminism and Psychology,* 2: 325–51.

hooks, b. (1984) *Feminist Theory: From Margin to Center*. Boston, MA: South End Press.

Jayaratne, T. and Stewart, A. (1995) 'Quantitative and qualitative methods in the social sciences: feminist issues and practical strategies', in J. Holland, M. Blair and S. Sheldon (eds), *Debates and Issues in Feminist Research and Pedagogy*. Clevedon: Multilingual Matters, pp. 217–34.

Kelly, L., Regan, L. and Burton, S. (1995) 'Defending the indefensible? Quantitative methods and feminist research', in J. Holland, M. Blair and S. Sheldon (eds), *Debates and Issues in Feminist Research and Pedagogy*. Clevedon: Multilingual Matters, pp. 235–47.

Kenway, J. and Willis, S. with Blackmore, J. and Rennie, L. (1998) *Answering Back. Girls, Boys and Feminism in Schools*. London and New York: Routledge.

Lennon, K. and Whitford, M. (eds) (1994) *Knowing the Difference: Feminist Perspectives in Epistemology*. London: Routledge.

Mies, M. (1983) 'Towards a methodology of feminist research', in G. Bowles and R.G. Klein (eds), *Theories of Women's Studies*. London: Routledge & Kegan Paul, pp. 117–39.

Nicholson, L. (ed.) (1997) *The Second Wave. A Reader in Feminist Theory*. New York: Routledge.

Oakley, A. (1981) 'Interviewing women: a contradiction in terms', in H. Roberts (ed.), *Doing Feminist Research*. London: Routledge & Kegan Paul.

Patai, D. (1994) 'When method becomes power', in A. Gitlin (ed.), *Power and Method*. New York: Routledge, pp. 61–73.

Riessman, C. (1993) *Narrative Analysis*. Thousand Oaks, CA: Sage.

Skeggs, B. (1997) *Formations of Class and Gender*. London: Sage.

Spender, D. (1982) *Invisible Women: The Schooling Scandal*. London: Writers & Readers

Stacey, J. (1991) 'Can there be a feminist ethnography?', in S.B. Gluck and D. Patai (eds), *Women's Words: The Feminist Practice of Oral History*. New York: Routledge, pp. 110–20.

Stanley, L. and Wise, S. (1993) *Breaking out Again: Feminist Ontology and Epistemology*. London: Routledge.

Weedon, C. (1987) *Feminist Practice and Poststructuralist Theory*. Oxford: Blackwell.

Weedon, C. (1999) *Feminism, Theory and the Politics of Difference*. Oxford: Blackwell.

Weiner, G. (1994) *Feminisms in Education: An Introduction*. Buckingham: Open University Press.

CHAPTER
8

CRITICAL THEORIES OF RACE

Laurence Parker
Department of Educational Policy Studies, University of Illinois at Urbana-Champaign, USA
Lorna Roberts
Education and Social Research Institute, Manchester Metropolitan University, UK

Key concepts[1]

Laurence Parker

Racism is a normal daily fact of life in society and the ideology and assumptions of racism are so ingrained in the political and legal structures as to be almost unrecognizable. Legal racial designations have complex, historical and socially constructed meanings that insure the location of political superiority of racially marginalized groups. *A critical study of race and ethnicity* objects to the experience of White Europeans and White Americans as the normative standard; rather, the critical study of race and ethnicity, broadly conceived, centres its conceptual framework in the distinctive contextual experiences of people of colour and racial oppression through the use of literary narrative knowledge, storytelling or other forms of qualitative and quantitative data gathering to challenge the existing assumptions about the social construction of race. A critical study of race and ethnicity is critical of liberalism and its belief in the law to create an equitable just society. The critical study of race and ethnicity centres race in the research study but also examines its connection to and conflict with other areas such as class and sexual orientation. It is also an interdisciplinary and international framework rooted in philosophical, historical and sociological critiques of oppression such as postmodernism-poststructuralism, Marxism, feminist theory, postcolonialism and queer theory. The critical study of race and ethnicity explores these connections and conflicts in both a domestic context and in other countries where race plays out differently in social relations and education policy and as a transformative project that seeks to obtain social justice with respect to combating racism and racialism.

Critical studies of race in education (particularly *critical race theory* in the US) have pointed to the frustrating legal pace of meaningful reform that has eliminated blatant hateful expressions of racism, but has kept intact exclusionary relations of power as exemplified by the legal conservative backlash of the courts, legislative bodies, voters and so on against 'special rights for racially marginalized groups'. Critical race theory (CRT), as a critique of racism in the law and society, emerged as an outgrowth of the critical legal studies movement that took place at the Harvard Law School in the early 1980s. The law professors and students in this group began to question the objective rationalist nature of the law and the process of adjudication in the US legal system. They criticized the way in which the real effects of the law served to privilege the wealthy and powerful in US society while having a deleterious impact on the rights of the poor to use the courts as a means of redress. Out of this growing critique of the role of law in society, a strand of critical scholarship emerged through the writings of Derrick Bell (1980), Richard Delgado (2003), Angela Harris (1993) and Kimberlie Crenshaw et al. (1995). These scholars argued that the critical legal studies movement did not go far enough in challenging the specific racialized nature of the law and its impact on persons of colour. Bell, Delgado, Harris, Crenshaw and other early critical race theorists argued that the law, particularly civil rights law of the 1960s, was targeted to combat classical racism. This type of racism was characterized by acts such as grossly offensive behaviour toward others because of their race, legal segregation and discrimination by public bodies, or overt acts of racial violence. The moral authority of the civil rights movement served to weaken this form of racism in the US and the power of the law was a vital tool in helping to eliminate classical racism so most white European Americans now abhor these actions against any racial group. However, one of the main tenets of CRT has been that while classical racism has subsided, everyday racism has remained alive. This type of racism can be characterized as those mundane practices and events that are infused with varying degrees of racism. The actions associated with everyday racism are subtle, automatic, non-verbal exchanges that are seen as derogatory slights by African Americans. Furthermore, everyday racism, in the form of micro aggressions, is incessant and cumulative as practised in everyday actions by individuals and groups and in institutional policy rules and administrative procedures. Critical race theory sought to expose the flaws in the colour-blind view of everyday social relations and the administering of law, by positing that the legal hope of ending discrimination and racism has not made a difference because of the contradiction in a professed belief in equality and justice but a societal willingness to tolerate and accept racial inequality and inequity.

Critical race theory's roots can also be partially traced to previous social science race-based critiques related to the epistemological and ontological construction of race and racialism within modernity (Stanfield, 1999; Winant, 2001). The legal theories related to race share commonalities with other critical theoretical positions related to race and history, philosophy and the social sciences. For example, in order to understand modernity and its evolution, one has to understand race and racialism and how race played a fundamental role in shaping philosophical, political and later scientific thought. In race-centred nation-states (for example, the US, United Kingdom, South Africa, Brazil) the sociological myth of racial categories is a powerful primary socialization tool that has a tremendous impact on social perceptions, social status and social identity of all societal members. Racial categorization is a part of cognitive psychological thinking in that it refers to the ways people think about humans defined in terms of races. It links social and cultural attributes to physical attributes. Therefore, reasoning is based on racial categories and it is more or less commonly accepted along with the rhetoric of progressive social justice through colour-blindness and acceptance of all that is used as a pretext to continue to justify hierarchical racial categories. We can see part of this in the UK, for example, through the work of Sewell (2000) and his

description of the popularization of Black youth culture which creates conflict in British schools when Black males 'act out' Black youth culture and white teachers are overtly threatened by what they view as Black male predatory behaviour that has to be disciplined. Racial micro aggressions also continue in many education institutions by creating differing degrees of hostile environmental encounters for African Americans that result in 'cumulative racism', or a convergence of all the subtle yet still prejudicial 'put-downs' or actions that groups such as African Americans, Latinos/Latinas, Chicanos/Chicanas, Asian/Pacific Island Americans experience in some higher education settings because of their race. All of these examples are illustrative of how other critical research centring on race connects to CRT, resulting in a powerful and encompassing framework of racial theory from a critical interdisciplinary perspective. These critical race-based positions developed in other fields, when coupled with CRT, have given the theory expanding explanatory power to address the myriad elements of race, its role in shaping law and the nation state, personal and group identity, the distribution of goods and services, and institutional practices and policies.

Since its inception, CRT has not locked itself into a singular line of criticism against the law and society regarding race. In the USA, CRT has evolved from its early focus on African Americans and the impact of the law on Black–white European American relations, to examining how issues related to the law and immigration, national origin, language, globalization and colonization related to race. From this line of critique formed the LatCrit and critical Asian American legal studies movement that called for a type of critical race theory specific to these groups of colour. For example, LatCrit has drawn similarities with CRT regarding the racism within US law. Yet, the LatCrit movement sees itself grounded more in documenting through narrative-storytelling how other aspects of race, ethnicity, language, and national origin converge to make it so that Latino-Latinas are seen as other within the US racial context. Asian American critical race theory borrows from poststructuralism for a critical reading and tracing of the use of language/discourse and the law to create Asian Americans as 'honorary whites' whose fears can be played against other groups of colour regarding affirmative action and admissions to elite public universities in California. Yet these groups can also have the law used against them, as it was in the Japanese internment camps during the Second World War and in current immigration law.

CRT has served as an evolving theoretical framework that has been useful to think about research, policy and race. Critical race feminism has also emerged as an area of study with respect to women of colour and their connection to the law and public policy's impact on their lives as women, both in the US and in other parts of the world. Critical race theory has also evolved to make more links with social class analysis and criticism in terms of seeing that racism and class discrimination are interconnected and that both need to be fought on multiple levels as global capitalism creates greater inequalities between poor persons of colour in many nations and the wealthy (Parker and Stovall, in press).

Epistemological racism

In order to understand modernity and postmodernity and how the disciplines developed and evolved, one has to look squarely at race and how it played a central part in shaping the world and nation-states and was central to capital formation and accumulation as well as how it served as an ontological and organizing foundation in shaping how one thinks about and does research. This was popularized by the work of Scheurich and Young (1997), but other scholars of colour have made similar assertions about the bias of centring a white Eurocentric perspective in social science research and instead looking to the rich research traditions and perspectives of scholars of colour in the communities where they live in terms of racial social justice (Lomawaima, 2000; Tyson, 1998).

Implications for research design

Studies that adopt a critical race theory approach involve a theoretical sensitivity to race as a personal quality of the researcher and acknowledge an awareness of the various meanings of the data or situations where race and ethnicity are central to the study of the issue. The research process involves reviewing the existing research on race and ethnicity; looking at one's own professional experience with race, and one's own personal experience with race. Solórzano and Yosso (2002) developed critical race methodology in terms of its utility as an analytical framework to ask research questions, review literature, analyse data and form conclusions and recommendations. They discussed five tenets of a CRT methodology: (1) placing

race and its intersectionality with other forms of subordination (e.g. gender, social class, etc.), at the centre of research; (2) using race in research to challenge the dominant scientific norms of objectivity and neutrality; (3) connecting the research with social justice concerns and potential praxis with ongoing efforts in communities; (4) making experiential knowledge central to the study and linking this knowledge to other critical research and interpretive perspectives on race and racism; and (5) acknowledging the importance of transdisciplinary perspectives that are based in other fields (for example, ethnic studies, women's studies, African American studies, Chicano/a-Latino/a studies, history, sociology) to enhance understanding of the effects of racism and other forms of discrimination on persons of colour. Critical race theory, or other critical perspectives on race in social science research, places race at the centre of the research analysis. Placing race in the centre is important not only to frame the research issues to study but also to interpret the evidence and provide a lens of focus for racial equity implications. A critical race methodology seeks to ask research questions focused on gaining an understanding of how, for example, students construct multiple identities based on their race, gender, social class, national origin and other aspects of youth culture, but institutions such as schools operate under tight structural interpretations of rigid racial categories that have biases associated with them which in turn cause conflict between the students and schools. A critical race theory perspective also has an element of being extremely sensitive to community issues. For instance, researchers who are committed to a community over a long period of time and gain trust with that community of colour develop a unique degree of sensitivity to racial equity issues, which combined with their knowledge of the research from relevant literature, theoretical understandings and history of race and racism in the particular context, allow the researcher to use race and cultural intuition to give meaning to the data (Delgado Bernal, 2002). Finally, Tillman (2002) offers her view that a culturally sensitive approach to race-based research is what researchers need to think about in terms of doing work in communities of colour. She uses the African American US experience to claim that most African Americans share a similar culture and heritage in the communities in which they live and a shared experience of racism and struggle against white supremacy and Black self-determination, and that these aspects of Black cultural thought need to be a part of education research studies conducted on/with US Black communities.

Stories from the Field

Lorna Roberts

A small girl and her mother passed a statue depicting a European man who had barehandedly subdued a ferocious lion. The little girl stopped, looked puzzled and asked, 'Mama, something's wrong with that statue. Everybody knows that a man can't whip a lion.' 'But darling,' her mother replied, 'you must remember that the man made the statue.' (Cannon, cited in Collins, 1990: 201)

It is widely accepted that our perceptions of the world are framed by our positioning in the world. When one particular world view becomes accepted as the norm, other ways of seeing become effaced. Earlier in this chapter, my co-author Laurence Parker indicated the significant role the social construct 'race' has played in shaping the world and our understanding of it. The story of the little girl and the statue reinforces this point. This has implications for the nature of the research topic, the way in which the research question is framed, the way in which research subjects are constituted and the ways in which data are interpreted. Consequently undertaking research in race/ethnicity issues as a Black researcher within a predominantly white institution can be fraught with difficulties. My story from the field concerns my experiences as one of two minority ethnic team members working on a project exploring issues related to the retention of minority ethnic trainee teachers. The account is very much from an 'insider' perspective, as someone who was actively involved in a piece of research and who is an African Caribbean woman; it is a personal report of the dilemmas I faced in the field therefore the views expressed are mine alone. The story is offered as a contribution to the debate, as an invitation to confront the unease and silences engendered by 'race' and racism and to think through/disrupt the ways in which 'race' constructs, positions and shapes actions.

This is a story about power dynamics, emotional turmoil, intrigue and discovery – too much to cram into this limited space. What follows are the 'highlights' to illustrate the dilemmas faced by a novice researcher emotionally attached to a particular area of research.

About 18 months into my PhD I was invited to participate in a small-scale project exploring issues related to the retention of minority ethnic trainee teachers. Within the institution where I was based tutors had noted a worrying drop-out trend among particular groups of students. It was my understanding that the research sought to determine factors that might have contributed to trainees' failure/drop-out or intercalation with a view to reforming the initial teacher training course, providing support to 'at risk' students and arriving at recommendations to feed into a nationally funded project examining retention more globally.

Of course I was initially delighted to be considered as part of the project team. However, doubts began to creep in. I started wondering if I had been asked to do the research because of the possible greater access afforded by virtue of my ethnicity rather than my ability as an interviewer. I discussed the issue with a friend who felt that the reasons for being asked were minor – of far greater significance was the role I could play in impacting positively on the situation. I therefore laid my concerns aside and decided to proceed with the project.

I was not involved in the initial discussions to shape the scope of the project or identify the trainee sample. The areas to be investigated were informed by the findings from previous research and tutors' own perceptions of likely difficulties. There was a desire to gain an understanding of the religious and cultural barriers. From my perception of discussions there seemed to be an impression that the minority ethnic trainees at risk of failing, repeating or intercalating tended to be mature students with alternative entry qualifications to the traditional 'A' levels (formal assessments undertaken in the UK, post-16) and those who had to negotiate family and course commitments.

Previous research in the area had identified a number of barriers to the retention of minority ethnic trainees including feelings of isolation in a predominantly white environment, lack of awareness of cultural and religious issues and racial discrimination. I did not want to make assumptions about the possible barriers but felt that racism might be at the heart of the problem. I felt that focusing on cultural and religious barriers somehow placed the emphasis on the trainees and ignored the issue of racism. I was very mindful of the fact of my own background and how this could impinge upon my framing of the situation. Although racism was foregrounded in my mind, I was aware that minority ethnic trainees are not a homogenous group and that a number of other factors could be at play, hence I did not want to limit the field of vision. I wanted to encourage trainees to tell their own story rather than what I thought their story would be. I also needed to bear in mind concerns tutors had raised. I therefore designed the interview schedule to be as open as possible to encourage trainees' own narratives. I asked interviewees to tell me about experiences at university and in placement schools, and I also asked students to tell me how they would define their own identity.

I drafted a letter of introduction to invite trainees to participate in the research. I briefly outlined my background and explained the aims of the project. It was suggested that my picture be included on the letter to provide a personal touch. I remember feeling some embarrassment but finally agreed. Would this 'personal' touch have been suggested if the project had not been focused on 'race' and ethnicity? The letters were sent to 22 individuals: some were active students including a certain number who were repeating a year; some had successfully completed the course and some had withdrawn. I experienced some difficulties contacting a small number of students. Nineteen agreed to participate; some were quite exasperated at the prospect of yet another study into minority ethnic issues. A few expressed anger that it had taken so long before their experiences had been investigated. In one case a student had agreed to participate because of my ethnicity; had I been white she would have refused.

I found interviewing in some cases distressing and would on occasions leave interviews feeling angry. I could not be a dispassionate observer as I sympathized with the struggles some of the participants were experiencing, having had similar experiences myself. On two occasions trainees were reduced to tears as they recalled experiences during their school placement block. Some trainees reported incidences of covert or overt racism. One student spoke about instances which displayed the perceived 'ignorance' and prejudice' of her white peers. She raised her concerns and had been referred to a tutor within the department who was seen as 'the expert' on such matters. The tutor was 'a professor ... white ... middle class' and had 'written loads of books'. They had 'this high brow conversation, picking up and dissecting everything' the trainee had said. The trainee was told 'basically ... without evidence you can't say whether that's racism or not.' The trainee tried to explain that 'unless you have got this badge on and you have got to walk with it everyday you won't know. Half the time these subtle things you won't be aware of.' The trainee was left feeling 'paranoid like [she] was the one with the problem because [she] had highlighted it.' In some instances trainees spoke about ways in which they were made invisible: for instance, there were examples of teachers in placement schools who avoided making eye contact with minority ethnic trainees, instead focusing attention on their white peers, thereby excluding the minority ethnic trainee from the discussion. At other times some trainees were made to feel very visible as a result of their perceived difference. One trainee told of an overtly racist incident which had occurred beyond the school gates in an area known for its racism. The school itself had been very supportive, 'the teachers were brilliant', 'the staff was absolutely excellent ... really facilitating'; but there were perceived tensions with parents and the local community: 'the parents ... just stare in such a demeaning way, they've just got those stereotypical views ...' Not all the experiences had been negative; a number of trainees spoke very positively about the training declaring that they had not encountered any racism. In many ways experiences were very similar to the majority ethnic group. The research dispelled a number of myths about the type of student who might fail or drop out, but raised a number of questions in my mind about the nature of racism, and the implications for minority ethnic researchers engaging in 'race'-based research in predominantly white institutions.

Personal dilemmas faced during the research process

I was fully committed to this piece of research, not as an academic exercise but for its potential to make a real difference to the trainees' lives. My earlier conviction that I could feed into a process of change soon waned and I began to feel uncomfortable with my role as researcher. Despite my feelings of powerlessness as I listened to the more disturbing accounts, some trainees actually looked to me as someone who could impact directly on their situation. Because I could empathize, I think I was trusted and many trainees opened up, releasing a lot of the tensions and frustrations they had had to keep bottled up. This raised all sorts of ethical issues related to how respondents are co-opted into the research, what is done with the data – particularly very sensitive information – and the relationship between the researcher and respondents.

I was far more emotionally attached to the participants in the research and had a strong investment in my particular understanding of the research aims. This possibly narrowed my vision to some extent. I could not escape the feeling of being 'the outsider' when discussing certain issues with fellow researchers. Certainly I felt that maybe I read the data differently. My perception was that the trainees' voices had been silenced – revealing their stories to me was one way of being heard and I wanted them to have that voice. Some of the data generated by the research made for uncomfortable reading. I was uncomfortable with writing protocols for reporting findings which had the effect of 'toning down' the language. In my mind this was another way of silencing the trainees' voices. I would have presented the data differently had I had sole control.

I have found this research problematic in many ways. Research into minority ethnic experiences of education – be it pupils' educational attainment or issues to do with trainee teachers – has been punctuated by silences and inertia. This is revealed in the fact that, in the UK, some twenty plus years on since the first studies were undertaken, the same questions are being posed with the same sort of data being generated. I find myself involved in yet another project looking at why minority ethnic trainee teachers leave teacher training, this time on a national scale rather than confined to an individual institution. Why is it that there is no movement forwards, just a seemingly endless recycling of the same issues? Is the 'need' for research part of a structural inertia, itself an aspect of institutional racism?

The way forward

Interrogating 'race'-based issues and questions of ethnicity is an extremely sensitive enterprise. It is very easy to attack or be defensive, but the way forward is not about attack or defence, rather it is about engaging in a critical dialogue. The issues need to be confronted head on and dealt with rather than sidelined or cushioned in more palatable language. For me this entails acknowledging self as a Black researcher as opposed to a researcher. It means allowing minority ethnic communities to tell their narratives in their own voices, and for those accounts to be heard and acknowledged. It means looking critically at how group identities are constructed and daily practices are informed by the notion of 'race' and the process of racism. The processes are hidden, difficult to detect, yet are clearly felt. Critical race theory offers a possible method to begin to interrogate daily practices and begin to make sense of the dilemmas I encountered.

Notes

1. This section draws on material first published in L. Parker (2003) 'Critical race theory and its implications for methodology and policy analysis in higher education desegregation', *Interrogating Racism in Qualitative Research Methodology.* by L. Parker in G.R. Lopez and L. Parker (eds), New York: Peter Lang, pp. 145–80.

Annotated bibliography

Bell, D.A. Jr (1980) 'Brown v. Board of Education and the interest-convergence dilemma', *Harvard Law Review*, 93: 518–33.
Delgado, R. (2003) 'White interests and civil rights realism: Rodrigo's bittersweet epiphany', *Michigan Law Review*, 10(5): 1201–24.
Harris, A.P. (1994) 'Forward: the jurisprudence of reconstruction', *California Law Review*, 82(4): 741–86.
Harris, C.I. (1993) 'Whiteness as property', *Harvard Law Review*, 106(8): 1709–91.
Johnson, A.M. Jr (1994) 'Defending the use of narrative and giving content to the voice of color: rejecting the imposition of process theory in legal scholarship', *Iowa Law Review*, 79(4): 803–52.
Lawrence, C.R. III (1995) 'The id, the ego, and equal protection: reckoning with unconscious racism', *Stanford Law Review*, 47(5): 819–48.
Lopez, I.F. (1997) 'Race, ethnicity, erasure: the salience of race to LatCrit theory', *California Law Review*, 85(5): 57–125.
Thomas, C. (2000) 'Critical race theory and postcolonial development theory: observations on methodology', *Villanova Law Review*, 45(5): 1195–220.

Wing, A. and Weselmann, L. (1999) 'Transcending traditional notions of mothering: the need for critical race feminist praxis', *Journal of Gender, Race, and Justice*, 3(1): 257–82.

These first nine references are selected works by the major authors who have defined critical race theory in the US legal theory context. These works give a solid overview of what the field is and how it has evolved, particularly in the areas of feminism and race and globalization studies.

Ladson-Billings, G. (1998) 'Just what is critical race theory and what's it doing in a nice field like education?', *International Journal of Qualitative Studies in Education*, 11(1): 7–24.

Solórzano, D.G. and Yosso, T.J. (2002) 'Critical race methodology: counter-storytelling as an analytical framework for education research', *Qualitative Inquiry*, 8(1): 23–44.

Tate, W.F. IV (1997) 'Critical race theory & education: history, theory, and implications', in M. Apple (ed.), *Review of Research in Education Volume 22*. Washington DC: American Educational Research Association. pp.195–247.

These three references provide key information regarding how critical race theory has been defined and used in education research and in qualitative research studies. Solórzano and Yosso in particular presents important information and examples of what a critical race methodology looks like and how it can be used in a research study.

Gunaratnam, Y. (2003) *Researching 'Race' and Ethnicity: Methods, Knowledge and Power*. London, Thousand Oaks, New Delhi: Sage Publications.

Using ethnographic data, this text explores methodological, epistemological and ethical dilemmas involved in doing qualitative research on 'race' and ethnicity within a UK context. The book is 'process oriented' and invites the reader to think through knowledge production about difference. The author draws on post-structuralist, feminist, critical 'race' and post-colonial theory to examine the ways in which racial and ethnic categories reinforce and reproduce racial thinking.

Further references

Collins, P. (1990) *Black Feminist Thought: Knowledge, Consciousness, and the Politics of Empowerment*. Boston, MA and London: Unwin Hyman.

Crenshaw, K., Gotanda, N., Peller, G. and Thomas, K. (eds) (1995) *Critical Race Theory: Key Writings that Formed the Movement*. New York: New Press.

Delgado Bernal, D. (2002) 'Critical race theory, Latino critical theory, and critical raced-gendered epistemologies: recognizing students of color as holders and creators of knowledge', *Qualitative Inquiry*, 8(1): 105–26.

Lomawaima, K.T. (2000) 'Tribal sovereigns: reframing research in American Indian education', *Harvard Educational Review*, 70(1): 1–21.

Parker, L. and Stovall, D.O. (2004) 'Actions following words: critical race theory connects to critical pedagogy', *Educational Philosophy and Theory*, 36(2): 167–82.

Scheurich, J.J. and Young, M.D. (1997) 'Coloring epistemologies: are our research epistemologies racially biased?', *Educational Researcher*, 26(4): 4–16.

Sewell, T. (2000) *Black Masculinities and Schooling: How Black Boys Survive Modern Schooling*. Stoke on Trent: Trentham Books.

Stanfield, J.H. II (1999) 'Slipping through the front door: relevant social scientific evaluation in the people of color century', *American Journal of Evaluation*, 20(3): 415–31.

Tillman, L.C. (2002) 'Culturally sensitive research approaches: an African American perspective', *Educational Researcher*, 31(9): 3–12.

Tyson, C.A. (1998) 'A response to "Coloring epistemologies: are our qualitative research epistemologies racially biased?"', *Educational Researcher*, 27(9): 21–3.

Winant, H. (2001) *The World is a Ghetto: Race and Democracy since World War II*. New York: Basic Books.

9

QUEER THEORY/LESBIAN AND GAY APPROACHES

Gloria Filax
Department of Secondary Education, Faculty of Education, University of Alberta, Canada
Dennis Sumara
Department of Secondary Education, Faculty of Education, University of Alberta, Canada
Brent Davis
Department of Secondary Education, Faculty of Education, University of Alberta, Canada
Debra Shogan
Faculty of Physical Education and Recreation, University of Alberta, Canada

Key concepts

Gloria Filax and Debra Shogan

Queer theory addresses the problem of a two-sex, two-gender, one-sexuality ordering, which systematically categorizes and then divides humans into what counts as normal and deviant. The idea of *normalization* is integral to understanding the significance of queer theory. Research processes that draw on queer theory pay close attention to processes of normalization including those that construct categories of race, class, able-bodiness and age along with the context of place, culture and time in researching experiences, discourses and identities related to this normalizing sexual order. Queer theory problematizes and historicizes the foundational assumptions of all categories which human science research mostly takes for granted. Queer theory borrows from and has close theoretical and political affiliations with feminist, gay and lesbian theories and studies.

Introducing the word 'queer' into academic discourses suggests both a rupture as well as continuity with the older categories of lesbian and gay. 'Queer', as reclaimed identification, was given intellectual capital at a conference theorizing lesbian and gay sexualities held at the University of California, Santa Cruz in February 1990. The conference was based on the speculative premise that homosexuality is no longer defined either by opposition or homology to a dominant, stable form of sexuality (heterosexuality) or as merely transgressive or deviant in relation to a proper or natural sexuality. Participants were invited to reconceptualize male and female homosexualities as social and cultural forms in their own right, even if under-coded and discursively dependent on more established forms of sexuality. In the words of Teresa de Lauretis:

> [R]ather than marking the limits of the social space by designating a place at the edge of culture, gay sexuality in its specific female and male cultural (or subcultural) forms acts as an agency of social process whose mode of functioning is both interactive and yet resistant, both participatory and yet distinct, claiming at once equality and difference, demanding political representation while insisting on its material and historical specificity. (1991: 3)

While 'queer' has come to stand in for a range of subjectivities that defy 'the normal', including lesbian, gay, bisexual, transsexual and transgender, specifically queer theory works to problematize, transgress or transcend the ideological baggage of distinctions produced by the terms lesbian, homosexual and gay. 'Queer' is contentious and many refuse to be contained by 'queer' because it is perceived to be Euro-Western, white, male and therefore exclusionary.

Queer theory brings a perspective to social science research, which has been influenced by how *poststructuralism* conceptualizes *subjectivity* and *discourse*. Post-structural theory provides a critique of the human subject or individual and calls into question the stability or fixedness of categories that are normally assumed. Subjectivity represents the poststructuralist notion that a human being is formed or produced through discourse. Poststructuralist theories of subjectivity insist there is no fixed, unified, biological, essential or pre-discursive self. Instead human subjects are born into language, culture and discourse. How we talk, act, think, what is said, what can be said, who is authorized to speak, when and where, and the ways in which our lives are organized, constitute unified ways of thinking about things, people, culture and events. An example of a discourse is gender. Gender is a systematic way of organizing and thinking about humans, which has the effect of producing male and female subjects. How bodies are produced as male and female through discursive practices of gender include: ways of dressing, family arrangements, laws regarding who can marry and inherit, appropriate leisure and work activities, and emotional responses and responsibilities. Discourses are multiple, overlapping, and contradictory. Queer theory is interested in how gender, sex, desire and sexuality organize all human behaviour including religion, education, family and kinship, politics, work and so on. By destabilizing categories, queer theoretical reworkings of poststructuralist theories of subjectivity reveal that human identity is a constellation of multiple and unstable positions.

Four overlapping principles operate in relation to queer theory.

1.   Queer theory works to problematize identity categories by showing how the assumptions on which they are based are falsely normalizing, reifying, homogenizing, naturalizing and totalizing. Queering the norm or standard (Shogan, 1999) reveals the arbitrariness of all social categories. Further, queer theory shows how fixed categories like lesbian or gay, even when these are used as a corrective to heteronormativity, leave heteronormative discourse unaltered and that 'gay' and 'lesbian' specify sexual identities that reproduce the ideology of heterosexual society. The effect of these categories is to fix a normal human identity in a two-sex, two-gender, one-sexual orientation system in what Warner calls the 'sexual order' (1993: x–xi). Because the sexual order permeates all social institutions (family, religion, work, leisure, law, education), challenging this order has the effect of challenging common-sense ideology about what it means to be a human being. To theorize

sexualities outside of the heterosexuality/homosexuality binary is to proliferate sexual categories. Bisexuality, transgender, transexuality, third sex and queer-straight are just some terms to capture sexuality and gender category proliferations. These, in turn, are proliferated by problematizing racial categories.

Finally, it is because sexuality is so inevitably personal, because it so inextricably entwines the self with others, fantasy with representation, the subjective with the social, that racial as well as gender differences are a crucial area of concern for queer theory, and one where critical dialogue alone can provide a better understanding of the specificity and partiality of our respective histories, as well as the stakes of some common struggles. (de Lauretis, 1991: xi)

To sexuality, race and gender we add class, physicality, religion, age, colonial, postcolonial and culture. Each of these is unstable and further destabilizes fixed sexual identities by proliferating categories. Differences are interlocking, producing hyphenated identities. Different perspectives, histories, experiences and different terms make crucial the reformulation of questions posed by queer theory. For example, *tombois and lesbi* in West Sumatra (Blackwood, 1999) and *two-spirited* for some indigenous peoples in North America (Wilson, 1996) are contemporary categories informed by sexuality, culture, gender, colonialism, racism, ethnocentrism and postcolonialism.

Two theorists are of particular importance in understanding the disruption of identity categories. Eve Sedgwick's *Epistemology of the Closet* (1990) troubles the assumed connection between gender and sexuality as well as troubling the open secret of the closet, an awareness of the existence of homosexuality alongside exclusion, denial and silence about homosexuality. Judith Butler's *Gender Trouble* (1990) problematizes the assumption that sex is a biological given which prefigures a cultural gender.

2.   Queer theory works to problematize *heteronormativity* as the dominating form of sexuality. This problematization challenges and destabilizes how normalization works by exposing incoherencies between gender, chromosomal sex, sexuality and sexual desire (Jagose, 1996: 3). Rather than see heterosexuality as the original or that from which homosexuality deviates, both are seen as mutually productive of one another. They are both effects of each other's

exclusions. Processes of normalization produce all other sexuality categories as outside the norm, that is as abnormal or deviant. To understand the myriad ways in which heteronormativity organizes and structures everyday life, queer theory explores how education, law, religion, psychiatry, family, and any other area of human activity all embed assumptions of what counts as normal and are normalizing mechanisms in human relations. As Warner writes: 'Realization that themes of *homophobia* and *heterosexism* may be read in almost any document of our culture means that we are only beginning to have an idea of how widespread those institutions and accounts are' (1993: xiii, our emphasis). For example, accounts of proper age-stage models of maturation embedded in educational, legal and family discourses assume a standard family form as well as normal sexual development in youth towards heterosexuality.

3.   Queer theory opens up possibilities for human relations by producing and/or noticing other ways of living and thinking differences. The least known and represented forms of desire may produce new and different forms of identity, community and social relations (de Lauretis, 1991). Living differently will be productive of different sorts of hierarchies whose effects cannot be predicted in advance. For some, queer theory shuts down potential as it reproduces another generic identity: white, colonial, male, well resourced, Euro-Western, gay, adult, United States. For others, queer is a word that cannot be reclaimed and symbolizes horrific forms of homophobia. Taking up queer theory obligates a researcher to work within what Hutcheon calls *complicitous critique* (1989) and Flax calls recognization of one's own *non-innocent* forms of knowledge (1992). This requires researchers to be vigilant about how their own assumptions are an ongoing site of conflict, ambivalence and power/knowledge.

4.   Queer theory mostly draws on three specific forms of analysis. These are *Foucauldian discourse analysis*, *deconstruction* and *psychoanalysis*.

Foucault offers a method which traces *conditions of possibility* (1970) or what he has termed as a *history of the present* (1979) which reveals the myriad ways in which discourses overlap and reinforce one another to produce particular kinds of human subjects. In *The History of Sexuality, Volume I*, Foucault (1980) described ways in which human sciences of sexuality create an imperative for people to know the Truth about themselves and others through 'knowing' and confessing sexual practices. Indeed, knowing one's self

and others through sexual practices, 'in modern Western culture [is] the most meaning intensive of human activities' (Sedgwick, 1990: 5). Through confessional technologies and their supporting discourses, sexual identities are created and regulated which, in turn, are central to the constitution of the subject as both subject to and subject of sexual (and other) discourses (Foucault, 1980). Both identity and consciousness of identity take place in contexts that constrain available identity categories. To problematize identity, then, is to interrogate ways in which individuals take up identity categories, as well as ways in which categories are socially produced.

In order for heterosexuality to function as the normal, natural and given, it must have its abnormal, unnatural, absent other: the homosexual. Both deconstruction and psychoanalytic theory make it possible to expose the ways in which heteronormativity is constructed through *exclusion* of the queer '*other*'. Deconstruction interrogates a category's 'construction as a pregiven or foundationalist premise' (Butler, 1992: 9) and demonstrates 'how the very establishment of the system as a system implies a beyond to it, precisely by virtue of what it excludes' (Cornell, 1992: 1). Deconstruction calls into question, problematizes and 'opens up' a category for 'a reusage or redeployment that previously has not been authorized' (Butler, 1992: 15). Homosexuality is not a stable or autonomous term but a supplement to the definition of the heterosexual. 'The homosexual' functions as a means of stabilizing heterosexual identity and, as such, is the *limit* or the beyond of 'the heterosexual'.

Psychoanalytic theory makes it possible to see 'the homosexual' as an *imaginary other* whose flamboyant difference deflects attention from the contradictions inherent in the construction of heterosexuality. Often this deflection is through a demonization process in which the actions of queer people are always already perverse in the negative sense by virtue of being queer. Perverse actions then become the defining features of what is queer. Heterosexuality is able to thrive precisely by preserving and consolidating its internal contradictions at the same time as it preserves and consolidates ignorance of them.

Implications for research design
Dennis Sumara and Brent Davies

Research informed by queer theory can utilize many established social science research methods, although most research is multi-methodological.

Because queer theory is primarily interested in how particular orderings of sexuality and gendering have been given primacy over others, the questions that guide research focus on both the constructions of and the experiences of personal and collective identities. These questions might be sociological: how are gay, lesbian, transgendered and heterosexual identities socially structured and policed? How have capitalism and globalization influenced the development of a two-sex, two-gender, one-sexuality ordering? They might be anthropological: what meanings do those who identify in different sexuality categories bring to their daily, lived experiences? They might be historical: what social and cultural circumstances have led to particular views of sexuality and gender? Or psychoanalytic: how does trauma and repression contribute to the organizing of sexualized and gendered identities? While all these methods are used, most research informed by queer theory is primarily interested in expressing historical and cultural perspectives: how do human beings experience the way sexuality and sexual identities are shaped by discourses of race, class, gender, etc.? How are these experiences of identity influential to the organization of societies and cultures?

Research informed by queer theory generally views the posing of research questions, the development of data-gathering activities and the processes of analysis and interpretation as iterative and recursive. That is, all aspects of research informed by queer theory continue to shift as the research develops. For example, in the 'Stories from the Field' section below, the research began with questions about how gay and lesbian teachers develop their pedagogical practices but, over time, evolved to include more fine-grained analyses of how minority sexuality categories can develop hierarchies of what is considered normal and deviant.

Outcomes from research developed with queer theory can be as varied as the different methodologies employed. However, what all research shares is a commitment to revealing the usually-not-perceived relationships between experiences of human sociality and culture, and expressions and experiences of sexuality. All outcomes of research informed by queer theory must in some way illuminate the ways in which sex, sexualities, sexual identities are both influenced by and influence individual and/or collective experiences.

The outcomes of research informed by queer theory can be presented in what are now considered to be traditional qualitative research forms (e.g. anthropological or sociological reports, case studies, reports of action research). However, in keeping with the queer theoretical imperative to interrupt status quo discourses and practices, the use of alternative representational forms such as literary, narrative, new journalism and other creative non-fiction that are able to more fully represent the complexity of human identities is encouraged.

Stories from the Field – troubling identities with literary forms: action research informed by queer theory
Dennis Sumara and Brent Davis

From 1995 to 1997 we conducted an action research project with eight teachers who identified as gay, lesbian and transsexual. The purpose of our research was to try to gain some insight into what it meant to occupy a minority sexuality identity category and be a public school teacher. All eight participants in the research were experienced teachers in a large Canadian urban centre. Four were men, three were women and one was transsexual in the process of transitioning from male to female.

Our reading of the theoretical literature in queer theory had suggested to us that we needed to create a research methodology that was collaborative and, at the same time, that remained critically aware of how collaboration, in itself, functioned to reproduce structures we were trying to interrogate. For us, this meant developing methods that not only allowed for a representation of the identities that participated in research processes, but, as well, of the ways in which the forming of a research collective functions to reproduce particular sorts of identities and not others. As well, we needed to create research processes that highlighted the complex ways in which identities continually shift and proliferate through processes of identification and representation. Therefore, although telephone and face-to-face interviews were initially used to gather demographic and autobiographical information about participants in the research, these were not considered to be central to our 'data gathering'. Instead, we aimed to create research structures that we hoped might help all participants in this collaborative research (including ourselves as the university-based researchers) to continually call into question the ways in which we presented and represented our identities as human beings and as human beings who were also teachers. Our reading of poststructural theories had helped us to understand the ways our identities were structured by various discursive practices (including, for example, the discourse of gender, class, race, age, ability, schooling, teaching). Our reading of queer theory had elaborated these insights by reminding us that the normal/deviant binary has been supported by a two-sex, two-gender, one-sexuality ordering, which assumes the 'naturalness' of a narrow view of heterosexuality and the 'unnaturalness' of any other presentation of identity that departs from this normalized version of human identity.

Following methods developed by Sumara (2002) we used shared readings of literary texts as sites for critical inquiry in order to interrupt the usual ways in which identities are both experienced and re-presented during processes of interpretive inquiry. These reading activities required readers to form literary identifications with characters and situations that challenged and expanded remembered and currently lived experiences. By working with our co-researchers to interpret these literary identifications, moments of insight occurred that often interrupted the transparent structures of our perceptions and our thinking. For us, these shared responses to literary texts create possibilities for what Iser (1993) has called 'literary anthropology' – an interpretive activity where the relationships among memory, history and experiences of subjectivity were made available for analysis. Because we all read the same texts, and identified in 'minority' identity categories, we predicted that our responses would be similar. Of course, this proved not to be the case.

In reading and responding to Audre Lorde's (1982) *Zami: A New Spelling of My Name*, for example, we discovered that no two members of our group identified similarly. Not only were the responses noticeably structured by learned gender differences, they were also clearly influenced by the members' racial and ethnic backgrounds. Some of the responses, particularly from several male participants of the group, were puzzling in that they seemed unable to acknowledge that anger and frustration was very much part of the experience of women depicted in the novel. As Jim explained:

I just don't understand why the main character is always so angry. Surely, things were not as bad for women as is suggested. Even if they were, I think that maybe some of what she is experiencing she is bringing on herself.

Here it became clear that, although some male members of the group expressed the need to unite under the banner of same-sex identification, many of their responses were structured by a profound and largely unnoticed (by them) misogyny. The women in the group, however, did notice and, for them, these responses confirmed past experiences with gay men. As Jan explained:

I guess I shouldn't be surprised by some of the things I hear from the men in the group. I mean, that's one of the reasons that lesbians must have their own communities. Gay men can be just as sexist as straight men.

These curious experiences of identification and non-identification continued in our group's reading and discussion of Califia's (1995) short story, 'The surprise party', where we learned that personally familiar erotic identifications can become restructured by literary identifications: As Sandy explained:

After reading this story, I had some vivid dreams that include sex of the kind the characters had in the story ... I didn't think that I could be interested in that kind of sex.

These responses to literary fiction informed our understanding about the relationships between and among expressed and experienced identities, regulated and disciplined forms of sociality, and experiences of pleasure, desire and imagination. Although it is obvious that human beings experience events of identification and pleasure that are not necessarily understood as 'normally' heterosexual, the various technologies of regulation around gender and sexuality force open secrets about what constitutes both identification and pleasure. And, although 'the closet' is usually understood as the place where queer identities simultaneously hide and make themselves comprehensible to themselves, we suggest that the closet's boundaries must be understood to include the polymorphous ways in which identification and pleasure are produced. It is important to note that we used queer theory to analyse any identity that defines itself as counter-to-normative constructions of heterosexuality, including those who sexually identify with members of the opposite sex and/or gender, but not in ways that are heteronormative. If sexuality is understood as a category of experience that emerges from various and overlapping technologies of self-creation and re-creation, then the cultural mythologies of what constitutes the categories that are understood as 'normal' – particularly the category heterosexual – must be critically interrogated.

At first, calling into question the construction of heterosexuality seemed easy for those of us in the research group who identified with minority sexuality positions. As we discussed our responses to literary characters who identified as both heterosexual and 'not-heterosexual' we were able to deconstruct the ways in which what is considered a 'normal hetero-sexual' identity is represented in almost every structure that we could identify, including everyday uses of language. What we eventually came to learn, however, was that 'normalization' occurs at every level of culture, including the gay, lesbian and cultural groups with which we identified.

Most surprising in this research were insights that emerged from the presence of Terry, our transsexual research group member. In her mid-fifties, Terry joined our group in the middle of her three-year programme of transitioning from a male to female identity. Terry suggested to us that her 25 year history as a husband and a father meant that she had had no history of involvement with the gay and lesbian communities and therefore felt like an outsider in our group. During most meetings, Terry continually attempted to represent the ways in which she did and did not identify with male/female gender systems or with straight/gay identity categories. During one of our meetings, Terry suggested that if our group was to be called the 'queer teachers study group' then she was the 'queerest' of us all.

The primary challenge for those of us who initiated this research and who were most familiar with the theoretical structures that guided the methodologies we were using, was to continually publicly surface and analyse the ways in which our research was reproducing the very normative structures that we were trying to both understand and undermine. As our group continued to meet, it became clear that the 'normal/not-normal' binary was being created in our group – those who presented unambiguous gay or lesbian identities and Terry who presented a much more fluid and ambivalent identity – one that continued to have features (both physiological and psychological) shift as she moved through her sex-reassignment transition. Some members of our group confided privately to us that they were not comfortable having Terry in our group:

> She continues to insist that she is a woman and I'm trying to see her that way. But she continues to respond to the women in the group like a man, and she insists that she was a heterosexual man. Well, I just can't accept that! To me, Terry is just not a woman and never will be, no matter what sorts of surgical and hormonal interventions are made.

Terry had her own responses to the group:

> You all seem to be so sure about your identities and you seem to have friends and activities that support who you are. I have none of that. When I was married and raising children I did not feel like I was a 'proper' heterosexual man and now that I'm doing what feels right to me, I don't feel like I'm a 'proper' member of this queer research group.

Terry's presence in our research group helped us to understand how strong the impulse to create fixed identity categories can be, and how easy it is for individuals and groups to make decisions about what counts as a 'normal' identity and what will be designated 'deviant'. While all members of our research group identified as activists for the civil rights of all members of society, we continued to make judgements about how the normal/not-normal binary was to be structured within our study/research group.

These issues were never fully resolved. Most members continued to feel dissonance with the different ways identities and experiences were presented within the context of group meetings. However, in final interviews with Sumara, it was clear that everyone had a much more well-developed consciousness of how processes of normalization are reproduced at all levels of cultural involvement, even when there is an awareness of how these structures are created and enacted. As persons who identified as 'queer' and who were also teachers, we realized that we needed to abandon the idea that we could draw a neat line between different ways people identify and how others experience those identities. In fact, what this research showed us was that not only could we not make a correlation between features of our experienced and expressed identities, but that we couldn't even be certain that we knew exactly what we meant when we used signifiers like 'gay', 'lesbian', 'transsexual' or 'heterosexual' to represent our and other identities. While these identity markers did help to connect us with historical and contemporary cultures and communities, at the same time, close identification with any of them seemed to require a reproduction of processes of normalization that we, as persons working within a queer theoretical framework, aimed to avoid. However, we did learn that participating in literary identifications helped us to render more visible the usually transparent ways in which we both identified others and created identities

for ourselves. In order to conduct research that is informed by queer theory, we learned that we as researchers must consciously and conscientiously continue to queer the ways in which we are involved in language forms that explicitly aim to produce heteronormativity. For us, this did not mean merely bringing a critical eye and ear to the ways in which language and cultural practices function to produce normalized identities. It also meant creating research structures that deliberately aimed to interrupt familiar ways of presenting, representing, and interpreting knowledge and knowing identities.

Annotated bibliography

Abelove, H., Barale, M. and Halperin, D. (eds) (1993) *The Lesbian and Gay Studies Reader.* New York: Routledge.
This is an early edited and comprehensive volume (7 sections, 42 chapters, 666 pages), which includes essential readings from work in lesbian, gay and early queer studies and theory.

Butler, J. (1990) *Gender Trouble.* New York: Routledge.
Taking up deconstruction, psychoanalytic theory and Foucauldian discourse analysis, Butler shows how gender and sex are productive of one another, effectively disrupting the notion that sex is a prior and more biological moment in identity formation.

De Lauretis, Te. (1991) 'Queer theory: lesbian and gay sexualities: an introduction', *differences*, 3(2): iii–xviii.
A tight, insightful introduction to the interface between queer, lesbian, gay and feminist theory and studies.

Duberman, M. (ed.) (1997) *A Queer World.* New York: New York University Press.
This edited book (5 sections, 52 chapters, 705 pages) showcases a range of scholarship which embraces queer theory and methods.

Foucault, M. (1980) *The History of Sexuality, Volume 1. An Introduction.* New York: Vintage.
A key reading in which Foucault traces the conditions of possibility that have given rise to modernisms' sexualized identities and subjectivities. Prior to the mid-nineteenth century diverse sexual practices existed but no corresponding identities. With the rise of the human sciences (*scientia sexualis*), both an accumulation of knowledge and a continuous refining of detail about identity categories were linked to behaviours which were labelled normal or deviant, and became fixed, hardened and productive of forms of human identities.

Hammonds, E. (1997) 'Black (w)holes and the geometry of black female sexuality', in E. Weed and N. Schor (eds), *Feminism Meets Queer Theory.* Bloomington and Indianapolis, IN: Indiana University Press. pp. 136–56.
This article critiques the hegemony of white thinking in queer theory. Essential reading pointing to the possibilities and limits of existing scholarship.

Jagose, A. (1996) *Queer Theory: An Introduction.* New York: New York University Press.
Excellent overview of the history of thinking from lesbian and gay studies which inform as well as remain distinct from queer studies. The tensions, problems and strategic reasons of the perennial debate within queer communities between integration (fitting in) and separation are reviewed.

Sedgwick, E.K. (1990) *Epistemology of the Closet.* Berkeley, CA: University of California Press.
The introduction is absolutely essential reading, setting out Sedgwick's six axioms which have become central to much queer research.

Sumara, D. and Davis, B. (1999) 'Interrupting heteronormativity: toward a queer curriculum theory', *Curriculum Inquiry*, 29(2): 191–208.

This article interrupts education as usual by applying queer theory to questions regarding curriculum. The authors demonstrate how interrupting heteronormative thinking is important to both social justice issues and broadening possibilities for interrupting singular and familiar patterns of thinking.

Wilson, A. (1996) 'How we find ourselves: identity development and Two-Spirit people', *Harvard Educational Review*, 66: 303–17.

This article points to the intersection of sexuality studies, aboriginal cultural practices and colonial legacies, showing how these cannot be understood separate from one another. This article is important because of the disruption to dominant white narratives and research in sexuality studies.

Further references

Blackwood, E. (1999) '*Tombois* in West Sumatra: constructing masculinity and erotic desire', in E. Blackwood and S. Wieringa (eds), *Same-Sex Relations and Female Desires*. New York: Columbia University Press, pp. 181–205.

Butler, J. (1992) 'Contingent foundations', in J. Butler and J. Scot (eds), *Feminists Theorize the Political*. New York: Routledge, pp. 3–21.

Califia, P. (1995) 'The surprise party', in P. Califia and J. Fuller (eds), *Forbidden Passages: Writings Banned in Canada*. San Francisco, CA: Cleis Press, pp. 110–24.

Cornell, D. (1992) *The Philosophy of the Limit*. New York: Routledge.

Flax, J. (1992) 'The end of innocence', in J. Butler and J. Scott (eds), *Feminists Theorize the Political*. New York: Routledge, pp. 445–63.

Foucault, M. (1970) *The Order of Things*. trans. A. Sheridan. New York: Pantheon.

Foucault, M. (1979) *Discipline and Punish*. trans. A. Sheridan. New York: Vintage.

Hutcheon, L. (1989) *The Politics of Postmodernism*. New York: Routledge.

Iser, W. (1993) *The Fictive and the Imaginary: Charting Literary Anthropology*. Baltimore, MD: Johns Hopkins University Press.

Lorde, A. (1982) *Zami: A New Spelling of My Name*. Freedom, CA: Crossing Press.

Shogan, D. (1999) *The Making of High-Performance Athletes*. Toronto: University of Toronto Press.

Sumara, D. (2002) Creating commonplaces for interpretation: literary anthropology and literacy education research', *Journal of Literacy Research*, 34(2): 237–60.

Warner, M. (1994) 'Introduction', in M. Warner (ed.), *Fear of a Queer Planet*. Minneapolis, MN: University of Minnesota Press.

CHAPTER

10

ACTION RESEARCH

Susan Noffke
Department of Curriculum and Instruction, College of Education, University of Illinois at Urbana-Champaign, USA
Bridget Somekh
Education and Social Research Institute, Manchester Metropolitan University, UK

Key concepts

Bridget Somekh

Action research directly addresses the problem of the division between theory and practice. Rather than research being a linear process of producing knowledge which is later applied to practice settings, action research integrates the development of practice with the construction of research knowledge in a cyclical process. Instead of being research *on* a social setting and the people within it, it is research *from inside* that setting carried out either by the participants themselves or researchers working in collaboration with them. It has an immediate impact since it is an integral part of day-to-day work.

The earliest action research took place in the 1940s and 1950s, led by Lewin (1988), a psychologist refugee from Germany, who worked with community groups in the USA to resolve social problems such as prejudice; Trist, influenced by Lewin, worked in a similar way at the Tavistock Institute in London, focusing during the 1950s on experimental work in organizations to help them address their practical problems (see Pasmore, 2001). Lewin's theory of action research divides the work into distinct stages within a series of cycles, starting with 'reconnaissance' and moving on to the collection of data, analysis and the development of 'hypotheses' to inform action. This then leads into the second cycle in which the hypotheses are tested in practice and the changes evaluated. The cyclical process of action research does not come to a natural conclusion, although at some point it is necessary to bring it to a close and publish the outcomes in some form.

In the USA, action research flowered briefly in education during the 1950s, but then attracted criti-

cism from established researchers and declined. In the UK, it first became important in education as a result of Stenhouse's Humanities Project and Elliott's Ford Teaching Project during the 1970s (Elliott, 2001; Stenhouse, 1975). These projects were concerned with curriculum development, the former with developing innovative ways of teaching moral issues and the latter with reform in the teaching of science using 'discovery learning' methods. Stenhouse saw research as a necessary component of the work of every teacher and his definition of curriculum as a set of processes and interactions rather than a specification of subject content led to his belief that curriculum development was an impossibility without the involvement of teachers-as-researchers. In Australia, Kemmis, Robin McTaggart and colleagues established a significant base of action research at Deakin University (Carr and Kemmis, 1983). In Austria, through the work of Peter Posch and colleagues at the University of Klagenfurt, action research has made a significant impact on government policy for education (Altrichter, 2001). Since the mid-1980s there has been a resurgence of interest in action research in the USA. Of particular importance has been the development of a sustained tradition of teacher research focused on improving learning and teaching (Cochran-Smith and Lytle, 1999; Zeichner, 2003), and more recently a tradition of self-study by teacher educators (Feldman, 2003). Another important strand has been the development of participatory action research (PAR) in organizational settings and the work of non-governmental organizations (Whyte, 1991). Emanating from South America, a different tradition of PAR has been influenced by the work of Paulo Freire. Starting out as a grassroots movement carrying out small-scale work in local 'popular education' settings (Torres, 1992), PAR has become a movement 'search[ing] for a new type of scientific plus activist/emancipatory work' (see Borda, 2001).

Some see action research as being carried out by practitioners – whether in a professional group or university – to understand and improve their own practice. This tradition places importance on an outside facilitator who has expertise in supporting the practitioner-researchers. The relationship between the facilitator and 'insiders', such as nurses, social workers or teachers, is crucially important but it raises ethical issues related to their differential power. Sometimes the whole research process (identification of the problem, data collection and analysis, writing up and presentation at conferences and in publications) is carried out by insiders. The facilitators' research focus is 'second order', concerned with improving their own practice as facilitators rather than the 'first-order' issues of practice. Another approach is for the action research to be led by a participant who comes into the practice situation from outside and negotiates the boundaries and parameters of the study with the participants, involving them as co-researchers without expecting them to undertake substantial amounts of additional work. The 'outsider' may be a professional who has become a graduate-student or a university-based researcher working on a funded project. Again, there will be imbalances of power and control so that the working relationship will need to be carefully negotiated. In all cases it may be useful to develop an agreed code of practice to ensure that ethical issues are discussed and addressed in advance.

There is a wide range of different approaches to action research. Noffke (1997) groups these within three dimensions: the professional, the personal and the political. The first focuses on improving what is offered to clients in professional settings, the second is concerned with social action to combat oppression. The third, the personal, not necessarily separated from either of the others, is concerned with factors such as developing 'greater self-knowledge' and 'a deeper understanding of one's own practice.' Noffke presents these categories as being of equal status, whereas Grundy's (1982) earlier categorization suggests a hierarchy of status: the 'technical', the 'practical' and the 'critical'. Based on the three kinds of knowledge in Aristotle's *Ethics*, the technical focuses upon making a better product (for example more efficient and effective practice), the practical focuses upon developing the 'practical judgement' of the

participant-researcher grounded in experience and self-reflection, and the critical leads to 'emancipatory' action research. The latter, which is characterized as 'more powerful' than the other two, involves group reflection and action to 'emancipat[e] the participants in the action from the dictates of compulsions of tradition, precedent, habit, coercion, as well as from self-deception'. Grundy, like Kemmis, with whom she worked closely at Deakin University, grounded her conceptualization of action research in the critical theory of Habermas. More recently, Kemmis (2001) has reconceptualized the relationship between action research and critical theory in the light of 'attacks on modernist theory from postmodernists and poststructuralists'. Drawing on the later work of Habermas, he reaffirms his belief in the importance of theory, and in particular critical theory, as a resource for conceptualizing action research.

Including the work already cited, a considerable body of writing has supported the development of action research, theorizing its similarities to, and differences from, other forms of research, and exploring the special value of generating theories as an integral part of development work in social settings. Much of this has focused upon the nature of practitioner knowledge and the special contribution it makes to research (Cochran-Smith and Lytle, 1993; Elliott, 1994; Winter, 1998). Action research is closely linked by many writers with the concept of 'reflective practice' which has its roots in the work of Dewey (1933) who saw one kind of reflection as leading to the testing of hypotheses in action. In the UK and Austria the work of Schön (1983) has been influential in developing concepts of reflection-in-action and reflection-on-action as core attributes of expert professional practice. While it is true that action researchers necessarily engage in reflective practice, it is not true conversely that all reflective practitioners are action researchers. Crucially, action research involves a process of the collection and analysis of data that provides the practitioner with some objectivity and distance, looking at his or her own practice from another point of view, sometimes through bringing to bear more than one kind of data in a process of triangulation. By comparison with action learning where the emphasis is on groups supporting reflection based on the perceptions and memories of individuals, action research is based on consideration of data collected during practice, freeing interpretation from some of the constraints of memory and individual perceptions.

Action research is always rooted in the values of the participants. Somekh (1995) points out that its close links with the values of practice tend to mean that action research methodology adapts and develops in rather different ways within different social groups. Action research among nurses, for example, is strongly influenced by the need to establish credibility alongside the research of the medical profession so it tends to conform rather more to standards of traditional research rigour. In the UK, much action research in education has focused on the professional development of teachers and teacher educators (Dadds, 1995; O'Hanlon, 2001). In the USA, an important strand of participatory action research, originating in the civil rights movement of the 1960s, has contributed significantly to social action to promote social justice. Noffke (1997) opens with a quotation from Martin Luther King inviting researchers to 'make society's problems your laboratory'. She points to the key role played by writers such as DuBois (1973) and Horton (1990) in building this tradition. A particularly interesting recent example is the work of Hinsdale et al. (1995) who addressed the need for impoverished communities to identify their own resources for economic, educational and social redevelopment. Similarly, action research in South Africa, with its roots in the struggle against oppression in the time of apartheid, was often overtly political with a strong emphasis on issues of social justice (Walker, 1998). For writers working in a feminist tradition, such as Griffiths in the UK (1998) and Berge and Ve in Sweden (2000), social justice concerns have become paramount within a holistic process of inquiry and personal–professional development.

Implications for research design

It will already be clear from the account of Lewin's traditional model above that action research frequently does not start with a research question. The driving force will be an impetus for change/innovation through deepening the participants' understanding of social processes and developing strategies to bring about improvement. There will be a focus on some aspect of the social setting in which the work will take place, but the starting point may be something rather vague, such as a feeling of dissatisfaction without being sure of the reason, or a desire to understand some aspect of activity more deeply. There can be multiple starting points and there is unlikely to be an

orderly progress through Lewin's cyclical stages. Many writers have developed variants of Lewin's model, for example McNiff (1988) adds small spirals of sub-activity breaking away from the main cycles. Altrichter et al. (1993) offer a four-step process of 'finding a starting point', 'clarifying the situation', developing action strategies/putting them into practice' and 'making teachers' knowledge public', in which the two middle steps are repeated as many times as necessary before moving to publication. However, the main point to remember is that models are only intended as rough planning tools, not exact representations of a process.

At the start it will be necessary to make some broad decisions. First, who will be involved? This will depend on whether the action research will be a study of one individual's practice in a clearly defined setting such as a hospital ward, or a study of organizational change, for example in a school or hospital. In either case, a lot will depend on who is prepared to volunteer. A partner prepared to act as an observer will be invaluable in providing a different point of view and enabling triangulation of data. Participatory action research may have the aim of drawing more and more people into the process as the work progresses. In practice, this approach is likely to lead to the initiator losing some control over the direction of the project and it is important to be prepared for this or it may create considerable stress. Collaboration is never easy, so ethical issues need to be clearly identified and working principles agreed in advance to safeguard the interests of all. As in all research, analysis of the data is the most difficult as well as the most interesting aspect of the work, but in action research it is an ongoing process which is integral with reflection during data collection. The development of action strategies and their implementation, based on the findings of the initial stage of the research, needs to be followed by further data collection to evaluate them, as the validation of action research outcomes involves testing them out as the basis for new actions to see if the expected improvement results.

Stories from the Field
Susan Noffke

Action research can begin in multiple settings, with multiple levels of participants. These 'stories from the field' are representations of how one action research issue, parent involvement in the education of school children, can emerge from differing perspectives which, in turn, affect the process as well as the outcomes of the research. Yet in each story, the process of research is cyclical and focused both on producing new knowledge and on creating actions which will affect directly the social situation in which the issue emerges. It is temporal, as well as cumulative.

This series of small 'stories' is built from actual experiences. It also embodies plans for future action research projects. Theory plays a role, both 'academic' and those theories generated from the hopes and dreams of those most closely connected to practice. Change and thereby improvement in the immediate social situation is a goal, alongside the generation of better understanding of the social context – hence, action and research.

The teachers' story

Many conceptions of action research focus initially on an individual teacher's concerns, but then move on to collaborative projects:

> I wonder about some of my students who are not doing as well as they could. If parents could be more 'partners' in the educational process, these children could do so much better in school.

After dialogue between colleagues and with administration, and a search of some of the relevant literature, the group devises a survey to gather information on both parent and teacher views on the issue of participation. While the survey results reveal much in terms of teacher attitudes, the parent response rate is small, involving primarily parents who are already involved in school activities. For some teachers, this response 'proves' their belief that 'these parents just don't care'. For others, who know parents and community members outside the school setting, that clearly is not the case. It makes no common sense for parents not to want their children to do well in school.

In the next cycle they design a focus group protocol, make use of their personal contacts and invite parents to discussions at local community sites at times when parents would be likely to be able to attend. Childcare is provided as well as refreshments. This time there is wide participation. The field notes taken were analysed and the patterns that emerged

provided a basis for staff development, but the results were also shared with other schools in the area.

An administrator's story

A school administrator has a parallel concern:

> The school staff is highly qualified, and very successful with many of the students, especially those who come from backgrounds similar to their own. Yet they constantly talk about parents and children in ways that I feel are a reflection of their lack of understanding of the local community culture. They seek to explain gaps and weaknesses and not find strengths on which to build.

Together with the school advisory committee, which includes teachers, paraprofessionals, parents and other local community members as well as participants from a local university teacher education programme, they brainstorm ways to bring the various segments of the staff and community closer together. They decide to make 'community' a theme for project work for the year. Each grade level team designs inquiry activities that will provide opportunities for families and community members to share stories and local history. As the work emerges, the school staff begins to see parents and children in a new light, especially through collecting information over time (interviews, student work, parent comments, attendance and achievement records) and using it as a focal point for team discussions of learning plans.

A parent and community story

A similar goal looks somewhat different from a parent and community perspective:

> I know that our son could be doing better at school, but I have a hard time finding out how to help. The regular progress reports and parent–teacher conferences are helpful, but I often feel that as long as my child isn't causing problems in class, there is little offered in terms of really tapping into what he could do. A 'C', or average grade, seems to the teachers to mean that everything is fine. But isn't more than that needed if he wants to go to college?

The parent talks with friends and other community members and starts a focus group, meeting in a local church. She learns that her concerns were widely shared. Together, they work out a network of parents sharing their concerns and develop a plan for bringing their initial concerns closer to a deeper understanding of the nature of the problem, as well as closer to concrete actions for change. Teachers known to be very successful, with high expectations for students, are invited to participate. Over the next year, they meet regularly, collecting data through interviews, meeting notes and field notes, hold focus group discussions with parents and teachers, and examine school documents. As they sort and analyse their data, their understanding of 'meaningful parental involvement' emerges over time. Both teachers and parents take on leadership roles and all gain research skills. They share their findings by producing a booklet that other groups can use in assessing their school's family–school relationships, including suggested actions for each of the seven points of their findings (Tellin' Stories Project, 2000).

A community organizing story

A community activist and research group has long been interested in addressing the widely acknowledged gaps in achievement between various racial/ethnic and socio-economic groups. Building on long-standing traditions of community organizing, with direct links to the ideas of people like Myles Horton and Saul Alinsky (two well-known USA community organizers), they work at developing a broad sense of parent involvement that includes not only attention at the school level to curriculum and teaching but participation in the policy-making and also budget-making processes.

Many educators say that they cannot do the work of educating children alone, particularly low- and moderate-income children and children of color. Unfortunately, there are few mechanisms that allow parents and community members in low-income neighborhoods to play a meaningful role in the education of their children. For many people involved in education, parent participation is not seen as important or meaningful. As Lucy Ruiz, a parent and organizer with the Alliance Organizing Project in Philadelphia put it, 'Parents are seen as the pretzel sellers'. The common viewpoint is that parents are seen as the people who drop their kids off at school, conduct fundraisers, and occasionally volunteer time in a classroom. Community organiz-

ing seeks to change that dynamic. (Gold et al., 2002: 4)

Such groups work with the assumption that public schools are neither equitable nor effective for all students. Unlike other contemporary efforts, which focus on 'standards' and high-stakes testing of students, these efforts begin with building a large base of members with solid relationships and shared responsibilities. Through such efforts, leadership emerges not from the professional community alone, but from community residents, taking charge of the education of their own children through democratic processes. In this way, the organizing efforts are also educative efforts, which build a power base for the communities through knowledge and action linkages.

Information gathering plays a major role, as parents share concerns about the safety of the school buildings their children attend and ask questions such as 'Why do our children have to drink out of lead fountains, and play in dirt? Why do some communities have better facilities and more programmes than ours does?' Instead of ending with the listing of grievances, the process reveals a need to research the questions, to document the disparities, to analyse budgets, to make plans to present findings to governing bodies, to take field notes on their responses. Such data are used to further understand the issues, but also to plan strategic actions for improvement. Work following this model has included a large number of projects with different targets. For example, groups have lobbied for funding changes, worked for the creation of after-school programmes, documented school safety issues, addressed issues related to the racial climate in schools, and sponsored new kinds of staff development programmes for teachers and administrators. While the particular issues vary by community, the overall goal stays constant – building knowledge within communities, with a form of knowledge that assumes a direct connection between understanding and action. That knowledge also connects to a long-term project: that of building a new theory of change, one that emphasizes community capacity building alongside school improvement.

A student story

Very few educational action research projects look at issues from the standpoint of the students, although teaching students to be systematic enquirers is a frequent goal for schooling. A student voice might start an action research project as well:

It's so boring. But it's also confusing. I think that I know what I'm supposed to be doing and learning, but then the tests don't seem to match. I want to do well, but every time I study, it seems like it just doesn't work. When I learn things at home, from my family, it's so clear. They tell stories, show me how to do things, let me practice, and enjoy the products when we're finished. It's a group effort, not just me under the spotlight.

Working with an after-school group and its leader – a local graduate student – the children share similar stories and note a common theme of how their families help them learn in different ways than the school does. They want to know more about how their parents see learning at home and learning at school. The group generates a list of possible avenues to pursue, and agrees to begin with a 'family stories of school' project.

The students learn to develop interview protocols and use audio recording and digital cameras to gather parents' views on learning and schools. As the interviews are being completed, students learn how to analyse the material for recurrent themes and patterns. These are in turn used to organize excerpts for public sharing. Vignettes of family 'learning times' – covering a wide range of skills and contexts (for example, housework, childcare, construction, automotive work, the arts; in churches, libraries, businesses) are included.

Overall, the data showed a tendency to work collaboratively on a concrete task which had mutual benefits, with the students learning as they worked. They also showed the many ways in which families support their children's schooling. But another theme emerged as parents moved from concrete conversations about family learning to remembrances of their own experiences with schooling. Many parents, most often parents of colour or those from low-income families shared stories that spoke of alienation – times when as children they felt and even today feel disrespect or a lack of cultural awareness by school staff. Their anger and hurt came through as powerful indicators of their commitment to their children's education: they worked with and encouraged the children despite these experiences.

When the research was shared with school personnel, the impact was mixed. Some were angry and 'tired of being called a racist'. Others, though, wanted to find out more about how they could learn to teach in new ways, how to interact with the communities differently. A small group said, 'Finally. Now perhaps we can move forward.'

Each of these stories highlights different communities of researchers and thereby embodies differing values which are, in turn, related to different ideological orientations. In that way, all of the projects share a concern with a particular political agenda, although one group might identify this as a professional concern while another articulates the concern in terms of its sense of community. Likewise, all of the 'stories' involve a personal dimension in the sense that they all require rethinking of one's actions in the world and revaluating their worth and effectiveness. The projects do not emerge in a linear fashion from research questions derived solely from academic definitions of researchable topics. Rather they revolve around questions that are integrally tied to practice; they are formed from a need for change which is driven by, and in the process generative of, new knowledge. They are research from 'inside', but at the same time show how the participants in the research, through the cycles of research, often define and often redefine who counts as an insider and who an outsider. All of the stories too work toward a new form of theory–practice relationship, in some cases through including 'popular' as well as 'academic' knowledge forms.

Annotated bibliography

Altrichter, H., Posch, P. and Somekh, B. (1993) *Teachers Investigate Their Work*. London: Routledge.

Provides information on research methods and practical exercises in a readable form. It draws on education, but the ideas can easily be adapted.

Binnie, A. and Titchen, A. (1998) *Patient-centred Nursing: An Action Research Study of Practice Development in an Acute Medical Unit*. London: National Institute for Nursing.

Presents a major action research project carried out in a hospital ward. A good example of an insider/outsider partnership.

CARN website (Collaborative Action Research Network): < http://www.did.stu.mmu.ac.uk/carn/ >

CARN is an international network founded in 1976 which hosts an annual conference. Membership includes a free subscription to *Educational Action Research*.

Carr, W. and Kemmis, S. (1983) *Becoming Critical: Knowing through Action Research*. Victoria: Deakin University Press, republished by Falmer Press.

A detailed rationale for action research as a way of putting into practice ideas from critical theory.

Cochran-Smith, M. and Lytle, S.L. (1993) *Inside Outside: Teacher Research and Knowledge*. New York and London: Teachers College, Columbia University.

Part one provides a detailed rationale for teacher research. Part two comprises 21 examples of teachers' research writing.

Dadds, M. (1995) *Passionate Enquiry and School Development: A Story about Teacher Action Research*. London and Bristol, PA: Falmer Press.

Through a detailed account of one teacher's action research and the reflections of her tutor (the author), this book gives unusual insights to the processes of action research and professional development.

Educational Action Research (EAR)

EAR, founded in 1991, is an international journal which defines action research broadly and includes a wide range of contributions from practitioners' accounts of action research projects to scholarly articles on methodology.

Elliott, J. (1991) *Action Research for Educational Change*. Buckingham, UK and Bristol, PA: Open University Press.

The short autobiographical introduction explaining Elliott's commitment to curriculum change is followed by case studies of teachers' professional learning.

Hollingsworth, S. (ed.) (1997) *International Action Research: A Casebook for Educational Reform*. London and Washington, DC: Falmer Press.

An excellent collection of articles on action research drawn from many countries and professional settings.

Noffke, S. (1997) 'Professional, personal, and political dimensions of action research', *Review of Research in Education*, 2: 305–43.

A comprehensive scholarly review of action research from the earliest days to the mid-1990s.

Reason, P. and Bradbury, H. (eds) (2001) *Handbook of Action Research: Participative Inquiry and Practice*. London and Thousand Oaks, CA: Sage.

Spans action research across the social sciences. It is divided into four parts ('groundings', 'practices', 'exemplars' and 'skills').

Winter, R. and Munn-Giddings, C. (eds) (2001) *A Handbook for Action Research in Health and Social Care*. London: Routledge/Taylor & Francis.

A key resource for those carrying out action research in health and social care settings.

Further references

Altrichter, H. (2001) 'Practitioners, higher education and government initiatives in the development of action research: the case of Austria', in S. Hollingsworth (ed.), *International Action Research: A Casebook for Educational Reform*. London and Washington, DC: Falmer Press, pp. 30–9.

Berge, B.-M. and Ve, H. (2000) *Action Research for Gender Equity*. Buckingham: Open University Press.

Borda, O.F. (2001) 'Participatory (action) research in social theory: origins and challenges', in P. Reason and H. Bradbury (eds), *Handbook of Action Research: Participative Inquiry and Practice*. London and Thousand Oaks, CA: Sage, pp. 27–37.

Cochran-Smith, M. and Lytle, S.L. (1999) 'The teacher research movement: a decade later', *Educational Researcher*, 28(7): 15–25.

Dewey, J. (1933) *How We Think*. New York: Heath.

DuBois, W.E.B. (1973) *The Education of Black People? Ten Critiques*. Amherst, MA: University of Massachusetts Press.

Elliott, J. (1994) 'Research on teachers' knowledge and action research', *Educational Action Research*, 2(1): 133–7.

Elliot, J. (2001) 'School-based curriculum development and action research in the United Kingdom,' in S. Hollingsworth (ed.), *International Action Research: A Casebook for Educational Reform*. London and Washington, DC: Falmer Press, pp. 17–29.

Feldman, A. (2003) 'Validity and quality in self-study', *Educational Researcher*, 32(3): 26-8.

Gold, E., Simon, E. and Brown, C. (2002) *Strong Neighborhoods, Strong Schools: The Indicators Project on Education Organizing*. Chicago: Cross City Campaign for Urban School Reform.

Griffiths, M. (1998) *Educational Research for Social Justice: Getting Off the Fence*. Buckingham: Open University Press.

Grundy, S. (1982) 'Three modes of action research', *Curriculum Perspectives*, 2(3): 23–34.

Hinsdale, M.A., Lewis, H.M. and Waller, S.M. (1995) *It Comes from the People*. Philadelphia, PA: Temple University Press.

Horton, M. (1990) *The Long Haul: An Autobiography*. New York: Doubleday.

Lewin, K. (1988) 'Group decision and social change', in S. Kemmis (ed.) *The Action Research Reader*. Victoria, Australia: Deakin University Press, pp. 47–56.

McNiff, J. (1988) *Action Research: Principles and Practice*. London: Macmillan Education.

O'Hanlon, C. (2001) 'The professional journal, genres and personal development', in S. Hollingsworth (ed.), *International Action Research: A Casebook for Educational Reform*. London and Washington, DC: Falmer Press, pp. 168–78.

Pasmore, W. (2001). 'Action research in the workplace: the socio-technical perspective', in P. Reason and H. Bradbury (eds), *Handbook of Action Research: Participative Inquiry and Practice*. London and Thousand Oaks, CA: Sage, pp. 38–47.

Schön, D.A. (1983) *The Reflective Practitioner*. New York: Basic Books.

Somekh, B. (1995) 'The contribution of action research to development in social endeavours: a position paper on action research methodology', *British Educational Research Journal*, 21(3): 339–55.

Stenhouse, L. (1975) *An Introduction to Curriculum Research and Development*. London: Heinemann Educational Books.

The Tellin' Stories Project Action Research Group (2000) *Between Families and Schools: Creating Meaningful Relationships*. Washington, DC: Network of Educators on the Americas.

Torres, C.A. (1992) 'Participatory action research and popular education in Latin America', *Qualitative Studies in Education*, 5(1): 51–62.

Walker, M. (1998) 'Academic identitites: women on a South African landscape', *British Journal of Sociology of Education*, 19(3): 335–54.

Whyte, W.F. (ed.) (1991) *Participatory Action Research*. Newbury Park, CA and London: Sage.

Winter, R. (1998) 'Managers, spectators and citizens: where does "theory" come from in action research?', *Educational Action Research*, 6(3): 361–276.

Zeichner, Kenneth M. (2003) 'Teacher research as professional development for P-12 educators in the USA', *Educational Action Research*, 11(2): 301–26.

11

RESEARCHING POLICY

Jill Blackmore
School of Education, Deakin University, Australia
Hugh Lauder
Department of Education, University of Bath, UK

Key concepts

Jill Blackmore

What is policy?

Policy studies is a highly contested field in terms of how policy should be understood, the role of policy researchers and who does policy research (Ozga, 2000). Policy is more than 'official' texts produced by and on the authority of governmental or executive power. Policy has multiple dimensions within any field of activity, whether education, health or welfare. Policy could be considered to be a text, a process, a discourse, a political decision, a programme, even an outcome. Policy is a 'form of social action both intended and actual', and it is 'inevitably incomplete in terms of how it maps into practice' (Ball, 1994: 10). Policy is also normative. Policy-makers seek to change behaviours through the distribution of scarce resources and in so doing change values (Le Grand, 1997). Whether it is at the state or institutional level, policy is 'the authoritative allocation of values' (Prunty, quoted in Taylor et al., 1997: 1).

The issues for policy researchers are about how and why certain policies come to be developed in particular contexts, by who, for whom, based on what assumptions and with what effect. On whose authority is policy produced and disseminated, what are the principles of allocation, whose values are being promoted, who wins and who loses?

Understanding the 'field' of policy research

In the twentieth century policy studies emerged as a discipline that sought legitimacy by claiming to be a 'science'. This *'rational' model of policy analysis*, which dominated until the 1970s, was premised upon statistical techniques, large population samples and linear hierarchical processes. In this model, research was done by experts, and policy was developed by government and then disseminated/implemented by practitioners. Any failures were blamed on technical problems rather than the assumptions underlying the policy. Poor dissemination/communication, failed implementation and flaws in statistical procedures and sampling were also possible 'culprits'. Government has historically favoured such 'rational or technocratic models' based on quantitative research because it claims to be generalizable, objective and offers simple ways of understanding a problem. This rational model was often associated with an incrementalist position in which policy is perceived as a pluralist, consensual process mediated by the state in relatively benign ways. If policy is seen as proceeding by consensus through a benign state then underlying assumptions about inequalities in power and who will win and lose as a result of a policy(s) need not be interrogated.

However, these rational models were coming under increasing criticism as the period of postwar reconstruction and 'consensus' was challenged by questions of social class, gender and ethnicity. By 1986, Dale (1986: 68) named three main orientations to policy analysis, particularly in education, arising from three fields of activity: those of social administration (prescriptive and ameliorative), of policy analysis (pragmatic and problem-solving) and of social science (theoretical and relatively distant from the action).

The new sociology of knowledge and the rise of a critical social science and feminism during the 1970s, informed by the work of cultural studies, critical theorists and Gramsci's notions of hegemony, questioned the value neutrality of the research methods underpinning the rational model and its claims to generalizability. This critical tradition perceived policy sceptically: rather than being about social justice it was about social control because the state was seen as complicit with the power of entrenched interests. In essence, policy was a product of political contestation and negotiation between stakeholders with unequal political power.

However, during the 1980s and 1990s, globalization on the one hand and democratic demands of diverse populations on the other, challenged the conception of the state as a unitary, monolithic source of power (Dale, 1986). But social theorists increasingly conceptualized the state as a contested site of political action, in which a set of, often contradictory, processes and relationships mediated policy production, simultaneously producing new opportunities and closing down others for particular groups. This approach has highlighted the importance of theorizing policy in terms of local/global relations. It has also led to reconceptualizing the nature of policy as 'new forms of public administration' which have given rise to a new managerial class of multi-skilled generic managers who 'wrote policy' but whose loyalty was to ministers rather than an 'imagined public'(Yeatman, 1998). At the heart of the reconstruction of the post-welfare state has been the notion of *performativity*: the idea that each institution would have targets against which performance could be measured. Behind such targets was a new social technology of control involving accountability systems, strategic planning, quality assurance and performance management. This social technology raised a new set of policy questions ranging from the obvious – do systems of performativity, such as external standards regimes imposed on the professions, improve performance? – to examining the related questions concerning the way performativity reconstructs professional identities, motivations and effectiveness. For example, in health a new cadre of managers was introduced to make resource and organizational decisions which were taken out of the hands of clinicians in order to gain financial efficiencies. But this strategy changed the professional identities of clinicians because priorities were determined by 'targets' rather than by their experience and judgement.

The above 'critical' analysis draws upon what has been termed the 'new policy sociology'. The new policy sociology, itself a product of the critical tradition, emerged in the context of the rise of the dominance of New Right policies in many Anglopho-ne nation-states during the 1980s on the one hand, and poststructuralist theory in the academy on the other (e.g. Ball, 1994). The focus here widened policy concerns from the production, reception and effects of policy to how discourse, language and text set the context for how policy questions are framed.

To better analyse these discursive shifts in policy in the field of education, Ball (1994) distinguishes between the notion of *policy-as-text* and *policy-as-discourse*. *Policy-as-text* distinguishes between more open-ended 'readerly' texts that allow for interpretation by policy actors, and more closed 'writerly' policy texts that are more prescriptive and constraining of re-interpretation by teachers. In both cases policy texts are seen as inherently ambiguous and open to degrees of interpretation. *Policy-as-discourse* sees policy as part of a wider system of social relations, framing what is said and thought. Policy texts simultaneously emerge out of, but also produce, particular policy discourses. Groups and individuals position themselves, and are positioned by, these texts and discourses, and their acceptance, rejection or modification is shaped, in part, by them. Discourse analysis, therefore requires policy researchers to uncover the normative nature of decisions that appear to be obvious, inevitable or natural, to test judgements about truth claims, and to consider alternative more socially just ways of developing policies and practice.

However, a theme running through policy studies concerns the nature of the links between policy as intended by policy-makers and its relationship to what actually happens in practice. Do the recipients of policy initiatives faithfully do as they are bid? A more radical interpretation of the disjuncture between the community of policy-makers and practitioners has been provided by Ladwig (1994). He utilizes Bourdieu's notions of field and habitus to argue that educational policy has little to do with what goes on in education systems and schools because education *policy* as a social field is marked out by players outside education --universities, journals, researchers (public and private), commercial providers, ministerial departments – which only partially overlaps with education as a field in which teachers, parents and students are the actors. Policy research is a relatively autonomous field with its own rules, hierarchies and players with their own predispositions seeking to position themselves optimally. Policy actors in this perspective both protect and advance the field but its relationship to practitioners may be only tenuous. This approach would explain why practitioners are often alienated by policy initiatives since policy-makers may have little understanding of the day-to-day realities of practitioners and understand less about their senses of professional identity.

These approaches also highlight how policy also has a *wider representational or symbolic power*. Recent policy research has focused on the role of the media in mediating policy, exemplified in how the New Right were able to mobilize popular opinion by producing 'de facto' policies (more standardized literacy testing, increased reporting of unemployed) in response to 'de facto' problems (e.g. literacy crisis, welfare cheating) through the media. Governments, through the media, test public opinion about policies and provide policy solutions (often under-researched, under-resourced and poorly timed).

The problem of the lack of articulation between policy and practice has been extended by globalization. Globalization has also led to a focus on the *articulation of policy transnationally* with the phenomenon of 'travelling policies' between nation-states during the 1990s, for example new public administration, devolution and privatization. Here the questions are: why have some policies been taken up in different nation-states, how appropriate is policy importation and in whose interests is it undertaken, and what have been the differential effects of such importation? Here again, Bourdieu's notion of policy 'fields' has been useful in conceptualizing the emergence of overlapping 'global policy communities', for example the OECD, UNESCO, international financial organizations such as the IMF and World Bank and non-governmental organizations (Henry et al., 2001). But while there may be overlapping views held by these multilateral agencies, their policy prescriptions hatched high up in the glass towers of New York and Washington may have little relevance to solving social problems on the ground.

Feminist critical theorists similarly view policy research as contested, socially constructed, 'situated' and value laden. *Critical feminist policy studies* focus on how gender permeates the categories of analysis in policy and the organizational contexts in which policies are produced, the need for interdisciplinary and multiple theoretical and methodological approaches and the power relationships between researchers and researched. They identify the gendered silences and gaps in policy texts and discourses, unpack the categories and assumptions underpinning policy, and consider the effects of policies on marginalized groups. For example, health, welfare and education policies often ignore the reality of women being the primary carers of the aged, sick and young, thus positioning women to take up the slack of the post-welfare state's withdrawal from responsibility. Critical feminist policy analysis has been particularly effective in criticizing the dominant New Right policies because they assume a human capital theory premised upon the self-maximizing, freely-choosing, autonomous individual who is a man, *homo economicus*. Yet individual choices are framed by material conditions and relationships of interdependency with different cultural and social capital – there is no race, gender and class neutral individual. Feminist policy researchers, particularly in Australia, New Zealand and Scandinavia, have contested the *state-centric view* of policy that focused on male policy elites. Feminist bureaucrats (femocrats) working through the state conceptualize policy as a 'dialogue' between the policy actors in the state and grass-roots social movements in particular policy communities (Yeatman, 1998).

Poststructuralist theories of policy, therefore, have addressed the fundamental question of whether the recipients and readers of policies have a sense of agency. On this basis we can construct more powerful explanatory theories of how social change occurs. The notion of discourse draws attention to the idea that power works through institutionalized discursive hierarchies in which some policy discourses are treated as 'truths' while more radical perspectives are marginalized. Questions for policy researchers are:

- How do some discourses become hegemonic or commonsensical, and under what conditions and with what effects?
- How are policies mediated through the state and articulated globally/nationally/locally, and with what unexpected outcomes?
- How are discourses appropriated and reworked?

This review of approaches to policy research has highlighted the importance of discourses and the theories they produce and the critical analysis and testing of the theoretical assumptions underlying policy initiatives (Lauder et al., 2004). It has also emphasized the different ways in which there may be a disjuncture between what policy-makers intend and what occurs in practice, which may give rise to unintended consequences.

Implications for research design

Doing policy research requires a notion of the intentions for undertaking policy research, a capacity to frame the policy 'problem' and some clarity about the boundaries. One way of locating oneself in the field of policy research is to make the distinction as to whether you are doing 'research for policy' and/or 'research about policy'. A second question is whether you are an 'outsider' or an 'insider', the latter more likely to be the case if you are a practitioner-researcher undertaking a workplace-based professional doctorate, and how that shapes your approach. Third, is your investigation about all or any of the processes of policy production, dissemination and implementation or policy effects? Finally, is your focus at the global, macro (e.g. governmental), meso (regional) or micro (e.g. hospital, employment agency, school) level or the articulation between levels?

Research for policy

The question for policy researchers is whether they are doing 'policy critique' or 'policy service'. While these are not necessarily mutually exclusive, each approach creates different ethical issues about definitions of the problem, ownership, outcomes and intended use. Researchers can warn policy-makers about problems, inform them of possible policy options, assist them in reframing policy problems or provide policy-makers *post hoc* with rationalizations of politically desired policy options. Your relation with key policy-makers may determine what you can research and what can be published in the public domain. The rise of contract research means that policy researchers may be restricted from publishing material as controversial reports are 'shelved'.

Research about policy

Ozga (2000: 1) states that '... the orientation of a policy researcher towards a policy problem is likely to have consequences for the kinds of investigations he or she carries out'. Action research is often appropriate for practitioner-researchers who wish to develop policy within their own workplace. Here policy critique and policy service can provide a useful tension but require high levels of reflexivity on the part of researchers. Feminist policy researchers overtly seek to be interventionist and visionary and provide alternative ways of conceptualizing a problem or doing policy, what Yeatman (1998) refers to as 'policy activism'.

What is the policy problem here?

Policies define a problem in a particular way and then set up categories and certain logics that typically go unquestioned. Policy is often less about 'problem-solving' and as much about 'problem-setting' in terms of setting up an agenda for social action (Yeatman, 1998). Bacchi's (1999) 'What is the problem?' approach explores 'strategic representations' of the policy problem and argues that 'policy solution' approaches of rational models close down debate. It is important, therefore, not to take official definitions of a problem at face value but to ask how that definition was generated and how it fits into the state's agenda for social programmes.

Multiple methods

The primary issue is what constitutes a policy question – is it defined by government, by research or by stakeholders? In turn, the policy question impacts on how one does the research. Policy studies does not have a distinctive set of methodologies, but calls upon a range of methodological positions and methods in order to achieve the most powerful explanations for policy questions. The strong tradition of large-scale statistical models continues to have greater influence among policy-makers because of its perceived generalizability and a belief that 'hard quantifiable data' has greater validity than what is perceived as 'anecdotal' case study or qualitative research. This falls into the trap that sees quantitative research providing 'real data' and qualitative research 'the colour' (Ozga, 2000: 91–2). Increasingly, the complexity of social problems has led to recognition that quantitative analysis often provides inadequate responses to many policy questions. Large-scale quantitative data sets tend to view individuals as 'averages' or as exhibiting ideal type behaviours and cannot always be contextualized in terms of particular locations or communities (Lauder et al., 2004). Equally, such studies can identify a problem and make associations between particular factors, but often cannot explain the phenomena. The complexity of the 'problem' is often best addressed by in-depth qualitative analysis. Quantitative and qualitative methods can augment one another to flesh out this complexity. Ideological positions that equate particular methods with particular policy ideologies or perspectives should be rejected.

The following case study explores and explicates some of these traditional aims of policy research and the often 'mysterious' processes by which research moves from a phase of creation to one of presentation.

Stories from the Field — a story of serendipity in the field of policy research

Hugh Lauder

This case study indicates the gap between official policy discourses about the knowledge economy that are being used (often *post hoc*) to justify workplace restructuring and new technology and the actuality of what happens on the ground. My work in the policy field has always sought to link the quantitative and qualitative to investigate such gaps. This story is based on an interview with my banking relations manager. Fitting the interview into the broader statistical picture about the changing demand for skills helped to challenge the dominant policy discourse about the relationship of education to the economy. It also helped to provide an alternative explanation of the links between the two and, more controversially, raise the question of whether the middle class is safe in its investments in higher education or whether as the novelist J.G. Ballard has suggested they will become *the new proletariat*.

For the past year I have been working with Phil Brown on the links between globalization, the knowledge economy and higher education. The general hypothesis we are investigating is that the knowledge economy will not deliver on the rhetoric of policy-makers by providing increasing numbers of highly skilled jobs. Indeed, we take the view that all the indications are that there will be a decline in opportunities for the middle class. Our aim, therefore, is to test the truth claims underlying the rhetoric that is taken as common sense or a natural part of the post-industrial landscape. Broadly speaking, most of the evidence marshalled in the resulting (Brown and Lauder, 2003) paper is quantitative. However, the chance to engage in some small-scale qualitative research enhanced the explanatory power of the paper.

One aspect of the study involved an idea first developed by Brint (2001) that the view taken by policy-makers of the knowledge economy is a-contextual and a-historical. Brint had noted that knowledge-based jobs in the previous century had over time with

the development and transfer of 'best practice' become routinized. The consequence was that many jobs that originally required a high degree of knowledge and skill no longer required that level of skill.

Could such an analysis be applied to some of the knowledge economy sectors today? Around the time that I was pondering this question I took time off to phone my personal relations banking manager. I wanted a loan to buy a second-hand car. In the past, let us call him Henry, had the discretion to loan up to £30,000. In this case I was only after a fraction of that sum and was expecting him to agree to it over the phone but he did not.

'It's a bit more difficult these days,' Henry explained. 'I don't have that kind of discretion anymore to agree the loan on the nod. You're going to have to fill in some paperwork and we'll have to send it up the line to get the loan agreed.'

I was surprised and asked him what was going on. Henry was close to forty, had worked in the same bank for a long time and was perceived as successful with strong knowledge of his local customer base.

'It's all changed,' he said, 'since we've been taken over.'

There was a pause on the line and then he said he'd send the paper-work out to me. I replaced the receiver and went back to the research but something had triggered a connection between Henry and my present preoccupation. The forms duly arrived and I filled them in, although most of the information should already have been with the bank. As I went to post the forms back to him, the hunch or intuition that had been working away at the back of my mind clearly presented itself. I should say that walking, as I had to the Post Office, is one way in which ideas present themselves; it's precisely when I am away from writing and doing something totally different that they seem to emerge.

Returning home I read back through some of the literature on national skills profiles in the UK. Sure enough the quantitative research showed that the banking industry was one where employees reported that their discretion in making judgements on the job was being reduced. One of the reasons why an economy would want better educated workers and especially more graduates is precisely that they are able to make independent judgements. After all, in order to study for a degree a high level of autonomy is required. However, the process of management delayering that started in the 1980s enabled many middle management jobs to be stripped out with closer communications between senior managers and workers. What facilitated this process was the new technology related to the introduction of the PC. In turn this has meant that many in intermediate positions – and indeed those in lower positions – now have to cope with greater complexity. However, greater complexity does not entail greater discretion and judgement over the tasks undertaken.

The assumption that policy-makers have made is that the introduction of new electronic technologies will create an increased demand for skills. But it 'ain't necessarily so'. Technology and skill can be used in a complementary way in order to raise productivity but electronic technology can also be used for purposes of surveillance and control. Initially it was thought that because banks had invested in new technology they would become a paradigm of the new knowledge economy. But what I had read, fired by Henry's comments, suggested otherwise. I needed to know what lay behind the figures on skill in the banking industry.

Within a week I was in Henry's office with a tape recorder, our usual positions reversed because I was now interviewing him. Henry was frustrated by what had happened to his job and he was happy to spend some time, in fact two hours, talking about it.

He took me through my personal file and showed me the paperwork involved in my loan application. What had come back from the 'credit controller' was effectively a computer printout that contained a series of criteria by which my application was judged. Interestingly, these included my postcode area and the percentage of those in the postcode that had defaulted on loans. Somehow my creditworthiness was to be judged against where I lived and the 'honesty' of my neighbours.

However, it emerged that this 'credit controller' is, in the first instance, a computer program that automatically assesses a loan application according to pre-specified criteria. Only in appealing against the credit controller's judgement, as represented by the computer program, does Henry have a role. But even here there is no indication that his judgement will carry weight. Effectively, the role of the personal relations manager is no more than one of 'front of office' sociability. As Henry put it to me, 'a junior with a ready smile could do my job now'. And, in this particular case, juniors on far lower salaries are being introduced to do the job. Indeed, salespeople were being hired from the next door clothes chain which was closing down.

But this was not the limit to the control and surveillance that had reduced Henry's ability to make independent judgements. His job now was one of mainly selling the bank's products to customers. Here he was a given a script that he was meant to follow based presumably on what was supposed to work and including various ways of manipulating potential customers' emotions. It was a script that Henry ignored. But there were many aspects of his job where that was impossible. His PC was brim full of manuals that governed the processes that had to be adopted for every conceivable problem or question that might arise. Failure to follow the manual would be subject to disciplinary procedures or a slap on the wrist depending on the gravity of the 'offence'.

But this was not all. The bank worked a five-day week which started on Fridays not Mondays. Every Friday his area manager, with data on Henry's performance on his PC screen, would phone him to review his performance for the week and whether he was on target to meet his annual financial goals. Starting a week on a Friday is psychologically telling because it could leave Henry with the weekend to worry about how his performance could be improved if he was not meeting his targets. Henry was actually very successful in what he did and the bank used him to convey best practice to his colleagues but the changes in his job left him with a dilemma. He enjoyed that part of the job where he could meet people and, where possible, help them with their financial problems. But the devaluing of his knowledge and experience by the systems of control and surveillance that had been installed was another matter and he was considering leaving the bank.

Henry had given me rich insights into how the introduction of new technology had changed his job and to some extent his life. But when linked to the quantitative data patterns thrown up by the national surveys on skill, his interview filled out important aspects of the wider picture by providing an explanation of why corporations had restructured his job and many like it.

Corporations were using the new technology to create as consistent and predictable outcomes as possible. It ensured that the variables leading to under- or over-performance could more easily be measured and therefore identified. No one could escape from this computer-driven micro management. By this process, the bank was able to calculate the practices that could minimize risk while maximizing profits. It reduced workers' discretion and left decision-making to those at the top who processed the information coming up to them and then through manuals developed codes of best practice.

This piece of the jigsaw also fitted in with another odd 'fact' about the knowledge-based economic revolution: it is not generating the productivity gains that might be expected given that this economic revolution, supposedly, is meant to be as significant as the Industrial Revolution.

The interview with Henry linked to the statistical data patterns we had analysed showed that our picture of the knowledge-based economy is not the one that policy-makers like to paint. It also raises further questions about who benefits from the official picture.

Annotated bibliography

Bacchi, C. (1999) *Women, Policy and Politics. The Construction of Policy Problems.* London and Thousand Oaks, CA: Sage.

Overviews traditional and current approaches to policy studies. Uses feminist and post-positivist theories to develop a conceptual framework for policy analysis that starts with the question 'what is the problem here?'

Ball, S. (1994) *Education Reform: A Critical and Post-structural Approach.* Buckingham: Open University Press.

An early explication of the new policy sociology drawn from poststructuralist theory through a policy analysis of Thatcher's education reforms in the UK.

Brint, S. (2001) 'Professionals and the "knowledge economy": rethinking the theory of post industrial society', *Current Sociology*, 49(4): 101–32.

Challenges the view that knowledge jobs will remain creative and rewarding, arguing that such a view is a-contextual and a-historical. Many such jobs will become routinized.

Henry, M., Lingard, B., Rizvi, F. and Taylor, S. (2001) *OECD, Globalisation and Internationalisation.* Sydney: Allen & Unwin.

Maps the changing role of the OECD as part of an emerging global policy field in education.

Ladwig, J. (1994) 'For whom this reform? Outlining educational policy as a social field', *British Journal of Sociology of Education*, 15(3): 341–63

Uses Bourdieu's notions of field, habitus and discourse to analyse policy in the US context.

Lauder, H., Brown, P., and Halsey, A.H. (2004, in press) 'Sociology and political arithmetic: some principles of a new policy science', *British Journal of Sociology*.

This paper argues that we can learn from the tradition of political arithmetic about rules by which we can best view theories and judge between them.

Le Grand, J. (1997) 'Knights, knaves or pawns? Human behaviour and social policy', *Journal of Social Policy*, 26(2): 149–69.

Argues that policies assume that people are either knights who have a sense of duty, knaves who operate out of self-interest, or pawns who are simply passive and therefore act accordingly.

Ozga, J. (2000) *Policy Research in Educational Settings. A Contested Terrain.* Buckingham: Open University Press.

Makes a case for developing the teacher's capacity to critically research and analyse policy.

Taylor, S., Rizvi, F., Lingard, B. and Henry, M. (1997) *Educational Policy and the Politics of Change.* London: Routledge.

Comprehensive analysis of the changing role of the state and the nature of the education policy field.

Troyna. B. and Halpin, B. (1996) *Researching Education Policy: Ethical and Methodological Issues*. London: Falmer Press.

Case studies in the UK explicating various policy research issues arising from a critical social science perspective (studying elites, feminist and anti-racist approaches).

Yeatman, A. (ed.) (1998) *Activism and the Policy Process.* Sydney: Allen & Unwin.

Case studies in the fields of health, welfare and education illustrating how activists work to change policy. Framed within earlier conceptual work on policy discourses, educational change, gender equity and Australian femocracy.

Further references

Brown, P. and Lauder, H. (2003) *Globalisation and the Knowledge Economy: Some Observations on Recent Trends in Employment, Education and the Labour Market*, Keynote Address to the BAICE/BERA Conference on Globalisation. Bristol University, June.

Dale, R. (1986) *Introducing Education Policy: Principles and Perspectives*. Buckingham: Open University Press.

CHAPTER

12

THE PRACTICE AND POLITICS OF SPONSORED EVALUATIONS

Tineke Abma

Health Care Ethics and Philosophy, University of Maastricht, The Netherlands

Thomas A. Schwandt

Department of Educational Psychology, College of Education, University of Illinois at Urbana-Champaign, USA

Key concepts

Thomas A. Schwandt

Evaluation is a professional social practice concerned with determining the value (merit, worth, significance) of a programme, policy or project. Much evaluation work is for hire, with contracts issued by national and international agencies, private foundations and public agencies. Evaluation is undertaken in a variety of fields including education, healthcare and nutrition, technology, economic development, social welfare (e.g. poverty, family assistance, youth development), transportation, energy, the environment and agriculture. It is practised by academics whose first affiliation is university-based research and by privately employed professional evaluators. Generally – as with any form of disciplined, systematic investigation of human affairs – evaluation requires expertise in methodologies for generating and analysing both qualitative and quantitative data as well as knowledge of substantive issues implicated in the policy or programme that is being evaluated. Audiences for evaluation reports vary but include the client commissioning the study and different groups with a vested interest in the success or failure of a programme or policy (i.e. stakeholders), including programme developers and managers, programme participants, government officials, politicians, legislators and the public at large.

Although there is nominal agreement among evaluators that the purpose of their practice is to determine value, there is considerable disagreement on just what that means and how it should be accomplished; hence, there are a variety of views on the purposes,

perspectives and methods of the undertaking (Chelmisky and Shadish, 1997; Donaldson and Scriven, 2003). This is far more than a simple debate over the choice of methods for doing evaluation; it concerns the very definition of the social practice of evaluation and its role in society.

Several of the more prominent, though not necessarily mutually exclusive, persuasions on the purpose and role of the practice include the following:

- *Evaluation to improve performance and accountability* is a view influenced by neo-liberalism and the programme and ideology of new public management that holds that evaluation is about the assessment and measurement of performance. The rationale here is that performance in public (and non-profit) organizations requires improvement (e.g., services should be more effective, efficient and transparently accountable to users, clients or customers) and the best way to achieve that is by adopting a results-oriented or outcomes-based approach.
- *Evaluation for knowledge building* defines evaluation as a scientific undertaking that generates explanations of how and why a programme or policy works and under what circumstances. Various methodologies and perspectives are employed here under the rubrics of theory-driven evaluation, scientific realist evaluation and social experimentation.
- In *evaluation for development* the evaluator partners or consults with an organization engaged in programme or organizational development.

Evaluation is focused on organizational learning and capacity building, on facilitating engagement of members in the task of development, enhancing their sense of ownership for the process and its results, and so on. Utilization-focused, participatory and collaborative, and empowerment evaluation are among the types of practices focused on development.

- *Evaluation for understanding* envisions evaluation as primarily a pedagogical rather than a technical undertaking. It is oriented to the practices of teachers, healthcare workers, social workers and the like. It aims at enhancing these practitioners' grasp of issues and concerns surrounding the judgement of the quality of their practice and their understandings of the meanings they attach to their practice and it often employs both dialogic and narrative strategies to accomplish these goals. It may be primarily descriptive and illuminative in intent and/or transformative. Fourth-generation evaluation, responsive evaluation, evaluation informed by hermeneutics and practical philosophy as well as some forms of case study evaluation are of this kind.

- *Evaluation for social critique and transformation* is a close cousin to the foregoing view and differs primarily in its avowed focus on power and the reduction or elimination of exploitation, inequality and oppression in social relations. Evaluation approaches of this kind are informed by the tradition of critical hermeneutics, feminist theories and social action perspectives.

Several significant debates within the field swirl around the very meaning of the words 'evaluate', 'value' and 'politics'. One important discussion deals with the proposition that evaluation *ought* to be concerned with making value judgements and just what making a value judgement means. Some evaluators argue that their responsibility is primarily scientific description and explanation. Thus, if the object in question is a drug-treatment programme (X), they would describe its features – what is done, by whom, how often, to whom, when, and so on. They would also determine the relationship between X and its desired outcomes (Y, Z) taking into account factors (e.g. B and C) that might mitigate or confound that relationship. They might also consider whether X achieves its desired outcomes efficiently (i.e. consider costs). Having done this they would render a judgement to the effect that 'X (under conditions B and C)

leads to Y and Z.' Judging value here is synonymous with scientific appraisal or explanation of what happened and why. A generous interpretation of this way of thinking is that evaluation involves judgement of the *instrumental* value of X, namely whether X is effective and efficient in achieving its desired purpose(s).

Other evaluators argue that scientific appraisal is not equivalent to evaluation. They claim that judging the value of a programme or policy means taking into account a variety of value considerations beyond utility (or beyond whether the programme is effective). For example, the evaluator must judge the value of the desired purpose(s) of the programme and the conduct of the staff in view of legal and ethical considerations, and determine the basis for saying that the programme has utility or instrumental value (for example, is the criterion one of the greatest good for the greatest number?), and so on. In sum, these evaluators argue that the judgement of value extends well beyond the matter of scientific appraisal of whether and how a programme works.

This dispute relates to concerns over whether value judgements are an objective or subjective matter. The *subjectivist* holds that value judgments are in the eye of the beholder, so to speak. They are nothing more than expressions of personal or political preferences, tastes, emotions or attitudes on the part of individuals or groups. They are to be distinguished from statements based on facts that describe and explain some state of affairs. The facts of the matter are capable of being rationally debated and resolved, and hence descriptions and explanations can be judged as either true or false. Thus determining the utility (effectiveness, outcomes) of a programme – whether it is instrumental in achieving its intended objectives – is really the only 'judgement' that can be 'objective' because that assessment rests solely on the facts of the matter. Judgements of value, because they are subjective, can never be resolved by rational means; they will be endlessly argued. This subjectivist position is typically held by evaluators who claim it is the primary *responsibility of stakeholders*, not the evaluator, to make the judgement of value. The evaluator's responsibility is limited to, at best, describing and reporting the various value positions at stake in what is being evaluated and making descriptive statements to the effect that 'if you value A, then B is the case'. Evaluators who assume that their task is primarily one of scientific appraisal and explanation often take this position.

The *objectivist* disagrees and holds that value judgements (e.g. 'X is a good, poor, corrupt, programme') are rationally defensible and that disputes over whether such statements are true and objective are resolvable. Thus there are such things as moral disagreement, moral deliberation and moral decision. Objectivists disagree on the procedure for objectively determining value questions. Some claim that it is primarily the *evaluator's responsibility* to render a judgement of value by taking into account all relevant values bearing on the merit, worth or significance of what is being evaluated. These evaluators identify and synthesize various pertinent sources of value – for example, needs assessments, professional standards for a practice, legal and regulatory considerations, programme objectives and relevant comparisons – in each particular evaluation. There is disagreement on just how this synthesis and judgement is to be made. Different procedures are defended including clinical inference, an all-things-considered synthesis that provides the most coherent and defensible account of value, a heuristic qualitative weight and sum procedure and non-deductive reasoning to develop an argument scheme. Other objectivists argue that determining the value of a programme or policy should not be undertaken exclusively by the evaluation expert but via some kind of democratic procedure or forum in which *stakeholders and the evaluator jointly discuss and deliberate* the matter of value and reach agreement or consensus. At issue here is the role evaluator expertise is accorded in the determination of value.

The relationship between evaluation and politics is also contested, in large part, because the 'political' is defined in different ways. A common assumption is that politics is about power, or more precisely the wrong kind of power – power in the form of guile, imposition, partisanship, threat, authority and command. Evaluation practice and its results are surely implicated in this political arena of bargaining, negotiating and deal making. The inevitability of this state of affairs is due to the facts that: (1) programmes are created and maintained by political forces; (2) higher echelons of government, which make decisions about programmes, are embedded in politics; (3) the very act of evaluation has political connotations (Weiss, 1991). Yet, despite the fact that evaluation practice inescapably brushes against this world of politics, steps must be taken so that politics of this kind do not taint or influence evaluation practice. Thus, in the politics of negotiating evaluation contracts, including access to and control of data, as well as the politics involved in the myriad types of interactions between evaluator, sponsor, client and stakeholders, every effort must be made to avoid polluting the evaluation process with the wrong kind of power politics. In other words, an evaluation must be planned and conducted in such a way that the cooperation of stakeholders is obtained, while any efforts by these groups to curtail or otherwise influence the conduct or conclusions of the evaluation are averted or counteracted.

In this way of thinking, the milieu and discourse of politics – conceived in terms of norms, values, ideology, power, influence, authority and so forth – is contrasted with the world of science – pictured in terms of facts, objectivity, and empirically warranted descriptions and explanations. The world of politics and values lies outside of the scientific practice of evaluation and presents a threat to its legitimate exercise of authority and persuasion grounded in information and scientific analysis. The findings of evaluation might well enter the arena of politics and become part of political rationality, but evaluators ought to take steps to minimize the contamination of scientific rationality by political influences. In a nutshell, this is the doctrine of value-free science as applied to evaluation (Proctor, 1991). This relationship between politics and evaluation neatly fits the representative liberal model of democratic theory (Ferree et al., 2002) in which disinterested, apolitical experts inform public decision-making in a detached (i.e. emotion- and value-free) manner thereby enhancing both the rationality and the civility of the debate about a suitable course of action in the free marketplace of ideas.

A different view holds that politics is primarily a matter of practical problem-solving. In this technocratic view of politics, the 'political' is paradoxically transformed into an outwardly apolitical phenomenon – a style of formalized accountability that becomes the new ethical and political principle of governance (Power, 1997). In this way of thinking, social service practices (education, healthcare, etc.) are treated as devices or technologies for engineering desired levels of output. Targets are set for practices to achieve. Evaluation becomes a means for quality assurance – it measures the *performativity* (efficiency) of practices against *indicators* of success in achieving the targets – and it takes on the characteristics of an engineering practice, aiming to exert direct influence on action in social and educational policy and practice by generating evidence of what works (Elliott, 2001).

A third view holds that politics is critical reflection on value-rational questions – where are we going? Is this desirable? What should be done? Who gains and who loses, by which mechanisms of power? (Flyv-bjerg, 2001). Here, evaluation practice is not envisioned as engineering or applied science concerned with establishing the rigour and reliability of its assessments of programme and policy performance. Rather, it is recast as a process of deliberation about values embodied in social action and human experiences (Schwandt, 2002). Evaluators are not neutral brokers of scientific information that informs public decision-making, rather they are more like deliberative practitioners connecting the worlds of is and ought, politics and ethics, in order to help clients and stakeholders 'learn not only about technique but about value; how we can change our minds about what is important, change our understanding and appreciation of what matters, and more, change our practical sense about what we can do together' (Forester, 1999: 62).

Implications for research design

Evaluation 'problems' do not come ready made, such that one can neatly select a design and set of tools to solve the problem. What comprises an acceptable study design and appropriate means of investigation depends greatly on how the 'object' of evaluation is framed and what one thinks the activity of evaluation should be. For example, when evaluations are viewed primarily as the scientific study of cause and effect, then designs follow standard principles of experimental and quasi-experimental studies; case study designs are often (but not exclusively) used by evaluators committed to evaluation as a form of understanding; evaluation as performance assessment employs a logic that entails precise specification of goals as tangible and measurable outcomes or targets, objective means with which to measure actual performance and standards against which the quality of the performance can be judged. Choices among various means of generating data (e.g. unstructured interviews or open-ended questions on surveys, questionnaires, structured or unstructured observations, archival data, document and record analysis, focus groups) and analysing/interpreting those data (e.g. constant–comparative method, cluster analysis, narrative portrayal, factor analysis) are determined in light of the kind of evaluation undertaken as well as practically in view of available resources and logistics. It is difficult to spell out a definitive list of design principles applicable to all evaluations beyond a list of epistemological virtues whose meaning is only determin-

able in context. This list includes (but is not necessarily limited to): responsiveness to client/stakeholders' needs and interests; open-mindedness; responsible use of means for generating and analysing data; honesty; objectivity (understood as the willingness and ability to provide reasons and evidence for one's claims); fallibility (accepting that one's claims are always corrigible and subject to reinterpretation); and a commitment to making one's study useful and its findings comprehensible to clients and stakeholders.

Stories from the Field – the politics of responsive evaluation
Tineke Abma

This is a story about the politics of evaluation and subtle mechanisms of exclusion. A few years ago, an executive manager at Welterhof, a psychiatric hospital in the South of the Netherlands, approached me to conduct a responsive evaluation of a vocational rehabilitation project. The project was meant to assist and train (ex-) psychiatric patients in their search for a meaningful day activity or job. Project participants wanted to start on a small experimental scale in the garden and greenhouse. 'Learning-by-doing' was their motto, and they also reasoned that this 'development along the way' might profit from an evaluation. The purpose of the evaluation was not to assess the project on the basis of its effectiveness, but to motivate participants to reflect on their actions and to improve their practice. I considered the evaluation a wonderful opportunity to gather material for my PhD on responsive evaluation. A responsive approach to evaluation focuses on stakeholder issues and a dialogue between stakeholders (Greene and Abma, 2001; Guba and Lincoln, 1989). The approach requires a certain power balance to give all stakeholders equal opportunities as participants in the process. The challenge was how to conduct a responsive evaluation in a situation characterized by asymmetrical relationships.

Managers and staff

A creative therapist, who worked on a part-time basis for the project, assisted me in the evaluation. The first question we confronted was with whom to start. The assistant suggested that the people who were most directly involved in the development of the project should be interviewed first, in this case the members of a specially formed task force. She had the feeling that some members were afraid that their work was not acknowledged while the manager was taking the credit for it. I took this observation seriously, because I did not want to ignore the *invisible work* of those who actually do the work. Being blind to these activities would be to succumb to the perils of managerialism.

The task force consisted of a heterogeneous group of practitioners with differing disciplinary backgrounds. Including them in a task force was uncommon in the hospital. Usually, projects were developed by a relatively homogeneous group of professional people. They would present their plans to the decision-makers and, what to do having been decided, the plans would be carried out by practitioners. The manager, who was relatively new in the hospital, considered this a very traditional leadership style. Her motto was participation: 'Involve people and share responsibility!' She liked to emphasize that 'involvement' was part of her participatory management philosophy, and that this also corresponded with the rehabilitation philosophy. In her own words: 'Not an expert-role towards the practitioner or an expert-role towards the patient, but jointly seeking the way.'

The vision of the manager differed remarkably from the experience of some of the members in the task force. We interviewed the staff and their stories suggested that they were not very happy with this new, participatory style of management. They liked being involved, but there were also signs that they did not like it. Some said, for example, that they wanted to be told what to do. Others interpreted the involvement as a delegation of work that needed to be carried out by them but that was not acknowledged. These paradoxical responses did not surprise us, because the message of the manager was also very paradoxical. On the one hand, people were invited to share responsibility; on the other hand several things were already predetermined. The manager, for example, preordained the planning: 'The first year to experiment, the second year to improve, and third year to make a "go–no go" decision.' The members accepted these time-constraints as hard and fast deadlines that could not be changed. This caused a feeling of panic especially among those who actually had to carry out the project: 'We haven't enough time to do the things that are needed to realize the quality we want.'

The imposition of the timeframe formed a *hidden conflict* between the manager and staff because the available time for the 'experiment' would have serious implications for their work. Compared to the hidden emotional response there was only slight overt resistance and this was only aired in private to a colleague of mine (Martin, 1992). The fact is that the staff did not encounter an overt conflict related to their self-definition. They did not consider themselves active 'subjects' who could influence the planning; rather, they behaved as if they were merely passive 'objects' that had to adapt to the situations that confronted them.

As evaluators we decided to support the staff by suggesting to them that they should draw attention to their problem. Since my colleague was also a member of the task force she could join the little coalition. Furthermore, we brought the subject up in one of the occasional meetings with the manager. We told the manager about the pressures of time that task force members felt under and asked her to adjust her deadlines to the rhythms of the people who were actually doing the project. Although this idea was at first contested, eventually the manager loosened her grip on the original plans. The negotiations over the planning and particularly the allocation of time to different phases were reopened.

Therapists and patients

The members of the task force were very eager to know what the patients thought of the project. 'Are they satisfied with what we are doing?' they asked. As evaluators we also found it important to take the patient perspective into account and wondered how we could make their silenced voices audible (Lincoln, 1993). We were very aware of the fact that madness was excluded from society the very moment that modern reason was born (Foucault, 1961/1984). How could we, as evaluators, let madness speak for itself? How could we talk with the silenced in their (silenced) language? I was not satisfied with the procedural rules offered by Guba and Lincoln (1989: 17, 150). These excluded all those actors – young children, mentally handicapped, psychotics – who lack communicational skills, but who in fact only lack the skills that are required in a specific context created by evaluators to succeed with their chosen method. I thought that if one sticks to an 'academic marketplace of ideas' then metaphorical, playful and embodied aspects of everyday speech would be excluded. Furthermore, I was afraid that a rational debate would only reproduce the process of 'othering' instead of emancipating them.

In line with Schwandt's (1994: 4) proposal for an 'ethics of care' that required 'attention to particular others in actual contexts' we began to participate in the activities of the group of patients who were taking part in the project. Initially we felt like voyeurs looking at people, but soon we began to forget about our role as 'observer'. Both of us liked gardening and got caught up in the work. We developed a relationship with the patients and their facilitator, and learned about their activities, their lives and their concerns. 'Patients,' the facilitator (gardener) said, 'are much more spontaneous in their reactions when they actually do something.' We recognized this ourselves; sitting or kneeling near someone's body on the ground with your hands in the mud is less threatening than a face-to-face situation where one is interviewing the other. One could say that the question–answer method – even if the tone is nice – is always feeding dualism.

The facilitator was not the only one who was sensitive to the connection between knowledge and power. The managers, for example, remarked that 'screening' was not an appropriate word in the context of rehabilitation because it maintained the *distance* between professional and patient. Ironically, the manager was also the one who promoted the development and standardization of new methods and techniques to test and screen people. Most of the therapists embraced this proposal under the cloak that it would enhance the quality of their work. We showed them that observational methods also (or primarily) served another purpose: they established and maintained the professional power of therapists who are literally disciplining the bodies of those who are the subjects of these experts. A therapist tried to explain what this meant: 'You create a different sort of relation. I mean, the relation therapist–patient is still there . . . and the patient does not need to be dependent . . . though . . . I have some expertise and that I find important too.' There was still another even more subtle way by which therapists tried to hold power. We discovered this mechanism only later when we confronted them with our ideas about approaching patients.

After having developed a trusting relationship we decided to do a group interview with the patients.

This was not encouraged; members of the task force reminded us that we had to take all the precautions required by the law that protected the rights of patients. We felt in two minds about this. We could not bypass the ethical commission, but it was somewhat patronizing that the patients could not decide for themselves whether to participate in the evaluation. While discussing the form of the group interview we suddenly came up with the idea of a picnic. This was less threatening than an individual interview. Moreover, we found it important to meet the patients in surroundings where they felt comfortable – in this case, nature. Again the task group warned us with the sentence 'They might become psychotic!' We interpreted this caution as a resistance to share power, because asking patients what they think is indirectly an attack on the power-expertise of the professional. No longer would they (the professionals) be the ones who knew what was best for the patients. Therefore we remained convinced of our idea and had a picnic. To everyone's surprise the outcome surpassed all expectations. Patients were capable of expressing their wishes and their dissatisfaction once we adjusted to their world and language. The task force members acknowledged they had underestimated the patients. The picnic as a different interaction with patients stimulated reflection and reopened fixated social relations between staff and patients.

In this story I have discussed the politics among project participants and how we as evaluators dealt with subtle mechanisms of exclusion as well as conflicts. Responsive evaluators have to be extra sensitive to power relations given the deliberate attempt to acknowledge plurality of interests and values and the genuine dialogue they want to facilitate (Abma et al., 2001; Koch, 2000; Wadsworth, 2001). In the case under consideration we as evaluators deliberately attempted to give voice to people and groups that are less powerful. We conducted in-depth interviews that acknowledge the personal identity of people and created a safe environment where people felt comfortable to speak up. These stories and voices were amplified in the process. The discrepancy between what was said and actually done stimulated reflection on the side of both managers and therapists.

Annotated bibliography

Donaldson, S.I. and Scriven, M. (eds.) (2003) *Evaluating Social Programs and Problems: Visions for the New Millenium*. Mahwah, NJ: Lawrence Erlbaum Associates.

Some leading North American theorists' views of evaluation and its social agenda including a transdisciplinary view, performance evaluation, empowerment evaluation, fourth-generation evaluation, a social activist approach, theory-driven evaluation and culturally sensitive evaluation.

Guba, E.G. and Lincoln, Y.S. (1989) *Fourth-Generation Evaluation*. Newbury Park, CA: Sage.

Although dated, this book has had a remarkable influence in shaping conceptions of the issues and practices of a social constructivist approach to evaluation.

House, E.R. (1993) *Professional Evaluation: Social Impact and Political Consequences*. Newbury Park, CA: Sage.

Explores evaluation as a modern social institution and its role in shaping society.

House, E.R. and Howe, K.R. (1999) *Values in Evaluation and Social Research*. Thousand Oaks, CA: Sage.

Explores the meaning and use of the concept of value in evaluation theory and practice. Advances a view of evaluation as wedded to deliberative democratic theory.

Kellaghan, T. and Stufflebeam, D.L. (eds) (2002) *International Handbook of Educational Evaluation*. Dordrecht, The Netherlands: Kluwer.

Coverage of key concepts, methods and areas of application in diverse national contexts.

Kushner, S. (2000) *Personalizing Evaluation*. London: Sage.

A unique way of looking at the relationship of people to programme in evaluation; instead of viewing programmes as the contexts in which participants' experiences are read, it argues that participants' experiences are the context in which social programmes and their significance are to be understood.

Patton, M.Q. (1997) *Utilization-focused Evaluation*. Thousand Oaks, CA: Sage.

Extensive explication of the theoretical and practical view that evaluations should be judged by their utility and actual use, where use includes both the application of evaluation findings and the value of participating in the process of evaluation. Also covers other forms of development evaluation.

Pawson, R. and Tilley, N. (1997) *Realistic Evaluation*. London: Sage.

A strong critique of current evaluation practice and an equally strong defence and explanation of evaluation methodology grounded in scientific realism.

Russon, C. and Russon, K. (eds) (2000) *The Annotated Bibliography of International Program Evaluation*. Dordrecht, the Netherlands: Kluwer.

Annotated bibliographies on evaluation theory and practice for Africa, Asia, Australasia, Europe, Latin America, the Middle East and North America written by authors with extensive work experience in the respective regions. Approximately 700 references are discussed.

Schwandt, T.A. (2002) *Evaluation Practice Reconsidered*. New York: Peter Lang.

A series of essays criticizing a narrow conception of evaluation as scientific methodology and arguing that evaluation practice ought to be redefined as a form of practical philosophy informed by the tradition of philosophical hermeneutics.

Stake, R.E. (2004) *Standards-Based and Responsive Evaluation*. Thousand Oaks, CA: Sage.

This book offers a balanced treatment of the choices evaluators face in framing programme evaluation in terms of standards and performance or in terms of activities, aspirations, and accomplishments of programme participants.

Weiss, C.H. (1998) *Evaluation: Methods for Studying Programs and Policies*. 2nd edn. Upper Saddle River, NJ: Prentice Hall.

A pragmatic approach to preparing for, designing and conducting evaluations in the complex political context of social programming.

Further references

Abma, T.A., Greene, J., Karlsson, O., Ryan, K., Schwandt, T.A. and Widdershoven, G. (2001) 'Dialogue on dialogue', *Evaluation*, 7(2): 164–80.

Chelmisky, E. and Shadish, W.R. (1997) *Evaluation for the 21st Century*. Thousand Oaks, CA: Sage.

Elliott, J. (2001) 'Making evidence-based practice educational', *British Educational Research Journal*, 27(5): 555–74.

Ferree, M.M., Gamson, W.A., Gerhards, J. and Rucht, D. (2002) 'Four models of the public sphere in modern democracies', *Theory and Society*, 31: 289–324.

Flyvbjerg, B. (2001) *Making Social Science Matter*. Cambridge: Cambridge University Press.

Forester, J. (1999) *The Deliberative Practitioner*. Cambridge, MA: MIT Press.

Foucault, M. (1984/1961) *De geschiedenis van de waanzin* (translation of *Folie et déraison: histoire de la folie à l'age classique*) (Published in English translation as *Madness and Civilization: A History of Insanity in the Age of Reason*). Amsterdam: Boom.

Greene, J.C and Abma, T.A. (eds) (2001) *Responsive Evaluation*. New Directions for Evaluation No. 92. San Francisco: Jossey-Bass.

Koch, T. (2000) '"Having a say": negotiation in fourth generation evaluation', *Journal of Advanced Nursing*, 31(1): 117–25.

Lincoln, Y.S. (1993) 'I and Thou: method, voice, and roles in research with the silenced', in D. McLaughlin and W. Tierney (eds), *Naming Silenced Lives*. New York: Routledge, pp. 29–47.

Martin, J. (1992) 'The suppression of gender conflict', in D.M. Kolb and J.M. Burtunek (eds), *Hidden Conflict in Organizations, Uncovering Behind-the-scenes Disputes*. Newbury Park, CA: Sage, pp. 165–86.

Power, M. (1997) *The Audit Society: Rituals of Verification*. Oxford: Oxford University Press.

Proctor, R.N. (1991) *Value-Free Science? Purity and Power in Modern Knowledge*. Cambridge, MA: Harvard University Press.

Schwandt, T. (1994) *On Reconceptualizing Interpretive Educational Inquiry as a Normative Undertaking*. Paper presented at the annual meeting of American Educational Research Association, New Orleans, LA.

Wadsworth, Y. (2001) 'Becoming responsive – and some consequences for evaluation as dialogue across distance', in J.C. Greene and T.A. Abma (eds), *Responsive Evaluation*, New Directions for Evaluation, No. 92. San Francisco: Jossey-Bass, pp. 45–58.

Weiss, C.H. (1991) 'Evaluation research in the political context: sixteen years and four administrations later', in M.W. McLaughlin and D.C. Phillips (eds), *Evaluation and Education: At Quarter Century*. Chicago: University of Chicago Press, pp. 211–31.

PART IV

OBSERVING, QUERYING, INTERPRETING

Introduction

This part of the book returns to the approaches and ideas presented in Part II and focuses more deeply on making meaning from human experience and social interactions in relation to different ways of understanding the nature of being (ontology) and knowledge (epistemology). The chapters stem from philosophical foundations and are primarily concerned with observing people, interactions, discourses and activities in naturalistic settings. These data are then interpreted to present rich stories about people and the world they live in from their perspective rather than that of the researcher. The first chapter provides an introduction to different philosophical stances that can shape the researcher's thinking and approach to data collection together with an introduction to hermeneutics, a theory of interpretation originally applied to biblical texts. The two chapters that follow describe methodological approaches which place emphasis on interpreting phenomena as experienced by research participants (or informants) in natural world settings. The chapter on observation provides an insight into how different ontological and epistemological starting points result in the collection of very different kinds of data, ranging from numerical records of instances of particular behaviours to reflexive accounts that involve the researcher in an interpretive dialogue with data recorded holistically. Finally, there is a chapter on discourse analysis, an analytical tool used to make sense of human communication through written and oral texts – interpreting and constructing meaning – going beyond apparent surface meanings to uncover the connotations of power and emotion that lie beneath.

Observation is a valuable tool used in many research approaches, whether quantitative or qualitative. But in Part IV the focus is mainly on immersion in the field, gathering data intensively from a variety of sources in naturalistic – as opposed to experimental – contexts, drawing on the researcher's direct experience and often attempting to view participants' experience from the inside (whether directly or indirectly). Interwoven with observation is querying or questioning, but not only questioning the participants or people upon whom the research is focused. A crucial aspect of the researcher as data gatherer is the capacity to question him/herself through a reflexive approach that takes account of the role of the self as a research instrument. How has the role of the researcher framed and shaped the interpretation through philosophical stances, insider/outsider approaches and prior experiences for example? Interpretation also needs to take careful account of the context in which the data were collected or recorded and the effects of interactions. In discourse analysis for example, Bakhtin's approach to the study of language is that words cannot be understood as transparent but rather as responsive – dialogic – and contextually embedded.

Once again, these chapters cross-refer to chapters in other parts of the book. Hermeneutics and phenomenology are philosophical approaches which have strongly influenced the practices of researchers using ethnography and case study (Part II). Ethical issues are of paramount importance when studying people, either directly through participation and shared experience, or indirectly through an independent, outsider's view (Part II). There are also obvious cross-links to Parts VI and VII where observation reappears as an important method of recording quantitative data and some of the stories from the field (see Crook and Garratt, in this volume) focus on the collection of observation data within naturalistic settings.

13

PHILOSOPHY AND HERMENEUTICS

David Heywood
Education and Social Research Institute, Manchester Metropolitan University, UK
Ian Stronach
Education and Social Research Institute, Manchester Metropolitan University, UK

Key concepts

Ian Stronach

This introduction is about philosophy. But what is philosophy, and how can we say what it is? If I say 'philosophy is X', then there is an immediate problem. Statements like 'philosophy is X' themselves already make assumptions about what kind of a thing philosophy must be, for example an entity that has a being, that can be defined as a system of beliefs, that offers persuasive argument as to its correctness and so on. A suspicion emerges. Every philosophy hides another philosophy behind, underneath or above itself. Put it another way: every philosophy tries to start at the beginning, and fails?

Try out the above problem by thinking about Descartes's famous philosophical conclusion: 'cogito ergo sum' (I think therefore I am). That philosophy reaches a conclusion, about mind/body dualism, that is also its unacknowledged starting point. The argument, or so it has often been claimed, is circular. Why is it so difficult for philosophies to begin or end decisively?

This raises a general and fundamental problem variously faced by all philosophies: how to make philosophical statements which avoid some kind of unacknowledged appeal to hidden grounds in order to justify themselves. This is a problem often couched as a transcendental or foundational appeal (e.g. to god, ego, Reason, consciousness, the Real). Or, indeed, to Method. Each of these offers an unexplicated 'philosophy' of the philosophy. Not as part of the argument, but as an unacknowledged axiom. This is why we have to deal with philosophical problems in relation to the 'identity' of researchers, their 'agency' in the research process, the methodological systems they

invoke in order to generate and interpret data, and the nature of the 'stories', 'concepts' or 'theories' that they generate.

In particular people fresh to research often assume a realist position. After all, we all practise our lives 'in the real'. And some statements about our lives seem very certain, like, 'today is Wednesday'. Given calendrical confirmation, no reasonable person can doubt that assertion. Yet if we ask: 'is it Wednesday everywhere in the world?' we begin to have to think of 'Wednesday' as a temporal envelope periodically sweeping across the world, a fleeting motion rather than a fact, ephemeral rather than enduring. If we add 'is it Wednesday on Mars?' the concept is spatially as well as temporally shattered. So the question 'is Wednesday real?' isn't always a daft one. It depends on your perspective:

> Every inquiry is a seeking. Every seeking gets guided beforehand by what is sought. (Heidegger, 1962: 24)

What is the relevance of this to educational research? Think of a 'feminist research' that would appeal as a foundation to a political standpoint, and therefore claim a standpoint epistemology (epistemology: theory of knowledge). Or think of an 'educational science' that would appeal as a foundation to its own internal methodological purity. What are the epistemological implications of these 'ghosts', the Feminist, the Scientist? Who are your ghosts? What are they whispering behind your back, and mine?

A little more about the 'philosophy of philosophy' problem. One solution would be to include the 'philosophy of philosophy' (P2 of P1) in our thinking. So if P1 has to be understood also in terms of P2 (which it assumes), then so be it. The problem is that if we claim that any P1 will always presume a P2, we have a problem of infinite regress. Won't P3 (etc.) always be round the corner, and doesn't that take us towards a dangerous relativism? A different and almost opposite sort of solution is to devise a system of ideas can be regarded as 'science'. There will then be no need for a P2. Education as 'science' is currently being promoted in this way by the UK government, although the philosophical belief system with which they support such a view is unknown. So here's a central dilemma. On the one hand, there is a view of philosophy as offering no better than a guarantee of incompletion and provisionality – there can be no certainty (Smith, 1989). On the other hand, there is the promise of educational and social research as cumulative science and increasing certainty. Between these possibilities, there is much thinking to be done by educational researchers.

As a matter of initial intuition, where do you stand on these issues of certainty? Your first answer may well be influenced by your own subject discipline, or indeed by your moral or political stance.

Meantime, then, work at clarifying five issues – what 'philosophy' can mean, issues of infinite regress, transcendental moves and the limits of certainty. They are philosophical problems intrinsic to any social research, any methodological move or any interpretive account. You can ignore them, but they will not ignore you.

Let's now try a different approach to the question 'What is philosophy?' In *Keywords* Raymond Williams answers that question historically. Philosophy began as the 'love of wisdom', and then took on 'subsidiary senses' (1976: 235) as in the post-classical sense of 'practical wisdom'. He contrasts 'philosophy' as a 'system of ideas' with its recent incorporation into managerial talk where philosophy can mean policy. This is philosophy as mission or vision.

Williams's view is that philosophical debates are not separate from culture and history. The word itself shifts in meaning, just as systems of belief do. Hold on to the idea that philosophy is somehow 'situated' in time and space (like 'Wednesday'), and look at how the versions of 'hermeneutics' relate to any possible 'science' of educational knowledge or scientific approach to educational research.

Hermeneutics (*Shorter Oxford English Dictionary*: 'the art or science of interpretation') emerged from biblical studies: it aspired to be a science of interpretation. Philosophically, hermeneutics rejected the correspondence theory of truth. Roughly speaking, correspondence theories separated facts from values via methodology, offered the researcher as a neutral or objective figure, and sought verification of phenomena in the generalizability and regularity of occurrences. Hermeneutics, on the other hand, tended to reject that there was a truth 'out there' with which 'facts' corresponded. Instead, it emphasized understanding as a situated event in terms of individuals and their situations – an inevitably prejudiced viewpoint. Some 'perspectives' were more defensible than others, but the idea of objective truth was an illusion.

Try that contrast by imagining the concept 'table' from a correspondence theory perspective, and then from a hermeneutic one. At first sight the 'table' is the most obvious candidate for the correspondence theory: of course the sign 'table' corresponds with that four legged, flat-topped thing over there in the real world. Is that so undeniable that any other possibility is silly? Now try the same trick with the concept 'education'.

Now for objectivity and subjectivity, realism and idealism. The table may be held to be really there (objective, real), or merely a cultural construct (subjective, ideal). If we follow Gadamer's version of hermeneutics (Gadamer, 1976) we argue that tables belong to a tradition which decides issues of 'tableness' as opposed to 'chairness' (etc.) and recognizes that the Absolute Table does not exist. It belongs instead to a continuum, blurred at its boundaries (table/shelf/breakfast bar). Again, it all sounds a bit silly, but if you substitute 'table' for 'education', and think how politicians often refer to 'education' as if it were a commodity, measurable, definable, countable (a league table!), you begin to see that issues of subjectivity, objectivity and what is to count as the 'real' are philosophical issues that are often assumed to be 'common sense' (Stronach, 1999). Again, we can try to avoid philosophical issues, but they will not avoid us.

There are a number of different approaches to 'hermeneutics' and no firm agreement about such categories. Most hermeneutic approaches in education refer to Gadamer and Ricoeur (see Elliott, 1991, for the former, and Brown and Roberts, 2000, for an example of the latter). Rather less often (in the 1980s and 1990s) writers refer to the 'critical hermeneutics' of Habermas (see Carr and Kemmis, 1983). It is sometimes the case that so-called 'postmodernist' approaches are referred to as 'radical hermeneutics' (e.g. Derrida, Lyotard). It may be best, at this stage, to read commentaries rather than originals since all the above original authors are difficult, and there are educational researchers who draw on their work and are more accessible (and therefore of course more simplistic.)

Most new researchers tend to start from philosophical positions that match their already existing political inclinations: very crudely – and many would place these attributions differently – Habermas for the soft-left; Gadamer for liberals; Derrida for conservatives and/or anarchists; and Marxian approaches for the standpoint epistemologists. There's lots of cross-overs, but where are you starting from?

It's important to understand the weakness of this kind of preliminary excursion into methodological para-digms, philosophical positions and epistemological distinctions. Typically, in this account, simplicity is achieved by making things into opposites, like posi-tivism/hermeneutics, objective/subjective, real/ideal, and so on. Or by making concepts more solid and coherent than they really are: hermeneutics/positiv-ism. Each word conjures a boundary, a distinction, and also a kind of seductive labelling that prevents certain movements of thought. Philosophers, there-fore, must try to live outside the house they live within, and remember to throw stones in all direc-tions. (Philosophers in glass houses should throw stones.) So this text, too, can't start at the beginning, may well be disguising a 'standpoint' or undertaking its own regressions. It also needs to be read suspi-ciously.

Finally, we might represent these different philo-sophical approaches to truth-telling through a number of different metaphors. Positivism describes that process, implicitly, as an arrow of meaning which does or does not hit its target (the truth). Management performance ideologies that centre on 'target-setting' are often implicitly positivist and reductive in that a very broad, plural and contested notion like 'educa-tion' is reduced to a narrow indicator against which various performances are compared. The metaphori-cal nature of that reduction (a part stands for a whole) is often ignored and the mathematical relationships predominate. Nevertheless, such reductions enable statistical measures to be made. Hermeneutics, on the other hand, is a circle rather than an arrow, moving from the detailed to the general, the local to the global in a series of trials of understanding, circling the

business of knowing in a series of refining rather then defining approximations. Geertz (1975) is a good exemplar of this kind of thinking. In his account of the Balinese cockfight, he considers the minutiae of the action, the spectators, the betting, in a constant toing and froing between the micro-events of that action and the nature of the culture that provokes and sanctions such displays. He links these two levels of analysis via the notion of 'deep play' – an attempt to show that what lies at the heart of the action is not 'profit' (the winners and losers in a betting game) so much as it is a matter of displaying both status and the cultural threats to its maintenance.

Difficult ideas everywhere, and they're only the welcoming committee! But the important thing is to learn to play with them, explore their meaning, how they connect with what you already believe, and how these beliefs might be challenged. From that, some learning, and on that, some more.

Implications for research design: 'talking dirty'

The positivist template for research design in social science inquiry is well known. It is linear and starts with a literature review and the identification of research questions for hypotheses. Then there's the question of a sample, a methodology to generate data and analyse it appropriately. Thence to the con-clusion, confirming or refuting hypotheses.

How would a hermeneutic approach differ? How do central notions like reflexivity, emergent themes and dialectical reasoning apply? Let's think about that by entering a recent research situation. You're in a classroom of 10-year-olds. They're doing 'sex educa-tion' and the class is being led by a school nurse rather than the teacher. The course is very explicit and you listen to the kids giggling a bit. You note that there are 'giggle words' and 'non-giggle words'. 'Vagina' draws no response, 'period' is a minor giggle word, but the biggest response is to the phrase 'erect penis'. Now you have an *emergent theme* – what is it about some words or phrases that provoke sup-pressed mirth? You start thinking of a literature that might inform your thinking. Mary Douglas's work on 'purity' and 'danger' comes to mind. So too does Austin's notion of words being 'performative' – of doing in some sense what they say. Note that the data begins to provoke this kind of reading – they act in a *dialectic*, as a mutual and recursive provocation. The worksheets even have a diagram of an ejaculating erect penis. The 10-year-old boy you're sitting next to says, 'what do you think of that?' 'Mmm,' you say, as non-commitally as you can. 'Mine's 12 inches,' he says. 'Now what's going on?' you ask yourself in *reflexive mode*. What constructs that 'macho' response? The 'erect penis' scenario within the class is the only place in the school where this diagram will not be read as an obscene graffito. A taboo seems to be breached by this – it's like 'purity' and 'danger' have changed places. The 'dirty' enters the classroom and is spoken about by the adults (in the worksheet, on the video). A *theory of taboo* might be a way of thinking further about these events, and you are encouraged in this when your case study is sent to the Department of Health Steering Committee – some of them cannot receive the electronic version because 'these words' are screened out by the system. The Department of Health is adamant – yes, they are dedicated to doing something about teenage pregnancy rates, but, no, the words 'erect penis' cannot go on their website, let alone the diagram of an ejaculating same (which we suggest to them both to wind them up and to see how they respond). What is 'adult' enough for the 10-year-olds is too adult for the adults. Is that right? Time to interview them about that . . .

In this way, the research emerges as a dialectical tacking between theory and data, between the local and the global – and the voice of the researcher and the voices of the other.

Stories from the Field

David Heywood

In this account I want to present a rather different conceptualization of research in science education. In this story I suggest that it is legitimate for teachers of science to grapple (and indeed struggle) with subject knowledge and suggest that such an endeavour should be encouraged and considered integral to professional discourse. I further contend that this places the teacher in a unique position as the principle interpreter of ideas in science and that this affords opportunity to explore notions as to what constitutes research.

In this short 'story from the field' I will attempt to raise some insight into the way in which research in science learning and teaching can affect perceptions of science subject knowledge and orientate our conceptualizations as to what science learning and teaching is. The account is a description of my own

emerging understanding in the first instance with regard to subject knowledge and latterly pedagogy with a conclusion concerning the synthesis of these two elements.

Whilst working with students on simple electric circuits I developed some ideas about the most appropriate way to tackle this particularly abstract phenomenon and explored the literature to determine how I might structure the session to support learners in developing their understanding. Teachers know that the responsibility of explaining ideas to someone else focuses the mind on grappling with the problem in earnest. The 'trawling' of literature and sharing ideas with colleagues, considered good practice, is less easily recognized as research. However, I contend that this process is illustrative of the synthesis of teaching and research.

Traditionally, simple electric circuits are taught through analogy and a central tenet of analogical reasoning is the relation between parts to whole and whole to parts. Analogical reasoning is a process in which developing understanding involves the juxtaposition of what is termed the *base domain of reasoning* (that which we have experience, knowledge and understanding of) with the *target domain of reasoning* (the phenomenon that we are trying to make sense of). This is necessary for most learners and teachers because phenomena are often abstract and explanations for them in texts counterintuitive. In order to make sense of the manifestations of electricity in simple electric circuits (such as a bulb lighting) there is a need to break the problem down and relate the abstract phenomena to something we have experience of.

One commonly used analogy attributes anthropomorphic status to electrons travelling around the circuit. Variations on this metaphor include a notion of electrons as 'moving crowds' (Gentner and Gentner, 1983) where the flow of electrons within a circuit is conceptualized in terms of people/vehicles moving around a circuit meeting resistance at certain points with subsequent observable effects (e.g. a bulb lighting). Other analogies use the idea of water in which the 'current' is analogous to water flow and the potential difference (voltage) and resistance are conceptualized in terms of pressure difference caused by constriction in the pipes around the closed water circuit. In this case, electricity comes with a built-in metaphor of both understanding and misunderstanding (i.e. 'current' as in the flow of water/electricity).

During the teaching session in question I used an analogy to explain a single bulb lighting in a circuit in terms of a 'friction' model of resistance in which the bulb in the circuit was conceptualized as a 'tunnel' through which the electrons pass generating enough heat (because of the constricted space) to make a bulb glow. (This is a variation on the 'moving crowds' metaphor.)

I planned the teaching session to investigate simple electric circuits through taking ammeter and voltmeter readings for single bulbs of different voltage ratings and for two bulbs wired in series. In terms of coherence in applying the 'tunnel' analogy for a frictional (heat generating) model, the difference in brightness for the various bulbs can be explained in terms of the 'tunnel' thickness (or length): the narrower (or longer) the tunnel, the greater the *resistance* to the 'movement' of the electrons therefore the more heat – and light – generated as they are 'pushed through'. Alternatively, the reduced thickness of the 'tunnel' (wire) could be explained as less current flowing and therefore fewer electrons to cause friction with the consequent opposite effect that the bulb glows less brightly. As I grappled with the ideas I became increasingly aware of the range of possible explanations of empirical evidence that seemed to contradict coherence in applying the analogy. With some trepidation I decided to present the analogy in a teaching session with the explicit purpose of sharing the limitations at various stages with the students to record their responses. I explained that I would be collecting ideas as we went through the learning process to determine their thinking at certain critical junctures (as decided by me) during the session. I knew that if the students found the analogy useful in explaining the causal mechanism for the single bulb lighting in the circuit they would meet with problems in attempting to apply this to two bulbs of different brightness.

In the teaching session I asked a group of students to apply the analogy to explain observations of two bulbs in a series circuit (analogies of this type tend to promote a sequential view of a circuit (Driver, 1994), a problem in itself), where one bulb was brighter than the other. Most reasoned that the electrons travel around the circuit meeting the brighter bulb first (using up most of the energy) and the less bright second because there is not enough energy left by the time the electrons reach this point in the circuit. The way to 'test this conjecture' is to swap the position of the bulbs in the circuit. The less bright bulb should now be the brighter. On discovering that this does not happen one student noted:

You can only apply the analogy [to two bulbs in a circuit] if you are saying the tunnel sometimes becomes larger – you need to *view* the circuit as a *single entity* – and the analogy *doesn't allow* you to do this. [my italics]

This particular statement raised an important question as to how we think *with* and *about* analogies. I also noticed that the students generated more questions and engaged more productively with ideas when the analogy broke down. There are a number of ways to respond to this. The process of reflecting on the teaching–learning dynamic I consider illustrates a synthesis of teaching and research as integral elements. Whilst too involved to report here (for more detail see Heywood and Parker, 1997; Heywood, 2001). the experience resulted in further work and a conclusion that the pedagogic task is less concerned with the search for the holy grail of analogies to satiate learners' needs for causal mechanisms than with the recognition that when analogies break down there is a significant opportunity to generate deeper thinking.

More significantly, analogies considered as metaphors, linguistic overlays that filter the way in which we resonate with phenomena, would support the view that direct experience with the world (or at least the way in which we make sense of it) is mediated *through* language. This rests uneasily with the presentation of science knowledge in the curriculum. There is always the 'authority of the text' to contend with, the notion that meaning is somehow situated outside of this process. Take, for example, the following account of a physicist's view of an electric circuit by Black:

Briefly, a physicist's view of electric circuits runs as follows. Charge does not pile up in conducting circuits, so current is conserved. Potential difference (p.d.), which is a measure of the field acting, is apportional around items in a series circuit according to their resistance. Free energy is transformed at a rate determined by the product 'current times p.d.' If one asks how the energy is transferred from (say) a dry cell to a small bulb, the best answer is that it is transferred through the electric and magnetic fields that surround the wire when a current flows: these fields are the means by which parts of the circuit wiring remote from the cell terminals 'know' that the current is to flow when the switch is closed: the effect of closing a switch is seen almost instantaneously (in fact it propagates at the speed of light) and does not travel around by means of shunting collisions of the electrons in the wires. The electrons travel quite slowly, and in an A/C mains circuit they jiggle backwards and forwards with amplitudes of less than a millimetre. Thus no material substance enters one's house along the mains supply cable; the flux of surrounding fields delivers the energy. (Black and Harten, 1993: 221)

Is this how electricity in a circuit really 'is'? Consider the manner in which science as knowledge of the world is represented here. What is the significance of terms such as 'free energy' and 'electrical and magnetic fields'? Since 'no material substance enters the house' is it reasonable to ask what is being paid for? Such questions challenge assumptions about the nature of knowing in science and the representation of science knowledge in the curriculum. In one sense we can consider the 'authority' of the science text as describing how things are and the pedagogic task as making accessible the ideas inherent in the description offered by the text. This assumes that understanding and meaning are 'out there' awaiting linguistic expression and here we meet a particular difficulty in respect of the 'science' knowledge that is represented in science texts because both implicitly and explicitly it perpetuates the idea of a fundamental knowledge that we can obtain, a referent that assumes a direct ontological relation to the real world. This assumes that it is possible to access the world directly via the language we use to describe it. In challenging this I have offered a hermeneutic approach with a conceptualization that language both allows us *possibilities* in accessing the world while at the same time presenting a *constraint*, as exemplified in the student remark regarding the fact that the analogy (quite literally) does not allow you to do this.

It is reasonable to ask where this leaves us in terms of knowledge representation and learning and teaching. In response to this it is necessary to review what we consider science learning to be about. A colleague reviewing the presentation of the same phenomenon at a research seminar wrote:

As the session progressed metaphor after metaphor broke down at some crucial juncture; frustration drove me to wonder if it would not be easier to dispense with the metaphor and just tell the children how it was! I was left to contemplate my naiveté for slipping into the all too seductive fantasy of believing that empirical objects, even intangible ones like electricity, must be uniquely apprehensible. (McNamara, 1995: 214)

In this sense we might consider that ideas in science are *uniquely individual* rather than *uniquely apprehensible*. This could lead to the charge of solipsism except that there is no suggestion here that there are not certain concepts in electricity to which we would subscribe (e.g. current conservation, resistance, potential difference, energy transfer). What I am suggesting is that meaning is quite literally dependent on the constant juxtaposition between the *possibilities* that language offers us and the *constraints* that language imposes on us. It is necessarily a process of interpretation, the explicit acknowledgement of which presents the potential for teaching as a research enterprise.

Annotated bibliography

There are no easy ways into philosophy. The following are generally difficult texts. A consoling thought: it is more by failing to understand such texts that we learn; it is only necessary that the failure be not total, and the reading not final.

Bernstein, R. (1986) *Philosophical Profiles. Essays in a Pragmatic Mode.* Cambridge: Polity.

It's a contrast between Gadamer (hermeneuticist in our potted account), Habermas (critical theorist) and Rorty (postmodernist in some interpretations of his work).

Deleuze, G. and Guattari, F. (1994) *What Is Philosophy?* London: Verso.

French bestseller in the last few years. Really difficult, but try the Introduction and the chapter 'What is a concept?'.

Feyerabend, P. (1975) *Against Method. Outline of an Anarchistic Theory of Knowledge.* London: Verso.

This is at the more relativist end of the game, and of course important to consider as a blow against the whole business of methodology as directing our enquiries in some *a priori* and unproblematic way.

Flew, A. (1985) *Thinking about Social Thinking: The Philosophy of the Social Sciences*. Oxford: Blackwell.
This is objective chalk to Feyerabend's cheese. A different kind of difficult.

Geertz, C. (1983) *Local Knowledge: Further Essays in Interpretive Anthropology*. New York: Basic Books.
Hermeneuticist. Based on Dilthey, and a notion of understanding as a 'continuous dialectic' between the local and the global. Writes very well as a bonus. His earlier book *Interpretation of Cultures* (1973) is wonderful as well – see especially the interpretation of the Balinese cockfight and the notion of 'thick description'.

Glaser, B. and Strauss, A. (1967) *The Discovery of Grounded Theory*. Chicago: Aldine.
This is the founding text of phenomenological studies in the social 'sciences' and in educational research. Still ritually invoked in ethnographic types of study.

Kimball, S. and Garrison, J. (1996) 'Hermeneutic listening: an approach to understanding in multicultural conversations', *Studies in Philosophy and Education*, 15: 51–96.
This is an interestingly practical translation of hermeneutics into interviewing techniques and approaches.

Lather, P. (1993) 'Fertile obsession: validity after poststructuralism', *Sociological Quarterly*, 34(4): 673–93.
Influential article building a bridge from a standpoint epistemology (feminism) to a more relativist (radical hermeneuticist) position. Like Judith Butler, she looks to bring relativist and subjectivist accounts into a radical and deconstructive critique.

MacLure, M. (2003) *Discourse in Educational and Social Research*. Buckingham: Open University Press.
Wonderfully clear treatment of difficult issues in interpreting texts – from political diatribes against educational research to parent–teacher exchanges and media accounts of education. A deconstructive approach.

Further references

Carr, W. and Kemmis, S. (1983) *Becoming Critical: Knowing through Action Research*. Victoria: Deakin University Press; published by Falmer Press.
Black, P.J. and Harlen, W. (1993) 'How can we specify concepts for primary science?', in P.J. Black and A.H. Lucas (eds), *Children's Informal Ideas in Science*. London: Routledge.
Black, P.J. and Lucas, A.M. (eds) (1993) *Children's Informal Ideas in Science*. London: Routledge.
Brown, T. and Roberts, L. (2000) 'Memories are made of this: temporality and practitioner research', *British Educational Research Journal*, 26(5): 649–59.
Driver, R. (1994) 'Children's ideas about physical processes: electricity', in R. Driver, A. Squires, P. Rushworth and V. Wood-Robinson (eds), *Making Sense of Secondary Science*. Routledge: London.
Elliott J. (1991) *Action Research for Educational Change*. Buckingham: Open University Press.
Gadamer, H.-G. (1976) *Philosophical hermeneutics*. Berkeley, CA: University of California Press.
Geertz C. (1975) *The Interpretation of Cultures. Selected essays*. London: Heinemann.
Gentner, D. and Gentner, D.R. (1983) 'Flowing water or teeming crowds: mental models of electricity', in D. Gentner and A. Stevens (eds), *Mental Models*. Englewood Cliffs, NJ: Lawrence Erlbaum Associates, pp. 61–93.
Heidegger, M. (1962) *Being and Time*. trans. J. Macquarie and E. Robinson. London: SCM Press.
Heywood, D. (2002) 'The role of analogies in science', *Cambridge Journal of Education*, 32(2): 233–47.
Heywood, D. and Parker, J. (1997) 'Confronting the analogy: primary teachers exploring the usefulness of analogies in the teaching and learning of electricity', *International Journal of Science Education*, 19(8): 869–85.
McNamara, O. (1995) 'The Construction of Knowledge in Mathematics Education'. Unpublished PhD thesis, Manchester Metropolitan University
Stronach, I. (1999) 'Shouting theatre in a crowded fire: "Educational Effectiveness" as cultural performance', *Evaluation*, 5(2): 173–93.
Williams, R. (1976) *Keywords: A Vocabulary of Culture and Society*. London: Fontana.

CHAPTER
14

PHENOMENOLOGY

Angie Titchen
*Senior Research and Practice Development Fellow, Royal College of Nursing Institute, UK
and joint Clinical Chair, Knowledge Centre for Evidence-Based Practice, Fontys University,
The Netherlands*
Dawn Hobson
Visiting Lecturer, St Bartholomew School of Nursing and Midwifery, City University, UK

Key concepts

Angie Titchen

ANGIE: *We need to understand phenomenology through reverse perspectives.*

DAWN: *Angie, that sounds like a riddle!*

ANGIE: *What I mean is that there are two very different approaches in phenomenological research to look at the same phenomenon. The first approach is direct – looking at the phenomenon, as it presents itself in the consciousness of the people who live it. The researcher is on the outside, looking in. The second approach is to get inside the social context of the phenomenon, to live it oneself, as it were, and look at the phenomenon more indirectly. I like the way we sometimes understand things by reading between the lines. So the key message I want to get across in this section is that researchers have to be very clear about the distinctive philosophical roots of each approach to enable them to choose between the two (or even to choose both for one study). Clarity is essential because these roots determine the nature of the research questions, the kind of research products and the whole research methodology and design. It's that different!*

DAWN: *I agree. In my study everything hung on the philosophical stance I used, for example the observer role I developed. The philosophical stance is like the acorn from which the oak tree grows in all its diversity.*

ANGIE: *Exactly. I want to use two perspectives, as a device, to show these differences. The first perspective is holistic, using metaphor and imagery. The second separates out the key concepts through a comparative analysis.*

DAWN: *OK. Will you start?*

Phenomenology is the study of lived, human phenomena within the everyday social contexts in which the phenomena occur from the perspective of those who experience them. Phenomena comprise any thing that human beings live/experience. Increasingly, the value of examining the phenomena of professional practice has been emphasized. For example, Dawn and I have both studied nursing phenomena, that is nurses' ethical decision-making when their patients were dying (Hobson, 2003) and patient-centred nursing and its development (Titchen, 2000).

Phenomena can be *directly* researched by exploring human *knowing*, through accessing consciousness, and *indirectly* by investigating human *being*, through accessing the senses and shared background meanings and practices (Figure 14.1). This is where the idea of different perspectives comes in, the perspectives being the foreground and the background of the phenomenon. It is as if the researcher shines a light **on** the foreground (white circle in Figure 14.1 (direct approach)) or **within** the background (white ring in Figure 14.1 (indirect approach)).

People can usually talk easily about the foreground because they have personal knowledge of it in their heads. So the uninvolved, detached researcher using a *direct approach* shines a light on the foreground of the phenomenon to engage in a systematic study of participants' mental representations of the phenomenon as they experience it. For example, the researcher asks participants questions about their rational actions when nursing patients, teaching students or whatever, exploring their underpinning logic, intentions, rationale, choices, decisions and so on. The researcher's detached observation and contemplation, throughout data gathering, analysis and interpretation, can be understood by remembering that to

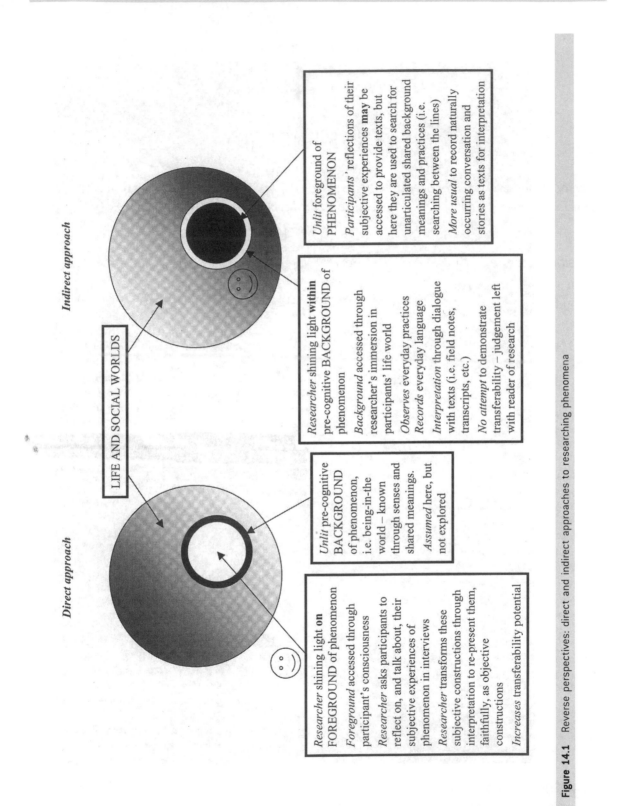

Figure 14.1 Reverse perspectives: direct and indirect approaches to researching phenomena

shine a light *on* some 'thing', we have to be outside of the 'thing'. Researchers, in this approach, may know about the pre-cognitive background, so much a part of us that it goes unnoticed and not talked about because it is transparent to us, just like the air we breathe. But they are not interested in it, so it remains dark, in the shadows (black ring).

In contrast, researchers using the *indirect approach* reverse perspectives and light up the background (white ring). This light is shone from *within* the life and social worlds of the participants, rather than from a distance. Researchers adopt an involved, connected observer stance and immerse themselves, literally, in the concrete, everyday world they are studying, so that they can better understand participants' intuitions, shared looks of unarticulated understanding and undisclosed, shared meanings between the words and in the practices. They engage in dialogue with the data emerging from the background.

DAWN: *This observer stance is exactly the one I adopted and it wasn't easy at all! But I must wait until I tell my story.*

Another way of looking at this reversal of perspectives is to think of studying the light around you that enables you to see this book (symbol of a phenomenon), rather than investigating the book (phenomenon) itself. Without the light, you would be unable to read this chapter at all and so it is here.

> It is only the pre-cognitive, transparent background that enables us to experience the foreground and know it cognitively. The background is, therefore, a prerequisite for human knowing.

Before reversing perspectives to undertake a comparative analysis of the two approaches, I outline their origins.

Origins

During the 1800s and reacting to ways of construing the world only through empiricism, German philosophers began the search for a new interpretive science. Their ideas were based on the investigation of the life and social worlds through the study of context and individuals' own constructions and meanings within that context. This work led to the development of two philosophical frameworks that influence interpretive research methodologies today.

Edmund Husserl (1859–1938) founded phenomenology, premised on epistemological concerns, so the starting point of his framework is the separation of a conscious actor in a world of objects (Husserl, 1964). This is the root of the *direct approach* in which researchers investigate the foreground of the phenomenon, and so develop research questions that lead to the systematic study of the mental content of individuals' inner worlds, for example Carol Edwards's (Edwards and Titchen, 2003) question, 'How do patients reflect on their healthcare experiences?'

While accepting this epistemological premise, Husserl's student, Martin Heidegger, did not see it as the starting point (Heidegger, 1962). Rather, he saw that we are first and foremost rooted, immersed in the world and not separate from it. So, the ultimate goal for Heidegger's phenomenology is to deepen our understanding of what it is to be. His concern is, therefore, ontological. The *indirect approach,* used to study the background of the phenomenon, grows from this root. Research questions here ask how participants interpret and make sense/seek meaning of their worlds. For example, 'What is the meaning of autonomy in a relationship between a nurse and an older patient?' (McCormack, 2001).

Neither Husserl nor Heidegger nor the philosophical giants who followed them, for example Hans-Georg Gadamer, Jean-Paul Sartre and Maurice Merleau-Ponty, developed methodological frameworks and procedures. This work fell to others, for example, in sociology (e.g. Schutz, 1970), psychology (e.g. Giorgi, 1985) and nursing (Benner, 1994).

Reverse perspectives: a comparative analysis

In this section, I offer an analytical perspective on the direct and indirect approaches that builds on the philosophical and methodological ideas above. In a sense, this is another reverse of perspectives, that is from the holistic (i.e. metaphorical and visual) perspective in Figure 14.1 to an analytic perspective which separates out key concepts. To give focus, I have used an analysis of Schutz's phenomenological sociology and Heideggerian/Gadamerian existential phenomenology.

Table 14.1 shows the baseline, empirical and methodological differences between the two approaches. Note that the decontextualized product (i.e. theory) in Schutz's phenomenological sociology *can* be contextualized through grounding typifications in rich description (see Titchen, 2000).

Table 14.1   Baseline, empirical and methodological differences

	DIRECT APPROACH *Phenomenological Sociology*	*INDIRECT APPROACH* *Existential Phenomenology*
CENTRAL CONCERNS	Looking for shared intersubjective meanings among participants Generation of general types of subjective experience	Analysis of everyday, masterful, practical know-how Interpretation of human beings as essentially self-interpreting
CONCEPTS	Consciousness, acting in the outer world, experience, rational action, subjective meanings, meaningful intersubjectivity	Dasein, i.e. being-in-the-world, being with, shared background meanings, involved coping in world
UNDERSTANDING	Rational understanding Verstehen – finding out what participant means in his/her action, in contrast to the meaning this action may have for someone else (including a neutral observer)	Ontological understanding – suspension of conventions of common logic/hermeneutics Background pre-reflective understanding in pragmatic, involved activity Understanding of being is embedded in language, social practices, cultural conventions and historical understandings
LIFE WORLD	Natural attitude (cognitive setting of the life world) which is embodied in the processes of subjective human experiences of the phenomenon Acting in the life world	Shared background practices Involved coping with the world
SOCIAL WORLD	Intersubjectivity 'We-relationship' (shared stream of consciousness) 'They-relationship' (adopted by the researcher because of need for objectivity)	Being with Shared, social, situated way of being
EMPIRICAL DIFFERENCES	Description and interpretation of social action through typification Empirical questions about knowledge and meaning attached to 'inner worlds', e.g. what is the nature of the professional craft knowledge of person-centred nursing? Development of abstract practical knowledge, decontextualized universals or theory, e.g. a conceptual framework for person-centred nursing	Description and interpretation of human being Empirical questions about shared meanings, e.g. what does it mean to be a person-centred nurse? Development of contextualized, practical knowledge and situated, relational and temporal meanings, e.g. interpretations that illuminate the meaning of being a person-centred nurse
METHODOLOGICAL DIFFERENCES	Separation: – subjective and objective – truth discovered through detached contemplation Everyday language as a key to getting at subjective meaning context of individual Researcher concerned with rational thinking of the actor Analysis of data to develop decontextualized 'ideal-types'	Holism: – notions of subjectivity and objectivity abandoned – truth discovered through involved contemplation Everyday language as a key to getting at background meanings, practices, social context Researcher concerned with intuitive thinking; embodied, non-verbal knowing Synthesis according to hermeneutic principles to uncover pre-cognitive evidence

Adapted from Titchen (2000: 47, 51).

Implications for research design

Weaving throughout both holistic and analytic perspectives above, significant clues have been laid to illuminate the design of research using direct and indirect approaches. The nature of research questions and product are summarized in the empirical differences in Table 14.1 and examples given both there and at the beginning of the chapter. The nature of observing, questioning and interpreting from a methodological standpoint has also been illuminated. Table 14.2 gives a summary of their implications for gathering data through, for example, participant observation, unstructured interviews, storytelling and written reflections, clinical supervision notes, photographs, video-recordings, poems, paintings and music. Data analysis, synthesis and interpretation through an approach (Titchen and McIntyre, 1993) shaped by Schutz's (1970) ideas and a hermeneutic approach inspired by Gadamer's (1981) 'fusion of horizons' are also summarized.

Resting place

Distinctions between *direct* and *indirect* phenomenological approaches have been shown using holistic and analytical perspectives. While researchers tend to adopt one or other approach due to the philosophical and methodological oppositions, the methodological distinctions are not as sharp as they have been made out to be. Being fully aware of the distinctions and their implications, I reconciled their differences and used them in complementary ways in my research to give a fuller picture of the phenomenon (Titchen, 2000). Reflexivity, in particular the ability to reflect upon one's own epistemological and ontological authenticity, is key in enabling the adoption of different stances and roles and using different observing, questioning and interpreting methods within them.

Stories from the Field

Dawn Hobson

This is a story about the collection and subsequent analysis of 18 months' worth of observational and interview data using the 'indirect approach' in phenomenology. The story highlights the great benefits of such an involved research focus for environments where many of the working challenges are not explicit. It also explores the difficulties of such a close integration. The challenges of allowing phenomenological principles to drive the management of a large and complex data set are also explored.

The study formed the basis of my PhD thesis (Hobson, 2003) and aimed to explore individual nurses' engagement with perceived moral problems as they occurred on an acute cancer unit. The backdrop to the study was an inadequate empirical base in ethical decision-making. Existing evidence demonstrated a lack of focus on clinical practice, with a subsequent lack of insight into the encounter between the nurse and a moral question. I felt that this indicated a participative research approach where nurses' intuitive ethical judgements were the focus of the study. It was apparent from the literature that such judgements were difficult for nurses to put into words and were likely to be hidden within day-to-day clinical practice.

I therefore needed an approach that would preserve the 'voices' of individual participants by a process of rich description both of their perceived and embodied values. I found the philosophical approach of Heidegger especially useful in this regard. Studying the involved practical viewpoint of people in situations in order to examine meaning and significance was exactly what I wanted to do. I chose an existential phenomenological approach for this reason.

Data collection was undertaken over a period of 18 months, based on one acute cancer treatment ward at a London teaching hospital between 1999 and 2001. During this time, observation participation was employed to gain access to the everyday experience of nurses on the ward. Informal interviews later explored nurses' perception of ethical issues occurring on the ward.

Access to the 'everyday'

As Angie describes in Figure 14.1, the indirect approach in phenomenology examines the pre-cognitive background of participants in order to illuminate aspects of their life and social worlds. I participated in the work of the ward to gain familiarity with the everyday experiences of nurses, and also to develop trusting relationships. My own training as a registered nurse gave me initial understanding of the language and types of activities undertaken. I also enjoyed easier access to the nurses' shared background practices and involved coping with the world (Table 14.1). These aspects of integration into the ward facilitated access to nurses' expressed and enacted values, and particularly to the ways in which they attached ethical significance to certain aspects of patient care.

I was interested both in accessing nurses' consciousness of their ethical values and their embodied

Table 14.2   Differences in research methods

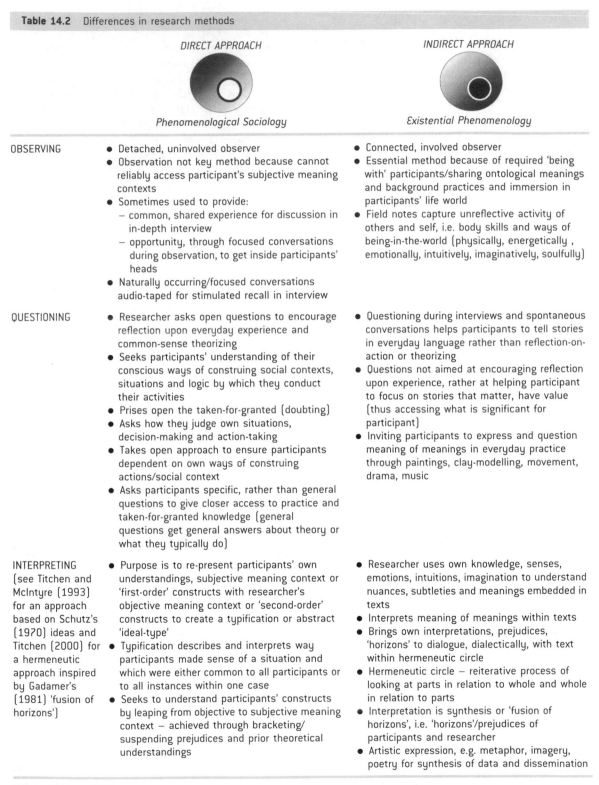

	DIRECT APPROACH *Phenomenological Sociology*	INDIRECT APPROACH *Existential Phenomenology*

OBSERVING	• Detached, uninvolved observer
	• Observation not key method because cannot reliably access participant's subjective meaning contexts
	• Sometimes used to provide:
	  – common, shared experience for discussion in in-depth interview
	  – opportunity, through focused conversations during observation, to get inside participants' heads
	• Naturally occurring/focused conversations audio-taped for stimulated recall in interview
		• Connected, involved observer
		• Essential method because of required 'being with' participants/sharing ontological meanings and background practices and immersion in participants' life world
		• Field notes capture unreflective activity of others and self, i.e. body skills and ways of being-in-the-world (physically, energetically, emotionally, intuitively, imaginatively, soulfully)

QUESTIONING	• Researcher asks open questions to encourage reflection upon everyday experience and common-sense theorizing • Seeks participants' understanding of their conscious ways of construing social contexts, situations and logic by which they conduct their activities • Prises open the taken-for-granted (doubting) • Asks how they judge own situations, decision-making and action-taking • Takes open approach to ensure participants dependent on own ways of construing actions/social context • Asks participants specific, rather than general questions to give closer access to practice and taken-for-granted knowledge (general questions get general answers about theory or what they typically do)	• Questioning during interviews and spontaneous conversations helps participants to tell stories in everyday language rather than reflection-on-action or theorizing • Questions not aimed at encouraging reflection upon experience, rather at helping participant to focus on stories that matter, have value (thus accessing what is significant for participant) • Inviting participants to express and question meaning of meanings in everyday practice through paintings, clay-modelling, movement, drama, music
INTERPRETING (see Titchen and McIntyre (1993) for an approach based on Schutz's (1970) ideas and Titchen (2000) for a hermeneutic approach inspired by Gadamer's (1981) 'fusion of horizons')	• Purpose is to re-present participants' own understandings, subjective meaning context or 'first-order' constructs with researcher's objective meaning context or 'second-order' constructs to create a typification or abstract 'ideal-type' • Typification describes and interprets way participants made sense of a situation and which were either common to all participants or to all instances within one case • Seeks to understand participants' constructs by leaping from objective to subjective meaning context – achieved through bracketing/suspending prejudices and prior theoretical understandings	• Researcher uses own knowledge, senses, emotions, intuitions, imagination to understand nuances, subtleties and meanings embedded in texts • Interprets meaning of meanings within texts • Brings own interpretations, prejudices, 'horizons' to dialogue, dialectically, with text within hermeneutic circle • Hermeneutic circle – reiterative process of looking at parts in relation to whole and whole in relation to parts • Interpretation is synthesis or 'fusion of horizons', i.e. 'horizons'/prejudices of participants and researcher • Artistic expression, e.g. metaphor, imagery, poetry for synthesis of data and dissemination

Source: Titchen, 2000.

values. Nurses' expressed values were known cognitively and I accessed them by questioning (see Table 14.2 – questioning). Their enacted values were accessed by observing through 'being with' in a shared, social situated way of being (Table 14.1). In practice this meant hearing nurses' everyday language with patients, their stories told to colleagues and what they emphasized at key times of information exchange in order to understand what was ethically significant for them.

Gaining their trust

An initial hurdle to becoming accepted on the ward was the difficulty in negotiating access to the real world of nurses and the care they provided. I came to the ward with the explicit aim of becoming a participant and entering a dialogue with the nurses on the ward about their practice. I was not prepared for the difficulty in negotiating a kind of 'being with' research relationship with the nurses.

Nurses had readily signed consent forms following information-giving meetings and an initial four month period of my attendance at ward handovers and meetings. However, when I was on the ward, nurses avoided my presence. Although very friendly and courteous, I was aware of being politely excluded from nurses' conversations and the delivery of care. I decided to do familiar jobs on the ward that did not require specialist knowledge, such as making beds, delivering meals, running to the pharmacy and delivering commodes or bedpans. After a few days of this, the ward bedpan washer broke. I spent the whole shift ferrying a series of bedpans to the next ward's washer. During this time, I had more questions about the research from nurses than I had had in the entire period of attempted integration. In order to achieve 'shared, social and situated ways of being with' participants (Table 14.1) I needed to be willing to do the things the nurses had to do, and to experience for myself the background practices and social context of the nurses. Only then did they see me as having any right to ask questions, because only then did I share in the situation in which they were operating.

Nurses then began to be more searching in their questions about what I was trying to achieve. I began to have a welcome place in informal coffee room discussions and a place in care planning meetings for patients. Nurses would actively seek me out if they thought I should be attending a particular event. Very often, it was interesting just to see what they thought was important for me to hear. As a result, I was able to access what was significant for them (Table 14.2 – listening and questioning). Individual nurses began to discuss with me their reactions to medical decisions with which they disagreed. They also began to share more private feelings about patients and their relatives. In this way, access to the everyday world of nurses facilitated further access to their 'ethical stories', revealing what they felt to be morally significant.

I took extensive field notes during this period of working alongside the nurses. These involved an account of events, records of conversations and impressions of how nurses had responded to particular events. These were collated in a qualitative analysis software package, called Nud.Ist (Non-numerical unstructured data: Indexing, searching and theorizing). I chose this because it allowed the coding and storage of data, line by line, around central analytical concepts called nodes. In practice this meant that I could first group data around individual nurses and from this develop further shared categories to build the analysis.

Interviews took place with the same 18 nurses I had been working alongside, who already felt familiar with me and able to discuss their feelings freely. I returned to working with them after the interview so that contextual data would provide a commentary on what had been shared. The interviews provided an opportunity for nurses to talk further and explore areas of concern in their field of practice.

During the interviews, questions and responses were developed and shaped by dialogue between us. I don't mean that I was sharing *my* experiences but that by listening to the answers to questions, it was possible to see their interpretation of the question and to let this shade the meaning constructed. Questions became part of a circular process in this way. In other words, both through observing and questioning, the participants and I entered a hermeneutic circle and were interpreting meanings through a synthesis or 'fusion of horizons' (Table 14.2 – interpreting), a process that I continued throughout data interpretation. Recording details such as pauses and emphasis in the subsequent transcription enabled this process and the developing meaning to become clearer. After the interview I would return to working alongside the nurses. In this way a broader understanding could be gained (see Table 14.2 interpreting: first bullet point).

Dealing with the data

Observational and interview data were interlinked in order to achieve a contextual account of individual nurses' ways of being. This enabled the analysis to draw on an integrated understanding of nurses' experiences, where different types of data were interlinked rather than used to critically review the other. The interview transcripts and field notes were used to create a text for each nurse, whereby key experiences connected with ethical concerns were identified. The fact that I had shared in the events in question provided insight into the nuanced meanings attributed by nurses in such situations. The synthesis of nurses' texts led to the identification of shared experiences between nurses.

The length of time spent in coming alongside individual nurses and the level of access it allowed meant that the study was able to examine the many barriers to ethical decision-making. Perceived ethical issues were avoided, both by individual nurses and by the medical team as a whole. Nurses often did not feel able to ask questions about the care in which they were involved, and their coping strategy of emotional distancing appeared to contribute to a lack of moral engagement with patients. This finding was a product of having been involved with participants' life world (Table 14.1).

The lack of a credible ethical language in practice and the effects of hierarchical decision-making also hindered open discussion of ethical issues. These discoveries were first made at the individual level, and then as the study progressed it was impossible not to notice that they were shared across the nurses, and and to broader issues in the treatment of dying patients.

At the same time, the pattern of my involvement in the ward began to affect my ability to remain a researcher as well as a participant. There were costs associated with being an involved, connected researcher (Table 14.2).

Costs of emotional involvement

I had realized that ethical issues were not discussed and that decisions about them did not appear to get made. However, I was not asking critical questions about this because, having shared so much with the nurses, I identified with them very strongly. I was therefore not following crucial lines of enquiry. Instead, there was some temptation to abandon all pretence at research in order to be totally involved and just help out. Writing and reviewing journal entries and field notes during this time proved to be a crucial means by which I realized what was

happening. I saw that I was becoming too immersed in the surroundings to be able to function effectively as a researcher.

I had heard and read about the benefits of clinical supervision and as a result sought to find an appropriate mentor. Fortunately there was a senior researcher within my university who had significant clinical experience in oncology and was not involved with either the research or the site. This meant that she could remain impartial while understanding the nature of patient care on the unit. She listened to my accounts of events on the ward and reflected with me on my responses to them. This strategy proved to be very effective in regaining a participant stance as opposed to one of unquestioning involvement. It enabled me to plan the focus of data collection more clearly.

Doing existential phenomenological research requires emotionally mature, reflexive researchers who can maintain a critical stance while living the daily experience of those they are alongside. Good emotional and intellectual support is crucial. A good research supervisor will provide this to some extent, but further emotional support is of great value in keeping the researcher on the road.

However, the benefits of an involved research stance, with a focus on the individual's construction of what is significant, were to lay bare what many nurses felt to be 'under the carpet'. Events taking place in the everyday were articulated for the first time, offering the potential for healthcare staff to openly confront ethical issues.

Resting place

My research methodology was tailor-made for the questions at hand. I was interested both in accessing nurses' consciousness of their values and their embodied values. However, I decided to locate the study firmly in existential phenomenology because of the need for an involved, connected observer stance in order to access practical ethical concerns. I also wanted to interpret data arising from expressed values, as described in Figure 14.1 as 'searching between the lines'. As Angie points out, methodological distinctions can be reconciled given a transparent epistemological and ontological position.

The method I used had great benefits for eliciting unarticulated concerns hidden in the everyday. It also had pitfalls for reflexivity during periods of intense exposure to participants' social worlds.

Annotated bibliography

Benner, P. (ed.) (1994) *Interpretive Phenomenology: Embodiment, Caring, and Ethics in Health and Illness*. London: Sage.

Provides theoretical and practical support for all stages of Heideggerian hermeneutic inquiry, e.g. how to dialogue with texts through the development of paradigm cases, exemplars and thematic analyses.

Crotty, M. (1996) *Phenomenology and Nursing Research*. Melbourne: Churchill Livingstone.

This book has provoked an interesting, critical debate about phenomenological research in nursing.

Dey, I. (1993) *Qualitative Data Analysis*. London and New York: Routledge.

I (DH) used this book to help me use qualitative data analysis software without prejudicing the phenomenological approach.

Edwards, C. and Titchen, A. (2003) 'Research into patients' perspectives: relevance and usefulness of phenomenological sociology', *Journal of Advanced Nursing*, 44(5): 450–60.

Demonstrates the close fit between investigation of the patient's perspective and Schutz's phenomenological sociology. Pinpoints similarities and differences between phenomenological sociology and symbolic interactionism.

Gadamer, H.-G. (1981) *Reason in the Age of Science*. London: MIT Press.

Gadamer's development of Heidegger's phenomenology has been key in enabling researchers to develop hermeneutic data analysis and interpretation approaches, more related to artistic appreciation and interpretation than scientific method.

McNiff, S. (1998) *Art-Based Research*. London: Jessica Kingsley.

Immersing self in the hermeneutic circle requires us to create open spaces, let go of clutter, suspend conventions of common logic and engage in processes more akin to artistic appreciation and expression. This book could provide a trigger for researchers to find their own ways.

Magee, B. (ed.) (1987) *The Great Philosophers: An Introduction to Western Philosophy*. London: BBC Books.

Hubert Dreyfus, in critical conversation with Brian Magee (pp. 254–77), lucidly explains the key ideas of, and differences between, Husserl's and Heidegger's phenomenologies.

Riessman, C.K. (1993) *Narrative Analysis. Qualitative Research Methods Series 30*. Thousand Oaks, CA, London and New Delhi: Sage.

An excellent insight into the hermeneutic analysis of interview transcripts.

Schutz, A. (1970) *On Phenomenology and Social Relations*. ed. H.R. Wagner. London: University of Chicago Press.

Sets out a system of sociological thought and procedure in accessible language with concepts that can be used by researchers to develop systematic data gathering and analysis strategies.

Titchen, A. and McIntyre, D. (1993) 'A phenomenological approach to qualitative data analysis in nursing research', in A. Titchen (ed.), *Changing Nursing Practice through Action Research*, Report No. 6, Oxford: National Institute for Nursing, pp. 29–48.

Describes a data analysis approach built on Schutz's concepts of first- and second-order constructs and bracketing. Compares this approach with structured and grounded theory approaches.

Van Maanen, M. (1990) *Researching Lived Experience: Human Science for an Action Sensitive Pedagogy*. New York: State University of New York.

A must read for researchers exploring contemporary understandings of phenomenology.

Further references

Giorgi, A. (ed.) (1985) *Phenomenology and Psychological Research*. Pittsburgh, PA: Duquesne University Press.

Heidegger, M. (1962) *Being and Time*. New York: Harper & Row (1st edn, 1927).

Hobson, D. (2003) *Moral Silence? Nurses' Experiences of Ethical Decision-Making at the End of Life*. PhD Dissertation, City University, London.

Husserl, E. (1964) *The Idea of Phenomenology*. trans. W. Aston and G. Nakhikan. The Hague: Nijhoff.

McCormack, B. (2001) *Negotiating Partnerships with Older People: A Person-centred Approach*. Aldershot: Ashgate.

Titchen, A. (2000) *Professional Craft Knowledge in Patient-Centred Nursing and the Facilitation of Its Development*, University of Oxford DPhil Dissertation. Kidlington, Oxon.: Ashdale Press.

CHAPTER
15

NATURALISTIC INQUIRY

Nigel Norris
Centre for Applied Research in Education, University of East Anglia, UK
Rob Walker
Centre for Applied Research in Education, University of East Anglia, UK

Key concepts

Nigel Norris

Buford Junker's *Field Work: An Introduction to the Social Sciences* (University of Chicago Press, 1960) was one of the first books to systematically address fieldwork. The book was the culmination of a project that looked at what had been learnt about fieldwork by both experienced researchers and by students who had been engaged in fieldwork as part of a course they took with Everett C. Hughes. In his introduction to the book Hughes wrote that fieldwork refers 'to observation of people in situ, finding them where they are, staying with them in some role which, while acceptable to them, will allow both intimate observation of certain parts of their behavior, and reporting it in ways useful to social science.' Hughes studied with Robert Ezra Park and his colleague Ernest Burgess in the sociology department of the University of Chicago, and this is one strand of the complex lineage and varied intellectual roots of naturalistic enquiry.[1]

William Isaac Thomas asked Park to join the University of Chicago in 1914. It was Thomas, with Florian Znaniecki, who worked on the monumental and iconic study of the Polish peasant in Europe and America (Thomas and Znaniecki, 1918–20). Park had been taught by John Dewey at the University of Michigan, Ann Arbor and by William James at Harvard. He had been at various times a city reporter and editor in Minneapolis, Detroit, Denver, New York and Chicago and for some eight years was at the Tuskegee Institute as aide to Booker T. Washington, the black civil rights activist. Park was known for his investigative style of journalism (Lindner, 1996). He had also studied in Berlin where he attended lectures by Georg Simmel among others. Studying under the philosopher Windelband, Park got his PhD from Heidelberg. The subject of his thesis was 'the crowd and the public' (Barker, 1973: 255).

Park was committed to empirical research, to the gathering of data through direct experience, as opposed to the speculative theorizing that had characterized much early sociology. For Park the first-hand study of Chicago was the research programme of the sociology department. According to Hammersley (1989: 78) Park advocated the investigation of the natural areas of Chicago and the cultures associated with them, 'not simply as a descriptive exercise but rather as a series of case studies exemplifying basic sociological processes.' The centrality of empirical field-based research rather than analytic theorizing as a basis for sociology was later an important theme in the development of grounded theory (Glaser and Strauss, 1967). Many of the graduate students that were taught by Park, Burgess, Znaniecki and Thomas went on to produce the major case studies of Chicago life that exemplify the naturalistic approach and are a testament to the rich sociological activity that is often referred to as the Chicago School: studies such as Nels Anderson's *The Hobo*, Harvey Warren Zorbaugh's *The Gold Coast and the Slum*, Paul Cressey's *The Taxi-Dance Hall* and Clifford Shaw's life history of a mugger, *The Jack Roller* (Becker, 1999).

Another related strand of development can be traced back to Norman Denzin's paper 'The logic of naturalistic enquiry' published in *Social Forces* in 1971. This was one of the first systematic explorations of naturalistic methodology. He takes as his starting point the philosophy of George Herbert Mead and the symbolic interactionism of Herbert Blumer. Denzin (1971: 166) defined what he called 'naturalistic behaviourism' to mean 'the studied commitment to actively enter the worlds of native people and to render those worlds understandable from the standpoint of a theory that is grounded in the behaviours, languages, definitions, attitudes and feelings of those studied.' According to Denzin naturalistic behaviourism 'places the sociological observer squarely in the centre of the research act'. He goes on to say:

> It recognizes the observer for what he or she is and takes note of the fact that all sociological work somehow reflects the unique stance of the investigator. It assumes that all studies begin in some fashion from a problem, or set of problems, deeply troubling to the sociologist; whether this be the character of alienation, the socialization of one's own children or an attempt to understand how mental hospitals create mental illness. (1971:167)

Following Charles Cooley's (1926) remarks about the role of introspection in sociological analysis, Denzin says of naturalistic enquirers that their reflections on self and other and their conduct in interaction become central pieces of data. Here the self is not just an instrument for collecting data but is also part of the interpretive frame.

More recent contributors to the naturalistic enquiry family have been Yvonna Lincoln and Egon Guba who, through a number of popular texts, have been strong advocates of naturalistic approaches to applied research and evaluation. Lincoln and Guba's 1985 book might be thought of as representing the metaphysical turn in constructs of naturalistic enquiry. They contrast the naturalistic paradigm with the positivist paradigm in social research. For them the naturalistic paradigm treats realities as multiple, constructed and holistic, the knower and the known are seen as interactive and inseparable. The naturalistic enquirer eschews generalization and believes that the aim of enquiry is to produce working hypotheses and case-based knowledge (Lincoln and Guba, 1985: 37).

There are a number of core ideas which have become associated with naturalistic enquiry. Naturalistic enquiry evokes the idea of the 'real' or 'natural' world as the setting for social research as opposed to the laboratory or other artificially constructed circumstances or the library armchair. The emphasis on the 'natural world' or 'natural context' can be overwrought since the dividing line between the natural and the artificial is not altogether easy to draw categorically. Nonetheless, naturalistic enquiry starts from the assumption that phenomena should be studied in their natural setting. Another student of the Chicago sociology department, Irvine Goffman (1959), reminds us that social life is not always what it seems, that what appears to be natural can in fact be an act, a staged performance. The natural can be a treacherous beast.

Naturalistic enquiry is related to ethnography (Vidich and Lyman, 2000). It shares with ethnography a commitment to detailed description. Foremost naturalistic enquiry strives to be true to the nature of the phenomena under study, 'to tell it like it is' as some have said. Lohman (1937: 891) notes that participant observation has been employed in community studies to 'obviate the bias of another cultural order'. Vidich (1955: 354) says that participant observation enables the researcher 'to secure data within the mediums, symbols, and experiential worlds which have meaning' to respondents, with the 'intent to prevent imposing alien meanings upon the actions of the subjects'. Denzin (1971: 168) talks about naturalism implying 'a profound respect for the character of the empirical world'. Being 'true' to the phenomena, 'telling it like it is', is, of course, not without its epistemological hazards: it is a bold claim.

Researching natural settings might be thought to depend on not disturbing too much the social processes through the obvious presence of the researcher. Florence Kluckhohn (1940: 331), for example, writes that the purpose of participant observation is to 'obtain data about behavior through direct contact and in terms of specific situations in which the distortion that results from the investigator's being an outside agent is reduced to a minimum'. Conventional participant observation is based on consent and is interventive, overt and reactive. In so far as naturalistic enquiry makes claims about being true to the social processes to be studied, apprehending and appreciating the natural social world as it is, then the researcher has to think carefully about the unintended consequences of being there. Not all social research projects can be overt and based on informed consent. There is sometimes no alternative than to engage in covert research, to be what Gold (1958) and Junker (1960) refer to as the 'complete participant'. This field research role offers the considerable advantage of avoiding the risk of disturbing the setting and 'studying an artefact of your presence rather than normal behaviour' (Fielding, 1993: 159).

As with ethnography more generally, naturalistic enquiry raises questions about representation. There are issues to do with how people are portrayed and whether they are represented in ways that are fair, accurate and reasonable. As I have noted, Lincoln and Guba (1985: 37), for example, argue that for naturalistic enquiry it is axiomatic that realities are multiple and constructed. Regardless of whether you share Lincoln and Guba's penchant for metaphysics, there are issues to do with how the poly-vocal many-sided nature of social life is captured, represented and read in narratives. In understanding others naturalistic enquiry tries as far as possible to keep close to the language, meanings, thoughts, activities and contexts of the people who are the participants in the study and to represent them in commonplace ways they would understand and would be understandable to others.

There are too questions about the capacity to empathize, to be in the shoes of another, if you are not like the other. Can a white middle-class Spanish male learn how it feels and what it means to be an Asian woman living in a community in London? To use another example: can heterosexual men understand the world from the perspective of gay men or women? While it is clear that people have the capacity to understand others and are able to empathize with others even when there are marked differences, nonetheless for any one individual the capacity for empathy is likely to have its limits.

Implications for research design

Because of the importance of context naturalistic enquiry is often best conceived as case study. It is not possible to pre-specify in detail the design for a naturalistic enquiry. The naturalistic enquirer has to go with the flow of social action, so to speak. The design of a naturalistic enquiry unfolds as the study progresses. The preferred methods of research are observation, sometimes participant observation, interview and the collection of documents and other social artefacts. Naturalistic enquiry emphasizes the importance of face-to-face rather than remote forms of data collection. The self is thought of as the research and interpretive instrument.

Naturalistic enquiry should be intensive. As Harry Wolcott (1995: 67) notes there is a significant difference between doing fieldwork and borrowing a fieldwork technique or two. Naturalistic enquiry requires significant amounts of time spent in the field becoming familiar, collecting data, understanding what things mean for people in situ and representing the social world in which people live and interpret their lives. In their discussion of the methods used to study the undergraduate college of the University of Kansas, Howard Becker, Blanche Geer and Everett Hughes (1968: 13) say that the 'participant observer follows those he studies through their daily round of life, seeing what they do, when, with whom, and under what circumstances, and querying them about the meaning of their actions'. To this extent naturalistic enquiry is up close and personal. It tends towards intimacy. It demands empathy. It needs the researcher to theorize with people rather than about them. This last point is perhaps critical to the project of naturalistic enquiry.

The up close and personal nature of naturalistic enquiry can raise particular ethical issues. Most obviously there are risks to individuals and groups of exposure or inadvertent disclosure. Given the importance of context and meaning in naturalistic enquiry, special efforts must be made to maintain confidentiality and guarantee anonymity.

Field workers often feel that there is something not quite right about their relationships with people, that they are using people, that their friendliness, their closeness to people is conditioned by the fact that they are doing research, collecting data. How data is recorded and analysed is critical to the success of naturalistic enquiry.

As Buford Junker (1960: 138) notes, 'field work and learning to do it are at bottom distinctly individual enterprises'. Naturalistic enquiry is a very personal thing. Who you think you are and how others see you make a big difference to what you can do and learn through naturalistic enquiry. It demands a certain amount of self knowledge, a capacity to observe one's self and critically analyse your own experience. Let me end on an equally personal note and with a question. Do I do naturalistic inquiry? Even though I do fieldwork, I don't think I do. I have borrowed from the thinking that informs naturalistic inquiry and its close relations, but thus far I have not had the time for such long-term wholehearted commitment. Given what I've written, I have dabbled but not done.

Stories from the Field – Alice on the Line

Rob Walker

Introduction

This account is extracted and abridged from one of a set of case studies of environmental education in

133

Australia (Robottom et al., 2000).[2] In 1995, there were political moves in Australia to establish a 'National Curriculum'. In this project we wrote case studies in a number of settings, focusing on the importance of local resources and local contexts. It seemed to us at the time (and still does) that environmental education is particularly dependent on local circumstances if it is to be education 'for' and 'in' the environment, and not just 'about' the environment. *Alice on the Line* was of interest because it was history-based and used the built environment, being a local project in which schools recreated the lives of the Bradshaw family who manned the Telegraph Station in the early 1900s.

The way this case was written places the observer at the centre of the story. In naturalistic enquiry, I believe, the case imposes its own authority and the researcher has to follow, even when the story might seem to be headed in unexpected directions, including here aspects of the local community and its history.

I have selected sections that cover several types of data – reflective description, reported observation and an interview.

What you will read here is a short extract from the case without the context of policy development and curriculum theorizing to be found in the full report. This can only give a brief taste of the style and not the evidence to evaluate its effectiveness.

First images

Among the dot paintings that represent the landscape of Central Australia, a common motif is the arrangement of irregular shaped blocks, each of dots of a particular colour, spread across a whole canvas to give a jigaw like effect. The explanation usually given for this effect is that these images are essentially aerial views of the landscape and the different colours represent different plants and shrubs. The intricate mosaic patterns are caused by the traditional practice of patch burning, for the burning of small areas on a regular basis allowed small animals to seek shelter from fire in nearby unburnt areas, for new plants to grow after the fire and for a complex ecosystem to emerge in which there was movement and balance between recently burnt, unburnt and regenerating areas.

The decline of these traditional practices, and the loss of knowledge needed to sustain them, has led to the emergence of different fire patterns. In 1994 a fire burned unchecked in the Tanami Desert for several months, destroying an area the size of Victoria. It did

so because of the loss of the pattern of regular localized fire which used to accompany small groups of aboriginal people as they travelled through the desert. Instead, a large fuel burden accumulated and, once started in such an isolated area, the large fire could only be left to burn.

Flying into Alice Springs and looking down on a landscape that looks more and more like a dot painting than seems believable, it is difficult to resist seizing on these contrasting images of fire regimes as an appropriate way of depicting the contrast between small localized curriculum developments and the emergence of the National Curriculum. And to extend the metaphor, to see the need to attend to each class and each school in terms of a cycle of renewal and replacement as an urgent and vital task. Before we lose the knowledge to do so.

Bradshaw Primary School

The contrasts within Alice Springs are remarkable. Looking down the tree-lined suburban streets around Bradshaw Primary School, it could, almost, be anywhere in the mainstream of Australian suburban life. But lift your eyes a few degrees and there, immediately behind the green of the school oval, are the McDonnell Ranges, a wall of sandstone, orange-red in the midday sun, not a hint of a plant or of any colour but the bare rock, looking like the backdrop for a stage set . . . But once inside the building, school life takes over. Several teachers said to me how inward-looking the building was. Once you are inside you could (almost) be in a primary school anywhere . . .

Some of the children in Paul's class have been out observing wallabies in the wild, doing transects in their habitat but especially watching how the wallabies behave and how they move. Around the class are drawings, maps, pieces of writing – a lot of research. Some of the girls explain how, with Bronwyn's help, they worked up dance steps from the observations they had made of the rock wallabies, how they looked for patterns and sequences in the movements that they had observed, and then tried to copy the tilt of the head that they had noticed among the wallabies when they were disturbed. Bronwyn is a dancer and singer who has just spent some time back home between work in Sydney and America.

Paul tells me a little about the children. Two of the girls, he explains, a white girl who grew up on a mission and her friend who is aboriginal, both speak Arrente, and have begun teaching the language to children in grade two. They have been looking for a dictionary and Paul gets them to fax an agency he knows which will tell them what is available and where they can get it.

It is a remarkably talented class; some of the other children are good athletes, others academically able. Their lives seem full of promise but Paul is aware of the shadow that looms as they face adolescence. This is especially true for aboriginal children who will encounter the risks of binge drinking, teenage pregnancy and cultural demoralization. One of the first signs of these problems, Paul explains, is a feeling of embarrassment. Recently one of the girls, usually outgoing and extrovert, brought some indigenous plants into school, bush tucker, but instead of showing them to the class, only showed him when he was in the next room, alone at the photocopier, perhaps because of what others might say.

For the moment though the children have that feeling of being a special group which you sometimes find in a successful grade six class. I discover there is a history in this. Previously many of these children, especially the aboriginal children, attended another school in the town, Traeger Park, an aboriginal school that no longer exists. In 1991 the government announced the school was to close, arguing that 'it was not in the long-term interests of Aboriginal children, who have to learn to take their place in the wider community – they have to learn to compete, and they are going to compete with white children and white adults' (Northern Territory Education Minister Shane Stone on ABC Radio, 28 July 1991). Despite resistance from parents and others in the community and a Human Rights Commission report, the school was closed.

When people tell this story (not just the teachers but the town librarian and various other people in the town) one of the things that you cannot help notice is the distance *they* put between Darwin (where the government is located, far to the north) and Alice Springs. Not just the obvious physical distance, but in their intonation and phrasing there is an undeniable sense of 'them' and 'us'.

First reflections: the recent history of environmental education in Alice Springs

Lesa Cornock, the librarian/teacher at Bradshaw Primary School, told me about *Alice on the Line*. This project was based on the Old Telegraph Station, a collection of buildings just north of the town which,

at the turn of the century, was the home of the Bradshaw family. The Telegraph Station was a key relay in the overland wire which linked Australia to the world when long-distance communications were limited to transmissions in morse code. In the 1960s Doris Bradshaw Blackwell, who as a child had lived at the Telegraph Station, wrote an autobiography of her childhood which described day-to-day life on the Station and which became the main source document for the *Alice on the Line* Project.

The project was encouraged and promoted by the Conservation Commission, the organization responsible for the Telegraph Station site, especially through the involvement of its Education Officer, Stuart Traynor. In a small town, a single project of this kind can have a significant impact, and one of the long-term consequences of *Alice on the Line* has been to disrupt any assumptions that social history and environmental education are divisible. Teachers in Alice Springs talk of social education and environmental education as closely associated, even as virtually interchangeable terms . . .

Stuart Traynor's story

Stuart's name comes up in every conversation. Over the last twenty years he has been closely involved with all the key environmental education projects in Alice Springs. The 'best and worst' thing he ever did, he says, was get involved in starting up *Alice on the Line*. 'Best' because it has had a bigger impact on Alice Springs schools than anything else he has ever been involved in. 'Worst' because stress of this kind, plus another major project he began in 1988, 'turned his hair grey'.

I asked Stuart the question that Paul and Lesa had raised earlier: 'Does the Living History approach risk exposing children to racist views and attitudes that are no longer acceptable?' Stuart responded:

The Bradshaws were unusually enlightened for the time. Thomas Bradshaw succeeded Frank Gillen, who had a great interest in anthropology and had established a climate of enlightened attitudes and good relations with the local Arrente people. One of Thomas Bradshaw's responsibilities was to act as the local magistrate and protector of aborigines. The record shows that he tried to be fair. If the case was built around Barrow Creek Station (where two whites were speared in the 1870s), 'it would be a lot harder' to sustain this case.

Part of the aim of the programme is to reveal what attitudes and values were at the time and to help children explore these and come to terms with them. So confronting racism is an important part of the curriculum, which of course some teachers will find easier to do than others. On the whole, teachers are not trained to handle values and feelings in the classroom, and many find this difficult. They are good at teaching skills and knowledge, but values and emotions are more difficult.

Role play was intended to be the key teaching strategy for the programme. For instance at one point two aboriginal girls are arguing in the laundry and a copper of hot water is knocked over (not really!) badly burning one of them on the arm. (. . .) The telegraph officer (using morse code) asks a doctor for medical advice (. . .) The family comes with ironwood root (Acacia estrophiolata) (. . .) to administer traditional healing. This sets the scene for an exploration of alternative values.

Stuart sees the need to explore attitudes and values as a gap in the conventional curriculum. What *Alice on the Line* offers is the opportunity to 'feel' history rather than just learn about it. The project found that some teachers did this very well but others were content to engage more superficially. Some taught 'only the historical facts, not getting into attitudes and values'. This he feels is where the real impact on children lies – 'I hadn't realized what an effect it had until my own daughter, now in year 7, went through the programme and I saw how excited and involved in it she was'.

But some years on Stuart sees other questions:

Seeing your own children going through school, you realize that schools cannot do everything you would like them to do. I have come to see that what they do very well is give children basic knowledge and skills. This means that some things

are best approached by educating the family, or the child in the context of the family, rather than the child in a class. We began to do this in *Alice on the Line*, because each class had to involve four adults, who were usually parents. But I began to see the need to develop this approach to community education more systematically.

. . . At this point the extract stops rather than ends. There is not enough information here to begin thinking about an ending or conclusion or to draw lessons from the case. To do this requires more description, more comparison and contrast with the other cases and a better explication of the curriculum problem. What I have tried to provide is a sense of the narrative structure of naturalistic enquiry. This is what I take 'putting the researcher squarely at the centre of the research act' to imply in practice. Pursuing the logic of enquiry, understanding the nature of the case and relating it to the research question all takes more time and more space than is available.

Notes

1. The term 'naturalistic' has not always been used in the way that we now associate with naturalistic enquiry. In the past naturalism was used by some to imply the unity of science and the appropriateness of the scientific method for the study of the social world, and humanistic phenomena were contrasted with natural phenomena and humanistic researchers were contrasted with naturalistic scientists (Znaniecki, 1927; Znaniecki, 1934).

2. I have used the real names of people and places, with their consent. Alice Springs is a one-off town that is hard to anonymize and if you live and work there then there is little privacy for those in public positions as everyone knows everyone else.

Annotated bibliography

Becker, H. (1998) *Tricks of the Trade*. Chicago: University of Chicago Press.

This is a delightful book about ways to think about research. Becker says that in a certain way the book is a homage to the people who taught him, people like Everett C. Hughes and Herbert Blumer. The book covers such things as, imagery, sampling, concepts and logic. It is also a book about how to solve research problems.

Coffey, A. and Atkinson, P. (1996) *Making Sense of Qualitative Data*. London: Sage.

This book offers practical advice on the many ways to analyse qualitative data and construct research accounts.

Hammersley, M. and Atkinson, P. (1995) *Ethnography*, 2nd edn. London: Routledge.

This is a key explanatory text covering the principles and practice of ethnography. It is an excellent and accessible review of the methodological territory of contemporary ethnography.

Schatzman, L. and Strauss, A. (1973) *Field Research: Strategies for a Natural Sociology*. Englewood Cliffs, NJ: Prentice-Hall.

This is a short, easy-to-read book which focuses on practical strategies for doing field-based enquiry, including a consideration of the self as researcher.

Van Maanen, J. (1988) *Tales of the Field*. Chicago: University of Chicago Press.

Van Maanen says of *Tales of the Field* that it is about 'how one culture is portrayed in terms of another in an ethnography'. The book explores the narrative conventions and literary devices associated with writing about culture. It identifies three main types of story: realist tales, confessional tales and impressionist tales.

Further references

Anderson, N. (1923) *The Hobo: The Sociology of the Homeless Man*. Chicago: University of Chicago Press.

Barker, P. (1973) 'The life histories of W.I. Thomas and Robert E. Park', *American Journal of Sociology*, 79(2): 243–60.

Becker, H.S. (1999) 'The Chicago School, so-called', *Qualitative Sociology*, 22(1): 3–12. Also available at: <http://home.earthlink.net/hsbecker/>

Becker, H.S., Geer, B. and Hughes, E.C. (1968) *Making the Grade*. New York: John Wiley & Sons.

Cooley, C.H. (1926) 'The roots of social knowledge', *American Journal of Sociology*, 32(1): 59–79.

Cressey, P. (1932) *The Taxi-Dance Hall*. Chicago: University Chicago Press.

Denzin, N. (1971) 'The logic of naturalistic inquiry', *Social Forces*, 50(2): 166–82.

Fielding, N. (1993) 'Ethnography', in N. Gilbert (ed.), *Researching Social Life*. London: Sage, pp. 154–71.

Glaser, B. and Strauss, A. (1968) *The Discovery of Grounded Theory*. London: Weidenfeld & Nicolson.

Goffman, I. (1959) *The Presentation of Self in Everyday Life*. Garden City, NY: Doubleday.

Gold, R.L. (1958) 'Role in sociological field observations', *Social Forces*, 36(3): 217–23.

Hammersley, M. (1989) *The Dilemma of Qualitative Method*. London: Routledge.

Junker, B.(1960) *Field Work: An Introduction to the Social Sciences*. Chicago: University of Chicago Press.

Lincoln, Y. and Guba, E. (1985) *Naturalistic Inquiry*. London: Sage.

Lindner, R. (1996) *The Reportage of Urban Culture*. Cambridge: Cambridge University Press.

Lohman, J. (1937) 'The participant observer on community studies', *American Sociological Review*, 2(6): 890–7.

Kluckhohn, F.R. (1940) 'The participant-observer technique in small communities', *American Journal of Sociology*, 46(3): 331–43.

Reis, H. (ed.) (1983) *Naturalistic Approaches to Studying Social Interaction*. San Francisco: Jossey-Bass.

Robottom, I., Malone, K. and Walker, R. (2000) *Case Studies in Environmental Education: Policy and Practice*. Geelong, Victoria: Deakin University Press.

Shaw, C. (1930) *The Jack Roller*. Chicago: University of Chicago Press.

Thomas, W. and Znanieki, F. (1918–20) *The Polish Peasant in Europe and America*, 5 vols. Chicago: University of Chicago.

Vidich, A. (1955) 'Participant observation and the collection and interpretation of data', *American Journal of Sociology*, 60(4): 354–60.

Vidich, A. and Lyman, S. (2000) 'Qualitative methods: their history in sociology and anthropology', in N. Denzin and Y. Lincoln (eds), *Handbook of Qualitative Research*, 2nd edn. London: Sage. pp. 37–84.

Wolcott, H. (1995) *The Art of Fieldwork*. London: AltaMira Press.

Znaniecki, F. (1927) 'The object matter of sociology', *American Journal of Sociology*, 32(4): 529–84.

Znaniecki, F. (1968 and 1934) *The Method of Sociology*. New York: Octagon Books.

Zorbaugh, H. (1929) *The Gold Coast and the Slum*. Chicago: University of Chicago Press.

16

OBSERVATION

Liz Jones
Education and Social Research Institute, Manchester Metropolitan University, UK
Bridget Somekh
Education and Social Research Institute, Manchester Metropolitan University, UK

Key concepts

Bridget Somekh

Through the habit of observation, social science researchers become sensitized to the fascinations of observing people going about their daily lives. An interesting phenomenon in recent years is the behaviour of people using cell phones: as soon as they make a connection their voice volume, their discourse and their non-verbal behaviour all become appropriate to the person they are talking to 'virtually', and in varying degrees inappropriate to their physical environment and the people around them. Patterns are easily observable – they talk too loudly, they nearly always start by saying where they are ('I'm on the train . . .') and they reveal personal details of their lives and work in a way which often seems extraordinary to those nearby. We notice this because it is new. Other kinds of patterned behaviour are equally easy to observe if we set out to do so systematically.

Observation is one of the most important methods of data collection. It entails being present in a situation and making a record of one's impressions of what takes place. In observation the primary research instrument is the self, consciously gathering sensory data through sight, hearing, taste, smell and touch. By various means of record-keeping, traces of those impressions are stored for careful scrutiny and analysis after the event. An obvious problem is the enormous complexity of human behaviour, whether as individuals or in groups, and the impossibility of making a complete record of all the researcher's impressions. Add to this the subjectivity of the researcher who at the same time as collecting sensory data is actively engaged in making sense of impressions and interpreting the meaning of observed behaviour and events. The record of the observation becomes, necessarily, a product of choices about what to observe and what to record, made either at the time of the observation in response to impressions or in advance of the observation in an attempt prospectively to impose some order on the data.

Ways of seeing the world

What is observed is ontologically determined, that is it depends to a very great extent on how the observer conceptualizes the world and his or her place within it. For example, if the starting point is a positivist belief that the world is external to the observer, and that facts about people, locations and events can be recorded unproblematically (see Garratt and Lee, in this volume), the main methodological issues will relate to how to make accurate observations and reduce observer bias. Observation will need to be a systematic, structured process, so that data can later be categorized for quantitative and statistical analysis. A good example of observation data collected and analysed in this way would be the many studies carried out on the length of time that teachers in classrooms pause after asking a question before either rephrasing the question or answering it themselves. It is now recognized that the pause is almost universally too short to give students a real opportunity of replying if the answer requires thought. This important finding resulted from classroom observations that measured the amount of time taken up by teachers' and students' utterances and the exact length of pauses between utterances.

If, on the other hand, the starting point is the symbolic interactionist assumption that behaviour is constructed through interaction between individuals and groups, and that much of it is strongly patterned, or 'routinized', in a kind of symbolic action-response performance (Garfinkel, 1984; Goffman, 1959), the observer will be looking for – and thus is likely to see – 'patterns' of behaviour. The interpretation of teacher–student interaction given above would then incorporate recognition of the mutual performance that they are engaged in, with both parties expecting students' answers to be short (between three and five words) and given rapidly (without any need for prior thought) and expecting teachers who receive no response to quickly redirect their question to another student or answer it themselves. This would imply that observation should focus on collecting as full a record as possible of words and behaviours by means of tape or video recording and scrutinizing these in a search for patterns. These might be obvious because of their novelty (as in the case of cell phone users) or unnoticed till they emerge through analysis because they are embedded in the observer's prior experience (as in the case of teacher and student).

Yet again, if the research is underpinned by an ethnographic approach (see Stark and Torrance, in this volume), the process of observation will be highly participatory and the researcher will seek to observe in an open-ended way, screening nothing out and noting as many details as possible, guided by some overarching categories (e.g. the concepts of culture, gender and social class). The aim here is that, through immersion, the researcher will become able to interpret the cultural meanings inherent in verbal and non-verbal behaviour. Analysis of the observation data will then adopt what (Geertz, 1973: 24) calls the 'semiotic approach' to 'the interpretation of cultures', through making meaning from complexity. Geertz says of this kind of observation that 'the aim is to draw large conclusions from small, but very densely textured facts' (1973: 28).

If, however, the starting point is deconstruction (see Burman and Maclure, in this volume) the observer will be expecting to challenge any 'obvious' interpretation of what is observed, and seek for ways of revealing underlying layers of meaning. This approach is exemplified in Liz Jones's story from the field in the second part of this chapter.

Ways of observing

As we have seen, the methodological framework for the research will largely determine what is 'seen' and is, therefore, the key factor in the choice of observation method from the options set out below.

Structured observation

One approach is to structure the observation around a schedule prepared in advance. Schedules predetermine the categories of behaviour/talk that will be observed and are inevitably influenced by the researcher's expectations, so it is usually best to develop a schedule specifically for a particular research study. Flanders' Interaction Analysis Categories (FIAC), is an example of an observation schedule developed as a replicable method of observing teacher and student talk in classrooms with inter-observer reliability (i.e. minimal differences due to researcher bias) (see Figure 16.1).

The observer's job is to 'code' the observed talk by jotting one of the category numbers on an observation schedule at regular intervals (e.g. every five seconds). FIAC is an excellent tool for the purpose it

Teacher talk	Response	1. Accepts feeling (e.g. accepts and clarifies an attitude or the feeling tone of a pupil)
		2. Praises or encourages
		3. Accepts or uses ideas of pupils
	Initiation	4. Asks questions
		5. Lecturing
		6. Giving directions
		7. Criticizing or justifying authority
Pupil talk	Response	8. Pupil talk – response
	Initiation	9. Pupil talk – initiation
Silence		10. Silence or confusion

Figure 16.1   FIAC categories (taken from Flanders, 1970: 34)

was designed for, but it leads to highly selective observation. For example, there is no distinction made between 'closed' questions which expect a yes/no answer or recall of a fact, and 'open' questions which ask for an opinion. There is bias built into the FIAC categories since seven categories apply to teacher talk and only two to pupil talk, and in fact it works best in situations where the teacher is working with the whole class (and teacher talk is more likely to be dominant). In classrooms organized around group work with the teacher moving around the room, researchers have either to make a decision to observe and record only one group, or make very frequent use of category 10.

Unstructured observation

Another approach is to sit at the side or back of the room and make detailed notes. In this holistic approach, the researcher is guided by prior knowledge and experience and 'sees' through the unique lens of her own socio-culturally constructed values dependent upon life history and factors such as gender, ethnicity, social class and disciplinary and professional background. Broad decisions are usually made in advance about the kinds of things to be recorded, either on the basis of analysis of other data already collected (e.g. interview or questionnaire data) or derived from the focus of the research. It is best to record key utterances verbatim, as this reduces the extent to which intended meanings are obscured, and is usually quicker. It is useful to draw a 'map' to show the position of furniture, numbering participants and recording movements with dotted lines, arrows and secondary numbers (2a, 2b); the time can be noted in the left-hand margin to record the speed of the sequence of events.

Shadow studies

Here the researcher tracks one of the participants, with or without prior agreement (there are ethical considerations in the latter case). The purpose is either to study the person shadowed or to share that person's experiences. For example, in the latter case a shadow study might be carried out in a prison in an attempt to understand the nature of the experience of being a prisoner. If researchers go into role and imitate the general behaviour of the group they often attract surprisingly little attention and have relatively little impact on group behaviour.

Participant observation

Participant observers gain unique insights into the behaviour and activities of those they observe because they participate in their activities and, to some extent, are absorbed into the culture of the group. Disadvantages include that they may be distracted from their research purpose by tasks given to them by the group, and note-making becomes much more difficult and may have to be done after the event, ideally the same evening.

The impact of the observer on those observed

Observers always have some kind of impact on those they are observing who, at worst, may become tense and have a strong sense of performing, even of being inspected. Negative effects are reduced if the purposes of the observation, how the data will be used and who will be given access to them are made clear in advance. It helps if the clothing worn by the observer merges into the context and signals equality of status with those who are being observed.

Using technology to record observations

Neither audio- nor video-recording replaces the need to make field notes, since technology only keeps a partial record and cannot replace the sensitivity of the researcher's 'self', open to nuances of meaning and interpretation.

Tape-recording and transcribing

A good microphone is much more important than the recording equipment itself. Portable tape recorders with external microphones, particularly those with a noise reduction feature that focuses on the main speaker, are good. Other newer technologies such as 'mini discs' provide excellent quality recordings. Choose where to place the microphone, since this will determine what is recorded most clearly. Small tape recorders can be kept in a pocket (not necessarily the researcher's) with a lapel microphone attached to clothing at the most appropriate height (e.g. waist height when working with small children). In order to analyse the data, the tape recording has to be transcribed: either a full transcription of every utterance or a partial transcription of selected passages. In the latter case, listen first to the whole tape and make brief running notes of its contents before making the selection. Transcribing is very time-consuming but yields excellent data.

Video-recording

Digital video is very much more useful than traditional video-recording because editing is quicker and easier and individual frames can be easily selected for display or printing. Remember that the video-camera is pointed in one direction which screens out a considerable amount of activity. It can be placed on a tripod and set up to record continuously, which is a good way of reducing the impact on participants as well as preventing further 'screening out' through discontinuities in the recording. There is a balance to be achieved here, however, as the researcher has more control over what is observed if the camera is manually operated. As with audio-recording, considerable work needs to be done to prepare video data for analysis, including the transcription of talk and some means of sorting and coding the visual images.

Digital still images

A small digital camera with automatic focus and zoom facilities is ideal for recording still images. One approach is to use it to systematically record a sequence of events over a period of time (e.g. by taking one picture every minute). There is a big difference between taking pictures socially and taking them for research, so it may be useful to plan carefully in advance what kinds of images will be most useful as research data.

Implications for research design

The approach taken to collecting, recording and analysing observation data depends on the methodological framework for the research. How the researcher understands 'being in the world' (ontology) and the nature of knowledge (epistemology) will fundamentally shape both the observation process and analysis of the data collected. Regardless of the approach to observation, it is crucially important to prepare well in advance. In the case of structured observations, schedules need to be prepared to ensure that exactly the right data will be collected to explore specified research questions. In the case of unstructured observations, considerable thought should be given to the kind of relationship that needs to be established with participants – and how to present the researcher in order to achieve this. This will also

involve a number of practical decisions such as what to wear and how much information about the purpose of the research to give in advance. Fundamentally, all kinds of observation involve invading other people's space and constructing meanings from the experience of participating in their activities, rather than through the filter of their accounts about their activities. The key issue here is the well-known mismatch between intentions and effects (e.g. interviewees usually make claims of behaving in ways that are not fully corroborated by observation). This means that the researcher's construction of meaning from observation data is unlikely to match the participants' own constructions of meaning from their experience of taking part in what has been observed. Observation is, therefore, much more threatening than interviewing and gives rise to a number of ethical issues. Hence, it is of the utmost importance to seek 'informed consent' and negotiate a 'code of practice' governing ownership and use of the data, in advance of carrying out the observation (see Piper and Simons, this volume).

Stories from the Field – Undertaking observations within a practitioner researcher inquiry
Liz Jones

And because the stories were held in fluid form, they retained the ability to change, to become yet new stories, to join up with other stories and so become yet other stories. (Salman Rushdie, *Haroun and the Sea of Stories*, 1990: 73)

My aim is to illustrate how written observations, undertaken as part of a practitioner inquiry for doctorial studies, became a means for self-scrutiny. In general, teachers who work with very young children, as I did, spend considerable amounts of time observing them closely. Careful observations are the bedrock of good teaching, where current strengths and weaknesses of the children are identified so that subsequent learning can be mapped. Observations in this instance aim to be objective and can be seen as reflections of reality. But what are the reverberations if an alternative position is adopted regarding language and meaning? What are some of the consequences if a sceptical attitude is taken in relation to language and its capacity to tell us how it – including the nursery classroom – really is?

What follows tries to illustrate the dynamic interplay between observing events, writing about them and then subjecting these texts to practices of deconstruction. The consequences of such an engagement can be fruitful, where observations can become 'enabling stories' (Bernstein, 1983) that can be used to:

> understand ourselves reflexively as persons writing from particular situations at specific times. (Richardson, 1993: 516)

A reflexive reading has, I think, the capacity to foreground how certain personal blind spots (Lather, 1993: 91) work at blocking the vision necessary for creative thinking. In brief, I want to enact how one story changed and became a new story . . .

Observing the mercurial world of the nursery classroom

Research for the doctorate took place in a nursery that is part of an inner-city primary school situated in Manchester, England. A central aim of the research was to provide an account of how children's identifications, as evidenced in their use of language, contributed to their own evolving identity, with particular reference to gender. Specifically, this entailed collecting examples of interactions between the children and their teacher and the children and each other. Choosing which interactions to focus on was clearly an issue. Within the nursery classroom the children experienced a relatively large degree of physical autonomy. They were encouraged to take some control over their own learning and as a consequence the children often made their own decisions about where they wanted to be located in the room and the type of activity that they wanted to be engaged with. The mercurial nature of this particular context had implications for the way in which observations could be undertaken. Undertaking Masters work – which was also a piece of practitioner research – had helped to evolve my observational techniques. It was here, for example, I learned never to be without my research journal. In this, rough notes about aspects of classroom life were quickly noted, including descriptions of children's play and snatches of their conversations. Having worked for some time with young children I had also become quite skilled in being able to work alongside one group of children while simultaneously being able to 'eavesdrop' on others. At other times the children involved me in their play. As a consequence, there were opportunities to observe both as a participant and a non-participant and, because the research journal had become such a familiar feature – part of my teacher persona – its presence was readily accepted by the children. Thus I made on-the-spot observations and, at more leisurely points in the school day, added reflections to enrich and categorize the initial notes.

Clearly decisions were made about what should and should not be recorded. To imagine that such recordings could comprehensively capture everything was a nonsense. As Martin and Bateson note:

> The choice of which particular aspects to measure, and the way in which this is done, should reflect explicit questions. (1986: 12–13)

My own criteria for selecting particular phenomena did not, however, rest on 'explicit questions'. Rather, instances were selected where it seemed that the children, through their imaginary worlds, were exploring a range of 'social positionings' (Davies, 1989). Role-play was a rich data source. I also noted extracts of children's conversations where they demonstrated a capacity to move between everyday, matter-of-fact talk to more wishful, imaginative musings. I was particularly attracted to moments that worked at destabilizing my own understandings and assumptions that I inevitably brought to notions such as 'the child' and 'identity'. Moreover, I recorded examples that had, for a number of reasons, touched the ideological and theoretical baggage that accompanied me into the nursery.

The written observations functioned on two levels. First, they fleetingly captured features of classroom life and, secondly, they revealed aspects of myself including particular attachments to specific value systems. Deconstructing the observations helped me to tease apart these attachments and in so doing created a necessary conceptual space where more creative ways could be considered. What follows illustrates this process.

An observation from the field

(Journal entry)

Lisa and Michael are in the area where the dressing-up clothes are kept. Lisa ties a narrow band of cloth around Michael's head. He then does the same for her. Both children have now become karate fighters. There is no actual fighting between them. Just a lot of posturing, with arms, legs, hands and faces indicating that they are executing some form of martial arts. Michael declares that he's 'Leonardo'.[1] Lisa states, 'I'll be Leonardo's friend'. Michael responds 'girls can't be your mates'. At this point I intervene in order to reason with Michael. I try to point out to him that as he and Lisa had been 'playing so well together' then 'weren't they friends, so why couldn't Lisa be the mate?' Michael makes no verbal responses. He looks uncomfortable as if he is being told off. He shifts around, avoids my eyes and looks down at his feet. Lisa looks bewildered. I make one more appeal to Michael: 'Couldn't Lisa be the mate?' I move away from the children hoping that by so doing the situation will be resolved.

Ground-clearing activities

Clearly, given the position that has been articulated concerning language and meaning, the notion that the above is an unbiased account is untenable. Better perhaps to see the above story/observation more as an invention than a description (St Pierre, 1997: 368). So, what fuelled the above account? What libidinal investment helped in its enframing (Lather, 1991: 83)? Why did I intervene? I think my intervention was prompted because I perceived Lisa as being treated unjustly. That is, Michael was refusing Lisa an opportunity to be a mate and it was a refusal that was premised on her gender – 'girls can't be your mates'. His refusal confounded me because it seemed to me to be irrational and illogical. On the one hand it appeared that Michael could befriend a girl in that they could play together. They could share their collective knowledge of a television programme with Lisa introducing headbands into their play so that both she and Michael could undertake transformations into karate fighters. Michael therefore appears to be accepting of Lisa when she is in the guise of a karate fighter, but nevertheless he is disbarring her from being a 'mate'. My intervention was I think guided by a sense of wanting to right a wrong. However, retrospectively I now perceive my action not as an intervention but as an intrusion. In part, I think my interference was fuelled by disappointment. My reading of the children's play was filtered through a number of adult perspectives, including a feminist

one, and as a consequence I found it wanting. Michael's particular reading of friendship precludes not just Lisa but all girls. There is of course a certain irony in his declaration because in the interest of reproduction girls have to be your mate. But for Michael, and indeed for a great number of men, mate is the favoured term for a same-sex friend. So what within the context of the play does 'mate' signify for Michael? My infringement into their play prevented opportunities occurring whereby this question might have been addressed. As it was, by truncating their narrative I managed to close a gap that had briefly been opened and which had allowed some insight into a young child's perception of the social order.

The observation illustrates, I think, how both Michael and I are caught up in undertaking what Connell (1983) refers to as category maintenance work. Categories are used in order to impose order on the world but it is a practice that can have negative implications. They can, for example, work at narrowing conceptions of what is and is not acceptable. In this instance, Michael has established which groups can and cannot be your mate. Meanwhile my own investment in feminism prompts me to act in ways that are unproductive, where an over-readiness to intercede in the children's play curtailed opportunities to fathom or appreciate why girls can be a play mate (a partner in play) but not a mate.

Tentative conclusions

In general terms, researchers who undertake observations are involved in first looking at 'the field'. Their task is then to analyse: to establish the 'essential meaning in the raw data' and to begin to tame the chaos by using 'the lenses we have at our disposal at any given time' (Ely, 1991: 140–54). These lenses are those tried and tested modes of qualitative analysis that are 'perfectly learnable by any competent social researcher' (Strauss, 1987: xiii) and are, in effect, filing mechanisms that work at organizing and categorizing the data (Goetz and LeCompte, 1984; Strauss, 1987) so that the researcher is better placed to stake a claim for certainty and impose absolute frames of reference.

In contrast, what is being suggested here is a shift from observation of the classroom events to inquiry into the observation itself. As such, a 'generative' as opposed to a reductive methodology is proposed (Lather, 1993: 673). Texts within a generative methodology do not purport to be transparent, where explicit findings are available. Nor are they attempts to capture the real. Rather, they are 'reflexive explorations of our practices of representation' (Woolgar, 1988: 98). Moreover, they are attempts at struggling with those boundaries and categories that work at stipulating what it is to know and do. In all, they are textual undertakings that endeavour to dislocate mastery.

Notes

1. Leonardo is a cartoon character drawn from a children's television series *Teenage Mutant Ninja Turtles*. The characters are highly trained in karate skills that are used to ensure that good triumphs over evil.
2. Thanks to Dr Julia Gillen of the Open University, UK for assistance in developing this Annotated Bibliography.

Annotated bibliography[2]

Angrosino, M.V. and Mays-de-Perez, K.A. (2000) 'Rethinking observation', in N.K. Denzin and Y.S. Lincoln (eds), *Handbook of Qualitative Research*, 2nd edn. Thousand Oaks, CA and London: Sage, pp. 673–702.

A comprehensive and scholarly review of ethnographic and interactionist approaches to observation.

Brown, T. and Jones, L. (2001) *Action Research and Postmodernism: Congruence and Critique*. Buckingham: Open University Press.

Draws upon extensive examples of classroom-based observations. These are deconstructed in order to create a necessary conceptual space in which to think differently about – among other things – teaching, young children and their social worlds.

Croll, P. (1986) *Systematic Classroom Observation*. London and Philadelphia: Falmer Press.

Provides a clear, readable account of structured observation, including an account of FIAC, drawing on studies carried out in classrooms in England.

Galton, M.J., Hargreaves, L., Comber, C. and Wall, D. (1999) *Inside the Primary Classroom: 20 Years On*. London: Routledge.

Donna started school in 1965 and her daughter Hayley in 1996. This book charts the difference in their likely experiences based on detailed research into teaching in UK primary school classrooms, using an observation schedule. An excellent example of the strengths of this approach.

Geertz, C. (1973) *The Interpretation of Cultures*. London: Fontana (First published 1973, Basic Books: New York).

A classic text which is essential reading for those taking a socio-cultural approach to observation. The final chapter on Balinese cock-fighting is a treat.

Jackson, P.W. (1968) *Life in Classrooms*. New York: Holt, Rinehart & Winston.

Provides a good example of how participant observation can transform our understanding of social practices – in this case elementary school classrooms in the USA in the 1960s. A fascinating read.

Jones, L. and Brown, T. (2001) '"Reading" the nursery classroom: a Foucauldian perspective', *International Journal of Qualitative Studies in Education*, 14(6): 713–25.

Provides a means for appreciating how observation undertaken within the classroom can be the basis for reflexivity.

Rolfe, S.A. (2001) 'Direct observation', in G. MacNaughton, S.A. Rolfe and I. Siraj-Blatchford (eds), *Doing Early Childhood Research: International Perspectives on Theory and Practice*. Buckingham: Open University Press, pp. 224–39.

A comprehensive guide to undertaking observations in general but within early years specifically. This chapter would be of particular benefit to the novice researcher as it clarifies a number of fundamental issues, including, for example, the establishment of research questions.

Sanger, J. (1996) *The Compleat Observer? A Field Guide to Observation.* London: Falmer Press.

Izaac Walton (1593–1683) in *The Compleat Angler* wrote: 'I undertake to acquaint the Reader with many things that are not usually known to every angler.' Sanger's book sets out to do the same for observation and is full of unexpected delights.

Sparkes, A. (1995) 'Writing people: reflections on the dual crises of representation and legitimation in qualitative inquiry', *QUEST,* 47: 158–95.

A fascinating paper on the issues that lie behind the writing up of observations. Sparkes demonstrates how the 'objective, author-evacuated' of third-person scientific writing up of observations is a rhetorical device designed to persuade, and, as such, as deeply subjective a stand as any more ostensibly personalized style of writing up.

Webb, E.J., Campbell, D.T., Schwartz, R.D. and Sechrest, L. (1966) *Unobtrusive Measures: nonreactive research in the Social Sciences.* Chicago: Rand McNally.

A classic work. The authors organize their discussion of simple observation around five topics: (i) exterior physical signs; (ii) expressive movement; (iii) physical location; (iv) spontaneous conversations, randomly selected; and (v) behaviour associated with time.

Further references

Bernstein, R. (1983) *Beyond Objectivism and Relativism: Science, Hermeneutics and Praxis.* Philadelphia: University of Pennsylvania Press.

Connell, R.W. (1983) *Which Way is Up? Essays on Class, Sex and Culture.* Sydney: Allen & Unwin.

Davies, B. (1989) *Frogs and Snails and Feminist Tales: Preschool Children and Gender.* Sydney: Allen & Unwin.

Deleuze, G. and Guattari, F. (1987) *A Thousand Plateaus: Capitalism and Schizophrenia,* trans. B. Massumi. Minneapolis: University of Minnesota Press (original work published in 1980).

Ely, M. (1991) *Doing Qualitative Research.* Basingstoke: Falmer.

Flanders, N.A. (1970) *Analyzing Teaching Behavior.* Reading, MA and London: Addison-Wesley.

Garfinkel, H. (1984) *Studies in Ethnomethodology.* Cambridge and Oxford: Polity Press.

Goetz, J.P. and LeCompte, M.D. (1984) *Ethnography and Qualitative Design in Education Research.* Orlando, FL: Academic Press.

Goffman, E. (1959) *The Presentation of Self in Everyday Life.* London: Penguin.

Lather, P. (1991) *Getting Smart.* London: Routledge.

Lather, P. (1993) 'Fertile obsession: validity after poststructuralism', *Sociological Quarterly,* 34(4): 673–93.

Martin, P. and Bateson, P. (1986) *Measuring Behaviour: An Introductory Guide.* Cambridge: Cambridge University Press.

Richardson, L. (1993) 'Narrative and sociology', in J. Van Maanen (ed.), *Representation in Ethnography.* Thousand Oaks, CA: Sage, pp. 509–41.

Rushdie, S. (1990) *Houran and the Sea of Stories.* London: Granta Books.

St Pierre, E. (1997) 'Nomadic inquiry in the smooth spaces of the field: a preface', *Qualitative Studies in Education,* 10(3): 365–83.

Strauss, A. (1987) *Qualitative Analysis for Social Scientists.* Cambridge: Cambridge University Press.

Woolgar, S. (1988) 'The next step: an introduction to the reflexive project', in S. Woolgar (ed.), *Knowledge and Reflexivity.* London: Sage.

CHAPTER

17

DISCOURSE ANALYSIS

Julia Gillen
Centre for Language and Communications, The Open University, UK
Alan Petersen
School of Sociology, Politics and Law, University of Plymouth, UK

Key concepts

Julia Gillen

In his stimulating introduction to discourse analysis, Gee writes:

> Any method always goes with a theory. Method and theory cannot be separated, despite the fact that methods are often taught as if they could stand alone. Any method of research is a way to investigate some particular domain . . . There can be no sensible method to study a domain, unless one also has a theory of what the domain is. (1999: 5)

Discourse analysis is concerned with the investigation of language and one might reasonably expect linguistics, the discipline concerned with the study of language, to be the root for 'discourse analysis'. It can be surprising for the student to find that this is not necessarily so, even if branches of linguistics sometimes supply significant 'tools of the trade'. In fact discourse analysis is a term used to embrace many different methods in the investigation of human communication found across the humanities and social sciences. At one end of a continuum one might put the algorithmic approach to language processing that informs computer software such as voice recognition and translation software. At another end one might put the poststructuralist disruptions of belief in any notion of 'transparency' in language. Yet the glorious characteristic of discourse analysis as it can be encountered from the hybrid interdisciplinary meadow of the social sciences is that any such notion of a continuum fails to work. Any attempt to draw such ends finds them circling back on themselves, like a snake coming to life and swinging round, suddenly

snapping at its tail. In this section I will indicate some strands of thinking in discourse analysis. From the chapter in its entirety you should gain a sense of how discourse analysis might be applied to your own research interests in the social sciences.

Theories, methods and thus disciplinary practices arise from their histories. The traditional linguistics paradigm, with roots in philology, grammar and philosophy, took as data language constructions intuitively judged as correct by linguists (usually white, Anglo, middle-class men). Discourse analysis is immediately different, accepting as data any language *as it occurs*, whatever the channel or mode. For example, the repairs, hesitations and repetitions characteristic of spontaneous spoken language are approached seriously. Practitioners have examined everything from humour in the workplace to the semiotics of labels on jars of baby food. Another important distinction is that traditional mainstream linguistics works with the sentence as the largest unit of analysis whereas discourse analysis usually considers longer texts.

Of course there has been a relationship between many aspects of linguistic theory and the analysis of actual texts. Brown and Yule (1983) outline ways in which approaches emanating from linguistics can be drawn upon in discourse analysis. Sociolinguistics, the study of individual variation, is a notable field of endeavour. One influential theorist has been Michael Halliday (1985), proposing that all language has a dual function, communicating both 'ideational' meaning (regarding ideas and information) and 'interpersonal' meaning (furthering social relations in some sense with our interlocutor). In recent decades Mikhail Bakhtin's emphasis on the dialogicality of language has taken hold. He argues that linguistic meaning exists 'neither in the system of language nor in the objective reality surrounding us' (Bakhtin, 1986: 87). A specific utterance should be understood as always responsive, in the broadest sense, each element of it being spoken (or written) under the influence of the speaker's (or writer's) previous experiences of the words themselves and the discourses in which they are embedded.

Theoretical developments are affected by changes in material practices; technology is always an important influence in fields of interest, methods of data collection and, ultimately, insights generated. An important advance began in sociology at a time when prevailing trends were concerned with abstract, generalizable explanations for human conduct located in identifications of social structures. The advent of the tape recorder, in the hands of fresh thinkers, brought about a new approach to the study of spoken language that continues to proliferate fruitfully today.

In the 1960s a little-known sociology lecturer struggled for recognition of his candidate PhD thesis even within his own faculty. Harvey Sacks, like Erving Goffman, appeared to be turning his back on the 'big questions' to focus on seemingly trivial tiny details of how we lead our daily lives. No detail is too small to lead to fascinating insights into human culture and the performance of identity – whether it be the exchange of 'hellos' on the telephone or the circumstances in which it is not taboo to 'talk to oneself'.

As you read the previous sentence did the saying 'first sign of madness' come into your head? If so, why is there this association? Also, do you in fact ever talk to yourself: perhaps when driving or carrying out a task regarding fine coordination? Are you always alone or are there any circumstances when you might be 'caught' talking to yourself? Goffman argues that we avoid the imputation of madness if in certain circumstances we allow ourselves to be heard talking to ourselves but then ensure those witnesses hear us stop. In fact, there are a lot of sophisticated rules about talking to oneself; if someone follows them carefully then that person will be judged as avoiding any suggestion of madness yet simultaneously demonstrating awareness of the taboo while communicating aspects of their feelings to others in what is effectively a performance of identity.

A vast amount of analysis has gone into such a commonplace feature of social talk as the exchange of greetings on the telephone. One of Sacks's notable early exercises was an investigation of calls to a suicide prevention centre. What strategies did the telephone answerer use to endeavour, without directly asking, to find out the caller's name in order to establish the beginnings of a rapport? What strategies may be used in evasion? Here is perhaps the central concern of discourse analysis: to establish, or rather reveal, that in any communicative interaction we have not a single goal – to transmit a piece of information – but a multiplicity of concerns. The answerer, at a psychiatric emergency institution, wants to encourage the caller to talk, to remain calm and to give his (in this case) name – as this move towards intimacy makes sudden disengagement less likely. The caller 'seeks help' but is wary, unsure how much trust may be warranted. When we are engaged in any more everyday interaction, phoning a colleague, say, we too juggle a multiplicity of concerns, balancing them according to what we hear in return; our orientations may be revealed not just in analysis of the content of what we say, but in the split-second pauses and intakes of breath. The approach pioneered by Sacks (1992, published posthumously), and developed for example by Ten Have (1999) has become known as conversation analysis (CA). CA explicitly rejects the notion that you have to understand the context before you can approach texts.

In opposition are other strands of discourse analysis emerging from perspectives in social anthropology and indeed approaches within sociology that have embraced ethnography and an emphasis on reflexivity. So, many practitioners of discourse analysis argue that the more one understands about the socio-historical situation of a text, the more sensitive and insightful will be one's interpretation. Such an ideal has influenced much discourse analysis in educational settings, for example. In practice the boundary between discourse analysis and qualitative methodologies in general has sometimes become blurred where language data and the construction of meanings is the focus of intensive attention. In many empirical investigations centred on bounded discourse data – transcriptions of interactions, interviews and so on – software tools have been devised to assist in categorization and other tasks.

Analytical approaches endeavouring to bring insights together from discourse analysis to the study of authentic texts have also been given powerful new dimensions through the collection of computer corpora. These are vast databanks of written texts and/or transcripts – for example the International Corpus of English contains both spoken and written texts from Great Britain, East Africa and New Zealand (Meyer, 2002).

You might wonder, 'what use is the study of such corpora if I am going to be working with my own texts?' In fact, investigation of actual usages of a word or phrase, perhaps a key term in one's research, can lead to some surprising insights. The British National Corpus of over 100 million words tells us that 'man' is more than twice as common as 'woman' yet the plural 'women' is more commonly used than 'men' (Leech et al., 2001: x). A few years ago, when engaged in a project investigating teachers' perceptions of 'continuing professional development' I found that in the corpus overall this term had more often been applied to occupations such as architects, actuaries and lawyers than to teachers. Could the (then) relatively recent replacement of the term 'INSET (in-service training)' by 'continuing professional development' be an attempt to try to enhance by association the discursive power of the descriptive term for this activity?

Contemporary discourse analysis research is alive to an exciting multiplicity of influences. A significant motivation for many is to use linguistic analysis to unpeel layers of negative evaluation applied, often unconsciously, to the language of some speakers (and writers) positioned as low status or in some way vulnerable within a discourse setting. Hymes (1996), for example, demonstrates with the aid of ethnopoetics the subtle patternings of a tale told by a young girl in a classroom that was disregarded in a setting ignorant of the cultural practices she was drawing on. Hymes and Gee (1999) are proving particularly influential, concerned as they are with ideologies as reflected by/constructed in discourses. Their concern to use discourse analysis for critical purposes, particularly in respect of 'public' discourses, is shared by a group of contemporary scholars who term their approach critical discourse analysis (CDA) – Ruth Wodak and Norman Fairclough are probably the best known. (See Gotsbachner (2001) for an effective CDA-influenced small-scale study tracing how 'symbolic representations in xenophobic discourse ... sneak under the threshold of awareness' to disperse themselves in everyday talk — below you will find mention of his methods.) Conversation analysts are sometimes critical of critical discourse analysts for so explicitly bringing ideological positions into their approaches to data; CDA practitioners argue, I think with equal justice, that CA practitioners may be in danger of bringing too little reflexivity into their own approaches to data.

Discursive psychology is one of the most exciting arenas for discourse analysis today, combining incisive textual analysis with a concern for the construction of identity and use of a broad range of theoretical understandings when probing how ideologies are made manifest. An inspiring example, drawing on feminism, poststructuralism and education, is Bronwyn Davies's (1989) study of the play of young children. Poststructuralist/Foucauldian notions of discourse at the same time flood and distil texts, causing us to see them as fluid, against ever-changing backcloths of the conditions in which they were created and are read. Often therefore poststructuralist insights take researchers away from a focus on an 'authentic text' viewed as the product of the individual in society towards a sense of language as one of many facets of discourse, and thus, arguably, beyond, or at least apart from, the domain of discourse analysis.

Implications for research design

There are, essentially, two main ways in which discourse analysis may be relevant to your research. The first concerns your examination of data. Overwhelmingly the majority of research in the social sciences is likely to collect data some of which is in the form of texts that would benefit from close analysis. Barbara Johnstone (2002: 9) suggests that you might begin to construct a plan for such analysis from considering the following heuristic:

1 discourse is shaped by the world, and shapes the world;
2 discourse is shaped by language, and shapes language;
3 discourse is shaped by participants, and shapes participants;
4 discourse is shaped by prior discourse, and shapes the possibilities for future discourse;
5 discourse is shaped by its medium, and shapes the possibilities of its medium;
6 discourse is shaped by purpose, and shapes possible purposes.

I would suggest that in practice different approaches to discourse are operationalized by deciding, in the design, to restrict analysis, at least in the first instance, to a certain number of levels working from '6' up. If your perspective at all times endeavours to operate at level 1 (embracing the rest) then it is likely that contemporary poststructuralism has the most to say to you and you should turn to the works of Foucault, Butler, Kristeva and others interested in language through cultural theory (see Burke et al., 2000 for a marvellous introduction).

Conversation analysis, to take a contrasting approach, willingly restricts itself to levels 6 and 5, in the process unravelling skeins of talk effectively.

In your practice, you might try first to examine in what ways the participants orient to the particular demands of the channel and any 'ritualized constraints' associated with it – to use Goffman's helpful (1981) expression. In what ways do the participants reveal their multiplicity of goals and how, if at all, do they acknowledge others' and negotiate with them? You might analyse features of grammar and their effect. One telling detail in the analysis by Gotsbachner (2001) as mentioned above is his examination of pronouns. Who is included in 'we' and referred to by 'he' or 'they'? What characteristics are made or inferred in such generalizations? Another feature to look out for is the active vs. passive voice of verbs. Norman Blake (1996: 30), a professor of English language at Sheffield, queries the effect if he were to choose to post a notice beginning, 'I forbid students to . . .' as opposed to 'students are forbidden to . . .' as generally preferred in this genre. The passive voice can be used to disguise agency and impute an authoritative air.

The second major way of using discourse analysis is to make use of resources others have collated in order to investigate an issue, concept or term that is central to your overall research question. For example, the social psychologists Antaki and Naji (1987), interested in the phenomenon of explanations, made an early corpus-based study to reveal that 'general states of the world' more often than 'other people's single actions' were employed after the word 'because' in general conversations. This empirical finding had consequences for attribution theory.

Stories from the Field

Alan Petersen

My work is motivated by theoretical and political concerns rather than by the desire to use a particular method or methods. I use whatever methods I believe are appropriate for the problem or issue at hand. My discourse analysis (DA) work has focused on news media portrayals of genetics and medicine, on assumptions about sex or gender differences in documents produced for a specific readership, and on discourses pertaining to medicine and public health. I have explored how assumptions are manifest in texts and how a particular use of language may serve to make these assumptions seem natural. My empirical materials have included a range of texts, including newspaper articles, anatomical texts, psychological journal articles and various expert documents, for example government reports and health promotion literature. Depending on the particular question(s) explored, I may focus on the use of rhetorical devices, the narrative structure, the inclusion of quotations or citations and of drama (in the case of news), the positioning of text relative to other items and the use of accompanying illustrative material.

Although I have undertaken a great deal of DA-related work, I have never found DA to be straightforward. Although some scholars see DA as an easy research method option, there is rarely a clearly defined path for the researcher. This is a contested area and there are no blueprints as to how 'best' to proceed. Subjective evaluations impinge on every stage of the research process. In my experience, every new project requires one to rethink the issue of methods: how they relate to the aims and research questions, what empirical resources are likely to be most useful or illuminating, and how to 'operationalize' concepts (i.e. put them in a form that can be measured). DA has proved particularly valuable in my recent work on news media portrayals of genetics and medicine, which I will focus on here.

In recent years, versions of DA have been used by a number of scholars in analysing the portrayal of medical genetics issues in news media and other popular cultural texts. The rise of public interest in genetics in the 1990s corresponded with media interest in the Human Genome Project and, later, its 'race' with the rival Celera to map the human genome. I was following some of the debates in newspapers about discoveries of 'genes for' X, Y and Z and, in light of what seemed to be a kind of genetic determinism in these reports, I believed it would be interesting and useful to examine news reports in detail. Coming from a background in the sociology of health and illness, my concerns were informed by sociological questions about the formation of public discourse. That is, I was interested in how a particular 'framing' of issues may shape public responses to the issues being reported and thus potentially shape public policies. When I commenced study in this field, I had only a few writers as guides to the kinds of questions worth pursuing and how DA might 'work' in practice in relation to news media. However, I had developed some relevant expertise and insights through earlier research into the portrayal of research into genetic-based differences of sex and sexual orientation in 'popular' science journals (see Petersen, 1999).

My research materials included a national broadsheet newspaper (*The Australian*) and two state-based tabloid newspapers (*The Sydney Morning Herald* and *The West Australian*). Because these newspapers are owned by different proprietors, I felt that they were less likely to share news stories than newspapers that are owned by the same proprietors. They also have different format styles, being oriented to different audiences, and, as I discovered, had somewhat different ways of presenting medical genetics issues. I located news articles for these newspapers via a news monitoring service. One can now do this more easily online via Newsbank and Lexus-Nexus, though these sources don't include accompanying illustrative material and sometimes don't include page numbers, which I find useful when making assessments about the prominence and framing of issues. As a first step, I made note of the location of articles in the newspapers: on what page they appeared, where they were positioned relative to other articles, and whether they appeared in special sections (e.g. 'Health and Medicine'). I found that for all three newspapers, a large proportion of articles on genetics and medicine appeared in the first three pages, and the majority in the first ten pages, which suggested that these stories were seen by editors as highly 'newsworthy'.

Besides positioning, I also made a note of the type of news items (article, editorial, opinion piece, letter to the editor) and of the amount and kind of detail presented. I also recorded details of the authorship of articles – whether they were written by journalists, scientists, bio-ethicists or other writers – and of any evidence of authors' efforts to verify information and to present alternative or disconfirming information. Finally, I made a note of the news source(s), if this was stated. Again, such information was useful in assessing how stories were 'framed'. As I discovered, news stories did not always include details on the professional identity of writers. Consequently I was unable to draw firm conclusions about the impact of the author type on the content and style of stories. In *The Australian* and *SMH*, regular contributors of articles were sometimes described as either 'medical writer', 'science writer' or 'science correspondent'; however, in all three newspapers, such descriptions often did not appear in articles. In some articles, most notably in *The Australian*, only the news agency (e.g.

Reuters, AFP, AP or AAP) or another newspaper (e.g. *The Sunday Times*, *The Times*) that was the source for the news was cited. In others, most evidently in *The West*, neither the writer's name nor a news agency source appeared in the article.

I read and then reread each news item, taking note of use of titles, subtitles, and accompanying illustrative material that helped attract readers' attention and shape the portrayal of stories, and of words, phrases and metaphors that imported particular images and associations. I made note of themes and sub-themes, and recorded who was cited or quoted in stories. I discovered that in many articles the scientists themselves were often cited or quoted, which allowed them to place a particular interpretation on research and its implications. Quotations or citations from experts lent credibility to stories by conveying the impression that information was straight from the expert's mouth and hence irrefutable.

Many articles relied heavily on the scientist's own descriptions and generally positive evaluations of research and its significance. Since no other alternative information was presented, there was little reason for the reader to doubt the veracity of the scientist's claims. The use of quotes from experts is an important element in the framing of news stories on medical genetics. I discovered that scientists frequently use terms such as the 'killer cells' and analogies such as 'prospecting' in describing research which provided insight into how scientists may seek to 'popularize' scientific information for lay readers and emphasize the significance of their work. The research literature on science news production suggests that there are 'two cultures' of science and journalism and that this may lead to misunderstanding between scientists and journalists about the role of news reporting. One influential perspective on the production of science news, the so-called 'popularization' model, suggests that scientists generate objective knowledge which is then popularized for lay readers or audiences by the use of simple language, particular metaphors and rhetorical devices. It is argued that this may lead to the distortion or misrepresentation of science fact. However, along with other recent research, my own work suggests that this model, although useful, is too simplistic and does not take account of the more subtle ways in which scientists may seek to influence the media portrayal of science through, for example, the use of popular metaphors and the promotion of positive images of science and its applications.

I found that good news stories and stories about discovery figure prominently in medical genetics news and that stories tend to neglect non-genetic and 'multifactorial' explanations of disease, thereby tending to convey an overoptimistic impression of the potential of genetics. The frequent use of particular metaphors such as those of the book, map and code help to convey the nature and significance of research. For example, in one article a scientist is cited as saying that 'the new screening technique complemented black and white strips of DNA resembling bar codes used on shopping centre goods'. He is also quoted as saying, '*Without the maps you do not know where to go . . .* They have immediate applications in clinical work where *the colour bar codes* can identify changes or rearrangements in the chromosomes' (*The West*, 25 July 1997: 10, my italics). Military metaphors were also common and reinforce an image of scientists as heroes who are pitted against an evil enemy (a 'killer disease') which is seen to threaten the public's health. For example, an article, 'Resistance to drugs cracks' announced that '*Genetic scientists are on the verge of defeating life-threatening organisms* that have developed strong resistance to conventional antibiotics . . .' (*The Weekend Australian*, 18–19 July, 1998: 40, my italics). It was not always easy, however, to determine who originally introduced a particular metaphor – whether it was the scientist who was originally cited or quoted, or the journalist who wrote the story. This is something that would need to be explored through further research, by talking to quoted/cited scientists and journalists, and perhaps editors.

I found that news reports of medical genetics are not always unequivocally positive. The nature of portrayals depends on the nature of the issue. In my study of medical genetics news, and also in a related project on news media portrayals of cloning in the wake of Dolly the sheep, I have discovered a recurring tension between utopian and dystopian themes and images of genetics, particularly in relation to reproductive issues (see Petersen, 2001, 2002). Public reaction to Dolly, which reflected concerns about the applications of cloning technology to humans, led many scientists to make extensive use of the media to defend and explain their work. The torrent of news articles on cloning in the months after the announcement of Dolly made considerable reference to the views and predictions of scientists, who extolled the medical virtues of cloning research and emphasized the distinction between 'therapeutic cloning' and 'reproductive cloning'. As this research revealed, following the unfolding news stories of genetics and medicine over an extended period of time allows one to identify themes and patterns in styles of reporting that are unlikely to be evident within a short time frame.

While DA is very useful in revealing how news issues are portrayed, it doesn't tell us much about the social processes of news production, or about how readers engage with stories. One needs to 'get behind the news' and talk to journalists, editors and sources to understand why certain issues get reported and how they are portrayed. This is the subject of my current research. And, one needs to develop methods for studying how readers interact with, interpret and use information gleaned from news media in order to assess the impacts of stories. DA, however, can provide a useful starting point for exploring processes of news production and news reception. For me, the application of DA methods in the analysis of news media has proved extremely fruitful. It has generated new questions, and opened up new avenues for exploration, which is what all research should be about.

Annotated bibliography

Burke, L., Crowley, T. and Girvin, A. (2000) *The Routledge Language and Cultural Theory Reader*. London: Routledge.

Lives up to its blurb as a 'core introduction to the most innovative and influential writings that have shaped and defined the relations between language, culture and cultural identity in the twentieth century'.

Davies, B. (1989) *Frogs and Snails and Feminist Tales: Pre-school Children and Gender*. London: Allen & Unwin

A classic work integrating feminist and poststructuralist theory with close regard for empirical texts.

Gee, J.P. (1999) *An Introduction to Discourse Analysis: Theory and Method*. London: Routledge.

Gee's theory of discourses embeds language in social practices through which diverse social identities are formed and transformed. He presents analytic techniques with special reference to cross-cultural issues in communities and schools.

Goffman, E. (1981) *Forms of Talk*. Oxford: Blackwell

Goffman's work is unique, in that his eye and ear for how we interact as members of a society is unparalleled. This is no research manual, much less a book 'on' discourse analysis as such. What it may do is assist us as researchers towards new sensitivities.

Mercer, N. (2000) *Words and Minds: How We Use Language to Think Together*. London: Routledge.

A highly readable and versatile book that offers something of interest to most of us, whatever our previous knowledge of language-related issues.

Piller, Ingrid (2002) *Bilingual Couples Talk: The Discursive Construction of Hybridity*. Amsterdam and Philadelphia: John Benjamins.

Whether the linguistic practices of German- and English-speaking couples seems near or far to your own research interest, this book exemplifies a thoughtful, eclectic approach to methodology. Piller examines the ways in which ideologies and identities are performed and contested as public discourses invade, shape or shadow private practices.

Silverman, D. (2001) *Interpreting Qualitative Data: Methods for Analysing Talk, Texts and Interactions*, 2nd edn. London: Sage.

This book and others by Silverman, including his 1998 book on Harvey Sacks, are popular starting points for many researchers.

Swales, J.M. (1998) *Other Floors, Other Voices*. Mahwah, NJ: Lawrence Erlbaum Associates.

In this enthralling read, Swales examines the links between varied academic disciplines and social practices through the empirical study of three floors of a single building on a university campus.

Ten Have, P. (1999) *Doing Conversation Analysis: A Practical Guide*. London: Sage.

This book draws effectively on the legacy of earlier work in the field, while encouraging the reader from page 1 to try its techniques in one's own research.

Wetherell, M., Taylor, S. and Yates, S. (2001) *Discourse Theory and Practice: A Reader*. London: Sage.

These studies illustrate the range of data discourse analysts work with and the concepts which organize discourse investigations. Designed for the active researcher, especially in the fields of psychology, sociology, cultural studies and social policy.

Further references

Antaki, C. and Naji, S. (1987) 'Events explained in conversational "because" statements', *British Journal of Social Psychology*, 26: 119–26.

Bakhtin, M. (1986) *Speech Genres and Other Late Essays*, eds C.E Merson and M. Holquist. Austin, TX: University of Texas Press.

Blake, N.F. (1996) *A History of the English Language*. London: Macmillan.

Brown, G. and Yule, G. (1983) *Discourse Analysis*. Cambridge: Cambridge University Press.

Gotsbachner, E. (2001) 'Xenophobic normality: the discriminatory impact of habitualized discourse dynamics', *Discourse and Society*, 12(6): 729–59.

Halliday, M.A.K. (1985) *An Introduction to Functional Grammar*. London: Edward Arnold.

Hymes, D. (1996) *Ethnography, Linguistics, Narrative Inequality: Toward an Understanding of Voice*. London: Taylor & Francis.

Johnstone, B. (2002) *Discourse Analysis*. Oxford: Blackwell.

Leech, G., Rayson, P. and Wilson, A. (2001) *Word Frequencies in Written and Spoken English based on the British National Corpus*. London: Pearson.

Meyer, C. (2002) *English Corpus Linguistics: An Introduction*. Cambridge: Cambridge University Press.

Petersen, A. (1999) 'The portrayal of research into genetic-based differences of sex and sexual orientation: a study of "popular" science journals, 1980 to 1997', *Journal of Communication Inquiry*, 23(2): 163–82.

Petersen, A. (2001) 'Biofantasies: genetics and medicine in the print news media', *Social Science and Medicine*, 52(8): 1255–68.

Petersen, A. (2002) 'Replicating our bodies, losing our selves: news media portrayals of human cloning in the wake of Dolly', *Body & Society*, 8(4): 71–90.

Sacks, H. (1992) *Lectures on Conversation*, ed. G. Jefferson. Oxford: Blackwell.

PART V

READING AND REPRESENTING SOCIO-CULTURAL MEANINGS

Introduction

This part of the book brings the concept of 'culture' to the centre of research activity and meaning-making. It begins with life history and narrative approaches in a chapter which bridges between Mills's classic notion of the creative marrying of theory with empirical data in the 'sociological imagination' (first published 1959) and Bruner's insight (from 1987) that 'narrative imitates life, life imitates narrative'. This is followed by two chapters dealing with semiotic approaches to interpretation, together illustrating processes of inter-textuality and multimodality. The final two chapters focus on the overlapping theoretical frameworks of communities of practice and activity theory, both of which see human interaction, co-construction of meaning and mutual cooperation as central to human agency and empowerment.

An important common denominator for these chapters is that they are all concerned with the process of 'reading' socio-cultural data and making meaning. Most of them draw explicitly on the socio-cultural psychology of Vygotsky and are concerned with learning as a process of transformation through engaging in human activity. Experience and meaning-making are encultured and co-constructed, whether in daily life or through engaging in research. The emphasis on the visual – photography and drawings as research data – and multimodality as a norm of representation opens up new opportunities for qualitative research. The tyranny of the written text is particularly challenged in the chapter on social semiotics and multimodality.

These chapters also privilege the practical and focus on the integration of theoretical insights with

practical action – in some cases through a focus on community engagement and change processes, in others through in-depth interpretation of representations as both expressions of human identity and encultured artefacts. The Stories from the Field portray learners of all ages from small children, through adolescents, to employees in industry and teachers coming to terms with technology. In all cases they are portrayed as unique individuals whose identity is mediated and sustained by the socio-historical and cultural contexts in which their life experience is embedded.

Again, there are many cross-links between this part of the book and chapters in other parts. The chapter on life history and narrative should be read in relation to Interviewing in Part II; the chapter on semiotic engagements links forward to the chapter on deconstruction in Part VIII; the 'story from the field' in the communities of practice chapter illustrates the integration of qualitative and quantitative data described in several of the chapters in Part VII; and all of the chapters need to be read in the light of the chapter in Part II on ethical issues.

The socio-cultural-historical theories that underpin these chapters provide a useful alternative to some of the mainstays of qualitative research portrayed in Parts II–IV, such as hermeneutic interpretation on the one hand or critical engagement with political processes on the other. If these socio-cultural theories have a limitation it tends to be in their neglect of the political but this is specifically addressed by the chapter on activity theory.

CHAPTER

18

LIFE HISTORY AND NARRATIVE APPROACHES

Geoff Shacklock
School of Social and Cultural Studies in Education, Deakin University, Australia
Laurie Thorp
Environmental Studies, Michigan State University, USA

Key concepts

Geoff Shacklock

Narrative inquiry is concerned with the production, interpretation and representation of storied accounts of lived experience and is increasingly popular with researchers in many fields. When this interest in narrative inquiry joins with a desire to exercise the descriptive and analytic processes of the sociological imagination (Mills, 2000) researchers find themselves engaged in dialogue with others and stories of life that lead toward the construction of life histories. In this Key Concepts section I will explore the connections between what we understand as narrative and what we understand as life history, while in the 'story from the field' Laurie Thorp presents and discusses an exemplar of narrative inquiry.

To begin, a word of caution. Life history is both a blurred and problematic genre as research practice and in terms of research products and artefacts. It is not always easy to pin down what is a life history and what is not. For instance, the distinctions between life stories, oral histories, auto/biographies and life histories are not as clear as methodologists might desire or claim. Also, continuing debates surrounding the shift from modern to postmodern forms of social research present theoretical and methodological challenges that arise from close scrutiny of the nature of identity, truth, structure and agency, and claims about the veracity of individual and collective voices in the representation of lives and experience (Tierney, 2000).

Life story or life history?

A life story is a personal account in the teller's own words. They tend to be selective, contingent upon remembered events that are amenable to being told, and 'provide a clear and ordered record of a personal truth that, of necessity, consists of both "fact" and "fiction"' (Atkinson, 1995: 116).

What makes a narration of lived experience a life history? Hatch and Wisniewski (1995: 125) conclude, in their edited collection on life history and narrative, that 'an analysis of the social, historical, political and economic contexts of a life story by the researcher is what turns a life story into a life history'. At its simplest, a life history is a life story or oral history with additional dimensions (Casey, 1993).

By locating stories of experience with descriptions of the contexts in which they occur, we build a sense of how lives are not free floating but socially constructed so as 'not to come to terms with an individual cohesive identity, but rather to see the greater complexity that exists across societies, across individuals' (Tierney, 1999: 310). Anthropologist Ruth Behar describes how inclusion of social and cultural contexts allows a more complex telling than is otherwise permitted:

> Rather than looking at social and cultural systems solely as they impinge on a life, shape it, and turn it into an object, a life history should allow one to see how an actor makes culturally meaningful history . . . a life history narrative should allow one to see the subjective mapping of experience, the working out of a culture and a social system that is often obscured in a typified account. (1990: 225)

Life histories allow the inquirer to introduce additional anchor points for understanding the subjective and the structural as mutual informants in understanding our own and other people's lives.

Life history and narrative

Bruner (1987) has described how lives take on meaning through the means by which they are told and retold and the successive cycle of interpretation that goes with the continual process of (re)constructing an account of life. In saying that 'narrative imitates life, life imitates narrative' (1987: 13), Bruner is pointing out two things: firstly, that we build our narratives of self around our understanding of the episodic and temporal qualities of lived experience; and, secondly, that human beings live out their lives in ways that can be understood and communicated narratively.

This conceptualization of a mutual relationship between narrative and life is important to storytellers and historians of life because it enables life experience, identity and cultural formation to be epistemically located in a narrative frame. Hence, when Richardson (1997: 31) talks about narrative knowing and sociological telling and suggests that 'narrative creates the possibility of history beyond the personal', it is this possibility, the storied weave of the personal and the collective, that becomes the narrative business of the life historian.

Doing life history work

Empirical material for life histories can come from a range of sources but often an oral history or a story of experience told in an interview will be a primary source of data. The conduct of the life history inquiry is built upon recognition that stories of life are constructed through narrative and dialogue.

The emphasis on dialogue is important. For instance, life history interviews are different to other kinds of research interview. Life history interviews are not just about collecting facts or reports on life events, they are about constructing a language-practice place where a life story is put together by the participant-conversants (Chambon, 1995). Chase (1995: 3) says that in a life history interview participants must take narrative seriously, and that 'if we want to hear stories rather than reports then our task as interviewers is to invite others to tell their stories, to encourage them to take responsibility for the meaning of their talk ... our questions should be phrased in everyday rather than sociological language'. This point about taking narrative seriously should not be dismissed – it is the key to successful interviews in life history inquiry.

The life history inquiry is a dialogic event where participants act together in an ongoing, non-linear process that leads towards the construction of an account. Rigid demarcation of inquirer and inquiree roles is blurred in life history enquiry. The flexible boundary between participant roles and the joint construction of the life history through the dialogic interaction between enquiry conversants means that the account often says a lot about the researcher conversant as well.

This is an important issue for life history researchers, and it requires ongoing reflexive positioning throughout a life history project. For Behar (1990: 323) being reflexive means being able 'to tell the story of how I came to the privilege of my pen', and a recognition of 'the biography in the shadow'. It is about being up-front about how, as researcher, you came to be telling another's story in your words, and through an interpretive frame built upon your (other) experiences, assumptions and individual knowledge of human life.

Taking up the challenge of life history

Life history inquiry faces many challenges. Central among the challenges are those concerned with the authorial capacity of one person to *textualize* the life of another for vicarious and likely voyeuristic consumption by unknown readers.

One part of this challenge lies in recognition of the limits to what can be told – and represented – about a life in a text (whatever that text might be). There are two strands to this. Firstly, do individuals have knowledge about their own lives that lends itself to telling others and, secondly, there is the equally difficult question of whether inquirers can access such knowledge and construct accounts that have qualities which satisfy the desires of teller, writer and reader for narrative richness and sociological insight? A second part of the challenge of representation, of telling the lives of others, for multiple unknown audiences is attending to ethical responsibilities. What constitutes confidentiality, informed consent, joint authorship, non-exploitative participation? These are important and complex questions.

A modernist legacy exists in life history research to build narratives that give the reader a complete picture with linear progression from beginning to end. While this desire to present lives as seriated and coherent is powerful, it may not lead to narratives that reflect the complex interplay between parts of a life.

I know that I cannot 'collect' a life. Narrative does not provide a better way to locate truth, but in fact reminds us that all good stories are predicated on the quality of fiction. We live many lives. (Munro, 1998: 12)

This is an important admission about the messy and unsettled nature of life history enquiry and reflects the imperative felt by the postmodern life historian to present stories of life that do not collapse to the simplicity of a 'this and then that, start here and finish there' account. The challenge, according to Tierney (1999: 309), is 'not to make the individual into a cohesive self, but instead to create methodological and narrative strategies that will do justice to those multiple identities'.

My interest in life history inquiry focuses on how to construct narratives which recognize and reflect multiplicity in assemblage of life fragments that do not fit together in neat, predictable ways. It seems to me that life history narratives can easily become stuck in seductive modernist assumptions about the linear and chronological in the narrative accounting of lives.

How best to shift away from this is an open question to which a range of arts-informed research alternatives are providing some answers (Barone and Eisner, 1997; Cole and Knowles, 2001). Currently, I am gaining inspiration from sculptor Rosalie Gascoigne (1997). Her visual narratives of landscapes made from fragments of discarded and weathered objects – it has been called a poetry of trash – tell stories in unexpected ways.

This teaches me that a different story can be told, one which has unique and unexpected vigour, by disrupting the pattern, the seemingly logical and necessary order, so as to cause the intellect and emotions to stumble out of their comfort zones and into a new territory of narrative associations. Inspiration for experimentation also comes from novelist Eudora Welty who warns against the illusion of order to be found in rigorous temporal sorting:

The events in our lives happen in a sequence in time, but in their significance to ourselves they find their own order, a timetable not necessarily – perhaps not possibly – chronological. The time as we know it subjectively is often the chronology that stories and novels follow: it is a continuous thread of revelation. (1995: 68-9)

Implications for research design

We have chosen to write this section as if advising a researcher who is preparing to begin a life history research project. In so doing, we ask you to entertain the series of questions that follow as a way of thinking through the methodological implications for research design in life history or narrative inquiry.

What is the purpose of this study?

Establishing a philosophical foundation and unpacking its associated paradigmatic assumptions is all too often glossed over or ignored in the fevered pursuit of knowledge for the sake of knowledge. We ask you to take time to think deeply about the implication of this foundation for your knowledge-making intent. Is the *purpose* of your inquiry to report on social change? A vehicle for self-understanding? Theory building? Social critique? Your answer to this will affect the strategies and methods you employ. As you have seen there are differences between life history inquiry and other forms of narrative inquiry. Action researcher Peter Reason (1996) suggests that knowledge-making ought to contribute to human flourishing – that it be of use. The dominant system of research found in the academy answers this question of purpose quite simply as 'to contribute to the body of knowledge'. Is this enough? We think it important to ask: where, and with whom, will the knowledge I produce have impact?

Who controls the research process?

Before embarking on a life history inquiry we ask you to consider power relations. Does your source of funding control the research design? Your thesis committee or supervisory team? Do you? Who determines the research questions? It would serve you well to surface these issues and inform your research participants of any tensions.

What methods of data collection fit the study?

Life history research is often a 'dialogic event' – does the researcher have the skills to enter into this mutual participant relationship? It is important to consider how this develops within the context of the inquiry. It is our belief that this is not simply a matter of developing an interview protocol and scheduling interviews! Dialogue and storytelling unfolds over time, life history and narrative research is emergent and cannot be rushed to fit an imposed schedule. We suggest that you read life history accounts and explore the reflexive musings of life history researchers.

How will you represent the life history?

Laurel Richardson (1994) has said that qualitative research 'must be read' and good life history research demands good writing. Can you engage the reader? Think about whose voices will be heard and represented in the text.

How will we judge the validity or 'goodness' of the study?

Finally, we must think about criteria for judging the validity/trustworthiness/quality of a narrative inquiry. Who will establish these criteria and make judgements about the worth of your inquiry – your community of scholars, your co-participants, you? There exists a rich discourse concerning validity in qualitative research and we suggest that you consider the discussions of Lincoln (2001) and Piantanida and Garman (1999).

Stories from the Field – 'they almost always know what they want to know'

Laurie Thorp

The following 'story from the field' is offered as an illustration of narrative research. This is not intended to be an illustration of life history research.

This project began as my doctoral fieldwork in agricultural education. Ever the idealist, I arrived at this 'underperforming' elementary school thinking I could somehow save the day with a garden-based science curriculum, and found instead the wisdom of emergent and participatory research methodology. What these beautiful children and teachers taught me about constructivist methods (narrative included), indeterminate ontology/epistemology (lovingly referred to as 'planning in the doorway'), prolonged engagement ('Laurie, what's gonna happen if you get that job?') and the glorious smearing together of social (read love) with science is my 'story from the field'.

Situated just ten miles from a research-intensive university, Middleville Elementary is routinely utilized as a site for academic research. Early into my fieldwork at this school I had the good fortune to witness a 'typical' research relationship with the local schools. Gloria, who would become a key informant,

approached me one afternoon inviting me to attend a meeting with a researcher from the university. Seems this educational researcher was interested in studying how teachers plan. Gloria wanted to include me in this meeting in order to 'kill two birds with one stone' as she wanted to start writing up 'all these great lessons' that were emerging from the garden (my study) *and* she could use these lessons to participate in the other study. I was thrilled – not only had Gloria initiated the idea of writing up the garden lessons, she was granting me entrée into this 'other' world of research. As I reflect back on this moment it was a turning point in my research at Middleville Elementary – it was a moment of grace. This gift of affirmation from Gloria set my research on an entirely new trajectory; there was a paradigmatic shift from *my* research to *our* collaborative work. Self-doubt concerning my role in this project faded with this *validation*. My study had been deemed trustworthy enough to act upon – 'let's write up these great lessons'. This invitation to write up the lessons also represented the validation of voice. Gloria was attempting to communicate this meaningful experience to her colleagues in a teacher's most familiar written genre – the lesson plan.

One week later at 4:00 pm we sat in Gloria's classroom waiting for the researcher and planned the logistics for our upcoming salsa-making festival with her teaching partner Carol. Thirty minutes tardy, a flustered woman arrived, introduced herself as Sandy from the university and muttered something about getting lost. Sandy then spent the next few minutes fumbling around and testing her audio-taping equipment. These tired, over-scheduled teachers had now spent forty minutes waiting for this meeting to begin. Sandy then proceeded to tell these seasoned veterans what a 'good' lesson plan entails. I silently seethed and wondered how this could be an inquiry into how teachers plan? Sandy handed Gloria and Carol a two-page guide to lesson planning and requested they follow this guide for the *ten* lesson plans they were requested to produce. Anger and embarrassment churned inside of me: anger at the insensitivity of this researcher to the local knowledge in this school and embarrassment at this manifestation of the academy's perverse relationship with society.

The conversation that ensued following our meeting with Sandy was a critical point of departure in my development as a researcher. Our conversation marked that wondrous moment in participatory research when the lines between researcher and researched begin to blur, when relationships solidify and other voices emerge. Unable to withhold my comments, I blurted out, 'I am appalled at what I just witnessed. How can this be a study of how teachers plan when she has told you exactly how to plan?' I continued to bluster and huff about the glaring methodological gaps in Sandy's study when Carol in her usual calm and steady voice interrupted me and said, 'Yes, they always know what they want to know. Most academic research is curiosity taken to the extreme perversion of idiocy'. From that moment forward my commitment was to un-knowing, to staying open to an emergent process. How would I demonstrate to these women that I was not like the other researchers? How could I demonstrate that I was not going to take what I needed and leave? The answer was quite simple – it was what I was brought home to do. I must garden.

So garden I did. Within a very short time trust was built and dozens of sweaty little hands would find my every appendage and drag me out into the garden. 'Mrs Thorp, the wheat is up!' 'Laurie, will the sweet peas survive?' 'Look at the size of this turnip!' 'Please can I take this home?' Notepad and pen were left in my bag and soon my head was swimming with voices. Ruth Behar (1996) writes, participant observation is 'split at the root'. Indeed, this term carries with it the lineage of a divided and distanced science. The grammatical demarcation between subject and object makes me uncomfortable. How to reconcile this schism? Besides, there is too much observation going on in our schools: principals observing teachers, teachers observing students, parents observing teachers, professors observing student teachers – all this observation makes me nervous. Count me out. And really, there is just too much to do. I have yet to find a day when my hands, eyes and heart weren't fully engaged. It's too late for participant observation – I can't keep the distance.

Here too was a critical juncture in my research: fieldnotes became *retrospective* fieldnotes. After driving home on those warm spring days in the garden I would empty my brain onto a writing pad. Would these dirt-under-the-fingernails field notes 'count' as data? I would clear this with my dissertation committee later. Phenomenology, I had found, doesn't wait.

Field notes May 23: As I look around me I begin to see that we are all wounded; wounded children, wounded teachers, wounded families, wounded storyteller. The stories jump out at me so fast and furious I doubt my ability to capture them all – to get it right. I lay down these words in fits and jerks not knowing where they lead or understanding the pattern. Yet I know from my own experience it is in the telling and the retelling that our wounds can heal and some sense can be made of it all.

Some weeks later, I was invited to attend a Middleville staff meeting at which the topic of pending district-wide curricular changes was addressed. The local district curriculum advisor made a plea for input from the Middleville teachers regarding their views on the curriculum. A long and pregnant pause settled over the meeting. Again the advisor made a plea for input, this time followed by a comment that the district had solicited this information by paper survey with a dismal 5 per cent response rate. This comment broke the silence and the floodgates opened. Teachers voiced concerns regarding lack of trust, lack of time and lack of freedom to voice what they really wanted to say on the survey (see Patti Lather, 1993, for a discussion of transgressive validity). These women were calling out to be genuinely heard and not to be treated as yet another number in the education game. One cried out, 'They expect us to teach to the whole child but they don't model that behaviour when dealing with us!' These teachers wanted to fully participate in knowledge construction. What a violation it would be for me to simply 'collect data' from them. Did my research epistemology embrace the 'whole child' and what about the whole teacher? My predetermined interview protocol suddenly seemed stiff and lifeless. The interviews I had conducted for this study felt artificial, never quite capturing the *lived experience* of Middleville Elementary. I could ask for a story but I never got it. Jerome Bruner (1991) reminds us that narrative is not only representative of reality but it is also *constitutive* of reality, and there's the rub. I have found that stories are not simply low-hanging fruit to be plucked in the course of an interview – it is not just a matter of *asking for* stories or *listening to* stories, it is learning to *be with* stories. Stories unfold in relationship over time.

Learning to be with stories meant learning to find the culturally acceptable methods for data collection, that is, how might I best enter into this give and take relatedness necessary for the telling of a self? Working side by side with children in the freshly tilled soil I began to photograph our horticultural triumphs: the discovery of those first potato shoots pushing toward the sun, the children's fascination with earthworms, our sweetcorn harvest to mention a few. Shortly thereafter photographs began appearing in my mailbox at school with penned notes from the teachers. Children would hound me mercilessly to see their photograph. I had found that photographing the teachers and children in this project was one of the least obtrusive and most natural methods of data collection available to me. After sharing this observation with several teachers we agreed that having the children talk about the photos would not only serve as 'good' data for the study it could also serve as an immersion literacy activity. Douglas Harper (2000) describes photo elicitation as an underutilized qualitative method and encourages us as social scientists to construct a 'visual narrative.' Visual images add a layer of complexity to our stories and representations pointing to specific moments of human interaction. They are, as Barthes (1981) has said, 'moments of resurrection'.

As social scientists I believe we have a responsibility to hold the question: how are things going to unfold here? Without pushing for an answer the story retains its inherent mystery. Arthur Frank (1995) suggests that our current blind allegiance to the restitution narrative (a storyline with remedy and return to 'normal') serves as the master narrative to modernity. This modernist expectation that for every problem there is a remedy smothers the mystery, suffering, or chaos of lived experience. One can see the restitution narrative is education's institutionally preferred storyline. I feel an obligation to transgress this modernist move for happily ever after restitution. This is not the story I experience at Middleville; most days it borders on chaos. As I cobble together our/my (?) story I take comfort in Patti Lather's concept of 'getting lost' as a methodological stance. Sarah, one of my key informants, helps me 'get lost', talking rapid fire she says, 'The garden is very upsetting to me, upsetting because we are torn. Torn between what is good and right for the children, for ourselves, for the environment, for education, and yet, knowing full well what is rewarded in the system.' This is the story I must tell, retell and tell again.

I think it safe to say that somewhere in our schooling the hegemony of 'factual' science began to erode the intrinsic value of stories. We began to fear that stories were embellished half-truths, anecdotal, or worse, we ceased to listen to the storyteller at all. I take my cue from Stephen Crites (1971) that, when we give up the story, we give up a condition for moral human existence.

Annotated bibliography

Cole, A. and Knowles, G. (eds) (2001) *Lives in Context: The Art of Life History Research*. Walnut Creek, CA: AltaMira Press.

This collection contains an introduction about doing life history research and informative accounts from researchers of doing life history inquiry and the challenges met in specific contexts. These reflexive tales of messiness in the narrative study of lives make compelling reading for novitiate and seasoned inquirers alike. A strength of this volume is its attention to how conducting life history research leads to a joint construction of lived experience that says a lot about the researcher's life as well. Coles and Knowles describe how the influence of an emerging arts-based tradition in qualitative inquiry enables life history inquiry to pay 'explicit attention to the aesthetic' and how this unsettles the modernist, linear legacy (and its coterminous assumptions) of life history as social science.

Goodson, I. and Sikes, P. (2001) *Life History Research in Educational Settings: Learning from Lives*. Buckingham: Open University Press.

This book addresses the ubiquitous *how to do it* questions with clarity. It is only a small volume but deals with reasons for doing life history inquiry, how to collect and work with data, ethics and power relations, and how to bring the social context into play with life stories. This latter aspect, described by the authors as moving 'from narratives to genealogies of context', is important for the novice to appreciate and learn to put into practice. A strength of this book is the rich set of examples that are introduced throughout the chapters.

Hatch, J.A. and Wisniewski, R. (eds) (1995) *Life History and Narrative*. Lewes: Falmer Press.

This collection offers a survey of methodological approaches and epistemic rationales for life history as narrative inquiry at a time when the field was being energized by new associations and insights. The concluding chapter is an excellent place for the novice life history researcher to gain a sense of the range of intents, strategies and challenges on offer in this field of inquiry at that time. The reference lists throughout this collection are a historical goldmine.

Tierney, W. (1999) 'Writing life's history', *Qualitative Inquiry*, 5(3): 307–12.

Tierney, W. (2000) 'Undaunted courage: life history and the postmodern challenge', in N. Denzin and Y. Lincoln (eds), *The Handbook of Qualitative Research*, 2nd edn. Thousand Oaks, CA: Sage, pp. 537–54.

Tierney (1999) introduces a special issue of *Qualitative Inquiry* that provides another set of stances on opening up life history inquiry beyond modernist assumptions of what counts as narration of lived experience and its representation. The papers in this collection, along with Tierney's (2000) other observation on postmodern challenges to life history, are important in the issues and questions they raise rather than in the answers they give.

Further references

Atkinson, R. (1995) *The Gift of Stories: Practical and Spiritual Applications of Autobiography, Life Stories, and Personal Mythmaking*. Westport, CT: Bergin & Garvey.

Barone, T. and Eisner, E. (1997) 'Arts-based educational research', in R. Jaeger (ed.), *Complementary Methods for Research in Education*. 2nd edn. Washington, DC: American Educational Research Association, pp. 73–116.

Barthes, R. (1981) *Camera Lucida: Reflections on Photography*. New York: Hill & Wang.

Behar, R. (1990) 'Rage and redemption: reading the life story of a Mexican marketing woman', *Feminist Studies*, 16(2): 223–58.

Behar, R. (1994) *Translated Woman: Crossing the Border With Esperanza's Story*. Boston, MA: Beacon Press.

Behar, R. (1996) *The Vulnerable Observer: Anthropology That Breaks Your Heart*. Boston, MA: Beacon Press.

Bruner, J. (1987) 'Life as narrative', *Social Research*, 54: 11-32.

Bruner, J. (1991) 'The narrative construction of reality', *Critical Inquiry*, 18: 1–21.

Casey, K. (1993) *I Answer with My Life: Life Histories of Women Teachers Working for Social Change*. New York: Routledge.

Chambon, A. (1995) 'Life history as dialogical activity: "If you ask me the right questions, I could tell you"', *Current Sociology*, 43(2–3): 125–35.

Chase, S. (1995) 'Taking narrative seriously: consequences for method and theory in interview studies', in R. Josselson and A. Lieblich (eds), *Interpreting Experience: The Narrative Study of Lives*, Vol. 3. Thousand Oaks, CA: Sage, pp. 1–26.

Crites, S. (1971) 'The narrative quality of experience', *Journal of the American Academy of Religion*, 39: 291–311.

Frank, A. (1995) *The Wounded Storyteller*. Chicago, IL: University of Chicago Press.

Gascoigne, R. (1997) *The Poetry of Trash – An Interview*. Available online at: < http://www.abc.net.au/arts/visual/stories/s424392.htm > (accessed 9 December 2003).

Harper, D. (2000) 'Reimagining visual methods: Galileo to *Neuromancer*', in N. Denzin and Y. Lincoln (eds), *The Handbook of Qualitative Research*. 2nd edn. Thousand Oaks, CA: Sage, pp. 717–32.

Lather, P. (1993) 'Fertile obsession: validity after poststructuralism', *Sociological Quarterly*, 34(4): 673–93.

Lincoln, Y. (2001) 'Varieties of validity', in John Smart (ed.), *Higher Education Handbook of Theory and Research*, Vol. XVI. New York: Agathon Press, pp. 25–65.

Mills, C.W. (2000) *The Sociological Imagination*, 40th Anniversary Edition. New York: Oxford University Press.

Munro, P. (1998) *Subject to Fiction: Women Teachers' Life History Narratives and the Cultural Politics of Resistance*. Buckingham: Open University Press.

Piantanida, M. and Garman, N. (1999) *The Qualitative Dissertation: A Guide for Students and Faculty*. New York: Corwin.

Reason, P. (1996) 'Reflections on the purpose of human inquiry', *Qualitative Inquiry*, 2(1): 15–28.

Richardson, L. (1994) 'Writing: a method of inquiry', in N. Denzin and Y. Lincoln (eds), *Handbook of Qualitative Research*. Thousand Oaks, CA: Sage, pp. 516–29.

Richardson, L. (1997) *Fields of Play: Constructing an Academic Life*. New Brunswick, NJ: Rutgers University Press.

Welty, E. (1995) *One Writer's Beginnings*. Cambridge, MA: Belknap Press.

chapter 19

SEMIOTIC APPROACHES TO IMAGE-BASED RESEARCH

Terry Carson
Department of Secondary Education, The University of Alberta, Canada
Matthew Pearson
Education and Social Research Institute, Manchester Metropolitan University, UK
Ingrid Johnston
Department of Secondary Education, The University of Alberta, Canada
Jyoti Mangat
Department of Secondary Education, The University of Alberta, Canada
Jennifer Tupper
Department of Secondary Education, The University of Alberta, Canada
Terry Warburton
Education and Social Research Institute, Manchester Metropolitan University, UK

Key concepts

Matthew Pearson and Terry Warburton

Representation theory and visual sociology are concerned with the complex processes through which people produce, circulate and read information about the world. We live in a world where images and graphics are increasingly central to cognitive processes and theories of representation allow researchers to explore how people produce and consume images about themselves and the world they inhabit. It would be incorrect to assume that either representation or visual sociology are concerned with images alone. Much work in representation theory has been done using film and television, and visual sociology often takes artefacts where text and images are mixed as the object of study. Stuart Hall has argued that representation 'connects meaning and language with culture' (Hall, 1997: 15), and in this chapter we will be exploring how these connections are created and most importantly how social scientists can use semiotically based frameworks to examine the complex processes of representation which take place in human activity systems.

Representation theory makes the assumption that when people and objects are represented it is incorrect to assume that their portrayal is naturalistic and is merely reflecting the reality of the lived world. Rather than reflecting an unproblematic version of reality, representations are seen as being socially mediated and contingent on a number of complex factors which vary with each instance of the representation. This process is best understood initially through the example of photography. Photography appears to us as a simple capturing of reality – the camera is pointed, a snap is taken and the moment is frozen in time. There appears to be little which can get in the way of the picture and the reality it purports to be representing, the process appears transparent and in little need of extended thought. But further analysis demonstrates that a whole series of decisions were involved in the taking of the photograph which affect the way it will be interpreted. For instance, if the photograph is of human subjects, their expressions and the way they are posed for the picture will predispose the photograph to being 'read' in a certain kind of way. Even an artefact as seemingly straightforward in its representation as a class photograph of the kind taken by official photographers and sold to parents is created by a complex set of social and cultural processes. The positioning of the teacher in the photograph can tell us a great deal: is she or he in the centre or at the edge of the group? Is the teacher there at all? What expression does the teacher have on his or her face? These questions may seem trivial, but representation theory aims to unlock the seemingly mundane and provide researchers with ways to dig under surface meanings and get at the complex social and cultural narratives, which underpin how we represent things. This chapter's Story from the Field, authored by the spatial practices research group at the University of Alberta, outlines the complexities inherent in the taking of photographs and the use of images to record students' attitudes to school 'spaces'.

Representation theory and visual sociology share common roots in semiotics, which can be defined as the theory of signs and signification. Building on this, semiotics also seeks explanations of the ways in which social processes mediate the production and consumption of meaning.

Semiotics employs, in the first instance, concepts such as 'sign', 'sign-system', 'signifier' and 'signified'. These concepts were first circulated by the Swiss linguist Ferdinand de Saussure in his General Course in Linguistics (Saussure, 1966) originally published in 1916. Saussure argued that a word (either spoken or written) creates meaning in the minds of the readers or listeners because it is a binary structure. Firstly there is the sound of the word or the representation of the word in letters on the page. Linked to this is the mental image which the sound or pattern of letters will create in the reader's mind. Saussure used the word 'tree' to illustrate his point. The word itself is known as the 'signifier' and the mental image of a tree is the 'signified', both parts of the structure taken together being known as the 'sign'. Now these insights by themselves are not particularly revolutionary, but Saussure developed his ideas further by reflecting on how sign systems work.

One key insight of Saussure is the distinction between *langue* and *parole*. *Langue* is the entire system of language we can draw on when making an utterance, namely the words of the language and the rules (grammatical, syntactical, social) which govern its usage. *Parole* is an instance of speech or writing. So we draw on *langue* to create utterances which are *parole*, but as many commentators (including Barthes) have pointed out, *langue* can only ever be constituted by *parole*.

Saussure was the first theorist to develop the key idea that signs are arbitrary, that is there is no absolute linkage between a word and the mental image it creates. This means that the word for 'dog', com-posed of the three letters 'd', 'o' and 'g', has no real link with the animal itself. The letters do not look like the word dog, and the sound of the word does not sound like a dog (contrast this with some writing systems where pictorial representation is used). The arbitrary nature of signs is hard to grasp at first because of their conventional nature and the fact that moving seamlessly between signifiers and signifieds is something which we all do when we read or listen to language. Using semiotics effectively as a theoretical framework in research requires us to examine the social conventions which underlie language and begin to unpick the complex processes of social mediation which allow people and communities to communicate with each other.

A key concept in understanding how language works is 'difference'. Saussure argued that a word like 'dog' gets its meaning, not from any inherent properties of the word itself, but because it is different from all other words. So the words 'log' and 'doe' have completely different meanings which arise simply because one letter of the original word is changed. We can concede that in the case of onomatopoeia (words which sound like their meanings such as whizz and whoosh), the link between signifier and signified is not completely arbitrary, but words of this class are relatively rare and any onomatopoeic effects are secondary to the main business of creating meaning,[1] only functioning in the first place when words are spoken in contrast to being written down.

Saussure also argued that signs are arbitrary but it is self-evidently not the case that we can go round calling things whatever we want. This is because the meanings of words are captured in forms of social knowledge and a complex set of shared rules which allow members of a speech community to process language. We all know (if we speak English) what the word 'dog' means because the word existed before we were born and we were enculturated into a social system where the meanings of words have been largely fixed and which we learned as children.

Roland Barthes was one of the most influential theorists to take the initial work on semiotics developed by Saussure and to develop and elaborate it. One contribution Barthes made was to draw a distinction between denotation and connotation. Denotation is what we take as the literal meaning of a sign. So the words 'oak tree' will conjure up a type of tree. Connotation is the whole range of social and cultural meanings which can be attached to a sign. So for 'oak tree' we may think of: Englishness, solidity, history (besieged monarchs hiding in oak trees), wisdom (the tree of knowledge), tradition (furniture made of oak) and many other concepts which get smuggled into our consciousness along with the simple sign. From a research point of view, paying close attention to the connotations of signs can give us a tool to explore the multiple meanings which people can attach to words and begin to unpack the secondary meanings which float nebulously around the language we use everyday.

Barthes (1987) argued that in addition to the sign (signifier and signified), which is a first order of signification, there is a second-order of signification where signs themselves are used as signifiers. He called this second order of signification 'myth', and developed elaborate analyses of cultural, social and literary artefacts where the 'myths' are made explicit and subjected to scrutiny. In *Image – Music – Text*, originally published in 1977, Barthes extends and refines the original semiotic framework provided by Saussure using it as a tool to theorize our understanding of how narrative operates within cultures.

The concepts of difference and the arbitrary nature of signification led to the development of an approach to literary and cultural studies called structuralism (see also Lee et al., in this volume). Structuralism creates an epistemology for the social sciences, one in which meaning is never located absolutely anywhere, but is created out of the complex interplay of differences which are constructed in human meaning systems. It must be noted that the relationship between semiotics and structuralism is complex, and a variety of competing definitions are in circulation. Structuralism acknowledges explicitly that meaning is generated within systems through the exercise of difference rather than residing in some absolute or essential entity. Structuralism also makes great play of binary oppositions. These are pairs of contrasting concepts such as 'good and evil', 'wild and domesticated', 'raw and cooked', and structuralism seeks to lay bare the way that these oppositions structure and control our thinking. Structuralism has been extremely influential in the world of literary studies and is often used as a way of exploring narratives. It can also be used for research in the social sciences where an analysis of binary oppositions operating within sign systems can provide a fruitful line of enquiry and generate new perspectives on seemingly familiar or commonplace social practices.

So far this chapter has dealt with utterances which are verbal in nature, but one of the beauties of using semiotics to underpin a research methodology is its versatility and durability evidenced in its capacity to work with images, both still and moving. Because semiotics posits an approach to meaning where signs are always representing signifieds and the link between them is social and cognitive in character rather than absolute or theological, adaptation to non-verbal modes of communication is relatively easy. One rapidly expanding methodology for social science research is visual sociology which takes images, illustrations and diagrams as its objects of study, but also investigates how meaning is produced within a broad range of visual formats including the spaces of buildings and landscapes, objects and artefacts, and virtual and cybernetic forms of representation such as video games, mobile phone interfaces and computer screens. Chaplin's 1994 book is a key work in visual sociology. In it she investigates the work of a group of modern artists (the Systematic Constructive group) and makes sense of their work from beyond the confines of an aesthetically motivated fine-art sensibility, and draws on sociology, anthropology, ethnography and feminist theory to illuminate these works. Visual sociology connects the insights gained from a century of theorizing about semiotics with post-industrial cultures which are increasingly driven by images and graphical representations.

Implications for research design

Adopting these frameworks for research means looking closely at sign systems, methods and practices of representation and how they are created, constituted, maintained, challenged and disrupted. If you are analysing utterances (in either spoken or written form), the social conventions which underpin their usage and the forms of social mediation which make communication possible could be subjected to scrutiny. If you are working with visual or moving images, you will use the same essential 'grammar' to underpin your analysis and examine the ways in which social practices create meaning and how even the most natural seeming of representations will carry imprints of power. You may also study points of tension or conflict within a sign system, those telling times when various social groups interpret signs in different ways or one group appropriates a chain of signifiers to assert independence and agency or to mount resistance against dominant forms of knowledge. For instance, if you collect data on a series of parents evenings, you may realize after close analysis that parents and teachers are attaching different concepts (signifieds) to words (signifiers), for instance in how they define 'homework', and you may want to explore this subtle slippage between what is said and what is understood. Once you understand how semiotics operates, then it can open up fascinating vistas on a whole range of complex issues, and these can have resonances beyond the spoken or written word. For instance you may study school uniform and the resistance which pupils have to wearing the school sanctioned clothing. The pupils may, for instance, tie their neck ties in a provocative way by making the knots very small or very large. From a semiotic point of view, there is nothing inherently rebellious or confrontational about this way of wearing ties, just as there is nothing inherently respectable about an average size knot and length of tie – we are dealing with social conventions here. Because the ties are 'different' to the expected and socially sanctioned norm, a meaning of resistance to school authority is created, and an understanding of how sign systems operate could allow you to make a more theoretically informed account of what is happening.

From a theoretical standpoint, you may wish to explore how influential Saussure and other semioticians have been in helping us to understand the socially constructed status of language and meaning. Saussure's insights into the conventional nature of the linguistic sign points us towards the later work of the socio-cultural theorists and those working with ideas of communities of practice, where social mediation and the collective creation of meaning remain cardinal issues. Using representation theory and visual sociology and drawing on the insights of semiotics can lead to research which is genuinely critical and remains grounded in real-life processes of communication while simultaneously adopting a sophisticated and powerful theoretical stance.

Stories from the Field – semiotic engagements: photographing high school spaces[2]

Terry Carson, Ingrid Johnston, Jyoti Mangat and Jennifer Tupper

School spaces and identity

In this chapter we present a 'story from the field' that is drawn from a three-year research study exploring the relationships between schooling, students' spatial practices and identity formation. The study builds on previous research that links curriculum to identity construction and acknowledges that space and spatial practices play a constitutive role in the construction of individual and group identities (see, for example, Benko and Strohmayer, 1997; Goodson, 1998; Hurren, 2000; Schutz, 1999). An important aspect of the study involves high-school students using digital cameras to photograph significant spaces in the school. A collection of these photos then becomes the basis for individual tape-recorded interviews in which students describe their understandings of the significance of the photos for how spaces are negotiated in the school.

Our study, which is part of a larger regional study, is situated in a public high school in a Western Canadian city with a growing ethno-culturally diverse school population. Visitors to the school are immediately struck both by the obvious ethno-cultural diversity of the school and by its unique geography. It is a sprawling, windowless, single-story structure with a maze of hallways containing classrooms, laboratories, a library, a theatre, art studio, gymnasium and other facilities. At the centre of the school sits a large rotunda, which functions as one of the main gathering places for students.

Collaborative research

While the research on students' spatial practices sought perspectives from teachers, school counsellors, administrators and support staff, the major source of data was gathered from the students themselves. The research question was presented to classes of students who were in their first year at the school and who represented the variety of available programmes including the International Baccalaureate and academic and general diploma programmes. Students who agreed to participate completed surveys asking them to rate school spaces on scales of most to least preferred and most to least frequented. They were also asked to provide additional anecdotal information on school locations that were of particular significance to them. Following the survey, a small number of student volunteers were provided with digital cameras and invited to take a collection of photos of significant spaces in the school. These images then became the basis for individual tape-recorded interviews in which students described their understandings of the significance of the photos for how spaces are negotiated in the school.

Students as photographic researchers

The students have proven to be enthusiastic photo-graphic researchers. They were comfortable with visual culture and enjoyed using the digital camera to photograph familiar spaces in the school. For us, working with students as researchers opened up some interesting questions of collaboration. Teather (1999) suggests that power relationships emerge out of how we are positioned or located relative to others in space and place. This insight helped us to realize that, as university-based researchers, we have entered the school with questions that are derived from theories about the relationships between spaces, social interactions and identity formation. To this extent, we cannot help but relate to the school site, teachers and students as objects of investigation. For the students our questions and invitation to participate in the study became an opportunity to make explicit what they implicitly know about the spaces in the school, who it is that 'hangs out' there and with whom. Having taken up our initial invitation to participate in the research students became co-researchers with us, choosing freely the aspects of school space upon which to focus without the imposition of meaning by us as outside researchers. Nevertheless, we realized that power relations again became a factor as we began to share interpretations of the meanings of these spaces.

In choosing which places to photograph students recognized that they were not simply recording unmediated realities of the school space. It was clear to them, right from the beginning of the research, that they were already making interpretations about the meanings of places as they selected the areas to be photographed. Students were consciously making decisions about camera angles and about who or what to include in the picture in an effort to connote a range of social and cultural meanings. One example of this construction of meaning was the way in which they intentionally used connotations of darkness and light to convey the desirability or undesirability of certain spaces. One student took a picture of the library to illustrate why the library is a place she and her friends like to be. In discussing her photo she explained that 'the library is popular because of the natural light, bright colours, big tables and lots of work space'. In a building with no exterior windows, natural light, which shines through by virtue of a skylight that is located in the ceiling in the library, is a rare commodity. This student then went on to describe another series of photos which she had taken of the many school corridors to show how darkness and lightness contributed to the physicality and aesthetics of certain hallways that encouraged or discouraged students from being in these spaces.

Most students surveyed identified the rotunda in the centre of the school as the most socially active place in the building. Without exception, each student photographer chose the rotunda as an example of a significant school space. One student described the rotunda as 'just a big open space where everyone gets together'. Another said 'it's the centre of everything and you can get to any place from there'. Further discussions with student photographers suggested that the rotunda was a complex social space, function-ing as a kind of microcosm of the school. They described how identifications of and with groups of students were played out in the rotunda area. The student researchers explained that in the public space of the rotunda you could observe how students would group together along racial lines, 'the blacks tend to gather around that corner'; or make associations of common interests, 'the "jocks" are over there'; or represent social status, 'that's where the popular girls are'. But the student researchers also noted that these lines of identification can be fluid, individuals move between groups, but such movements also receive public notice in the open space of the rotunda.

The ethics of taking pictures

While student-produced images of the school reveal a particular physicality of space, in the first year of the research the most salient features (for the purposes of our investigation these were the social aspects) had been absent from the photographs. This was a major frustration that threatened to dampen the potential for using photographic images in research. Privacy legislation and increasingly stringent requirements of research ethics have made the use of photographs of students highly problematic. In Canada, most prov-inces have enacted legislation that requires public institutions and organizations to explicitly define, in advance, the uses that will be made of information, and to restrict the information only to these uses. Research funding bodies, as well as public institutions like schools and universities, have interpreted this legislation to mean that all persons depicted in research studies will have to provide informed con-sent and be guaranteed anonymity. Obviously, this interpretation places severe restrictions on the use of photography in research, particularly on studies such as ours, which places cameras in the hands of students.

Taking seriously our responsibility for assuring informed consent and anonymity, we encouraged the student researchers to take photos of places, not of people. Yet as the research progressed, we more keenly appreciated that it is the social elements more than any other that have a tendency to attract or deter student presence in particular school spaces. Gruenewald (2003: 5) confirms this observation, as he draws upon critical geographies of space to conclude that, 'places are social constructions filled with ideologies, and the experience of places … shapes cultural identities'. Viewing the initial sets of photos and discussing them with the students, we were struck by the irony of (mis)representing the school as a place without people. While people were missing from most of the photographs, they were not absent in the minds of the students taking the pictures or in the actual spaces of the school. Clearly the solution for our research would have to be something other than following a restrictive ethics based solely on protection from harm.

A provisional solution has been to digitally alter the faces in the photographs of the students so they cannot be individually identified. A longer-term solution must be a deeper consideration of the ethics and politics of representation in the use of photographic research. As university-based researchers our obligations are not limited to harm prevention; we are also responsible for ensuring fair representation and for the development of practices that will help to build genuinely democratic collaborative relationships with research participants. We are resolved to be guided by this deeper sense of obligation as we go forward in the next two years of the research on students' spatial practices.

Interpretive possibilities in photographic research

As we work with high-school students and staff to understand the relationship between schooling, spatial practices and identity formation, we are following two lines of inquiry. The first is semiotic, that is how are the students themselves, primarily, going about representing the meaningful spaces in the school? How do the photographs work to convey meaning, and what kinds of conversations are occasioned by the various pictures taken by the students? The second line of inquiry is hermeneutic, having to do with interpretive theory and its particular application to visual culture.

Our use of hermeneutics is inspired by Heywood and Sandywell's (1999) suggestion that hermeneutics might be employed as 'an analytic attitude toward the field of experience in which visual experience is approached as a socio-historical realm of interpretive practices' (p. xi).

The practical implication of visual hermeneutics for our research is that we are alerted to the fact that understanding is a creative process. As collaborators in this research project on spatial practices we are not simply interpreting what is already there in the photographs; rather we are also producing different meanings by virtue of our contrasting predispositions, or fore-structures of understanding. Thus we notice that students are already predisposed to identifying school spaces in terms of comfort/discomfort, or finding the places inviting/uninviting. They produce these meanings from the perspective of inhabiting the school. Contrastingly, as a university-based research team, we are already predisposed toward understanding spatial practices more theoretically in terms of how these contribute to citizenship and identity formation. In this connection, we notice how our attention is drawn to the school's concerns for safety and orderly conduct. In our conversations with the students we point out the security cameras, the bulletin boards that focus on character education, the use of piped-in music over the school's intercom and the signs posted in the corridors which discourage loitering and encourage the efficient movement of traffic in the hallways. The effect of visual hermeneutics is to produce a complex and nuanced interpretation of spatial practices that supports the semiotic engagements of the students taking pictures of school spaces.

Reflections on photographing school spaces

As we reflect on our past two years of research, we understand more clearly the potential and limitations of using photography to help make sense of students' subjective experiences of school spaces. We realize that photographs offer more than just a 'historical rendering of the setting and its participants' (Bogdan and Biklen, 1982: 103), and that, like all images, photographs are socially and technically constructed and 'often reveal unconscious beliefs behind the picture-taking process itself' (Taylor, 2002: 123).

We now see how our invitation to take photographs of their school spaces allowed them to become co-investigators with us in the research, effectively allowing them to exercise agency in seeing their school spatial experiences in new ways. Rather than being passive subjects of our study, participants worked with us in interpreting and analyzing the spaces of their school experience.

Notes

1   By way of illustration, take two onomatopoeic words, 'woof' (what dogs do), and 'whoosh' (what planes do). Both *can* be spoken in ways which emphasize the link between the sound of the words and their meaning but often are pronounced in ways which doesn't make this link explicit. In the absence of hissing sibilants and canine mimicry, the key meanings of these words are still conveyed through difference (one ends in an 'f', the other in a 'sh').

2   Our research is supported by the Social Sciences and Humanities Research Council of Canada (SSHRCC), Grant #410-2001-1614 (Wanda J. Hurren, Principal Investigator).

Annotated bibliography

Barthes, R. (1966) 'Introduction to the structural analysis of narratives', in B. Astley (ed.), (1997) *Reading Popular Narrative: A Source Book*. Leicester: Leicester University Press.

For Barthes this chapter is reasonably accessible, although a close reading will reveal the complexity of thought and analysis in play here. Originally from *Image – Music – Text* (1977), Barthes is at his structuralist zenith here, creating an elaborate system of analysis to explain the operation of narrative.

Barthes, R. (1964) *Elements of Semiology*. London: Noonday Press.

A key work in which Barthes fully explores the legacy of Saussure and provides much of the ground work to position semiotics as an influential academic discipline. This is a challenging text but will repay careful study.

Chaplin, E. (1994) *Sociology and Visual Representation*. London: Routledge.

The introduction is excellent in respect of theory and context generally. For the most part Elizabeth Chaplin uses painting and fine art as exemplar material and the quality of writing and the conceptual linkage between image production and sociological theory is very impressive in this work.

Fiske, J. (1982) *An Introduction to Communication Studies*. London: Routledge.

This book gives an overview and simplified version of semiotic approaches. It is very easy to follow and quite readable. It may not carry all the detail and depth of intellectual argument of *Elements of Semiology*, but, taken as an accompanying text, it is very useful indeed.

Hall, S. (ed.) (1997) *Representation: Cultural Representations and Signifying Practices*. London: Sage.

A readable and comprehensive guide through the complexities of representation theory. Hall and his fellow writers are engaging and provocative throughout and included are many 'worked through' examples to show theoretical ideas put into practice. This book combines many illustrations with lucid and theoretically sound analysis of visual artefacts. An ideal place to start to get a grounding in this field.

Prosser, J. (ed.) (1998) *Image-based Research: A Sourcebook for Qualitative Researchers*. London: Routledge.

The book is a comprehensive guide to different approaches to image-based research, and covers sociological, anthropological and ethnographic styles of working with images. This is vital reading for anyone wishing to use representation theory or visual sociology within their work.

Prosser, J. and Warburton, T. (1999) 'Visual sociology and school culture', in J. Prosser (ed.), *School Culture*. London: Paul Chapman Publishing.

The book charts the evolution of research into schools and classrooms as cultures. The chapter examines how visual sociology can be used as a tool to examine school culture. Photographs and cartoons are used to illustrate this approach and the writing demonstrates how the theoretical frameworks of visual sociology can be applied to empirical investigations.

Further references

Barthes (1987) *Image – Music – Text*. London: Fontana Press.

Benko, G. and U. Strohmayer (1997) *Space and Social Theory: Interpreting Modernity and Postmodernity*. Oxford, UK: Blackwell.

Bogdan, R.C. and Biklen, S.K. (1982) *Qualitative Research in Education*, 1st edn. Boston, MA: Allyn & Bacon (2nd edn, 1998).

Goodson, I. (1998) 'Storying the self: life politics and the study of the teachers' life and work', in W.F. Pinar (ed.), *Curriculum: Towards New Identities*. New York: Garland, pp. 3–20.

Gruenewald, D. (2003) 'The best of both worlds: a critical pedagogy of place', *Educational Researcher*, 32(4): 3–12.

Heywood, I. and Sandywell, B. (eds) (1999) *Interpreting Visual Culture: Explorations in the Hermeneutics of the Visual*. London: Routledge.

Hurren, W. (2000) *Line Dancing: An Atlas of Geography Curriculum and Poetic Possibilities*. New York: Peter Lang.

Saussure, F. (1966) *Course in General Linguistics*. New York: McGraw-Hill.

Schutz, A. (1999) 'Creating local "public spaces" in schools: Insights from Hannah Arendt and Maxine Greene', *Curriculum Inquiry*, 29(1): 77–98.

Taylor, E.W. (2002) 'Using still photography in making meaning of adult educators' teaching beliefs', *Studies in the Education of Adults*, 34(2): 123–40.

Teather, E. (1999) *Embodied Geographies: Spaces, Bodies and Rites of Passage*. London: Routledge.

CHAPTER 20

SOCIAL SEMIOTICS AND MULTIMODAL TEXTS

Gunther Kress
Institute of Education, University of London, UK
Diane Mavers
Education and Social Research Institute, Manchester Metropolitan University, UK

Key concepts

Gunther Kress

A need for new thinking

Language alone can no longer give us full access to the meanings of most contemporary messages, which are now constituted in several **modes**: on pages in the mode of *writing* and of *image*; on screens through CD-ROMs and on the Web; in *speech, music, image* – moving or still; in *gesture, colour* and *soundtrack*. In such *texts* each mode, language included, is a partial bearer of meaning only. The co-presence of modes other than speech or writing in a text raises the question of their function: are they merely replicating – echoing perhaps – what language already does? Are they ancillary, marginal, or do they play a full role in *representation*? If they do, is it the same role as that of writing, or is it different? And if they play a different role, is that because their different material make-up (say *sound* compared to *graphic matter*) and their differing cultural histories provide different potentials for making meaning? That is, does the *materiality* of mode provide different *affordances*, which may be taken up, worked on and used differently in different cultures?

If that were the case, we would need to look again at language – whether as *speech* or as *writing* – and ask: if all modes have specific potentials, then what are those of *speech* and of *writing*? What are their potentials, their limitations, their particular affordances? That is a new question to ask not just of language, but of all representation and communication. It is a question of near Copernican import, with its implication that language does not occupy the central and privileged place in the firmament of communication.

We deal with that issue from the perspective of a general theory of meaning (-making), that of **Social Semiotics**, and from the assumption that all modes – and not just those of *speech* and *writing* – have specific parts to play in the making of meaning, the perspective of **multimodality**. The shift of discipline from linguistics to **semiotics** is a move with two profound effects: one, it is a move from a *concern with one mode* to a *concern with many modes*; and two, it is a move from a *concern with form alone* to a *concern with form-and-meaning*. It is a move from a theory in which form (as grammar and syntax) is dealt with separately from meaning (as semantics and pragmatics). It challenges the assumption – implicitly or explicitly held – that linguistic theory can provide a satisfactory and generally applicable account of representation and communication, and posits that we need a theory which can account equally for *gesture, speech, image, writing, three-dimensional objects, colour, music* – a theory that applies to all modes – and that linguistics cannot provide an appropriate model.

Semiotics, sign-making and signs

For one of its founders, Ferdinand de Saussure (1857–1913), **Semiotics** was 'the science of the life of signs in society'. To get a grasp on that 'science' we need to understand the characteristics of the formation of signs of whatever kind, at all levels. (Social) semiotics provides categories which, at one level, apply to all modes equally, to *speech* as much as to *image*, to *gesture* as much as to *music*, to *writing* as much as to *three-dimensional objects*, and so on: categories such as **sign, text, genre, discourse**, or those of **metaphor** and **analogy**. At the same time we need descriptions which focus on the characteristics of specific modes, categories such as *verbs* or *vectors* (to deal with dynamism, action, movement), *subjects* or *salient entities* (to deal with grammar-like functions), *nouns* or *depictions* (to deal with the representation of object-like things). Throughout much of the twentieth century, mainstream linguistics had, by and large, dealt with language in highly abstracted ways. In semiotic terms, it had focused on form, on the *signifier*, while meaning was exported to peripheral enterprises – semantics, pragmatics, socio-linguistics, stylistics. Linguistics has been the science of the signifier, focused on form; semiotics has been the science of the sign, a fusion of form and meaning, of *signified* and *signifier*. In the multimodal social semiotic approach taken here, the language-modes – *speech* and *writing* – will also be described semiotically, as a part of the whole landscape of the many modes available for representation – though special still in that they have highly valued status in society, while speech certainly still carries the major load of communication.

In social semiotics, the idea of *sign-use* is replaced by *sign-making*, a move away from the conventionally accepted view that there are (relatively) stable signs which are *used* in representation and communication. Instead signs are seen as constantly newly made, out of the *interest* of the (socially and culturally formed and positioned) individual *sign-maker*. This interest gives shape to the signs made.

The relation of form to meaning in social semiotics is *iconic*, that is the signifier is apt for the 'shape' of the signified (that is, the shape of the signifier 'squiggly line' aptly indicates the look of what is signified – the line of writing). If we think in terms of the principles of connection, the relation is *motivated*, never *arbitrary* as it is assumed to be in the still dominant common sense in mainstream semiotics. 'Motivation' assumes that the form of the signifier is an apt expression of the content of the signified: what is being meant is indicated by the shape of that which means it: a circle 'meaning' wheel, the direction of an arrow 'meaning' the direction in which we are to move, and so on. If we look at the many signs in Figure 20.1 (see Diane Mavers' Story from the Field below) we can see these principles at work in a number of ways: in the *selections* (of functions of the technology) made by the child (music, Internet, games, email, work, website); or in the different ways in which each of these is realized or read as a sign – so for the music-function, for instance, the screen is blank, for the email function the screen is filled with squiggly lines to 'mean' written text; and the squiggly lines themselves are signs in which the signifier *squiggly line* means *line of alphabetic writing*, and so on. In Figure 20.1, in two cases the computer has a mouse attached – once the centrally depicted machine, and once the machine at work. The other signs of computer, which focus on specific functional aspects, do not have the mouse attached: that, it seems, is not an issue in the case of that sign. 'Mouse' is an apt signifier for meaning 'action', and that in turn is an apt signifier for 'this is about work', just as a squiggly line is an apt signifier for 'line of writing'.

Each of these signs is a (double) metaphor – 'mouse means action; action means work', or 'lines of writing look just like a horizontal line of quite similar squiggly marks'. These are motivated signs, where form and meaning are intrinsically connected, always in an iconic relation, always as metaphor; in fact they are always both. The interest of the sign-maker at the moment of making the sign leads to the selection of the criteria for representing that which is to be represented – 'action' say – and for selecting the signifier/form which most aptly, most plausibly represents it, the mouse.

Representation is never neutral: that which is represented in the sign, or in sign-complexes, realizes the interests, the perspectives, the positions and values of those who make signs. The outwardly-made sign functions in **communication**, and so it must necessarily fit into the structures of power which characterize situations of communication. In its forms, the sign must factor that in as well – it must be fit for its role in the social field of communication.

We can now ask about the relation of *the sign that is made* to *signs (like it) that were made before*: is the relation one of copying, of imitation, of imperfectly understood use? The shapes of the computers in Figure 20.1 have strong similarities to shapes that might conventionally indicate computers, and yet each differs in specific ways, actually indicating quite precisely the functions that the child sign-maker wished to indicate. In other words, the signs are not copies, not imitations, and are very well understood uses of existing signifier material. But they are, in each case, specific *transformations* of culturally available material. As transformations they are always new, specific and creative in a non-trivial sense: something that had not been there before is made from culturally available material. Such a view of sign-making has profound consequences for theories of meaning and therefore for theories of learning: the latter is not ever seen as mere acquisition, as imperfect copying, as deficient imitation, but as always the best possible new making from existing cultural material transformed in line with the sign-maker's interest.

The process of outward meaning-making has a transformative effect: the sign-maker's resources have been changed because the sign made outwardly is a new sign; the inner transformations produce learning, and learning is the shaping of the subjectivity of the maker of signs. The outward transformations produce new syntactic, textual forms, which play their role, however slightly, in the change of the resources which were used in making meaning. This is how semiotic and cultural change happens – whether in a change to writing, to speech, to gesture; it is also the way in which that semiotic change, the change in the modal resources, always reflects and tracks the values, structures, meanings of the social and cultural world of the meaning-maker; and it is the way in which engagement in these processes constantly transforms the subjectivity of the maker of signs.

The new technologies of information and communication facilitate the ready use of many modes together on the screen, and so choice of mode has become a crucial issue. *Mode* has material aspects, and it bears everywhere the stamp of past social-cultural work, among other things the stamp of regularity of organization. This regularity is what has traditionally been referred to as *grammar* and syntax. When we can choose mode easily the question about the characteristics of mode arises in a way that it has not done before: what can a specific mode do? What are its limitations and potentials? What are the *affordances* of a mode? And these bring up another, the central question of *design*.

One fundamental distinction in the potentials of modes – that of *space* and of *time* – is due to their materiality. *Time-based modes* – *speech, music* – have potentials for representation which differ from *space-based modes* – *image, layout, sculpture* and other *three-dimensional forms* such as *architectural arrangements, streetscapes*, as both differ from modes which combine time and space such as *dance, gesture, action*. The fundamental logics of these types of mode differ: the *logic of time* affords the possibilities for making meaning through the temporal succession of elements, their place in a sequence constituting a resource for meaning; the *logic of space* affords the possibilities for making meaning through the spatial distribution of simultaneously present elements, relations of elements

in space being a resource for meaning. These lead, in all modes, to preferred textual/generic forms: *narrative* in speech and writing; *display* in visual modes (and perhaps *displayed narrative* in the case of modes resting on both logics).

Multimodally constituted texts rest on *design*, with its question: what resource is best to achieve that which I wish to communicate now, for this audience? To answer that question we need to understand fully the potentials, the affordances, of the different modes – what can writing do best? What can image do best? But also the question: is my intended audience more likely to respond to image or to writing, to moving image, sound of various kinds (speech, music, soundtrack, etc.) on a screen rather than writing alone in a book?

Implications for research design
Diane Mavers

A strength of multimodality is that it opens up scope for studying signs beyond the linguistic. As yet in its infancy, a multimodal approach has been applied to an assorted range of studies, for example computer animation (Burn and Parker, 2003), conceptualization of the idea of 'bounce' in designing a computer game (Jewitt, 2003), drama (Franks, 2003) and bilingual children's bodily and cognitive engagement with script-learning in Chinese, Arabic and Spanish (Kenner, 2003). A social semiotic approach takes for granted that while the ways in which meanings are made are the same for all humans, the resources and the conditions in which meanings are made in one culture and society are not necessarily like those in another. Because multimodality is located in a socio-cultural approach to understanding semiosis, it can provide insights into culture-specific meaning-making. Typically in semiotics, one might ask the questions: what is the sign? What are the conditions and the resources with which it is made? What might it mean? Data might be captured by using video recording or photography, or gathering textual artefacts such as pieces of writing and/or drawing, electronic texts, paintings or three-dimensional models. Research questions using a multimodal approach can be wide-ranging and might be used as part of, for example, an ethnographic or case study. Suited to detailed analysis of small amounts of data, it can stand alone or be combined with other theoretically compatible forms of analysis, for example quantitative or phenomenographic analysis (Mavers et al., 2002).

Stories from the Field

Diane Mavers

Semiotic interpretation of image and writing

My particular research interest is in how children represent/communicate graphically. As I began to study children's writing and drawing semiotically I became interested in signs beyond those that are traditionally valued. For example, how text had been set out in a particular format appeared to carry meaning. Not attending to the full range of signs made in a graphic text seemed to me to be a partial analysis of all that the sign-maker had represented. I therefore began to draw on the methods of analysis developed by Gunther Kress and Theo van Leeuwen (1996). This provided me with an explicit analytical 'toolkit' with which to study children's texts in a systematic, rigorous and detailed way. Multimodality offered a means of accounting for the multiple modes in which signs can be made and of understanding more about the interrelationships between different modes in graphic texts. Of course, Nathalie's representations (examined below) are her interpretations of phenomena just as my 'reading' of the signs she made are interpretations. In presenting my work, I found that interpretation beyond or without the authentication of spoken or written words made people nervous. This is symptomatic of the view that language can give full access to meaning. Nevertheless, the mode of speech in interviewing enabled children to express how they thought about phenomena in a different way from diagrammatic drawing (Mavers et al., 2002). It is not that one mode is inferior and another superior but that each communicates different aspects of meaning.

Signs in image-based mind mapping

Sign-making on the page is a means of sharing ideas with others. The form – the way in which marks have been composed – carries the meanings of the sign-maker. In her mind map[1] Nathalie made a whole range of signs to communicate how she thought about 'Computers in My World'[2]. The aim of the task was to gain an understanding of children's 'secondary artefacts' or mental representations of the computer as a tool (Cole, 1999; Wartofsky, 1979). Scripted instructions asked the children to think about types of computers, where they can be found, if they are connected and the people who use them, and how.

Read out by the class teacher, the script informed Nathalie's class (9-and 10-year-olds) that image-based mind mapping would be a means of communicating with researchers. This framed the task in two ways. Firstly, the children's interest was shaped according to the particular communicational need. Implicitly, the inference was that the mind maps would be 'read' by unknown others and would therefore need to be readily 'readable' by them. An embedded aim was therefore to communicate effectively within a tight time limit of 20 minutes. Secondly, the direction to use image as the primary means of communication was significant for the meanings that could be made. This both enabled and disabled according to the 'functional specialization' (Kress and van Leeuwen, 2001: 64) of drawing. The instructions asked the children to draw ideas quickly as they came into their minds and to link them with lines: 'The order in which you do the drawings is not important but it is important that you draw lines between the drawings that you feel are linked.' They were also asked to 'write a few words to label any of your drawings' or to write a contents list. The spatiality of the page had implications for the signs Nathalie could make.

Drawing obliged Nathalie to show (Figure 20.1). Her representation of the Internet, like the website at the top of her map, is generalized rather than specific. It carries signs that communicate something about her conception of online texts. She shows that they include writing (represented as repeated horizontal text squiggles) and other textual framings (shown as rectangles), presumably images. Note how the 'email' and 'work' nodes (individual images), in contrast, contain only representations of writing. The implication is that words and image work visually as blocks that can be presented in different ways. This was not an accident. It carries meaning. Drawing compels ways of communicating, and therefore of thinking, in a different way from words. Other children in Nathalie's class represented the Internet as a surfboarder, as 'www.' inside a computer screen and as a globe. This gave a different emphasis, a different 'slant'. The drawings do not exclude each child's knowing about other characteristics of the Internet but signify the foregrounding of a particular idea at a particular moment in time (Marton and Booth, 1997: 123).

Nathalie's drawings are not reproductions. She transformed the three-dimensional world onto the flatness of the page. Bearing in mind the focus of the task and the intended audience, she chose and

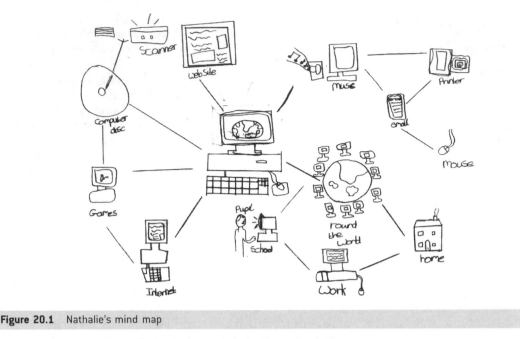

Figure 20.1   Nathalie's mind map

represented those features of electronic games equipment which she considered key to conveying her intended meanings (Mavers, 2003). With one exception each node is drawn frontally. Essentially diagrammatic rather than pictorial, this gives her map high modality (a term borrowed from linguistics to denote 'truth value'). Nathalie's map comprises 14 nodes. The majority are drawings of actual 'things'. However, to the right of her central node is a world image encircled by 10 computers. As a whole, this node is not something she has drawn directly from actuality. It is a bringing together of drawings of the world and computers to construct a visual metaphor. This carries particular conceptual meanings. Symbolically, Nathalie shows that computers are situated all around the world. Interestingly, there is a shift in how Nathalie made signs through her written label for this node. Whereas all the other labels in her map are identifiers (nouns), 'round the world' (preposition, definite article and noun) signifies something different from 'world' or 'our world'. It extends from identification to explanation. The meanings of this node expand when considered in relation to the central node. The image of the globe displayed on the computer screen suggests that the world is in some way contained in the computer. When these two nodes are looked at together, the joint implication is that computers are around the world and the world is

in the computer; technology is a worldwide resource and the global is accessible electronically.

Nathalie also made signs in her positioning and linking of nodes. The central computer works as the title or superordinate of the map to which all other nodes are linked either directly or indirectly as representations of Nathalie's ideas about 'Computers in My World'. With the exception of the scanner, the links to the left of her map connect drawings to the central node individually. However, to the right of her map, Nathalie created two discrete and internally interlinked groupings of nodes. The single links from the superordinate guide the 'reader' to these groups. The grouping to the bottom right suggests locations where computers are used – school, home, possibly the workplace and the world. The interlinked grouping of nodes to the top right is perhaps less transparent. The sounds of music are depicted through conventional representation as musical notes emanating from a computer speaker. This node is linked to a drawing of a printer with a just-printed image of a face. The text squiggles in the email node suggest writing. At the bottom of the grouping the mouse may imply control. These nodes might show the variety of modes available on computers: writing, sound, image and possibly the actional – their multimodal capacities.

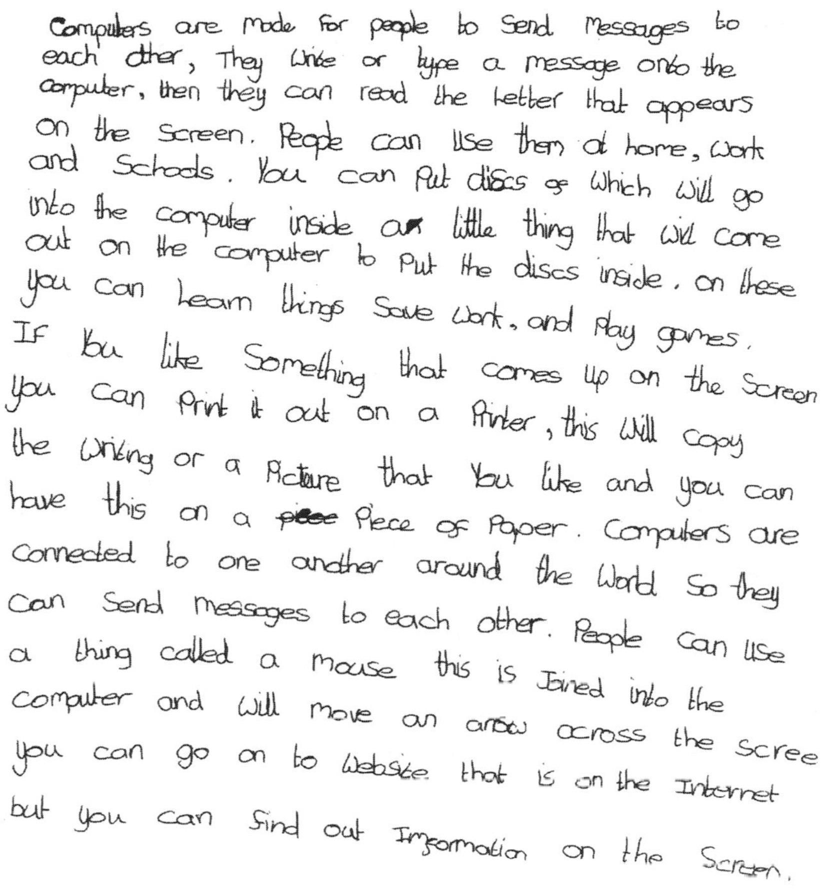

Computers are made for people to send messages to each other, They write or type a message onto the computer, then they can read the letter that appears on the screen. People can use them at home, work and schools. You can put discs of which will go into the computer inside a little thing that will come out on the computer to put the discs inside. on these you can learn things save work, and play games. If you like something that comes up on the screen you can print it out on a printer, this will copy the writing or a picture that you like and you can have this on a piece piece of paper. Computers are connected to one another around the world so they can send messages to each other. People can use a thing called a mouse this is joined into the computer and will move an arrow across the scree you can go on to website that is on the internet but you can find out information on the screen.

Figure 20.2   Nathalie's writing

Signs in writing

A 15-minute written task was undertaken on a separate occasion, around one week after the mind mapping. The children were asked to write about their maps but the maps were not returned to them. This was framed as talking to an Alien. The emphasis in the scripted instructions was on description and explanation, the closing words being 'What would the Alien need to know to understand computer systems in our world and what they can do?' In response, Nathalie's writing is shaped as an objective, factual piece. Her opening refers to 'people' and 'they'. On her fifth line (just under a quarter of the way through the text) Nathalie shifts to the personal pronoun 'you' which she retains apart from one further use of 'people'. Never is there slippage to 'I' or 'me'. This is a generalization where she notes regularities in human practices. It defines the text as an informational report rather than a personalized account.

Nathalie wrote 176 words in black biro on one side of A4 paper (see Figure 20.2). Her punctuation is of significance. She attends to seven different topics, each framed as a sentence ending with a full stop. There are just two exceptions. On one occasion a word overruns the edge of the page. On her seventh line she made two full stops but followed the first with a lower case letter as if to imply that the two parts of the topic are related (they are both to do with electronic information) but contain separate ideas (how to put a disk in a computer and different types of information for different purposes). She dealt with the wholeness of her opening topic by splitting clauses with commas rather than full stops. This may represent a transcription of speech in response to the

PART V   READING AND REPRESENTING SOCIO-CULTURAL MEANINGS

task instructions 'Write down what you would say if you were speaking to the Alien.'

The seven topics Nathalie addresses (communication, locations of use, electronic resources, medium, connectivity, control and information) are similar to the themes of her mind map. However, the mode of writing enabled her to communicate different meanings from drawing. Nathalie's written account includes statements of fact (for example, 'People can use a thing called a mouse'), descriptions of actions and processes (for example, 'You can put discs of which will go into the computer inside a little thing that will come out on the computer to put the discs inside') and explanations of purposes (for example, 'on these you can Learn things, save work and play games'). For the majority of topics the fact precedes the explanation, for example 'Computers are connected to one another around the world so they can send messages to each other'. Here 'so' implies a causal connection, as does 'and' elsewhere. The word 'can' appears ten times in Nathalie's text. On five occasions the succeeding verb is to do with functionality such as operating computer devices (for example, 'print', 'go on a web site'), three occurrences are cognitively related ('read', 'Learn', 'find information') and two suggest the affective ('play', 'like'), ideas particularly well suited to writing.

Issues arising

In both her mind map and her writing Nathalie endeavoured to communicate an accurate, factual account of computers in her world. Both were shaped by the set title and the scripted directions on content, and for the identified audience as she perceived it. The functional specializations of drawing and writing brought about different representations of meaning.

Drawing obliged her to show meanings in a way different from words. It enabled her to depict 'things' as aspects of 'Computers in My World' such as electronic equipment and locations. Her spatial arrangement through positioning and her links were also a means of communicating aspects of her conceptualization, as in her groupings of nodes. Something different happens in her writing. Here, she describes actions and processes, and explains reasons why and purposes for. The mode may have been prescribed but Nathalie made choices about how to shape meanings according to her individual interest within the potentialities of drawing or writing. Representation/communication in drawing and writing enabled Nathalie to make meaning in particular ways. It is not that one is more trustworthy than the other but that their different affordances enable different signs to be made. Her signs – how she connects signifiers and signifieds – were shaped by her interest and her intent to mean.

Notes

1. 'Mind mapping' was the term used to describe the genre in the scripted instructions. In other publications it has been referred to as 'concept mapping'.
2. This work draws on data from the ImpaCT2 evaluation funded by the UK Department for Education and Skills and managed by the British Educational and Communications Technology Agency. The team included: C. Harrison (Director), T. Fisher, K. Haw, E. Lunzer (University of Nottingham), P. Scrimshaw, C. Lewin (Open University), B. Somekh, D. Mavers (Manchester Metropolitan University).

Annotated bibliography

Hodge, R. and Kress, G. (1988) *Social Semiotics*. Cambridge: Polity Press.

In exploring how meaning systems are socially constituted and situated in social contexts, this book addresses power and ideology, space and time, and gender and class.

Jewitt, C. and Kress, G. (eds) (2003) *Multimodal Literacy*. New York: Peter Lang.

Using a range of diverse examples, this edited book explores how meaning-making is made through a variety of representational and communicational modes such as speech, image, writing, gaze, gesture and movement. It provides conceptual tools for understanding a multimodal approach to literacy and learning.

Kress, G. (1997) *Before Writing: Rethinking the Paths to Literacy.* London: Routledge.

In attending to a multitude of ways in which children make meaning, Gunther Kress explores key ideas in a social semiotic approach and challenges how early literacy is understood.

Kress, G. (2003) *Literacy in the New Media Age.* London: Routledge.

In this book Gunther Kress explores the need for a reconceptualization of what literacy is as a consequence of technological change. As new media signal the dominance of the screen, he considers social and cultural implications.

Kress, G., Jewitt, C., Ogborn, J. and Tsatsarelis, C. (2001) *Multimodal Teaching and Learning: The Rhetorics of the Science Classroom.* London: Continuum.

This book explores the different communicative modes that are used to make meaning in the secondary science classroom, going beyond language to image, three-dimensional models, gesture and movement.

Pahl, K. (1999) *Transformations: Meaning Making in Nursery Education.* Stoke on Trent: Trentham Books.

In this book, Kate Pahl explores the multiple ways in which nursery-aged children make meaning as they draw, write, cut out, stick together and model. She uses her detailed observations to explore their developing literacy.

van Leeuwen, T. and Jewitt, C. (eds) (2001) *Handbook of Visual Analysis.* London: Sage.

With a focus on visual analysis, this edited book covers a wide range of methods such as content analysis, psychoanalysis, social semiotic analysis and ethnomethodology. It provides examples such as advertisements, photographs, children's pictures and film.

Further references

Burn, A. and Parker, D. (2003) *Analysing Media Texts.* London: Continuum.

Cole, M. (1999) 'Cultural psychology: some general principles and a concrete example', in Y. Engeström, R. Miettinen and R.-L. Punamäki (eds), *Perspectives on Activity Theory.* Cambridge: Cambridge University Press, pp. 87–106.

Finnegan, R. (2002) *Communicating: The Multiple Modes of Human Interconnection.* London: Routledge.

Franks, A. (2003) 'Palmer's Kiss: Shakespeare, school drama and semiotics', in C. Jewitt and G. Kress (eds), *Multimodal Literacy.* New York: Peter Lang, pp. 155–72.

Jewitt, C. (2003) 'Computer-mediated learning: the multimodal construction of mathematical entities on screen', in C. Jewitt and G. Kress (eds), *Multimodal Literacy.* New York: Peter Lang, pp. 34–55.

Kenner, C. (2003) 'Embedded knowledges: young children's engagement with the act of writing', in C. Jewitt and G. Kress (eds), *Multimodal Literacy.* New York: Peter Lang, pp. 88–106.

Kress, G. and van Leeuwen, T. (1996) *Reading Images: The Grammar of Visual Design.* London: Routledge.

Kress, G. and van Leeuwen, T. (2001) *Multimodal Discourse: The Modes and Media of Contemporary Communication.* London: Arnold.

Marton, F. and Booth, S. (1997) *Learning and Awareness.* Mahwah, NJ: Lawrence Erlbaum Associates.

Mavers, D. (2003) 'Communicating meanings through image: composition, spatial arrangement and links in student mind maps', in C. Jewitt and G. Kress (eds), *Multimodal Literacy.* New York: Peter Lang, pp. 19–33.

Mavers, D., Somekh, B. and Restorick, J. (2002) 'Interpreting the externalised images of pupils' conceptions of ICT: methods for the analysis of concept maps', *Computers and Education,* 38:187–207.

Scollon, R. and Scollon, S. (2002) *Discourses in Place: Language in the Material World.* London: Routledge.

Wartofsky, M. (1979) *Models: Representation and Scientific Understanding.* Dordrecht: Reidel.

chapter 21

COMMUNITIES OF PRACTICE

David Benzie
College of St Mark and St John, Plymouth, UK
Diane Mavers
Education and Social Research Institute, Manchester Metropolitan University, UK
Bridget Somekh
Education and Social Research Institute, Manchester Metropolitan University, UK
Edith J. Cisneros-Cohernour
College of Education, Universidad Autonoma de Yucatan, Mexico

Key concepts

*Diane Mavers, Bridget Somekh and
Edith J. Cisneros-Cohernour*

The term 'community of practice' was created by Jean Lave and Etienne Wenger (1991) as a means of exploring the notion of situated learning within a particular domain of social practice. In this chapter we explore the ways in which these ideas can be used as a theoretical framework for research. We begin by discussing notions of 'situated cognition/situated learning' and 'distributed cognition', which have been highly influential in work on learning during the last twenty years. This is followed by a more detailed overview of the interrelated concepts of 'legitimate peripheral participation' and 'communities of practice'.

All these theories relate closely to the socio-cultural psychology of Bruner (1996), Cole (1996), Wertsch (1998) and Engeström et al. (1999) that builds upon the work of Vygotsky. A good summary of the general approach is provided by Lave in the introduction to the book she edited with Chaiklin: *Understanding Practice* (1996: 8). She sets out 'four premises concerning knowledge and learning in practice' that were agreed upon by all those who attended the working conferences which gave rise to the book.

1   Knowledge always undergoes construction and transformation in use.

2   Learning is an integral aspect of activity in and with the world at all times. That learning occurs is not problematic.

3   What is learned is always complexly problematic.

4   Acquisition of knowledge is not a simple matter of taking in knowledge; rather, things assumed to be natural categories, such as 'bodies of knowledge,' 'learners,' and 'cultural transmission,' require reconceptualization as cultural, social products.

The concept of 'situated cognition' is of great importance for pedagogy (Brown et al., 1989). Its central tenet is that learning is always contextualized. According to Brown et al., knowledge in the educational domain is commonly treated as abstract, neutral and decontextualized. They argue that the context in and activities through which learning takes place are an integral part of what is learned. Authentic activities, they contend, are made available in communities where members co-construct a particular view of the world through socially shared 'webs of belief' (1989: 33). The environment in which the learner engages in learning is an integral part of the learning experience and shapes that which is learned. For example, if a student learns science in a science laboratory working alongside professional scientists, the individual is immersed in that community's culture. A school science laboratory may not provide the features of 'authentic' activity and may therefore both fail to provide insights into the 'real' work of science and render learning school-specific rather than scientifically apt. If the situated nature of cognition is ignored, Brown et al. maintain, schooling is unable to provide robust, useable knowledge.

They provide examples, drawn from observation and interview data with secondary school students of mathematics, that demonstrate learning 'short-cuts' that may potentially interfere with the intended development of understanding. They strongly indicate that the school system has taught these students that the purpose of education is to make good use of short-term memory in preparation for tests. The school context is, therefore, likely to interfere with conceptual learning. Further, there is strong evidence that schools may provide structures which cause many children to develop a 'failing' identity. Lave, with reference to case studies of learning in *Understanding Practice*, writes: 'Paradoxically, learning craftwork may appear easy in the chapters in Part II [i.e. the workplace settings] whereas in Part III it often seems nearly impossible to learn in settings dedicated to education' [brackets added for this text] (1996: 9). She goes on to say:

[The case studies in educational settings] provide evidence of the socio-cultural production of failure to learn. [. . .] They are about how people learn identities and identify the situated meaning of what is to be learned, and the specific shaping of people's identities as learners. [. . .] Students who fail (and perhaps the most successful as well) are the sacrificial lambs whose fates give material form to legitimate knowledge. (1996: 10–11)

The concept of 'distributed cognition' (Salomon, 1993) originates in Vygotsky's notion that talk and interaction assist learning. It builds on his theory, for example, that inter-mental activity is internalized as intra-mental activity, and that, through interaction with a supportive adult or peer, learners can move beyond their current range of ability and function at a higher level within their 'zone of proximal development'. But 'distributed cognition' takes this further. What can be understood and achieved by a group of learners working together can often be more than any one learner could understand and achieve alone. Or, to take Hutchins and Klausen's example of airline pilots working in a team, not only was the pilots' knowledge distributed between themselves with variations in understanding and expertise, they also relied upon the representational instruments that were

available for their shared use. The researchers needed 'a unit of analysis' that 'must permit us to describe and explain the cognitive properties of the cockpit system that is composed of the pilots and their informational environment. We call this unit of analysis a system of distributed cognition' (Hutchins and Klausen, 1996: 17).

The concept of a 'community of practice' is used by Lave and Wenger (1991), and later by Wenger (1998), in slightly different ways. In some senses, in the earlier book it serves as a metaphor for an ideal learning context in which new members of the community can engage in 'legitimate peripheral participation' and be inducted into the community. However, in the second book, the two opening 'vignettes' of working environments are used as the basis for developing a descriptive framework for analysing the practices of any working group. While any community of practice will potentially be a supportive community in which 'apprentices' could engage in legitimate peripheral participation, this fuller description of a community of practice reflects the tensions of actual workplaces. These communities of practice are real cases, not ideal types.

'Legitimate peripheral participation' in a 'community of practice'

Legitimate peripheral participation as described by Lave and Wenger (1991) is about learning through a form of apprenticeship within a community of practice. Learners learn by participating in a community of practitioners; they undertake tasks which contribute to the productive activity of the enterprise. The newcomer is not just an observer but also a participant at increasingly multiple levels as a member of the community (1991: 98). As participants share understandings about what they are doing and what that means, the apprentice absorbs and is absorbed by the 'culture of practice' (1991: 95). 'Activities, tasks, functions, and understandings do not exist in isolation; they are part of broader systems of relations in which they have meaning' (1991: 53).

Acceptance by and interaction with 'acknowledged adept practitioners' (1991: 110) makes learning legitimate and of value for the apprentice. Legitimacy is a way of belonging and becoming. Peripherality is viewed positively; it is dynamic in the sense that it enables access to sources of understanding through growing involvement. Apprentices begin with basic tasks and gradually take on increasing responsibility when they are ready. Furthermore, 'benign community neglect' (1991: 93) provides the space to learn from other apprentices. In this way, individuals move from peripheral to more intensive participation, and towards full participation in the community (from newcomers to old timers). There are strong goals for learners because, as legitimate peripheral participants, they can develop a view of what the whole is about and what there is to be learned.

Legitimate peripheral participation is not just about goals, tasks and knowledge acquisition but also identity. In performing new tasks and demonstrating new understandings, learners' identities are transformed. Furthermore, this is a two-way process. Communities of practice exist of and depend on membership and the relationships, practices and biographies therein. As well as apprentices developing knowledgbably skilled identities through participating in the practices of the community, the community of practice is itself transformed. Thus a community is not complete in the sense of a closed domain of knowledge or collective practice. Learning involves the co-construction of identities.

Apprenticeship is more about learning than teaching. Unlike schooling where the focus is on individual progress, the (changing) person is not the central motive of the enterprise in which learning takes place. Engagement in practice is not an objective but the condition for effective learning. The community of practice itself provides the 'curriculum'. Learners learn from and in the presence of 'masters', for example 'expert' midwives, tailors and quartermasters (1991: 67–76). Nevertheless, a decentred view means that mastery resides not in an individual master but in the organization of the community of practice of which the master is part.

Wenger's community of practice as an analytic framework

In his 1998 book, Wenger develops the notion of community of practice into a fully described theoretical framework. His starting point is that 'a social theory of learning must [. . .] integrate the components necessary to characterize social participation as a process of learning and of knowing' (Wenger, 1998: 4–5). He lists these components as 'meaning', 'practice', 'community' and 'identity'. He then defines communities of practice as all those overlapping social groupings which are an integral part of our daily lives.

Meaning is constructed within communities of practice through the dual process of 'participation'

and 'reification'. It is important to note that whereas many writers use the word reification to describe loss of subjective meaning in a negative sense, for Wenger this process of depersonalizing ideas plays a key part in strengthening and developing the power of abstract thought. He argues that through participation we mutually construct our identities and through reification we identify and accord meanings to abstract concepts so that we can own them and manipulate them. 'Whereas in participation we reorganize ourselves in each other, in reification we project ourselves onto the world, and not having to recognize ourselves in those projections, we attribute to our meanings an independent existence' (1998: 58).

Community is constructed and made coherent by practice. There are three dimensions of this process: 'mutual engagement', 'a joint enterprise' and 'a shared repertoire' (1998: 73). After detailed analysis of how these operate in practice, Wenger points out that they are not always in place in a community of practice. However, he goes on:

> Still, most of us have experienced the kind of social energy that the combination of these three dimensions of shared practice can generate. Conversely, we may also have experienced how this social energy can prevent us from responding to new situations or from moving on. (1998: 85)

Wenger explores the implications of this concept of communities of practice, opening up fascinating insights into workplace experience and related learning. He focuses upon the individual's membership of multiple communities of practice and the way that the learning from across these communities overlaps or sets up boundaries. In the second half of the book the emphasis is on the impact on individual identity of membership in a community of practice, and the power implications and politics of membership. The framework provides a very useful tool for analysing the practice of groups or organizations. It also provides an excellent tool for analysing the context for legitimate peripheral participation, uncovering the positive features of some workplaces and the less ideal aspects of others as sites of participatory learning.

Implications for research design

The notion of a community of practice provides a very useful theoretical framework for research into the social processes of groups in contexts such as the home, the workplace or the local community. The starting point is likely to be broad, exploratory research questions rather than specific focused ones: for example, how do these people relate to each other? what is it like to become a member of this community? what is their joint enterprise? what is their shared history? how does membership of this community shape individual identity? what are different individuals learning? The research setting will be within the community itself and a wide range of data will be needed to enable holistic analysis of its structures, rituals, repertoires and relationships. Immersion in the community and observation 'from within' as a participant might be one approach; in-depth interviewing with a focus on eliciting detailed descriptions of activities might be another; a combination of both approaches probably better than either one or the other. In the 'story from the field' that follows the concept of 'overlapping' communities of practice leads to an extensive, complex analysis of individual identity, motivation and achievement. In the article by Somekh and Pearson (2002) vignettes describing group interactions at international meetings become the focus for holistic analysis of the workings of a project team drawn from several European countries undertaking collaborative research. Since a community of practice is defined by the details of its interactions, shared stories and memories, research reports are likely to include portrayals of persons and places.

Stories from the Field

David Benzie

Some of my students are really good with IT while others just don't get it. Why? And what can I do about it?

I teach students in higher education to use computers. In broad terms, the aim is to develop their information technology (IT) capability to the point where they are able to make effective personal and professional use of technology. Some of my students are aspiring school teachers and their courses take place in a context where there is considerable pressure to make effective use of computers in the classroom.

It was against this background that I decided to conduct a three-year longitudinal study of a cohort of undergraduate students with the initially stated aim of illuminating the way in which undergraduate students

perceive, acquire and deploy IT skills during the course of their study (Benzie, 2000). As with much practitioner research, it was not driven by the desire to explore the issue from a particular theoretical perspective. Rather, the driving force was a desire to provide an interpretation of the student experience that would be helpful to those who are responsible for teaching and supporting students in contexts where there is an IT dimension. What I failed to notice at the start, and for some considerable time, was the extent to which the implicit assumption that IT capability is an individual attribute and that the acquisition and deployment of IT skills are separate, albeit related, activities was framing my thinking. These assumptions were first exposed, and then rejected, as Lave and Wenger's (1991) and Wenger's (1998) theories slowly moved from off-stage to centre-stage during the main analytical phase of the research. The story of the research illustrates how and why this happened.

The starting assumption was that a number of research tools would be needed in order to track changes in IT skills and IT-related attitudes over time. (Literature suggested that the latter might be significant.) Additionally, it was assumed that instruments would be needed to illuminate the actual use of IT by students and to identify the contexts in which their learning occurred. Against this background an IT skills self-assessment questionnaire and three IT-related attitude scales were developed. These instruments also collected routine nominal data. In addition, an 'IT diary' was created which individual students used to record IT-related activities over a week. These diaries were themselves linked to a series of interviews. After 2½ years, 225 students had completed the questionnaires on three occasions. About 20 students kept IT diaries covering 182 distinct weeks. Eighty-three interviews were conducted, the majority being linked to a recently completed IT diary.

Early assumptions were also made about the relationship between the data from the different instruments. Foremost among the assumptions was the expectation that the large IT skills questionnaire and attitude data sets, together with coded quantitative data from the IT diaries, would be the main source of insight. The interviews were merely seen as having a role to play in assessing the reliability and validity of the IT diaries. But it did not turn out that way!

As the research progressed the stories from the interviews became ever more fascinating. An early change of perspective came when it became clear that the real power of the IT diary came from its ability to trigger interview dialogue. Attributing a code to the diary entry 'spent 2 hours word-processing an essay' and subsequently analysing many hundreds of similar entries is all very well, but it simply fails to catch the social reality that often lies behind such bald statements. It was not untypical, for example, for a diary entry like this to be the product of a complex social negotiation between family members who each wished to use the single available computer. In this situation, power relationships and value systems within the family led to one claim becoming privileged. Experiences like this had two important consequences. Firstly, the perceived relationship between diary and interview switched with the diary ultimately seen as an interview discussion starter. Secondly, the stories generated by the interviews began to highlight the profound significance of social context in shaping the way in which students interact with computers.

The full data set was available shortly after the self-assessment questionnaire and the attitude surveys were completed for the third time. By then it was clear that the interview data was going to be at least as significant as the quantitative data but it was not clear how the various data sets would finally relate to one another, or even how a single theoretical framework could be used to create a coherent account of all the available data. Against this background, an extensive exploration of the quantitative data set was undertaken and a number of statistically significant patterns did emerge. There was, however, one pivotal pattern that shifted the theoretical focus of the research. The quantitative data showed, with exceptional clarity, that patterns in the development of self-assessed IT skills varied tremendously from student to student. Some students who started their degree course with very low skills made huge progress while others made almost none. This pattern of differential progress was repeated for students at every level of initial skill.

The nominal variables of age, gender and degree course provided no accessible explanation for this pattern, though the nominal variables associated with attendance on an IT course and with computer ownership did point to other intriguing patterns. IT-focused courses, unsurprisingly, made a significant difference to self-assessed IT skills, but it was also clear that some students who did not attend a course also managed to make gains. Where and how was that learning taking place? What was more, attending an IT course did not appear to affect the future development of self-assessed IT skills. In other words, students did not appear to have learnt how to continue learning about IT.

It was at this stage, over three years into the research, that the full analytical focus switched to the qualitative data generated by the interviews. Could it explain the patterns evidenced in the quantitative data? The interview data had already been explored to some extent using Strauss and Corbin's (1990) approach to grounded theory and this acted as a powerful sensitizing agent. In particular, that exploration highlighted the significance, and complexity, of context-related features in shaping each individual's 'IT story' over a period of time. This experience, together with a preliminary reading of Lave and Wenger (1991), led to an 'informed guess'. The hunch was that Lave and Wenger's framework, with its focus on the situated nature of learning, might illuminate the data from a perspective that would lead to a coherent account of the patterns that had been observed.

The next stage in the research involved a close reading of Lave and Wenger (1991) with two main aims, the first being to immerse myself in their perspective and the second being to highlight key questions given what I already knew from the interview data. Those key questions included fundamental ones concerning the concept of a community of practice – how does it translate from the well-bounded contexts described by Lave and Wenger (1991) to the rather different settings that are found in higher education? Other key questions were less fundamental but equally intriguing. Lave and Wenger (1991: 57, 93), for example, draw passing attention to the role that near-peers play in learning yet the first reading of my data suggested this role was highly significant.

Following this, the full data sets (quantitative data, IT diaries and interviews) for two students, Adam and Hazel, were used as the basis for detailed case studies. These were designed to explore the questions that arose from the reading of Lave and Wenger (1991). Wenger's (1998) later book was published around this time, and from that point on it too had an impact on the analysis. The exploration of the experiences of these two students now moved to centre stage in the research. The quantitative data, originally seen as having the leading role, now moved to become part of the supporting cast.

Both stories provided challenges to theory while also affirming many key tenets. Communities of practice were clearly visible as discernable and useful analytic units in the stories of both students, though the demarcation of boundaries was more problematic than even Wenger (1998: 103) suggests. The experiences of Adam and Hazel, for example, suggest that the demarcation of a community is itself a situated act (Benzie, 2000: 163). Where a boundary is drawn depends on who is drawing the boundary and for what reason. This is particularly important to recognize when seeking to use this theory in settings where the unit labelled as a community is either transient or of secondary significance (or both) to those involved.

As the analysis proceeded it also became clear that Adam and Hazel's experiences could only be understood by recognizing that they were both members of multiple communities of practice and that they were both members of contemporary and historic communities. It also became clear that both students needed to be seen as active agents in multiple communities with their membership in each community having an impact on their membership in others. This in turn led to a theory of participation that suggests that the pattern of an individual's participation in a community of practice is shaped by the resulting force from three web-like structures. The first web concerns legitimacy: what are the values and rationales that a community uses to legitimate and promote certain activities? For a given individual these legitimating rationales have to be set against the legitimizing rationales that are available to them through their membership in other communities. Inevitably, the individual actively traverses this web of available rationales as they choose to engage or otherwise in community activity. The other webs concern power and motivation.

Hazel's story powerfully illustrates this theory of participation. She knew that playing and 'fiddling around' are leading legitimate activities in many IT-related communities yet deep in her value system was the notion that learning and playing are illegitimate bedfellows. She always struggled when her courses involved work with a computer. The explanation for the difficulties that she experienced is grounded in Lave and Wenger's (1991) and Wenger's (1998) theories. It illustrates how they can be used as a foundation for accounts of learning that respect social complexity.

There were two other significant outcomes from the research that could be directly attributed to the decision to use a theory concerning communities of practice. Firstly, a theory of IT capability was created that recognizes the mutually constitutive nature of a community and its members (Benzie, 2000: 190). A distinctive feature of the theory is its inclusion of IT capability descriptors for the community as well as for the individual. This symmetry is a consequence of working in a theoretical framework that relentlessly drives issues of context and relationship to the fore.

The second significant outcome was an explanatory model for the failure of some individuals to make effective use of IT. The distinctive feature of the model is that it explains failure without giving primacy to matters of individual cognitive inadequacy (Benzie, 2000: 217). Again, this arose because the underlying theory shifts the focus in discussion of learning from matters of cognition to ones of enculturation.

The strength of working with an analytical framework that has the concept of a community of practice at the centre is that it emphasizes the situated nature of knowledge and brings matters of context to the fore. It highlights relationships both between individuals and between individual and community. In this way, it is well suited to supporting accounts that capture social complexity.

Working with community of practice theory does, however, bring particular challenges. Any given community has a complex set of relationships with other communities and so consideration of its affairs inevitably requires matters in other contexts to be scrutinized. Wenger (1998) provides a comprehensive taxonomy of entities and concepts that assist analysis. The complexity of the terminology may be seen as a barrier but it does provide a vocabulary that enables social complexity to be probed.

There is a mutually constitutive relationship between a community of practice and the individuals who belong to it. In research terms, this is particularly powerful because it forces individual-centric studies to take account of social structures and provides the means to do so. Conversely, it forces studies that focus on social institutions and groupings to account for active individuals whose behaviours are shaped by their experiences in multiple contexts.

Annotated bibliography

Brown, J.S., Collins, A. and Duguid, P. (1989) 'Situated cognition and the culture of learning', *Educational Researcher*, 32(Jan.–Feb.): 32–42.

This is a seminal paper on the concept of situated learning. It presents an overview of theories developed at the end of the 1980s and argues for the importance of matching the context of learning to the subject of study.

Chaiklin, S. and Lave, J. (1996) *Understanding Practice: Perspectives on Activity and Context*. Cambridge, New York and Melbourne: Cambridge University Press.

This book originated in a two-part conference between researchers of learning in the USA and Europe (particularly Scandinavia). The opening chapter provides an excellent introduction to current thinking (in 1996) on the importance of the context of learning. The contributors' approaches are varied, but all agree on the situated nature of learning and the importance of creating supportive environments.

Hogan, K. (2002) 'Pitfalls of community-based learning: how power dynamics limit adolescents' trajectories of growth and participation', *Teachers College Record*, 104(3): 586–624.

In this article, situated learning theory is used to study the power dynamics that intervene as students move from peripheral to participants in an environmental management community.

Lave, J. and Wenger, E. (1991) *Situated Learning: Legitimate Peripheral Participation*. Cambridge, New York and Melbourne: Cambridge University Press.

This book describes how some elements of community-based learning can be accounted for socially, and provides a theory of apprenticeship that illustrates how people become part of a community.

Nardi, B. and O'Day, V. (1999) *Information Ecologies*. Cambridge, MA: MIT Press.

Although they do not use the term 'communities of practice' Nardi and O'Day's concept of an 'information ecology' provides a very similar framework to analyse the development of social practices mediated by on-line networks and communities of ICT users.

Salomon, G. (ed.) (1993) *Distributed Cognitions: Psychological and Educational Considerations*. Cambridge, New York and Melbourne: Cambridge University Press.

An excellent collection of papers by leading thinkers in the study of the mind, many of them relating their ideas to practical contexts.

Somekh, B. and Pearson, M. (2002) 'Inter-cultural learning arising from pan-European collaboration: a community of practice with a "hole in the middle" ', *British Educational Research Journal*, 28(4): 485–502.

In this article vignettes are used to provide insights into the relationships between team members working on an international collaborative research project. Analyses of relationships and intercultural learning are drawn out from these descriptive passages.

Wenger, E. (1998) *Communities of Practice: Learning, Meaning and Identity*. Cambridge, New York and Melbourne: Cambridge University Press.

This classic book on communities of practice is the successor to Lave and Wenger's earlier book on legitimate peripheral participation. The two concepts are closely related, but the ideas in the earlier book are considerably extended and adapted in this one.

Wenger, E., Snyder, W. and McDermott, R.A. (2002). *Cultivating Communities of Practice: A Guide to Managing Knowledge*. Cambridge, MA: Harvard Business School Press.

In this book Wenger and colleagues describe different steps and principles for building a community of practice and its evaluation.

Further references

Benzie, D.H. (2000) *A longitudinal study of the development of information technology capability by students in an institute of higher education*. PhD dissertation. University of Exeter. Available from <dbenzie@ marjon.ac.uk>.

Bourdieu, P. (1977) *Outline of a Theory of Practice*. Cambridge and New York: Cambridge University Press.

Bruner, J. (1996) *The Culture of Education*. Cambridge, MA and London: Harvard University Press.

Cole, M. (1996) *Cultural Psychology: A Once and Future Discipline*. Cambridge, MA and London: Belknap Press of Harvard University Press.

Engeström, Y., Miettinen, R. and Punamäki, R.-L. (eds) (1999) *Perspectives on Activity Theory. Learning in Doing: Social, Cognitive, and Computational Perspectives*. Cambridge, New York and Melbourne: Cambridge University Press.

Hutchins, E. and Klausen, T. (1996) 'Distributed cognition in an airline cockpit', in Y. Engeström and D. Middleton (eds), *Cognition and Communication at Work*. Cambridge, New York and Melbourne: Cambridge University Press, pp. 15–34.

Lave, J. (1996) 'The practice of learning. Understanding practice: perspectives on activity and context', in S. Chaiklin and J. Lave (eds), *Understanding Practice: Perspectives on Activity and Contex*. Cambridge, New York and Melbourne: Cambridge University Press.

Strauss, A. and Corbin, J. (1990) *Basics of Qualitative Research*. London: Sage.

Wertsch, J.V. (1998) *Mind as Action*. New York and Oxford: Oxford University Press.

chapter 22

ACTIVITY THEORY

Ines Langemeyer
Department of Psychology, Centre for Media Research, Freie Universität Berlin, Germany
Morten Nissen
Department of Psychology, University of Copenhagen, Denmark

Key concepts

Morten Nissen

CHAT – Cultural-Historical Activity Theory – was born when Lev Vygotsky, in the 1920s and 1930s, inspired by the Russian revolution, began to reformulate his research in linguistic and developmental psychology into an outline of principles for a psychology drawing on Marxist insights. Psychic phenomena, in particular the higher functions specific to humans, must be viewed primarily as social activities mediated by tools. Tools are cultural objects, social forms that develop historically, and language is the overall most important structure of social forms which organize thinking, perception, emotion, action and so on conceptually.

In psychology, these are highly controversial ideas, since psychology has typically attempted to establish itself by demarcating a field which is precisely not socio-cultural and historical. And if we try to spell out their implications in terms of research methods, we run into yet another provocation: while much psychology is strictly 'going through the movements' of what is perceived as a 'scientific' methodology, regardless of its object of study, CHAT is carried out in a wide variety of activities, many of which would normally not be recognizable as scientific methods at all. Nevertheless, this is what we will do – asking the reader to be prepared to question everything, even the concept of method itself.

The first implication is that of an inherently interdisciplinary approach to any phenomenon studied. This has been most outspoken at psychology's borders with philosophy and socio-cultural studies. In the latter case, various concepts have been adapted that serve to mediate phenomena which

appear to be features of individuals and their functions. Prominent among these have been broadly anthropological and socio-linguistic ideas such as Bakhtin's notion of dialogism (Wertsch, 1991) or, more recently, Latour's idea of actor-networks (Middleton and Brown, 2000). With the help of such mediators, thoughts and actions can be viewed as creations, appropriations and uses of cultural forms rather than merely 'natural' entities, and as forming part of wider social practices.

In relation to philosophy, Jensen (1999) has referred to CHAT as a 'science of categories', since it not only begins by reworking the categories that frame research, but also takes categories to be at the same time as cultural forms part of its subject matter. For reworking categories, a genuinely theoretical methodology is derived from the dialectical tradition of Hegel, Marx and their followers (Ilyenkov, 1977). According to this, the point is not to stipulate terms that 'match' things that exist. Rather, it is to create models which, in their conceptual hierarchies, reconstruct contradictory moments (or aspects) of development. Thus the theoretical questions are the likes of: 'How did this quality (this function, dimension, aspect of life, this feature) come to be? What does it presuppose? How does it transform, and how does it differentiate into opposing forms?'

This way of questioning leads us to the second implication for methodology: Vygotsky stressed the historical approach as the most fundamental principle:

To study some thing historically means to study it in the process of change; that is the dialectical method's basic demand. To encompass in research the process of a given thing's development in all its phases and changes – from birth to death –

fundamentally means to discover its nature, its essence, for 'It is only in movement that a body shows what it is'. (Vygotsky, 1978: 64–5)

In CHAT, we can distinguish at least three important historical dimensions. First, there is the all-encompassing history in which all forms of existence – such as the psyche, meaning, learning or play – were developed, even long before humanity. To gain a theoretical framework, we must reconstruct the emergence and transformations of such most basic qualities, using data from biology, paleontology, philosophical anthropology and so on, and the most decisive issue is how life changed with the advent of Humanity. For instance, 'learning' is no longer, as in apes, just building from experience or socialization into given norms but, as 'human learning', it is the appropriation of culture and the enhancement of participation in a proactive control of life circumstances. Secondly, there is the cultural history of any issue at hand; thus, for instance, studying the way the ideas and the forms of 'learning' changed when schools, and later school disciplines (subjects) were invented helps us understand how the issue itself has been framed, how learning is bound up with 'knowledge' and 'teaching', and how the 'scholastic' prejudices that arise from this may be overcome. Finally, investigating the specific histories of the living communities, individuals and activities studied forms the overall approach to live empirical data: in CHAT, all psychology is 'developmental psychology'.

The way this developmental approach is realized is itself another methodological implication of the basic ideas. If thinking is basically a social activity mediated by tools, and research is no exception, the implication is that we always gain understanding through intervention. This is true of natural processes and conditions, the general laws of which we conjecture from manipulating their particular instances. And it is even more obvious if we consider cultural forms: if the objects we study are socio-cultural creations, we do not stand outside them and watch, neither do we just manipulate them: we co-create them. In psychology, the understanding of research as basically interventionist leads to an experimental approach, and the understanding that intervention is basically productive leads to the idea of what Vygotsky called an 'experimental-genetic' method: studying 'higher mental functions' by creating them. Accordingly, the particular people and activities studied are not viewed as a sample but as a prototype. A prototype is different from a sample in that it is something new. And, as in the case of industrial design, the questions of generality and validity are important, of course, but they are subsumed to the idea of relevance, and thus allow and demand – and include in methodological reflection – all the adjustments and mediations on the way from the abstract idea (drawn from the prototype) to its various concrete realizations.

A striking early example was the expedition to Uzbekistan in the 1920s (Luria, 1976). Vygotsky was critical of developmental psychology, notably that of Piaget, for regarding cognitive functions as merely maturing or developing in the course of the individual's own activities. The developmental level of formal logical thinking was seen by Vygotsky to evolve through the social practice of schooling. So, his colleagues Luria and Leontiev accompanied the literacy campaign in Central Asia to contribute and record the historical development of this highest form of conceptual thinking, demonstrating qualitative differences between peasants' conceptual reasoning before and after learning to read, write and calculate.

The researchers not only documented events, but themselves suggested practical interventions. Sometimes, special arrangements were constructed for the sake of research itself – such as the cognitive tests the peasants were asked to perform – but in general, the prototype was the 'real-life' practice of teaching and learning. The core of the methodology was the ongoing reflections that connected the emerging practical prototype with general theorizing, leading to renewed practical changes and/or new tests and so on.

The implication of this process is that research methods develop as part of the social practices studied. This has been called a tool-and-result dialectics of method (Newman and Holzman, 1993), referring to a famous quote from Vygotsky:

The search for method becomes one of the most important problems of the entire enterprise of understanding the uniquely human forms of psychological activity. In this case, the method is simultaneously prerequisite and product, the tool and the result of the study. (Vygotsky, 1978: 65)

In other words, rather than a fixed set of rules or recipes to be followed, method is the ongoing theoretically informed reflection of the social practices in which research participates; yet method is also, still, a tool for research, a specific cultural object produced to form and transform that activity.

Objections have since been raised to the underlying colonial evolutionism of the Uzbekistan expedition which rendered the Russian cultural form as the 'highest'. But the expedition exemplifies the social engineering which lies at the heart of early CHAT. The project of understanding generic properties of the human psyche was closely connected with the project of creating the 'new man' of the 'new society' in the Soviet Union; the assumed general features of 'Humanity' were at once the overall determination, the germ cell from which later forms evolved and the ideal to be realized. This is, admittedly, a tricky idea, although essential to dialectics since Hegel. It has been much criticized as teleological and self-confirming dogmatism; it is often felt that understanding 'laws' and 'necessities' should be not only distinguished but kept apart from espousing 'values' or 'preferences'. Today, a CHAT scholar would reply that, while it is true that evolutionist ideas about a necessary development of our societies – such as the current belief that welfare states must succumb to a globalized neo-liberalism – are ideologies that obscure powerful interests, we would deceive ourselves if we were to think that laws can be studied with no values in mind, or that preferences are not subject to necessities. 'Teleology' is inescapable, but it should be regarded as the projects of people rather than of God, Spirit or History.

In other words, CHAT, methodologically, is a form of action research that stresses the integration of basic theoretical work with empirical-practical engagement. This integration is always a challenge, since it is a critical and inventive process – which implies some distance from the everyday. The idea of 'social engineering' suggests an inherent pitfall that sometimes has removed CHAT from the democratic standards of action research. Especially during Stalinism and the Cold War, political climates have nurtured elitist and technocratic conceptions of experimental-genetic methodology: dressed in the white cloaks of a 'science' aloof from controversial everyday life, researchers, in the East as in the West, could gain some protection from political censorships and still be funded to make a better world.

A strong counter-current emerged in the 1970s with the reception of CHAT into the context of the students' movement, the New Left and academic Marxism in the Western (European) countries. This was most outspoken in the 'critical psychology' which developed in West Germany and the Nordic countries. Here, the agenda was one of democratic

emancipation and, above all, critique of ideology: subjectivity as directly immersed in contentious social practice was the focus and the starting point for a process that would seek to reconstitute subjects as they reconstructed and transformed the cultural categories and conditions that shaped their lives (see Haug, 1999). In this context, building on CHAT as a Marxist foundation of psychology was an alternative to either abandoning psychology altogether as a form of 'bourgeois ideology' or developing it from critical psychoanalysis. The CHAT legacy implied a notion of subjectivity as a productive and reflective agency, but the irrevocable implication of ideology critique was an anchoring of research in participants' experience. This was elaborated in the seminal 'Foundation of Psychology' (Holzkamp, 1983), where the phenomenologically inspired consequence was drawn that people should never be made the objects of research, only its agent-subjects. Viewed in the larger framework of CHAT, this epitomizes a discernible general tendency toward employing hermeneutic methodologies – above all, the qualitative interview – to elicit participants' subjective perspectives. Sometimes this amounts to a pitfall opposite to that of technocratic experiments, responding in a different way to the challenge inherent in critical research: seeking to carve out a space of free inter-subjective communication and disavowing the objectification inherent to research as to any social practice. But on the whole, contemporary CHAT embraces the democratic lessons that date back to Aristotle's notion of phronesis, where each participant has something to contribute to the truth, while also maintaining that achieving this 'truth' is the practical production of a real-life prototype.

Implications for research design

Your first step – although these points should not be read as occurring in a linear sequence – is a historical reconstruction of the category studied. Although its dimensions vary from preliminary readings to full-blown research projects, this goes beyond the traditional state-of-the-art review in three ways: (1) it seeks out theoretical core problems and thus inevitably becomes interdisciplinary; (2) it transcends science to reconstruct the history of your category as a cultural element (not unlike a Foucauldian 'genealogy'); (3) it construes your topic as an instance of fundamental aspects of human life, reconstructing relevant concepts into this overall historical framework, and recasting the present issue critically in the light of these assumptions about what is human. For instance, if you want to understand 'humour', you might retrace the (historically recent) emergence of our current preparedness to consider humour legitimate in almost all spheres of life, read studies of anthropoid play behaviour or review theories of humour in philosophical anthropology in the light of basic CHAT ideas.

Your second step is to design or engage in a prototypical practice. Typically, of course, things work the opposite way around: various practical 'development projects' first exist and may or may not call for research. Either way, you should consider the relations of relevance between research problems and development problems: humour in learning may be an interesting topic, but it may not be the most promising approach to the problems faced in an urban secondary school. This is not simply a question of match; it is a ceaseless negotiation and developing of relevancies that runs parallel to your ongoing analysis of social conditions and is intimately connected with a 'political' dynamics of power balances, alliances and so on.

The third step is to objectify and inscribe the processes into data. Here, some relatively rigid discipline is required so that the structure of the transformations made can be retraced and critically reflected – whether your data are observation field notes, video or audio tapes, or samples of field materials (for example, school homework, official documents, websites, etc.). Specialized 'data production' activities may be useful as a deliberate part of both research and development of the prototype – such as interviews, diaries or documented reflection meetings and so on.

The fourth step is that of analysis, of objectifying activities into theoretically organized models which are constructed to challenge experience and theory (seek out contradictions), and to suggest ways to meet those challenges (mediate and resolve contradictions).

As far as possible, data and analyses should be produced and treated as the property of all participants, mediating a critical dialogue which transforms relevant cultural elements in participants' lives.

Finally, while analytical models are half-made artefacts used by all participants, academic writing achieves a closure that embodies the distances and tensions between the communities of your prototypical practice and of academia. Since this is likely to be both problematic and productive, itself conducive to

generalization, there are no stylistic conventions to cover that gap, but the gap, and the movements and transformations across it, is an important source of methodological reflection.

Stories from the Field
Ines Langemeyer

My story reports on a vocational course that provides a qualification in programming software tools, applications and data banks. This state-subsidized training programme was kept at low cost through adopting relatively self-dependent learning practices, among others 'e-learning' and 'training-on-the-job', in a 14-month-apprenticeship (which was partially financed by private companies). Several changes characterized the research field: the shift in the technological mode of production, the 'modernization' of the relations of production that include a political change towards a 'lean state' (analogous to 'lean production') and the current 'reforms' of the German public education system. By interviewing seven trainees four times (during 2002–3), I tried to reconstruct how each participant coped with the responsibility of learning under these conditions. My other focus was the notion of learning itself. To compare the trainees' with the teachers' perspectives I arranged a group discussion with the latter.

The first contact with the trainees was at the beginning of their apprenticeship after eight months on the course; two further interviews followed, and the last contact was after 15 months, one and a half months after they had finished the course. Their ages ranged from 27 to 52 and the ratio of five men to two women constituted an approximately representative sample of all the students on the course. My research aimed at a comparison of cases to analyse the particular developmental processes in relation to general societal transitions. It was motivated by specific theoretical results from former studies; nonetheless, the implications of the methods and the theoretical concepts that I referred to needed further reflection at every step of intervention and analysis.

My view of socio-technological change induced by information technologies was inspired by the Berlin research project on automation work (1972–87, directed by Haug – see PAQ, 1987) which can be summarized as follows: inventing, planning, executing and controlling were previously carried out within hierarchical organizations in which human involvement in the actual production process required above all physical power and manual skills. However, as a result of automation and computer technologies, work activities have become mainly intellectual: regulative, investigative, experimental and generally increasingly scientific. Procedures have merged into integral tasks and the former division of labour has become more or less obsolete. Due to a radical revision of the competences of, and demands on, the individual employee, industrial work has been partially 'humanized', but it also entails new contradictions and conflicts. The new, less hierarchical organization of work gives relative autonomy to the workers, but it is also experienced as an indirect form of coercion.

This contradiction became the starting point for a previous case study of programmers in 2000, in which I investigated subjective conflicts associated with this kind of autonomy (Langemeyer, 2003). To analyse interview data, I reconstructed how the new type of organization and regulation assigns a set ('dispositive') of various responsibilities to the employees. According to this, some of my interviewees had to think and act like entrepreneurs although they were not formally employed as such. These demands affected their motivation and commitment to working for the company. Thus some programmers undertook overtime willingly (or unwillingly) while others did not. The crucial question turned out to be whether, on the one hand, responsibilities had been 'individualized' or whether, on the other hand, cooperative and mutual support structures existed among the programmers. This clarified that the organization of responsibilities brings up power structures which foster the extensification and intensification of work.

In this study I challenged Holzkamp's (1983) view of competitive wage labour, in which he attributed constraints, such as the subordination of the self or self-adaptation to requirements (for example to work harder and faster than others), as indications of a 'restricted action potence', whereas the expansion of action possibilities and solidarity signified a tendency towards a 'generalized action potence'. His conceptualization suggested a dichotomy between a restricted and an extended range of action possibilities. But in my project where the programmers' conflict resulted from constraints arising from this new 'autonomy', analysis in terms of such a dichotomy would have been misleading.

Likewise, in this new research I challenged Holzkamp's analytical categories of learning. His foundation of a 'subject science of learning' (1993) focused

on the articulation of premises and motivations for learning. He assumed that contradictory educational practices resulted from whether someone learns 'defensively' or 'expansively'. He assumed a polarization between learners' efforts to adopt appropriate behaviours to avert negative effects (like bad grades) and positive endeavour that arises from learners' intentions to increase their power to learn. He argued that learning is not merely a mechanical internalization of ready-made facts, nor simply a performance of behaviour evoked by teaching. Rather, an individual always needs to be aware of a subjective problematic in order to start learning intentionally. Any institutionalized form of learning should take into account that the individual learners (subjects) need to recognize their own concerns within educational practice.

Although these reflections were quite useful, my interviews document that the conflicts did not stem from the power relations of a repressive institution that imposed its rules on the learners, but rather crystallized around the issue of responsibility. The trainees wanted to expand their opportunities for action and obtaining qualifications in information technology (IT), but faced a discrepancy between their desired and their actual performance and between planned achievements and any shortfall. Therefore, I decided to focus on the learning activities, their trajectories and boundaries, rather than conscious learning intentions. With regard to the scientific logic of IT, the interviewees reported how they organized their learning activities on their own. For them, it became paramount to identify a strategy to orientate their efforts, to collect the information that was relevant for solving a certain problem and to receive hints and suggestions for their problem-solving strategies. Most of the trainees discovered the convenience of addressing their questions to websites, chatrooms, newsgroups and also personally to their colleagues, yet during face-to-face meetings they were dissatisfied with their relationship with their teachers. The latter were organizing the programme as a team and in the group discussion they complained that poor communications among themselves had adversely affected the coordination of the programme, but that they did not see a way out. They said this was due to lack of time and blamed the trainees for deficiencies in 'social skills'. In interview, the trainees admitted being part of a 'difficult group'. On the other hand, they complained that the teachers neither kept their promises to support them individually nor managed to respond effectively to the wide disparity of aspiration levels during classes. In a few cases, the ineffectiveness of teaching did not affect the learners so badly, since their employers were able to arrange a support group at work. In 1999, in the beginning of this programme, successful employment after the apprenticeship assured the success of this shortened job training (22 months instead of three years), but the conditions did not remain the same. Because of a precarious economic situation, not many of the new trainees had prospects for employment. Since they needed to qualify for a tight labour market, they felt highly responsible for their own learning, but in view of the lack of job opportunities and the shortcomings of the programme they also gave up. The impact of this situation on their commitment nurtured permanent conflicts between trainees and teachers on the one hand and hassles among the classmates on the other. Repeatedly, conflicts arose about the methods and the organization of the course. These debates were symptomatic of a number of organizational inconsistencies and a rather 'mechanical' application of 'new' forms of learning. In spite of the potential for the trainees' critique to be instructive for the teachers, those debates did not cure the problematic situation, they rather impeded any improvement. Personal relationships seemed to be deadlocked. A 40-year-old trainee starkly pointed out that it was 'so stressful' for her to put up with 'stupid people' at the course and at work that she pretended to be sick in order to skip classes. She described experiencing a sense of 'being abandoned' on the one hand and 'not finding the right place in life' on the other. This not only indicates her suffering but also the resulting stalemate that made any development impossible – due to lack of support and her own loss of motivation.

During the research process, the generation of empirical methods or strategies and explanatory theoretical assumptions was intertwined. I constructed several theoretical perspectives that made the cases comparable as well as distinguishable: the mode of participation, the forms of cooperation, the formation of experience and personal development. While elaborating these perspectives as components of a theoretical explanation of the respective problems in practice, I also figured out what kinds of question were important for the next series of interviews and the next step of evaluation.

Through the analysis of conditions and relationships between specific educational practices, possibilities for development could be generated. Similar to Clot et al. (2001), I came to understand how generative structures of a learning culture not only depend on the material resources that are at someone's disposal but also on a certain kind of experience. As Clot et al. (2001: 23) explain, with reference to Vygotsky and Bakhtin, it is a new way of perceiving things and conditions that enables individuals to adopt new possibilities for action. This means that the personal activity process is generalized and its comprehension becomes richer by recontextualizing it. Thus, the individual (subject) gains the capability to reorganize his or her own activity. Of course, such a development is not achieved in isolation. Only in cooperation with others can subjects develop, on the basis of their spontaneous reactions, new cultural resources and a space for collective as well as individual reflexivity. This always takes place within the diversity of possible (realized and unrealized) activities, when someone focuses on an activity's distance from its potential advanced form, when individuals measure the distinction between an intended activity and its realization, when they understand the difference between isolated and cooperative engagement in an activity or learn about less and more adequate forms of cooperation, and so on. (Cooperation is not always identical with joint activity. Accordingly, collective forms of learning do not necessarily imply fruitful cooperations for learning activities.) Although I 'discovered' these generative structures by analysing and comparing the interview data, I did not initiate a process of joint reflection between interviewees on these available resources nor make any attempt to generate them in practice as Clot et al. did, for example, with their methodology of a 'crossed self-confrontation' – although this could have been a good way of extending this research project. Nevertheless, during the inquiry, I tried to support each interviewee to become aware of generative structures and common resources. For this purpose, the interviews were charactized by three major types of questions: first, questions to find out how the trainees relate themselves to the learning-demands and to the different learning practices; secondly, questions to let them report how they perceive and judge the activities and attitudes of their classmates, their teachers and their colleagues; third, questions to generate reflection on their own way of doing things and on alternative possibilities for changing practice.

The problems that emerged between the teachers and the course participants in relation to learning showed how important it is to develop those activities as an 'organic' whole in which its components (instrument, object, community, division of labour, and rules) are integrated, so that it forms a coherent complex (cf. Engeström, 1987: ch. 3.3) and thereby a cooperative power of action. Otherwise, it is likely that the subjects (those involved) internalize the respective contradictions, deal with them as internal conflicts and try – inevitably unsuccessfully – to solve them as individuals only.

Annotated bibliography

Chaiklin, S., Hedegaard, M. and Jensen, U.J. (eds) (1999) *Activity Theory and Social Practice: Cultural–Historical Approaches.* Aarhus: Aarhus University Press.

Papers by renowned authors centring mostly on philosophical and theoretical contributions. Useful in showing how CHAT is situated in contemporary off-mainstream psychology and cultural studies.

Daniels, H. (ed.) (1998) *An Introduction to Vygotsky.* London and New York: Routledge.

Accessible overview of Vygotsky's work combining reprints of key journal and text articles with editorial commentary and suggested further reading.

Engeström, Y. (1987) *Learning by Expanding: An Activity-Theoretical Approach to Developmental Research.* Helsinki: Orienta-Konsulit.

Provides an overview of CHAT approaches to learning and founds the approach to experimental-genetic studies of activity systems widely employed, especially at the Helsinki centre. Full text available at: <http://communication.ucsd.edu/LCHC/MCA/Paper/Engestrom/expanding/toc.htm>.

Ilyenkov, E.V. (1977) *Dialectical Logic. Essays on its History and Theory.* Moscow: Progress Publishers.

Reconstructs history of philosophy to achieve a dialectical understanding of the ideal as based on activity. Ilyenkov is one of the very few of the more recent Soviet philosophers who is still respected in today's philosophy. Full text available at: <http://www.marxists.org/archive/ilyenkov/works/essays/index.htm>.

Leont'ev A.N. (1981) *Problems of the Development of the Mind.* Moscow: Progress Publishers.

Systematic collection of papers from the 1930s and 1950s demonstrating general and specific research methodologies. This is the classic that introduces the overall historical approach to the psyche.

Tolman, C. and Maiers, W. (eds) (1991) *Critical Psychology. Contributions to an Historical Science of the Subject.* Cambridge: Cambridge University Press.

Central classical papers in the critical psychology branch of CHAT collected, introduced and contextualized for the English-speaking audience.

Vygotsky, L.S. (1962) *Thought and Language.* Boston: MIT Press.

The ultimate CHAT classic. Most of the text available as 'Thinking and Speaking' at: <http://www.marxists.org/archive/vygotsky/works/words/index.htm>.

Vygotsky, L.S. (1978) *Mind and Society.* Cambridge, MA: Harvard University Press.

Central text stating overall approach illustrated by experimental data. Most of the text available at: <http://www.marxists.org/archive/vygotsky/works/mind/index.htm>.

Wertsch, J.V. (1991) *Voices of the Mind. A Sociocultural Approach to Mediated Action.* Cambridge, MA: Harvard University Press.

Accessible general reconstruction of Vygotskian thinking into an American context, stressing socio-inguistic aspects and affiliation with Bakhtin.

Websites

The official website of the International Society for Cultural and Activity Research: <http://www.iscar.org>
The website for International Cultural-Historical Human Sciences: <http://www.ich-sciences.de>
Oldest and biggest international journal: *Mind, Culture & Activity*: <http://www.education.bham.ac.uk/research/ sat/publications/mca/default.htm>
Newer journal based in Denmark: *Outlines – Critical Social Studies*: <http://www.psy.ku.dk/forskning/Udgivelser/ Outlines/Outlines.html>
The Laboratory of Comparative Human Cognition (LCHC) at the University of California, San Diego, United States: <http://lchc.ucsd.edu/>
Centre for Sociocultural and Activity Theory Research (CSAT): <http://www.education.bham.ac.uk/research/sat/ default.htm>
Center for Activity Theory and Developmental Work Research (CATDWR): <http://www.edu.helsinki.fi/activity/>

Further references

Clot, Y., Prot, B. and Werthe, Chr. (2001) 'Special Issue: Clinique de l'activité et pouvoir d'agir', *Éducation permanente,* 146(1).

Haug, F. (1999) *Female Sexualisation. A Collective Work of Memory*. London: Verso.

Holzkamp, K. (1983) *Grundlegung der Psychologie*. Frankfurt am Main: Campus Verlag.

Holzkamp, K. (1993) *Lernen. Subjektwissenschaftliche Grundlegung*. Frankfurt amd Main: Campus.

Jensen, U.J. (1999) 'Categories in activity theory: Marx's philosophy just-in-time', in S. Chaiklin, M. Hedegaard and U.J. Jensen (eds), *Activity Theory and Social Practice: Cultural-Historical Approaches*. Aarhus: Aarhus University Press, pp. 79–99.

Langemeyer, I. (2003) 'Hyperlink zur Subjektivität. Verantwortung in der IT-Arbeit', in A. Dirbaumer and G. Steinhardt (eds), *Der flexibilisierte Mensch. Subjektivität und Solidarität im Wandel*. Heidelberg: Asanger, pp. 201–13.

Langemeyer, I. (2004) 'Widersprüche expansiven Lernens. Eine kritische Analyse neuer Lernformen in der Fachinformatikausbildung. Dissertation to be published.

Luria, A.R. (1976) *Cognitive Development: Its Cultural and Social Foundations*. Boston: Harvard University Press.

Middleton, D. and Brown, S. (2000) *Topologies of Durability and Transformation in Networks at Work: Exploring the Organization of Accountability and Agency in Neonatal Intensive Care*. Available online at: <http:// www.devpsy.lboro.ac.uk/psygroup/djm/BrazilDM%26SB.html>.

Newman, F. and Holzman, L. (1993) *Lev Vygotsky: Revolutionary Scientist*. London: Routledge.

PAQ (Projekt Automation Qualifikation) (1987) *Widersprüche der Automationsarbeit*. Berlin/W: Argument Verlag.

PART VI

SAMPLING, CLASSIFYING AND QUANTIFYING

Introduction

Part VI presents the theoretical origins of quantitative methods and an introduction to the wide range of tools and techniques that can now be applied in social science research. 'Quantitative methods' is a broad umbrella term for a huge range of specialized topics and approaches. Indeed there are many textbooks that focus entirely on one specific statistical technique and it is difficult to do any of them real justice in the space we have here. However, what we seek to do, as indeed we seek to do elsewhere in this book, is to provide a flavour of what is available and why it might (and should) be of interest to the social science researcher.

The first chapter describes the development of positivism (and post-positivism) which underpins quantitative methods in the social sciences, through the period of Enlightenment from theory testing grounded in reasoning and verification grounded in value-free observations to Popper's theory of falsification – the basis of many statistical tests today. The second chapter develops this further, highlighting the way in which positivism has been acknowledged by many as being important, and how it has been adapted within contemporary social science research in a variety of ways. Here, for example, the Story from the Field presents a combination of positivist and socio-cultural methods.

The third chapter serves as an introduction to many elements associated with quantitative methods, from defining basic terminology and underlying principles, to explaining sampling strategies, approaches to questionnaire design and statistical methods of organizing descriptive data. In the fourth chapter, techniques for identifying differences between groups (usually of people in the social sciences) and relationships between characteristics of a single group are presented. The fifth and final chapter discusses a range of approaches for modelling relationships between characteristics. In particular, multilevel modelling is introduced as a recent and important,

sophisticated yet flexible technique that has the potential to serve the needs of social scientists very well. It is based on the premise that analysis should take account of the similarities of members of a group (students in a class, nurses in a hospital and so on) because the contextual factors and influences are shared. Of course there will still be individual variation but this is also accounted for.

These latter three chapters seek to provide the reader with the language required to understand quantitative approaches and a flavour of what can be achieved with the diverse tools and techniques available, either in isolation or in combination with other methods. Stories from the Field which exemplify some of the techniques in practice, including multilevel modelling, and draw on elements from all three chapters are presented in Part VII.

There is a multiplicity of links between Part VI and others in the book. Part VI and Part VII are of course inextricably linked, the latter providing five 'stories from the field', and a chapter on mixed methodologies. Questionnaires are not exclusively quantitative and have a place in many qualitative and mixed method approaches. Sampling strategies are required in many spheres of research – how do you select which members of society should be interviewed for example? Holt (Corbin and Holt, in this volume) refers not only to sampling issues that he faced but describes his samples in terms of their average ages. Observation can be applied within quantitative research. Some techniques applied in discourse analysis involve counting occurrences of words in texts. In fact numbers occur in almost all research whether it be statistical analysis in a large-scale survey or reporting the number of people involved in an ethnographic study.

The editors would like to thank Peter F. Cuthbert, Business and Management Studies, Manchester Metropolitan University, for providing helpful comments and advice on drafts of Chapters 25–27.

23

THE FOUNDATIONS OF EXPERIMENTAL/EMPIRICAL RESEARCH METHODS

Dean Garratt
Education and Social Research Institute, Manchester Metropolitan University, UK
Yaojun Li
Department of Sociology, University of Birmingham, UK

Key concepts

Dean Garratt

The foundations of experimental/empirical research methods have a long and chequered past that can be traced to what is often, if somewhat indeterminately, referred to as the period of 'Enlightenment'. The mystique surrounding the 'Enlightenment Project' stems from its nebulous character, which is coloured by complexities of time, place and philosophical tradition. Conceptually, it is difficult to establish as a unitary social, political and/or philosophical movement, and any such attempt would amount to betraying its distinctively rich and diverse philosophical heritage. Over many years, writings have been produced for what have been termed as the 'French Enlightenment' (see Jimack, 1996), the 'Scottish Enlightenment' (see Stewart, 1996) and German 'Aufklärung' (see Kuehn, 1996). In real terms, none of these were completely isolated from, nor fully integrated with, their respective intellectual contemporaries. Rather, each movement had its own distinctive voice and thus made its own individual contribution to the Project. Yet, significantly, when taken together, all can be seen to share important common ground where the Enlightenment was perceived to stand for the 'rejection of traditional authority, especially that of the Church, . . . [the] bold and constructive attempt to understand and explain man and the universe, and in particular to define man's place and role in society, both as it was and as it should be' (Jimack, 1996: 228). Put simply, the Enlightenment may be conceived as the critical reaction towards, and purposeful examination of, previously accepted ideas from the point of view of reason.

The foremost exponent of 'reason' or 'rationalist thinking' was Descartes. Philosophically speaking, he paved the way for successive accounts of human knowledge (between 1637 and 1649) that were both broad ranging and incredibly complex (see, for example, Cottingham, 1998 for a lucid account of his work). Through the elaboration of a single 'method' (Sorrel, 1987), Descartes made a significant contribution to scientific thinking as we know it today. Interestingly, while on the one hand Descartes was often thought of as a rationalist in seeing knowledge as deriving from the intellect, on the other he was sometimes perceived as a keen experimenter, holding firm to the belief that experiment and observation were important preconditions in the quest for knowledge. As such, critics have argued as to whether his work contains considerable tensions (even contradictions) or interesting complementarities.

In contrast with Descartes, Locke (whose writings were published around 1690 to 1695) emerged from a different tradition of intellectuals – known collectively as 'empiricists'. Formed in Britain, empiricists believed that the source of all knowledge was not human reason but experience. However, while this movement was seen as separate and distinct from that of the 'rationalists', Locke's notion of ideas as 'whatsoever is the object of the understanding when a man thinks' (Locke, cited in Woolhouse, 1988: 80) and his conception of them as mind-dependent things might be easily viewed as Cartesian (i.e. deriving from Descartes). Moreover, like Descartes, Locke also believed that real knowledge must be certain and that mathematics, in its ability to provide essential proof and certainty, was the model of knowledge to which all other forms should sensibly aspire (Zaw, 1976). For Locke, then, all knowledge is based on ideas that are derived from experience or combinations of experiences, so that knowledge of social affairs is inextricably bound with our knowledge of physical phenomena. Finally, under the influence of Descartes, Locke also believed strongly in the idea that there is a duality of mind and matter, where the latter stands as a separate reality regardless of whether it is apprehended by the mind (Smith, 1989). This idea is at the heart of modern science where the outside world, viewed as separate from the senses, is to be discovered through systematic research and experimentation.

More than a century after Locke emerged the French social philosopher Auguste Comte (1798–1857). While it is debatable whether Comte was influenced directly by Locke, it is obvious that his elaboration of a positivist philosophy, as a basis for the practice of modern science, may be viewed as part of an overall empiricist tradition. As Smith suggests 'positivism provided a powerful statement for the unity of all the sciences and thus for the acceptability and necessity of employing the methods of the natural sciences in the study of social affairs' (1989: 40). The development of this conceptual framework, sketched by Comte, was influenced as much by the political mood of the moment as his undeniably distinctive philosophical thesis. Influenced by a group of French thinkers known as Encyclopedists (who predated Comte by some 50–75 years), noted for their hostility towards religion, disapproval of authority and rejection of the illusions of metaphysics in philosophy, Comte exalted the virtues of liberty, equality and an empiricist epistemology, the latter being undoubtedly influenced by the impact of the French Revolution. Comte saw the development of modern science as a panacea to a broad range of political and philosophical problems. Politically speaking, it would provide the basis for addressing what was often perceived as the 'disintegration' of society by establishing order, stability and social unity in response to an excessive and pernicious individualism. Philosophically speaking, it would provide the method for securing knowledge about society. By treating the social world in the same way as physical objects were treated by natural scientists, Comte believed that social researchers would develop their own practical mastery of knowledge, and thereby emulate the progress and success of the natural sciences. In meeting these requirements, it might then be possible for the social world to develop its own 'laws' of behaviour and in turn, from a utilitarian perspective, secure the preconditions for effective social engineering. This meant that in contrast with Descartes (who believed in the possibility of innate ideas and first principles), all positive knowledge, as certain and indubitable, should be grounded in observations and guided by the boundaries of our sensory experiences.

The legacy of Comtean positivism to the process of social inquiry has revealed a series of interrelated assumptions and methodological commitments. These are, namely, that theory is to be universal rather than specific or context-bound and principally concerned with the generation of scientific laws. Such laws are affirmed on predictions derived from the study of social phenomena, whose interrelated variables may be examined independently so as to provide plausible theories and conditionally predictable outcomes. A methodological commitment to researcher neutrality and the disinterested observation of events is included, as a regulative measure, to ensure that facts are free of values, opinions and personal interests. Together, these create a site for the production of disinterested knowledge and concomitant reliance upon mathematics in the process of theory construction (Sparkes, 1992; Popkewitz, 1984).

These points encapsulate the spirit of positivism and demonstrate clearly how the work of Descartes, Locke and the architects of the French Enlightenment had profound influence on Comte. Furthermore, they show how the study of social life deliberately employed the methodology of the natural sciences: a commitment to the discovery of social laws; the development of a methodology based on the observation of experiences and experiments; the separation of facts from values and, similarly, the cognizing subject from the object of cognition; and the reliance upon mathematics in the process of developing tested and proven knowledge (Smith, 1989).

In the years that followed came a forceful critical reaction to the assumptions that informed Comte's philosophy and, by association, against the entire edifice of empirical/experimental research. The legacy of positivism to contemporary social inquiry engendered an adherence to the strict separation of facts and values and compliance with the commitment to a disinterested science. During the early twentieth century this commitment was rehearsed and reshaped by a group of thinkers known as 'logical positivists'. For them, as with Comtean positivists, the project of science was predicated on empirical purity and logical reasoning. In keeping with the empiricist tradition of

Locke, logical positivists believed that all genuine knowledge (the product of scientific inquiry) could only be based on what is available to our senses, i.e. all that we observe. Opinions, values and metaphysical introspection were to be held separate from the process of the disinterested observation of events. Moreover, from within the Cartesian tradition, the concept of logical reasoning was employed as part of the language of an inductive science or the generation of ideas based on theoretical propositions or hypotheses. In this process observation would ultimately determine the falsity or truth of such propositions. All statements about the world commanded empirical verification (free of value judgements) in order for the 'facts' to be produced. This meant that all propositions must be proven beyond doubt before knowledge could be certified genuine.

By the mid-1950s philosophers began to acknowledge the frailty of this argument in recognizing that no proposition could be totally or completely verified through observation, and certainly not in the absence of an external referent that might adjudicate between truth claims. Recognizing the problems associated with induction and its methodological commitment to the verificationist model, Popper (1990, 1991, 1992) elaborated his own unique thesis. In contrast to his predecessors he suggested that while statements about the world can never be completely verified, they might nevertheless be tested and confirmed through scientific inquiry. For Popper, refutation rather than justification would become the regulatory ideal of modern science. Falsification is thus privileged over verification on the premise that, however much favourable evidence there might be to support a proposition, there can never be enough to completely verify any conclusion. More than this he suggested that the utilization of probabilities is equally problematic, since such appeals might be construed as being as much an inductive step as the verificationist model itself. In contrast, useful theories are selected on the basis of the degree of corroboration achieved by the theory. This means that only those with high explanatory power that have survived the most severe tests (those which have genuinely sought to refute rather than verify content), given current levels of knowledge and experience, can be temporarily confirmed.

Confirmation is thus predicated on high corroboration rather than high logical probability, and plausible theories are taken to be those that can withstand a harsh test. Such theories explain things about the world in ways that are persuasive and credible, and

which are supported by high levels of empirical evidence. This adds a qualitative dimension to the process of scientific reasoning, for it goes beyond the simple requirement of assigning credibility to a process of repeated testing. Indeed, repeated tests applied to a theory will not increase its respective content or degree of corroboration, simply because they lead to an increase in probability, which in Popper's terms is inductive rather than falsificationist. When comparing theories that seek to explain things about the same phenomena, Popper argues that each should be considered in terms of its verisimilitude (truth value) or relative degree of corroboration, neither of which are said to contain inductive nuances. In practice this means that in selecting particular theories we should seek those that contain greater empirical content (evidence to support the theory when tested) and which seem to offer greater precision and universality based on both retrospective and contemporary critical discussion.

This perspective, however, is itself wrought with deep philosophical tensions that ostensibly contain traces of inductive logic. For example, it is questionable whether Popper's notion of well-corroborated theories (those that have survived severe testing), representing an increase in truth-value, is completely immune to an inductive leap of faith. After all judgements concerning the nature of credible theories involve educated guesswork and speculation about the world, which in turn involve generating ideas that draw upon values and opinions that have predictive overtones. While arguments will undoubtedly continue, it is beyond the scope of this chapter to elaborate and extend the debate (for a detailed critical discussion of these issues see O'Hear, 1980).

Implications for research design
Yaojun Li

The discussion above carries important implications for empirical social research. As there has been much discussion on qualitative research in other chapters of this volume, we shall focus on the implications for quantitative research.

The first task in a quantitative study is to identify and define research questions that are theoretically aware and empirically testable. To be theoretically aware means that the researcher needs to be familiar with existing research in the area. For instance, ethnic penalty in occupational attainment may be our research question. There is a large body of research findings in the area and we need to know where and how to contribute, i.e. what research hypotheses to formulate and how to formulate them in a way that is amenable to empirical investigations. To do this, we need to ask: what is being debated on ethnic penalties? What evidence is there? What are the shortcomings in existing research and how can we improve on them?

The research question should be specific and measurable, capable of rigorous statistical analysis. For instance, what do we mean by 'occupational attainment'? Do we mean earning powers or access to different class positions? And how do we know whether or not there exists an ethnic penalty with regard to occupational attainment? There is, of course, no definitive answer to the question, but rigorous analysis can give us solid evidence. As soon as we begin to think in these terms, we see that research questions must be capable of being measured as 'variables' in the data sets.

This brings us to the question of availability and suitability of data. What data can we use for the research? Is it feasible to collect our own data, or are there existing data sets with sufficient sample sizes and representativeness that can serve our research purposes? Take the example of 'ethnic penalty' again. Social surveys usually do not contain sufficient sizes of minority ethnic groups. However, samples of anonymized records (SARs) from the 1991 and the 2001 UK censuses each contain over a million records, with 5 per cent and 8 per cent respectively belonging to the minority ethnic groups. The data also contain a lot of socio-economic information which can meet many of our research needs (see Li, 2004). Indeed, social researchers concerned with patterns and/or trends of important social issues find it increasingly necessary to use large-scale national representative data as they simply cannot afford to collect their own data. Fortunately, there are many data sets collected by government agencies and the academic community over the past decades which are free for academic users.[1]

Once we have well-formulated research questions and appropriate data sets, we need to know how to use the data to answer our research questions. Data analysis is both a science and an art. Training in social statistics and in the use of computer packages such as SPSS or Stata is needed, as is practice. Depending on the research question at hand, we may need descriptive statistics and/or advanced statistical modelling of various forms.

Stories from the Field

Yaojun Li

I now turn to my 'story from the field', which seeks to locate itself within a broadly Popperian framework. It provides an empirical test of competing sociological theories. We show how to use large-scale national representative surveys to test theories. The analysis also aims to show how Popper's idea of falsification is behind much of quantitative sociological research.

Two highly influential theories have been in debate over the class position of professionals and managers in contemporary Britain. They are 'the employment relationship theory' (Goldthorpe, 1982, 1987; Erikson and Goldthorpe, 1992) and 'the assets theory' (Savage et al., 1992; see also Wright, 1997). The first theory holds that the two groups belong to the same social class while the second theory holds that they belong to two different classes.

The employment relationship theory argues that both professionals and managers are members of the 'service class' because of the common employment relationship they have with their employing organizations. They are 'service' experts who provide specialist knowledge to, or exercise delegated authority on behalf of, their employers. Both kinds of services are prerequisite for the smooth and efficient running of modern organizations. In return for the services, they are compensated with secure employment, attractive remuneration and distinctive prospects of career advancement. Once access to the class is obtained, both groups will have a high degree of career continuity and a very low degree of subsequent long-range downward mobility. Furthermore, professionals will, as a defining characteristic of the service-class career, tend to move into senior management as their careers progress, which will facilitate the professionalization of management and reduce the cultural gap between the two groups. Finally, the distinctive socio-cultural-economic advantages enjoyed by the service class will be shared by their family members and passed onto their children for the intergenerational preservation of class advantages. Overall, the theory holds that the service employment relationship will lead professionals and managers to form a distinctive and increasingly consolidated service class.

The employment relationship theory acknowledges differences within the service class just as within other broadly defined classes. Differences within the service class lie both between the higher and the lower grades or 'echelons' of the class (called Classes 'I' and 'II'), and between the professional and the managerial 'situses'. The echelon relations represent a social and the situs relations represent a technical division of labour. Both echelon and situs effects will manifest themselves in certain aspects of their work and non-work lives but the differences are of an *intra*-class kind unrelated to their common employment relationship. In other words, the differences among the service-class groupings will be fairly small and comparable to those observed within the other main classes and, as such, will not constitute major divisions of an *inter*-class kind.

Challenging this is the 'assets theory', which seeks to develop a new theoretical perspective to the understanding of middle-class formation and action. The theory argues that underlying professional and managerial careers are two fundamentally different assets: cultural assets possessed by professionals and organizational assets possessed by managers. Cultural assets are objectified in credentials, embodied in the habitus (Bourdieu, 1984) and transferable from one context to another whereas organizational assets are context-specific and non-transferable. As a result, professionals will form a stable and cohesive social collectivity but managers will be marginalized with large numbers subject to long-range downward mobility in their career trajectories. In other words, the professional and managerial relations are *inter*- rather than intra-class. The theory further predicts 'a deepening of the split between professionals and management' (Savage et al., 1992: 217).

The exponents of the theories have conducted empirical research to support their arguments. However, owing to the different theoretical and methodological frameworks they use, the results they report are rarely comparable. The very fact of the theories being in two analytical paradigms (Kuhn, 1970) also makes their adjudication difficult. In order to test their claims, we must use systematic and rigorous analysis based on the most appropriate data and methods. Given that the theories have wide-ranging predictions over *the patterns and the trends* of professional and managerial class formation, it would be inappropriate to resort to in-depth interviews or focus groups to test their validity as these techniques are not designed for such purposes. In other words, we must use large-scale national representative surveys, standardized class categories and appropriate statistical methods to discern patterns and trends on the basis of which to make judgements over their respective validity. It is also the case that the theories make

claims over many areas of professional and managerial lives. It is not feasible to test all such areas within the space of this chapter but we can still give some illustrations where such a study can be illuminating (see Li, 1997 and 2002 for further discussion). In the remainder of this section, I shall use the General Household Survey (GHS) in the UK for twenty consecutive years (1973–92) to analyse the patterns and trends of mate selection between professionals and managers, and the distributions of degree-holders in the different groupings of the 'service-class' positions, as a means of establishing the class character of the two groups.

The rationale for choosing these two aspects is their direct relevance to the debate between the theories. As Max Weber points out, 'The primary practical manifestations of status with respect to social stratification are connubium [and] commensality' (1994: 125). By connubium is meant 'who marries whom' and by commensality is meant 'who eats with whom'. If professionals tend to marry professionals rather than managers, they should be regarded as belonging to two status/class groups; otherwise, we can reasonably regard the evidence of 'status homogamy' or 'class endogamy' between the two groups as grounds for classifying them into the same social positions. In the same vein, if people with the highest levels of cultural capital tend to find themselves in professional rather than managerial positions, we may say that the two groups should, at least from the assets theoretical perspective, be viewed as constituting two social classes.

I shall first explore patterns and trends of conjugal partnership of men and women in Great Britain in the twenty consecutive years from 1973 to 1992 drawing data from the GHS as previously noted. The GHS is a unique source with reliable and representative data on, among other things, marriage patterns and trends in the two decades. The total sample size is 130, 573 couples. Our analysis is confined to respondents living in family units of their current marriage. It is noted here that what is revealed in each year is the current class distribution between married partners, not an analysis of the class position of the respondent at the time of marriage. But, on the other hand, it can be argued that the patterns and the trends of professional–managerial marriages over the twenty years constitute the very evidence that serves as the best barometer of the professional–managerial relations crucial for testing the predictions of the competing theories.

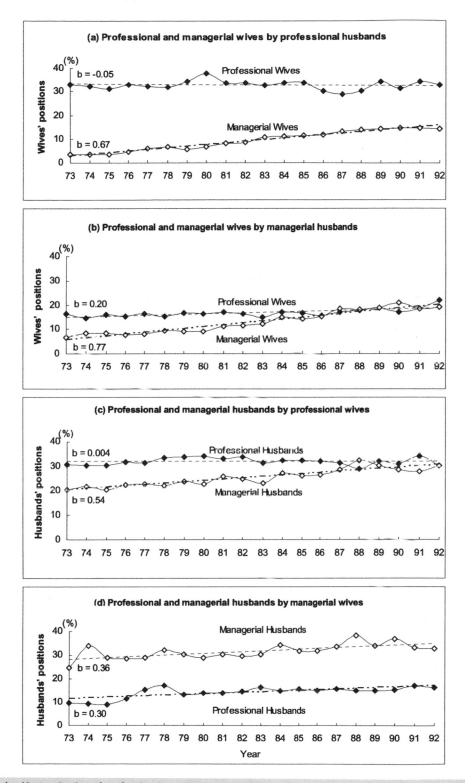

Figure 23.1 Mate selection of professionals and managers

Source: The General Household Survey (1973–1992).

The data in Figure 23.1 show that some of the expectations of the assets theory are supported: both male and female professionals had a much higher likelihood than managers of having professional spouses. Around 30 to 34 per cent of professional men had professional wives throughout the period (Panel (a)), but the figure for managerial men was less than 20 per cent (Panel (b)); around 30 per cent of professional women had husbands working in professional positions throughout the period (Panel (c)), but the figure for managers was only between 10 and 15 per cent (Panel (d)). Yet against this we find evidence of increasing managerial 'attraction' to professional women (Panel (c)), and the managerial men were throughout the period at least as likely to have professional as managerial wives (Panel (b)). Only in Panel (d) for women managers was the expectation of the assets theory fully supported.

If we view the evidence from the perspective of the employment relationship theory, the proposition of the professional–managerial integration in family formation holds good. In three of the four panels in the figure, we find not only a large number of professionals and managers married to each other, but also a clear convergence of such intermarriages. Professional men were increasingly more likely to marry managerial women (from less than 4 per cent in 1973 to nearly 15 per cent in 1992: Panel (a)); managerial men showed no less propensity to marry professional than managerial women (Panel (b)); and professional women were increasingly found to be married to managerial men (Panel (c)). Thus, for both men and women, professionals exhibited a constant likelihood of having professional spouses and an increasing likelihood of having managerial spouses while managerial men were as likely to have professional as they were to have managerial spouses throughout the period. Overall, the patterning of convergence in three of the four panels suggests more support for the service employment theory than for the assets theory.

Having explored patterns and trends of conjugal partnership, we shall now assess the relative 'attractiveness' of the service-class groupings by looking at the occupational orientations of degree-holders in these positions. As noted earlier, the employment relationship theory recognizes the echelon and situs differences as representing the social versus the technical division of labour within the class. The assets theory argues, on the other hand, that professionals are the carriers of cultural capital but managers have no cultural capital. As cultural capital is usually measured in terms of educational qualifications, we shall examine where those with the highest levels of cultural capital, namely with at least a first degree, tend to find themselves. If the assets theory holds true, people with cultural capital will find themselves in professional rather than managerial positions. For the employment relationship theory, its expectation of the professional progression into management will mean increased cultural assets of managers. We again base our analysis on data from the GHS (1973–92).

The data in Figure 23.2 show the patterns and trends of the distribution of degree-holders in British society from 1973 to 1992. The first thing to note is the fairly flat line at the top marked by professional and managerial, or service-class, positions. Around 90 per cent of people with degrees were found in service-class positions throughout the period. The lower lines show the flows of degree-holders to situs (professional–managerial) and echelon (Classes I and II) positions. Here we see a most interesting phenomenon. Whereas the distances between distributions to the echelons (higher and lower grades within the service-class) remained fairly constant, those between the situses (professional and managerial positions) were narrowing all the time, with the result that the much greater situs over echelon difference in 1973 became a much greater echelon over situs difference two decades later. In 1973, two-thirds of degree-holders were working in professional jobs and only one-fifth were found in managerial positions, with a gap of 45.7 percentage points (the gap between Classes I and II was 32.7 points in 1973). Yet as time went by, the distribution of degree-holders to professional positions went *down* at an average rate of 0.86 per cent, and that to managerial positions went *up* at a rate of 0.89 per cent, at a *convergence* rate of 1.75. The patterns and trends give direct and unequivocal evidence to the claims by the employment relationship theory and were completely unexpected by the assets theory.

1. The following websites will prove very useful: <http://www.data-archive.ac.uk/> for ordering data; <http://qb.soc.surrey.ac.uk/> for question banks and other support; <http://www.ccsr.ac.uk/> for getting SARs data and related help; and <http://www.esds.ac.uk/> for various services concerning the use of large-scale government data sets. For access to international macro- and micro-data sets, see <http://www.esds.ac.uk/international/access/>.

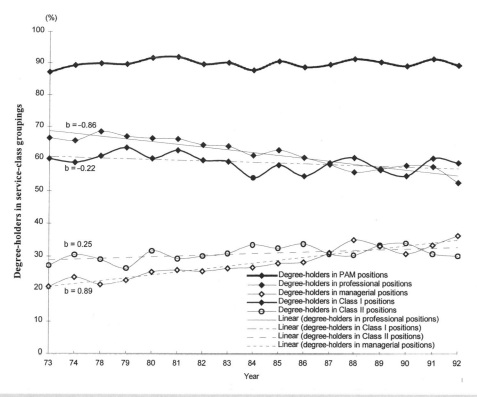

Figure 23.2 Class destinations of degree-holders (1973–92)

Source: The General Household Survey (1973–1992).

Annotated bibliography

Goldthorpe, J.H. with Llewellyn, C. and Payne, C. (1987) *Social Mobility and Class Structure in Modern Britain.* Oxford: Clarendon Press.

This book is a classic on social mobility and social stratification. The theoretical and methodological developments in the book have influenced mobility studies in Britain and many other countries.

O'Hear, A. (1980) *Karl Popper.* London: Routledge & Kegan Paul.

This text provides a lucid commentary on the work of Popper and his falsification thesis. It raises critical issues in relation to the tensions that exist between induction and verification.

Popper, K.R. (1990) *The Logic of Scientific Discovery* (14th impression). London: Unwin Hynam (I, II, pp. 27–56, IV, pp. 78–92).

This is Popper's seminal thesis on the scientific principle of falsification. This idea was responsible for reshaping the aspirations of modern science.

Savage, M., Barlow, J., Dickens, P. and Fielding, T. (1992) *Property, Bureaucracy and Culture: Middle-class Formation in Contemporary Britain.* London: Routledge.

This book offers a direct challenge to the fundamental principle of class formation and class action as contained in Goldthorpe (1987). It proposes a new, assets-based theory and argues for treating professionals and managers as two social classes.

Smith, J.K. (1989) *The Nature of Social and Educational Inquiry: Empiricism versus Interpretation.* New Jersey: Ablex (I, II, III, pp. 1–62).

This book provides an insightful commentary on the foundations of empiricism, mapping the evolution of scientific method and subsequent critical reaction.

Wright, E. O. (1997) *Class Counts.* Cambridge: Cambridge University Press.

This book is a comprehensive account of class relations from a Marxist perspective. Its discussion on professional and managerial positions is, however, closely related to Goldthorpe's treatment of the service class.

Zaw, S. (1976) *John Locke: The Foundations of Empiricism, Thought and Reality: Central Themes in Wittgenstein's Philosophy A402 units 3–4.* Buckingham: Open University Press (1–5, pp. 1–70).

This text elaborates the origins of modern, Western philosophy, paying particular attention to the vital distinctions between rationalist thinkers (Descartes, Plato) and empiricists (Locke, Berkeley and Hume).

Further references

Bourdieu, P. (1984) *Distinction: A Social Critique of the Judgment of Taste*, trans. R. Nice. London and New York: Routledge & Kegan Paul.

Cottingham, J. (ed.) (1998) *Descartes.* Oxford: Oxford University Press.

Erikson, R. and Goldthorpe, J.H. (1992) *The Constant Flux.* Oxford: Clarendon Press.

Goldthorpe, J.H. (1982) 'On the service class, its formation and future', in A. Giddens and G. Mackenzie (eds), *Social Class and the Division of Labour: Essays in Honour of Ilya Neustadt.* Cambridge: Cambridge University Press, pp. 162–85.

Jimack, P. (1996) 'The French Enlightenment II: deism, morality and politics', in S. Brown (ed.), *British Philosophy and the Age of Enlightenment.* Routledge History of Philosophy, Volume 5. London: Routledge.

Kuehn , M. (1996) 'The German Aufklärung and British philosophy', in S. Brown (ed.), *British Philosophy and the Age of Enlightenment.* Routledge History of Philosophy, Volume 5. London: Routledge.

Kuhn, T. (1970) *The Structure of Scientific Revolutions*, 2nd edn. Chicago: University of Chicago Press.

Li, Y. (1997) *The Service Class: Theoretical Debate and Sociological Value.* DPhil Dissertation, Nuffield College, Oxford University.

Li, Y. (2002) 'Falling off the ladder? Professional and managerial careers', *European Sociological Review*, 18(3): 253–70.

Li, Y. (2004) 'Samples of anonymised records (SARs) from the UK censuses: a unique source for social science research', *Sociology*, 38(3): 553–72.

Popkewitz, T. (1984) *Paradigm and Ideology in Educational Research: The Social Functions of the Intellectual.* Lewes, Sussex: Falmer Press.

Popper, K.R. (1991) *Conjectures and Refutations – The Growth of Scientific Knowledge*, 5th edn revised. London: Routledge.

Popper, K.R. (1992) 'Realism and the aim of science' (reprinted edition), in W.W. Bartley III (ed.), *Postscript to the logic of Scientific Discovery.* London: Routledge, II, III, IV, pp. 159–216.

Sorrel, T. (1987) *Descartes.* Oxford: Oxford University Press.

Sparkes, A.C. (1992) 'The paradigms debate: an extended review and a celebration of difference', in A.C. Sparkes (ed.), *Research in Physical Education and Sport.* Lewes: Falmer Press, pp. 9–60.

Stewart, M.A. (1996) 'The Scottish Enlightenment', in S. Brown (ed.), *British Philosophy and the Age of Enlightenment.* Routledge History of Philosophy, Volume 5. London: Routledge.

Weber, M. (1994) 'Status groups and classes', in D.B. Grusky (ed.), *Social Stratification in Sociological Perspective.* Boulder, CO: Westview Press, pp. 122–6.

Woolhouse, R.S. (1988) *The Empiricists, A History of Western Philosophy 5.* Oxford: Oxford University Press.

CHAPTER
24

THE POSITIVIST PARADIGM IN CONTEMPORARY SOCIAL SCIENCE RESEARCH

Charles Crook
Faculty of Education, The University of Nottingham, UK
Dean Garratt
Education and Social Research Institute, Manchester Metropolitan University, UK

Key concepts

Dean Garratt

The idea of a positivist *paradigm* in contemporary social research is a rather curious one and in many ways remarkably misleading. The fact that Comtean positivism argued for the unification of the sciences and employed a single method in order to achieve such certified knowledge positively rules out any notion of difference and with this the idea of simultaneously competing perspectives. At the core of this issue is an ambiguity of meaning associated with the term 'paradigm', which can be traced back to the work of Kuhn (1970). For Kuhn, 'paradigm' is connected with the set of beliefs, procedures and working practices that inform the dominant world view and which shape the context of modern science. A paradigm is nothing more or less than a conceptual framework, providing a model from which spring particular coherent traditions of scientific research – such as Newtonian physics or wave optics. Yet the essential point is that while Kuhn would acknowledge the presence of anomalies and inconsistencies in modern science, he would also emphasize that any 'normal period' of science is governed by the regulative ideals that constitute the prevailing view. Over time, of course, there will be issues that are difficult to solve and recurring problems for which the dominant scheme can offer no straightforward solution. A crisis then ensues and a new paradigm is born. The new framework is entirely incommensurable with the old one, since its standards and practices are at odds with the new, emerging rationality (Kuhn, 1970; Lakatos, 1984). What this 'crisis' or 'revolution-

ary period' suggests is that one paradigm is completely dominant until it is displaced by a new scheme, as there can never be any mutual tolerance of differing ideologies.

Over time this view has received a great deal of critical attention. For example, Guba (1990), reflecting on Masterman (1970), has argued that Kuhn himself used 'paradigm' in no fewer than 21 different ways, many of which were said to contain subtle variations of meaning. Indeed, it is perhaps not surprising that contemporary definitions within social and educational inquiry have exploited this ambiguity in order to exercise something subtly different. Patton, for example, employs a definition in which 'paradigm' represents a basic belief system or:

> ... world view, a general perspective, a way of breaking down the complexity of the real world ... paradigms are deeply embedded in the socialization of adherents and practitioners telling them what is important, what is legitimate, what is reasonable ... (1975: 9)

Similarly, Sparkes (1992) uses the term to suggest the possibility of different frameworks or perspectives containing contrasting sets of values, beliefs and assumptions. These factors are said to articulate with epistemological, ontological and methodological considerations in social enquiry, influencing and shaping the nature and conduct of research. They also assume the coexistence of different schemes that are often in conflict and where no single perspective is able to achieve total dominance over another. Of course, this idea contrasts radically with the Comtean scheme of science, which envisaged a system in which notions of unity and singularity would prevail. Indeed, the critical reaction against positivism has forced some serious conceptual modifications to be made, which have in turn allowed for a more encompassing definition of 'paradigm' within contemporary social research.

Of all the criticisms that have been lodged against the positivist philosophy of science, including debates surrounding the separation of facts from values, the idea of 'theory-free' data and the characterization of truth in correspondence terms (Smith, 1993), perhaps the two most enduring issues are associated with the burden of 'proof' or the verification of knowledge and the problem of sustaining a distinction between the researcher and that which is researched. Starting with the former, it is the work of Popper (1990) that arguably provides the ultimate undoing of the verificationist theory of knowledge. In *The Logic of Scientific Discovery,* Popper (1990) outlines his falsifiability thesis in which he effectively undermined induction – the logical basis on which science was affirmed and for which empiricism, as a foundational theory of knowledge, notably relied. Smith expresses this point well:

Popper convincingly pointed out that, no matter how many confirming or verifying instances have been accumulated for a theory, it is always possible that the next test of prediction will go astray. The problem is that induction does not allow one, with complete certitude, to predict the as yet unknown based on the known, or to predict the future based on what has happened in the past. Popper reversed the situation on traditional empiricism, so to speak, with his argument that one can never verify, but rather can only attempt to falsify, a hypothesis from a theory. A claim to knowledge must always stand as provisional in the sense that one can accept the claim only in so far as no one has been able to refute it or demonstrate it is false. (1993: 71)

As a consequence of Popper's work the idea of confirmation was effectively displaced by the plausible logic of his own theory of falsification. The second major issue that led to the demise of traditional empiricism, and by extension the emergence of various modifications to more recent 'positivistic' research, was the problem of correspondence or the distinction between the researcher and researched. The empiricist theory of knowledge rests, in part, on the possibility of realizing the Cartesian (deriving from Descartes) dualism that separates mind and matter. From this perspective, the object of research is to ensure that the researcher does not allow values and interests to interfere with the disinterested observation of events. Only if this is achieved can the researcher be sure of theory-free observation and hence be confident that knowledge is immunized and protected from the unwarranted intrusion of subjective ideas. Kuhn (1970), Putnam (1981) and Phillips (1987), to name but a few, have each pointed out that in practice this type of dualism is impossible to achieve. There is simply no 'God's Eye' perspective and hence possibility of 'brute data', nor any 'theory-free observation' or articulated account that stands separate from the influence of the researcher. As Smith (1995) has pointed out, it is impossible to know when what is inside of oneself leaves off and when what is on the outside begins, since such issues are lost to infinite reflexivity.

The implication of this reaction to traditional positivism is that some serious modifications have been made to the old empiricist model. This is reflected within the literature, where positivism is now often referred to as 'post-positivism', 'post-empiricism', 'subtle-realism' or 'neo-realism' (Hammersley, 1995; Smith, 1995; Sparkes, 1992), to indicate a shift away from the old scheme towards something less naive and more sophisticated. As new perspectives have emerged they have been forced to submit to the impossibility of employing a method that will lead to certain and indubitable knowledge. Instead, contemporary approaches have embraced the need for more subtle approximations of 'truth', where they have acknowledged that in the absence of the possibility of absolute truth, modern science may still adopt a fallibilistic approach to knowledge. One such sophisticated position is elaborated by Hammersley (1992) in which he examines in some detail the reasons for avoiding an abandonment of 'truth' as the regulative ideal for educational research. Others like Miles and Huberman (1994) and Kvale (1996) have resisted the pressure to reject conventional criteria as a means of guiding the practice of research. For them, the conventional criteria of validity, reliability and generalizability provide an important working model for the production of defensible research findings. Finally, Gage has made a similar plea for the reinterpretation of positivistic research, arguing that:

Being positive can mean being certain or being affirmative. Behavioural scientists should indeed reject trying to be positive in the sense of seeking a certainty that tolerates no exceptions to generalizations, a certainty that is logically unattainable not only in the behavioural sciences *but also* (according to Popper, 1965) *by the natural sciences*. But behavioural scientists should not reject trying to be positive in the sense of affirmativism, an attitude that affirms the value of the generalizations and theory thus far achieved and the value of the search for more. (1996: 14–15)

The positivist paradigm in contemporary social research, then, is one which has undergone some radical modifications, and yet as Popper has demonstrated in *Realism and Aim of Science* (1992) a non-justificationist theory of knowledge affirmed on the idea of falsification does not entirely abandon the legacy of the old empiricist tradition. On the contrary, it recognizes the value of positivism in ways that are logically defensible, practically feasible and, by necessity, epistemologically non-foundational.

Implications for research design

The changing face of positivism in contemporary social inquiry has generated some serious questions for the ways in which educational research is both conceptualized and conducted. Some of these implications have been discussed in Garratt and Li (in this volume) in terms of the various technical procedures that can be followed while carrying out empirical social research. These convey ideas that are broadly commensurate with the implications of positivism discussed here and their impact on research design.

Stepping back, it seems somewhat ironic that although within certain circles of sociology positivism has been declared 'dead' (Gartrell and Gartrell, 2002), and is conceived as an object of derision by leading theoreticians and authorities on the subject (Bryant, 1992; Gibbs, 1994), in practice it remains remarkably persuasive and continues to flourish in many aspects of social inquiry. In particular, the legacy of traditional positivism, modified and reconstructed, continues to permeate ways in which educational researchers set about their work. A dominant feature of its reappropriation can be observed in the way that high-profile, educational research projects are increasingly utilizing mixed methods, combining qualitative features, such as interviewing and observation, with quantitative statistical analysis. In one particular continuing professional development of teachers (CPD) project in the UK (Hustler et al., 2003), for example, the adopted

methodology displayed several characteristics of traditional positivism, including operational definitions/partial interpretation, formal language to express patterns between variables, variables that were related together empirically and extensive use of statistical techniques to underpin generated theories (Gartrell and Gartrell, 2002). In this particular funded project, such methods were employed to explore the views of a cross-section of the teaching force in England about CPD and its concomitant effects on their abilities to perform as classroom teachers and leaders in maintained schools in England. In the spirit of positivistic research or behaviourism more generally, the project also utilized broader generalizations predicated upon a relatively large dataset (Hustler et al., 2003).

Elsewhere more subtle flavours of positivism have emerged through social inquiry. In some quarters, quasi-experimental approaches have been adopted so that clearly expressed hypotheses may be tested through empirical investigation (see Bowler, 1997). Alternatively, some have made a concerted effort to locate ostensibly reductionist models of science (psychology) within more encompassing cultural frameworks of knowledge. Such approaches have typically combined loosely conceived positivistic ideas with more subtle socio-cultural perspectives. In the Story from the Field in this chapter, for example, psychological methods, operationalized as a 'toolkit', are blended with socio-cultural theory, so that two apparently disparate and diametrically opposed research orientations are imaginatively fused to present an intervention, 'perturbation' or disturbance of existing study practices with undergraduates engaged in full-time, higher education.

Ultimately, as long as researchers within education and the social sciences more generally continue to attempt to measure social phenomena in ways that articulate with the conventional criteria of validity, reliability and generalizability, the tradition of positivism, modified and reappropriated, will continue to influence research design in contemporary social inquiry.

Stories from the Field
Charles Crook

My background in psychology makes me sensitive to a suspicion that educational researchers feel towards the discipline. It is the research of psychologists that is expected to do most violence to the subtle nature of educational phenomena. It is psychologists that promote attitudes of objectivity, analysis by reduction and the methodology of control – as positivists. Yet, ironically, this critique of psychological research itself illustrates one of the problematic symptoms: namely, a readiness to circumscribe or decontextualize what people are doing. Perhaps some critics of psychological methods seize too willingly on the rhetoric of 'definitive experiment'. When judged as part of a bigger investigative picture, much psychological research in education can be seen to be making a distinctive and valuable contribution to the field.

The empirical toolkit of psychology has most often resourced my own practical work. Yet the theoretical orientation of that work has been very much socio-cultural. This might suggest a difficult tension to manage. For the supposed reductionist and impartial methods of psychology appear to sit uneasily with the supposed holistic and interpretative traditions of a cultural perspective. To be sure, if critics choose to detach studies arising from this methodology from the bigger picture of which they are often a part then this tension may be real enough. However, from my own perspective, any method/theory tension I have encountered as a researcher has been more empowering than debilitating.

There are three features of a research agenda that are important to cultivate at this interface of psychology method and socio-cultural theory. First, it is important to protect the *systemic* nature of complex human activity. So, the most useful research often succeeds by creating *perturbations* of an existing activity system – structured, perceptible but minimal forms of disturbance. Second, individual research projects are rarely 'definitive'; rather they are merely points on a trajectory of enquiry. For researchers (and their audience) they are pointers as to where to probe more tellingly next. They assist us in unfolding a problem. Finally, what is observed and reported by research can itself become a resource in our further engagements within the community of concern. That is to say, our research observations can serve as the focus of discourse and, thus, further enquiry within the community.

I will illustrate this with an empirical example: one of interest to educational practitioners. That is the contemporary ambitions to 'virtualize' areas of higher educational practice. Sometimes this is motivated by interests of inclusion or economy. But sometimes by beliefs about learning: say, the belief that virtual educational methods can liberate the student into greater autonomy of study. Now, the socio-cultural

tradition of educational theorizing should find these ambitions provocative. Not just because that theoretical tradition has focused on the *interpersonal* dimension of learning (and virtualization seems set to dilute that) but because the socio-cultural tradition theorizes learning (or, more telling, 'study') as cultural practice. And as a form of practice, study is likely to be resiliently grounded in a set of cultural resources: namely, those associated with particular institutions, places, routines, artefacts, and ways-with-words. If we shift learners away from this paraphernalia of cultural practice – shift them towards more virtual methods – then there may be trouble.

Of course, the visible success of some distance programmes might suggest that there are no serious obstacles to a virtualized university. Yet the equally visible rejection by school leavers of such routes into higher education surely presents a contrasting picture. What if we penetrate the established educational culture of these traditional undergraduates to explore this? What if we, as researchers, create a virtualizing perturbation in their system of activity? One good target for such meddling might be the lecture. We want to understand something about the status of this practice within the undergraduate's experience because, as virtualizing engineers, we want to redesign things. If so, then we must understand how the lecture integrates with the larger system of cultural practice in which undergraduates participate – as actors in a full-time, campus-oriented higher education. What we, as researchers, do *not* aim to do is conduct a self-contained little study that legislates on the general viability of substituting traditional lectures with something more virtual. So, what then counts as a disturbance of this system that is both credible and genuinely informative?

My own answer was pretty simple, at least at one level. It was straightforward in terms of what was to be done, what was to be observed, what was to be compared. Yet credibility depended on more subtle features of the overall design, such as protecting continuity between the experience of my interventions and the existing ecology of this community. The formal structure of this intervention involved no more than audio recording weekly lectures and making them immediately accessible as MP3 files on web pages – along with associated visual aids. What was then at stake as 'outcome' was the students' continued engagement with the live lectures – when compared with parallel classes they take. Yet our view about any outcome of all this depends on how we judge our meddling in relation to the larger context in which the activity is set.

In the present case, getting it right was a matter of the intervention (a virtualization of the lectures) being realized in a manner that was *legitimate* for the participants. That demanded that this new form of resourcing be seamlessly woven into existing practices. So it mattered that these students were in an institution where networked communication was strongly emphasized: where campus-based students (half the total number) enjoyed broadband access to that network in their study bedrooms, where every university module had a local website to which students naturally turned for routine course materials. It was also relevant that this intervention was perceived as an innocently conceived form of alternative resource – not an 'experiment' about which everyone might become rather self-conscious. In fact, it was originally designed merely to meet the legitimate need of one blind student requesting an audio record.

Against this background, the web-based lecture became an interesting disturbance of existing study practice: an interesting invitation for students to encounter a modest version of the autonomy promised by virtualization. However, attractive though this invitation might seem in the abstract, in practice it held little appeal. Compared to parallel and conventionally resourced lecture courses, attendance was no more or no less. This was reinforced by network system logs from the website. For although the course pages were visited frequently and most students accessed the recorded lectures, they typically only did so once and for lengths of time that suggested casual curiosity rather than engagement.

The example illustrates the three ambitions of empirical work noted above: first, structured observations making a useful 'perturbation' of a complex system; second, the construction of an outcome that becomes a point on a trajectory of enquiry (for it prompted further research – to be described below). But, finally, the work also furnishes a grounding for understanding changes in study practice by recruiting the sense-making interpretation of the participants themselves. In short, our intervention gives us something to talk with them about. The observations that make up the *results* of the intervention can themselves be recruited into discussion – to more effectively ground it. So we can talk about the documented stability of lecture attendance patterns and we can talk about the neglect of the audio web resource.

When we do this, we find students saying two kinds of thing. First, they make observations about lectures that concern the value added from simply attending. The corporate nature of the event seems reassuring, it affords casual (perhaps benchmarking) conversations with study peers, and it imposes a form of habitual or disciplined engagement with the curriculum. Second, they talk about the audio record being an 'uncomfortable' resource for studying. There is something unnatural about sitting down in one's room and listening to a recording of a lecture – even more so if the student endeavours to then take notes. This part of such conversations offered a helpful lever on understanding the resilience of existing study practices, the matter we set out to probe. But it was still just a point on a trajectory of enquiry: for it made us notice other forms of teaching practice disturbing the lecture format and we picked this up for further research.

A parallel course which provided on its website full written notes of the lectures did manifest a more noticeable attendance decline. This resource was much praised by these students and, interestingly, it did seem more continuous with students' preferred modes of private study. This tempts us to ask whether the experience of a course as a set of web-based lecture notes supports a different mode of study to the experience of a course as a sequence of live lectures. This is not an easy issue to address and, once again, there is no question here of invoking a 'definitive study' form of encounter with it. Yet structured observations are possible, again to discretely disturb existing systems of practice.

The heart of the matter now shifts. It still concerns migration of lectures to the Web, albeit in the form of *text* resources, rather than spoken ones. However, the issue now is whether this new form of mediation makes any difference to how learners study the material.

My approach invoked 'study practice' through the empirical device of orchestrating collaborative work sessions among peers. An advantage for the 'independently observing' researcher is that the resulting collaborative conversation makes more accessible the way in which students relate to certain study materials. The research was realized in something much more like a traditional experiment. What was at issue was the character of collaborative conversation under different circumstances of study resource. So some students revised together making use of a hypertextual set of web-based and lecturer-authored notes. Others talked around a linear (no hypertext links) version of those web documents. And still others talked around their *own* notes: of the same set of lectures that were documented by the web material. In brief, the students collaboratively studying around their own notes were much more animated, on-task and creative in their conversation. The packaged, authorized character of the web notes seemed to inhibit exploration around the lecture course ideas. Instead, topics discussed were strongly shaped by formal headings in the web texts, movements between topics were faster, and conversation dwelt more on what the lecturer wanted than on what the ideas themselves might amount to. Again, nothing is getting sewn up by this research. But the trajectory of enquiry does invite new forms of concern. It asks us to consider more carefully the mode of intellectual arousal that is supported by this kind of web resource – compared with personal records of live expositions.

This seems a rather classic form of psychological investigation. Participants are recruited into made-up associations; they are stage managed into 'sessions' – where they are closely monitored by 'independent observers'. Can this really advance understanding of issues arising out of new technology and higher educational practice? Again, our judgement about this requires that we look carefully at the larger ecology of this particular perturbation.

A critical onlooker might ask: are such participant pairings not the typical 'nonsense groups' of experimental social psychology? Not quite: students chose their own partners and, indeed, chose whether to volunteer or not. Most said they understood it to be an innocent evaluation of resources and wanted the opportunity to be forced into a bit of study anyway. Was what they were asked to do relevant to them in their role (as students)? Yes: they were just weeks away from a finals examination and all their time was currently given to one form of such revision or another. Were the circumstances of their activities in the research project alien to them? Hopefully not: a large, comfortable and familiar teaching room was used, with several pairings meeting at the same time in the same space. Coffee and snacks were always available and participants could stop, relax and start just as they might in more private settings. The

computer materials were similar to documents encountered for other courses. However, will there always remain a reflexivity problem inherent in observation? Well, not that the tapes themselves would suggest: some conversation was alarmingly frank and none suggested that the participants were inhibited by being recorded – or even consciously aware of it.

These observations converge on a general point that I hope is illustrated by these two interrelated examples. As researchers we will often position and equip ourselves to become well-resourced and well-positioned observers of events. Sometimes those events are flowing past us independently of our own design. Sometimes, our non-invasive role is complemented by us structuring our observations to afford relevant comparisons – say, between usefully contrasting flows of different events. But sometimes we do intervene and then we may configure such comparisons through our own engineering of events. I believe such interventions are a crucial ingredient of educational research and I have argued here that the issue for vigilance is the extent to which we manage them as 'perturbations to established activity systems' rather than controlled manipulations of variables. Finally, the status of 'observer' in these scenarios will often be judged inadequate. For often we may seem to deny ourselves access to the experience of those we observe – by our insistence on protecting a sense of distance. But this is not an inevitable requirement of research inspired by the psychological tradition. Here I have argued that the human *relationship* inherent within research remains an important concern. What we do when we exercise this concern is cultivate intersubjectivity: a mutual understanding with the participants in our research. Moreover, the achievement of intersubjectivity is often discursively resourced by making reference to other research observations we have made – albeit observations that may have engaged us with these participants from positions of greater interpersonal distance. In this way our 'impartial' observations of events often dovetail creatively with our need to resonate more closely with experiences in the community we are concerned to understand.

Annotated bibliography

Cole, M. (1996) *Cultural Psychology*. Cambridge, MA: Harvard University Press.

A distinguished introduction to making the cultural approach to psychology – with special attention to issues of cognitive development and educational practice.

Gage, N.L. (1996) 'Confronting counsels of despair for the behavioural sciences', *Educational Researcher,* 25(3): 5–15, 22.

This paper focuses on tensions that have arisen in the behavioural sciences as a result of their failure to produce long-lasting generalizations, and hence theories, from research. In 'Popperian' fashion, the paper concludes by suggesting that while the object of certainty is logically unattainable, researchers in the behavioural sciences may still display an attitude that affirms the value of generalizations and theory.

Hammersley, M. (1992) *What's wrong with Ethnography: Methodological Explorations*. London: Routledge, 4, pp. 57–82.

In this text, Hammersley develops a version of subtle realism that is both conventional and sophisticated, retaining a semblance of a correspondence theory of truth as a working model for assembling and judging ethnographic accounts.

Kuhn, T. (1970) *The Structure of Scientific Revolutions,* 2nd edn. Chicago: University of Chicago Press.

A seminal text on the relativity of scientific knowledge. In rejecting the idea that science grows by accumulation of truths, Kuhn presents his thesis of scientific paradigms.

Leigh Star, S. (ed.) (1995) *Ecologies of Knowledge*. Albany, NY: State University of New York Press.

Various papers that explore the consequences of approaching knowledge as embedded in local ecologies. Ranges widely and not exclusively on matters educational.

Newman, D., Griffin, P. et al. (1989) *The Construction Zone: Working for Cognitive Change in School*. Cambridge: Cambridge University Press.

The authors describe empirical work conceived to examine the problem of recognizing schooled cognition in out-of-school contexts. Their discussion of fieldwork thereby illustrates the challenges of adopting a cultural approach to cognition and educational practice.

Popper, K.R. (1992) 'Realism and the aim of science' (reprinted edition), in W.W. Bartley III (ed.), *Postscript to the Logic of Scientific Discovery*. London: Routledge, II, III, IV, pp. 159–216.

Popper elaborates his non-justificationist theory of knowledge, presenting the argument that while empirical science aims at true explanatory theories, it can never prove or finally establish any of its theories as true.

Roth, W.-M. (1998) *Designing Communities*. Dordrecht, Netherlands: Kluwer Academic Publishers.

The book explores an agenda of putting pupils at the heart of the educational enterprise by constructing a sense of learning community. The enterprise is discussed in terms of its rationale and the surrounding research is well illustrated.

Salomon, G. (ed.) (1993) *Distributed Cognitions: Psychological and Educational Considerations*. Cambridge: Cambridge University Press.

A collection of papers exploring the consequences of regarding human cognition in situated or distributed terms. While none are explicitly reports of empirical work, there is much discussion of such research and together these papers should give a strong sense of why human cognitive activity is best regarded as 'stretched' over social and material space and what implications this has for a research agenda.

Smith, J.K. (1993) *After the Demise of Empiricism – The Problem of Judging Social and Educational Inquiry.* New Jersey: Ablex.

This text explores the implications for contemporary social enquiry following the demise of traditional empiricism. Smith considers the problems and possibilities that are inherent to the process of judging social and educational enquiry.

Ward Schofield, J. (1995) *Computers and Classroom Culture.* Cambridge: Cambridge University Press.

An unusual book for its distinctive insistence on approaching educational computer use in a school from a cultural point of view – seeking to understand how patterns of using technology are related to the fabric of established traditions for institutional interactions. The book represents a full report of a substantial field study and gives insight into method and theory.

Further references

Bowler, J. (1997) 'Setting, social class and survival of the quickest', *British Educational Research Journal*, 23(5): 575–95.

Bryant, J. (1992) 'Positivism *redivivus?* A critique of recent uncritical proposals for reforming sociological theory (and related foibles)', *Canadian Journal of Sociology*, 17(1): 29–53.

Gartrell, C.D. and Gartrell, J.W. (2002) 'Positivism in sociological research: USA and UK (1966–1990)', *British Journal of Sociology*, 53(4): 639–57.

Gibbs, J. (1994) 'Resistance in sociology to formal theory construction', in J. Hage (ed.), *Formal Theory in Sociology: Opportunity or Pitfall?* Albany, NY: State University of New York Press.

Guba, E. (ed.) (1990) *The Paradigm Dialog.* London: Sage.

Hammersley, M. (1995) *The Politics of Social Research.* London: Sage.

Hustler, D., McNamara, O., Jarvis, J., Londra, M., and Campbell, A. (2003) *Teachers' Perceptions of Continuing Professional Development*, Research Report 429. London: DfES.

Kvale, S. (1996) *InterViews: An Introduction to Qualitative Research Interviewing.* London: Sage.

Lakatos, I. (1984) *The Methodology of Scientific Research Programmes*, reprinted. Cambridge: Cambridge University Press.

Masterman, M. (1970) 'The nature of the paradigm', in I. Lakatos and A. Musgrave (eds), *Criticism and Growth of Knowledge.* Cambridge: Cambridge University Press.

Miles, M.B. and Huberman, A.M. (1994) *Qualitative Data Analysis: An Extended Sourcebook*, 2nd edn. London: Sage, pp. 59–89.

Patton, M. (1975) *Alternative Evaluation of Research Paradigms.* Grand Forks, ND: University of North Dakota Press.

Phillips, D. (1987) *Philosophy, Science, and Social Inquiry.* Oxford: Pergamon Press.

Popper, K.R. (1990) *The Logic of Scientific Discovery* (14th impression). London, Unwin Hyman, I, II, pp. 27–56, IV, pp. 78–92.

Putnam, H. (1981) *Reason, Truth and History.* Cambridge: Cambridge University Press.

Smith, J.K. (1995) 'The ongoing problem of criteria', in T. Tiller, A.C. Sparkes, S. Tarhus and F. Darling Waess (eds), *The Qualitative Challenge: Reflections on Educational Research.* Bergen: Caspar Forlag, pp. 133–54.

Sparkes, A.C. (1992) 'The paradigms debate: an extended review and celebration of difference', in A.C. Sparkes (ed.), *Research and Physical Education and Sport.* Lewes: Falmer, pp. 9–60.

CHAPTER
25

ELEMENTARY QUANTITATIVE METHODS

Cathy Lewin

Education and Social Research Institute, Manchester Metropolitan University, UK

Key concepts

Statistical methods are a wide range of tools and techniques that can be used to describe and interpret data that are quantitative or can be measured numerically. Numerical data can make a valuable contribution in both quantitative and qualitative research whether it be simple percentages or the results of complicated techniques. The use of mixed methods (see Greene et al., in this volume) has become increasingly popular as a means to harness the strengths of both approaches, triangulate data and illuminate statistical findings with, for example, case studies and/or vignettes.

Quantitative researchers require knowledge of a range of very precise methods and procedures, all of which are associated with specific terminology and a range of principles arising from probability theory. This chapter seeks to provide the foundations required to understand quantitative research. The first section of the chapter provides the reader with an introduction to statistics – what can be measured and how – and introduces the concepts of reliability and validity. The second section covers sampling strategies, how to choose what will be included in quantitative studies in the social sciences. The third section provides an introduction to questionnaire design, a data collection instrument commonly used within quantitative paradigms to survey a large number of respondents. Finally, the last section explains how statistics can be used to describe and explore numerical data.

Introduction to statistics

What can be measured?

Statistics are applied to *variables* or measurements of attributes or characteristics of whatever is being studied, whether a person or an object, each of whom or which is often referred to as a *case*. Attributes can be real measurements or something that can be counted or quantified (for example age, height, income, test scores). Numbers can also be used to 'measure' opinions and attitudes through ranked responses to data collection methods such as survey questions or structured observations (for example educational level, socio-economic status, rating of services such as banking). Variables can also be assigned specific values (0, 1, 2 and so forth) to represent categorical attributes or characteristics that cannot be measured numerically or ranked in any way such as eye colour or gender.

How can statistics be used?

Statistics are particularly useful when asking questions of large numerical datasets, enabling researchers to summarize and make comparisons. *Descriptive statistics* are used to describe and summarize data and include measures of central tendency (average) and dispersion (the spread of data or how close each case is to the measure of central tendency). Descriptive statistics have an important role to play, enabling data to be explored before any further analysis is undertaken but also as a primary means of describing how things are rather than seeking to explain why phenomena occur.

Inferential statistics are used to identify differences between groups, look for relationships between attributes and create models in order to be able to make predictions. Inferential statistics are introduced and discussed in Barnes and Lewin (in this volume) and Jones (in Part VI, in this volume). Statistics can be applied to a single variable (univariate analysis), two variables (bivariate analysis) or more than two variables (multivariate analysis). The kind of statistical tool that can be used also depends on the type of data involved and whether specific conditions have been met. The *significance level* of a statistical test is also established, that is the likelihood that a difference or relationship has been identified when it does not truly exist. If the probability of this occurring is very small it means it is less likely that the result has occurred by chance and so the researcher can be more confident about the findings.

What do we mean by reliability and validity?

Reliability refers to the stability or consistency of measurements; that is whether or not the same results would be achieved if the test or measure was applied repeatedly. For example, a question may be worded ambiguously and answered differently on different occasions. *Validity* refers to whether or not the measurement collects the data required to answer the research question. A measure can be reliable (always generate the same result) but not valid (not measure the intended concept). However, if it is not reliable then it cannot be valid. There are various aspects of validity that should be considered when designing any measurement (see, for example, de Vaus, 1995, for more on this) and threats to validity can differ according to the statistical approach undertaken (see Jones, in Part VI in this volume, for a discussion of threats to validity in relation to modelling).

Causality can be inferred if it can be demonstrated that changing the value of one variable, the *independent variable*, has an effect on the value of another, the *dependent variable*. It is a means of explaining a phenomenon through its likely causes. *Internal validity* refers to the confidence that can be placed in causal inferences. There may be other (unaccounted for) variables at play. Some variables will have a direct effect on others while others may have an indirect effect. There are many threats to validity in quantitative research including history (circumstances changing over time), testing (test practice effects), mortality (attrition or being unable to collect data from all original participants) and maturation (developmental changes in participants). *Generalizability* or *external validity* refers to the possibility of expanding any claims of causality from the group or sample being studied to the population that the group represents – that is, that the same effect will be found in another group and/or in other contexts.

Quantitative designs

Quantitative research can employ a number of different designs, one of which is usually selected at the outset depending on the kind of research question being investigated. *Experimental design* is the primary approach in the positivist paradigm (see Garratt and Li, in this volume). This involves the manipulation of at least one independent variable to see whether or not it has any impact on the dependent variable. Tests can be conducted before the experiment begins – *pre-test* – and after it has been completed – *post-test* – or just at post-test. These data are used to identify differences between two or more groups on measurements of the dependent variable. *Laboratory experiments* take place in contrived settings but allow researchers to have more control whereas *field experiments* are conducted in naturalistic environments where it is often easier to recruit participants. Many argue that results achieved in laboratory settings are not generalizable to naturalistic settings casting doubt on the external validity of such experiments. Often in social science research, *quasi-experimental designs* are adopted when it is not possible to allocate individuals randomly to groups (see section on the principles of sampling below). For example, in educational research whole schools or whole classes are often assigned to groups (rather than individuals being randomly assigned to groups) because of practical and logistical issues.

Randomized controlled trials or RCTs are one form of experimental design in which participants are allocated truly randomly to an experimental group (for example, those exposed to the independent variable such as a new drug) and a control group (those not), enabling unmeasured or unknown variables to be taken into account and strengthening claims for internal validity. These approaches are expensive due to the large numbers of participants required. Furthermore, random allocation can be hard to achieve in social science research and there are ethical considerations that necessitate constraints. Nevertheless, there are often opportunities to set up randomized experiments when an experimental and control group occur naturally, for example when there is a limited number of places on a course and participants are selected randomly. RCTs are often referred to as the 'gold standard' for quantitative research although the value of such an approach is not universally accepted by social scientists.

A *cross-sectional design* is often used in survey research and involves the collection of quantitative data on at least two variables at one point in time and from a number of cases. These data are then used to look for patterns of association or relationships either in the group as a whole (all cases) or in subgroups sharing characteristics or attributes (females or males for example). It is problematic to establish causality in simple statistical tests of relationships (see Barnes and Lewin, in this volume) but causal inferences can be made using more sophisticated techniques such as regression analyses (see Jones, in part VI, in this volume).

A *longitudinal design*, often an extension of a cross-sectional design when a survey is administered repeatedly at regular time intervals over a number of years, can be used to more easily establish causality but is expensive to conduct.

Principles of sampling

Social science research can focus on a specific *population* or complete set of units being studied (for example, all state secondary schools in one country or all nurses working in a region) when time, costs and accessibility often prohibit the collection of data from every member or about every item. In these situations it is necessary to select a *representative sample* of the population, one in which the same range of characteristics or attributes can be found in similar proportions. It is only with a truly representative sample that you can *generalize* the research findings to the whole population. So judgements have to be made to ensure that the sample is as representative as possible adopting one of a number of different *sampling strategies* to go some way towards overcoming potential limitations. A *census* involves collecting data from all members of the population and is a true representation. Sampling, however, results in an estimate of population characteristics because the sample selected may not be truly representative. Researchers should explain the sampling strategies used in their research so that readers can make judgements about potential bias that might be introduced or other limitations. In *probability sampling* each member or item of the population has an equal or known chance of being selected. It is usually possible to generalize findings from analysis of data collected from such a sample to the population overall. *Non-probability sampling* covers all other approaches.

There are many ethical considerations that need to be addressed such as participant consent (see Piper and Simons, in this volume). Some samples will be easier to access than others by the nature of the population characteristics. For example, access to employees in companies will be easier than self-employed people working from home.

Probability or random sampling strategies

Simple random sampling is the simplest strategy in which each population member has an equal chance of selection through 'pulling names from a hat' or assigning each member a unique number and using random number generators (tables of random numbers or a computer program that generates random numbers within a specified range). However, a complete list of the population is required and this is not always available. *Systematic sampling* is similar but uses the *sampling frame* (a complete unordered list of all members of the population) rather than random numbers in the selection process. A member of the population is selected at regular intervals from the sampling frame. The sampling frame should not be ordered (names listed alphabetically for example) or there may be a bias in the selected sample.

Stratified sampling involves ordering the sampling frame by one or more characteristics and then selecting the same percentage of people or items from each subgroup either using simple random or systematic sampling. This will ensure that characteristics of the population are represented proportionately (for examples males and females). The more characteristics that are used, the more complex this procedure will be. Only characteristics that are considered to be likely to affect the data analysis should be considered.

When the population is large and widely dispersed it may be more appropriate to initially select subgroups such as geographical areas rather than randomly select from the whole population. This is known as *cluster sampling*. For example, a number of hospitals could be randomly selected from the list of all hospitals in a country and then the sample identified through a random sampling strategy (simple, systematic or stratified) applied to lists of nursing staff at those hospitals selected initially. An extension of cluster sampling is *stage sampling* in which more than one level of grouping is used to generate the sample such as selecting a region, then a school, then a class, then a number of students within that class.

Sampling error

Probability or random samples have less risk of bias (selecting subgroups disproportionately, for example twice as many men as women) but will still be subject to a degree of *sampling error* or the difference between attributes or characteristics of the sample and the

PART VI   SAMPLING, CLASSIFYING AND QUANTIFYING

population it is intended to represent. Consider a population of 15 female nurses and 15 male nurses from which you wish to select a representative sample of 10. Each randomly selected sample (choosing names from a hat) is likely to be different. Common selections will include five females and five males, six females and four males, and four females and six males. However, there is a small chance that you might select 10 females and no males or vice versa, which is clearly not representative of the group being sampled.

It is easy to calculate the sampling error when the characteristic being measured is truly numerical and an average or *mean* value can be calculated (for example, the average height of Chinese women). This is estimated using a statistic called the *standard error of the mean* which is a measure of the spread or distribution of all possible means of samples of a given size drawn randomly from a population. The smaller the standard error, the more closely grouped the possible means of all samples are and therefore the more likely it is that a single sample drawn from a population is representative. So the standard error is an estimate of how much the sample mean differs from the population mean. The *confidence interval* can be calculated from the standard error and represents the range of values between which the population mean is most likely to lie, enabling the researcher to estimate the population characteristics from the sample characteristics. This should be used in conjunction with the *confidence level,* which indicates the likelihood that the population mean lies within the specified interval. Common confidence levels that are used are 95 per cent and 99 per cent. The 95 per cent confidence level means that, 95 times out of 100, the population mean is likely be in the range specified by the confidence interval. The confidence interval will vary according to the confidence level used – the higher the confidence level, the wider the confidence interval. See Fowler (2002: 29–32) for a more detailed and mathematically grounded explanation of sampling error.

Sample size

The absolute size of the sample is the crucial factor rather than the relative size or the proportion of the population sampled. The larger the sample size the smaller the error will be in estimating the characteristic(s) of the whole population but the more it will cost to administer a survey and analyse the data. The

sample size will be dependent on the accuracy required and the likely variation of the population characteristics being investigated, as well as the kind of analysis to be conducted on the data. The larger a sample size becomes the smaller the impact on accuracy so there is a cut-off point beyond which the increased costs are not justified by the (small) improvement in accuracy; a sample size of 1,000 is often referred to as a cut-off point beyond which the rate of improvement in accuracy slows. Populations may be *homogenous* when the characteristics under investigation are largely similar or *heterogeneous* when the range of the characteristic is very diverse. It is good practice to overestimate rather than underestimate sample size to allow for attrition or non-response (participants withdrawing from research or failing to return a questionnaire for example).

The size of the sample is an issue for any researcher. Suggested minimum sizes for different approaches are as follows:

- In surveys, the sample should be sufficiently large so that any major subgroups contain at least 100 cases and minor subgroups contain between 20 and 50 (Fowler, 2002; Oppenheim, 1992).
- In correlational studies (looking at relationships between particular characteristics of a population, for example smoking and health), there should be at least 30 participants.
- In experimental designs, in which one or more variables are controlled and comparisons are made between two or more groups over a period of time, there should be at least 30 participants in each group.

Non-sampling error

A non-sampling error is one that relates to the sampling design or way in which data are collected. Such errors can occur in a variety of ways. For example, using a telephone directory as a sampling frame omits all members of the population who are ex-directory or do not own a landline. Or a poorly worded question may be interpreted in different ways by different respondents. Or the response from a question may be recorded incorrectly when preparing data for analysis.

Non-probability sampling

This approach is adopted when researchers target a particular group and are not always seeking to generalize findings to the population overall. This kind of approach is commonplace in small-scale research (particularly when costs need to be minimized) or qualitative approaches such as ethnography, case studies or action research. In fact, in the real world of social science research, non-probability sampling is widespread when time constraints and costs force the researcher to make compromises. The sample is often a group (a class, employees in a local company) that the researcher has easy access to or has selected for a particular reason. It is important to acknowledge the undoubted biases that will occur from this approach.

In *convenience sampling* or *opportunity sampling* easy access drives the selection process. For example, a local hospital or school is used, or a group with whom the researcher has an established relationship, or those who responded to a request for volunteers to participate in the research. *Quota sampling* is similar to stratified sampling but individuals are selected to fill quotas to represent relative proportions of specific characteristics. In *purposive sampling* cases are hand-picked for a specific reason such as use of a new product. In *snowball sampling* a small number of individuals are identified to represent a population with particular characteristics and they are subsequently used as informants to recommend similar individuals.

Questionnaire design

Questionnaires provide a way of gathering structured and unstructured data from respondents in a standardized way either as part of a *structured interview* or through *self-completion*. Often, the data collected are numerical (a measurement) or can be represented numerically (ranked in order of preference for example) and can thus be analysed using statistical techniques. Self-completion questionnaires are also a cost-effective way of collecting data from a large number of widely dispersed participants, particularly if postage costs can be avoided by, for example, asking individuals such as teachers or employers to supervise completion of questionnaires by groups. However, in questionnaire design there are many issues that need to be considered in order to (a) maximize the responses and (b) be confident that it is an instrument that is reliable and valid.

Thought needs to be given as to whether the questionnaire should be completed anonymously or not, depending on the sensitivity of the questions

being asked. Questionnaires may or may not be truly anonymized depending on the sampling strategy employed. Quota sampling can guarantee true anonymity for respondents whereas if a sampling frame has been used the researcher may know who the respondents are. Respondents can be asked to optionally give names and contact details if they agree to being willing to participate in the research further, for example through follow-up telephone interviews. It may be necessary to keep a record of who has and has not responded (in order to send reminders for example) in which case questionnaires can be part-anonymized by giving respondents a unique identifier. In such cases, respondents should be assured that the information identifying them will be destroyed at the data processing stage or not taken into account during analysis.

A questionnaire should have clear aims and objectives and be structured logically into sections and subsections (if necessary) with *filter questions* to ensure that respondents only answer relevant questions (for example, 'if yes, go to question 10'). The researcher should ensure that the data will be relevant and sufficient to answer the research questions as it is difficult to collect additional data after the questionnaires have been returned. It is often useful to include demographic data (those used to describe the population and its subgroups) such as gender, age and occupation. Often these questions appear at the beginning of the questionnaire because they can be answered easily and quickly although some (for example Oppenheim, 1992: 108–9) caution against this practice on the grounds that it can be seen as a personal intrusion by respondents and hence deter them from continuing. Either way, the first group of questions should be easy to answer. Be aware that if a limited amount of time is allocated to the completion of the questionnaire the respondent (for example young children) may not get to the end.

Highly structured *closed questions* are more suitable for large-scale surveys, as they are quick for respondents to answer and are easy to analyse using statistical techniques, enabling comparisons to be made across groups. Question types include: dichotomous questions (yes/no), multiple choice and Likert or rating scales (for example indicating how often an action is undertaken from 'always' to 'never'). In ratings, odd scales (3, 5, 7 points) allow respondents to remain neutral. Some respondents may avoid extreme responses (either end of the scales) in which case a 3-point scale may need to be avoided. Even scales (4, 6 points) force respondents to indicate which aspect they favour (for example, to agree or disagree with a statement). However, scales may force a particular response, may not include all possible options and do not always allow for additional comments. *Open-ended questions* are more suited to qualitative approaches allowing the respondent to give a free response in continuous text. Open-ended questions rather than closed questions can be more appropriate to elicit sensitive information. However, they are more difficult to code (categorize) and classify. In self-completion questionnaires, there should not be too many open-ended questions as they are more time-consuming to complete and respondents need adequate space to give their answers.

Questionnaires often have a combination of question types and collect data on facts, attitudes and beliefs. Questions can be direct or indirect. Attention must be given to the wording of the questions themselves in order to maximize reliability.

Questions should:

- be clear and unambiguous and not use technical language or language that is inappropriate for the respondents;
- not lead the respondents to particular answers;
- be simple rather than complex;
- avoid questions that are double-barrelled (ask more than one question simultaneously, for example 'do you own a mobile or a landline?' – if respondents say yes how do you know whether they own a mobile only, a landline only or both?);
- avoid the use of negatives and double negatives;
- ensure that in multiple choice questions and rating scales all categories are considered and are mutually exclusive (if a single response is required);
- avoid questions that may antagonize or irritate respondents or could be perceived to be threatening.

Instructions on how to complete the questionnaire should be explicit, clear and polite. It is good practice to repeat instructions for each section as often as necessary. Researchers should be aware that respondents will interpret imprecise words such 'sometimes', 'often', 'very little' differently, so whenever possible more precise terms should be used – for example, 'at least once a week'. Researchers should be aware that respondents may not always answer accurately or may give the answer that they feel is expected – this can occur both with children and adults. This will introduce an element of bias. Questions that introduce an element of cross-checking can be useful.

Questionnaires do not always have to rely on words to elicit information. With children and adults with poor literacy skills for example, pictures can be used to represent possible responses. Vignettes can be used to provide a context for a question and make it more meaningful and are often helpful for eliciting opinions and data relating to more sensitive issues. Use of graphics and colour can make questionnaires visually more interesting and stimulate responses, making completion more fun especially for children. Layout should be uncluttered and inviting with plenty of space for open-ended answers but also be consistent (all responses indicated by ticking a box or by circling the appropriate answer).

For self-completion questionnaires, length and ease of completion should be considered. It is helpful to indicate at the beginning or in a covering letter how long completion might take. It is beneficial to include a brief note at the end of the questionnaire to ask respondents to check that they have answered all questions, remind them of the date by which the questionnaire should be returned and thank them for their time.

Piloting a questionnaire (testing it with a limited number of individuals who are similar to the sample) is crucial and can highlight ambiguities and other potential pitfalls.

Questionnaire administration

Questionnaires can be administered face to face, via the telephone or via the post. Ethical issues need to be considered such as anonymity and confidentiality depending on the sensitive nature of the questions being asked (see Piper and Simons, in this volume, for a discussion of ethical considerations). A covering letter for postal questionnaires often improves intitial response rates to self-completion postal questionnaires and should outline the aims of the research, highlight the importance of an individual's contribution, assure respondents of confidentiality and encourage their replies. It should also state how the questionnaire can be returned (a stamped addressed envelope – known as an SAE – eliminates costs for the respondent and avoids addressing errors on the return envelope) and what to do if any uncertainties arise (contact name and number for queries for example). Questionnaires that are going to be administered by someone other than the researcher will require a clear and comprehensive set of administering instructions.

Questionnaires can be returned electronically or completed online, in which case data entry can be automated but may exclude some members of the sample (for example those without access to the Internet) introducing a bias. Costs can be lower (no postage, printing or data entry costs) but this will depend on the technical expertise required (costs of creating an online questionnaire).

A response rate of 40 per cent is typical to the original letter and questionnaire. Reminder letters can increase response rates and can be sent with a second copy of the questionnaire in case the respondent has mislaid the original. Three reminders can increase the response rate by up to 30 per cent. Offering incentives can also increase response rates (for example entering respondents into a draw for a highly sought after prize!). Response rates are likely to be lower in postal questionnaires than in face-to-face situations. Timing may need to be considered. A postal questionnaire in mid-December, for example, may not attract a high level of response in historically Christian countries. Non-responders should be considered and any resulting likely bias should be commented upon in reporting the research (for example poor literacy skills of a subgroup of respondents).

If the questionnaire is being administered through a structured interview, either face to face or over the telephone, care needs to be taken to ensure that the process is standardized for all respondents, particularly if more than one interviewer is involved. Interviewers should be briefed and trained prior to the data collection. There should be clear instructions to the interviewers on how to administer the questionnaire. For example, guidance should be provided on follow-up questions (probing or prompting) to ensure that the administration is consistent. It is also useful to hold a debriefing session for interviewers after the interviews have been completed to identify any matters which should be taken into consideration during analysis – questions that were unclear for example.

The final stage before quantitative analysis can begin is to ascribe numerical values to responses or code the data (for example, no = 0, yes = 1). Data from questionnaires can be pre-coded for closed questions. Where open-ended questions are to be coded, clear instructions need to be given to individuals undertaking this process, particularly if there is more than one person involved. A coding frame will be devised identifying how individual responses should be coded. There may initially be a number of queries relating to this process as new codes may emerge over time. Inter-rater reliability should be ascertained (the extent to which individuals make the same judgements about how to code a particular response). There should also be guidance on how to code variables when questions have been spoilt (more than one box ticked for example).

Describing and exploring data using statistics

As well as a wide range of statistical tests that can be applied to data, tables and graphical representations are often used as analytical tools. Tables can be used to present data in an easy-to-understand format. Graphs and charts can present data visually and often highlight patterns and issues that may be drawn out in interpretations of the data.

Many textbooks give detailed (mathematical) explanations of how each statistical test or tool is calculated. In reality, all calculations can be easily performed using computer-based tools such as the Statistical Package for the Social Sciences (SPSS). It is important to understand what tests are appropriate for the data that you have and why you might use them. It is not strictly necessary to understand the underlying mathematical principles but some researchers find this helpful. (Textbooks on statistical techniques in the social sciences vary, some pay lip service to the mathematics behind the tests while others provide detailed mathematical justifications.) You also need to be aware of any limitations that need to be acknowledged when interpreting results in relation to the kinds of data, the sample size and the sampling strategy that was followed. It is also helpful to have the same understanding of basic principles in order to be able to read the (quantitative) work of others and make judgements about whether or not their interpretations and conclusions are sound.

Data types

There are three main types of data that can be analysed statistically. *Nominal* data have no numerical meaning such as dichotomies (responses that have two options only such as yes/no, male/female) or categorical data (year group or ethnicity). *Ordinal* data have a rank order and are represented numerically but differences between values may not be equal hence there is no true numerical meaning. For example, the responses to a question on how often online banking is used could be represented by the number zero (never use online banking) to the number four (use online banking at least once a week). *Interval* data have true numerical values but have no true zero, for example a thermometer. *Ratio* data do have a true zero, for example distances travelled to work. Variables containing data of nominal or ordinal types are sometimes referred to as *discrete variables*. Variables containing data of the interval or ratio type are sometimes referred to as *continuous data*.

Descriptive statistics

Frequency distributions are used to describe data indicating the frequency of all categories or ranks, either in a tabular form or in a graphical form as a *bar chart*. The frequency distribution of two such variables can be compared with a *cross-tabulation* as long as each variable does not have too many categories and each category is mutually exclusive. This would generate a two-dimensional table with rows (the categories for the first chosen variable) and columns (the categories for the second chosen variable). So, for example, a cross-tabulation of gender with job category in healthcare would provide frequency counts for males and females according to their job (nurse, doctor and so on). Percentages are often used to represent the number of responses to a categorical question. Frequency distributions for interval data can be represented graphically with a *histogram*.

The *central tendency* is a measure of the most typical value or central value in a frequency distribution and can be measured in three ways: mode, median and mean. The *mode* is the most common value in a set of data (the value or category that occurs most frequently). It is not often used but it is the only measure of central tendency that is appropriate for nominal data. The *median* is the middle value if all responses are put in order from the highest to the lowest value such that 50 per cent of the distribution is below the median and 50 per cent is above. The *mean* is the average value, which is calculated by adding up all the values in the distribution and dividing the total by the number of values. The mean can be influenced by extreme values.

Measures of dispersion are used to describe the 'spread' of the data or the distribution of values. It is possible for two frequency distributions to have the same central tendency (that is the same mean, median or mode value) but to be very different in the distribution of individual items. A measure of dispersion that is small often indicates that measures of central tendency accurately represent the population from which the data were collected. A measure of dispersion that is large indicates a wide and diverse set of responses such that central tendency measures are less meaningful. The *range* is the difference between the highest and lowest value. The *quartiles* are the values found at quarterly intervals if the data are ordered from the lowest to the highest and the *interquartile range* is the difference between the upper quartile (the value that is three-quarters of the way through the ordered list) and the lower quartile (the value that is one-quarter of the way through). The *standard deviation* is a measure of the spread based on all values, measuring the 'average' amount by which all values differ from the mean. This is explained further below.

The two most commonly used measures for continuous variables are the mean and standard deviation.

Normal distributions

The *normal distribution* is represented by a bell-shaped curve or *normal curve* (Figure 25.1) and represents a set of values that are commonly clustered around the mean value (the point where the curve turns) with a smaller number of values at each end of the range. For example, female adult shoe sizes are normally distributed. In the UK, common sizes are between 4 and 6 with a mean of, say, 5. Some of the population have shoe sizes of 3 and 7, a small minority of the population have sizes less than 3 or greater than 7. Many variables that are studied are assumed to come from populations with a normal distribution. Many statistical tools assume a normal distribution. In a normal distribution the values of the mean and the median will be about the same. It is worth noting that the 'norm' varies in different populations, for example common shoe sizes were much smaller in China in 1989 when one of the editors of this book tried to buy a pair!

Standard deviation

As mentioned above, the *standard deviation* is a way of measuring the differences between each individual value of a variable and the mean value of the variable for the sample. It represents the spread of the data or

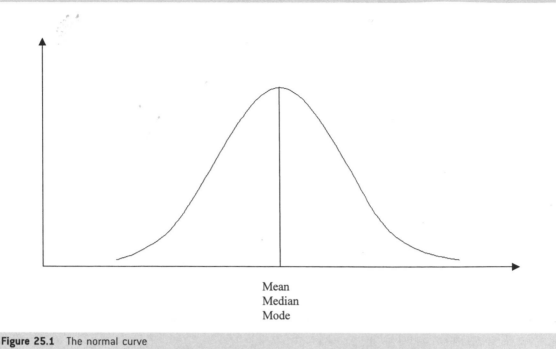

Mean
Median
Mode

Figure 25.1 The normal curve

the variability. In a picture of the normal distribution, the horizontal axis is usually measured in standard deviations. A normally distributed population with high variability (greater spread of differences from the mean) will be represented by a flatter bell-shaped curve (that is, with a lower central point) and a normally distributed population with a low variability will be represented by a thinner, higher curve, indicating a tighter clustering of individual values around the mean value. Mean values should always be considered alongside a measure of variability. The *variance* is the mean of the squared deviation of all scores or values for a variable from the mean value. The deviations are squared to eliminate any negative deviations (those that are less than the mean value) that would otherwise result in the total deviations adding up to zero, preventing the calculation of the mean deviation. The standard deviation is the square root of the variance (which is measured in squared units) providing a measure of variability in relation to the original unit of measurement (for example, average deviation from the mean salary in terms of salary rather than salary squared).

In a normal distribution two-thirds of all individual values of a variable will be within one standard deviation of the mean. Ninety-five per cent of all cases will lie within about two standard deviations either side of the mean (from $+1.96$ to -1.96 standard deviations). Ninety-nine per cent of all cases will lie within about two and a half standard deviations either side of the mean (from $+2.58$ to -2.58 standard deviations).

Hypotheses and statistical significance

A hypothesis in quantitative research has a particular meaning. It is the reformulation of a research question (grounded in theory and/or literature) to form a precise declarative statement including a prediction of the outcome such that it can be operationalized and tested statistically. That is, the requirements for data collection and measurement become explicit and it is clear which statistical technique should be applied. Two hypotheses are required: the *null hypothesis* and the *alternative hypothesis*.

The *null hypothesis* assumes that there is no real difference or relationship between two variables. So, for example, if the research question was 'Does smoking cigarettes negatively affect health?' the null hypothesis would be:

$H_0 =$ The scores achieved on a questionnaire assessing general health by a group of non-smokers will *not differ* from the scores achieved on the same questionnaire by a group of people who smoke at least 20 cigarettes a day.

The *alternative hypothesis* assumes that there is a difference or relationship. It can be non-directional if it is not possible to say whether one group will outperform a second group. In this example, the research question suggests that the difference will be directional, that is that the group of smokers will be less healthy than the non-smokers. So the alternative hypothesis would be:

H_1 = The scores achieved on a questionnaire assessing general health by a group of non-smokers will *be greater* than the scores achieved on the same questionnaire by a group of people who smoke at least 20 cigarettes a day.

Based on falsification theory (see Garratt and Li, in this volume) it is the null hypothesis that is tested rather than the alternative hypothesis (i.e. it is easier to prove that something is false than it is to prove that something is true). Statistical tests enable researchers to reject the null hypothesis (proving it to be false) based on specific probabilities. When there is no evidence to prove the null hypothesis is false it is accepted, but not 'proved' and the alternative hypothesis is rejected. *Statistical significance* is used to indicate the likelihood that a 'real' difference or relationship between two sets of data has been found. A test result that is significant at the 0.05 level means that there is evidence of a difference or relationship and that there is only a five in one hundred (which is the same as one in twenty) probability that it does not truly exist but the result has been obtained due to chance variation. A more confident interpretation would arise from a test result that was significant at the 0.01 level, when obtaining a result by chance may occur one in a hundred times. Another, yet more accurate interpretation would arise from a test result that was significant at the 0.001 level (one in a thousand). Significance testing is described in more detail in the chapter that follows (Barnes and Lewin, in this volume).

Implications for research design

While the approach to designing quantitative research is generally top-down, as Doig (in this volume) comments, it is wise to consider the intended outcomes from the outset. The research question(s) will drive the design of the study but the researcher does need to ensure that the right approach is undertaken and the relevant data are collected to provide the

answers. Does the study simply need to describe a population, as surveys such as the UK General Household Survey do? Or does it need to test a hypothesis regarding a potential difference or relationship? Or is the aim to develop a model enabling predictions to be made about a population? Which of these is the right approach to deal with the problem and be in a position to provide reliable answers? Other considerations are whether or not the chosen approach is feasible in relation to the constraints of the research project (such as available funds and time) and accessing the required population. Ethical and/or political issues may also need to be considered in quantitative approaches in social sciences research. It is arguably not ethical, for example, to study the impact of smoking by randomly assigning people to two groups, where the 'experimental' group smoke 20 cigarettes a day and the 'control' group do not. It would be more appropriate to identify a group of smokers and non-smokers and conduct a survey.

A sampling strategy needs to be considered and will be constrained by resource limitations (time and costs). Does the research need to be generalizable (as discussed in the section on reliability and validity above) and if so will a truly random design be feasible? And what about sample size? Here considerations include the combination of research methods that might be included in the research design, the variation in the characteristics under investigation and the required accuracy. What compromises will have to be made?

The next aspect to consider is how to collect the data. This chapter has provided an overview of questionnaire design as this research instrument is frequently employed in quantitative research, being a cost-effective way of collecting standardized data from large samples. Alternative approaches, however, may be more suitable such as observation, structured interviews or the use of secondary data sources (see Garratt and Li in this volume). A questionnaire needs to be reliable and valid (see the discussion of reliability and validity above). Threats to validity must be considered. The questions asked need to be appropriate and suitable to test the research hypothesis. Anticipating likely bias can be helpful. Steps could be taken, for example, to ensure that ethnic minorities are not underrepresented in a survey by providing the questionnaires in different languages. Non-response can be estimated in advance and sample sizes increased accordingly.

Descriptive statistics are helpful for providing a picture of the sample, whatever the design or approach. A measure of central tendency (appropriate for the kind of data collected) together with a measure of spread of the data can provide a useful summary. In addition, graphical tools and tables provide alternative means of summarizing the data. Descriptive methods can also be used to explore the data and identify outliers (extreme values) and to confirm that it is worth continuing with further data analysis.

Annotated bibliography

De Vaus, D.A. (1995) *Surveys in Social Research*, 4th edn. London: Routledge.

Chapter 5 provides a readable introduction to sampling. Chapters 6 and 7 provide details on questionnaire construction and design. Chapters 8 to 13 describe statistical analysis tools and techniques that are particularly relevant to survey research methods.

Diamond, I. and Jefferies, J. (2001) *Beginning Statistics: An Introduction for Social Scientists*. London: Sage.

This textbook assumes no mathematical or statistical background and places little emphasis on statistical formulae. Full of examples to explain concepts, it focuses on description and graphical displays of data, providing an excellent starting point. There are lots of practice questions with answers and explanations given in the back of the book. It also contains some very helpful appendices explaining commonly used mathematical notation and some basic mathematical principals. A very readable book that is easy to follow. Chapters 8 and 9 are very helpful introductions to sampling, the standard error, confidence intervals and confidence limits.

Fowler, F.J. (2002) *Survey Research Methods*, 3rd edn. London: Sage.

Chapter 2 covers the principles of sampling. Includes a detailed discussion of non-response and bias. Also includes aspects of Internet- and email-based surveys and particular issues arising from these approaches, although not in great detail.

Hinton, P.J. (1995) *Statistics Explained: A Guide for Social Science Students*. London: Routledge.

Another easy-to-read introduction to a whole range of statistical tests. Good use of examples to explain why and how statistical tests are used. Very easy to read and a useful reference text.

Kinnear, P.R. and Gray, C.D. (1999) *SPSS for Windows Made Simple*, 3rd edn. Hove: Psychology Press.

This is an excellent book, not only for easy-to-follow explanations of how to calculate statistical tests, but also for very clear and concise explanations of the main statistical concepts and how to choose an appropriate test. This book is updated regularly as more advanced versions of SPSS (Statistical Package for the Social Sciences) are released.

Oppenheim, A.N. (1992) *Questionnaire Design, Interviewing and Attitude Measurement*. London: Continuum.

A comprehensive and practical guide covering design and implementation of questionnaires in the context of survey research. Each chapter has a list of follow-up readings for those who wish greater detail on a particular aspect.

Rowntree, D. (1981) *Statistics without Tears: A Primer for Non-mathematicians*. London: Penguin.

A classic introduction to statistics, assuming no mathematical knowledge and explaining the ideas behind their use rather than getting heavily into calculations.

Salkind, N. (2000). *Statistics for People Who (Think They) Hate Statistics*. London: Sage.

Another helpful text for those who have limited experience of statistics or find the concepts difficult.

Sapsford, R. (1999) *Survey Research*. London: Sage.

Chapters 3 and 4 cover sampling. Again a very readable guide, full of helpful examples to illustrate the points being made. Key points and useful mathematical explanations are presented in boxes within each chapter. Chapters 5 to 7 discuss aspects of questionnaire design together with interviews and systematic observation techniques.

CHAPTER
26

AN INTRODUCTION TO INFERENTIAL STATISTICS: TESTING FOR DIFFERENCES AND RELATIONSHIPS

Sally Barnes
Graduate School of Education, University of Bristol
Cathy Lewin
Education and Social Research Institute, Manchester Metropolitan University, UK

Key concepts

Introduction to inferential statistics

Describing sets of data is often only the first step in data analysis. Frequently what we are most interested in doing is asking questions of the data, exploring relationships between different things we have measured. *Inferential statistics* cover all the techniques which allow us to explore in-depth relationships between variables. They provide a very powerful way of asking questions of numerical data. There are three main approaches: to explore differences; to explore the nature and extent of relationships; and to classify and make predictions (see Jones, in Part VI of this volume). The focus of this chapter is to introduce some of the key concepts and some of the most commonly used procedures in exploring differences and relationships. The use of a statistics package can take the strain of calculating the mathematics required for each technique. However, no statistical package can make the decision about which technique to use in a particular situation nor how to interpret what the results mean.

Inferential statistical procedures are divided into two main types: *parametric* and *non-parametric*. Parametric statistics are based on the principles of the normal curve (see Lewin, in this volume). Therefore, in order to be able to use parametric statistics, the data must be normally distributed and interval level data (some form of counting rather than categorical or a ranked response). Suggested sample sizes vary according to the kind of statistical test; a general rule of thumb is to have a minimum sample of about 30. When you have samples of less than 30 it is often better to use non-parametric statistics – or statistics which are distribution-free (that is, not based on the principles of the normal curve). Category variables, either nominal or ordinal (see Lewin, in this volume), are analysed using non-parametric techniques because the mean and standard deviation cannot be calculated.

One of the most difficult tasks in analysing data is to select the most appropriate statistical technique that both addresses the research question and fits the data you have collected. Howell (1997: 11) provides a useful diagram for selecting an appropriate technique according to:

- the type of data (categorical, ordinal, interval);
- whether testing for differences or relationships;
- number of groups of participants (two or more);
- whether the groups are *dependent* or *related* (a single group exposed to different conditions or tested at different points in time) or *independent* (two or more unrelated groups of participants);
- whether the test should be parametric or non-parametric.

Pallant (2001) also provides very clear guidance in chapter 10, *Choosing the right statistic*.

Evaluating statistical results

Carrying out a statistical procedure is a two-stage process. First, we carry out the appropriate statistical test; second we carry out the appropriate test of significance to see what the probability was of achieving the statistical result obtained. The test of statistical significance enables us to say how confident we are that the result achieved from the analysis of the data from the sample is a 'real' result or if it is as a result of 'chance'.

Probability theory allows us to ask what are the chances of achieving a similar result from another sample drawn from the same population. The better the chances the more confident we tend to be in thinking our result is valid. There are, of course, enormous implications behind significance testing (see Freedman et al., 1998) including two important assumptions. The first is that random selection needs to be used to select the original sample from a well-defined population. The second is that measurements need to be both valid and reliable – something often difficult to achieve in the social sciences.

Significance testing uses 'degrees of freedom', or 'df' as it is commonly written. See Howell (1997: 53–4) or Field (2000: 253–4) for clear mathematical explanations. It refers to the number of items in a set (values of a variable for example) which can vary and the calculation of this differs according to the statistical technique selected. In a classroom with 30 desks, the first student to arrive can choose where to sit, as can each of the following 28 students although from a decreasing number of possibilities each time. But the last student to arrive will have no choice because there will only be one empty desk left. So the degrees of freedom in this case will be the number of desks minus one: 29. In simplistic terms the degrees of freedom figure approximates to the sample size and so provides helpful information when reading quantitative research reports.

Every statistical procedure will have a formula for calculating the degrees of freedom. Often it is:

$n - 1$ (if there is only 1 group of people, $n =$ number in group)

or:

$n_1 + n_2 - 2$ (if there are 2 groups, $n_1 =$ number in group 1, $n_2 =$ number in group 2)

The results of statistical tests are written in conventional notation which typically include four pieces of information: the statistical test used, the actual result, the degrees of freedom and the probability that the result is a real or chance result (see Coolidge, 2000; Freedman et al., 1998; Salkind, 2000).

To evaluate the significance of results researchers present their findings in terms of different probability levels. The level of 0.05 ($p < 0.05$ – 'p' stands for probability value), for example, means that the probability that a difference or relationship has been detected in error is less than 5 times in 100. The probability values which we tend to use in the social sciences ($p < 0.05$, $p < 0.01$, $p < 0.001$) are based on the shape of the normal distribution curve.

There are a number of cautions about the interpretation of statistical results and their associated probabilities.

– The 0.05 and 0.01 levels of significance used throughout the research world are arbitrary. Their use is now common convention and that is the only reason they continue to be used. It actually makes more sense to state the actual probability value (p-value) rather than $p < 0.05$ – most statistical packages do now report the actual probability value.
– The p-value depends on sample size. The larger the sample the smaller the difference needed to reach statistical significance.
– Researchers should always summarize their data using descriptive statistics (see Lewin, in this volume) so that readers can draw their own conclusions about the importance of any statistically significant p-values. (For example it would be important to state the mean values for each group.)
– p-values are only relevant for samples as they are based on probability or chance models. When you have data from a whole population it is irrelevant to do a significance test as you would only be comparing the population with itself.
– Tests of significance do not check for design errors. So if a researcher has chosen the sample incorrectly or used invalid or unreliable measures, or used an inappropriate test, there is no way to identify this statistically.

(Adapted from Freedman et al., 1998)

One aspect of significance testing that is often difficult for new researchers is the idea of one- or two-tail tests of significance. In the normal curve there are two 'tails' one in either direction that stretch to infinity. If you have a research question that is very specific about the result you are testing (that is, looking for a greater mean value of a variable in one group in comparison to a second group) then you can use a one-tailed test of significance and only look for the specific result. For example, to answer the question 'Do boys complete more sit-ups in 5 minutes than girls?' is quite specific and we can look only to see if boys do complete more sit-ups than girls. However, if we phrase this question as 'Is there a difference in the number of sit-ups boys and girls complete in 5 minutes?' it suggests that we could have either group completing more sit-ups and here a two-tailed test is more appropriate. In this case, we cannot predict the direction of change so we consider both possibilities (boys may do more sit-ups than girls or girls may do more than boys).

Grounding analysis in inferential statistics: looking for differences

How different do two things have to be before we get all excited about the results? In other words is a difference between several groups real or did it occur by chance? To test this we carry out statistical tests that look at differences and then using methods of calculating statistical significance we evaluate the probability of arriving at a particular result.

Parametric techniques for identifying differences

For interval or ratio numbers the main parametric techniques are the t-test (when we have only two groups) and the analysis of variance or ANOVA when we have more than two groups.

We use the t-test when we wish to test and see if there is a significant difference between two sample means. In other words we are using this test to see if two samples can be thought of as coming from the same, or two different, population(s). Our null hypothesis is that there is no difference between the two sample means. Our alternative hypothesis is that there is a statistically significant difference between the means.

There are two t-test formulas to consider when you have independent samples (see Popham and Sirotnik, 1992), that is two groups of people which are totally unrelated (for example, males/females; doctors/patients; 10-year-olds/12-year-olds). The *separate model t-test* is used when each group has the same number of participants. The t-test formula to use when you have unequal sample sizes is called the *pooled variance model t-test*. The difference in the two formulas comes in the way that the variance (distribution of data around the mean) of each sample is calculated.

One assumption of the t-test is that the variances of the two groups are the same. SPSS also conducts a separate kind of test automatically to look for equality of variances or that the spread of values around the mean of each group being compared is similar. SPSS reports the Levene's test (so called because Levene invented it) based on the null hypothesis that the two variances are equal. If the results of Levene's test is significant at $p < 0.05$ then the null hypothesis is rejected and the alternative hypothesis is accepted; the variances are not equal. If the results of Levene's test are not significant then the null hypothesis is accepted; the variances are assumed to be equal. SPSS generates two different t-test results according to whether the variances are equal or not and provides the results for both of them, clearly labelled.

The result of the t-test is referred to as the t value. The larger the resulting value of t the greater the difference between the two means. To interpret the t value we check the probability value associated with that t for our sample, taking into account the sample size. Then we are able to interpret the finding and state whether or not there is likely to be a real difference between the two groups, and if so how confident we are that such a difference exists.

To report the results of t-tests it is important to specify which t-test formula was used; then state the outcomes including the degrees of freedom for this technique (df), for example:

$$t = 4.52, df = 40, p < 0.01$$

This tells us that there were 42 people altogether in the two samples as for this statistical technique the degrees of freedom are calculated by adding the number of people in each of the groups and deducting two (as there are two groups). It also tells us the actual t value is 4.52 and the probability of achieving that result by chance with 42 people is less than 1 in 100. Therefore we can conclude that the means of our two groups are different and that this difference is statistically significant.

There is a third t-test formula used when there is only one group of people when data are collected about the same participants under two different conditions (known as a *dependent* or *related* design). This is called the paired sample t-test and is most commonly used in pre-test/post-test designs. Teachers often give a class a test at the beginning of term to assess pupils' knowledge of a subject. At the

Table 26.1   Example of ANOVA results

	df	Sum of squares	Mean squares	F	p
Between Groups	2	198.38	99.19	12.45	<0.01
Within Groups	72	95.62	7.97		
Total	74				

end of the term the pupils are tested again. Obviously teachers hope that pupils will have performed better in the end of term test than the initial test and that there is a significant difference in the means suggesting great improvement.

When testing for differences between three or more groups analysis of variance (ANOVA) is used instead of a t-test (see Popham and Sirotnik, 1992; Salkind, 2000). An ANOVA will identify whether or not there is a significant difference in the means across a number of different groups. The null hypothesis for this test is that there is no difference in the means for the different groups. For example, an ANOVA would be required to test for any variation between three exam markers, each marking 100 exam scripts. Here the variable being tested would be the exam mark given to each student and the grouping variable would be the exam marker. In this case, we would hope not to find a difference (i.e. that the test result is non-significant) demonstrating that the exam markers are consistent with each other.

In the ANOVA we are looking to see if the difference between the groups is greater than the difference within the groups. The result of the ANOVA test is called the F ratio (after the creator of the statistic, Fisher). This ratio compares the variability (variance or sum of squares) between groups (the differences you might expect because of the grouping factor) to the variability within the groups (the differences that arise due to chance factors, irrespective of the group they are in). The larger the variability between groups and the smaller the variability within groups, the larger the F ratio will be and the more likely that the difference between the groups will be a real one.

For this technique two different degrees of freedom (df) calculations are required. The degrees of freedom for the between groups measure is the number of groups minus one. The degrees of freedom for the within groups measure is the total

number in the sample minus the degrees of freedom for the between groups measure. The results of the ANOVA are often presented in a table as shown in Table 26.1.

The ANOVA result tells us whether or not there is a significant difference in the means of the groups overall. But it does not tell us if the significance is between all of the groups or just between some of the groups. To find out which pairs of groups are significantly different we carry out a *post-hoc* analysis (an analysis after the initial analysis). The two most commonly used in the social sciences are the Tukey HSD test and the Scheffé test (see Field, 2000).

Non-parametric techniques for identifying differences

For nominal or ordinal data there are many non-parametric tests of difference (see Leach, 1979; Siegel and Castellon, 1988). Each technique has a specific purpose and each has specific requirements about level of measurement (that is nominal or ordinal data), number of categories, number of groups and type of difference explored. It is crucial to know what kinds of differences are being explored using what types of data in order to select the most appropriate technique. These techniques can also be used with interval data when you have very small samples or when there are violations of the assumptions which underlie parametric tests (for example, when data cannot be described as having a normal distribution – see Lewin, in this volume). Non-parametric tests typically use ranking of data to compare groups and are based on fewer assumptions. For example, they are distribution free, that is the data is not assumed to be normally distributed. The Mann-Whitney U test is the non-parametric equivalent of the independent sample t-test. The Wilcoxon signed-rank test is the non-parametric equivalent of the paired sample t-test.

Grounding analysis in inferential statistics: looking for relationships

When we explore the relationships between variables we are using a process called *correlation*. In social science research correlation procedures are very popular. We use them to compare groups of individuals on different tasks. For example, we may correlate two different groups of 10-year-olds' performance on a maths exam, or we might compare one group of children's literacy scores with their numeracy scores, or we could explore the relationship between height and weight, that is two characteristics of individuals in a single group. In all cases what we are exploring is how the shape of the distributions of two variables are related.

The correlation coefficient (r) tells us the degree of linear association between the two variables or the strength of the relationship. By linear we mean how straight a line they form when plotted on a graph showing their relationship. One of the implications of exploring linear relationships is that the things being measured must be continuous (i.e., interval or ratio) so they could theoretically form a straight line. Only interval and ratio numbers where means and standard deviations can be calculated can be used to explore linearity. Nominal data (named categories or types) cannot be measured linearly, so we use 'chi-square' and the measures of association for these. There are special correlation procedures (Spearman rank order correlation, Kendall's tau) to explore the relationships between ordinal or ranked data.

The correlation coefficient (r) will be somewhere between -1.0 and $+1.0$. When $r = 1$ or -1 it tells us the data fall in a perfect straight line. When r is positive then the correlation is positive meaning that scores on both variables increase together. When r is negative then the correlation is negative meaning that as the value of one variable increases the value of the other variable decreases. When $r = 0$ it tells us that there is no association between the two variables. Values of r between 0 and 1 show the different strength of the relationship between the two variables. Generally speaking if r is below 0.33 it is considered to be a weak relationship; if r is between 0.34 and 0.66 it indicates a medium strength relationship; and if r is between 0.67 and 0.99 it indicates a strong relationship.

Scatterplot techniques

One way to understand what we mean by linear relationships is to draw a scatterplot of the two

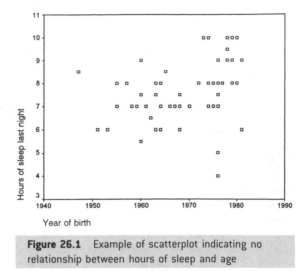

Figure 26.1 Example of scatterplot indicating no relationship between hours of sleep and age

variables. The more 'line' or cigar shaped a scatterplot looks the greater the linear relationship. If the scatterplot is a straight line that is a perfect correlation. For example, the scatterplot in Figure 26.1 shows a non-significant relationship between hours of sleep and year of birth among 53 people attending a statistics class.

When the scatterplot results in a mass of dots all over the paper there is unlikely to be a correlation and we would expect the resulting correlation coefficient to be very close to 0.

The next example in Figure 26.2 shows a linear relationship between a mark given for coursework and a final module mark for 193 students.

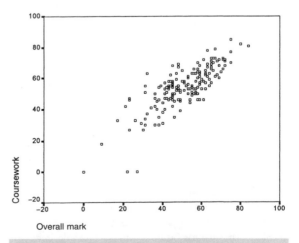

Figure 26.2 Example of scatterplot suggesting there may be a linear relationship between the mark given for coursework and the overall module mark

Correlations

		Coursework	Overall Mark
Coursework	Pearson Correlation	1	.908**
	Sig. (2-tailed)	.	.000
	N	193	193
Overall Mark	Pearson Correlation	.908**	1
	Sig. (2-tailed)	.000	.
	N	193	193

**Correlation is significant at the 0.01 level (2-tailed).

Figure 26.3   Example of SPSS output from correlation test

Calculation requirements

To calculate the correlation coefficient requires two samples of scores, often called the X and Y variables. The scores are paired in some way. In most cases in social science research this pairing is by individual, so we often have a set of people and scores for them on two things. For example, we might do a correlation on a particular class of students' performance on the first term exam and the second term exam. This would tell us the degree of association between the two exam results. In this case each individual would have two scores. Or if we gave the same exam two years in a row we could do a correlation between last year's students and this year's.

Another good example is the relationship between coursework mark and overall mark for 193 students. Here, you would expect there to be a strong relationship and the SPSS output in Figure 26.3 shows that:

$$r = 0.908, \, n = 193, \, p < 0.01$$

In this case the size of the sample (n) is normally quoted instead of the degrees of freedom. (Sometimes the degrees of freedom figure is given instead which is calculated as the number of pairs -2; in this case the df $= 191$. It is important to give the sample size as it strongly effects the statistical significance of the correlation (see Figure 26.3).

There are a number of correlational methods. Which method is used depends on the scale of measurement of the two variables. The most commonly used method of calculating correlation is the *Pearson product-moment correlation coefficient* called Pearson's r. We use this method when both variables are

interval or ratio, such as test scores, height, number of correct answers, proportions and so on. The correlational method appropriate when one or both variables are ordinal (ranked) is the *Spearman rank order correlation coefficient*, called Spearman's rho, or if the data set is small with many observations equally ranked, Kendall's tau (see Field, 2000: 91–3). These techniques can also be used when assumptions for parametric tests are violated (i.e. the data is not normally distributed). There are also correlational methods to use with nominal data (chi-square – see below).

Interpreting correlations

To interpret a correlation we use a minimum of three pieces of information: r (the correlation coefficient indicating the strength of the relationship, described above); the statistical significance of r (the probability value); and the size of the sample. To interpret correlations all these factors can be taken into account. Clearly, statistical significance is relevant but so is the strength of the relationship. Correlation is greatly affected by sample size. With very large samples weak correlation coefficients may be statistically significant; with small samples only very strong correlations will reach statistical significance.

The significance of r

As with other tests, we first decide if we are hypothesizing a result in a particular direction or not – so do we use a one- or two-tailed level of significance? We then decide what is the minimum level of significance we are prepared to accept – 0.05, 0.01, 0.001 or whatever. The choice about what level

GENDER* Use a computer outside school Crosstabulation

Count

		Use a computer outside school		Total
		No	Yes	
GENDER	Male	322	2963	3285
	Female	288	2566	2854
Total		610	5529	6139

Figure 26.4   Example of a simple cross-tabulation

of significance to use as the standard for a particular study depends on the reliability and validity of the data being analysed as well as the original research question being addressed. Always, your reasons for the decisions taken will need to be explained when reporting the outcomes.

Chi-square

Chi-square is one of the most used techniques to explore relationships using nominal and/or ordinal data. It is a very unusual statistic because it does two things in one test. It is a test of independence and also a test of association. In chi-square we formally are testing the null hypothesis that two things are independent. If we reject the null hypothesis because we have significant results we can do further analysis to look at the kind of relationship that exists between two variables and the strength of that relationship.

The first step in interpreting a significant chi-square is to look carefully at the values and/or percentages in the frequency table as a way of understanding the association between different variables. The frequency table indicates how many cases (people for example) exhibit each of the possible combinations of the two nominal variables being tested. The example in Figure 26.4 shows how many boys and how many girls use computers outside school and how many do not. By using the 'Crosstab' procedure in SPSS it is possible to produce this two-way frequency table (or contingency table as it is often called).

However, by also using SPSS to display the percentages in each column and row as in Figure 26.5 it is easier to interpret the relationship between gender and out-of school use of computers in this sample.

The percentages help us to take into account that there are many more pupils reporting use of computers out of school than not, and slightly more boys than girls in this sample. SPSS chi-square output produces the results of many tests. The most commonly used chi-square statistic is the *Pearson chi-square* (χ^2). In this case (see Figure 26.6):

$$\chi^2 = 0.142, df = 1, p = 0.706$$

GENDER* Use a computer outside school Crosstabulation

			Use a computer outside school		Total
			No	Yes	
GENDER	Male	Count	322	2963	3285
		% with GENDER	9.8%	90.2%	100.0%
		% within Use a computer outside school	52.8%	53.6%	53.5%
GENDER	Female	Count	288	2566	2854
		% with GENDER	10.1%	89.9%	100.0%
		% within Use a computer outside school	47.2%	46.4%	46.5%
Total		Count	610	5529	6139
		% with GENDER	9.9%	90.1%	100.0%
		% within Use a computer outside school	100.0%	100.0%	100.0%

Figure 26.5   Example of a cross-tabulation with row and column percentages

Chi-Square Tests

	Value	df	Asymp. Sig. (2-sided)	Exact Sig. (2-sided)	Exact Sig. (1-sided)
Pearson Chi-Square	.142[b]	1	.706		
Continuity Correlation[a]	.112	1	.738		
Likelihood Ratio	.142	1	.706		
Fisher's Exact Test				.732	.369
Linear-by-Linear Association	.142	1	.706		
N of Valid Cases	6139				

[a]Computed only for 2 × 2 table.
[b]0 cells (.0%) have expected count less than 5. The minimum expected count is 283.59.

Figure 26.6   SPSS output for chi-square test

The df for chi-square is (number of rows −1) multiplied by (number of columns −1). For a table with two rows and two columns (a 2 × 2 table) the df = 1. It also tells us that the probability of achieving a $\chi^2 = 0.142$ is totally by chance because p > 0.05 (p = 0.706). Therefore there is no relationship between gender and reported use of computers outside of school.

The chi-square statistic is the most used and most abused statistic in social science research. The abuse comes from researchers making interpretations about the association between variables beyond what the result indicates. In and of itself chi-square only tells us if there is an association between two things or if there is independence. To explore the strength of relationship requires using one of the *post-hoc* analyses in measures of association such as phi or Cramer's V (see Field, 2000: 67). Similarly to correlation coefficients, these give a measure of strength between 0.0 and 1.0; the closer to 1.0 this statistic is, the stronger the association.

Implications for research design

One of the main issues to consider either when testing for differences or for relationships is whether or not to choose a parametric test or a non-parametric test.

Parametric tests are more sophisticated and many argue are more sensitive than non-parametric tests (and so are likely to detect differences) but can only be used with interval or ratio level data and only if certain assumptions are met. The data should be normally distributed (see Lewin, in this volume). This can be determined by using statistical procedures such

as the Kolmogorov-Smirnov test (see Field, 2000: 46–9). And, the variability of values in each group should be approximately the same – known as *homogeneity of variance*. This is tested in different ways for different procedures.

Non-parametric tests are more robust but less sensitive. They are sometimes referred to as assumption-free tests. The techniques are based on ranking rather than exact differences, that is whether scores or variable values are higher or lower than others. Non-parametric tests are appropriate for ordinal and nominal data. They can also be used when the necessary parameters for parametric tests are not in place (for example, the distribution of the sample is not a normal distribution).

Chi-square, while being a non-parametric test, does depend on assumptions that need to be met. Firstly, each case or person must only contribute to one cell in the contingency table (i.e. the characteristics for each variable must be mutually exclusive). Often this can be tested logically. If we collect information about gender and eye colour from 100 students you would expect the responses to each question to elicit only one answer (each student will be classified as being of one type of gender and having eyes of one particular colour). Secondly, the chi-square test works by comparing the distribution of observations in the cells of the contingency table with the distribution that might have been expected if there was no association, generating an *expected count* in each cell. If any of the expected counts are less than 5 then the chi-square test may be invalid although with large contingency tables accepting no more than 20 per cent of cells with expected counts less than 5 is acceptable.

Prediction and causation – a caution

One of the most common mistakes researchers make when using correlations is to talk about cause and effect. If there is an association between two variables that does not necessarily mean that one causes the other. There are three conditions, which must be satisfied in order to prove cause and effect relationships:

● There must be a significant correlation between the 'cause' and 'effect' variables.
● The correlation must be 'real', not due to some other factor (we call this spurious).
● The cause variable must precede the effect variable in real time.

A significant correlation, on its own, does not provide any evidence for causality. For example, there is a positive association between height and weight – taller people tend to weigh more than shorter people or people who weigh less tend to be shorter than people who weigh more. We cannot say that tall people weigh more because they eat more because it is equally possible that they weigh more because they grow taller and need to eat more. Association does not mean causation.

Also, the significant correlation between the variables must be seen to be 'real'. Freedman and Pisani (1998) use the example of searching for the cause of polio back in the 1950s where there was a worldwide epidemic. Researchers gathered massive amounts of information from polio victims and their families and discovered two very significant correlations:

● an increase in the incidence of polio and an increase of drinking soft drinks;
● an increase in the incidence of polio and an increase in temperature.

Only one of these is a 'real' relationship. The other is 'spurious'. The polio virus spreads as the temperature rises and so that is a real relationship. However, as the temperature rises we tend to drink more liquids and so the connection between polio and soft drinks is spurious because it is connected to temperature and doesn't exist on its own.

The final condition which must be met to examine prediction and causality is that the cause variables must precede the effect variable. For example, an intervention to improve the teaching of reading must take place before the test measuring reading ability is undertaken. However, sometimes in the social sciences the cause and effect is harder to unravel. Think about the relationship between job satisfaction and productivity. Which comes first?

Annotated bibliography

Coolidge, F.L. (2000) *Statistics: A Gentle Introduction*. London: Sage.

The book offers a good introduction to statistics and their underlying principles. Coolidge's examples and writing make some of these difficult concepts more easily approachable. His description of the ins and outs of t-test (Chapter 7) and ANOVA (Chapter 9) are good. His step-by-step calculations may help the reader to understand what these tests actually do. He uses a style of notation which many people find accessible.

Field, A. (2000) *Discovering Statistics Using SPSS for Windows*. London: Sage.

An excellent, friendly, accessible book which leads the novice researcher into the ins and outs of using statistics on SPSS.

Freedman, D., Pisani, R. and Purves, R. (1998) *Statistics*, 3rd edn. New York: Norton.

This is an excellent book which focuses on probability and significance testing and the use of root mean square (RMS) in developing statistical sophistication.

Howell, D.C. (1997) *Statistical Methods for Psychology*, 4th edn. Belmont, CA: Duxbury Press.

This is a very comprehensive text with careful conceptual and mathematical explanations together with helpful examples. It takes the reader through the underlying principles of statistical techniques to advanced methods such as multiple regression.

Leach, C. (1979) *Introduction to Statistics: A Nonparametric Approach for the Social Sciences*. Chichester: John Wiley & Sons.

Mendenhall, W. (1987) *Introduction to Probability and Statistics*. Boston: Duxbury Press, Chapter 1: 'What is statistics'.

Mendenhall uses a case study to present his key concepts. So he develops the idea and use of inferential statistics in sections 1.2, 1.3 and 1.4 and then applies them to his case study in 1.5. An interesting and useful technique.

Pallant, J. (2001) *SPSS Survival Manual*. Buckingham: Open University Press.

Written in a friendly, detailed style. Covers almost everything. One of the best features of this book are the tables of statistical tests with when they can be used and how.

Popham, W.J. and Sirotnik, K.A. (1992) *Understanding Statistics in Education*. Itasca, IL: F.E. Peacock.

An excellent introductory statistics book which describes each statistical technique across two chapters. The first in conceptual form and the second through computation.

Salkind, N.J. (2000) *Statistics for People Who (Think They) Hate Statistics*. London: Sage.

For beginners this book is the place to start. It is friendly, easy to understand and full of useful information. Chapters are in good, clear English with easy step-by-step procedures. Starts with the assumption that people don't know and may not want to know what they need to know about! The three chapters on t-test and ANOVA are a good progression. Highly recommended.

Siegel, S. and Castellon, J. (1988) *Non-parametric Statistics for the Social Sciences*, 2nd edn. New York: McGraw-Hill.

Siegel wrote the definitive guide to non-parametric statistics in the 1950s. It is a classic. The current text is an update on the original and though it is written in a statistical way most tests you will ever use are described and explained.

CHAPTER
27

AN INTRODUCTION TO STATISTICAL MODELLING

Kelvyn Jones
School of Geographical Sciences, University of Bristol, UK

Statistical modelling is a huge subject. In the space we have available I will concentrate on why you do modelling and what can be achieved. I consider what sort of questions it can answer, what sort of data looks like a 'regression' problem and what steps we can take to ensure we get valid results. I have written this introduction from the advanced perspective of the generalized linear model (McCullagh and Nelder, 1989) and have included a substantial discussion on the developing approach of multilevel modelling because of its major potential in the analysis of social research questions.

Regression Modelling

In the social sciences we research 'cause and effect' relations that are neither necessary (the outcome occurs only if the causal factor has operated) nor sufficient (the action of a factor always produces the outcome). Moreover, inherent variation or 'noise' may swamp the 'signal' and we need quantitative techniques to uncover the underlying patterns to produce credible evidence of a relation. A good exemplar comes from epidemiology. There are lung-cancer victims who have never smoked, and people who have smoked for a lifetime without a day's illness. The link was once doubted but we now have unequivocal evidence. Men who smoke increase their risk of death from lung cancer by more than 22 times (a staggering 2,200 per cent higher). The estimate is that one cigarette reduces your life on average by 11 minutes (*British Medical Journal*, 2000, 320: 53).

To illustrate the arguments I will use a research problem of assessing the evidence for discrimination in legal firms. In that context, statistical modelling provides the following:

- a quantitative assessment of the size of the effect – for example, the difference in salary between blacks and whites is £5,000 per annum;

- a quantitative assessment after taking account of other variables – for example, a black worker earns £6,500 less after taking account of years of experience; this *conditioning* on other variables distinguishes modelling from 'testing for differences' (see Barnes and Lewin, in this volume);

- a measure of uncertainty for the size of effect – for example, we can be 95 per cent confident that the black–white difference in salary to be found generally in the population from which our sample is drawn is likely to lie between £4,400 and £5,500 (see Lewin, in this volume, for an explanation of confidence intervals).

We can use regression modelling in a number of modes: as description (what is the average salary for different ethnic groups?); as part of causal inferences (does being black result in a lower salary?); and in predictive mode ('what happens if' questions). The latter can be very difficult to achieve because change may be so systemic that the underlying relations themselves are altered, and past empirical regularities captured by the modelling no longer hold in a period of regime change (Lucas, 1976).

Data for modelling

Modelling requires a quantifiable outcome measure to assess the effects of discrimination. Table 27.1 provides several, differentiated by the nature of the measurement: a continuous measure of salary; the binary categorical outcome of promoted or not; the three-category outcome (promoted, not promoted, not even considered); a count of the number of times rejected for promotion; and a time-to-event measure, the length of time that it has taken to promotion, where a '+' indicates that the event has not yet taken place. All of these outcomes can be analysed in a generalized linear model, but different techniques are

Table 27.1 A dataframe for regression modelling for the discrimination study

Respondent number	Responses					Predictors			
	Salary (£k)	Promotion (2 category)	Promotion (3 category)	Number of rejections	Time to promotion (yrs)	Gender	Ethnicity	Years of education	Years of service
1	32.4	No	No	1	6.2+	Female	White	<11	9.1
2	40.1	Yes	Yes	0	3.2	Male	White	11-13	6.2
3	65.2	Yes	Yes	0	2.9	Male	Asian	14-16	4.9
4	32.1	No	No	2	8.2+	Female	Black	>16	8.2
5	21.6	No	Not	4	6.7+	Female	Unknown	11-13	6.7
6	25.4	No	Not	3	4.2+	Male	Black	<11	4.2
7	32.7	No	No	1	5.1+	Female	White	14-16	5.1
8	51.7	Yes	Yes	0	3.9	Male	White	<11	4.8
9	44.0	Yes	Yes	0	4.2	Female	Asian	14-16	7.2
10	32.6	No	No	1	3.9+	Female	Black	14-16	3.9
11	41.7	Yes	Yes	0	4.9	Male	White	11-13	9.7
.	.	.	.	.	.	.	.	.	.
.	.	.	.	.	.	.	.	.	.
.	.	.	.	.	.	.	.	.	.
500	39.7	No	No	2	5.2	Male	Unknown	14-16	8.1

required for different scales of measurement. Suitable models going from left to right across the table are normal-theory, logit, multinomial, Poisson and Cox regression but they all share fundamental characteristics of the general family (Retherford and Choe, 1993). Also shown in the table are a number of 'explanatory' or predictor variables, again with different scales of measurement. Gender is measured as two categories, ethnicity as four, education as a set of ordered categories and years of employment on a continuous scale. All of these scales can be analysed in the general framework.

Relations

Figure 27.1 displays a range of relations between a response, salary, on the vertical axis and predictor variables on the horizontal. In (a) there is a sizeable difference between the male and female average income. In (b) to (d) we see a number of straight-line relations between salary and years of service. The first (b) is a positive one – the longer you have worked for the firm, the more money you get. The second (c) is the flat one of no relation; there is no effect of length of employment on pay (think fast-food outlets!). The third (d) shows a negative relation, the longer you have been there, the less you get paid (this can happen in physically demanding jobs).

A non-linear relation between salary and length of employment is shown in (e) – an initial steep rise tails off indicating that the full salary is reached rapidly. In (f) salary increments get steeper and steeper with experience, and in (g) there is a curvilinear relation such that salary increases for the first six years then tails away. An interaction between gender and length of employment is shown in (h). At appointment there is no gender gap but this opens up the longer you are employed. The distinctive feature of (i) is that in addition to the solid lines displaying averages for the four categories of ethnicity, there are dashed lines representing the confidence interval (see Lewin, in this volume). We can be 95 per cent confident that the true population value will fall within this interval given our sample data. Here, the average white salary is estimated with the greatest reliability and has the narrowest band. The Asian band is the widest – we are unsure what the average for this group is. While the black salary is unequivocally lower than the white as the confidence intervals do not overlap, the evidence is not sufficient to decide on white–Asian differences, nor on Asian–black differences. The

unknown group looks indistinguishable from the white group, with a slightly wider confidence interval. The final graph (j) is a *three-way interaction* between gender, ethnicity and length of employment. At the outset, there are substantial differences between the groups and as time proceeds black women would appear to be doubly discriminated against.

Conditioning

We may be interested in the effect of just one variable (gender) on another (salary) but we need to take account of other variables as they may compromise the results. We can recognize three distinct cases:

- Inflation of a relation when not taking into account extraneous variables: a substantial gender effect could be reduced after taking account of ethnicity – this is because the female labour force is predominantly non-white and it is this group that is characterized by poor pay.
- Suppression of a relation: an apparent small gender gap could increase when account is taken of years of employment, women having longer service and poorer pay.
- No confounding: the original relation remains substantially unaltered when account is taken of other variables.

While modelling can usually assess the partial relationship between two variables taking account of others, this cannot be achieved when predictor variables are so highly correlated that we have no effective way of telling them apart. In the pathological case of exact collinearity (complete dependence between a pair or more of variables) a separate effect cannot be estimated. For example, if all Asians in the survey are women, we cannot determine the gender gap for Asians. More generally, collinearity is a matter of degree and as the correlation between predictor variables increases, so do the confidence intervals as there is insufficient distinctive information for reliable estimation.

Form of the model

All statistical models have a common form:

Response = Systematic part + Random part

The systematic part is the average relation between the response and the predictors while the random part

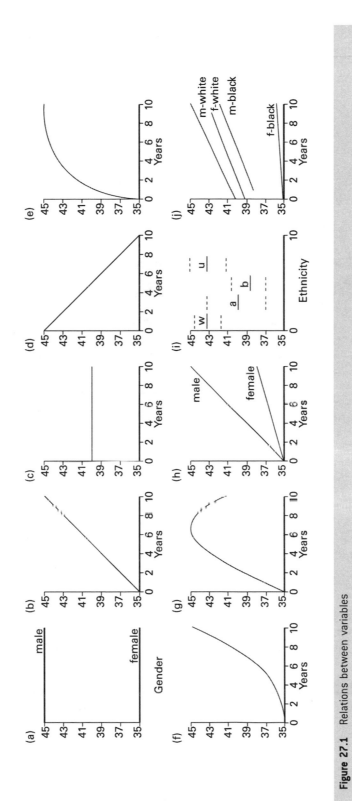

Figure 27.1   Relations between variables

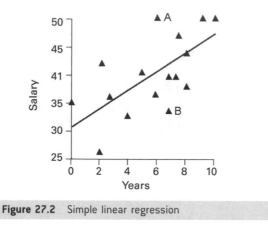

Figure 27.2   Simple linear regression

is the variation in the response after taking account of all the included predictors. Figure 27.2 displays the values representing the data for 16 respondents and a straight line we have threaded through the points to represent the systematic relation between salary and length of employment. The line represents fitted values – if you have ten years' service you are predicted to have a salary of about £45,000.

All equations of the straight line involving two variables have the same form:

Fitted value = Intercept + (Slope × Predictor)

which here is:

Predicted salary = Intercept + (Slope × Years of service)

which (say) we estimate to be:

Predicted salary = 30.3 + (1.7 × Length of service)

The intercept gives the predicted value of the response when the predictor takes on the value of zero, so we are predicting that the average salary on appointment (when years of service is 0) is £30,000. The slope gives the marginal change in the response variable for a unit change in the predictor variable. For every extra year with the firm, salary increases by £1,700. Importantly, the increase in salary consequent from staying 0 to 1 years in service is the same as from 5 to 6 years of service. This is a direct consequence of assuming that the underlying functional form of the model is linear and fitting a linear equation.

The term random means 'allowed to vary' and, in relation to Figure 27.2, the random part is the variation in salary that is not accounted for by the underlying average relationship with years. Some people are paid more and some less given the time they have been with the firm. We see that person A has an income above the line while B is below. The difference between the actual and predicted salary is known as the residual. In fitting the line we have minimized these residuals so that the line goes through the middle of the data points. Here we have used a technique called *ordinary least squares* in which the sum of the squared residuals is minimized. Responses with other scales of measurement require other techniques, but all of them are based on the same underlying principle of minimizing the 'poorness of fit' between the actual data points and the fitted line.

In some cases there will be a close fit between the actual and fitted values but in other cases there may be a lot of 'noise', so that for any given length of employment there is a wide range of salaries. It is helpful to characterize this residual variability. To do so requires us to make some assumptions. We need to conceive of the residuals as coming from a particular distribution. Given that salary is a continuous variable, we can assume that the residuals come from a normal distribution (other scales would suggest other distributions). If we further assume that there is the same variability for short and long length of service (that is homoscedasticity) we can summarize the variability in a single statistic, the standard deviation of the residuals. For Figure 27.2 this value is 6, and we can anticipate (given the known properties of a normal distribution) that the income for 95 per cent of employees on appointment will lie roughly 2 standard deviations around the mean value of £30,000. Most people will have an initial income between £18,000 and £42,000. This rather wide spread of values is due to inherent uncertainty in the system and the small number (16) of observations we have used. Another key summary statistic is the R-squared value which gives the correspondence between actual and fitted values, on a scale between zero (no correspondence) and 100 (complete correspondence).

The model we have so far discussed is a 'simple' one with only one predictor. In a multiple regression model there is more than one predictor (there can be any combination of continuous and categorical variables) with the following differences:

- *Intercept*: this is now the average value for the response when all the predictors take the value zero.
- *Slope*: there is one for each predictor and this summarizes the conditional or partial relationship as the change in the response for a unit change in a particular predictor, holding all the other predictors constant.
- *Residual*: the difference between the actual and fitted values based on all the predictors.
- *R-squared*: the percentage of the total variation of the response variable that is accounted for by all predictors taken simultaneously.

Figure 27.1 (h) to (j) are all examples of multiple regression models, the key to their specification being the coding of predictor variables. A comprehensive discussion of how to do this can be found at: <http://www.ats.ucla.edu/stat/stata/webbooks/reg/chapter5/>.

Implications for research design

We can recognize two broad classes of design that will produce suitable data for regression modelling: experiments where we intervene and observational studies. Experiments are artificial settings in which we change the predictor variable and see what happens to the response while keeping other variables 'controlled'. We can also randomly allocate each case to an 'intervention' or not, thereby guaranteeing that any detectable change in the response is due to the intervention. Because of this control of unknown factors, experiments are a very strong procedure for causal inference. It is often thought that experiments are more or less impossible in most social sciences due to ethics and relations being disposition-response, not stimulus-response. You cannot easily change a person's gender and keep everything else the same! But with some ingenuity we could get something like the data we need. If we are interested in how ethnicity affects whether a person is promoted or not, we could write scripts for an interview, varying some elements such as length of employment but keeping all the rest the same. Actors of different ethnicity could record these, and the videos played to managers to see what decision they would come to. Modelling would then identify the size of the effect of ethnicity in relation to years of employment. This is a very strong design for causal inference but the external validity may be weak due to the artificiality of the process so that everyone gets promoted!

Observational designs are less strong for causal inference, but if attention is paid to scientific sampling so that each member of the population has a known chance of inclusion, they can be highly representative. We can recognize four broad groups of design, each with their own strengths and weaknesses: administrative data, cross-sectional surveys, case-comparison study and panel design (see Jones and Moon, 1987). All of these designs can yield data that can be modelled by regression analysis, the choice of design being determined by the type of question being asked and the resources available. There is one golden rule that must be followed, however: 'the specifics of the design must be taken account of in the modelling'. For example, a panel survey (where people are tracked periodically) will generate data for respondents that will be patterned across time (salary now will be similar to what it was last year and the year before), and this 'non-independence' must be explicitly modelled.

Our aim in designing how we are going to collect the data and how we are going to analyse them is to get valid results. We can recognize two broad areas of validity that particularly apply to the analysis and the design of a model-based study, and we will discuss these issues using regression in causal mode.[1]

Conclusion validity

This is concerned with analysis and asks if the conclusions we have reached about relationships in our data are credible. We can be wrong in two ways: missing a real relation, and finding a relation where there is none.

The key threats to this sort of validity (and what to do about them) are.

- The assumptions of the systematic part (for example, in terms of linearity) and the random part (in terms of the nature of the distribution and such properties as homoscedasticity, that is equal variance, and independence[2]) must be met. This amounts to the systematic part of the model fully capturing the generalities of the world; equivalently the random part is just 'trendless' fluctuations. We can use 'diagnostics' to assess assumptions and robust procedures with less demanding assumptions. A useful guide to both these approaches is to be found in Cook and Weisberg (1999).
- Fishing for results: this is analysing the data repeatedly under slightly differing conditions or

assumptions, dropping these cases, transforming this variable, trying out a very large number of different predictor variables, or including every possible interaction to maximize the R-squared. If we do this, we are more or less bound to find something. But the status of what we have found is problematic – we cannot tell whether what we have found is idiosyncratic noise or generalizable signal. The best advice is to focus on a single topic. We should ask not the vague 'what determines salary', but 'is there discrimination by ethnicity in annual salary when account is taken of gender and length of employment?' If you do undertake some fishing (because of the lack of theory), keep it limited, be honest in your write-up, adjust your level of significance to take account of multiple hypothesis testing and use a hold-out sample as an independent test of the model.

- Lack of statistical power so that the sample is too small a sample to detect a real relationship. The required number of observations is determined by three factors: noisy systems need more observations, so do predictor variables lacking variability and collinear predictors. As a very rough rule of thumb, you would not usually have more than ten predictor variables in a single model, and you might plan on collecting at least 25 observations for each. Software is available (e.g. < http://www.insp.mx/dinf/stat_list.html >) which indicates required sample size for a given power. A common rule of thumb is a power of 0.8 – at least an 80 per cent chance of finding a relationship when there is one.

- Measurement error: we can have imprecise measurements and we can have systematically biased measurements. In general, biased measurements will produce biased estimates of effects unless all variables are off target by the same amount. Non-systematic errors in the dependent variable will require additional observations for the same power, while such errors in the key predictor variable usually biases estimates by attenuating them to zero. We can do a sensitivity analysis to appreciate the effects of measurement error, while during collection we can use a pilot survey to assess reliability and bias. Developing a consistent protocol, training the interviewers and careful wording of questions can all help.

Internal validity

This second type of validity addresses the question of whether the relationship we have found is a causal one. The key threats to validity (and what to do about them) are:

- *Omitted variables bias* refers to an alternative explanation of the results: to be problematic, such variables must be related to *both* the response and the included predictor variable. Specification error tests are available (Hendry, 2000), but while these may indicate a problem, they cannot suggest what variable is missing. This is the Achilles heel of regression modelling with observational data; with an experiment employing randomization this should not be a problem. The best possible advice is to think hard about the research problem and include all the relevant variables. At the same time you do no want to include irrelevant variables, as this will reduce the power of the design to detect real effects. It can help a great deal to classify possible predictors into direct causes, indirect causes, moderating variables and mediating variables (Miles and Shevlin, 2001).

- *Endogeneity* is a fancy term for having a predictor variable that is directly influenced by the response, such that income is determined by health and health by income. In an experiment, this problem is ruled out by design as you can manipulate the predictors and see the subsequent effects. With observational designs there are specialist techniques such as instrumental variables and structural equations models for improved estimation. Panel designs can also be vital here. In some situations it is possible to rule out this problem *a priori* – it is unlikely for example that gender or ethnicity are determined by salary!

- *Selection bias* is when we have selected our respondents so as to in some way systematically distort the relation between the predictor and the outcome. The problem is such that any selection rule correlated with the response variable will attenuate estimates of an effect towards zero. For example, if we had only been able to collect data on those above an income threshold, we would have attenuated the relation between salary and years of experience. People who do not return your questionnaire may be different, in some important way, to the people who did. Strict adherence to sampling protocols, well-trained interviewers and intensive follow-up to a pilot can help minimize this problem. There are also analytical techniques than can adjust the estimates to take account of this bias.

It is worth stressing in concluding this section what regression modelling is trying to do. It aims at generality and generalizable results. We are not primarily interested why this specific person did or did not get a salary rise but what is happening to females as a group. We can only collect sample data but we wish to infer quite generally what is going on across the country. Once identified, this generality throws into stronger relief any unusual cases. We are continually searching for evidence that supports/ challenges alternative explanations and we are always looking for the empirical implications of our theory to subject it to rigorous evaluation.

Multilevel Modelling

Multilevel modelling is a recently developed procedure that is only now seeing widespread use. It is given a separate section here because of its potential for handling a wide variety of research designs. Although it grows out of regression, the approach represents a considerable increase in sophistication. We begin with a specific problem, and then show how this relates to different forms of multilevel structures and associated research designs.

A multilevel problem

My university (in the UK) like others has been keen to widen its participation. It may be that if an able student goes to a poorly performing school, their A-level score at entry is an underestimate of their potential.[3] Alternatively, if they go to a fee-paying, highly resourced school, their score has been temporarily boosted and this does not carry over to their degree performance. If we can identify such situations we may justifiably recruit students with a lower point score on the basis of greater potential. But what is the evidence for such a policy? We can set this up as a regression-type problem in which the response of the degree result of the student is related to three predictors: A-level score, the school average performance and an indicator of school type.

But there is a difficulty because we are dealing with a problem with a multilevel structure. Student and school are not at the same level in that (many)

students are nested in (fewer) schools. Moreover, students belonging to the same school are more likely to be alike than students from different schools. If this 'auto-correlation' or 'non-independence' is not taken into account, we have fewer observations than we think we have and we run the risk of finding significant relationships where none exist. Technically the effective degrees of freedom (see Barnes and Lewin, in this volume) are lower than we think they are. But this is more than a technical problem, for there are several sources of variation that need to be taken into account for a proper analysis. Thus there is the between-student variation, between-school variation and, extending the analysis, between-university and between-discipline variations. In relation to the latter there may be disciplines where the A-level score is a very poor guide to degree performance and should not be used as the main entry requirement. Thus the effect of an A-level score on performance is not fixed but varies from context to context, where context is provided by the different levels in the structure. In comparison to standard regression models, multilevel models have a more complex random part.

Research designs and multilevel structures

It turns out that a very large array of research questions can be seen as combinations of just three types of multilevel structure that can now be routinely handled by computer-intensive procedures. The simplest structure is the hierarchy in which a lower-level unit nests in only one higher level unit (see Figure 27.3). The classic example (a) is the two-level model in which pupils are nested in schools. This can readily be extended so that pupils at level 1 can be nested within classes (level 2) within schools (level 3) within local education authorities (level 4). This strict hierarchy includes a number of research designs that you might not initially conceive as multilevel problems. A panel design is shown in Figure 27.3(b) where repeated measures (at level 1) are elicited for voting behaviour for individuals (level 2) who are nested in constituencies (level 3). In Figure 27.3(c), there is a multivariate design in which three responses measuring health-related behaviour (at level 1) are nested within individuals (level 2) within places (level 3); the responses are seen as repeated measurements of individuals, and individuals are repeated measures of places. Other examples with such a hierarchical structure include an experimental design in which the intervention is not made for individuals (at level 1)

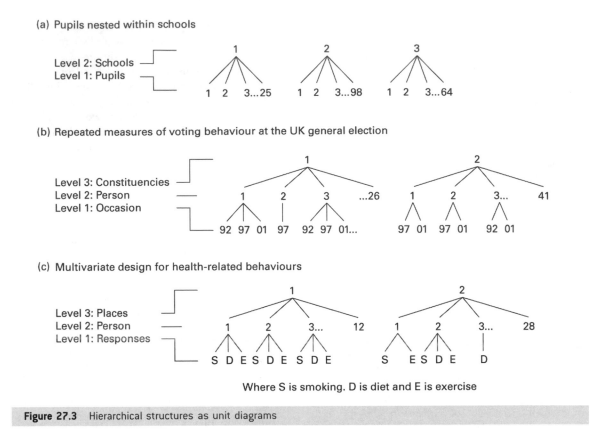

Figure 27.3   Hierarchical structures as unit diagrams

but for communities (level 2); an observational design in which there is a two-stage sampling process, first areas (which then become level 2) and then respondents within them (at level 1).

The other types of multilevel structure are two different non-hierarchical structures. The classic example (see Figure 27.4(a)) of a cross-classification is students (level 1) being nested within neighbourhoods and also schools (both at level 2). Not all the students in a neighbourhood go to a particular school and a school draws its pupils from more than one neighbourhood. Thus schools and neighbourhoods are not nested but crossed. The final structure is the multiple membership in which a lower level unit 'belongs' to more than one higher level unit (see Figure 27.4(b)). Thus a student (at level 1) may be nested within teachers (level 2) but each student may be taught by more than one teacher. We might include in the analysis a 'weight' to reflect the proportion of time each pupil spends with a teacher, so that student 2 spends 50 per cent of their time with teacher 1 and 50 per cent with teacher 2. Again a large number of

problems can be cast within this framework, for example a dynamic household study in which individuals 'belong' to more than one household over time. A less obvious example is a spatial model in which individuals are affected by the neighbourhood in which they live and also by surrounding neighbourhoods, the weight in the multiple-membership structure being some function of distance from the home neighbourhood to the surrounding neighbourhoods. These models can be extended to look at pupil achievement in situations where there is 'competition' between the higher level units, such as schools with overlapping catchments, perhaps differentiated by school types.

An alternative way of conceiving and visualizing structures is as classifications. A 'classification diagram' is particularly helpful for complex problems. Figure 27.5 shows some examples of hierarchical and non-hierarchical structures using this type of diagram: (a) is a three-level hierarchical problem; (b) is a cross-classified design; (c) is a multiple membership structure; and (d) shows a spatial structure. Boxes

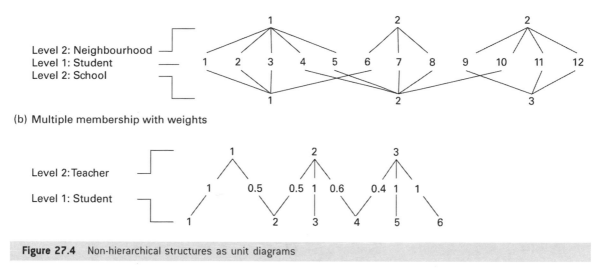

Figure 27.4   Non-hierarchical structures as unit diagrams

represent each classification with arrows representing nesting, single arrows for single membership and double arrows for multiple membership. Returning to the student performance example, we can see it as a combination of these three types of structure (Figure 27.5(e)). Students are nested within schools, and students are nested within disciplines within universities. Schools and universities are crossed because not all the students from a school go to one university. While the student/school relation might be conceived as a strict hierarchy (the last school attended) the university/discipline structure can be seen as a multiple membership one, in that students move between subjects and universities after starting courses.

Importance of structures

Is all this realism and complexity necessary? It is important to realize that a simple model tells you little about a more complex model, but a more complex model provides information about the simpler models embedded within it. Such complexity is not being sought for its own sake, but if the real world operates like this, then a simpler under-specified model can lead to inferential error.

There are in fact two key aspects of statistical complexity. We have so far concentrated on *dependencies arising from structures*. Once groupings are established, even if their establishment is random, they will tend to become differentiated as people are in-

fluenced by the group membership. To ignore this relationship risks overlooking the importance of group effects and may also render invalid many of the traditional statistical analysis techniques used for studying relationships. An example is Aitkin et al.'s (1981) re-analysis of the 'teaching styles' study. The original analysis had suggested that children's academic achievement was higher if a 'formal' teacher using all-class activities taught them. When the structure of children into classes was taken into account, the significant differences disappeared and 'formally' taught children could not be shown to differ from the others. Some data, such as repeated measures and individuals within households, can be expected to be highly auto-correlated, and it is essential this dependency is taken fully into account.

The second aspect is *complexity arising from the measurement process* such as having 'missing' data or having multiple measuring instruments. In an observational study we can expect that there will be a different number of pupils measured at each school as shown in the unit diagram of Figure 27.3(a). In a panel study, each person may not respond every year, while in the multivariate design not all people respond to all questions that form the outcome variables. A defining case of the latter is the matrix sample design where all students are asked a core set of questions on say mathematics but different random subsets of pupils are asked detailed questions on either trigonometry, algebra

(a) 3-level hierarchical structure

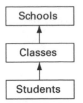

(b) Cross-classified structure

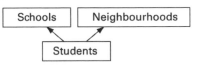

(c) Multiple membership structure

(d) Spatial structure

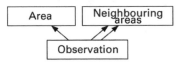

(e) Widening participation research problem as a classification diagram

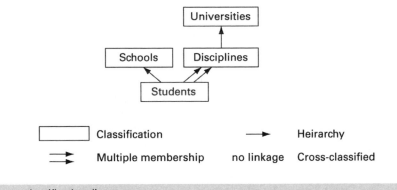

Figure 27.5   Structures as classification diagrams

or set theory. Treating this design as a hierarchical structure allows the analysis of the full set of data in an overall model.

Prior to the development of the multilevel approach, the analyst was faced with mis-applying single-level models, either aggregating to the single level of the school and risking the ecological fallacy of transferring aggregate results to individuals, or working only at the pupil level and committing the atomistic fallacy of ignoring context. The standard model is mainly concerned with averages and the general effect, where reality is often heterogeneous and complex. Thus females may not only perform better than males in terms of degree results, but they may also be more consistent (more homogenous) in their performance. It is this analysis of structures, contextual effects and heterogeneity that is tackled by multilevel models.

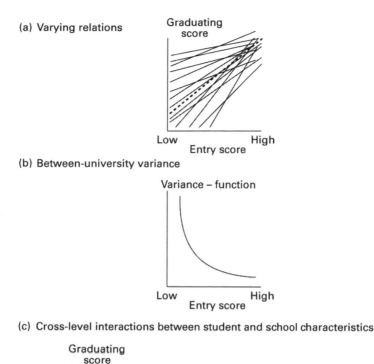

(a) Varying relations

(b) Between-university variance

(c) Cross-level interactions between student and school characteristics

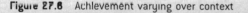

Figure 27.6 Achievement varying over context

Figure 27.6 portrays graphically some elements of the widening participation problem in terms of this heterogeneity and contextuality. In (a), the vertical axis is the final year points score of graduating university students, while the horizontal axis is the points score on entry. The lines shown are the different sampled universities. There is a noticeable 'fanning-in' so that highly qualified students on entry achieve the same excellence irrespective of where they study. But for those with a low score at initial entry, it makes a great deal of difference where they study. This varying relation between pre-score and post-score is shown in an alternative form as a variance function in Figure 27.6(b) with the same horizontal axis, but the vertical axis is now between-university variance. As the pre-entry score increases, the be-

tween-university variation decreases. Finally, Figure 27.6(c) shows what is known as a cross-level interaction: the axes are the same as (a), but the four lines represent fee-paying and non-fee-paying schools for male and female students. The cross-level interaction is between a school-level variable (fee-paying or not) and two individual-level variables (gender and pre-entry score). The noticeable result in terms of our research question is that students who have attended fee-paying schools do less well across the entry range, but this is most marked for males, especially those with relatively low entry scores. If these results were confirmed, a university may be justified in taking students with lower entry grades from non-fee paying schools, particularly for males, if it wished to pursue a policy of equal opportunity.

Implications for research design

A major difference between the design of multilevel and single-level studies is in the requirements for sufficient power to detect effects. It is not the overall number of observations but the number at each level that is important. Advice depends on the amount of underlying variation in the 'system' being modelled and what are the main aims of the analysis. Thus in planning a school-effects study an absolute minimum would be 25 pupils in each of 25 schools, preferably 100 schools. Any less of the higher units will give poor estimates of the between-school differences, particularly if school effects are being examined on several dimensions, for example in relation to high- and low-ability pupils. At level 1 the number of pupils within a school is an important determinant of what can be reliably inferred about a particular school. Little can be said about a particular school if only a few students have been sampled. In contrast, if the higher-level unit is a household, there would be very few containing 25 individuals! But this is not a problem for we are unlikely to want to infer to a named household. Instead, we want to know about between-household variability in general, and that is determined by the number of households, and not by the number of people in a household. Finally, if we only sample one person in each household we would be totally unable to separate household effects from individual effects. Hox (2002) provides an accessible discussion of statistical power in multilevel models.

Conclusion

Social reality is complex and structured. Recent developments in multilevel models provide a formal framework of analysis whose complexity of structure matches that of the system being studied. Modern software allows the estimation of very complex problems with multiple levels of nesting, and many units such as hundreds of thousands of students. Some examples of this approach are given in Jones (this volume); the usefulness of multilevel models in reality in addressing the widening participation issue can be seen from a study entitled 'Schooling effects on higher education achievement' available at <http://www.hefce.ac.uk/pubs/hefce/>, while Raudenbush and Bryk (2001) provide extensive discussion of modelling school effects.

Notes

1. Space precludes a discussion of construct validity (the extent to which variables faithfully measure concepts) and external validity (the extent to which we are able to generalize from our study).
2. To estimate correctly the confidence intervals for an effect requires that the residuals are independent, that is knowing the value of one should tell you nothing about the value of another.
3. A-levels are public examinations taken in the final year of secondary education, usually at 18 years; good scores are normally required to secure a university place.

Annotated Bibliography

Regression modelling

Allison, P.D. (1999) *Multiple Regression: A Primer*. Thousand Oaks, CA: Pine Forge Press.

An excellent primer which introduces the underlying concepts with a minimum of algebra while covering a wide range of models and their motivation.

Cook, R.D. and Weisberg, S. (1999) *Applied Regression Including Computing and Graphics*. New York: Wiley Interscience.

This stresses regression as conditional modelling and diagnostics, which are implemented in their freely available ARC software (at: <http://www.stat.umn.edu/arc/>).

Fox, J. (1997) *Applied Regression Analysis, Linear Models, and Related Methods*. Thousand Oaks, CA: Sage Publications.

An intermediate text which provides a thorough course in standard regression modelling for social scientists.

King, G., Keohabe, R.O. Verba, S. (1994) *Designing Social Inquiry*. Princeton, NJ: Princeton University Press.

An innovative text that discusses validity and design issues in quantitative and qualitative studies.

Retherford, R.D. and Choe, M.K. (1993) *Statistical Models for Causal Analysis*. New York: Wiley & Sons.

A very approachable account of generalized linear models in which the response can be categorical or time to an event.

Tacq, J. (1997) *Multivariate Analysis Techniques in Social Science Research: From Problem to Analysis*. London: Sage.

Discusses quantitative analysis in the context of specific research problems.

Trochim, W. (2000) *The Research Methods Knowledge Base*. Cincinnati: Atomic Dog Publishing (<http://trochim.human.cornell.edu/kb/>).

Available in printed form or as a web-site, this 'knowledge-base' provides a lot of useful advice on minimizing threats to validity in observational and experimental studies.

Venables, W. and Ripley, B. (2002) *Modern Applied Statistics*. New York: Springer Verlag.

One of the most comprehensive and up-to-date accounts of all sorts of developments in regression-like modelling with substantial on-line resources (see: <http://www.stats.ox.ac.uk/pub/MASS4/>) that can be used in the 'free' Open-source R software environment (see: <http://www.r-project.org/>).

Multilevel modelling

Goldstein, H. (2003) *Multilevel Statistical Models*, 3rd edn. London: Arnold.

This is the definitive (but rather demanding) text. The author's team maintain a comprehensive website at: <http://multilevel.ioe.ac.uk/>.

Hox, J. (2002) *Multilevel Analysis: Techniques and Applications*. Mahwah, NJ: Lawrence Erlbaum Associates.

Provides a well-written and approachable introduction to multilevel modelling.

Raudenbush, S.W. and Bryk, A.S. (2001). *Hierarchical Linear Models*, 2nd edn. Newbury Park, CA: Sage.

Written by two American pioneers of multilevel modelling, this provides a detailed treatment that is linked to their HLM software.

Singer, J.D. and Willets, J.B. (2003) *Applied Longitudinal Data Analysis: Modelling Change and Event Occurrence*. Oxford: Oxford University Press.

A very gradual account that shows in detail how the multilevel model can be used in the analysis of repeated measures; their worked examples in a number of different software packages are provided at: <http://www.ats.ucla.edu/stat/mlm/>.

Further references

Aitkin, M., Anderson, D. and Hinde, J. (1981) 'Statistical modelling of data on teaching styles (with discussion)', *Journal of the Royal Statistical Society, Series A*, 144: 148-61.

Hendry, D.F. (2000) *Econometrics: Alchemy or Science*. Buckingham: Open University Press.

Jones, K. and Moon, G. (1987) *Health, Disease and Society*. London: Routledge.

Lucas, R.E. (1976) 'Econometric policy evaluation: a critique', in K. Brunner and A.H. Meltzer (eds), *The Phillips Curve and Labor Markets*, Carnegie-Rochester Conference Series on Public Policy, 1: 19–46.

McCullagh, P. and Nelder, J.A. (1989). *Generalized Linear Models*, 2nd edn. London: Chapman & Hall.

Miles, J. and Shevlin, M. (2001) *Applied Regression and Correlation Analysis in Psychology: A Student's Guide*. London: Sage.

PART VII

QUANTITATIVE METHODS IN ACTION

Introduction

Part VII consists of five Stories from the Field providing examples of some of the quantitative tools and techniques presented in Part VI together with a chapter on mixed methodologies. The application of quantitative methods across the social sciences highlights a number of issues, demonstrating that the shift from theory to practice is not a smooth path.

Some authors in Part VII raise issues in relation to sampling which are of central concern for any quantitative researcher. Pelgrum describes the difficulties inherent in international comparisons in defining what is meant by the population to be studied. In addition, he discusses the impact of sampling strategy and non-response in relation to sample size and representativeness. Ainley notes the difficulties of sampling in a school context when attrition (students moving to another school for example, or being absent during data collection) can be high. Greene et al. stress that sampling strategies in mixed methods (which can be separate or integrated) need to take account of the study design.

Addressing the issue of validity, several authors discuss the need to be clear about what is being measured. Pelgrum looks at problems of comparability in the design of questionnaires to be used internationally when language translation effects, curriculum differences and cultural interpretations all have potential to introduce bias. Underwood and Dillon argue that the validity of their reusable instrument has been strengthened through consultation with practitioners and they also plan to use statistical analysis to help them to fine-tune their model. Doig describes how he used a model which 'preserved and reported all responses' in order to measure increasing levels of sophistication in students' understanding of science concepts when analysing data in which there was 'no single, correct response'.

One common theme throughout these chapters is the need to take account of context. Jones challenges the need for quantitative researchers to seek universal truths and instead uses multilevel modelling to tease out contextual differences in an analysis of voting behaviour in the UK. He argues that acknowledging context within modelling allows the quantitative researcher to build bridges with the qualitative researcher. Pelgrum, as has been noted earlier, shows how contextual issues such as national and regional differences in curriculum specification and delivery must be taken into account when designing international comparative assessments. Underwood and Dillon describe the development of a new instrument specifically designed to take into account contextual differences when evaluating the impact of new technologies in education on six dimensions. Ainley describes how multilevel modelling was again used to take account of contextual factors, this time in educational research in Australia. This story, while focusing on quantitative methods, refers to the mixed method approach he adopted in order to be able to describe classroom practice and interpret the quantitative findings in relation to context. In Greene et al.'s chapter on mixed methods in the social sciences the integration of contextual understanding forms one of the multiple perspectives adopted and serves to aid triangulation.

The contributions in Part VII illustrate that boundaries between quantitative and qualitative approaches are blurring in contemporary social science research. The five Stories from the Field, commissioned as examples of quantitative research in practice, illustrate this, signalled by words such as 'rich description', 'context', 'case study' and 'interpret'. The final chapter on mixed methodologies highlights the benefits of drawing together multiple perspectives, not only the underlying theories informing research designs, but also multiple approaches to both data collection and analysis which may be integrated to varying degrees. This enables the social scientist to develop a more comprehensive understanding of human phenomena in our world, through multiple lenses, numbers and words working together in harmony.

28

RANDOM REFLECTIONS ON MODELLING, GEOGRAPHY AND VOTING

Kelvyn Jones

School of Geographical Sciences, University of Bristol, UK

Stories from the Field

Introduction

This short piece is about applying quantitative modelling to a dispute about the importance of area effects in understanding voting behaviour in the UK. In particular it uses multilevel modelling to assess the nature and extent of place effects and thereby challenges the familiar critique of quantification that in pursuing generality it ignores specificity. In that context, I try to bring two general standpoints to my work:

- a realist philosophy (Sayer, 2000) which encourages both intensive (qualitative) and extensive (quantitative) empirical work, but rejects the positivist position that causation equates with regularity, and replaces this with

$$Outcomes = Mechanism + Context$$

so that there are no 'universal' laws in social science that are independent of the context in which they are embedded;

- the importance of place – as a geographer I see local specificity as integral to explanations of general social processes. I see people and places existing in a recursive relationship. People create structures in the context of places; those structures then condition the making of people. This is a large claim for it means that geography matters so much that human processes cannot be understood without being informed by a geographical imagination.

These standpoints influence how I undertake statistical modelling in a way, I hope, that is far-removed from the anti-positivist caricature that is often given of quantification. In standard regression models, local specificity is often regarded as deviation which must be minimized during calibration. Attention is solely focused on the underlying generality and not the departures from this generality. Standard models deny geography and history in fitting an 'average' model to all places and times. However, the multilevel model (Jones, in this volume), in developing the random part of the model, allows relations to vary from place to place. These two standpoints and approach to modelling informed some research with colleagues that contributed to a key debate on voting behaviour (Jones et al., 1992).[1]

Voting behaviour in context?

The crux of the argument is that geography does not make a *contextual* difference, but it is merely *compositional*. Thus, the strong support for Labour in South Wales is simply due to a high percentage of that population being low social class who, irrespective of place, generally vote Labour. These arguments have been strongly expressed:

> Contextual variables have little or nothing to add. (Tate, 1974: 1662)

> Where a voter lives is of very little relevance. (Rose and McAllister, 1990: 124)

Other researchers, however, contend that context does matter. According to a social-contact model, Conservatives gets their core support from the controllers of society (employers and managers), and while few individuals belong to this 'core' class, voting is related to the local contacts with them. Others have argued that core class is an important element of the local milieu in which people are politically socialized. In a society that is spatially segregated by class, place is a continually self-reinforcing context for political socialization (Johnston, 1986).

Evaluating alternatives

To enter such debates, we need:

- *To be able to set out the empirical implications of alternative theories.* If geography is contextually unimportant, as we model composition by including individual characteristics of voters, any place effects should attenuate. If geography is important, people of similar characteristics should vote differently in different places.
- *To set out a plausible model that is a fair test of the alternative theories.* Much of the literature is rendered problematic by including attitudinal variables measuring voters' political values as an explanation of actual voting, and then claiming that there is no evidence for contextual effects. If the dependent variable is voting Conservative or not, surely it makes little sense to include right-wing ideology as an explanatory attitudinal variable and then to conclude that there is no 'residual' geography.[2] Consequently the model should include a range of individual characteristics for socio-economic and demographic position in society, but not attitudinal variables *per se*.
- *Good reliable empirical evidence from a range of different contexts.* Data are required on voting choice, individual and place characteristics. This is provided by the British Electoral Study, which is undertaken contemporaneously with the General Election. The survey has a multistage design with individuals at level 1 nested in constituencies at level 2.
- *An appropriate modelling framework.* Much of the research in this area has been undertaken using traditional modelling working at a single level, but this debate can only be addressed by recognizing that individuals and constituencies form different levels in a hierarchical structure, with multilevel modelling as the appropriate method.

Some results

We undertook an analysis of the 1987 and 1992 General Elections. For the latter we modelled 2,275 respondents nested within 218 constituencies with a binary outcome, the probability of voting Labour as opposed to Conservative. Crucially, the differences between constituencies remained substantial even when age, sex, tenure, income, qualifications and class were taken into account. The probability of voting Labour for the 'stereotypical' individual (a middle-aged woman with low qualifications living in an owner-occupied household whose head is unskilled working class and receiving a 'middle' annual income) ranges from 0.22 in Nottingham East to 0.70 in Renfrew West. These are not small differences.

Going beyond crude composition/contextual debates, Figure 28.1 shows results when modelling the interaction between individual and place characteristics. In each of the graphs, the vertical axis is the probability of voting Labour, while the lines on the graph portray the relation for eight 'fractions' of individual class. The horizontal axis in each graph is a different measure of constituency characteristics. In (a) there are marked individual class effects (lowest support from the petty bourgeoisie, highest from unskilled manual workers), but these do not change in relation to the tenure characteristics of the constituency. Local geography in the form of tenure is not important.

A more complex picture is found in (b) in which the horizontal axis is the percentage of the constituency labour force who are in employment. Voting Labour is related to employment levels more markedly for working-class than non-working-class individuals. While the latter are somewhat immune to the economic situation of the local area, the working class are affected by the local economic environment. Graph (c) shows a strong place effect, which takes a consensual form in that both individual and constituency class (represented by the percentage of employers and managers in an electoral constituency) are mutually reinforcing. Where this core class forms a sizeable proportion of the population, more or less everyone, irrespective of their individual class, votes Conservative.

Another aspect of the importance of geography is shown in Figure 28.2 where the relation between variables is allowed to vary from place to place. Underlying the graph is a three-level model of people in constituencies in regions. The outcome variable on the vertical axis is the choice between Labour and Conservative for the 1987 General Election.[3] The horizontal axis is the percentage of the constituency labour force employed as coal miners as measured by the 1981 census. The lines on the graphs show the relation between Labour voting and employment in

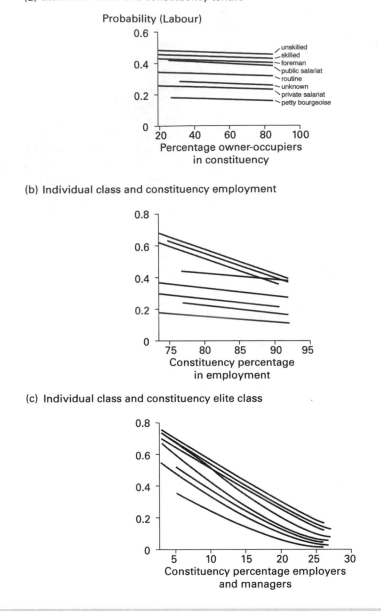

(a) Individual class and constituency tenure

Probability (Labour)

unskilled
skilled
foreman
public salariat
routine
unknown
private salariat
petty bourgeoise

Percentage owner-occupiers
in constituency

(b) Individual class and constituency employment

Constituency percentage
in employment

(c) Individual class and constituency elite class

Constituency percentage employers
and managers

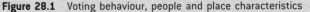

Figure 28.1   Voting behaviour, people and place characteristics

coal mining for each region in the UK after conditioning on individual class, tenure, employment and demographic characteristics. The most marked contrast is between South Wales and the East Midlands. South Wales is a pro-Labour area, and this support increases as the economy of the constituency is more involved with mining. The opposite is found in the East Midlands, where the most anti-Labour areas are the coal-mining constituencies! Places that appear to be outwardly the same (they both were coal-mining areas) are shown to be quite different when the analysis is sensitive to place differences. The East Midlands mining area known as the Dukeries has a distinct history of working traditions, cultural practi-

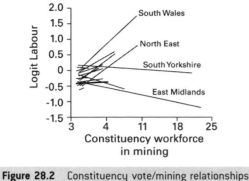

Figure 28.2 Constituency vote/mining relationships varying over region

ces and social relations that differ from other coalfield areas to the extent of electing a Conservative MP in 1987.

These results show that any analysis of British voting that does not take place into account is at best partial. Voting depends not only on who you are (class and age), what you have (tenure and employment), but also on where you live in the context of the history and traditions of that place.

Conclusions

For me, there are several aspects of this 'story from the field' that are important. There is a need in quantitative research work to pay *simultaneous* attention to theory ('what do we mean by a contextual effect?'), operationalization ('what are fair tests of alternative

theories?'), data collection ('what is reliable and appropriate data?') and data analysis ('what is the appropriate technique that addresses the research question taking account of the structure of the data?'). Moreover, in reality of course there is also no simple neat linear narrative which leads inexorably to a set of conclusions. Along the way we fitted a range of models, trying all the time to see if the sizeable contextual effects were simply an outcome of specifying the wrong model.

Developments in random-coefficient modelling mean that we can now address more sophisticated questions. Indeed, the complexity of the world is not ignored in the pursuit of a single universal equation (as has been done in much previous modelling) but the specifics of people and places are retained in a model, which still has a capacity for generalization. Keeping contexts in the model allows the possibility of bridge-building with qualitative researchers posing such questions as 'what is it about areas such as the East Midlands that has allowed a distinct local political culture to develop?'

Notes

1. More recent developments are reported at: <http://www.ccsr.ac.uk/methods/>.
2. It is like saying there is no geography of death when we take account of those who are mortally ill!
3. Modelled for technical reasons in a logit form.

References

Johnston, R.J. (1986) 'The neighbourhood effect revisited', *Society and Space*, 4: 41–56.

Jones, K., Johnston, R.L. and Pattie, C.J. (1992) 'People, places and regions: exploring the use of multilevel modelling in the analysis of electoral data', *British Journal of Political Science*, 22: 343–80.

Rose, R. and McAllister, I. (1990) *The Loyalties of Voters*. London: Sage.

Sayer, A. (2000) *Realism and Social Science*. London: Sage.

Tate, C.N. (1974) 'Individual and contextual variables in British voting behaviour', *American Political Science Review*, 68: 1656–62.

chapter 29

METHODOLOGICAL ISSUES IN INTERNATIONAL COMPARATIVE ASSESSMENTS OF EDUCATIONAL PROGRESS

W.J. Pelgrum

Department of Curriculum Technology, Faculty for Behavioural Sciences, University of Twente, The Netherlands

Stories from the Field

Introduction

The history of international comparative statistical assessments of educational progress started around 1960, when the International Association for the Evaluation of Educational Achievement (IEA) ran a first study among 10,000 students from twelve education systems to explore the feasibility of conducting international comparative assessments. The results were positive (Foshay, 1962) and from then onwards a regular series of assessments has been conducted by the IEA in mathematics, science, reading, writing, civics and information and communications technology. Since 1999 the Organization for Economic Cooperation and Development (OECD) has also conducted international comparative assessments of student achievement in mathematics, science and reading every three years.

The interest of countries in participating in large-scale international comparative assessments has considerably increased over the past thirty years. This development illustrates that in particular among policy-makers a need exists to collect hard data on educational progress. This need may be motivated by various considerations, including economic and accountability factors or the need for educational improvement. Although in the past international comparative assessments were the domain of a relatively small in-crowd of researchers, nowadays the huge databases can also be processed with relatively small computers and are available for the educational research community at large. Based on the author's more than twenty years of experience in international comparative assessments, this chapter provides a description of a number of methodological issues related to international comparative assessments and the way that the data from these assessments can be accessed.

Conceptualization of international comparative assessments

The conceptual frameworks of the various assessments that were conducted by the IEA contain generic elements such as those shown in Figure 29.1, where a distinction is made between input, process and output characteristics of education systems and interdependencies between several components of the system are hypothesized.

In practice, the hypothesized models are much more complex than the one which is presented in Figure 29.1. The investigation of which models can be fitted to the data is particularly important for advancing our theoretical knowledge on how education systems function. In general this is realized through secondary analyses (e.g. Robitaille and Beaton, 2002), but especially through doctoral theses of which hundreds[1] have been produced over the last decade.

Design issues

One of the greatest challenges for international comparative assessments is the issue of comparability. How can instruments and samples be designed so that the international statistics are comparable? Several aspects of this comparability issue are reviewed in more detail below.

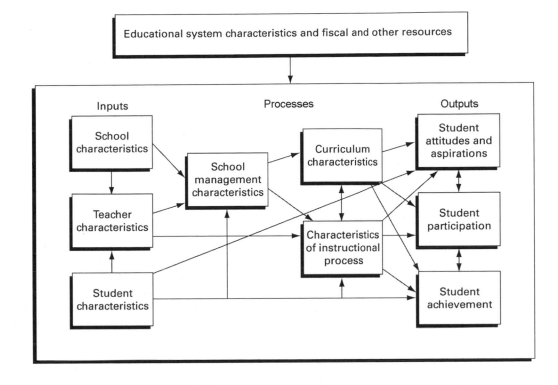

Figure 29.1   Elements of an educational monitoring system containing indicators of educational quality on different levels

The comparability of achievement tests

The average country scores on international achievement have usually attracted the greatest attention from policy-makers and in particular the press. Quite often the criticism of international assessments is that an attempt is made to compare the incomparable. Incomparability would stem from differences in educational contexts and national curricula. The international test designers are usually very much aware of this potential fallacy and have tried through several mechanisms to minimize this problem, for instance by:

- Conducting curriculum analyses in order to determine the overlap between intended curricula of the participating countries, as a basis for the definition of the domain and for test construction.
- Including so-called opportunity to learn (OTL) measures in the testing programme, by letting teachers judge to what extent the items in a test cover the implemented curriculum. These measures can be used to determine *post hoc* to

what extent comparisons between particular groups of countries are warranted or may be biased to the advantage of some countries.
- Conducting analyses of differential item-functioning (DIF). This may be caused by the fact that in some countries the curriculum very heavily emphasizes the content that is needed to answer some items correctly.

It may be of interest to note that quite often the potential incomparability of tests is mainly mentioned in the context of international comparative assessments. However, the lessons learnt from these international assessments may be of particular value also for national assessments, from which quite often comparisons are made between states, districts and even schools. Here also the comparability issue needs to be examined because within countries different schools (or alternatively districts or states) may implement a curriculum in substantially different ways. Although it is to be expected that such differences in particular will exist in decentralized education systems, past research has shown that also in centralized systems there may be quite huge differences between schools in terms of OTL.

The comparability of questionnaires

During international assessment projects the participating researchers create, on the basis of a common conceptual framework, questionnaires that are meant to tap the intended concepts. These (English-language) questionnaires are then translated into national languages and extensively pilot-tested in order to determine their measurement characteristics. It is obvious that translation errors can seriously affect the comparability of these measures. Therefore translation verification is an important activity to try to minimize this risk. Translation verification can take place in several forms, such as:

- *Independent back translations.* This is a very costly activity because professional translators need to be contracted who can translate the national versions of questionnaires back to English in order to be compared with the original version. Any deviation between the original and the back-translated version may point to translation problems and, hence, these deviations need to be examined in detail in order to determine how the national translation needs to be adapted. The option of back translation is usually (because of the associated costs) only applied for the items in the achievement tests.
- *National verification.* This option consists of checking the national translations against the original English version by a group of people who are independent of the group that was involved in the translation. Obviously a simultaneous mastery of English and the native language is crucial for recruiting people who can do this. In some countries it has proved to be quite difficult to find such people and, hence, this would be a circumstance that would need to be taken into account when interpreting the data.
- *Data-analytical techniques.* Once the data from international assessments are collected they are verified in a variety of ways. Data-checking and data-cleaning software is applied to extensively check whether potential inconsistencies exist in the data. Such inconsistencies may result from different sources of which translation error is one (other potential sources are data-entry errors and, inconsistency of the respondents). An example of a potential inconsistency is when a substantial number of respondents in a particular country indicate that they value highly the use of computers in school while at the same time saying that computers are useless for educational purposes.

The comparability of samples

International comparisons are made on the basis of estimates from data that result from national samples of students, teachers and schools. If the samples are incomparable obviously the comparability of the estimates is at stake. There are a number of aspects that need to be taken into account when national samples are defined and selected, namely:

- *The comparability of the nationally defined target population with the international definition.* As a first step to maximize the chance of getting comparable samples from countries, in international comparative assessments the researchers agree upon an international population definition. Such a definition may be: *all students that have reached a particular age on a particular date during the school year,* or: *all students at a particular grade level in the school system that is comparable in terms of student age composition.*
- *The accuracy of the population statistics.* Population statistics are estimated from sample data. Depending on the size of the sample these statistics have a particular accuracy (that is, the confidence interval – see Lewin, in this volume). In international comparative assessments these confidence intervals are defined before national sampling plans are created. This is usually done by using the criterion that the national estimates of statistics based on student data should have the same accuracy as a simple random sample of 400 students from an infinite population. Due to the fact that most countries cannot draw simple random samples but instead need to apply more complex sampling designs (for instance, first selecting schools and next selecting students within schools), in practice the sample sizes need to be much higher than 400, usually by a factor of ten. An important implication of the complex sampling designs is that statistical tests from standard statistical programs (such as SPSS or SAS) can no longer be applied and that more sophisticated techniques for estimating sampling error need to be applied (such as jack-knifing: Gonzalez and Foy, 2000).

- *The representativeness of the sample.* A sample is representative if every element in the population has a known chance of being selected. These chances are not known if considerable non-response occurs. Therefore currently most international assessments have strict rules for the percentage of non-response that can be accepted in order to include the data from a country in the international reports.

Reporting

The international reports that result from assessments of the IEA or OECD are available at the websites of these organizations[2] where information can also be found regarding the accessibility of the data. Several types of reports are distinguished, such as descriptive reports, secondary analyses and technical reports.

International assessment databases and their potential uses

International comparative assessments result in huge data sets (50 countries with on average 5,000 students per country is not abnormal) that are nowadays easily accessible for several purposes. Also the background documents on design and methodological issues (sampling, technical standards, psychometrics) reflect how researchers in the field apply theoretical insights from educational methodology. These data can be of value for examining and illustrating several methodological topics that have been addressed throughout this book, such as:

- *Conceptualization: concepts and indicators.* When students at universities (for instance from departments of educational sciences) are being trained in creating conceptual frameworks, the international assessments may offer them plenty of examples of concepts and indicators that have been defined to reflect these concepts.
- *Questionnaire development.* By critically examining questionnaires that have been used in international assessments, forming hypotheses about the strong and weak points and analysing the data to find evidence for these hypotheses, much can be learned about issues that concern questionnaire development.
- *Sampling.* Several issues are worth examining and discovering in the international data files, such as:
  - Is the accuracy of the population estimates comparable to theoretical expectations?
  - Do education systems where streaming occurs have higher intra-class correlations than systems where this is not the case?
- *Data collection.* International comparative assessment projects have over the past thirty years developed a whole set of tips and tricks for collecting high-quality data from large samples of students, teachers and schools in a country.
- *Data analysis.* International comparative data sets nowadays offer a wealth of opportunities to investigate how certain measures behave under different circumstances. For example, questions like: Do attitude measures from Japanese and UK data show the same underlying dimensions?' may be posed.
- *Substantive questions.* International comparative assessments typically cover a broad range of topics. For instance, the tests for measuring student achievement may contain hundreds of questions covering a large part of the mathematics domain. Detailed examination of these items may reveal much more than the overall tests statistics which are published in the international reports.

Notes

1. At one small university in the Netherlands we have already counted ten theses based on international assessment data over the past ten years.
2. Access to the reports and databases of the IEA and/or OECD can be acquired via, respectively, <www.iea.nl> and <www.oecd.org>.

References

Foshay, A.W. (ed.) (1962) *Educational Achievements of 13-year-olds in Twelve Countries.* Hamburg: UNESCO Institute for Education.

Gonzalez, E. and Foy, P. (2000) 'Estimation of sampling variance', in M.O. Martin, K.D. Gregory, K.M. O'Connor and S.E. Stemler (eds), *TIMSS 1999 Benchmarking Technical Report.* Chestnut Hill, MA: Boston College.

Robitaille, D.F. and Beaton, A.E. (eds) (2002) *Secondary Analyses of the TIMSS Data.* Dordrecht: Kluwer Academic.

CHAPTER
30

CAPTURING COMPLEXITY THROUGH MATURITY MODELLING

Jean Underwood
Division of Psychology, Nottingham Trent University, UK
Gayle Dillon
Division of Psychology, Nottingham Trent University, UK

Stories from the Field

Why is it so difficult to capture the educational benefits of new technologies?

The evaluation of any educational innovation raises theoretical and conceptual issues. In our review of the research on integrated learning systems (ILSs) in UK schools a decade ago, we argued that:

> we need, but do not currently possess, a well-founded 'language' which we can use to classify, relate and communicate about the different kinds of tasks we use to assess learning, so that we can refine our claims about the impact of teaching and learning outcomes and our assessment of what a 'learning gain' means. (Wood et al., 1999: 99)

Although many teachers and pupils in the UK ILS evaluation and similar international studies recorded strong positive attitudinal and motivational changes to learning (Haitiva, 1989; Lawson et al., 1997), while at the same time also reporting a strong belief that learning gains were substantial (Barrett and Underwood, 1997), there was no evidence of ILSs conferring benefits on the standard indices of school and pupil achievement in the UK such as National Tests (compulsory for children at 7/8, 10/11 and 12/13 years) or GCSE scores (exams normally taken prior to the end of compulsory formal education at age 16).

A partial explanation of the discrepancies exemplified by the ILS evaluation is that we were measuring the wrong thing. Perhaps new technologies are delivering new forms of learning for which we have yet to develop adequate assessment techniques. However, a second argument is that we are not so much failing to capture new types of learning as failing to capture causal variables which impinge on that learning. Information and Communication Technology (ICT) effects are difficult to assess in the classroom because technology is generally not a direct cause of change but rather a facilitator or amplifier of various educational practices. The underpinning infrastructure or environment into which ICT is placed may or may not be adequate to allow the beneficial effects of the technology to emerge. Learning is context-bound and we must understand the context in all its richness if we are to understand the extent and quality of the learning that may ensue.

Here we present our current thinking on how to capture the complexity of the educative process with the view to providing more informative evaluations that resonate with the everyday experiential evidence of practitioners in the field. This research framework is being developed for the evaluation of the Test Bed project[1] which seeks to establish the educational costs and benefits of new technologies in environments across primary, secondary and tertiary institutions, when 'sufficient' technology is present. All institutions have received significant funding to top up their ICT provision. The focus here is on the evaluation approach and not the Test Bed project *per se* which is in its initiation stage.

The evaluation approach started with three assumptions:

1. New approaches to educational research are needed to capture the rich interplay of variables

when a complex innovatory cycle such as Test Bed is to be monitored.

2. The evaluation needs to be grounded on a model of how actions in particular contexts produce observable outcomes.

3. Technology effects can be directly causal but more often are indirectly causal of change as the technology acts as a facilitator or amplifier of various educational practices.

This cross-institutional and cross-sector project required a research design which could assure that both the strengths and weaknesses of the impacts of new technologies were recorded and understood in order to allow lessons learnt from the target institutions to be disseminated to the wider community. The approach taken is 'maturity modelling', drawn from organizational research where it has been shown that it is possible to score organizations to reflect the level of maturity at which they operate (Curtis, et al., 1995). Maturity model (MM) frameworks permit a rich description of an intervention over time, which allows us to ask whether the designated institutions are so resourced and have the appropriate structures to deliver effective educational experiences using ICT.

Building the maturity model

The first goal of any such model is to describe and assess the complex environments in which innovations are to function. We began our model building by designing a number of sub-models or dimensions (see Figure 30.1). These sub-models were integral to the Test Bed evaluation, although the picture, as represented here, is not the final overall model. Here we present five dimensions: technological, curriculum, workforce, leadership and management, and communications and linkage maturity. These are key factors in effective ICT innovation and usage. It goes without saying that other models might have been developed, for example there is no learner MM in this framework. Many will find this disturbing, arguing that the student should be at the centre of the learning process. However, learners are pervasive throughout the sub-models. This is apparent in the way they should and do impact on and are in turn empowered or otherwise by pedagogic practice which encompasses teachers' skills, needs and technology knowledge and requirements.

Once the sub-models were defined we established framework descriptions of maturity along key fea-

tures. For each feature a set of levels or stages was constructed with the clear assumption that any institution would evolve through the stages in order. For example, one feature of technological maturity would be the presence of action plans for the renewal and maintenance of the system year on year and also after the Test Bed funding has ended. Further examples of features and levels are presented in Figures 30.2 and 30.3. The levels provide a scoring rubric that will allow the evaluation team to record the progress of the institution on that feature. The score for each feature is designed to provide, with the other features within the sub-models, a snapshot of the institution's progress on each key dimensional sub-model.

Building an effective MM is an iterative process. Initial work on constructing the models was completed by the evaluation team following in-depth interviews with some 20 expert stakeholders. Once the initial model was created, an expert seminar was organized to critically assess the model so far. Again some 20-plus expert stakeholders attended this meeting. The resulting discussions led to a revision of the model that is now being re-evaluated by our experts. The experts, collectively over 30 in number, were drawn from a range of stakeholders, including government agencies, leading research and development groups in ICT in education, members of the Test Bed project core team and ICT leaders in local education authorities and schools.

The model is also being field trialled by ten institutions known to be active ICT users. The purpose of these field trials is to check the usability of the models and also, crucially, to verify the scaling of the levels. As this is a medium-term project we need to know that institutions are not already sitting at level 4 or 5 (the highest level) on too many features. There has to be room for institutional growth in each of the models.

What makes a difference?

Interesting though it is to capture the complexity of the educational process this is only a first stage of the analysis. We intend to use the emerging measures from MM in a series of exploratory factor analyses both within each model and across the six models to identify how the features within and across models relate to one another. These data will then be used in a regression model to seek what predicts (contributes to) educational outcomes, that is to test the predictions of causality summarily indicated in Figure 30.1. The outcomes will include standard scores such as

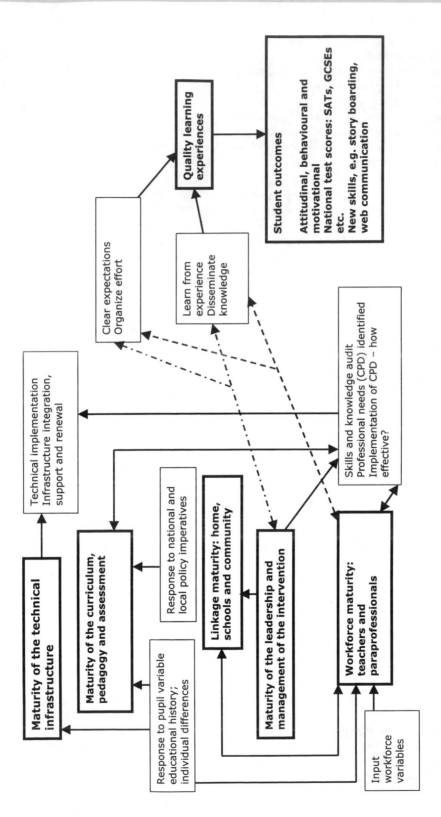

Figure 30.1   Causal modelling of the Test Bed intervention (after Lesgold, 2000)

- **Feature:** Extent of connectivity
- **Feature levels:**
  1. Most computers are stand-alone. External link by low-speed connection.
  2. There is a networked central resource or some clusters which are networked with low speed connection shared across the network.
  3. Most computers are networked with a shared broadband institutional access but there are impediments to the flow of data between the management and curricula sectors.
  4. All systems (management and curricula) are networked together allowing the sharing of resources and data. Regular backups are made.
  5. All systems (management and curricula) are networked together allowing the sharing of resources and data. Differential internal and external access to the network. Awareness of need for security. Options such as wireless networks are used in addition to, or as a replacement of, fixed networks.

Figure 30.2 Technological maturity

- **Feature:** Embedding teaching and learning with ICT
- **Feature levels:**
  1. Few staff use ICT in their teaching.
  2. Some staff use ICT in some of their subject teaching. Some schemes of work may include explicit ICT activities.
  3. Most staff use ICT in their teaching but there is no overall guidance of how this should be done. ICT is an add-on to the curriculum.
  4. Collective agreement on key uses and on embedding of ICT within the curriculum.
  5. ICT has been embedded into all schemes of work, which in turn is evidenced in the classroom. Active monitoring of the implication of technology change on educational activities, including audit of child- and teacher-based usage.

Figure 30.3 Curriculum maturity

National Tests and GCSE results and also less direct but educationally significant data such as school attendance or truancy levels. In this way we are seeking to identify key indicator factors and patterns of factors that make a difference to the effective use of ICT for the benefit of students' learning.

Advantages of the maturity model approach

Perhaps the key advantage is that it sets such an innovation to be evaluated in context and is therefore in tune with current educational thinking (Lave and Wenger, 1991). It allows not only a rich description of the intervention over time, but also an assessment of the degree of implementation. In tracking the contextual variables that are likely to affect the levels of implementation or outcomes the MMs should allow us to understand the processes of innovation leading us to an informed assessment of the reasons for high and low implementation and impact over time.

As is apparent from our description of the building of the model, one of the key advantages of this approach is that it allows the relevant stakeholder communities to participate directly in the discussions of the appropriate features to be included in the models. In constructing our models we have called on experts from a wide and representative range of stakeholders.

We would also argue that the models themselves can act as a guide providing specific goals which educational institutions can aspire to and work towards. As we seek to triangulate evidence of maturity we will be asking each institution to conduct a self-assessment using the MM framework.

One final advantage, attested to in the business community, is that although the initial development cost in time and effort can be, and in our case has been, extensive, reuse costs, including the costs of adapting the model to different circumstances or purposes, should prove relatively inexpensive – these are durable instruments.

The MM presented here is one response to the need to understand the ICT innovation cycle. A critical step to setting up the models at first was the involvement of the educational community through the use of experts from across the relevant spectrum to refine the model and to tune the mechanisms. It is anticipated that the model will provide the 'backbone' of the evaluation over a period of years, alongside which a number of microstudies will be conducted to confirm findings about the influences of different maturity aspects on each other.

Note

1. The ICT Test Bed Evaluation, funded by the UK government's Department for Education and Skills, is a joint project of Manchester Metropolitan and Nottingham Trent Universities. The research team comprises: A. Convery, G. Dillon, S. Forrest, C. Lewin, D. Mavers, D. Saxon, B. Somekh and J. Underwood.

References

Barrett, J. and Underwood, J. (1997) 'Beyond numeracy', in J. Underwood and J. Brown (eds), *Integrated Learning Systems: Potential into Practice.* London: Heinemann.

Curtis, B., Hefley, W.E. and Miller, S. (1995) *Overview of the People Maturity Model^{SM}*, Technical Report CMU/SEI-95-MM-01. Pittsburgh, PA: Carnegie Mellon University, Software Engineering Institute.

Haitiva, N. (1989) 'Students' conceptions and attitudes towards specific features of a CAI system', *Journal of Computer-Based Instruction*, 19: 56–63.

Lave, J. and Wenger, E. (1991) *Situated Learning: Legitimate Peripheral Participation.* Cambridge: Cambridge University Press.

Lawson, T., Underwood, J., Cavendish, S. and Dowling, S. (1997) 'Tutor responses to integrated learning systems', in J. Underwood and J. Brown (eds), *Integrated Learning Systems: Potential into Practice.* London: Heinemann.

Lesgold, A. (2000) *Determining the Effects of Technology in Complex School Environments.* Available online at: < http://www.publishers.org.uk > (accessed 15 June 2001).

Wood, D., Underwood, J. and Avis, P. (1999) 'Integrated learning systems in the classroom', *Computers and Education*, 33: 91–108.

CHAPTER

31

EVALUATING LITERACY ADVANCE IN THE EARLY YEARS OF SCHOOL

John Ainley

Australian Council for Educational Research

Stories from the Field

Literacy Advance was a systemic reform of the Catholic Education Commission of Victoria that began in 1998 with the purpose of improving the literacy development of students, especially in the early years of schooling. Over a period of five years we conducted a parallel Literacy Advance Research Project using longitudinal, multilevel and multimethod approaches to evaluate the impact of the initiative on student learning. This chapter provides an outline of what we did. Our results are described in greater detail in the reports of the study (Ainley and Fleming, 2000; Ainley et al., 2002, Ainley and Fleming, in press).

Background

Literacy Advance operates through the support of programmes in schools, emphasizing a whole-school approach to programme design, mandated professional development for teachers, designated blocks of time for literacy in schools, intervention programmes for students needing additional assistance and the systematic evaluation of student learning. The strategy arose out of a renewed interest in literacy and large-scale educational reform similar to developments elsewhere. Each school proposed a plan for the improvement of literacy and, on the basis of these plans, schools received additional funds. Key requirements included the appointment of a literacy coordinator, systematic monitoring of children's progress and assessment of all Year 1 students. Each school plan nominated a focus for its literacy teaching in the early years of school. These included: Western Australian First Steps (WAFS), the Children's Literacy Success Strategy (CLaSS), and the Early Years Liter-

acy Programme (EYLP). In addition, schools could nominate an Approved School Design (ASD) programme.

Design

The Literacy Advance Research Project began in 1998 and involved more than 150 schools in the Catholic education system of Victoria. We made a number of key design decisions at the beginning but modified details (such as particular instruments) during the course of the project depending on our analysis at each point. We collected information at student, classroom and school level for two cohorts of students: the first entered Year 1 (following a preparatory year in school) in 1998 and the second in 2000. From the beginning our focus was on achievement growth in literacy so we chose to develop a longitudinal design in which individuals could be followed over their primary school years. For our first cohort we initially sampled students within schools but when we confronted the complexities of various transfers we realized it was more sound to include all students from the designated Year level in each school. Furthermore, since we were interested in influences that operated at the individual level (such as intervention programmes), the classroom level (such as approach to teaching) and the school level (such as contextual influences) we planned to analyse our data using multilevel methods. Figure 31.1 outlines the overall design of our study. We didn't conduct any assessments during 2001, which means that there are no assessment data in Year 2 for the second cohort.

Measures

Student achievement was assessed at the beginning and end of Years 1 and 2 and at the end of Year 3.

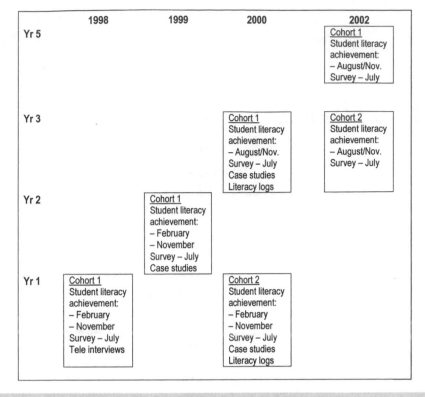

Figure 31.1   Design of the Literary Advance Research Project

Teachers provided information about each student during each year. In addition, we gathered information about school and classroom organization, programmes and approaches by means of questionnaires. From the analyses of these data it was possible for us to evaluate the extent to which the factors influencing student literacy development had changed as a result of the implementation of Literacy Advance.

Student progress in literacy

In general we made use of assessment data that were being collected as part of the regular operation of Literacy Advance and supplemented these with other assessments. Assessment in Year 1 was based on the Burt Word Reading Test, Text Level and components of the Clay Observation Schedule. In Years 3 and 5 the Burt Word Reading Test and the Reading, Writing and Spelling components of the statewide assessment programme were used to assess student literacy proficiency. At each point in the study we combined the individual assessment components to form a composite measure (using confirmatory factor analy-

sis to establish the appropriate weights for each component).

Influences on literacy growth

We analysed student achievement in a series of multilevel analyses using student-level data (such as initial achievement, participation in individual programmes such as Reading Recovery, engagement, as well as social and language background) and school/classroom-level data (such as approach to literacy teaching, time allocation to literacy, interruptions in the literacy block, school and classroom characteristics). In the analysis we found it necessary to combine school- and classroom-level data because, where there are multiple classrooms for each Year, students often change classes from one year to the next and because many schools had just one classroom for each Year.

Results

Cohort comparison

When we compared word recognition scores over Year 1 for the 1998 cohort and the 2000 cohort we found that Year 1 students in 2000 began with higher average scores than did their counterparts in 1998: equivalent to one quarter of a year's growth in word recognition. This initial advantage was maintained over the course of Year 1 and through to the end of Year 3. In addition Year 1 students in 2000 began Year 1 with higher text level scores than Year 1 students in 1998. We found that the sustained advantage for the second cohort was corroborated in the reading scores on the state-wide assessment for the two cohorts and there was a consistent difference between the two cohorts in the ratings given by teachers for each of the skills listed in the profiles. Thus from several perspectives we were able to conclude that there had been an improvement between 1998 and 2000 that was sustained as students progressed through school.

Analysis of influences on Year 1 reading growth

In our analysis of reading growth in Year 1 we used two-level regression analysis of end-of-year literacy achievement to allow us to investigate influences at the school or classroom level at the same time as influences at the individual level.

Not surprisingly we found that the strongest influence on end-of-year achievement was achievement at the beginning of the year. This highlights the importance of what happens before Year 1, either in the preparatory year or in the pre-school years. Because we included initial achievement the analysis of the other variables refers to achievement growth. We found several individual-level factors that influenced achievement growth. Attentiveness, as measured by a rating scale completed by teachers (Rowe and Rowe, 1999), was strongly related to progress in reading over Year 1. We also found that participation in Reading Recovery had an effect on reading development of the Year 1 students who participated in it for both cohorts, but more for the 1998 cohort.

At school and classroom level we found a significant effect for the CLaSS approach compared with other approaches but the magnitude was smaller in 2000 than in 1998. Information about characteristics of the literacy block was only available for the 2000 cohort (because we did not develop adequate measures for the first cohort). For that cohort we found a significant positive effect on reading growth of the time allocated to the literacy block and there was a negative effect of interruptions in that time.

Influences on literacy to the end of Year 3

We conducted similar analyses using the literacy outcome measures at the end of Year 3 for both cohorts of students. Our intention was to explore the extent to which the factors that influenced Year 1 reading in a beneficial way had enduring effects through to Year 3.

We found again that reading proficiency at the beginning of Year 1 strongly influenced literacy achievement at the end of Year 3. This reinforces the importance of the early years in providing a strong basis for development. We also found that student attentiveness had a lasting influence on Year 3 achievement and that engagement (measured in Year 3) had an even stronger influence. We also found that, on average, participation in Reading Recovery did not appear to have a significant influence on literacy achievement in Year 3. We concluded that the benefits of Reading Recovery in Year 1 did not endure over time.

We found that the benefits from the CLaSS approach in Year 1 did endure. Other things equal, students from CLaSS did better in Year 3 literacy than students from other Year 1 programmes. It appears that what occurs in the first year of schooling can make a difference to literacy development. When we reflected on these results we remembered that in the 1998 cohort schools that became part of the CLaSS approach were from socio-economically disadvantaged schools. They were achieving below their capacity at the beginning of Year 1 and intensive attention to literacy development resulted in substantial gains that endured.

Influences on literacy at the end of Year 5

We also analysed influences on literacy outcome measures at the end of Year 5 for the 1998 cohort of students. We found that the strongest influence on achievement at the end of Year 5 was achievement at the beginning of Year 1; the influence of attentiveness measured in Year 1 persisted through to Year 5; and engagement measured in Year 5 had an influence on literacy achievement. We found no lasting effect of participation in Reading Recovery through to the end of Year 5. We did find a significant effect for the CLaSS approach compared with other approaches, although the magnitude of that effect was less than that in Year 3.

Reflections

The assessment of school and programme influences on student learning needs to be based on measures of achievement growth rather than single static measures (Willet, 1994). In this study we successfully measured changes in literacy achievement over time using composite measures of achievement that were robust. Indeed, we were able to study changes over an extended time and thereby evaluate enduring as well as immediate outcomes from different approaches to teaching. The fact that the study extended over several years meant that for many analyses it was not possible to examine school- and classroom-level factors separately (because classes typically change each year). However, our design enabled us to compare effects at the time of and subsequent to an initiative and so provide a basis for inferences about the effects of the intervention and the main elements within the intervention (such as broad approach to teaching and individual interventions).

We were less successful in capturing more detailed aspects of classroom practice and the influence of those practices on student learning. It seems that this may be partly due to the absence of an established conceptual framework of classroom practice and partly because survey research methods based on questionnaires may not provide sufficiently sensitive measures of practice. It may also be that variable-focused analytic methods do not capture enough of the contingencies and interactions that are important aspects of classroom influences on learning. The use of classroom- or person-focused analyses could help to identify clusters of factors that in combination shape student learning. In this study we made use of case studies and teacher logs to capture more detail of classroom practice but we used these for descriptive purposes. The potential of such methods is likely to be more fully realized when they are linked to quantitative analyses of the type conducted in this study and are used to interpret the broader patterns established from the survey analyses.

References

Ainley, J. and Fleming, M. (2000). *Learning to Read in the Early Years of School*. Melbourne: Catholic Education Commission of Victoria.

Ainley, J. and Fleming, M. (in press). *Five Years On: Literacy Advance in the Primary Years*. Melbourne: Catholic Education Commission of Victoria.

Ainley, J., Fleming, M. and McGregor, M. (2002). *Three Years On: Literacy Advance in the Early and Middle Primary Years*. Melbourne: Catholic Education Commission of Victoria.

Rowe, K.J. and Rowe, K.S. (1999) 'Investigating the relationship between students' *attentive-inattentive* behaviors in the classroom and their literacy progress', *International Journal of Educational Research*, 31(2): 1–138.

Willett, J.B. (1994) 'Measurement of change', in T. Husen and N. Postlethwaite (eds), *Encyclopedia of Educational Research*. Oxford: Pergamon Press.

CHAPTER

32

WORKING BACKWARDS: THE ROAD LESS TRAVELLED IN QUANTITATIVE METHODOLOGY

Brian Doig

Faculty of Education, Deakin University, Australia

Stories from the Field

Context

The context of this example of quantitative researchers in action is set in the early 1990s in Victoria, Australia. The Victorian Department of Education requested the Australian Council for Educational Research (ACER) to investigate the science achievements of Victorian school students at Year 5 (9- to 10-year-olds) and Year 9 (13- to 14-year-olds). Thus the variable of interest, science achievement, was quite clear, as was the population.

However, at that time the Department of Education did not know what the content of the school science curriculum was, especially in primary schools. Secondary school science, on the other hand, was better known as the popular science textbooks gave some indication of what was being taught. This had come about because the Department had made a decision, in the early 1980s, to have schools develop their own curricula without central overseeing by the Department. This was promoted at the time as a way to make curricula appropriate to local needs.

The dilemma facing the research team was how to report on students' science achievement when it was unknown what students had been taught and there was no time or funds available to ascertain this.

Methodology

The methodology used to achieve the desired outcomes of this research project was typical of quantitative research in other contexts. Good practice in quantitative research suggests that you should start where you want to end up and work backwards. This means that you should:

- decide how the findings can be reported most usefully for your audience; then
- select the analytic approach that will provide the results in a form suitable for this form of reporting; and finally
- prepare to collect data that can be analysed in your chosen way.

The relationship between the last two steps is never completely one-way, as there are contextual aspects of the data collection that may influence your choice of analysis. While this 'start at the end' strategy may appear simplistic, it does ensure that you finish with data that can be analysed in a way for you to report the findings usefully.

Reporting

In the example being discussed here, we turned, as one should, to the research literature on students' achievements in science to provide a context for our research and the reporting of its results. At the time, there had been a considerable amount of international investigation of student understandings of science concepts. This research has been variously characterized as 'children's science' or 'misconception research' because of its focus on children's misunderstandings of scientific phenomena. (For an overview, see, for example, Driver and Easley, 1978; Osborne and Freyberg, 1985.) At the time, most of this research had been conducted through clinical (one-to-one) interviews using a variety of stimuli, and the findings provided insights into a range of understandings held by children for a range of different aspects of science. We argued, then, that we should report on students' conceptual understandings, as these are independent of the curriculum studied, and the Department agreed that this should be done.

Analysis

The literature on children's science made it obvious to us that we should report on the full range of understandings in the student population. We were interested in being able to describe the understandings of students at different points along a continuum of understandings, from the naive to the most sophisticated. Clearly, an analysis that allowed higher 'scores' for more scientifically sophisticated responses to a stimulus was needed.

The analytic approach we adopted was an item response theory (IRT) model, that of Masters (Masters, 1982; Masters, 1988; Wright and Masters, 1982). Masters's partial credit model (PCM) is an extension of the Rasch model (Rasch, 1960). The PCM analysis has two distinct features that make it eminently suitable for analysing data for which there is no single, correct response. First, it allows a range of responses, from the least to the most sophisticated, to be preserved: that is, it does not place all 'incorrect' responses into a single 'wrong' class but preserves and reports all responses and, in this case, places them in order of scientific sophistication. The second feature of the PCM is that it places student total scores and student responses on the same scale, which means that it is possible to estimate, for any given student total score, the likely response of a student with that score to any question. (See Bond and Fox (2001) for a detailed explanation of item response theory and its applications.)

The intention was that students would respond to a stimulus and provide written responses that could be categorized into levels of increasing scientific understanding. The PCM analysis would then scale the students' performance in terms of their scientific understandings, and the categories of response would describe the development of these. At no stage would ideas of 'correct' or 'incorrect' responses be used, but instead there was to be a continuum of increasingly sophisticated science understanding.

Data source

After much debate and reflection we decided to create pseudo-interviews, that is written questionnaires that would, as far as possible, emulate the clinical (one-on-one) interviews found in the literature. In this way, we believed, our results could be comparable to those found in the literature, and also add to knowledge in the field. A series of short written stories was created, based on the typical questions and results described in the 'children's science' literature. There were six of these stories in all, each assessing students' beliefs about a particular topic in science. This set of stories was entitled *Tapping Students' Science Beliefs* (TSSB). The six stories were:

- *The Day We Cooked Pancakes at School* – a cartoon story that had a focus on the structure of matter.
- *What Hhappened Last Night* – a short story that is a conversation between a child and an alien visitor and focuses on the Earth and Space.
- *Skateboard News* – this was a newsletter about skateboarding with a focus on force and motion.
- *Children's Week* – this was a role-play, where the focus was on various aspects of light and sight.
- *Our School Garden* – a cartoon story with a focus on living things.
- *Environmental Impact Survey* – this was a role-play that had a focus on living things and the environment.

(See Doig and Adams, 1993, for details of the TSSB assessment units.)

Figure 32.1 shows Question 4 from the *Our School Garden* TSSB.

The practice

The official report of the research project (Adams et al., 1991) provides details of the analysis and the findings. For this discussion it is useful to examine how the three aspects – report, analysis and data – were implemented. For the sake of clarity, the description of this is in the reverse order to the project's design, that is it starts with the data collection and concludes with the report.

A sample of students, at Year 5 and Year 9, were administered a battery of surveys as well as the TSSB instruments – see Adams et al. (1991) for details of the sample of students involved in the project.

The design of the questions in the TSSB booklets meant that, in most cases, students at both year levels were administered the same TSSB booklets. Each student completed two booklets.

When the completed TSSB scripts were returned from schools, two of the researchers took a random sample of 100 of each booklet. Student responses

Adams, R.J., Doig, B.A. and Rosier, M. (1991) *Science Learning in Victorian Schools: 1990*, ACER Research Monograph No. 41 (ACER: Camberwell, 1991). Reproduced with the permission of the Australian Council for Educational Research.

Figure 32.1   Question 4 from the *Our School Garden* TSSB assessment unit (Adams et al., 1991: 124)

were examined on a question-by-question basis, and responses that indicated 'like' responses were grouped together. Descriptions of these 'like' categories of response were made, and the two collections of scripts swapped between the researchers. Each researcher then used the other's category descriptions to categorize the same set of student responses. Whenever a response was not able to 'fit' into a category, discussion between the researchers led to either a new category being established or the description of an existing category being revised. This iterative process was continued until all student responses to the questions were categorized. The number of categories of response to any question was dependent on the range of understandings indicated by the student responses, and there was no attempt made to force a set number of categories. The refined descriptions were used by a group of trained markers on the remaining student scripts.

Categorized student responses were analysed using Masters's partial credit model, a scale established and students' total scores placed on the scale to show levels of understanding. So that the report would show clearly how the scientific understandings developed and how students' levels of understanding were

distributed, a continuum of understanding was constructed for each TSSB.

Figure 32.2 shows the continuum for Light and Sight (Adams et al., 1991: 25). The distributions, of Year 5 and Year 9 students by total score are at the extreme left and right, respectively, while the description of levels of scientific understanding are in the central column. The highest level of understanding displayed represents the highest level of understanding displayed by the students sampled. The total score scale range (50 to 70) was selected to avoid confusion or misinterpretation with percentages particularly, 50 per cent being taken as some sort of 'pass' score.

This continuum shows that, of the students sampled, those whose total score on the *Children's Week* TSSB booklet was 56 are likely to believe that light is directly associated with its source and it is not an entity. On the other hand, those students whose total score was, say, about 64, regard light as an entity that can travel. Clearly, learning experiences provided for these two groups of students need to be very different.

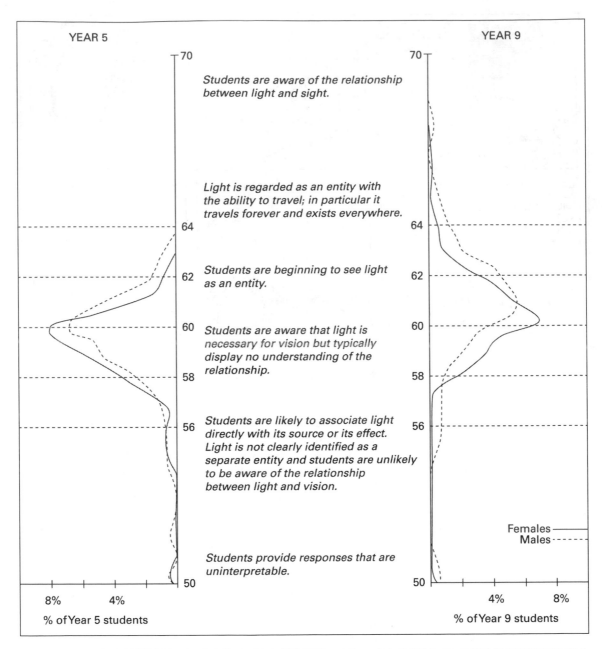

YEAR 5

Students are aware of the relationship between light and sight.

Light is regarded as an entity with the ability to travel; in particular it travels forever and exists everywhere.

Students are beginning to see light as an entity.

Students are aware that light is necessary for vision but typically display no understanding of the relationship.

Students are likely to associate light directly with its source or its effect. Light is not clearly identified as a separate entity and students are unlikely to be aware of the relationship between light and vision.

Students provide responses that are uninterpretable.

YEAR 9

Females ———
Males - - - - -

8%   4%
% of Year 5 students

4%   8%
% of Year 9 students

Adams, R.J., Doig, B.A. and Rosier, M. (1991) *Science Learning in Victorian Schools: 1990*, ACER Research Monograph No. 41 (ACER: Camberwell, 1991). Reproduced by permission of the Australian Council for Educational Research.

Figure 32.2   The *Light and Sight* continuum (Adams et al., 1991: 25)

Conclusion

Quantitative methodology is unforgiving, as all statistical procedures rely on you and your data addressing the assumptions underlying the procedures. My message is: if you don't know what you wish to say in your report when you begin, you run the risk of having data that you cannot analyse in a manner that allows you to report usefully. Plan ahead – but work backwards!

References

Adams, R.J., Doig, B.A. and Rosier, M. (1991) *Science Learning in Victorian Schools: 1990*, ACER Monograph No. 41. Melbourne: Australian Council for Educational Research.

Bond, T.G. and Fox, C.M. (2001) *Applying the Rasch Model: Fundamental Measurement in the Human Sciences*. Mahwah, NJ: Lawrence Erlbaum Associates.

Doig, B. and Adams, R.J. (1993) *Tapping Students' Science Beliefs*. Hawthorn: Australian Council for Educational Research.

Driver, R. and Easley, J. (1978) 'Pupils and paradigms: a review of literature related to concept development in adolescent science students', *Studies in Science Education*, 5: 61–84.

Masters, G.N. (1982) 'A Rasch model for partial credit scoring', *Psychometrika*, 47: 149–74.

Masters, G.N. (1988) 'Partial credit model', in J.P. Keeves (ed.), *Educational Research, Methodology, and Measurement*. Oxford: Pergamon Press, pp. 292–7.

Osborne, R. and Freyberg, P. (eds) (1985) *Learning in Science: The Implications of Children's Science*. Auckland: Heinemann.

Rasch, G. (1960) *Probabilistic Models for Some Intelligence and Attainment Tests*. Copenhagen: Danmarks Paedogogiske Institut.

Wright, B.D. and Masters, G.N. (1982) *Rating Scale Analysis*. Chicago: MESA Press.

CHAPTER

33

COMBINING QUALITATIVE AND QUANTITATIVE METHODS IN SOCIAL INQUIRY

Jennifer C. Greene
Department of Educational Psychology, University of Illinois, Urbana-Champaign, USA
Holly Kreider
Harvard Family Research Project, Harvard Graduate School of Education, USA
Ellen Mayer
Harvard Family Research Project, Harvard Graduate School of Education, USA

Key concepts

Jennifer C. Greene

Mixed-method approaches to social inquiry[1] involve the planned use of two or more different kinds of data gathering and analysis techniques, and more rarely different kinds of inquiry designs within the same study or project. Using methods that gather and represent human phenomena with numbers (such as standardized questionnaires and structured observation protocols), along with methods that gather and represent human phenomena with words (such as open-ended interviews and unstructured observations), are classic instances of mixing data gathering and analysis techniques. Examples of mixing overall inquiry designs include the combined use of an experiment and ethnography or the mix of a survey design with a case study. Although what constitutes important dimensions of difference in mixed-method inquiry is contested, there is general agreement that what is importantly mixed in mixed-method inquiry extends beyond the numerical/quantitative or narrative/qualitative character of the different methods used to include other dimensions of method. These other dimensions include the degree of standardization and structure (for example, deciding in advance what specific questions to ask of all respondents or allowing different questions to emerge during interviews with different people), and the degree of desired generalizability or particularity (extending the inquiry findings to other sites and populations or emphasizing an in-depth understanding of the particular contexts and people studied).

The roots of the mixed-method conversation

The early roots of mixed-method social inquiry are found partly in the construct of triangulation, which involves the use of multiple methods – each representing a different perspective or lens – to assess a given phenomenon in order to enhance confidence in the validity of the findings. If, for example, data from a self-report instrument and data from an external observation converge, the overall results are more likely to be valid, credible and warranted. Interestingly, triangulation has an honoured history in multiple methodological traditions (Denzin, 1978; Webb et al., 1966).

Other roots of the contemporary interest in mixing methods are embedded in the infamous qualitative–quantitative debate that raged in the social sciences during the latter quarter of the twentieth century. This debate was most often about method, but also invoked deeper questions of what philosophical paradigms or what sets of assumptions about the social world and our knowledge of it are appropriate for the social sciences. Quantitative proponents aspired to realism, objectivity, causal explanation and universal truth, while qualitative advocates emphasized the interpretive, value-laden, contextual and contingent nature of social knowledge. With rapprochement came a general acceptance of the legitimacy of multiple philosophical traditions for social inquiry and an opening for inquirers to eschew allegiance to one in favour of taking advantage of social science's full methodological repertoire.

Why mix methods?

Early on, mixed-method approaches to social inquiry were advanced as uniquely able to generate *better understanding* than studies bounded by a single methodological tradition (Greene, in press). Over time, a set of *purposes for mixed-method inquiry* evolved from these early beginnings, each offering a different form of better understanding: (1) understanding more defensibly, with stronger validity or credibility and less known bias, as with the classic approach of triangulation; (2) understanding more comprehensively, developing more complete and full portraits of our social world through the use of multiple perspectives and lenses; (3) understanding more insightfully, with new ideas, fresh perspectives, creative concepts and meanings, as when findings diverge and thus require reconciliation via further analysis, reframing or some other shift in perspective; and (4) understanding with greater value consciousness and with greater diversity of values, stances and positions through the inclusion of different methods that themselves advance different values.

Because practice is characteristically quite a bit more complex than theory, many mixed-method studies incorporate several of these mixed-method purposes within a given set of methods. For example, let's take a study of the barriers, facilitators and meanings of 'inclusion' in pre-school settings, where inclusion refers to the grouping of children with and without disabilities in the same classroom. In this study, structured classroom observations could be paired with a qualitative analysis of programme documents, aiming for convergence of information about programme structure, routines, instructional philosophy and so forth (purpose 1). These same structured observations could also be paired with open-ended teacher interviews, seeking a more comprehensive and complete understanding of the character of the interactions among children in the classroom setting (purpose 2). And the teacher interviews could be, in turn, paired with a structured parent questionnaire or a set of qualitative parent focus groups, in an effort to surface multiple and diverse perspectives on the key values of and rationales for inclusion at the pre-school level (purpose 4). The different mixed-method purposes are reflected in the various pairings of the set of methods chosen and would be intentionally pursued during the analysis stage of the study. (This example was adapted from Li et al., 2000.)

Beyond method, what else is mixed in mixed-method inquiry?

But, beyond type of method and data, what else is being mixed when we mix methods in social inquiry? And what else *should* be mixed? The legacies of the qualitative–quantitative debate demonstrated that while social scientific methods are not tightly bound to a given philosophical tradition, methods are indeed framed by the philosophical world view of the inquirer. Within this world view, key assumptions include views of the social world (for example, realism or constructionism), perspectives regarding the nature of social knowledge (for example, objective or value-laden) and positions regarding what is most important to know (for example, generalizable causal relationships or contextual meaningfulness). The controversial issues here are thus: when social enquirers mix methods, are they also mixing philosophical assumptions, and should they?

There are currently three primary stances on this issue. First, proponents of *a-paradigmatic stances* argue that philosophical assumptions are useful conceptual tools but they should not drive practice decisions. Rather, practical decisions about design and method should be steered by the demands of the context or by the requirements of the substantive constructs being studied. Michael Patton (2002) has long been an eloquent spokesperson for this practical stance. Second, proponents of a *dialectic stance* argue in favour of intentionally mixing philosophical assumptions while mixing methods, because philosophical assumptions should meaningfully influence practice decisions. And because all sets of philosophical assumptions are partial and limited, more comprehensive and insightful mixes are attained via the intentional inclusion of more than one philosophical framework. In this dialectic perspective, possible tensions and dissonance from different sets of assumptions are especially welcomed as generative of new insights and fresh perspectives. The work of Greene and Caracelli (1997) well illustrates this dialectic stance. Third, proponents of *pragmatic stances* advance an alternative, inclusive philosophical framework within which multiple assumptions and diverse methods can comfortably reside. In this third stance, like the first, differences in philosophical traditions are de-emphasized and thereby not considered either particularly beneficial or problematic in mixed-method work. Various forms of contemporary realism and American pragmatism are the most popular alternative frameworks advanced within this pragmatic perspective. The work of Creswell (2003) and that of Tashakkori and Teddlie (1998, 2003) exemplify this alternative paradigm stance.

Mixed-method practice

Beyond purpose and paradigm stance, the practicalities of mixed-method inquiry are still being developed. Again, because practice is always so much more complex than theory, it is unlikely that a single prescriptive guide can ever capture the myriad combinations and facets of possible mixed-method design, analysis, quality considerations and write-up. Rather, the practice of mixed-method social inquiry is likely to continue to be conceptualized in terms of typologies, stances and dimensions to consider.

With respect to *designing a mixed-method study*, several key dimensions of importance have been consistently identified. One is whether the methods are integrated throughout the study or rather kept separate until the end, at which point conclusions and inferences are compared or connected. In an integrated design, data from various methods can inform the design of a particular instrument or the sampling plan for another, and data of different types become iteratively merged or blended in analysis, yielding a unique set of results and inferences in which the different data forms are possibly no longer distinct or recognizably different in origin. In a component design, data retain their original form and character throughout, and conclusions and inferences seek harmony and connection rather than full blending or integration. Clearly, analysis and quality considerations are quite different in integrated versus component designs. A second important design dimension is whether the different methods involved are considered of relatively equal importance and weight or one methodology is dominant and the other less dominant. Designs with one dominant methodology tend to adhere to the traditional guidelines of that methodology, while the more practically challenging mixed-method designs are those where the different methods have relative parity in importance. Third, different methods can be implemented concurrently or sequentially, either for important conceptual reasons or for reasons of practicality.

Ideas about *mixed-method data analysis* are substantially less codified at this time, especially for integrated designs. Here are some examples of how social inquirers are currently grappling with the challenges

of mixed-method analysis. Li et al. (2000) identified three different approaches to analysis in their mixed-method study of pre-school inclusion policies and practices: parallel tracks for component designs, and either cross-over tracks or a single track for integrated designs. In a cross-over track analysis, analyses are initiated in separate qualitative and quantitative tracks, and then data in one track can be transformed and then crossed over to the other track for comparison and further analysis. For example, quantitative frequencies could be summarized in narrative form and then crossed over to the qualitative track for comparison with interview themes. Other cross-over strategies include typology development, or using the mid-stream results of one track of data analysis to generate a typology (a set of substantive categories) that is then used as a framework for analysing the other data track, and extreme case analysis, or using the results of one track of data analysis to identify 'extreme cases' for further analysis with the other track of data. In a single track analysis, the data from diverse methods are merged into one stream as the analysis proceeds, for example through a process of consolidated coding whereby a new data set is created from a joint review of both qualitative and quantitative data. (See Caracelli and Greene, 1993, for illustrations of these analytic strategies.)

Other challenges of mixed-method practice remain in development. Criteria and procedures for judging the *quality of mixed-method social inquiry* remain problematic, particularly when the studies include stances from different methodological traditions, different methods of relatively equal importance and efforts at integration. Setting aside traditional criteria in favour of constructs and criteria of broader relevance is a promising approach, as illustrated by Teddlie and Taskakkori's (2003) notions of 'inference quality'. And finally, some enquirers are experimenting with using *mixed representational forms to report* the results from mixed-method social inquiry (Chin, 2003; Goodyear, 2001). In addition to standard textual and tabular presentations, stories, poems, cartoons and performances can all help to capture and re-present the broader, deeper and more nuanced results that are themselves the 'better understandings' of mixed-method inquiry.

Implications for research design

Planning a mixed-method study involves an iterative negotiation of macro and micro lenses, perhaps best accomplished by grounding this process in the various constructs or variables to be assessed in an inquiry. For example, in an evaluation of a substance abuse prevention programme for youth, one key outcome to be assessed is substance abuse behaviour. The evaluator envisions using both a standardized questionnaire and an innovative role-play method to assess this outcome, with the methods equally weighted and implemented concurrently and their analysis highly integrated under a dialectic mixed-method purpose of initiation (more insightful understanding). The evaluator then repeats this design process for the next construct to be assessed, making adjustments in her mixed-method plans for the first construct as necessary. And so forth, balancing micro plans for each construct with the macro need for a coherent, sensible and practically feasible overall plan. An important aspect of this approach to mixed-method planning is to ensure that methods are selected and implemented in the service of inquiry questions rather than vice versa. Flexibility, creativity, resourcefulness – rather than a priori methodological elegance – are the hallmarks of good mixed-method design.

The presentation above focuses on dimensions, typologies and categorical lists of various stances and strategies for mixed-method inquiry. An alternative is to approach mixed-method inquiry more holistically. For example, Maxwell and Loomis (2003) proposed an interactive framework for mixed-method inquiry composed of five parts: inquiry purposes, conceptual framework, inquiry questions, methods and validity. This approach emphasizes the ways in which these five components influence one another, both during planning and implementation, thereby highlighting the iterative, dynamic and holistic nature of design decisions. In another holistic example, Smith (1997) iteratively reviewed multiple sets of quantitative and qualitative data all together to generate final inquiry assertions that could be fully warranted by the data, both qualitative and quantitative.

Stories from the Field

Holly Kreider and Ellen Mayer

This is a story of a mixed-method analysis journey into a large and complex mixed data set. The story highlights conceptual and practical challenges of integrative mixed-method analysis and thereby adds case study data to our emerging understanding of how to productively work simultaneously with different data sources and forms.

The first few waves of data had been collected in the School Transition Study (STS),[2] when we, together with other researchers[3] at the Harvard Family Research Project (HFRP) began an early mixed-method analysis examining family educational involvement. The STS was a complex mixed-method investigation following approximately 400 ethnically diverse children in low-income families from kindergarten through fifth grade across three different sites in the US. The study's purpose was to understand school, community and familial influences on successful pathways through middle childhood. Data collection included both a range of quantitative instruments and assessments, such as surveys of the children's primary caregivers and teachers, as well as in-depth qualitative case studies of a representative sample of 23 children over their first and second grade years. Our HFRP contingent had just completed overseeing a collection of the case study data. We added a quantitative researcher to our qualitative team and embarked on our first mixed-method analysis.

Where to begin?

In hopes of broadening our understanding of the nature of educational involvement of low-income families, we first listened to our rich qualitative case study data, as qualitative data are often well suited to exploratory analysis and generative of new understanding. We deliberately followed unexpected and surprising themes as they emerged.

> We don't even have a [Parent-Teacher Association] at this school ... I have often wondered if PTA will become a thing of the past, because parents are too busy just trying to make ends meet and get dinner on the table, and occasionally wash a pair of socks. (Second grade teacher)

> ... I think every parent should have time for their kids, no matter how much work you have? ... When I want to talk to [my child's teacher], I just fax him something to school, from my job, or I call him. (Mother of a second grader)

Our case study interview protocols focused primarily on family educational involvement issues, without directly exploring parental work and its relationship to family involvement. Yet no matter who we asked – whether teacher, parent or principal – and no matter what aspect of involvement we asked about – whether it was about the level of parent involvement at school, parent–teacher communication or what could help children succeed – we heard reference to parents' work in the qualitative data.

The surprising salience of this theme seemed to warrant further analysis, but we carefully thought through the mixed-method potential of this line of analysis before deciding to pursue it. First we narrowed our consideration to *maternal* work, largely because the vast majority of STS primary caregiver respondents were mothers. We then reviewed prior research, identifying only a few studies on the connections between maternal work and family involvement and concluding that this limited understanding could be especially strengthened through a mixed-method analysis. Specifically, we could move beyond the existing research emphasis on negative associations between work and involvement, especially for low-income mothers, to also examine parental strengths and strategies. Most existing literature also lacked a strong empirical base, relying on theory, advice, anecdotal information or singular methods, whereas our data set offered the potential of an integrated mixed-method analysis. With this reassurance, we felt ready to follow this discovery much the same way as other researchers have been pulled in unexpected directions (Rabinow, 1977; Skinner, 1956).

To systematically explore the connection between work and family involvement, we deliberately crafted guiding research questions that required reaching into both quantitative and qualitative data sources to be answered: how does maternal work influence low-income mothers' involvement in children's education? What strategies enable low-income working mothers to become or stay involved in their children's education?

How to work together?

We chose a team approach to analysis for practical reasons. Specifically, we had far too many data for one person to handle, a team structure already in place from data collection and a larger organizational culture of team-based work.

We put several structures and processes in place to create a space for qualitative and quantitative researchers to talk together. We set up clear team procedures that would support the necessary intentional reflexivity. These included regular team meetings and two sets of written logs, one to track substantive findings and another to record thoughts about our mixed-method process. Reading through the shared logs kept team members in daily touch with the work of others and later helped us gain a more coherent understanding of the analysis journey we had taken.

Norms of extensive and respectful dialogue also were crucial to supporting our ability to work together. A stance of openness and discovery is one inherent to mixed-methods, which actively seeks multiple routes to enhanced understanding (Cook, 1985). This openness to other views and perspectives includes not just rival explanatory hypotheses, but more profoundly rival ways of thinking and valuing. As qualitative and quantitative researchers we approached our work together with openness and curiosity not only about the others' methodology and findings, but also about the others' different paradigmatic assumptions and traditions. The interdisciplinary nature of our team, which brought together disparate disciplines of psychology, education and sociology, also made open dialogue critical.

In addition, we developed structured analytic exercises to start this new mixed-method process and generate hypotheses – exercises that honoured our different ways of thinking about and analysing empirical data. We each explored the core construct of work by scouring a particular quantitative or qualitative data source and generating a list of knowledge claims about work. Then we reconvened to discuss these claims, as well as our understandings of the strengths and weaknesses of each particular data source. This led us – as a team – to understand work as linked to a variety of supports for mothers' work and family lives. Among the familial supports we identified, parent initiative emerged as important for mothers' strategies in balancing work and family involvement.

How to plan?

First, the team generated a rough mixed-methods analysis plan. As neophytes in this enterprise, we diligently read the literature about mixed-methods analysis and settled on the notion of iterative or 'cross-over tracks' analysis to guide our initial analytic planning and analysis (Li et al., 2000). In this approach, an intentional and iterative interplay exists between the separate analyses of qualitative and quantitative data sets, such that mixing and integration happen throughout the analysis.

However, we soon found ourselves in uncodified territory with our integrative mixed-method analysis – the cross-over tracks approach provided only minimal guidance. In reality, our work process was fluid and intuitive. For example, the quantitative analyst brought her factor analysis results to qualitative team members for interpretation and validation. Qualitative analysts drew from their long-time internalized stores of case study knowledge to see if the factors passed the grounded 'this makes sense' test, and whether revised factor analyses were appropriate or necessary.

These and other discussions often began by pitting objective reality and contextual nuance, numbers and words, against one another. Over time and through discussion, we found ourselves relaxing our different paradigm assumptions. For example, we took a primary caregiver survey that had always been viewed as a 'quantitative' instrument and approached it anew as a source of qualitative data. We read the survey transcripts holistically, and discovered for example a rich new layer of narrative in the spontaneous talk of primary caregivers, talk which occurred as the interviewer moved from one survey question to another.

How to interpret our contradictory findings?

Interesting mixed-method analyses are likely to be replete with both convergent and divergent results. In our work, we took care to be open to both, privileging neither. Our first descriptive quantitative analyses showed parental work as a perceived *barrier* to family involvement. When asked 'What barriers to parent involvement do you see among your parents?' 89.5 per cent of the kindergarten teachers surveyed named parents' work schedule as somewhat of a problem or a serious problem. Yet early case study analyses suggested that work perhaps had some *positive* connections with involvement – witness the mother who contacted her child's teacher by fax from her workplace.

We turned more systematically to our case study data, developing case portraits of the involvement patterns of the 20 mothers who worked and conducting a cross-case analysis. We discovered that work could present opportunities and resources for involvement. Four strategies emerged that these working mothers used to become or stay involved in their children's learning. First, they described *promoting a kith and kin network*, overseeing a complex support system of helpers, including family members and co-workers, to support their children's learning. Second, they *used their workplace as a home base* for a variety of involvement activities, such as taking their children to work for stop-gap child-care or enrichment purposes. Third, they intentionally *garnered other resources from work* such as summer camp fees, educational advice from fellow workers or clients, or homework help for their children. Finally, they described *conquering time and space challenges* by negotiating transitions and adaptively finding time to be involved in their children's education, such as by selecting jobs near or even in their children's school.

These divergent findings between quantitative and qualitative data sources led us to a more expansive and complete understanding of educational involvement among low-income working mothers. We also stayed open to divergences in later iterations of quantitative analyses. For example, quantitative findings continued to show maternal work as a barrier to family involvement, but also began to suggest its opportunities. Univariate analyses of maternal reports showed that full-time working mothers reported attending significantly fewer events at their children's schools (such as parent-teacher conferences and open houses) than those who were not employed or employed part-time ($\chi^2 = 19.02$, df = 9, N = 216, p < 0.05). However, part-time working mothers reported the most involvement of any group, suggesting that the time demands of full-time work may interfere with involvement in school activities, but that work in general may provide opportunities for selective involvement. In this way, our quantitative findings converged with our qualitative findings to strengthen our interpretation of maternal work as a potential resource for educational involvement.

By mixing methods we had arrived at a unique, complex and nuanced understanding of low-income mothers' employment as both obstacle and opportunity for their family educational involvement. We had also arrived at an appreciation of mixing methods as a challenging but imminently worthwhile approach.[4]

Notes

1. The term 'social inquiry' is used in this chapter to refer to both research and evaluation.
2. STS, directed by Deborah Stipek and Heather Weiss, was supported by a grant from the John D. and Catherine T. MacArthur Foundation, with supplementary funds from the W.T. Grant Foundation. We thank STS ethnographers for data collection. See <www.hfrp.org> for a fuller description.

3. Other researchers were Heather Weiss, Margaret Vaughan, Rebecca Hencke and Kristina Pinto. We thank Jennifer Greene, STS steering committee member, for inspiration as we began this analysis.

4. More detailed accounts are available of the substantive findings (Weiss, et al., 2003) and mixed-method analytic process (Weiss, et al., in press).

Annotated bibliography

Cook, T.D. (1985) 'Postpositivist critical multiplism', in R.L. Shotland and M.M. Mark (eds), *Social Science and Social Policy*. Thousand Oaks, CA: Sage, pp. 21–62.

This important statement on the fallibility of post-positivist (traditionally quantitative) approaches to applied social science anchors contemporary thinking about using multiple methods in order to enhance validity.

Cook, T.D. and Reichardt, C.S. (eds) (1979) *Qualitative and Quantitative Methods in Evaluation Research*. Thousand Oaks, CA: Sage.

This is an early statement about being pragmatic in mixed-method evaluation and downplaying the importance of philosophical differences. This small volume includes several historic case examples.

Creswell, J.W. (2003) *Research Design: Qualitative, Quantitative, and Mixed Methods Approaches*. Thousand Oaks, CA: Sage.

Creswell has been a steady contributor to the mixed-method conversation, particularly of the pragmatic sort.

Greene, J.C. and Caracelli, V.J. (eds) (1997) *Advances in Mixed-Method Evaluation: The Challenges and Benefits of Integrating Diverse Paradigms, New Directions for Evaluation* No. 74. San Francisco: Jossey-Bass.

This volume engages the paradigm issue in mixed-method evaluation, offers descriptions and rationales for several different stances and includes exemplary mixed-method evaluations illustrative of each stance.

Greene, J.C., Caracelli, V.J. and Graham, W.F. (1989) 'Toward a conceptual framework for mixed-method evaluation designs', *Educational Evaluation and Policy Analysis*, 11(3): 255–74.

Greene and her colleagues seriously launched their mixed-method journey with this conceptual analysis of their review of 55 empirical mixed-method evaluation studies.

Li, S., Marquart, J.M. and Zercher, C. (2000) 'Conceptual issues and analytic strategies in mixed-method studies of preschool inclusion', *Journal of Early Intervention*, 23: 116–32.

Already a classic mixed-method case example, noted especially for its creativity and reflexiveness in both design and analysis.

Ragin, C.C. (1989) *The Comparative Method: Moving Beyond Qualitative and Quantitative Strategies*. Berkeley, CA: University of California Press.

International comparative researcher Ragin frames mixed-method work as mixing variable-oriented and case-oriented approaches to social science. He also offers a Boolean algebraic approach to data analysis, updated more recently with a computer programme and a second book.

Reichardt, C.S. and Rallis, S.F. (eds) (1994) *The Qualitative–Quantitative Debate: New Perspectives, New Directions for Evaluation* No. 61. San Francisco: Jossey-Bass.

This small volume presents highlights from the 1992 American Evaluation Association Conference, dedicated to healing the qualitative–quantitative rift so divisive at that time.

Tashakkori, A. and Teddlie, C. (1998) *Mixed Methodology: Combining Qualitative and Quantitative Approaches*. Thousand Oaks, CA: Sage.

This book offers a strong pragmatic statement about mixed-method work, including an extension beyond method to mixing discovery and validation models for social research.

Tashakkori, A. and Teddlie, C. (eds) (2003) *Handbook of Mixed Methods in Social and Behavioral Research.* Thousand Oaks, CA: Sage.

This comprehensive volume incorporates multiple perspectives on mixing methods in each of several sections devoted to frameworks and rationales, purposes and designs, and analysis strategies. Chapters on mixing methods in various domains of social science are also featured.

Weisner, T.S. (ed.) (in press) *Discovering Successful Pathways in Children's Development: New Methods in the Study of Childhood and Family Life.* Chicago: University of Chicago Press.

This exciting volume offers papers from a 2001 working conference on mixing methods in the study of children's development — in family, school and community locales. The key question addressed was, what did a mixed-method approach uniquely contribute to our understanding about children's developmental pathways?

Further references

Caracelli, V.J. and Greene, J.C. (1993) 'Data analysis strategies for mixed-method evaluation designs', *Educational Evaluation and Policy Analysis*, 15(2): 195–207.

Chin, M.C. (2003) *An investigation into the impact of using poetry and cartoons as alternative representational forms in evaluation reporting.* PhD dissertation, Florida State University.

Denzin, N.K. (1978) *The Research Act: An Introduction to Sociological Methods.* New York: McGraw-Hill.

Goodyear, L. (2001) *Representational form and audience understanding in evaluation: advancing use and engaging postmodern pluralism.* PhD dissertation, Cornell University.

Greene, J.C. (in press) 'A reprise on mixing methods: Why and how', in T.S. Weisner (ed.), *Discovering Successful Pathways in Children's Development: New Methods in the Study of Childhood and Family Life.* Chicago: University of Chicago Press.

Maxwell, J.A. and Loomis, D.A. (2003) 'Mixed-methods design: an alternative approach', in A. Tashakkori and C. Teddlie (eds), *Handbook of Mixed Methods in Social and Behavioral Research.* Thousand Oaks, CA: Sage, pp. 241–71.

Patton, M.Q. (2002) *Qualitative Research and Evaluation Methods,* 3rd edn. Thousand Oaks, CA: Sage.

Rabinow, P. (1977) *Reflections on Fieldwork in Morocco.* Berkeley, CA: University of California Press.

Skinner, B.F. (1956) 'Case history in scientific method', *American Psychologist*, 11: 221–33.

Smith, M.L. (1997) 'Mixing and matching: methods and models', in J.C. Greene and V. J. Caracelli (eds), *Advances in Mixed Method Evaluation: The Challenges and Benefits of Integrating Diverse Paradigms, New Directions for Evaluation* No. 74. San Francisco: Jossey-Bass, pp. 73–85.

Teddlie, C. and Tashakkori, A. (2003) 'Major issues and controversies in the use of mixed-methods in the social and behavioral sciences', in A. Tashakkori and C. Teddlie (eds), *Handbook of Mixed Methods in Social and Behavioral Research.* Thousand Oaks, CA: Sage, pp. 3–50.

Webb, E.J., Campbell, D.T., Schwartz, R.D. and Sechrest, L. (1966) *Unobtrusive Measures: Nonreactive Research in the Social Sciences.* Chicago: Rand McNally.

Weiss, H.B., Mayer, E., Kreider, H., Vaughan, M., Dearing, E., Hencke, R. and Pinto, K. (2003) 'Making it work: low-income working mothers' involvement in their children's education', *American Educational Research Journal* 40(4): 879–901.

Weiss, H.B., Kreider, H., Mayer, E., Hencke, R. and Vaughan, M. (in press) 'Working it out: the chronicle of a mixed-method analysis', in T.S. Weisner (ed.), *Discovering Successful Pathways in Children's Development: New Methods in the Study of Childhood and Family Life.* Chicago: University of Chicago Press.

PART VIII

RESEARCHING IN POSTMODERN CONTEXTS

Introduction

The chapters in this part of the book do not divide so neatly into separately demarcated methodologies and methods as those in the earlier sections; instead they overlap with one another, visiting and revisiting a number of core themes, resisting the notion of certainties in the construction and production of research knowledge and challenging the very notion that there are clearly defined methodological territories. This is signified by three of the chapters having hybrid titles (e.g. *From Hermeneutics to Poststructuralism*) and one incorporating in the title an intentional 'strike through' to denote that deconstruction can only be talked about as a method 'under erasure'. The final chapter begins by describing and analysing current research practices in virtual realities which relate directly to 'mainstream' methods and methodologies, but moves in its final section to present a 'discursive construction of research more organically "at home with" or "inside" – cyberspace.'

All the chapters explore the implications for social science research of the linguistic theories which developed during the twentieth century, beginning with Saussure and culminating with Derrida, involving a fundamental challenge to Enlightenment rationalism through recognition that all meaning is represented by signs which are arbitrary. These theories are important in destabilizing certainty and reconstructing knowledge as partial and contingent rather than valid and reliable. They resist traditional processes of data collection, analysis and interpretation grounded in assumptions of established procedures of induction and deduction in moving between 'the field' and 'theories'. These chapters adopt a Foucauldian analysis of knowledge produced and represented in discourses emanating from the development of systems and categories which instantiate power in social groups.

Put more simply, the theories presented in this section are important because they have given social science research a means of resisting the assumption that knowledge relating to human experience and behaviour can be developed using very similar methods to those which have been so spectacularly successful in the natural sciences (e.g. in producing planes that fly and materials that the body tolerates in hip replacements). The chapters do this in two ways – first by radically challenging much that has been presented and discussed in the earlier chapters in the book, and second by taking ideas from these earlier chapters and exploring them through a different lens. The process can perhaps best be understood through the metaphor of music organized in the form of a theme and variations. Hence the theme presented in the chapter on semiotic engagements in Part V is re-presented in a playful variation in 'From structuralism to poststructuralism'; and the themes presented in the chapters on feminist methodologies and queer theory in Part III are re-presented in the chapter on 'Feminism/poststructuralism'. As with the music, the delight for readers may be in identifying the interplay of ideas between theme and variations.

Some of the ideas contained in these chapters are difficult to grasp on first encounter, but they are presented here with considerable clarity. Rather than being seen as 'authentic' narratives of the present which mimic the voice of 'unwritten' texts, the Stories from the Field should be read as playful conversations with the Key Concepts sections. Part VIII as a whole might be seen as providing a critique on the book itself, destabilizing and deconstructing its categories and certainties.

CHAPTER

34

DECONSTRUCTION ~~AS A METHOD OF RESEARCH~~

Erica Burman
Research Institute of Health and Social Change, Manchester Metropolitan University, UK
Maggie MacLure
Education and Social Research Institute, Manchester Metropolitan University, UK

Key concepts

Maggie MacLure

Today is, among other things, the day where we have lost our 'metaphysical comfort'. (Biesta and Egéa-Kuehne, 2001: 50)

Pre-amble: 'key concepts' in the text below are dark yet starry, thus: '****différance****'. The 'strike-through' in the title is intentional and is explained below.

Perhaps the most important proposition of deconstruction is that our dealings with the world are *unrelievedly textual*. This is in contrast to many other philosophies or theories, which dream of a 'binary' universe of fundamental things on the one hand (reality, truth, thought, identity, etc.), and the textual or sign systems that convey these on the other. For these latter kinds of theories, texts (e.g. writing, speech or pictures) are a kind of unfortunate, pragmatic necessity. They are merely *mediators* whose function is to give us access to those fundamentals, origins or first principles that, if we only could, we would access directly, without mediation. Deconstruction challenges such 'metaphysical' thinking. In a famous phrase, Derrida wrote that 'there is no outside-text'.[1] In other words, there is no vantage point external to text, or discourse, that would give us an unmediated access to truth, ethics, being, etc. The world is always 'mediated', always-already textualized.[2]

Deconstruction is difficult to define further because definitions presuppose some kind of contract between words and meanings. But as I have already hinted, deconstruction tangles with, and tangles up, pairings such as word/meaning. It provides a sus-

tained, philosophical interrogation of this and other ****binary oppositions**** that have underpinned Western thought – truth/error; reality/representation; cause/effect; thought/language; essence/appearance; Man/woman; presence/absence; nature/culture; mind/body; reason/emotion; universal/particular, world/text, original/copy and so on.

There is always a hierarchy in these oppositions. One term always represents some higher principle or ideal or ****presence****, while the other is always a kind of ****supplement**** – something lesser and subordinate. This binary logic has been deployed by many different philosophical systems in their enduring preoccupation with fundamentals and first principles. Derrida refers to this preoccupation as the 'metaphysics of presence'. He describes it as:

> the enterprise of returning 'strategically', in idealization, to an origin or to a 'priority' seen as simple, intact, normal, pure, standard, self-identical [i.e. *presence*], in order *then* to conceive of derivation, complication, deterioration, accident, etc. [. . .] good before evil, the positive before the negative, the pure before the impure, the simple before the imitation, etc. (1988: 236; original emphasis)

You might think the metaphysics of presence is just an arcane practice of philosophers; but it is central to the way we make sense of the world. Consider these remarks from a former UK Chief Inspector of Schools with a beef about research journals:

> I used to try to read these journals. Life is too short. There is too much to do in the real world with real teachers in real schools to worry about methodological quarrels or to waste time decoding

unintelligible, jargon-ridden prose to reach (if one is lucky) a conclusion that is often so transparently partisan as to be worthless. (Quoted in MacLure, 2003: 11–12)

Do you see the hierarchy that privileges presence? The *real* (real world, real teachers, real schools) is opposed to the *written* (i.e. the debased jargon of the academics). Another example of 'presencing' underpins the very structure of this book, whose central chapters are organized in terms of 'Key Concepts' followed by 'Stories from the Field'. The Key Concepts set out the general principles or the ideas – that is to say the ground of 'presence' – while the Stories from the Field provide examples or particulars. That is why (if you read in a linear way) you will find yourself reading 'me' first and 'Erica' later. Deconstruction would interfere with these oppositions – as indeed Erica does in her 'stories from the field', which complicate the very notion of story, and of field.

Derrida shows how the binary law of presence always contains the seeds of its own undoing. It will always break down under pressure. Indeed, deconstruction could be described as the act of bringing pressure to bear on the cherished oppositions that are woven into texts, forcing/allowing them to reveal their blind spots or **aporias** – that is to say points of impasse – where the integrity of the oppositions is fatally compromised, and an excess of disorderly and contradictory meanings and resonances is released. Erica's examples 'below' apply just that sort of pressure to ostensibly simple texts relating to childhood and children, opening these texts up to a 'perplexing surplus of contested and conflicting meanings'.

One of Derrida's primary targets for deconstruction, which he has returned to many times, is the opposition between *speech* and *writing*, in which writing is generally the lesser partner. This ancient and persistent bias in Western philosophy is one manifestation of **logocentrism** – the belief in orders of meaning, reason or logic that exist independently of language or text. In privileging speech over writing philosophers have assumed that we are closer to thought, meaning, imagination, logic, our inner selves, other people or external reality when we speak than when we write. Writing has been accused of many crimes. It appears derivative, lifeless and artificial, in contrast to 'living' speech with its seeming proximity to presence as thought, consciousness or intention. It

stands for the 'bad' side of the nature/culture divide, as the disfiguring mark of alienated, 'civilized' societies, in contrast to the authenticity and apparent 'self-presence' of oral cultures. Lacking the supposed 'transparency' of speech, and its real-time connectivity between speaker and addressee, writing seems to offer too many chances for messages to go astray or for meanings to be distorted or for the stylistic vanities of writers to pervert the truth. This is the threat to presence that the Chief Inspector perceived (above). In many different ways, then, writing has been considered the pre-eminent threat to presence. It stands for secondariness, distance, non-identity, absence, exteriority and mediation. Writing seems to deflect or to *come between* us and the important stuff.

Deconstruction interferes with the hierarchy of opposition between speech and writing, to show how speech is no less troubled by distance, difference and delay than writing, and therefore no more secure a guarantor of presence. Those extralinguistic desirables such as meaning, reason and so on are still brought to us – made present to us – via *signs*, which refer to other signs, in a chain of endless substitutions or differences. We will never arrive at the end of the chain, to claim the prize of unmediated access to reality, truth, etc. Something always intervenes or deflects. The world is always mediated. Always *written*. Thus Derrida reverses the hierarchy of privilege, to show that speech has the same qualities of writtenness, as it were, as writing. In so doing, he invests the word **Writing** (sometimes called **arche-writing**) with a new, quasi-technical status, as the mark of all those qualities of secondariness, distance, displacement, textuality, absence that mediate the world. Writing (under deconstruction) institutes a paradoxical logic very different from the orderly economy of presence. It brings you closer to what you desire – reality, meaning, truth, origins, other people, the 'self' – by condemning you also always to be separated from it. Separated by the very words, or signs, that make the world possible.

In place of origins or essences, deconstruction thus finds **différance** – the term coined by Derrida which, in French, contains traces of both difference and deferral, and can only be distinguished from the conventional French *différence* in its written form. 'Différance' thus embodies a little joke or allusion to the priority of writing over speech, as the figure of the absence/difference/deferral that lies at the 'heart' of meaning. Sometimes also referred to as **spacing**, différance is the irreducible gap that allows meaning, reality, identity, etc. to come to definition in contrast to their opposites (words, representation, otherness). But the spacing is always uncanny – a matter of opening a space between things that cannot, yet must have, existed prior to the movement of opening.

Derrida says that philosophy's longing for presence arises from the desire to escape from the **play** of différance – to 'arrest', for example, the flickering relays of differences amongst signs that produce, but also endlessly defer, meaning. Why not go along with that project? Why not try to make a wobbly world more stable? Derrida's argument is that the binary hierarchies of presence are always *violent* (Derrida, 1972: 41). The stability that is (temporarily) achieved is always at the cost of suppression of some 'other' – of whatever is banished to the 'wrong' side of the binary. This can be seen very clearly with binaries such as white/black, Man/woman, adult/child, as Erica's Stories 'below' show. There is always power, authority and violence at play in the stratagems of presence. This is not to say that we can ever entirely escape it. The 'closure' of metaphysics is too deeply wired into our ways of being. But we can continually try to glimpse the **trace** of what has been silenced, or 'othered' in order to provide us with our metaphysical 'comforts of mastery' (Johnson, 1987:13). This is, says Derrida, an *ethical* stance of responsibility to the 'other': that is, to whatever remains silent, unthought or 'untruthed' so that presence can come into being. *Education* is pre-eminently a scene where ethical responsibility is demanded (see Biesta and Egéa-Kuehne, 2001).

Can deconstruction be a 'method' of research?

Derrida would say No. You can see why: to call it a method or theory is to conjure another metaphysical opposition, between an external world and deconstruction, as if this were something separate which could be 'applied'. Deconstruction is always inextricably tangled up with whatever is its object.[3] Moreover, to reduce it to a set of procedures ('Spot the binary, reverse the binary, displace the binary') would be to remove its capacity to engage with the unpredictable Other that is its focus. So, if we are to talk of deconstruction as a method, we need to do so **under erasure** – that is, in the acknowledgement that it is one of those impossible things that we cannot do without. The strike-through notation, as used in the title of this chapter, is the mark of

something put under erasure. (In the case of the title, it is the im/possibility of deconstruction as 'a method' that is put under erasure.)

With the foregoing warnings in mind, I offer some precepts (or perhaps pretexts) for doing deconstruction. They are annoyingly gnomic. They should be read alongside instances of deconstruction such as Erica's, 'below', and the texts in the Annotated Bibliography.

- See the world, your data and yourself as *text*, with all that that implies. For example, that there is no direct access to reality, other people or even one's self. Think of such things as 'the classroom', 'the child', 'the researcher' with invisible quotation marks around them: they are not 'natural', not self-evident and *never* innocent.
- Look for the binary oppositions in texts (which might be interview transcripts, observation notes, questionnaire returns, documents, your own biases and assumptions) and worry away at them. Put pressure on them. This is what Erica does in her Stories 'below'.
- Challenge the taken-for-granted – not in a destructive spirit, nor in the hope that you will reveal some deeper truth. But in order to *open up* textual spaces that seem closed or, contrariwise, to *tangle up* or confound things that seem too intent on keeping their distance.

Implications for research design

If deconstruction has implications for design, these are not so much about the paraphernalia of methods or sampling – which might look pretty conventional – as about our ways of engaging with the world and the status that we accord such things as 'data', 'analysis', 'subjects' and so on. Perhaps the primary insight that deconstruction affords is that methods are typically *devices for policing 'presence'*. Method – qualitative or quantitative – is about ensuring that we come as close as possible to truth, trustworthiness, generalizability, authenticity, justice, knowledge or ethical propriety. As we have seen, deconstruction puts all these concepts 'under erasure'. Here are a few examples of the boundaries that are policed by Method, which deconstruction would problematize.

Researcher/researched

Think of all the methods that are designed to dissolve the boundaries between the researcher and her 'subjects' or to bring their different worlds into closer proximity. This would include 'conversational' interview techniques and narrative or life-history methods, which try to speak to subjects in their own vernacular and thus to bridge the gap of power and alienation that has been such a trouble for social research. It would include action research, with its prioritizing of practitioners' experience over academics' theories. These examples prioritize the world of the research subjects as the ground of presence, in contrast to that of the researchers, which is external, alien, cold, un-natural. Deconstruction would not, of course, prioritize their opposites, or suggest abandoning these 'vernacular' methods (cf. MacLure, 2003: chapter 7). But it would argue that these methods exhibit a 'drive to innocent knowing' (Lather, 1996) which can never uncomplicatedly deliver the warmth of presence that it seeks, and often leaves power and inequity intact. Researchers will always be knottily entangled with their subjects and ambiguously positioned both inside and outside various worlds and realities.

Fieldwork/theorywork

Erica will have more to say about the field below. For the moment, notice how in ethnography 'the field' generally stands for subjects' real, unmediated experience, and for the place where the researcher has her/his direct contact with that experience. While academic monographs may carry the authority (i.e. the presence) bestowed by science, or the higher-order abstractions of theoretical knowledge, that knowledge is always insufficient or incomplete without the alternative, if lesser, legitimacy granted to the researchers and their research by their Stories from the Field (Clifford, 1990). Think of the special status of field notes or snatches of conversation which, when inserted into reports, seem to bring a little piece of the real into the written. As Erica shows, 'the field' is no less a textualized, power-infused space than that of theory, though its contours are different.

Research/writing

Deconstruction denies, of course, that these are two entirely separate things. One of the more specific implications for research design is that researchers might experiment with novel, 'playful' forms of writing and reporting, with the aim of producing knowledge that is more surprising and less masterful than is often the case.

Attempting to summarize, deconstruction raises questions. What counts as analysis? How do phenomena come to be 'data'? What would be an 'ethical' stance towards the Other? What is the status of the knowledge produced by research? How are the selves of researchers and subjects fabricated – that is to say fashioned and knotted together – in research?

Stories from the Field

Erica Burman

Deconstructing stories

'Stories from the field' seem oddly modernist and objectivist, the agricultural metaphor suggestive of the discourse of data flourishing 'out there' (where? anywhere that is not 'here', perhaps?), awaiting collection like ripe fruit. 'Stories' – after Benjamin (1955/1973a) – evoke the oral tradition of spoken wisdom countering the dead weight of sterile information in an industrial age, at a time that has forgotten how to communicate. Here the discourse of 'what methodology books don't/can't tell you' meets a long-standing preoccupation that links voyeurism with the intimacy of informal/illicit knowledge.

Pausing to consider the kinds of relations presumed by the discourse of stories invites consideration of who is deemed worthy to tell and to hear stories. Typically the dominant stories, or received histories, have been produced by those who have won progress' competitions (capitalism, patriarchy, colonialism . . .). History – or what we know as history – is therefore the story of the winners. 'The storyteller is the figure in which the righteous man [sic] encounters himself' (Benjamin, 1955/1973b: 106). There is a project of implicitly masculine (self-)recognition structured into storytelling that evokes not only the Enlightenment subject of humanism but also its implicit correlate: victorious heroic struggle.

Meeting points/engendering the field

So telling 'stories from the field' seems a suspect activity, replete with gendered, age and colonial relations. Indeed such notions remain alive and kicking – for those with the money, gender and class status and leisure to 'play':

THE FIELD is the world's original country and fieldsports magazine . . . For nearly 150 years, THE FIELD has been the first choice for those that love the British country sports tradition. And if you love gameshooting, flyfishing, hunting, dogs and the land, it will be your natural choice too. (Editorial statement <http://www.countrylife.co.uk/thefield/who.htm>)

Indeed, the genre of stories can often be a place to disclose the 'off-takes', the tales of 'not always getting it right' that the rigours of published academic research seem to demand. But here even the traditional sporting advice has pre-emptively usurped the genre to reinstate itself again. Hence we see traditional hegemonic Western masculinity get a laddish facelift in *The Field* editorial, from the man who always does his country sports right, to a less severe and more playful and altogether more (self-)indulgent and fallible character:

Well, we almost always do the right thing. Sometimes our labradors and spaniels forget their manners and riot, badly. Sometimes, among friends, we cannot resist shooting the high, curling bird that is rightfully theirs. Sometimes we find ourselves in Irish bars after a day's salmon fishing, drinking too much Guinness, laughing too loud, having another cigarette when we've promised we'd given up. (Editorial statement <http://www.countrylife.co.uk/thefield/who.htm>)

'Who am I to write this?' is a necessary question, but not necessarily a paralysing one. Instead of pretending the position of disembodied, omniscient (culturally masculine) knower or even its feminine/feminist autobiographical variety (which sheds its subjectivity by virtue of, instead of denying, its reflexive status), we can attempt research stories that highlight the ambiguities and instabilities of the identities of researcher and researched, and attend to shifting convergences and contests over respective agendas that are structured within any encounter. At stake is the impossibility of attaining that secure place of 'knowing' that characterized the modernist methodological and interpretive project.

Picturing children

Childhood is an uneven and troubled 'field' from which researchers are always partly exiled by virtue of having grown up. This field is often conceptualized as an enclosed space of domesticated nature from which 'we' (adults) originated. What do the prevailing discourses of 'innocence' or 'primitiveness' or 'development' conceal or suppress about children's experiences and their unequal power relations with adults?

Rather than striving to close the gap between 'us' and 'them', our research 'others', we should analyse what is being covered over. What follows is an attempt to create some space to reflect upon the construction of stories of childhood, to promote moments of radical political possibility as '... brief truces ... wrest out of history' (Rajan,1993: 143). Precisely because of their naturalized and abstracted status, representations of childhood offer a repository of some of our most deeply held precepts. Hence these stories highlight the perplexing surplus of contested and conflicting meanings mobilized by and around children (and childhoods), and the impossibility of separating the object from the subject of the research. In terms of form, they also stretch the notion of 'story' to move from and between the 'privatized/feminized' sphere of personal account to seemingly more authoritative, public statements. Rather than proposing a specific 'moral' the stories are accompanied by questions that highlight dilemmas produced by prevailing, but limited, binary polarities structuring children and their others. Such questions are inevitably 'leading', but quite where they go is another matter.

Methodologically speaking, in various of these accounts I deploy the following tactics:

- displacing the high/low culture binary: expertise vs. the everyday (I do not 'speak as' – only – an academic psychologist, but 'as' a woman (therefore) with non/motherhood status and racialized and classed positioning – cf. Burman, 1998);
- highlighting the materiality of the context of production of academic knowledge (personal/ academic identities and settings);
- displacing the privileging of specific disciplinary authority (e.g. psychological knowledge of children) – by drawing on other (e.g. anthropological) sources;
- presence/absence and the temporal relations of the (narration of the) research space;
- the identification and allocation of separate spaces: us and them, and how these are constituted;
- the Rights and Wrongs of childhood: childhood as a site of indulgence vs. exploitation, but for which children?
- intertextuality: how the different texts of childhood relate to each other, and each elaborate, distinct subject positions for other constituencies around children.

Stories of risk

Far from being a benign space of sport and entertainment, 'the field' has become somewhere to be protected from. Discourses of 'risk' have emerged as the contemporary response to and expression of vulnerability – and the ways we position children index this.

Story I: PURITY AND DANGER

At the public swimming baths, the changing rooms are locked. Why, I ask? Because the schools are using them, when they come for lessons. But can't I use them at the same time, I persist? The attendant says, 'We're not allowed to – child protection'. This appears to signal an absolute stopping point for that line of inquiry. So he tells me I should use the 'disabled' shower room instead. But, I say (since I have tried this already), these are kept locked too. 'Oh yes,' he says, 'we have to keep them locked 'cos kids vandalize them'.[4] *(February 2003)*

Some questions:

1   Am I a potential child abuser, or a victim of vandalism?
2   What are the ambiguities about who or what is being protected?
3   How is this coded by the opposition between 'children' and 'kids'?
4   What concatenations of identity categories are at play, and with what effects?
5   What institutional relations structure those identity categories?

Some reflections:

● Between commonsense and expertise.
● Particularly useful to challenge psychological authority which peddles received cultural norms back to parents, and educators and health professionals, dressed up in jargon.
● Risk as the mode to express vulnerability – with significant consequences for the elaboration of the individual/state relationship (in terms of discourses of responsibility and scrutiny).
● Children in particular function as tokens in this cultural economy of 'risk', with consequences for 'our' positioning in relation to them.

Story II: ACCESS AND LIABILITY

About a year ago, the following notice appeared on the noticeboards and corridor walls of my university (and is still on display):

> *the*
> Manchester
> Metropolitan
> University
>
> IMPORTANT NOTICE
>
> CHILDREN
>
> The University is concerned that small children (under 10) may be at risk from falls from height from staircases and landings in buildings that have not been designed with children's safety in mind.
>
> Therefore until further notice **children under 10 are prohibited from University buildings**.
>
> Staff, students and visitors are expected to co-operate with the University in the interest of preventing accidents and injuries.
>
> I.W. Hallam
> Personnel Director

(Typeface and emphasis following the original)

Some questions:

1   Who does this 'notice' address (Is it 'children under 10')?
2   Who or what is the 'speaker'?
3   What kinds of 'concern' are being expressed?
4   Which kinds of (gendered, classed, aged) 'staff/students/visitors' are likely to be most affected by such measures?
5   What penalties follow from failure to comply with such prescriptions? How can it be regulated or enforced?

Some reflections:

● This is a story of self-regulation.
● 'Small' conflates size with immaturity and irresponsibility.
● Children as a distraction/obstacle to the education/work business.
● The welfare of children is assimilated to a health and safety issue.

Story III: *CHILDHOOD LOST AND REGAINED*

A 1999 Virgin Entertainment advertisement on hoardings and at bus stops announces in large blue and yellow letters: 'DELAY BECOMING YOUR PARENTS'. The small print at the bottom of the poster reads: 'www.virgin.net movies, music, travel, shopping' and on the next line: 'make the most of your free time'.

Some questions:

1   What characteristics of parents are implied?
2   What characteristics of children are implied?
3   What assumptions (and psychological models) underlie the notion that 'we' will eventually 'become' our parents, and that all we can do is to 'defer' this?
4   Who are 'we'?
5   What age, class, gender and cultural assumptions are set in circulation?

Some reflections:

● Becoming 'old' before your time?
● (Modern) childhood as the space of (freedom, irresponsibility and) play.
● Cultivating 'your' 'inner child' as the route to ward off this process.
● Consumption as the most visible measure of success in this project.

Story IV: *EXPLOITATION OR EDUCATION?*

'No Job Too Dirty' [accompanying picture of girl on knees, scrubbing floor]
cleans quietly and efficiently

This is the kind of work Farida does 17 hours a day, 7 days a week. It could be worse. In parts of the world, children as young as 6 are being sold into prostitution or hazardous work. All because they are desperately poor and desperately vulnerable.

UNICEF is working to end the exploitation of children. With your help we can make sure they get a proper education. We can help their families to earn an income. And we can lobby governments to protect them by law.

CHILDREN LIKE FARIDA CAN'T ASK YOU FOR HELP, SO WE ARE. PLEASE, SEND AS MUCH AS YOU CAN TODAY

(UNICEF, typeface as in the *Guardian* – 6 February 2003)

Some questions:

1   Does this ad resist or reiterate prevailing representations of childhood?
2   What happens when the discourses of sentiment and human rights are rubbed up against each other – indulgence vs. exploitation?
3   How mandatory are the measures being advocated?
4   What kind of appropriate childhoods, family and state relations are implied here?
5   What kind of relationships between donor and recipient(s) are elaborated?

Some reflections:

● Child labour incites controversy but the ad side-steps this by the ambiguity of whether all working children are exploited.
● 1st/3rd World relations elaborated via polarized discourse around child labour ('1st W': 'working to play' (Mizen and Pole, 2000) vs. '3rd W': 'working to live').
● Positioning of children as 'desperate' (× 2), in need of 'help' (× 2) and 'protect[ion]' (× 2) does not seem to allow for agency and decision-making (notwithstanding how these do not reflect young people's actual engagement within, for example, International Labour Organization debates).
● The girl child as the quintessential (deserving?) victim.

Notes

1. 'Il n'y a pas de hors-texte' (Derrida, 1978: 158). Frequently translated as 'There is nothing outside of the text', this aphorism has been widely misunderstood by critics of deconstruction as a statement of relativism and nihilism.

2. Such a view – that realities are mediated through text or discourse – places deconstruction within that broad strand of intellectual work known as *poststructuralism* – see Stronach, Miller and Lee, in this volume.

3. This makes deconstruction a form of *immanent* theory or critique.

4. A fuller version of this story would include how: (a) the staff indicated that there had been a design

fault in the plans for the new complex by failing to include non-public showers; (b) that in lieu of this staff had arrived at an arrangement to open up the disabled shower rooms on request, which clearly posed problems on capacity, highlighted my middle-class status as having the cultural capital to have discovered this arrangement and posed questions about how adequately they would be able to cater for disabled bathers.

Annotated Bibliography

Reading instructions

Derrida's writing is notoriously difficult. His work assumes a familiarity with European philosophy and is full of puns, word-plays, digressions and complications. The two texts recommended here happen to have excellent introductions. Culler also provides a good companion. There are also useful digests on the internet from university departments of literary theory or philosophy. Typing your keywords into the Google search engine will usually throw up several useful sites.

Texts by Derrida

Derrida, J. (1978) 'Nature', 'Culture', 'Writing', in *Of Grammatology*, trans. and intro. Gayatri C. Spivak. Baltimore, MD: Johns Hopkins University Press.

Deconstruction of speech and writing via Rousseau and Levi-Strauss. Hard-going, with a challenging introduction by Spivak, but this sets out and explains the basic terrain and concepts of deconstruction.

Derrida, J. (1981) 'Plato's pharmacy', in *Dissemination*, trans. and intro. Barbara Johnson. London: Athlone.

Deconstruction of speech and writing via Plato. Relatively accessible and entertaining, with a wonderful closing section where the Pharmacist becomes overwhelmed by the dissemination of meaning.

Commentaries/expositions

Culler, J. (1983) *On Deconstruction*. London: Routledge.

Bit elderly now, so not up on the latest work. Focused primarily on literary theory. But a trusty and accessible guide.

Johnson, B. (1987) *A World of Difference*. Baltimore, MD: Johns Hopkins University Press.

Collection of essays, including a helpful one trying to show what's special about deconstruction. Again literary examples, but a clear and engaging approach.

Deconstruction and social research

Biesta, G.J.J and Egéa-Kuehne, D. (2001) *Derrida and Education*. London: Routledge.

Edited collection by educationalists who know their Derrida.

Brown, T. and Jones, L. (2001) *Action Research and Postmodernism: Congruence and Critique*. Buckingham: Open University Press.

Thoughtful deconstruction of the nursery classroom and the discourses of child development, gender and action research.

Lather, P. (2003) 'Applied Derrida: (Mis)reading the work of mourning in educational research', *Educational Philosophy and Theory*, 35(3): 256–70.

Short article by one of the best-known writers on deconstruction and educational research, outlining some important issues.

MacLure, M. (2003) *Discourse in Educational and Social Research.* Buckingham: Open University Press.

Methodological implications of deconstruction for social and educational research, via topics including parents' evenings, women's writing and life history interviews.

Rambo Ronai, C. (1998) 'Sketching with Derrida: an ethnography of a researcher/exotic dancer', *Qualitative Inquiry*, 4(3): 405–21.

Complicates the boundaries between researcher/researched, self/other, emancipation/exploitation while still saying something about difficult lives that resist reduction to simple truths.

Stronach, I. and MacLure, M. (1997) *Educational Research Undone: The Postmodern Embrace.* Buckingham: Open University Press.

Engagements between deconstruction and educational research, in the context of a range of research and evaluation projects with which the authors were involved.

Further references

Benjamin, W. (1955/1973a) 'The storyteller', in *Illuminations.* London: Jonathan Cape, pp. 83–107.

Benjamin, W. (1955/1973b) 'Theses on the philosophy of history', in *Illuminations*. London: Jonathan Cape, pp. 245–55.

Burman, E. (1998) 'The child, the woman and the cyborg: (im)possibilities of a feminist developmental psychology', in C. Griffin, K. Henwood and A. Phoenix (eds), *Standpoints and Differences*. London: Sage, pp. 210–32.

Mizen, P. and Pole, C. (2000) *Why Work at the Edge? Motivations for working among School Age Workers in Britain*. Paper presented at 'Working Children's Challenge to the Social Sciences' conference, Bondy, France.

Rajan, R.S. (1993) *Real and Imagined Women*. London and New York: Routledge.

CHAPTER

35

FROM HERMENEUTICS TO POSTSTRUCTURALISM TO PSYCHOANALYSIS

Tony Brown
School of Education, University of Waikato, New Zealand
Daniel Heggs
School of Health and Social Sciences, University of Wales Institute, Cardiff, UK

Key concepts

Tony Brown

The issues to be discussed in this section relate to the question: how does language shape the life it seeks to describe and how does life shape language? This circularity is an example of the 'hermeneutic circle', where 'hermeneutics' might be understood simply as the process of interpretation. The notion of hermeneutics is often combined with the term 'phenomenology': the logic of the world as experienced. In this perspective the focus is on how people experience the world and make sense of it rather than with any notion of underlying truth. We consider these terms here in relation to how humans experience the world and offer statements to encapsulate this experience.

Gallagher (1992) categorizes four forms of hermeneutics:

Conservative hermeneutics

This early conception of hermeneutics is exemplified in the task of reading a text, where the primary objective is to understand the author in the way the author intended. Gallagher draws an analogy with schooling where the learner's task is restricted to understanding what the teacher intends. As Scheleimacher puts it, this understanding of hermeneutics involves a 're-cognition and re-construction of a meaning (towards) prepar(ing) the individual for common participation in the state, the church, free society, and academia' (cited in Gallagher, 1992: 213).

Moderate hermeneutics

Leading modern exponents of hermeneutics are Gadamer and Ricoeur (e.g. 1981). For these writers, whose work has included a strongly theological dimension, there are certain truths that orientate our way of seeing things. Gadamer's moderate hermeneutics does not see tradition as fixed, but rather sees it as being transformed through an educative process. The components of tradition are not seen as fully constituted objects to behold but rather tradition is something of which one is part.

Hermeneutics permits a range of interpretations, some of which may be seen as being closer to the truth. However, no interpretation is ever final. Hermeneutical understanding never arrives at its object directly; one's approach is always conditioned by the interpretations explored on the way. Here there is an attempt to capture the continuity of understanding in discrete forms, as explanations. But these explanations then inform the continuous experience of understanding. While one's own understanding may become 'fixed' in an explanation for the time being, such fixity is always contingent. In choosing to act as if my explanation is correct, the world may resist my actions in a slightly unexpected way, giving rise to a new understanding, resulting in a revised explanation, providing a new context for acting and so on. This circularity between explanation and understanding is another encapsulation of the *hermeneutic circle*.

Critical hermeneutics (or critical social theory)

Within critical hermeneutics research is seen as a transformative process, primarily concerned with the 'emancipation' from the ideological structures that govern our actions. Such an attitude leans on the work of Habermas, who is generally regarded as a contemporary Enlightenment philosopher in so far as his work is predicated on achieving rationality. Here we have a conception of human behaviour understood in relation to certain social consensus of universal principles (e.g. moral perspectives, the existence of God) that can be called upon in the event of some supposed divergence from rational behaviour. Habermas aims for unconstrained language but sets out by supposing that in most societies language has become distorted as a result of the interplay of alternative forms of political power. Habermas seeks 'Ideal' communication without the 'hidden exercise of force' (Ricoeur, 1981) resulting from supposed ideological distortion. His reflecting subject has a conception of the universal principles at work and a conception of how any in-built contradictions to these can be overcome. The human subject is thus trying to find ways of making things better from some supposed deficit position. A caricature of Habermas is that this points to a supposed emancipatory interest whereby these contradictions are confronted and action is designed to remove them.

Radical hermeneutics (or poststructuralism)

All my books . . . are, if you like, little tool boxes. If people want to open them, or to use this sentence or that idea as a screwdriver or spanner to short-circuit, discredit or smash systems of power, including eventually those from which my books have emerged . . . so much the better. (Foucault, cited in Patton and Meaghan, 1979: 115)

Foucault (e.g. Rabinow, 1991), although generally supportive of Habermas, rejects the idea of human activity being governed by universal principles and specifically rejects Habermas's notion of communication based around these.

The idea that there could exist a state of communication that would allow games of truth to circulate freely, without any constraints seems utopian to me. This is precisely a failure to see that power relations are not something that is bad in itself, that we have to break free of. I do not think a society can live without power relations, if by that one means the strategies by which individuals try to direct and control the conduct of others. (Foucault, 1997: 298)

For Foucault (1998: 448) 'no given form of rationality is actually reason'. Habermas, discussing Foucault's work after the latter's death, sums up this move by Foucault. Habermas suggests that with the publication of the *Birth of the Clinic* Foucault elected to abstain from dealing with texts through commentary and to give up all hermeneutics, no matter how deeply it might penetrate below the surface of the text. He no longer (as he did in *Madness and Civilisation*) seeks madness itself behind the discourse about madness. As such there are no universal rules to be located beneath the surface of human activity. Each individual then is responsible for his or her own self-mastery without reference to universal rules. The individual must harmonize any perceived antagonisms to create a 'balanced' person.

Another leading writer often identified with poststructuralism is Derrida. Derrida has discussed how our understandings of the present are conditioned by the media through which we receive depictions of it. He claims that actuality is *made* and that virtuality ('virtual images, virtual spaces, and therefore virtual outcomes') is no longer distinguishable from actual reality. 'The "reality" of "actuality" – however individual, irreducible, stubborn, painful or tragic it may be – only reaches us through fictional devices' (Derrida, 1994: 29).

And then to psychoanalysis

If phenomenology is logic of world as experienced, how do we understand the 'person' 'experiencing'? Also, how do people use language in describing the world around them and by implication the way they see themselves fitting in?

Freud is at the root of contemporary psychoanalysis. In the following extract Habermas characterizes the importance of Freud's contribution:

Freud dealt with the occurrence of systematically deformed communication in order to define the scope of specifically incomprehensible acts and utterances. He always envisaged the dream as the standard example of such phenomena, the latter including everything from harmless, everyday pseudo-communication and Freudian slips to pathological manifestations of neurosis, psychosis, and psychosomatic disturbance. In his essays on cultural theory, Freud broadened the range of phenomena which could be conceived as being part of systematically distorted communication. He employed the insights gained from clinical phenomena as the key to pseudo-normality, that is to the hidden pathology of collective behaviour and entire social systems. (Habermas, 1976: 349)

Thus Freud's work underpinned Habermas's critical quest to detect the faults in society more generally and find ways of repairing them. Freud's psychoanalytic sessions were predicated on a supposed cure achieved through 'helping the subject to overcome the distortions that are the source of self-misunderstanding' (Ricoeur, 1981: 265). But Freud also provides an understanding of how we as individuals in contemporary society understand ourselves fitting into a world where social roles are not clearly set out before us. Society itself has an image of how it conducts itself and promotes particular understandings of normality. Such socially derived understandings provide a backdrop to individuals making sense of their own lives within this frame.

Giddens discusses this:

Self identity has to be created and recreated on a more active basis than before. This explains why therapy and counselling of all kinds have become so popular in Western countries. When he initiated modern psychoanalysis, Freud thought that he was establishing a scientific treatment for neurosis. What he was in effect doing was constructing a method for the renewal of self identity ... what happens in psychoanalysis is that the individual revisits his or her past in order to create more autonomy for the future. Much the same is true in the self-help groups that have become so common in Western societies. At Alcoholics Anonymous meetings, for instance, individuals recount their life histories, and receive support from others present in stating their desire to change. They recover from their addiction essentially through re-writing the story line of their lives. (1999: 47–8)

Perhaps this account of Freud provides a helpful metaphor for those of us carrying out practitioner research in which the practitioner researcher is seen as a psychoanalyst's client who lies back on a couch and talks of her life, her motivations, fears and aspirations. And in pinpointing these motivations, fears and aspirations, in words spoken to the psychoanalyst, they somehow become more real and tangible. As such they emerge as guiding principles for how the client lives her life thereafter. The words

and the way they are put together become part of her. The story that the client tells of her life shapes her actual experience by providing a framework against which she understands what she is doing. Nevertheless, this reification of lived experience can deceive as well as enlighten. Some versions of self are more comfortable than others, and a client may choose a version that she feels she can work with.

An alternative to Freud's quest for a cure, is possibly to be found in the writings of Lacan. Lacan (e.g. Lacan, 1977; Leader and Groves, 1995) sees the human subject as caught in a never ending attempt to capture an understanding of his or her self in relation to the world in which he or she lives. The human subject is always incomplete and remains so, where identifications of oneself are captured in a supposed image, an image of which, Lacan insists, we should always be wary. Here the individual is forever on a quest to complete the picture she has of herself in relation to the world around her and the others who also inhabit it. She responds to the fantasy she has of the Other and the fantasy she imagines the Other having of her. The identity thus created evolves through a series of interpretations (and mis-recognitions) through interactions with others.

In the context of practitioner research, for example, reflective writing may provide a forum for building such a narrative layer in which the researcher acts as her own analyst as it were (Brown and England, 2004). The images constructed in such a process provide material for the researcher to interrogate herself. In this perspective we might see the flow of narrative as an ongoing construction of a reflective/constructive/disruptive layer that feeds while growing alongside the life it seeks to portray.

Implications for research design

These theoretical frameworks can be used in a wide range of research contexts. However, they are particularly powerful as a means of deepening self-understanding and have often underpinned practitioner research in its many guises. An example of an approach that might be suggested in this context could be guided by a conception of action research shaped around *reflective* analysis, targeted at stimulating a process of 'professional development', but also following a cyclical *reflexive* model in which new understandings of self emerge during the research process. This approach, however, might be adapted to accommodate a more fluid association between the researcher and the researched. Here the practitioner researcher forges, and reflects upon, a professional trajectory within which the research situation is recognized as being a function of her evolving perspective, resulting from successive encapsulations of herself created within the research process.

The procedure would be shaped primarily around the researcher writing autobiographically about herself, over a period of time, in relation to the world she occupies. An analogy might be drawn between this and a sequence of psychoanalytic sessions. Here, the researcher, in creating reflective writing, would be producing accounts of herself. This might be directly, through descriptions of herself and of her actions, or indirectly through the revelation of her particular perspectives. That is, this writing, produced as part of the research process, would be seen as providing declarations by the teacher of who she was and of what she was trying to achieve. A key aspect of this would be some awareness that she is addressing these writings to a future version of herself, a proxy for an analyst, who would be making sense of data produced in this way later on in the research process. The writings would provide framings of the past and possible formats for crafting the future. Ongoing analysis could provide points of reference for her in constructing an account of who she was at different points in time and in different situations. Through this later analysis the researcher could provide an account of her own evolving self as a professional and as a researcher. This research approach is discussed more fully by Brown and Jones (2001).

The questions to be asked along the way might include: What version of myself do I feel comfortable with? What fantasies do I have about myself, the place I work and the people I work with? How do I understand the broader social context within which this takes place? What stories do I tell to justify my actions?

Through this process the researcher creates an image of herself. This version of events, however, is perhaps haunted by the bits that she chooses not to see. As seen above, the relationship between word and image is not always straightforward. The image might be seen as a cover story for things the researcher is finding difficult to address. At the same time the researcher has to reconcile her own image with the image others seem to have of her and also how the tasks she faces seem to be framed for her by others. The research might then become an attempt to address these difficult issues.

Stories from the Field
Daniel Heggs

I have read comic books for as long as I can remember and have associated them with fleeting, simple pleasures. A general history of the medium might focus on humorous newspaper strips, American superheroes and children's comics and these dominate our common perceptions of what is suitable material for a comic. Here the relationship between word and image is seen as straightforward. Knowledge of the typical content then regulates understandings of the form. So, the '. . . silly medium, suitable only for children' (Barker, 1984: 6) is hampered by a restricted message, in spite of having '. . . a highly developed narrative grammar and vocabulary based on an inextricable combination of verbal and visual elements' (Witek, 1989: 3). Comics are texts in which representations are held in the blend of words and pictures and so recognition of their hybrid form is an important first step in their analysis. Yet to try to focus solely on a text is problematic. Popular characters have a longevity that has seen them be updated for new generations. Moreover, many characters have successfully transferred to other media. Dennis the Menace has become a popular cartoon, and Batman and Superman have both moved into film, television, radio and cartoon. Our cultural knowledge of the characters and settings must be taken into consideration when looking at them critically as our preconceptions influence how a reading might progress.

The research from which this section is derived took Superman and Batman comic books as its main object of enquiry. These American superheroes have long and intriguing histories (Brooker, 2001). They have become cultural icons that signify different meanings in different contexts. They have been updated, translated for various media and always in print in comic book form. It was important, then, to develop and employ a theoretically informed approach to the analysis of these hybrid texts that would remain sensitive to their signifying properties, that would provide a methodical and checkable approach and that would look to the function of the texts in broad cultural contexts. Conceptual developments from narrative analysis, discourse analysis and psychoanalysis were employed in the readings of Batman and Superman texts in order that no single theoretical orientation dominated interpretation. I will now briefly outline what I take from these three interlocking areas of theory before offering an example reading.

Narrative analysis allows the general features of a plot to be explored and the particular narratives of the characters to be emphasized, and so I employed narrative analysis to focus on surface features of stories to be examined. Discourse analysis was used to identify key themes but in a way that went beyond the detection of salient narrative features. I preferred a Foucauldian approach for its emphasis on representation and meaning, which made its application to hybrid texts appropriate. Finally psychoanalysis was employed through the readings derived from discourse and narrative. Two broad areas, the Oedipus complex and the structure of fantasy, as described by Lacan, were used. These two interlinking aspects of psychoanalytic theory enable issues of subjectivity to be explored and look to the relationship between the intersubjective and the intrasubjective. In this dimension the connections between the social and the individual are paramount, and these are grasped through an understanding of fantasy as a screen for desire.

Each of these areas of theory could be employed independently, yet together they enable analyses to combine different perspectives so that meaning is not closed down through the application of a particular theoretical frame. As such the eclectic analysis I offer moves from poststructuralist, or radical, hermeneutics to psychoanalysis.

Example reading

Superman first appeared in the first issue of *Action Comics* in June 1938 and, much to the surprise of the publishers (McCue, 1992), was an instant success. Less than a year later, in issue 27 of *Detective Comics*, Batman had his debut. Although both characters have certain similarities – caped costumes and secret identities – it is the contrasts that provoke fascination. As a comic book author and illustrator put it '[t]heir primal, complementary qualities have given rise to the entire field [of superheroes] and, arguably, have defined its parameters' (Gibbons, 1992: Intro.). These can be grasped clearly through the origin stories for the characters. These stories provide a psychological backdrop for the motivations of the characters, offering accounts as to why young orphaned boys would take up the fight against crime or injustice while dressed in outlandish costumes. Superman's origin story was told with his first appearance, and Batman's was told six issues after he debuted. Since then the stories have been repeated many times in

different contexts. The retellings allow for different interpretations of the characters, yet also delimit the possible range of character representations. The origin stories might then be said to provide an immanent textual surveillance of the characters, conferring authenticity on the figures represented and so guaranteeing that a genuine Batman or Superman is illustrated.

The text I chose for the example reading is from *Superman and Batman: World's Finest* (Gibbons and Rude, 1992). It is a two-page spread (see Figure 35.1) that contrasts the origin stories for both heroes, and as such it highlights some of their structural similarities. Two main factors have influenced the selection of the text. First, it is not from the mainstream continuity of either character, but was from a special edition three-part series. The appearance of the characters deliberately harks back to the early Shuster and Kane versions and so recognizes the nostalgic appeal of the characters and their longevity as it pays homage to the 'team-up' titles of the 1940s and 1950s. Secondly, the juxtaposition of the two versions of the origin stories does some of the analytic work for a critical reader by illustrating the opposition of the characters in a complementary fashion.

The general approach I used is based upon Eco's semiotic reading of comic strips (Eco, 1987), but not in order to search for the meaning of the text so much as to look at the way that meaning is signified. Key sections are selected and focused upon. In this instance the selection is from a sequence in which Batman and Superman dream their origin stories in parallel, following Clark Kent's and Bruce Wayne's attendance at a fund-raising event for an orphanage. This device reminds us that both characters are orphans and that they passed through a traumatic event that makes sense of their superheroic actions. The panels are juxtaposed, with Superman's origins being shown in sepia coloured panels on the left-hand side of the page and Batman's in dark blue on the right-hand side. Reading the sequence over the two pages the breakdown of the central edge of each panel can be seen. Rather than simply offering a straight edge to the panels' contents the panels also represent meaning. Here a jagged pattern that becomes stronger through the sequence can be seen, indicating increasing agitation and disturbance on the part of the dreamers until they wake in the final two panels. As such, these origin stories are shown to be disturbing and powerful and maintaining an influence on the characters' actions.

The first frames show concerned and caring parents and the actions they take to protect their

Figure 35.1 *World's Finest* (1992: 22/23).

children, placing a child in a rocket to escape destruction or pushing him out of the way of a gunman. On the second page the first two panels depict the moments in which the course of the characters' lives are irrevocably altered with the launch of the rocket and the pulling of the trigger. The subsequent panels contain the consequences of the freeze-framed irreversible moments. A small child is held in the arms of a woman while a man behind her fights to put out a fire; a young boy is led away by a policeman while another searches for a pen and readies his notebook. Visible in the background of each panel is what has been lost by the characters, their biological parents. In the foreground are indications of their future roles. Such dreams are disturbing. Bruce Wayne and Clark Kent wake.

The sequence depicting the origin stories appears early in the story, once we have been introduced to the cities and main protagonists. We know that the heroes are different, fighting different problems. The unwitting recollection of the origin stories implies a more complex relation and reaction to the orphanage than mere altruistic concern. There is an identification between the heroes and orphans in the loss of parents, and it is the circumstances of this loss that have led to the adoption of vigilante identities and distance from family life. Now, having described the selected text, I will look to the three theoretical terms to show how they can be employed in the analysis of the sequence.

The repetition of the origin stories ties the characters back into the superhero narratives that return to the late 1930s. It suggests that we are getting the real thing. Moreover, it ties the heroes into an identification with the orphans – an important aspect as the orphanage plays a key role in the events of the story. The orphans need care and protection. Finally, the juxtaposition of the two stories shows them to be equivalent, but also illustrates the key differences between them, one a superpowered alien the other a determined human. Looking at this discursively, the role of the family comes to the fore. Loss of biological parents is contrasted to an ideal of a caring and protective family life. A discourse on family helps

to make sense of the character's actions. Further, a discourse of the lone hero might be discerned in this as individual figures emerge from the traumatic loss of parents, showing them to be alone, even when they have the support of others. This can be further understood through psychoanalytic theory. I argue that the origin stories can be understood as *primal scene fantasies* as they are concerned with the origins of the superhero subject. The conflation of *primal scene* and *primal fantasy* alludes to the manner in which an important originary moment for the subject can be understood as not necessarily having taken place for them to be psychically effective, but that is interpreted by the child as an act of violence by the father toward the mother. This can be grasped through Freud's elaborations of the Oedipus complex. First, the origin stories relate a crisis in the Oedipal situation in which the child is wrenched from the familial support network through an act of supreme violence. The adoption of the superhero role, then, is an attempt to resolve a crisis caused by the failure to enter into full symbolic relationship with the other. Second, Freud argued, in *Totem and Taboo* (Freud, 1913), that the Oedipus complex was a repeat of a much earlier clan transgression that took place in pre-history. Without accepting Freud's claims, this idea of pre-history can be applied to the use of origin stories for the two heroes, where the origins are re-enacted in pre-history in dream-like time (Reiff, 1963). The origin stories describe two single events that took place in pre-history and that constitute the hero in the present so that the scene from the past becomes what it always was. As such we can see the way that origin stories can be repeated and give a coherence to the multiple versions of Superman and Batman.

From this brief and superficial analysis the way that narrative, discourse and psychoanalysis come together to show the functioning of a text has been illustrated. Narrative has highlighted how key events can be grasped and described, discourse analysis has shown how immanent features help to make sense of the narratives, and psychoanalysis has brought these two aspects together to offer an account for the importance and repetition of the origin stories.

Annotated Bibliography

Brown, T. and Jones L. (2001) *Action Research and Postmodernism*. Buckingham: Open University Press.

This book offers detailed discussion of practitioner research carried out in the context of masters and doctoral degrees. It focuses in particular on hermeneutic enquiry in which reflective writing generated by the researcher builds towards an assertion of professional identity through which professional demands are mediated.

Butler, J. (1993) *Bodies That Matter*. New York and London: Routledge.

An early book by a leading feminist writer that tackles some core concepts in identity.

Gallagher, S. (1992) *Hermeneutics and Education*. Albany, NY: State University of New York Press.

This book offers an excellent overview of theoretical perspectives. It provides an examination of how education offers a productive paradigm for work more generally in the social sciences.

Habermas, J. (1976) 'Systematically distorted communication', in P. Connerton (ed.), *Critical Sociology*. London: Penguin.

This is an accessible chapter by a difficult leading author. It shows how the work of Freud and his emphasis on individuals might apply to society more generally. How do we as a society talk about ourselves so that we conceal the bits that we would rather keep quiet about?

Hall, S. (1997) *Representation: Cultural Representations and Signifying Practices*. Buckingham: Open University.

An excellent and accessible introduction to this area of theory in the context of social science.

Harvey, D. (1992) *The Condition of Postmodernity*. Oxford and Cambridge, MA: Blackwell.

This book offers a clear exposition of postmodernity from the perspective of a geographer. It presents an interesting account of how conceptions of time and space themselves evolve through time and how this impacts on individual and social values.

Lacan, J. (1977) *Ecrits: A Selection*. London: Routledge.

This book provides a good selection of Lacan's own original writing.

Leader, D. and Groves, J. (1995) *Lacan for Beginners*. Cambridge: Ikon.

Lacan's own writing is notoriously slippery – this is an entertaining introduction written by a leading expert on Lacan.

McLaren, P. (1995) *Critical Pedagogy and Predatory Culture*. London: Routledge.

This text provides a good introduction to how deconstructionism is being embraced by more politically oriented writers in the social sciences. McLaren is a leading contemporary writer in a critical education tradition embracing Freire, Giroux and Apple.

Rabinow, P. (ed.) (1991) *The Foucault Reader*. London: Penguin.

This edited collection gathers together a good selection of Foucault's work from different periods in his varied and influential writing.

Ricoeur, P. (1981) *Hermeneutics and the Human Sciences*. Cambridge: Cambridge University Press.

This collection provides some key writings by Ricoeur applicable in a broad range of social scientific disciplines. Centred on discussion of how understandings are processed as explanations, it offers detailed examination of how language conditions the ways in which humans make sense of their world.

Further references

Barker, M. (1984) *A Haunt of Fears: The Strange History of the British Horror Comics Campaign*. London: Pluto Press.

Brooker, W. (2001) *Batman Unmasked: Analyzing a Cultural Icon*. London: Continuum.

Brown, T. and England, J. (2004) 'Revisiting emancipatory teacher research: a psychoanalytic perspective', *British Journal of Sociology of Education*, 25(1): 67–80.

Derrida, J. (1994) 'The deconstruction of actuality', *Radical Philosophy*, 68: 28–41.

Eco, U. (1987) 'A reading of Steve Canyon', in S. Wagstaff (ed.), *Comic Iconoclasm*. London: Institute of Contemporary Arts.

Foucault, M. (1997) *Ethics*. London: Penguin.

Foucault, M. (1998) *Aesthetics*. London: Penguin.

Freud, S. (ed.) (1913) *Totem and Taboo*, Penguin Freud Library 13. London: Penguin.

Gibbons, D. (1992) 'Introduction', in D. Gibbons and S. Rude, *Superman and Batman: World's Finest*. New York: DC Comics.

Gibbons, D. and Rude, S. (1992) *Superman and Batman: World's Finest*. New York: DC Comics.

Giddens, A. (1999) *Runaway World: How Globalisation Is Reshaping Our Lives*. London: Profile Books.

McCue, G. (1992) *Dark Knights: The New Comics in Context*. London: Pluto Press.

Patton, P. and Meaghan, M. (1979) *Michel Foucault: Power, Truth, Strategy*. Sydney: Feral Publications.

Reiff, P. (1963) 'Meaning of history and religion in Freud's thought', in B. Mazlish (ed.), *Psychoanalysis and History*. Englewood Cliffs, NJ: Prentice Hall.

Witek, J. (1989) *Comic Books as History: The Narrative Art of Jack Jackson, Art Spiegelman and Harvey Pekar*. Jackson, MS and London: University Press of Mississippi.

36

POSTMODERNIST PERSPECTIVES

Julianne Cheek
Division of Health Sciences, University of South Australia, Australia
Noel Gough
Faculty of Education, Deakin University, Victoria, Australia

Key concepts

Noel Gough

This brief introduction to postmodernist perspectives in social inquiry is necessarily partial and imprecise. Words that refer to complex areas of human understanding cannot be reduced to unambiguous definitions. We can no more provide a straightforward definition of 'postmodernism' than stipulate the meanings of 'love' or 'justice' – these terms are perpetual foci of speculation and debate. Readers of research methods texts who are confused by this ambiguity and imprecision should heed Morwenna Griffiths's advice: 'If you ... can't find one clear definition that works for everything you read, then you need to know that you can abandon the search. Instead, you need to develop an understanding of the range of use, and to be clear about your own understanding, as a result' (1998: 43).

The concepts of *modern* and *postmodern* recur through fields as diverse as art, architecture, advertising, economics, literature, music, politics, popular media, science, social philosophy and theology. The term 'postmodernism' has been used to describe conceptual movements in many of these fields for more than a century.[1] In *The Postmodern Condition*, Jean-François Lyotard uses the term 'modern' to designate 'any science that legitimates itself with reference to a metadiscourse' or that makes 'an explicit appeal to some grand narrative, such as the dialectics of Spirit, the hermeneutics of meaning, the emancipation of the rational or working subject, or the creation of wealth' (1984: xxiii). Lyotard critiques what he calls '*grands récits*' (variously translated as grand narratives, master narratives, metanarratives or metadiscourse): 'Simplifying to the extreme, I define

postmodern as incredulity toward metanarratives' (1984: xxiv). As Cherryholmes explains:

The modern attitude is part of the Enlightenment tradition. It is concerned with rational control of our lives, beliefs, values, and aesthetic sensibilities ...

Modern, analytic, and structural thought seek rationality, linearity, progress, and control by discovering, developing, and inventing metanarratives, metadiscourse, and metacritiques that define rationality, linearity, progress, and control. Postmodern, postanalytic, and poststructural thought are skeptical and incredulous about the possibility of such metanarratives. (1988: 10–11)

The prefix *meta-* signifies 'behind, after (*metaphysics*)' or 'of a higher or second-order kind (*metalanguage*)'[2] and is 'used in the name of a discipline to designate a new but related discipline designed to deal critically with the original one'.[3] Metanarratives guide a discipline by specifying rules and conditions for producing knowledge, such as the positivist metanarrative which extended a 'story or set of rules characterizing positive knowledge' (Cherryholmes, 1988: 9) from the natural to the social sciences. Postmodernism can be understood as a generic label for the erosion of trust in such metanarratives across various disciplines.

For example, in the physical sciences, the metanarratives of empiricism and experimentalism specified the rules and conditions for producing knowledge from Newton's era until the late 1880s when the discovery of radioactivity began to undermine experimental physicists' categorical distinctions between theory and observation. The 'new physics' did not result from direct observations of sub-atomic structures and processes but from physicists inventing new concepts such as sub-atomic particles to guide their enquiries. According to Joseph Schwab, by the mid-twentieth century most scientists were working in this post-positivist way: 'Today ... [a] fresh line of scientific research has its origin not in objective facts alone, but in a conception, a deliberate construction of the mind ... [this conception] tells us what facts to look for in the research. It tells us what meaning to assign these facts' (1962: 198). In effect, Schwab is describing the emergence of postmodernist perspectives in the natural sciences, which include treating the perceptions, interpretations and explanations that constitute our experience and understandings of 'reality' as meanings fashioned by human actors from the social and cultural resources available to them rather than as 'facts' (as modern science conceived them).

It is important to emphasize that understanding 'reality' (and our knowledge of it) as socially constructed is *not* an 'antirealist' position (as some critics of postmodernism argue). What is at issue here is not *belief* in the real but confidence in its representation. As Richard Rorty writes, 'to deny the power to "describe" reality is not to deny reality' (1979: 375); 'the world is out there, but descriptions of the world are not' (Rorty, 1989: 5). Representations of the world are effects and artefacts of *discourses* produced in a particular time and place by the *discursive practices* that regulate 'what is said and written and passes for more or less orderly thought and exchange of ideas' (Cherryholmes, 1988: 2). In Michel Foucault's words a discursive practice is 'a body of anonymous, historical rules, always determined in the time and space that have defined a given period, and for a given social, economic, geographical, or linguistic area, the conditions of operation of the enunciative function' (1972: 117).

The term 'discourse' itself illustrates this specificity of discourses to particular times and places. Sara Mills notes that in disciplines such as sociology, linguistics, philosophy, literary theory and cultural studies, 'discourse' is 'common currency' and has 'perhaps the widest range of possible significations of any term', yet within theoretical texts 'it is frequently left undefined, as if its usage were simply common knowledge' (1997: 1). For example, some linguists use 'discourse' to signify an object of analysis, such as the context in which certain utterances occur (e.g. legal discourse, medical discourse) and assume that this understanding is 'common knowledge' within their disciplinary community. This usage is different from (say) Foucault's, for whom discourses cannot be analysed in isolation because they are 'practices that systematically form the objects of which they speak' (1972: 49) and can only be detected by what they produce as utterances, concepts or effects. For example, to paraphrase Foucault, in the first part of the twentieth century, atomic theorists systematically formed the objects of which they spoke as particles rather than as waves. One result of this formation is that we now represent the speed with which information can be transmitted through silicon chips as a function of how fast electrons move through semiconductors. If these same physicists had formed their theories using the concept of waves (which they soon found to be equally fruitful) then we might now be talking about indices of resistance and patterns of refraction rather than electrons and semiconductors. Asserting that electrons and semiconductors are social constructions does not deny the 'reality' of an information speed limit through silicon chips. The limit is no less 'real' for being social constructed.

Postmodernist perspectives in social inquiry are not a uniform set of shared assumptions but, rather, a loose collection of ways of thinking about how to go beyond modernist perspectives without producing alternative metanarratives. For example, Jane Flax identifies several Enlightenment beliefs that postmodernist philosophers 'seek to throw into radical doubt', namely that:

- 'language is in some sense transparent';
- there is 'a stable, coherent self';
- 'reason and its "science" – philosophy – can provide an objective, reliable, and universal foundation of knowledge';
- 'knowledge acquired from the right use of reason will be "true" ';
- 'by grounding claims to authority in reason, the conflicts between truth, knowledge, and power can be overcome';
- 'freedom consists of obedience to laws that conform to the necessary results of the right use of reason' (1990: 41–2).

However, as Judith Butler writes, such doubts (and many other characterizations) 'are variously imputed to postmodernism or poststructuralism, which are conflated with each other and sometimes conflated with deconstruction' (1992: 4). Patti Lather offers a way of distinguishing between postmodernism and poststructuralism that resists 'fixing' the meanings of either concept:

> I generally use the term *postmodern* to mean the shift in material conditions of advanced monopoly capitalism brought on by the microelectronic revolution in information technology, the fissures of a global, multinational hyper-capitalism and the global uprising of the marginalised . . . The code name for the crisis of confidence in western conceptual systems, postmodernism is borne out of our sense of the limits of Enlightenment rationality . . .
>
> I generally use *post-structural* to mean the working out of academic theory within the culture of postmodernism, but I also sometimes use the terms interchangeably. (1992: 90)

Implications for research design

Some of the methodological implications of postmodernist perspectives for research design can be appreciated by comparing social inquiry to the work of fictional detectives (Gough, 2002).

For more than a century, detective fiction has simultaneously modelled and critiqued culturally privileged forms of social inquiry, but even a superficial analysis reveals that social researchers have not necessarily kept pace with their fictional counterparts. Many social researchers still privilege scientific rationalism, but Sherlock Holmes and other heroes of the classic 'logic and deduction' detective story are no longer the dominant models of how we should obtain worthwhile knowledge of the social world. During the 1920s and 1930s the detachment and 'objectivity' of Holmes's methods began to give way to a variety of more involved and subjective approaches. For example, Agatha Christie's Miss Marple is more like an ethnographer: by closely observing life in St Mary Mead she produced grounded theories of human behaviour that she used to solve mysteries both within her village and elsewhere. 'Hard-boiled' detectives like Raymond Chandler's Philip Marlowe demonstrate another type of involvement and subjectivity by deeply implicating themselves as actors rather than spectators in the mysteries they try to unravel. Marlowe and many of his successors also told their stories in the first person, a change in narrative perspective that further problematized the role of the researcher in the dialectic of truth versus deception decades before interpretivist inquiry seriously challenged positivist social science. More recently, fic-

tional detectives have adopted socially critical standpoints such as feminism, exemplified by Amanda Cross's Kate Fansler and Sara Paretsky's V.I. Warshawski.

Some literary critics see the detective story as the characteristic genre of modernist storytelling. For example, Brian McHale argues that modernist fiction usually involves 'a quest for a missing or hidden item of knowledge' (1992: 146) and that 'a modernist novel looks like a detective story', centrally concerned with 'problems of the accessibility and circulation of knowledge, the individual mind's grappling with an elusive or occluded reality' (1992: 147). The detective is the archetypal modernist subject, a quest(ion)ing 'cognitive hero', an 'agent of *re*cognitions . . . reduced synecdochically to the organ of visual perception, the (private) eye' (1992: 147), seeking to understand a unified and objective world.

The postmodern turn in detective fiction (which may have preceded an analogous transformation of social research) is signalled by the emergence of 'anti-detective' stories that evoke the impulse to 'detect' in order to frustrate it by refusing to solve the crime. One of the most celebrated anti-detective stories is Umberto Eco's *The Name of the Rose* (1983) which takes some well-known examples of generic detective fiction as its intertextual models, but – as Eco himself puts it – 'is a mystery in which very little is discovered and the detective is defeated' (1984: 54). In *The Name of the Rose*, Eco uses the form of detective fiction to deconstruct, disrupt and undermine the rationality of the models of conjecture conventionally provided by the form – which is why, as Eco writes, his 'basic story (whodunit?) ramifies into so many other stories, all stories of other conjectures, all linked with the structure of conjecture as such' (1984: 57). Eco provides a physical model of conjecturality in the abbey's labyrinthine library but also demonstrates that his detective – William of Baskerville – cannot decipher the complex social milieu of the abbey by assuming that it has a comparably logical (albeit complicated) structure. Following Deleuze and Guattari (1987), Eco likens 'the structure of conjecture' to the infinite networks of a rhizome rather than to the finite and hierarchical roots and branches of a tree:

> The rhizome is so constructed that every path can be connected with every other one. It has no center, no periphery, no exit, because it is potentially infinite. The space of conjecture is a rhizome space . . . the world in which William realizes he is

living already has a rhizome structure: that is, it can be structured but is never structured definitively . . . it is impossible for there to be *a* story. (1984: 57–8)

Thus the anti-detective story not only subverts the rationality of the investigatory methods modelled by conventional detective fiction but also denies the defensibility of the dominant cultural expectations that animate such enquiries, namely 'the longing for "one true story" that has been the psychic motor for [modern] Western science' (Harding, 1986: 193).

Eco's story of William's 'failure' as a (modernist) detective is riddled with implicit and explicit references to postmodernist inquiry strategies, as in the following conversation between William and his 'Watson', Adso:

'What I did not understand was the relation among signs . . . I behaved stubbornly, pursuing a semblance of order, when I should have known well that there is no order in the universe.'

'But in imagining an erroneous order you still found something . . .'

'What you say is very fine Adso, and I thank you. The order that our mind imagines is like a net, or like a ladder, built to attain something. But afterward you must throw the ladder away, because you discover that, even if it was useful, it was meaningless . . . The only truths that are useful are instruments to be thrown away.' (1983: 492)

The Name of the Rose is itself such an 'erroneous order', which Eco emphasizes by using metafictional narrative strategies to expose its status as fiction and draw attention to the processes by which it is constructed both as a world to be explored and the means of its own exploration.

Thus the more appropriate models for postmodernist social researchers are not detectives like Sherlock Holmes, Miss Marple, Philip Marlowe or Kate Fansler, but authors like Umberto Eco. Our work is to fathom the mysteries *we* inscribe.

Stories from the Field

Julianne Cheek

Postmodern approaches are about challenging, interrupting and interrogating aspects of reality that are so central or entrenched in our understandings of what is 'normal' that we can come to take them for granted

(Cheek, 2000). In the Stories from the Field that follow, I focus on two pieces of research which challenge aspects of the everyday reality of healthcare. As both have been published elsewhere I do not report the research findings per se in the way that we have come to understand such reporting – itself a discursive construct. Rather, I use the studies to give insights into how postmodern thought shaped the research at all points: from the questions asked to the analysis produced. In many respects what follows is as much about the research process itself as it is about the texts that form the product of the studies undertaken. Although the studies focused on aspects of healthcare, which reflects the location from which I research, the insights can be extrapolated to any substantive focus where the challenge and goal is to better understand how things came to be the way they are and what operates to sustain this.

One Sunday morning I was reading the local newspaper and discovered a section where readers' comments about their role as parents were published. One response was from a parent who wrote: 'I rang a hospital once at night to ask advice about my baby when she was crying and pulling at her ears, fearing that she had earache. The head nurse/matron said that the baby was too young to know if she had earache or not and her condescending attitude made me feel incompetent' (*Sunday Mail*, 1996: 29). This comment intrigued me. What appeared to be going on here was that the point of view of the parent seemed to be able to be excluded by that of the nurse. Questions I began asking myself included: What enabled this exchange to occur? How was it that the nurse was able to say what she did? Why did the parent use the term 'incompetent'? What assumptions were being made in this particular exchange about healthcare? My thinking about the comment, and when formulating these questions, was influenced by Foucauldian thought, particularly the idea of discourse, where 'a discourse provides a set of possible statements about a given area, and organizes and gives structure to the manner in which a particular topic, object, process is to be talked about' (Kress, 1985: 7).

A comment in the local newspaper thus comprised the data for this study. Similarly, De Montigny (1995) reports exploring a specific textual fragment in social workers' case notes about a client, namely 'the apartment smelled of urine' (1995: 209). He was interested in exploring what enabled a social worker to determine that an apartment did smell of urine in the first place, and the way that this became 'truth' or fact in the notes, thereby precipitating a series of events that were only possible as a result of this truth – 'the smell was inscribed into a professional code as a matter indicating potential failure and therefore as properly deserving social work attention' (1995: 211). In the same way, in the specific textual fragment that was the focus of my study, I was interested in exploring what enabled the nurse to say what she did, and how that allowed the participants in the exchange to be positioned relative to each other.

What immediately struck me was the power of the health professional to determine what counts as knowledge and what experience is 'real'. Drawing on dominant discourses of science and medicine, the nurse is able to exclude, or at least relegate to the margins, the parent's understandings of the situation. Professional expertise premised on scientific/medical discourse about the 'facts' positions the parent as amateur and non-authoritative whose account is non-factual. In this instance an effect of power is the ability to claim presence (Fox, 1994), or as De Montigny puts it 'Power is realised as social workers [read health professionals more generally] construct their accounts about clients' lives and thereby appropriate for themselves the right to tell the story and to decide what gets counted as relevant' (1995: 219). Thus it is a 'fact' that the baby is too young to know it has earache. Premised on this 'truth' a cascade of actions and events can follow. This includes the parent being positioned at the margins in terms of whose account and knowledge is afforded mainframe (or centre stage).

Yet it was clear that the parent did not simply accept this position. Writing the comment and sending it in to the paper is indicative of resistance on the parent's part to the position created for them by 'expert' discourse. Thus I was as much interested in the fact that the parent wrote the comment at all as I was in the actual comment itself. It would be too simplistic to portray the nurse as having power and the parent not. Of interest to me was: Whose voice is heard?; Whose is not and when?; How this is able to happen?; and what the effects of this are. In such an analysis, explorations of communication between health professionals and their clients are moved beyond focusing on content, turn taking and the need for 'better' communication, to highlight that communication itself is a discursive construction. The focus is on how texts represent rather than on what they represent (Starn, 1989).

* * *

In the second 'story from the field', the substantive focus was on the way that a relatively new health phenomenon, toxic shock syndrome (TSS),[4] was represented in print-based media between 1979 and 1995. Again Foucauldian perspectives informed the research, particularly notions of discourse and governmentality. In addition I approached this from the position of newspapers not being simply conveyors of information, but rather constructed by, and in turn constructing, understandings including those pertaining to aspects of health and healthcare. I was particularly interested in how understandings of TSS were constructed. How did knowledge about TSS become 'stabilised, emerging as fact'? (Guillemin, 1996: 42).

In this study the data were all articles published in four purposively selected print-based popular media – the purposiveness relating to choosing media with diverse readerships and likely to be information rich in terms of reporting of TSS (see Cheek, 1997). Frequency of reporting and a number of other features of the articles were analysed, and a chronology of the reporting of TSS in these sources was developed (Cheek, 1997: 188–9). At this stage the analysis remained at the descriptive level. I then applied a Foucauldian influenced lens to the articles to 'examine the discourses competing to create meaning at the site of Australian press accounts' (Lupton, 1994: 74). As I read each article I asked myself (drawing on Workman, 1996) what 'are the discourses that shape the representation of, and understandings about, TSS, and ultimately discipline the dialogue about it? How is seriousness assigned, truth fixed, understanding domesticated and discussion routinized about the relatively recent health phenomenon?' (Cheek, 1997: 191).

Three major discursive frames emerged from this analysis and questioning. They were the discourse of concealment, scientific/medical discourse, and discourse about individual responsibility for health. The discourse of concealment was largely framed by the unmentionable nature of menstruation and menstrual products. Tensions were evident in affording TSS mainframe (or centre stage) in terms of the public reporting of the syndrome, yet at the same time having to acknowledge its link with such unmentionables usually relegated to the margins. The impact of scientific/medical discourse in both defining TSS itself and in assigning seriousness of risk also was present throughout the period of the reporting. At the outset (1980) some medical authorities are quoted as decrying TSS as 'trivial' and as 'another American beat up to scare the nation's females' (see Cheek, 1997: 193). In later reporting TSS is established as a 'legitimate' disease, but only according to medical/scientific discourses – 'the syndrome of toxic shock is based on a constellation of strict diagnostic criteria' (Garland and Peel, 1995: 8).

With respect to the third discursive frame, namely individual responsibility for health, many early articles were about the need for hygiene on the part of individual women and girls. Thus 'TSS early on is transformed into an issue of neglect of care for the self, and of carelessness on the part of individual women' (Cheek, 1997: 196). The effect of this was to relegate questions about the manufacturing and testing of tampons to the margins. The problem is thus framed as one of individual hygiene, not production processes. Olesen (1986: 57-8) notes that 'the toxic-shock phenomenon poses critical questions in the definition and construction of the issues'. My research confirmed this.

Both 'stories from the field' presented here enable different possibilities and ways of viewing health and healthcare practice to emerge. Thus research informed by postmodern approaches enables us to open to scrutiny and contestation understandings of any aspect of reality. For me it has been to open up to scrutiny aspects of healthcare that previously may have seemed innocuous and neutral. This is the subtext from these 'stories from the field'. None of this is to privilege the position that I have constructed in writing this text, nor is it necessarily to argue against particular healthcare practices. Rather it is to open up possibilities, new ways of looking at practices

that may be so familiar to us as to be invisible in terms of where they came from, the assumptions they make and the effects that they have.

In concluding I need to acknowledge that these stories, and the understanding of the 'field' that they employ, reflect a position that I-as-researcher have adopted in relation to postmodern thought. What position(s) a researcher takes up in the somewhat fluid and diverse understandings that can be broadly called postmodern shapes and frames the research undertaken, and is therefore as much a part of the story from the field as the methods employed or the analyses done.

Notes

1. For example, Charles Jencks credits British artist John Watkins Chapman with using 'postmodern' in 1870 to refer to painting after Impressionism (see Appignanesi et al., 1995: 3).
2. *The Concise Oxford Dictionary of Current English.*
3. *Webster's Seventh Collegiate Dictionary.*
4. The specific causative agent of TSS is the bacterium staphylococcus aureus. It usually affects menstruating women and is linked with tampon use (although this is disputed).
5. Rosenau suggests that decisions to hyphenate postmodernism (or not) might signal a position: 'The absence of the hyphen has come to imply a certain sympathy with post-modernism [*sic*] and a recognition of its legitimacy, whereas the hyphen indicates a critical posture' (1992: 18).

Annotated bibliography

Appignanesi, R., Garratt, C., Sardar, Z. and Curry, P. (1995) *Postmodernism for Beginners*. Cambridge: Icon Books.

An illustrated introduction to key players and events in the history of postmodernism in Western culture that traces its multiple genealogies in popular and academic arts and disciplines. It also includes brief accounts of Islamic and 'Third World' postmodernisms.

Cheek, J. (2000) *Postmodern and Poststructural Approaches to Nursing Research*, 2nd edn. Thousand Oaks, CA: Sage.

A clear account of how Foucauldian analyses of power/knowledge and critical discourse analysis can inform health and nursing research. More than half the book focuses on case studies and examples.

Deleuze, G. and Guattari, F. (1987) *A Thousand Plateaus: Capitalism and Schizophrenia*, trans. B. Massumi. Minneapolis, MN: University of Minnesota Press.

Deleuze and Guattari contrast modernist 'arborescent' thought, organized systematically and hierarchically as branches of knowledge grounded in firm foundations, with postmodernist 'rhizomatic' thought. *A Thousand Plateaus* 'walks the talk': it is written as a rhizome.

Foucault, M. (1980) *Power/Knowledge: Selected Interviews and Other Writings 1972–1977*, trans. C. Gordon. New York: Harvester Wheatsheaf.

Foucault's guide to Foucault. These accessible essays and interviews demonstrate how his investigations of prisons, schools, barracks, hospitals, factories, cities, families, social justice and the history of sexuality contribute to understanding the mechanisms through which power pervades our discourses, learning processes and everyday lives.

Gough, N. (2002) 'Fictions for representing and generating semiotic consciousness: the crime story and educational inquiry', *International Journal of Applied Semiotics*, 3(2): 59–76.

A detailed elaboration of the intertextual connections and parallels between crime fiction and social inquiry and their implications for designing and doing educational research.

Rosenau, P.M. (1992) *Post-Modernism and the Social Sciences: Insights, Inroads, and Intrusions*. Princeton, NJ: Princeton University Press.

Traces the disciplinary histories and applications of 'post-modernism'[5] and shows how postmodernist critiques of rationality affect such academic fields as anthropology, economics, geography, history, international relations, law, planning, political science, psychology, sociology, urban studies and women's studies, and how it has inspired alternative political, social and cultural movements.

Further references

Butler, J. (1992) 'Contingent foundations: feminism and the question of "postmodernism" ', in J. Butler and J.W. Scott (eds), *Feminists Theorize the Political*. New York: Routledge, pp. 3–21.

Cheek, J. (1997) '(Con)textualizing toxic shock syndrome: selected media representations of the emergence of a health phenomenon', *Health: An Interdisciplinary Journal for the Social Study of Health, Illness and Medicine*, 1(2): 183–203.

Cherryholmes, C. (1988) *Power and Criticism: Poststructural Investigations in Education*. New York: Teachers College Press.

De Montigny, G.A. (1995) 'The power of being professional', in M. Campbell and A. Manicom (eds), *Knowledge, Experience, and Ruling Relations: Studies in the Social Organization of Knowledge*. Toronto: University of Toronto Press, pp. 209–20.

Eco, U. (1983) *The Name of the Rose*, trans. William Weaver. London: Secker & Warburg. (Original work published 1980).

Eco, U. (1984) *Postscript to The Name of the Rose*. trans. William Weaver. New York: Harcourt, Brace & Jovanovich.

Flax, J. (1990) 'Postmodernism and gender relations in feminist theory', in Linda J. Nicholson (ed.), *Feminism/Postmodernism*. New York: Routledge, pp. 39–62.

Foucault, M. (1972) *The Archeology of Knowledge*, trans. A.M. Sheridan Smith. New York: Pantheon (original work published 1969).

Fox, N. (1994) *Postmodernism, Sociology and Health*. Buckingham: Open University Press.

Garland, S. and Peel, M. (1995) 'Tampons and toxic shock syndrome', *Medical Journal of Australia*, 163: 8–9.

Griffiths, M. (1998) *Educational Research for Social Justice: Getting off the Fence*. Buckingham: Open University Press.

Guillemin, M. (1996) 'Constructing menopause knowledge through socio-material practice', *Annual Review of Health Social Sciences*, 6: 41–56.

Kress, G. (1985) *Linguistic Processes in Sociocultural Practice*. Victoria: Deakin University Press.

Lather, P. (1992) 'Critical frames in educational research: feminist and post-structural perspectives', *Theory into Practice*, 31(2): 87–99.

Lupton, D. (1994) 'Femininity, responsibility and the technological imperative: discourses on breast cancer in the Australian press', *International Journal of Health Services*, 24: 73–89.

Lyotard, J.-F. (1984) *The Postmodern Condition: A Report on Knowledge*, trans. G. Bennington and B. Massumi. Minneapolis, MN: University of Minnesota Press (original work published 1979).

McHale, B. (1992) *Constructing Postmodernism*. London and New York: Routledge.

Harding, S. (1986) *The Science Question in Feminism*. Ithaca, NY: Cornell University Press.

Mills, S. (1997) *Discourse*. London and New York: Routledge.

Olesen, V. (1986) 'Analysing emergent trends in women's health: the case of toxic shock syndrome', in V. Olesen and N. Woods (eds), *Culture, Society and Menstruation*. New York: Hemisphere, pp. 51–62.

Rorty, R. (1979) *Philosophy and the Mirror of Nature*. Princeton, NJ: Princeton University Press.

Rorty, R. (1989) *Contingency, Irony, and Solidarity*. Cambridge, MA: Cambridge University Press.

Schwab, J.J. (1962) 'The concept of the structure of a discipline', *Educational Record*, 43: 197–205.

Starn, R. (1989) 'Seeing culture in a room for a renaissance price', in L. Hunt (ed.), *The New Cultural History*. Berkeley and Los Angeles, CA: University of California Press, pp. 205–32.

Sunday Mail (1996) 'Please believe the children', 28 January: 29 (South Australia).

Workman, T. (1996) *Banking on Deception: The Discourse of Fiscal Crisis*. Nova Scotia: Fernwood Publishing.

CHAPTER 37

FROM STRUCTURALISM TO POSTSTRUCTURALISM

Lee Miller
Performance Studies Division, University College Northampton, UK
Joanne 'Bob' Whalley
Performance Studies Division, University College Northampton, UK
Ian Stronach
Institute of Education, Manchester Metropolitan University, UK

Key concepts

Ian Stronach

A boundary is not that at which something stops but, as the Greeks recognized, the boundary is that from which something begins its presencing. (Heidegger, 1971: 152–3)

Think of a table. Flat top, four legs, standing there. Where? Here. In the centre of the table, there is a vase of flowers. What is the relation between the vase of flowers, the four legs and the tabletop? Do the legs and top need the vase for the table to work as 'table'? Does the vase 'perform' the table as table? Is the vase a part of the structure we call 'table', or is it merely decorative from a structural perspective?

One way of sorting out some of the preliminary complexities of vase-sits-on-table-with-four-legs-but-what-the-hell-is-going-on-epistemologically is to think of the table in terms of *structures* and *functions*. They are different. The tabletop 'needs' the legs in a way that it does not need the vase: the legs are structural necessities for the tabletop. One less and it wobbles. Two less and it falls. And with it its 'tablehood'? Yet the vase may be just as necessary for the table to be a table – rather than a stool, or something to stand on. The vase, then, defines the table as table in a quite different way. The vase is an object on the table just as knives and forks, or pens and phones might be. Their presence (culturally circumscribed as always, but we will ignore that for the moment) indicates that the object, which may or may not look structurally like

the conventional range of objects that we call table, is being used *as* a table. Think of 'as' in the last sentence. It means 'in the function of'.

Where does that take us? A table is never wholly defined or undefined by its conventional structures: there is always an aspect of function that may disrupt or confirm the object-as-named object. The two notions work together either to define, disconfirm or at least make us uncertain about the object in its 'true' nature and 'proper' definition.

Now imagine that we all want to be 'tablologists'. One way of doing that would be to develop a line of thinking that was mostly oriented towards the structural properties of tables. A typology would soon emerge since snooker tables, for example, have very different properties and underlying dynamics than coffee tables and card tables. But in all cases we would hope to be able to find some deep, perhaps hidden properties of tables that constitute them as such. A universal theory of tables could then be derived from these commonalities. The theory might identify what essentially defines tables, moving from the descriptive to the analytical, the real to the ideal. In so doing, it would subordinate instances of variation to the status of peripheral and unimportant differences, or at least those unthreatening to the developing core epistemology of 'tablologists'.

Before we move on from this train of thought, let's take an example from Education, moving metaphorically not very far from the 'table' to the 'timetable', another object that can be held to have regular structures and definitive functions that constitute it as such.

Bernstein's famous paper 'On the classification and framing of educational knowledge' (1971) saw the curriculum as a kind of table. The timetable was compartmentalized into a number of boxes, usually containing 'subject' contents. These boxes were more or less cut off from each other. The degree to which they overlapped or were distinct encouraged Bernstein to develop concepts that expressed these features, like 'classification' and 'framing', either of which could be 'weak' or 'strong'. From these he claimed to have derived the underlying principles which shaped them and which in turn were related to broader social and political influences. We're not really concerned here with this theory as such but with its structural properties, indeed with the theory as a carefully worked through instance of *structuralism*. Fortunately, Bernstein was explicit about his methodology and so leaves a clear trace of his thinking:

1   I shall first distinguish between two types of curricula: collection and integrated.
2   I shall build upon the basis of this distinction in order to establish a more general set of concepts: classification and frame.
3   A typology of educational codes will then be derived.
4   Sociological aspects of two very different educational codes will then be explored.
5   This will lead on to a discussion of educational codes and problems of order.
6   Finally, there will be a brief discussion of the reasons for changes in educational codes. (Bernstein, 1971: 48)

Without going into too much detail, we can see that what begins the inquiry is the inspection of surface phenomena (classes, teaching, learning, assessing, timetables, subjects, and so on). Beneath these, the theorist sees the *structural properties* of the curriculum or the pedagogical and assessment relations. He distinguishes between structural properties (like classification and framing) and those which in terms of the 'vase' analogy would be dismissed as decorative or unimportant. To the theorist, the actual content of the 'History' box doesn't matter: to the 'tabulist', it doesn't matter what kind of flowers. Both express interest only in the structural properties as 'deeper' markers that indicate hidden relations. Bernstein shows how knowledge can be 'classified' and 'framed' in different ways, either 'strongly' or 'weakly'. These concepts are not part of the surface description,

although they are derived from it. Participants may not recognize them at all. He then relates those structures to still deeper and more general notions like 'code' and links the whole thing as a kind of *functioning*, where events at the broadest level (e.g. society) can be related to events at the microsocial (e.g. classroom). *By tracing the structural properties of the system, he is able to show its functional nature.* This clarification of hidden functioning by structural identification typified much of radical educational theorizing in the USA and the UK in the 1970s–1980s. Its purpose was often expressed in terms of words like 'demystification', the unmasking of the ways in which power operated (*structures*) in educational systems to the ultimate benefit (*functions*) of economic elites.

It is of course only one example of structuralism. Bernstein was a classic theorist of this kind of approach, although there were others who took a Marxist approach. There are numerous examples of this kind of structural thinking, some of which you will already know. For example, Piaget claimed to have found some of the deep structures of learning, to have typologized stages of development (concepts like 'concrete'/'abstract').[1] Freud explored the mind in terms of its alleged structures. Similarly Marx made claims about being able to explain surface phenomena with relation to underlying stages of economic development. Each is quite different, politically, but each makes the same 'radical' move, offering to get to the root of things. As Raymond Williams points out, these are all examples of structuralism as an explanatory system:

> It is here, especially, that *structuralism* joins with particular tendencies in psychology (when Id, Ego, Superego, Libido or Death-Wish function as primary characters, which actual human beings perform in already structured ways). (1983: 306, emphasis in original)

Williams raised a problem for this kind of structuralism which it never satisfactorily resolved:

> . . . it is a very fine point, in relation to any system or structure, whether emphasis is put on the *relations* between people and things, or on the *relationships*, which include the relations and the people and things related. (1983: 306, emphasis in original)

The issue raised here concerns relations (which happen to us) and relationships (which we make). To go back to our analogy of the table, the problem was that tables don't have intentions and desires, but people do – in and out of the timetable. Thus issues of 'agency' as opposed to 'structure' grow more insistent. If relations do not wholly determine action and thought for people, then what is the role of active 'relationship' against the 'relations' in which people find themselves? This was an issue on which structuralism was apparently weaker, and which other 'isms' like phenomenology or 'social interactionism' placed in the foreground. They were, after all, primarily concerned with agency, interaction and consciousness.

A further problem emerged. Universalist theories (e.g. of deep structures, elaborate connected systems that could explain all phenomena) developed a history of inconsistency over time, inconstancy over place, unpredictability over circumstance. Piaget, Marx, Freud all came under attack for the certainty and determinacy of their systems of thought, even by those who were sympathetic to their underlying concerns for child development, economic justice or psychic health. Worse still, such epistemologies relied on subjects whose identities would be regular in their development, constant in their nature and so capable of an 'authentic' expression (once whatever mystifications had been cleared up).

But before we get further into the problems of structuralism and the solutions (or really non-solutions) of poststructuralism, let's go back to the table and think about some of the instabilities that our structural/functional thinking suppressed.

The first of these was signalled by the unexplained interjection in line 1 of this account, '. . . there. Where? Here.' It was an attempt to remind the reader that, (a) there *is* no table there, only the writing of 'table', and, (b) that the no-table – let's call it a 'writing-desk' by way of a pun – is available to you only in imagination as a 'reading-desk', and on my say-so, though you may resist that say-so if you notice it as such, and that (c) the time and circumstance of 'writing-desk' is always political, pedagogically strategic, culturally coloured, quietly privileging.

So what's the problem? The table is not there. It is only someone writing 'table'.[2] The table is performed rather than represented and it is a command performance ('Think of a table'!). Writing performs the table, and positions the self who will read. The failure of the

table ever to be neutrally *there* is repressed, and the impossibility of 'going back' to it is denied. The active engagement of the reader in this masquerade is demanded. The acceptance of the heuristic is imposed rather than proposed. What at first sight can seem to be an innocent attempt to recruit the reader to a new possibility in thinking can simultaneously be exposed as shot through with power-play, inauthenticity, manipulation and misrepresentation. This is what has often been called the 'linguistic turn' – an acceptance that these 'flaws' no longer seem open to correction. We have to live with the mess – there can be no recourse to a level of discourse where 'pure' structures/concepts/theories really tidy up the everyday nature of complexity and contradiction:

> What is profoundly unresolved, even erased, in the discourses of poststructuralism is that perspective of depth through which the authenticity of identity comes to be reflected in the glassy metaphorics of the mirror and its mimetic or realist perspectives. (Bhabha, 1994: 48)

Now we're thinking poststructurally, and maybe you can feel the difference. For a start *you're* here with me, as a paradox of that impossibility of which you have to be reflexively aware:

> You and I, we will never be here, and yet here we are. (Stronach, 2002: 294)

Perhaps that undermines the 'authenticity of identity', the 'easy realism' of writing, the unproblematic relation of author to reader. It makes them part of what we have to think about in the uneasy equations of writing and reading. The rest of Bhabha's claim is difficult to understand, but important. The 'glassy metaphorics' of the 'mirror' refers to Rorty's postmodernist account in 'Philosophy and the mirror of nature' (Rorty, 1980). In his account language can only pretend to 'mirror' nature. Structuralism sought a new language that would mirror the 'true' depth of things. Poststructuralism casts doubt on such projects, seriously modifies their ambitions and pretensions to clarity, challenges them as utopian, or eventually totalitarian in tendency. Here's a poststructuralist mirror to look into instead:

> The mirror takes place – try to think out the taking-place of a mirror – as something designed to be broken. (Derrida, 1981: 315)

Just as phenomenology sought out a favoured ground of 'presence' and structuralism sought insight through 'depth', so too (if any nutshell can do it) did poststructuralism draw most insistently on notions of 'difference'. With that term, a whole range of splits, disjunctions, displacements and provisionalities come to the surface. Poststructuralism claims they were always the hidden disasters, tragedies and crimes of the 'systems' of social and cultural thinking that preceded it, including, among others, structuralism. For such systems of thought, poststructuralism offers the last word, not in terms of definition, but in terms of irresolution. It is the last word for last words.

Which takes us back to the first quote. If poststructuralism *were* the last word in a definitive and arresting sense, it would be the latest paradigm. It would claim to set the boundary of what we can know, culturally, socially, educationally. But it is a different kind of boundary which refuses to think in separate states and insists on attending to the 'border-crossings'. It is more like the Heidegger quote with which we began, 'boundary' as an opening-out, a new 'presencing':

> We should be done once and for all with the search for an outside, a standpoint that imagines a purity for our politics. (Hardt and Negri, 2000: 57)

Implications for research practices

Imagine a 'structuralist' at work in research. Firstly he (they mostly were) would collect data, as speech, documents, etc. Next, he might look for structural properties suggested by the data. And he would decide what sorts of theories (psychological, anthropological, linguistic, etc.) addressed his purposes in collecting such data. These would emerge, metaphorically, as 'depth' generalizations – stages of learning (Piaget) or grieving (Kubler-Ross), theories of 'id' (Freud), types of organization (Handy). The surface would be sifted, gathered together and analysed until it yielded its secrets. Note that the 'secret' has the property of being 'already there', awaiting discovery. And 'discovery' is a central metaphor for the structuralist in search of his hidden depths. This is not, then, a constructivist model.

Now for the poststructuralist. She will also collect data. But the process is a little different. There is a similar eye on what the subjects are saying, writing, doing. But the other eye, a cock-eye, is on what is not said, what discourses make it impossible to say, what

practical or theoretical logics hide away from sight. The interest here, following Foucault, is in how power is intrinsically present in all forms of knowledge. It's a theory, therefore, that denies 'depth' its 'purity'. It says if you want to be profound, attend profoundly to the surfaces and pot-holes of discourses. And that attention implies a reflexive methodology:

> . . . the formation and accumulation of knowledge – methods of observation, techniques of registration, procedures for investigation and research, apparatuses of control. [. . .] All this means that power, when it is exercised through these subtle mechanisims, cannot but evolve, organize and put into circulation a knowledge, or rather apparatuses of knowledge, which are not ideological constructs. (Foucault, 1980: 102)

Are you exercising on the apparatus of knowledge, or are you merely its sweat?

Stories from the Field – 'taking the piss': notes on collaborative practice as research

Lee Miller and Joanne 'Bob' Whalley

On behalf of Roadchef, may I first of all say how thrilled we were to allow Lee and Bob permission to renew their wedding vows here at Sandbach. It's probably a landmark occasion for the motorway industry. (Peter Kinder, Site Director, Roadchef Sandbach Services)

This story focuses upon a doctoral project in the domain of Performance Studies comprised of an originally devised, site-specific performance centred on Joanne 'Bob' Whalley and Lee Miller's renewing of their wedding vows. The one-off performance took place at Roadchef Sandbach Services on the M6 Motorway on 20 September 2002 in the UK.

When writing about their collaborative research, Deleuze commented on his work with Guattari thus: '[s]ince each of us is several, there was already quite a crowd' (Deleuze and Guattari, 1988: 3). This sentiment accurately articulates our collaborative research and practice, because the research in which we are currently engaged lies in the interstices between us, a product of manifold conversations, arguments and dialogues.

Our collaborative practice as research has its origins in the chance observation of what appeared to be a bottle of urine, lying abandoned on the hard shoulder of the M6 motorway. In order to confirm our suspicions, we stopped to collect it, and having seen one bottle, we began to see them at regular intervals along the hard shoulder. Knowing that these bottles and their contents were the product of fellow travellers, Bob felt uncomfortable about simply taking them, and so it was decided that we needed to make some sort of exchange. At first we left behind whatever we had in our pockets (coins, tissues, paid utility bills), but this developed into keeping a selection of items in the car, gifts that had been given to us, things with some provenance, things we could exchange for the bottles of urine we found on our travels.

Because of the illegality of stopping unnecessarily on the hard shoulder, a ritualized behaviour developed which performed the outward signifiers of mechanical failure. Lee would activate the car's hazard warning lights, open the bonnet, stand in front of the car and scratch his head. Throughout this, Bob would be executing the exchange, collecting the bottle and leaving the treasured item behind. Following the discovery of the first discarded bottle of urine and as a result of the many subsequent exchanges executed, we began to explore the position that the motorway occupied in current cultural perception. This found articulation in the writing of French sociologist Marc Augé, who conceptualizes spaces such as the motorway, the airport lounge and the shopping mall as 'non-places'. Augé remarks that:

> [i]f a place can be defined as relational, historical and concerned with identity, then a space which cannot be defined as relational, or historical, or concerned with identity will be a non-place. (1995: 78)

We felt that this was only a partial account of the motorway, one that ignored possible subversions of its 'normative' use, and so we sought to qualify Augé's thesis. On Friday, 20 September 2002 we invited fifty family, friends and interested parties to the Roadchef Sandbach Services between junctions 16 and 17 of the M6 for the performance event *Partly Cloudy, Chance of Rain*. Between the hours of 11 am and 4 pm, ten performers in wedding dresses, ten performers in morning suits, a six strong choir, a three-piece jazz-funk band, a keyboard player and a priest occupied the site. At 12:30, we renewed our wedding

vows in a ceremony that was open to all the users of the service station. After the ceremony, our guests were taken on a guided tour of the site, and users of the service station were witness to a variety of performative actions.

> It might not seem appropriate, but I want to tell you a tale of heartbreak and tragedy. It is reputed that a ghost stalks this very bridge, this bridge that spans the northbound and southbound carriageways of the M6. Legend has it that Electric Suzy (a girl named for the multicoloured spiralled wire that connects the cab with the truck) walks the bridge, awaiting the day when an Eddie Stobart lorry emblazoned with her name will set her free. It is said that she sings to pass the time and on a still day, it is possible to hear the strains of *Ave Maria*. (text from *Partly Cloudy, Chance of Rain* 2002)

Within a postmodern context, the incursion into the service station provided by *Partly Cloudy, Chance of Rain* can be articulated as redundant, since the multi-accented sign already accounts for a multiplicity of readings, thus ensuring that place and non-place are given equal primacy. However, an acceptance of 'habitus' (Bourdieu, 1994) developed out of the functional need for a sedimentation of meaning suggests that our incursion into the non-place was necessary. The project accounts for *both* a recognition of the slipperiness of language *and* a recognition of the need for a sedimentation of use, thus ensuring a dialogic both-and position is maintained.

The role of the vow renewal ceremony was to function as both parodic and sincere, to provide the audience with an experience that could not simply be reduced to the position of either/or, and thus support the creation of an exoteric/esoteric aesthetic. It was both a sincere event and a parody, and in this respect conforms to Hutcheon's definition of the postmodern in which she states:

> [p]ostmodernism offers precisely that 'certain use of irony and parody' [...] As form of ironic representation, parody is doubly coded in political terms: it both legitimizes and subverts that which it parodies. (1989: 101)

In order that our qualification of Augé's non-place might be successful, it was necessary to provide space for the wedding ceremony to function as a sincere event. However, at the same time we needed to provide space for the event to read as parodic, to ensure that we were not simply replacing one monologic conception of space with another. In this way, the employing of parody can be articulated as a postmodern strategy of resistance, subverting and affirming that which is represented. By employing parody and sincerity within the same moment, we were ensuring that both the exoteric and esoteric aesthetics were accounted for.

As part of this site-specific performance work, we made tapes and CDs which were sent to the guests who would be attending the renewal of our wedding vows. The central paradox comes from locating the aesthetic of self-hypnosis tapes to the interior landscape of the car on a motorway journey:

Close your eyes. Visualize a picture in your mind. Think of the most beautiful service station you have ever seen. Imagine a lovely service station in the sun. The car park lights are so tall and radiant. Graceful, beautiful floodlights. There are lovely golden fast-food outlets that are so completely unspoilt. There are wild and exotic plants. Some of them plastic. And the toilets are so clean, so clean, so clear, so calm.

The sun is shining from a perfect sky. It's a beautiful island. A service station that is private, belonging to you. Your own private service station.

In Augé's thesis, the motorway is a (non-)place of transit, a scape to be traversed, lacking coordinates with the everyday world. The hypnosis text was intended to encourage the listener to recognize that, rather than the binary suggested by Augé (place/non-place), the experience of using the motorway is both dislocating and familiar at the same time. The taped narratives were thus encouraging the listener to engage in theory at the same time as experiencing that which the theory conceptualized.

The concept of 'situated cognition' (Brown et al., 1989) has been influential in shaping our approach to research and practice, allowing us to develop the concept we have termed 'operational knowledge'. 'Operational knowledge' refers to knowledges developed through intuition and experience, as much as through the objective analysis of data. Thus *Partly Cloudy, Chance of Rain* sought to generate operational knowledge through the location of a site-specific performance within the quotidian space of the motorway service station, and was characterized by the user of the space encountering a challenge *to* the space she is using, *in* the space she is using.

While the general users of the space do not necessarily have access to the vocabulary of Augé, their use of the space suggests that they are familiar with the concept, at least at an operational level. Thus, to provide a challenge without engaging solely in academic discourse, our research presented a context-specific qualification of Augé's thesis, one that would encourage the development of operational knowledge in the users of the service station. This explicit engagement with the thesis of Augé suggests that this project is both theory aware and knowledge producing, which led us to question for whom such knowledges are intended:

Interviewee One: I prefer a more traditional method myself.
Interviewee Two: What, with everybody taking tea and coffee and all that … breakfast and dinner and … no I don't think so.
(*Granada Reports*, 6.30 pm, 20 September 2002)

These two users of the Sandbach Service Station on the M6 were interviewed as part of *Granada Reports*, a regional television news bulletin for the North West. They were questioned about their experience of the location of a 'wedding ceremony' in the quotidian space of the service station.

The responses of the two interviewees, while not necessarily representative of all the users of the service station on that day, serve as useful markers of the position that the service station occupies in current cultural perception. The fact that both men responded negatively to the location of an explicitly anthropological event within the service station suggests that Augé's articulation of the non-place is operationally valid. The responses of the two men indicate that there is a certain sedimentation in culture of the public's attitude to the service station. Although the users of the space may not be consciously aware of the habitus of the service station, nonetheless they occupy the space according to a set of acculturated principles. Whilst it is fair to assume that the two men interviewed were unlikely to be familiar with the arguments and terminology of Augé, their responses suggest that they have an operational understanding of the habitus of the service station.

While it is possible to construct an entirely written thesis to qualify the way in which Augé articulates the operation of non-places within society, this qualification would provide no account of the way in which the 'non-place' is used. The aim of *Partly Cloudy,*

Chance of Rain was to go beyond a qualification of Augé within his own terms. Instead, it sought to provide an operational alternative to the habitus articulated in the responses of the two men interviewed for *Granada Reports*. While we can articulate our conceptual framework and challenge Augé in an appropriately academic manner, this sort of academic discourse is not enough if the aim of our research is to affect some sort of operational shift. The location of *Partly Cloudy, Chance of Rain* at the Roadchef Sandbach Services on the M6 motorway was in part an attempt to provide a challenge to the concept of the non-place at an operational level. This strategy provided us with the opportunity to challenge a habitus of how the motorway is perceived by the users of such spaces, thus allowing the motorway to be the site of both a contestation and a generation of knowledge.

Notes

1. Those interested in education in England might like to mark the irony that school effectiveness claims no affiliation to 'theory'. It is about what works. Yet the notion of 'key stages' (structuring education around age ranges 5–7, 7–11, 11–14 and 14–16) is based on a 'common-sense' notion that relies somewhat on the spinning corpse of Piaget.
2. Note the irony: I have to use speech marks to indicate 'writing marks' – for which we have no sign.

Annotated bibliography

Atkinson, P. (1985) *Language, Structure and Reproduction. An Introduction to the Sociology of Basil Bernstein.* London: Methuen.

Paul Atkinson is a leading sociologist of education in the UK. He has long complained of the neglect accorded Bernstein's work in recent years. In Chapter 2, 'A structuralist anthropology of schooling', Atkinson outlines what he takes Bernstein's position to be: you will find that it clashes with the account implied above in that he finds Bernstein to be 'suggestive' rather than 'definitive' in his theorizing. Chapter 7 may interest you: in it Bernstein meets Foucault, or, if you like, structuralism meets poststructuralism.

Foucault, M. (1979) *Discipline and Punish. The Birth of the Prison.* London: Penguin.

Foucault was a prominent thinker about the nature of the 'social', whether that's about clinics and the medical gaze, the nature of knowledge down the ages, or in this case – his earliest poststructuralist work – the nature of discipline. Try reading 'The means of correct training' to get a flavour of the difference between his style, which is much more historical and genealogical, and that of Bernstein.

Hardt, M. and Negri, A. (2000) *Empire.* Cambridge, MA: Harvard University Press.

If Foucault's *Discipline and Punish* is early poststructuralism, this book travels through what it argues are the final positive achievements of poststructuralism and deconstruction, and arrives at a new revolutionary state based 'not on the basis of resemblances but on the basis of differences: a communication of singularities' (2000: 57). I have my doubts but the first 50 pages take you through the outline of the journey.

Stronach, I., Halsall, R. and Hustler, D. (2002) 'Future imperfect. Evaluation in dystopian times', in K. Ryan and T. Schwandt (eds), *Exploring Evaluator Role and Identity.* Greenwich, CT: IAP, pp. 167–92.

The chapter offers a broad view of the contemporary condition of knowledge in 'postmodern' times. It offers three dystopias. The first concerns educational discourse as global spectacle. The second investigates the 'policy hysteria' that characterizes responses to the spectacle. The third dystopia concerns the effects on educational research and evaluation methodologies. The approach is broadly poststructuralist.

Further reference

Augé, M. (1995) *Non Places: An Anthology of Super-modernity*, trans. J. Howe. London and New York: Verso.

Bernstein, B. (1971) 'On the classification and framing of educational knowledge', in M. Young (ed.), *Knowledge and Control. New Directions for the Sociology of Education*. London: Collier-Macmillan, pp. 47–69.

Bhabha, H. (1994) *The Location of Culture*. London: Routledge.

Bourdieu, P. (1994) *Distinction: A Social Critique of the Judgement of Taste*, trans. R. Nice, 2nd edn. London: Routledge (1st edn, 1984).

Brown, J.S., Collins, A. and Duguid, P. (1989) 'Situated cognition and the culture of learning', *Educational Researcher*, 18(1): 32–42.

Deleuze, G. and Guattari, F. (1988) *A Thousand Plateaus: Capitalism and Schizophrenia*, trans. B. Massumi. London: Athlone Press.

Derrida, J. (1981) *Dissemination*, trans. B. Johnson, 2nd edn. London: Athlone Press (1st edn, 1972).

Foucault, M. (1980) 'Power/knowledge', in C. Gordon (ed.), *Selected Interviews and Other Writings 1972–77*. Brighton: Harvester, pp. 170–94.

Heidegger, M. (1971) *Poetry, Language, Thought*. New York: Harper & Row.

Hutcheon, L. (1989) *The Politics of Postmodernism*. London and New York: Routledge.

Rorty, R. (1980) *Philosophy and the Mirror of Nature*. Oxford: Blackwell.

Stronach, I. (2002) 'This space is not yet blank: anthropologies for a future action research', *Educational Action Research*, 10(2): 291–307.

Williams, R. (1983) *Keywords. A Vocabulary of Culture and Society*. London: Fontana.

CHAPTER
38

FEMINISM/POSTSTRUCTURALISM

Bronwyn Davies
Education, University of Western Sydney, Australia
Susanne Gannon
Education, University of Western Sydney, Australia

Key concepts

Feminist poststructuralist theory can be taken as a third feminism, historically following on from, but not replacing, liberal feminism and radical feminism (Kristeva, 1981). Whereas liberal feminism mobilizes a discourse of individual rights in order to gain access to the public domain, and radical feminism celebrates and essentializes womanhood in order to counteract the negative constructions of women and girls in masculinist discourse, feminist poststructuralism seeks to trouble the very categories male and female, to make visible the way they are constituted and to question their inevitability.

Poststructuralist analysis focuses on discourse and discursive and regulatory practices. It seeks to transcend the individual/social divide and to find the ways in which the social worlds we inhabit, and the possibilities for existence within them, are actively spoken into existence. The central focus of feminist poststructuralist theorizing is on the processes of gendered *subjectification*. By subjectification we mean the historically specific processes whereby one is subjected to the discursive regimes and regulatory frameworks through which gendered individuals and their social contexts are also, and through the same processes, constructed (Butler, 1992; Foucault, 1980).

Feminist poststructuralism makes visible, analysable and revisable, in particular, the binaries male/female and straight/lesbian. It shows how relations of power are constructed and maintained by granting normality, rationality and naturalness to the dominant half of any binary, and in contrast, how the subordinate term is marked as other, as lacking, as not rational. Through examining the ways the social inscribes itself on the individual, and by calling into

question the construction of the individual in the essentializing terms of humanist theories, poststructuralist theory shows how it is that power works not just to force us into particular ways of being but to make those ways of being desirable such that we actively take them up as our own.

This very different approach troubles 'foundational ontologies, methodologies, and epistemologies' (St Pierre and Pillow, 2000: 2) and opens up the possibility of a different kind of agency. The subject is inscribed, not just from outside of herself, but through actively taking up the values, norms and desires that make her into a recognizable, legitimate member of her social group. To the extent that she is actively and reflexively engaged in that process she can act to disrupt the signifying processes through which she is constituted. As Butler (1992: 13) says, the 'subject is neither a ground nor a product, but the permanent possibility of a certain resignifying process'.

In this way poststructuralist feminism breaks with theoretical frameworks in which gender and sexuality are understood as inevitable, as determined through structures of language, social structure and cognition. It also breaks with theoretical frameworks that define power as that which can be held by certain groups and individuals (Foucault, 1980). The *agency* that feminist poststructuralism opens up does not presume freedom from discursive constitution and regulation of self (Davies, 2000a). Rather it is the capacity to recognize that constitution as historically specific and socially regulated, and thus as able to be called into question. Discourse turns out, upon examination, to be filled with contradictory possibilities, particularly in terms of the complex relations between gender, ethnicity and class. Agency, thus, entails the capacity to recognize multiple readings such that no discursive practice, or positioning within it by powerful others, can capture and control one's identity.

Poststructuralist writing practices open up strategies for resisting, subverting, decomposing the discourses themselves through which one is being constituted (Barthes, 1977). The rational conscious subject is decentred, and the play of desire and the unconscious are made relevant. Old ways of knowing such as through master or grand narratives are resisted as arbiters of meaning, though they may still have constitutive force. It is not that the grand narratives with their humanist heroes are no longer there, but their meanings may be taken up against the grain of dominant ways of seeing and new subjectivities may be generated. New subjectivities are not opened up through simple acts of opposition and resistance but through a series of escapes, of small slides, of plays, of crossings, of flights – that open (an other, slippery) understanding (Cixous and Derrida, 2001). Agency in poststructuralist writing is not understood, then, in terms of an individual standing outside or against social structures and processes. Agency becomes instead a recognition of the power of discourse, a recognition of one's love of, immersion in and indebtedness to that discourse, and also a fascination with the capacity to create new life-forms, life-forms capable of disrupting old meanings of gender, even potentially overwriting or eclipsing them. Poetic and multilayered writing becomes a central tool in those attempts to both recognize and eclipse gendered discourses and regulatory practices through which we are constituted.

Feminist poststructuralist research is focused on the possibility of moving beyond what is already known and understood. Its task is not to document difference between men and women, but to multiply possibilities, to demassify ways of thinking about 'male' and 'female' – to play with the possibility of subjectivities that are both and neither – to understand power as discursively constructed. The following principles are central to a feminist poststructuralist analysis of gendered texts:

1   'Data' do not stand as transparent *evidence* of that which is real. Accounts or descriptions or performances of gendered ways of being reveal *the ways in which sense is being made of gender*, or *the way gender is being performed* in that particular text, rather than an underlying essential truth about sex or gender.

2   The way that sense is made of gender in accounts or descriptions or performances is not of interest because it might reveal something about the essence of the individual sense maker, or about his or her motives or intentions. Rather, interest lies in *the processes of subjectification and the kinds of gendered subjectivities that are available* within a particular discourse.

3   Gendered discourses are neither transparent nor innocent. What subjects describe of what they see and think may be taken as evidence of the ways in which the world outside themselves has forcefully shaped them. Ways of making sense of that which is taken to be real do not spring from one's breast, but are an intrusion from outside of ourselves. *At the same time and through the same processes* we come to see them as our own, to defend them, to desire their maintenance, to understand ourselves in terms of them. Subjectification involves the simultaneous imposition and active take-up of the gendered conditions of existence (Butler, 1997).

4   The language as it is presented in texts produced as data is not respected as if it did reveal 'the real' but may be deconstructed and broken open to show *the ways in which the real is constructed*, for example through binary pairs, and an argument is made for seeing the limiting effect of the binary and suggesting ways of going beyond it – in particular through the method of deconstruction.

5   Researchers are not separate from their data, nor should they be. The complexity of the movement between knowledge, power and subjectivity *requires researchers to survey gender from within itself*. They use their own bodies and emotions as texts to be read, as in collective biography (Davies, 2000b; Davies et al., 2001; Davies et al., 2002; Davies et al., 2004), or to read the gendered texts produced by others, in order to see gender as it is produced through and in relation to such texts.

6   Science is perceived as *systems of discourse that produce knowledge in certain ways*, rather than as a hallowed discourse that is necessarily better than others (Haraway, 1991). The psy-sciences are themselves implicated in the production of the liberal humanist gendered subject (Henriques et al., 1998).

7   *Neither the gendered subject who produces the texts to be read, nor the researcher, is the final arbiter of meanings*

in any text being read. It is the task of those who work with poststructuralist theory to use and develop the concepts they find in gendered texts as a source of creative possibilities.

8   The point of a feminist poststructuralist analysis is not to expose the hidden truth of sex/gender in all its simplicity, but to *disrupt that which is taken as stable/unquestionable truth*.

9   Gendered subjects exist at the points of intersection of multiple discursive practices, those points being conceptualized as subject positions. *The individual is not fixed at any one of these points or locations*. Not only does the individual shift locations or positions, but what each location or position might mean shifts over space and time and contexts. This understanding is central to the fluidity and multiplicity of subjectivities that is central to feminist poststructuralist thinking about change and agency.

10   Gendered experience is understood as being constituted through multiple discourses which give rise to *ambivalent understandings and emotions*. Understanding gendered experience (one's own and that of others) is very often through the recognition of ambivalence and contradiction. The insistence on interpretations cleansed of doubleness, oppositions and multiplicity is a strategy through which the illusion of the rational subject is constituted.

11   Power is understood in terms of lines of force. It is not the property of one gender. Its *strategies, its manoeuvres, its tactics and techniques* are always contingent and unstable (Deleuze, 1988; Foucault, 1980).

12   Feminist poststructuralist theory is interested in the folding and unfolding of history, in the movement from one configuration of feminism (Kristeva, 1981) or of gender (Davies, 2003) to another, *in the lines of flight that make new realities*. The researcher working with poststructuralist theory may contribute to those lines of flight rather than remain simply an observer of others' lines of flight (Deleuze, 1988).

Implications for research design

Feminist poststructuralist researchers ask questions that destabilize taken-for-granted knowledges. They might ask: How do feminist stories reiterate and re-instantiate the male/female binary? How do they open up other imagined subject positionings, discursive practices and desires? How are transsexual identities negotiated in relation to the male/female binary? How is the desiring transsexual subject constituted and reconstituted as he/she moves among masculinities and femininities? Within a particular setting of interest, such as a school, how do gender discourses intersect with discourses of race, ethnicity, religion, socio-economic status and (multi)culturalism? How do these discourses work as an absent presence even when not being spoken into existence?

Any setting where discourses are being mobilized, either in speech or in writing, can be chosen for research. Where a particular category of subject is of interest, any settings where that category of subject is to be found speaking or writing or somehow bringing that category into existence may be chosen. Where speech is the preferred discursive medium, subjects may be willing subjects who agree to enter with the researcher into an investigation of their own discourses and subjectivities, or they may have produced discourse for another purpose, for example as a documentary, radio interview or novel. Researchers may interrogate their own subjectivities and/or their own use of discourses.

Data may include accounts produced by interviewees about the topic in question, any kind of spoken or written text relevant to the concept or category under investigation, observation of social scenes in which the subject under investigation is being produced discursively or in some other form of practice. Data are examined not as if they described or explained an independently existing 'real world' but as constitutive work that itself is implicated in the production of 'the real'. Those data are analysed in terms of the binary categories and discursive regimes at play. The researcher might ask: how does the interviewer or the speaker constitute herself in this text? How does s/he constitute the other? How do they each discursively and interactively constitute the topic under examination? What regulatory regimes have what effects? What discursive strategies are taken up? How is subjection or governmentality accomplished? The point of analysis is not to reveal the individual subject but to investigate the processes of subjectification.

The theoretical concepts of the (sexed) subject, subjectification, and discourse are central to any analysis. Theory is not separate from any stage of the project: from asking questions to choosing data and writing up the data, each moment is informed by the theoretical possibilities opened up in feminist poststructural writing.

The practice of writing poststructuralist texts is not simple reporting, since the writing itself is understood as a constitutive act, as is the collection and analysis of data. The text may not follow predicted patterns of report writing but may set out to deconstruct or disrupt report writing itself (Neilsen, 1998; Richardson, 1997). The subject of the author will not be removed from the writing but will be evidently at work in the text that is produced.

Stories from the Field

In the workshop from which we draw these 'stories from the field' we went back to 'the subject' in/of poststructuralist discourse in order to re-examine the relation between the humanist subject and the processes of subjectification through which the poststructuralist subject is constituted. We each contributed to selecting theoretical readings prior to the workshop. Participants were located throughout Australia and in Sweden, so preliminary analytical and imaginative work took place by email before we met in person. We came together in Sydney, Australia, for three intensive days during which we generated and began to analyse our early memories. Subsequently, we returned to our various homes and continued our collaborative work. The process from beginning to end in this case took in excess of twelve months.

Our approach was one of collective biography, an explicitly poststructuralist methodology developed from Haug et al.'s (1987) memory work. Haug's research group met for several years, but we found that even in one day many memories can be generated, and we were able to engage in collaborative analysis and writing up of those memories within the overall design of our workshop.

We wished to examine the 'break' between humanism and poststructuralism, since several of us had noted the persistence of humanism despite (and even within) poststructuralist discourses in our own writing and thinking. During the workshop sessions we generated memories around themes that had emerged from our preliminary readings and discussions. We used these themes as triggers for memories of 'being someone', of 'being hailed as someone in a way that felt good', of 'being misrecognized' and of 'changing'. They enabled us to re-remember particular moments when we recognized ourselves (and others recognized us) as *particular* selves, as unique and unitary individuals differentiated from others – qualities that we saw

as productive of humanist subjects. In the workshop sessions we each told one or two memories to the group, wrote them, read them aloud and began collectively interrogating the sorts of 'selves' we produced ourselves as in these memories. After we had parted, analysis continued in virtual space as we typed up and annotated the final versions of our memory stories. Finally, we took turns with the evolving draft of an analytical text using the memories as data. We moved back and forth between personal and collective knowledge, between lived experience and theoretical understanding, and between narrative and analytic texts as we continued to struggle towards a paper to which we could all put our names.

The paper reviews early feminist poststructural texts that claim a radical break with the humanist subject which becomes the 'other' against which poststructuralist theorizing of subjectivity might be understood (Henriques et al., 1998; Weedon, 1997). The two kinds of subjects were theorized in a binary with each other, taking their meaning in opposition to each other. We were interested in moving beyond this binary. Although we begin by noting the 'break' marked in these texts that had been influential in our own intellectual autobiographies, we are aware that theoretical 'progress' is itself a grand narrative, and are wary of assumptions that 'new' theories of the (poststructuralist) subject have displaced the 'old' humanist subject.

While liberal humanism might read our stories as snapshots of progress towards a more or less stable and self-contained personhood, reading through a feminist poststructuralist lens enables us to read them as stories of (in)appropriate(d) femininity, providing instances of the ways in which discursive regimes constitute these particular (sexed) subjects at these particular moments in these particular social contexts. We found as we wrote that though instability and slippage mark poststructuralist analyses, they do not erase or displace the humanist analyses that are always already there, part of us, the very 'air we breathe' (St Pierre, 2000: 478). The two memories analysed below demonstrate our way of working with memory texts as well as the precarious tangled subjectivities we constructed within them.

My school report card had arrived. My parents silently read the comments written in neat careful handwriting in each of the boxes. The report card was passed over to me to read. There was a comment in relation to each subject. Then at the bottom, in the seven or so lines of overall comments, the word 'conscientious' appeared. I'd never heard the word, or read it before. I wondered what it meant. I asked, and when my mum told me, I thought it sounded good. I had my own special word. I felt proud and important. I read it over and over to myself. I liked having that word on my report card. I savoured the word, the sound of it, the speaking of it, the meaning of it. There was no discussion about my coming first in the class. Then my father pointed out to me that I shouldn't think I was better than my big sister. She was in the B grade at her boarding school solely because of subject preference. She wanted to study art. And dressmaking was useful for a girl. She was coming near the top of her class, and she was excelling at tennis, which was very pleasing to him. She might be chosen to represent her school. I felt shamed about feeling proud, shamed that I was not good at tennis. But I liked that word, conscientious, its curious spelling, the sound of it, the virtuous feeling of it. I went around saying it to myself over and over.

This memory, generated in response to 'being hailed as someone in a way that felt good', can be understood in a liberal humanist reading as indicative of developmental progress. A school psychologist, for example, might conclude that the girl is emotionally well adjusted and from a good family. She is succeeding at school and her parents take care to ensure that she is sensitive to the needs and skills of other family members. The words on the page are taken as clues to the (real) existence of the individual subject with a particular eye to her adjustment to the social world and to any possible areas where her capacity to adjust might be flawed and in need of remediation. From a poststructuralist perspective the story might be read in terms of the process of subjection to the term *conscientious*: 'Subjection exploits the desire for existence, where existence is always conferred from elsewhere; it marks a primary vulnerability to the Other in order to be' (Butler, 1997: 20). The child experiences herself as willingly embracing the term, despite the lecture she receives from her father about not thinking she is better than her sister. She can therefore be read as the resisting subject, as well as the desiring subject. She can also be read as being taught by her father the precise and detailed embodiment of pleasure in her achievement – it will be quiet, not displaying itself as superior. She takes up

these limitations on the correct form of desire and attitude and bodily comportment in the dual act of being recognized and recognizing herself. In order to be, she is vulnerable to the report writing teacher and the father. The story shows the process as *both* an imposition *and* an act of agency in which she seeks out and lives the meaning of herself, her subjecthood, within the terms made available to her. The girl did not first experience herself as conscientious and then learn the word for it. In hearing herself described as such, her experience is constituted as such. She is constituted (subjected) as conscientious and she actively takes up the constitution of herself inside the new term that she understands as a desirable way of being. At the same time she reads herself as already that kind of person.

In the second story, told in response to the prompt of 'misrecognition', a young teacher is called into an undesired and abject naming by a student:

. . . She asked a question and looked across the hands thrust up into the air to Alex over by the window, up to something, as usual. 'Alex,' she said, calling him back to attention, 'what do you think of blah blah blah?' Suddenly, Roslyn stood up in the centre of the room and shouted 'You only ask the boys questions,' she said, 'because they've got penises.' Everyone stared at her as she stood at the front of the class, the tears in a burning rush up behind her eyes and her throat choking. She wanted to say, 'No, you've misunderstood.' Or 'No, that is the last thing I would want to do.' But she thought she would collapse, or explode, and she couldn't speak through her horror at these words. She turned and walked out of the classroom before they could see what they'd done to her, she marched briskly up the path, heart thumping, feeling like she might throw up. She marched straight into the staff toilets where she locked the door and sat on the seat and sobbed and sobbed until the bell rang.

This story enters volatile terrain. The teacher sees herself as sensitive and responsive to the needs of students, as professional and reasonable, as equitable. Yet, in her classroom practice, she falls into an old gender trap where – for diverse reasons – teachers tend to interact more with boys than with girls in classrooms. Although the teacher has the 'power' to select this student (Alex) rather than that one (Roslyn) to participate in the discussion, her authority is tenuous and depends on the more or less willing subjection of students to the disciplinary regimes of the school and the classroom. Roslyn refuses this subjection and assumes authority in the class, bodily by 'standing up' and 'shouting' into a space where she is not authorized to stand or speak, discursively constituting the teacher as one who only attends to boys. The humanist question the teacher might ask herself in that moment is 'Am I really that person?' and she struggles to do this by examining her conscience and her practice and beginning to rehearse answers to that question. But it is not possible to answer from this unspeakable place. These students are 15 years old, young men and women. Roslyn's accusation is that her excessive interest in the boys is because of their male genitals. She cannot debate this rationally with Roslyn/the class. It is a dangerous moment, as the violent reaction of her body reveals. In feminist poststructuralism, this embodied response is as relevant as the words that are spoken in mapping ì(the dynamic relations and effects of power. In contrast to the humanist question about how she 'really feels' as a teacher/person/individual/woman, poststructuralism questions the workings of relations of power – between the teacher and Alex, between the teacher and Roslyn, between the rest of the class and these subjects – and how they are constituted in the moment to moment interactions of that intense social space.

Binary categories slip and slide through this story. The teacher reads Roslyn as equal to 'the students'. Although only one student speaks, the teacher leaves the room 'before *they* could see what *they* had done to her'. She positions herself in binary opposition to the whole class (whom she imagines aligned with Roslyn,

though they too may be stunned into silence). Another binary fracture exists between the rational reflective teacher of her imagination and the capricious, lascivious woman that Roslyn names her as. In this story, she is not willing in her subjection to Roslyn's conferral of this new subject position, but she lacks resources to resist. She *has* been favouring the boys. She *is* sexist in her practice, in effect if not in intention. And because her way of 'being' has been named in that way, so too her way of thinking (about herself, her practice, her students) is cast in that moment in terms of sex/gender rather than through any other possible categories. The binary shifts from teacher/students to women/men. 'Woman' entails the unteacherly characteristics of emotionality and susceptibility to desire. But she *is* a woman as well as a teacher and, as in other spheres of her life, these multiple subject positions are in delicate balance, fluid and precariously achieved.

We could say much more about these stories but for now note that our analyses demonstrate the sorts of issues and approaches we are interested in as feminist poststructuralist researchers. Using lived experience as the ground for theorizing is central to feminist research, as is our particular interest in examining discourses of sex/gender. Poststructuralism enables us to attend to processes of subjectification and discursive regimes. In our analyses of the speaking subjects of these stories, traces of the self-contained liberal humanist subject remain in some readings but our subjects are called into existence in social spaces where power and knowledge circulate unpredictably and where subjects are always tenuous, in process, vulnerable and prone to decomposition.

Annotated bibliography

Butler, J. (1993) *Bodies that Matter: On the Discursive Limits of Sex.* New York: Routledge.
Gender performativity is a reiterative and citational set of discursive practices that produces sexed subjects that are always under threat, unstable, at risk, dependent on the simultaneous recognition and exclusion of 'abject' others.

Davies, B. (2000b) *(In)scribing Body/Landscape Relations.* Walnut Creek, CA: AltaMira Press.
Collective biography, interviews, journal/personal/poetic writing and literary analysis are used to deconstruct body/landscape binaries and generate writing 'against the grain' of dominant discourses.

Grosz, E. (1994) *Volatile Bodies: Towards a Corporeal Feminism.* Bloomington, IN: Indiana University Press.
Bodily boundaries are decomposed as women's corporeality is theorized as 'flows' and 'intensities'.

Haraway, D. (1991) *Simians, Cyborgs and Women: The Reinvention of Nature.* New York: Routledge.

Haraway theorizes 'situated knowledge' and deconstructs nature, culture, experience, gender, truth and scientificity itself.

Haug, F. et al. (1987) *Female Sexualization*, 1st edn. London: Verso (2nd edn, 1999).

Collective memory-work brings theory and lived experience together as early memories are used to unpick discursive regimes of femininity that are deeply inscribed and embodied.

Henriques, J., Hollway, W., Urwin, C., Venn, C. and Walkerdine, V. (1998) *Changing the Subject: Psychology, Social Regulation and Subjectivity*, 2nd edn. London: Methuen (1st edn, 1984).

Poststructural theory comes to education and the social sciences. Psychology is deconstructed as a regime of truth that produces the very subjects in which it is interested.

Lather, P. (1991) *Getting Smart: Feminist Research and Pedagogy with/in the Postmodern.* New York: Routledge.

Lather articulates poststructuralism with feminist praxis and emancipatory discourses. She maps modernist and postmodernist paradigms, interrogates 'validity' and scans the field of social inquiry for new research possibilities.

Richardson, L. (1997) *Fields of Play: Constituting an Academic Life.* New Brunswick, NJ: Rutgers University Press.

Epistemological implications of re-presenting data as poetry, drama, autobiography and fiction are examined in terms of poststructural challenges to knowledge production in the social sciences.

St Pierre, E.A. (2000) 'Poststructural feminism in education: an overview', *Qualitative Studies in Education*, 13(5): 477–515.

Key philosophical terms (language; discourse; rationality; power, resistance, and freedom; knowledge and truth; and the subject) are discussed in terms of how they are understood differently in humanism and feminist poststructuralism.

St Pierre, E.A. and Pillow, W. (eds) (2000) *Working the Ruins. Feminist Poststructural Theory and Methods in Education.* New York: Routledge.

This collection demonstrates the creativity and breadth of research undertaken by feminist poststructuralist educators.

Walkerdine, V. (1990) *Schoolgirl Fictions.* London: Verso.

Gendered relations of power and patterns of desire are analysed through psychoanalytically inflected poststructuralism. Research contexts include the production of 'the child' in progressivist pedagogy, femininity in popular culture and (the desire for) heterosexual marriage.

Weedon, C. (1997) *Feminist Practice and Poststructural Theory*, 2nd edn. Oxford: Blackwell (1st edn, 1987).

Psychoanalytic and discursive versions of poststructuralism are elaborated as Weedon explores the necessary and productive discomfort entailed in conjoining feminism and poststructuralism.

Further references

Barthes, R. (1977) *Roland Barthes.* Berkeley, CA: University of California Press.
Butler, J. (1992) 'Contingent foundations', in J. Butler and J.W. Scott (eds), *Feminists Theorize the Political.* New York: Routledge, pp. 3–21.
Butler, J. (1997) *The Psychic Life of Power.* Stanford, CA: Stanford University Press.
Cixous, H. and Derrida, J. (2001) *Veils: Cultural Memory in the Present.* Stanford, CA: Stanford University Press.
Davies, B. (2000a) *A Body of Writing.* Walnut Creek, CA: AltaMira Press.
Davies, B. (2003) *Shards of Glass. Children Reading and Writing Beyond Gendered Identities*, 2nd edn. Cresskill, NJ: Hampton Press (1st edn, 1993).

Davies, B., Dormer, S., Gannon, S., Laws, C., Taguchi, H.L., McCann, H. and Rocco, S. (2001) 'Becoming schoolgirls: the ambivalent process of subjectification', *Gender and Education,* 13(2): 167–82.

Davies, B., Flemmen, A.-B., Gannon, S., Laws, C. and Watson, B. (2002) 'Working on the ground. A collective biography of feminine subjectivities: mapping the traces of power and knowledge', *Social Semiotics*, 12(3): 291–313.

Davies, B., Browne, J., Gannon, S., Honan, E., Laws, C., Müller-Rockstroh, B. and Petersen, E.B. (2004) 'The ambivalent practices of reflexivity', *Qualitative Inquiry*, 10(3): 360–89.

Deleuze, G. (1988) *Foucault*. London: Athlone Press.

Foucault, M. (1980) *Power/Knowledge.* Brighton: Harvester Press.

Kristeva, J. (1981) 'Women's time', trans. A. Jardine, *Signs*, 7(1): 13–35.

Neilsen, L. (1998) *Knowing Her Place*. San Francisco: Caddo Gap Press.

CHAPTER 39

SOCIAL SCIENCE RESEARCH IN VIRTUAL REALITIES

Colin Lankshear

School of Education, University of Ballarat, Australia

Kevin M. Leander

Department of Teaching and Learning, Vanderbilt University, Nashville, Tennessee, USA

Key concepts

Virtual realities

Brill (1994) distinguishes seven types of virtual reality (VR) along a continuum. At one end is 'Immersive First Person VR' of the 'helmet, goggles and glove' variety that provides 'an immediate first-person experience' of being and acting inside a simulated environment that looks, feels and behaves as though it were *real*. At the other is 'Cyberspace', where one 'is' when connected to a computer network or electronic database – or even, perhaps, when talking on the telephone.

Between these poles Brill locates variants like Desktop VR, which provides non-immersive first-person experiences, and a range of virtual realities offering second-person experiences.

Most conventional published social science research conducted within so-called virtual realities is concerned with human activities in cyberspace: spaces on the Internet. This, accordingly, is our focus here.

Research in cyberspace

Research in cyberspace involves the Internet in a dual capacity: as a 'research tool' and as 'a social medium' presenting phenomena to be researched (Jones, 1999: x). Notwithstanding the existence of interesting outlier forms (see, for example, Costigan et al., 2002), social science research and discussion of issues about research design and methodology in cyberspace have to date been dominated by a handful of research 'types':

- *Ethnographic and other participant observation-based studies* of social practices within online spaces and

'communities': for example, Kendall (1999), Hine (2000), Miller and Slater (2000).

- *Text and discourse analytic studies* of communication and interaction in text-based online spaces, Multi User Domains (MUDs), Multi User Domains Object Oriented (MOOs), and Internet Relay Chat (IRC). Typical examples include studies by Marvin (1995) and Vallis (2001).

- *Interview-based studies* of online social practices (see, for example, Markham, 1998).

- *Surveys* of diverse social phenomena pertaining to offline as well as online environments using online questionnaires (see, for example, Smith, 1997).

- *Document-based research* which uses the Internet mainly as a tool for collecting data and/or for engaging in analysis and interpretation (often collaboratively). Such research – whether primary or secondary – draws on burgeoning online archives and databases to circumvent laborious searches in physical libraries and to maximize data pools.

Recognized issues and challenges in cyberspace research

Within these contexts and types of research (generally published in conventional forums like commercial books and book chapters, and refereed academic print-based and online journals), problems of the design and conduct of social science research in cyberspace have become 'legion' (Leander, 2003: 396). The following are typical.

- Many social interactions in cyberspace are conveyed solely by text, or otherwise without any kind of embodied presence, creating issues for researchers and researched alike. Participants in online worlds and exchanges often have to be taken at face value in terms of the identity they (choose to) present within that space. Identity play and experimentation are common online. Thus researchers face challenges of authenticity and validation with respect to gathering, analysing and interpreting data. But just as researchers can be 'fed a line' without knowing it, so the researched can be 'under observation' without knowing it.

Further questions arise around how to capture nuance when text is all there is to go on, and how to fairly represent participants. Likewise, precisely what counts as the *site* or *field* (e.g., of 'field notes') becomes dispersed and nebulous. How can 'the site' be construed and bounded? What sense and integrity can be given to key concepts like 'community' within cyberspace?

- Relations between online and offline lives and environments are complex, varied and uncertain. This raises questions about the extent to which we can understand online social phenomena independently of their offline extensions (Kendall, 1999), and challenges many researcher assumptions about 'atom space' (the physical world) and 'bit space' (virtual space of digitally coded data) being radically separate (Hine, 2000).
- Online information space is highly unregulated. From conventional academic perspectives this creates issues for assessing credentials and credibility of online sources: veracity, verifiability and authority (Burbules and Callister, 2000). The sheer amount of information available online and the impressive capacity of search engines to deliver it exacerbate this issue.
- Researchers identify a range of logistical difficulties involved in collecting *qualitative* data and achieving 'data saturation' (see Stories from the Field below; Markham, 1998).
- Quantitative social researchers identify logistical issues associated with conducting survey research online. These include sampling in contexts where participant authenticity is practically impossible to establish, difficulties with obtaining adequate response rates from online communities and developing appropriate survey instruments for online environments.
- Online spaces are notoriously non-permanent and transient. How can researchers be confident they will be left with a study in a month's time, let alone in a year?

- In many traditional research settings, ethnographers' work might actually be supported by their initial actual or assumed naivety and lack of cultural knowledge. Conversely, many online environments are extremely status conscious and can prove punishing to 'outsiders'. Knowledge of Internet practices often becomes very important for obtaining and maintaining access to informants within online settings (Leander and McKim, 2003).

Implications for research design

As with the issues identified above, the following description of design and methodology implications is selective, yet *indicative*.

- When contemplating research of an online space researchers should attend to the age and stability of that space, and the likelihood it will endure at least until data collection is complete. For participant research, investigators should present themselves as sufficiently technologically and culturally capable to establish credibility within the online world being studied (Leander, 2003).
- Opinions vary among researchers about what counts as ethical conduct around issues like observing as a 'lurker' and appropriating texts available in online archives as data for analysis and interpretation. Researchers should be especially alert and sensitive to the ease with which it is possible to participate fully within virtual worlds without alerting others to one's research status and intentions (Leander and McKim, 2003). Barbara Sharf (1999: 254) states what are probably majority views when she suggests researchers should (i) introduce themselves clearly to online groups or individuals who are the intended focus of study with respect to their identities, roles and purposes; (ii) make concerted efforts to contact directly and obtain consent from individuals who have posted messages they want to use as data; and (iii) 'seek ways to maintain an openness to feedback from the e-mail participants who are being studied'.
- The radically dispersed, distributed, yet 'placeless' nature of the 'field' entails different ways of thinking about participant observation and the bounding of sites from traditional conceptions associated with ethnographic and other forms of fieldwork. For example, online observations of

necessity draw on 'connections rather than location' in defining their object or focus (Hine, 2000: 10).

- Similarly, the complex relations between online and offline environments and lives incline researchers like Kendall (1999) to argue that all social research on interactive online forums should include participant observation, even where researchers wish to prioritize other methods. Leander and McKim (2003) recommend developing methods that 'follow the moving, traveling practices' of participants online and offline to clarify relations between practice, context and identity.
- To help validate participant identity and authenticity and to validate data about their online practices, some researchers choose to interview and observe participants offline while they participate online (Turkle, 1995).
- Quantitative concerns about online surveying have spawned ongoing experimentation with various combinations of questionnaire design and format and modes of administering questionnaires (for example 'snail mail' plus online distribution).

Stories from the Field

Unlike other chapters, ours does not end with stories from the field. We think the issues that have mainly interested social scientists to date represent just one set of possibilities for '*research* in cyberspace'. This section presents three representative stories from researchers working within an academic research mainstream. These are followed by a statement introducing a different perspective or orientation we believe lies outside the mainstream of social science research in cyberspace. This alternative perspective is viable, has its own integrity and might actually constitute a discursive construction of research more organically 'at home with' – or 'inside' – cyberspace than the presently prevalent 'mainstream'.

Some challenges facing the ethnographic study of literacy practices among youth in on- and offline settings
Kevin Leander

Our research ('Synchrony') aims to enhance understanding of (a) the use of literacy practices for identity and social networks, (b) the 'situatedness' of literacy

or, in other terms, how to understand literacy in relation to space-time, and (c) reflexively, new methodologies for conducting research across online and offline contexts by tracing how the participants use a range of new information and communications technologies (ICTs). These include instant messaging, chat, email, searching the Internet and building websites, and gaming.

We initially hoped to enrol a diverse group of youth who were intensive users of ICTs as key informants. We wanted to observe them in English and Social Studies classes in US secondary schools at least once weekly over several months, and online in their homes bi-weekly, using screen capture software to record their interactions. We aimed also to collect classroom artefacts (mostly written work) and to interview informants and their teachers about their schoolwork. Moreover, we wanted to enrol additional participants in the study as it moved along – friends of the key informants (either offline friends or those known only in cyberspace) – in order to move from cases of individuals to cases of entire social-technical-literate networks, across online/offline boundaries.

Access has been a key challenge. Obtaining human subjects ethics approval from the university, locating a school district willing to participate and then finding individuals willing to participate provided challenges from the outset. We eventually identified and studied seven key informants.

Further issues of access, more nuanced and fine-grained than those involved in locating participants, have subsequently emerged. For example, one of our informants was willing to participate, including home visits and the like, but would not allow us access to certain parts of her online world. In particular, this participant ('Angie') was continually involved in playing some sort of online game during the school day, and was likely involved in other online interactions, using her laptop in a wireless environment. While we continually observed her participating in this activity (during classroom observations), and 'mode-switching' between gaming and coursework, she would not discuss this with us. Rather, Angie seemed set on presenting more of a student persona about her work in school.

Similarly, 'Brian', who is an intense gamer at home, allowed us access to his gaming, but little to his Instant Messaging, and seemingly offered us a sanitized version of his online life. My hunch about this stems from bits of interaction captured by the screen capture software that were of an entirely different discourse than the interactions Brian made available to us. For instance, Brian nearly never would curse online (or offline) while being observed yet he would use screen passwords something like 'Ufuckoff.'

Another important issue of access involved enrolling online and offline friends in the study so as to better trace social networks. We have had some success in that some of our original key participants are friends, but we have not moved far in truly mapping online and offline social relations in a way that can be institutionally authorized by gaining consent from every participant. In many cases we have one-sided 'authorized' data in interactions. We were cautious with our participants, who were already being pushed in terms of their involvement, and did not want their social relationships to feel under pressure. We continue to work on this issue and think about it during the follow-up stage and as we establish more history with some key participants.

Another predictable challenge of the study has involved trying to scale up to multi-site research with a very small team of people. Even the study of seven key participants gets very large when this is multiplied by two classroom visits per week (in diverse classrooms in two schools, 20 miles apart), home visits, managing digital data capture, interview schedules, photocopying coursework, consent processes, and so on. I conducted this study with two graduate students, who were working on it for their part-time assistantships during this past academic year. As such, time resources were always stretched thin and we found ourselves having to jettison some of our original goals, including the kinds of visits we had hoped to make to informal peer contexts (parties, shopping centres and the like). In the end, we focused on home (online) activity and school (typically but not always offline) activity.

We now present two stories that we have extrapolated from published research in cyberspace.

Some challenges facing an interview-based study of online experiences

In *Life Online* (1998: Chapter 2) Annette Markham describes issues she faced studying – principally by means of online interviews – how people experience cyberspace. How do Internet users make sense of identity and reality in computer-mediated contexts?

Markham describes herself facing the inevitable struggle associated with qualitative research generally

between wanting to be 'open and flexible' yet having to 'design and justify a study'. This played out in her study through the tension between wanting to learn how people experience cyberspace and trying to fit their experiences into her own 'conceptual and grounded understandings of social life' (Markham, 1998: 62).

The following two excerpted 'moments' from Markham's account of her research echo in resounding ways the experiences of many social scientists trying to forge mainstream research paths into cyberspace, as well as of many researching in conventional sites.

(a) Markham says her interview protocol changed considerably during the interviewing period. 'Because I concentrated more on the conversation with the participants and less on the protocol, I ended up with richer discourse' (1998: 77). She worried for some time about possible methodological problems arising from departing from the interview protocol: 'many methods teachers had warned me against such deviations' (1998: 78). After completing data collection and spending time looking through the transcripts, Markham admits to not quite knowing 'if I am more interested in what they say about [the study's] issues of reality and identity, or what they do while they're online and what they think about their online experiences. I'm not sure, but it seems I am not getting what I thought I wanted out of the interviews' (1998: 79).

(b) After accepting that the interviews did not tell her what she thought they would, Markham began identifying possible themes in the transcripts. One theme was that each user is 'different and unique' (1998: 80). Her informants did *not* talk about the same issues. They were all different. This posed problems for identifying similarities. If saying something meaningful about 'users of online communities' as some kind of a group is what the research calls for, how can this be done in light of the primacy of differences?

> By conducting 'User in The Net' interviews, I am addressing the question 'How do users make sense of identity and reality?' If I am pressed, I say I'm looking for themes or patterns in their discourse, otherwise, what's the point? (1998: 80)

Yet Markham found this goal seemingly 'incommensurate' with the kinds of interviews she conducted.

> If my goal is to find themes and patterns, and I don't seem to be finding any in [what] I have

collected, can I really say anything meaningful with these texts? Do I just present eight stories, eight sets of sense-making practices? (1998: 80)

When she sought advice it was suggested that she keep interviewing until she could see patterns repeating – a widely held view among qualitative researchers. This crystallized as a problem for attaining 'data saturation' and, indeed, of knowing what could count as 'data saturation' for her kind of study purposes. Markham comments:

> . . . more interviews might yield critical insights that tie the rest of the interviews together. [Also] doing more interviews would be a strategy to gain some credibility for what I did eventually decide to say. [But] . . . how many interviews . . . does it take to validate the results of a qualitative study? (1998: 80)

Some challenges facing an Internet-based survey research project

Christine Smith's (1997) paper 'Casting the Net' was an early attempt to provide a scholarly appraisal of the prospects of using self-administered questionnaire surveys with Internet populations. Smith wanted to survey opinions from within the 'web presence provider' (or 'professional webmaster') industry. Her main purpose was to obtain adequate and sufficient responses to questionnaire items. She also wanted to compare the relative efficacy and experiences of administering online surveys by two different means: via email questionnaires and via web-based surveys.

Her study design was complex. The email questionnaire mode involved drawing a sample of 300 providers from an international directory of web consultants. This was divided into two groups of 150, using accepted selection procedures. The first group received the email questionnaire unsolicited. The second received by email a 'call for participation' message without the questionnaire.

The web-based survey mode involved sending a blanket coverage 'call for participation' message to subscribers of several web-content oriented email mailing lists, calculated to have around 8,000 subscribers in total. (Smith documents an array of implementation problems experienced using the web format.)

In terms of her *efficacy* purpose, Smith reports an 8 per cent response rate from the 'push' email population (11 valid responses from 150 recipients – some

messages bounced) and 13.3 per cent from the email 'call for participation population'. Thirty-nine per cent of the email sample provided responses to the follow-up poll. From the estimated 8,000 recipients of the web survey call for participation, Smith received 161 valid responses (under 2 per cent) and 86 follow-up poll responses (under 1 per cent). Smith's total 'catch' across the two modes was 2.3 per cent. She comments as follows:

> I am of two minds on the issue of the obtained response rate. Based on the potential 8000 participants from the mailing lists on which my CFP [call for participation] appeared, and the 300 person e-mail sample, one could call 2.3% (192) a truly dismal catch . . . However, I feel I have more than enough data to take the baseline pulse of the industry [particularly since two-thirds of the respondents worked in enterprises involving two or more people, all of whom probably subscribe to the same mailing lists. Hence, the proportion of web presence providers actually 'present' in the data would be higher than 2.3% of the companies represented in the mailing lists].

With respect to her *comparative* purpose, Smith offers several observations that are pertinent here. First, she says that one person 'accused me of spamming him' – that is, of sending a mass message unsolicited by recipients – and copied his message to Smith's Internet service provider to indicate that he thought she had used her service provision inappropriately. Notwithstanding this response, Smith says:

> Netiquette proscribes e-mailing large surveys unannounced, but this practice, I would argue, is still valid for the purposes of survey design and methodological research. Survey length has been an issue . . . and while we know there is such a thing as 'too long' we do not yet know its dimensions.

Second, Smith acknowledges 'the practical impossibility of probability sampling' using Internet-based surveying. In formal quantitative research terms, this means 'one can only tentatively generalize to a very specific population'. Moreover, 'there is no precise and reliable means of determining response rate' when using web-administered surveys.

Third, trying to contrast email and web survey administration techniques involved some major logistical and related methodological problems relative to

Smith's paradigm. Form submission and browser incompatibility problems 'raised real concerns about whether I could gather enough data'. These resulted in Smith making 'concerted efforts to publicize the survey beyond the initial calls for participants and followup polls'. This response, however, 'somewhat muddies the . . . analysis of the web-based phase'.

Finally, Smith opines that the new technologies of email and the Internet present survey researchers with 'a spate of new problems'. These include 'sheer competition from marketers, journalists and other researchers'. While email 'is a wonderful tool for impromptu polling on timely issues' and is 'an extremely useful tool for building a potential sample', Smith questions 'its utility for anything more' in an 'age of "infoglut" and pervasive e-mail spamming by unscrupulous marketers'. Not the least of challenges facing Internet researchers is the fact that 'an aura of suspicion often surrounds any stranger-to-stranger communication in cyberspace, even when the declared topic is of mutual interest'.

Alternative perspectives and discursive colonization

The emergence of cyberspace as a tool and context for social science research invites (re)consideration of two quite different orientations. In many ways these echo themes raised by Lyotard's (1984) account of knowledge in the postmodern condition – particularly the idea that the postmodern condition privileges knowledge as an *exchange* rather than a *use* value.

The first orientation focuses on the extent to which established social science norms and procedures could comport satisfactorily to cyberspace, and how far new or modified ones need to be developed, in order to do 'good quality research' relative to conventional discourses of scientific knowledge. Of course, 'established social science norms and procedures' are not monolithic. For example, recent constructions of 'validity' and 'reliability' within qualitative research and associated concerns over 'representation' and approaches to 'interpretation' differ markedly from more strictly 'positivist' and 'post-positivist' versions, as well as from those associated with interpretivist and interactionist currents within sociology and anthropology of just 15–20 years ago.

For all their differences, however, such discursive variants of scientific knowledge share important common features. They emphasize conformity to

norms and rules fought out around practices like peer review, apprenticeship to disciplined inquiry, preservation of standards, deference to experts and recognized (academic) authority and so on. They are predicated on beliefs that doing research 'this way rather than that' will produce better results in terms of 'fidelity' to the object of inquiry understood as some kind of *use* value.

In some cases, this is knowledge as a kind of 'truth'. In others it is knowledge in the form of demonstrated commitment to providing good audit trails – so that readers can identify points where disagreement arises – in search of 'qualitatively better understandings or interpretations'. All such cases invoke some idea of scientific knowledge as *an end in itself* and worthy of all rigour and 'fidelity' – with whatever discursive variations these might entail.

Most of the ideas and issues we have surveyed above reflect this broad perspective. They participate in the commitment to finding the best ways to ensure that researching cyberspace as a social medium and/or using the Internet as a tool for social science inquiry preserves the best of our constructions to date of research in 'atom space'.

In the second orientation – which has strong purchase within everyday practices in cyberspace – 'knowledge' is no longer an end in itself. Rather, knowledge is produced in diverse shapes and forms in order to be sold or exchanged for all manner of 'goods' ranging from economic gain or winning attention to straightforward experiences of affirmation, kudos or being able to identify yourself as an active participant in some affinity group.

Under this sign, research as a 'knowledge game' is broad-based, multiple in the extreme and plays by very different rules to those that characterize conventional (academic) social science research. Almost anything social becomes 'researchable' and 'reportable' – from the production of 'cheats' for computer games to the objects of zany fetishes that spawn countless electronic zines (do-it-yourself publications of a popular culture magazine variety), weblogs (permanently updatable websites that often have a daily journal format), websites and other online 'reporting and publishing' media. The respective 'knowledges' of the two modes could hardly be less alike. Neither could the 'presses' used to report them.

Furthermore, whereas research and knowledge within the first (conventional) orientation emphasizes conformity and fidelity to recognized norms, rules and procedures, research and knowledge within the second orientation emphasizes *originality* that is often best served by breaking rules and procedures, changing them, inventing new ones and, particularly, being adept at making up the rules and procedures for new knowledge games 'on the fly'. Jeff Bezos (CEO amazon.com) captures this difference in his distinction between first- and second-phase automation. First-phase automation uses new technologies to do familiar things, only more efficiently. Second-phase automation takes new technologies as pretexts for envisaging entirely new and different things to do. This involves an 'enactive' logic of research and knowledge, whose emphasis is not on fidelity toward unveiling what is in some sense (or from some perspective) *already there* but, rather, on bringing entirely new and unforeseen practices and artefacts into *existence* – as 'productions' that can be exchanged. Fidelity to established norms and procedures yields to a restless search for 'originality that works' that gets validated by people 'picking it up and running with it'.

Interestingly, in so far as 'truth' can still be seen to be at stake in research and knowledge, cyberspace enables the restoration of a radically different (indeed, *premodern*) mode of 'truth bearing' from that which typifies conventional scientific research. The multimedia realm of ICTs is making the radical convergence of text, image and sound *normal* in ways that break down the primacy of propositional forms of truth bearing. While many images and sounds transmitted and received in virtual realities still stand in for propositional information, many do not. They can behave in very different epistemological ways from talk and text – evoking, attacking us sensually, shifting and evolving constantly. In cyberspace, meaning and truth arrive in spatial as well as textual expressions. Michael Heim (1999) argues that as new digital media displace older forms of type and printed word, questions about how truth is made present through processes that are closer to rituals and iconographies than to propositions and text re-emerge in similar forms to those discussed by theologians since medieval times.

In many ways, then, the question about social science in virtual realities might be seen as a struggle between these two orientations to shape and define concepts and practices of research in cyberspace.

Acknowledgment

The authors acknowledge helpful discussion with Chris Bigum and Michele Knobel in preparing this chapter.

Annotated bibliography

Brill, L. (1994) 'Cyber software: designing, authoring and toolkit', *Virtual Reality World*, 2(4): 41–7.

Contains a model that distinguishes seven kinds of virtual reality, including physically immersive and non-physically immersive varieties.

Burbules, N. and Callister, T. (2000) *Watch IT: The Risks and Promises of Information Technologies for Education*. Boulder, CO: Westview Press.

Contains discussion of issues involved in discerning and establishing credibility online and criteria for deciding which resources to take seriously (or not) as information and knowledge.

Costigan, J., Johnson, A. and Jones, S. (2002) 'Comparison of remote user representation in a collaborative learning environment', *Journal of Virtual Environments*, 6(1).

Reports a study in which a remote instructor appearing via a video window and a remote instructor sharing the virtual space via an avatar body are compared against an instructor sharing local virtual space with the student. Available online at: < http://www.brandeis.edu/pubs/jove/HTML/V6/costigan.html > (accessed 19 September 2003).

Heim, M. (1999) *Transmogrifications*. Available online at: < http://mheim.com/html/transmog/transmog.htm > (accessed 21 March 2002).

Heim discusses the construction of avatar worlds by online users of VR software to express their visions of virtual reality as a form of truth and describes 'the new mode of truth' he believes will be realized in the twenty-first century.

Hine, C. (2000) *Virtual Ethnography*. London: Sage.

Argues that researching the Internet, as both a site for cultural formations and a cultural artefact shaped by our understandings, requires a new kind of ethnography.

Jones, S. (ed.) (1999) *Doing Internet Research: Critical Issues and Methods for Examining the Net*. Thousand Oaks, CA: Sage.

Discusses key issues of Internet research from a wide-ranging academic standpoint.

Kendall, L. (1999) 'Reconceptualizing "cyberspace": methodological considerations for online research', in S. Jones (ed.), *Doing Internet Research: Critical Issues and Methods for Examining the Net*. Thousand Oaks, CA: Sage, pp. 57–74.

Focusing on research about on-line forums, this chapter argues for the importance of participant observation as a key means for understanding how participants gain access, blend their on-line and off-line lives, reproduce aspects of the Internet's history and culture, and develop cultural practices unique to specific on-line groups.

Leander, K. (2003) 'Writing travellers' tales on new literacyscapes', *Reading Research Quarterly*, 38(1): 392–97.

Discusses ethical and methodological issues associated with new practices, involving literacy and identity, and with researching these practices.

Leander, K. and McKim, K. (2003) 'Tracing the everyday "sitings" of adolescents on the Internet', *Education, Communication and Information*, 3(2): 211–40.

Argues that ethnographers studying adolescents' Internet practices must move beyond place-based ethnography and develop methods that follow participants online and offline.

Lyotard, J.-F. (1984) *The Postmodern Condition: A Report on Knowledge*. Minneapolis, MN: University of Minnesota Press.

Seminal account of how the status of knowledge changes with advances in electronic information technologies.

Markham, A. (1998) *Life Online*. Walnut Creek, CA: AltaMira Press.

Describes issues and challenges of undertaking formal online research about how users create, negotiate and make sense of their online social experiences.

Marvin, L. (1995) 'Spoof, spam, lurk and lag: the aesthetics of text-based virtual realities', *Journal of Computer-Mediated Communication*, 1(2).

Uses four jargon terms to explore communication practices in six MUUs, asking what these terms communicate about interaction aesthetics. Available online at <http://www.ascusc.org/jcmc/vol1/issue2/> (accessed 26 November 2003).

Miller, D. and Slater, D. (2000) *The Internet: An Ethnographic Approach*. New York: Berg.

Ethnographic study of Trinidadians at home and abroad using the Internet for diverse social and relationship purposes.

Sharf, B. (1999) 'Beyond netiquette: the ethics of doing naturalistic discourse research on the Internet', in S. Jones (ed.), *Doing Internet Research: Critical Issues and Methods for Examining the Net*. Thousand Oaks, CA: Sage, pp. 243–56.

Drawing on research into the Breast Cancer Online list, Sharf advances five ethical guidelines for using data available on publicly accessible Internet forums.

Smith, C. (1997) 'Casting the Net: surveying an Internet population', *Journal of Computer-Mediated Communication*, 3(1).

Reviews literature on postal and email surveying and reports a study involving email and web-based surveying, highlighting practical difficulties experienced. Available online at: <http://www.ascusc.org/jcmc/vol3/issue1/> (accessed 19 September 2003).

Turkle, S. (1995) *Life on the Screen: Identity in the Age of the Internet*. New York: Simon & Schuster.

Classic interview-based study of identity and subjectivity in online environments from a psychological perspective.

Vallis, R. (2001) 'Applying membership categorization analysis to chat-room talk', in A. McHoul and M. Rapley (eds), *How to Analyse Talk in Institutional Settings: A Casebook of Methods*. London: Continuum, pp. 86–99.

Conversation analysis of how 'speakers' in a chat room achieve identities for themselves, others and absent parties through membership categorization.

PART IX

PARTICIPATING IN THE RESEARCH COMMUNITY

Bridget Somekh
Education and Social Research Institute, Manchester Metropolitan University, UK
Ian Stronach
Education and Social Research Institute, Manchester Metropolitan University, UK
Cathy Lewin
Education and Social Research Institute, Manchester Metropolitan University, UK
Máire Nolan
Enterprise and Commercialisation Division, Lancaster University, UK
Jeffrey E. Stake
Indiana University School of Law – Bloomington, USA

The authors would like to thank Marshall Leaffer, Distin-guished Scholar in Intellectual Property Law, and Ann J. Gellis, Professor of Law, Indiana University School of Law, Bloomington, for providing advice on the legal issues dealt with in this chapter.

Ensuring the impact of research

> Research is systematic inquiry made public. (Sten-house, 1981)

The purpose of all research is always ultimately to have an impact on ideas/opinions and influence action through the generation of knowledge and understanding. In this sense, whatever its method-ological stance on the important debates that sur-round notions of subjectivity and objectivity, research is never truly impartial and always involves re-searchers in positioning their work socio-politically and engaging in communicative dialogues. Some social science research has been hugely influential. For example, in the 1970s Cronbach (1981) developed an approach to the evaluation of publicly funded pro-grammes in the USA which overturned previous

assumptions about the application of quantitative methods to social organizations and shaped pro-gramme evaluation practice for at least the next two decades; and research into assessment of learning in schools, carried out by Paul Black and colleagues at King's College London at the turn of the century, has had a major impact on both policy and practice in the UK (Black and Wiliam 1998a, 1998b; Wiliam and Black, 2002). More frequently, however, the impact of research takes place over time and is harder to establish. The effect is cumulative over a very large number of studies rather than unambiguously the outcome of one or two studies. It is diffused through inter-personal networks over time. Examples of this more diffuse and incremental process can be seen in the wave of acceptance of 'reflective practice' as a key strategy for professional development across the disciplines during the 1980s in which the work of Schön (1983) was one significant influence; and of 'constructivist' approaches to knowledge and learning as the dominant concept for policy-makers and practitioners in the USA during the 1990s, in which the work of Bruner (1986), drawing upon Vygostkian theories of mind, was one significant influence.

STRATEGIES FOR MAKING SURE YOUR RESEARCH HAS IMPACT

- Engage with practitioners, build trust and confidence, present your work orally and encourage feedback, get into dialogue.
- Engage with policy-makers and public officials, for example by responding to consultation documents or bidding to undertake research contracts on their behalf.
- Engage with the media – write articles about your research for popular and professional journals/magazines.
- Develop your website pages, if possible within your institutional website which signals the status of your research. Take trouble to keep it up to date with a copy of your CV and examples of recent and current work.
- Write books about your research or chapters in books edited by other people, as these are often more widely read than academic journals.
- Seek out opportunities to present your work at conferences, both to academic and non-academic audiences.

Designing and carrying out a research project

The earlier chapters in this book have introduced a wide range of social science research methodologies and methods and these are always the starting point for carrying out research. If you are going to spend a substantial amount of time (perhaps three years or more of your life) undertaking an inquiry you need to feel passionate about it. So the first step in choosing a research focus is to find something you care about deeply and move from there to investigating what methodologies or methods accord with your way of seeing the world – ask yourself the big questions: what for me is the nature of being (ontology), of knowledge (epistemology) and of truth (philosophy)? We hope you will begin to start answering these questions with the help of reading this book.

In reality you are very unlikely to be working alone. You may have been hired to join a research team which already has funding to carry out the work, or you may be embarking on a PhD under the supervision of a well-known academic – either way you are likely to find yourself expected to work within a particular methodological tradition as part of a research community which is mutually supportive. At this early stage, we suggest you read Alison Lurie's novel, *Imaginary Friends* (Lurie, 1978), as a fun way of getting a sense of the larger arena in which you are about to play out your own personal research game. It tells the story of a young researcher embarking on an ethnographic study in partnership with an eminent academic. It gives a fascinating multilayered analysis of relationships within a research project and might be a good way of reducing any uncomfortable sense of being overawed! The novel is loosely based on a famous – some would say infamous – piece of research conducted by Leon Festinger in the 1950s. He and his team infiltrated a religious sect who believed in the imminent end of the world and the coming of a Saviour. The researchers cut a lot of ethical corners in order to test and confirm their hypothesis – deception, lying, interference with their 'subjects' were all part of the stratagem. Their conclusion? 'Although there is a limit beyond which belief will not withstand disconfirmation, it is clear that the introduction of contrary evidence can serve to increase the conviction and enthusiasm of a believer' (Festinger et al., 1956: 23).

Even before you have made definite decisions about your research focus and methodology, you need to start planning your research as a project with start and end dates, work stages and deadlines. A major personal project such as writing a book or doing a PhD requires a combination of creativity and good time management. You need to start to understand the key levers for your own motivation in a process that perhaps could be called personal meta-psychology. How do you work best? What strategies can you adopt to keep your motivation levels high and maximize your opportunities to be creative? A support group or partnership, drawn from your research team or fellow graduate students, can be hugely important. You will also need to plan opportunities for publications to come out of your work, negotiating these with colleagues if you are working in a research team. A good strategy is to make commitments to present strands (or discrete sections) of your work as conference papers. There are many ways of organizing your research so that you feel you are making progress and your motivation levels remain high, but the basic idea is to plan to carry out the work in stages and seek out opportunities to give yourself real deadlines for completing each stage.

An important part of research is the reading which opens up for you other research and sheds an interesting light on your own. For us, the secret is to treat reading irreverently. We suggest you read widely rather than narrowly – often tangentially to your main topic – so that you bring to your work insights from key thinkers from both your own discipline and interdisciplinary sources. Whatever your project, you will need two strands to your reading – a systematic survey of the research carried out in your substantive subject area over the past five or ten years, and an in-depth exploration of the methodological literature relevant to your research approach. Reading has an important secondary function in giving you (subliminally) models of language for your own writing. For us the first step to writing a paper is always a day immersed in the library, reading to stimulate our thinking and soak up models of discourse.

If reading is undertaken as a creative process, with a focus on making notes of your own ideas triggered by what you have read, the transition from reading to writing a 'review of the literature' should not be problematic. But let's start with a warning! A written review of the literature will be very boring to read if it does no more than summarize what has been said in a large number of books and articles. This is not what a good literature review is about. The point of the reading is to stimulate your thinking and enable you to approach your empirical research sensitized to the issues and alert to what is likely to be significant. So the first step in writing about your reading might be to make a flow chart of the development of your thinking since the inception of your research. Start by identifying the two or three books or articles which have been seminal to developing your ideas. From these trace out the strands of your thinking which have developed in the course of your reading and research. From the developing flow chart you should be able to identify what speakers of German call the 'red thread' of your main argument. This will form a sequence of your ideas and developing understanding as they emerged in response to your reading, and you can use this as the plan for your literature review – in effect the backbone on which you will hang a critical reading of each text. For a reader, the effect should be of sitting in on a dialogue between you and your reading, with sufficient summaries of key ideas in the texts to make it possible to understand the questions they raised for you. Brief quotations from the texts will help to emphasize key points that you have found interesting or with which you wish to disagree, but use these to illustrate points you have made rather than relying on them to carry your argument forward – readers should be able to skip the quotations and still follow your argument.

There are some pitfalls to reviewing the literature which can become serious handicaps as you get more deeply into your research. All of these stem from failing to keep adequate notes. Even texts which make a deep impression when you read them will fade into the recesses of memory after a period of time. At a minimum you need to note the complete citation for each publication and make notes of the main points which have stimulated your thinking, together with notes of your own responses (clearly marked so that you can tell the difference when you come back to read the notes at some future date). Direct quotations from the publication need to be marked and the page number noted – to avoid the classic problem of having to spend time later in tracking down a book or article to locate the page number of a quotation. We recommend EndNote software which can be loaded into your computer so that its commands appear in the Word 'Tools' menu. It is simple database software that prompts you to enter the full citation, attach keywords and make notes. As your EndNote library grows in size you can search to select items relating to particular strands of your research. Best of all, you can import citations from EndNote into Word files while you are writing so that the whole tedious business of producing reference lists is done for you automatically by the software – and these references can be automatically reorganized into different formats (e.g. endnotes rather than Harvard style) if you are requested to do this by a publisher.

The most creative part of research, and the part which paradoxically many people find the hardest, is analysis. Many of the chapters in this book give advice on analysis, which is a process deeply dependent on the methodological framework within which you are working. The one feature common to analysis in all social science research is that it is the core process whereby you begin to make sense of the data you have collected, interpret them, 'make meaning' and move towards the larger process of generating knowledge (in a form that will vary considerably depending upon your epistemological framework). Quantitative data analysis is a technical process which has become increasingly sophisticated in recent years with the advent of powerful computer software. It is now possible to carry out very complex statistical procedures on large quantities of data once they are entered into a software package, with the result that quantitative research in the social sciences is now capable of reaching a much more sophisticated understanding of data and their correlations with each other and with contextual variables. SPSS is the obvious starting point if you want to use quantitative methods. Data can be explored initially and described before being subjected to a variety of tests. Exploratory data analysis can be used to check the data. For example, outliers can be identified and checked in case they have occurred as a result of an error during data entry. The results of all analysis including graphing procedures are created in the SPSS Viewer window, which opens automatically, and this output can be saved as separate files for subsequent analysis or copied and pasted into other documents.

Qualitative data analysis is often a two-stage process of (1) making analytic memos in a research diary or field notebook and (2) undertaking a more systematic process of fragmenting the data and attaching concept labels to each separate piece as a first step in the construction of theory or 'interrogating' data to search for answers to questions and evidence to either support or refute emerging theories. Here too computer software which allows you to attach concept labels to sections of text can be very helpful, although it can be a less flexible and creative process than the old approach of cutting up photocopies and sorting fragments into groups, or marking up data with highlight pens. NVivo is the obvious starting point if you want to carry out computer-aided qualitative analysis, but it is worth remembering that for smaller-scale studies it may not be worth the effort.

STRATEGIES FOR DESIGNING AND CARRYING OUT A RESEARCH PROJECT

- Choose a focus about which you feel passionate.
- Use this book to help you find a methodological framework which is in accord with the way you see the world and use it as the basis for designing your research.
- Make a work plan that sets out all the stages of your research in a time-line, divided into stages with completion dates.

- Read widely and creatively, regarding your reading as a source of ideas and a stimulus for your thinking and never as texts to be memorized.
- Organize your literature review to reflect the development of your thinking in response to reading, with a clear 'red thread' of argument.
- Remember that data analysis is the fun part of research as well as the most difficult. Use this book to help you identify approaches to data analysis appropriate for your methodology.
- Don't be afraid to use your creativity in coming up with interpretations and making meanings, but remember that this creative stage needs to be followed by meticulous checking to see if you really have evidence to support your claims.

Carrying out sponsored research

It is a normal part of the process of being a social science researcher to write proposals seeking funding from sponsors. This is an important way of increasing the available funding for research, employing researchers and providing them with wide-ranging experience, and increasing the public profile of your university research centre. By definition, externally sponsored research is likely to have impact beyond your own organization but relationships with sponsors are always influenced by the sponsor's requirement that your work should enhance their public profile and reputation. In the case of evaluation research which sets out to explore the value of an initiative or organization, sponsors are usually in a position of power over the participants in the initiative and the researchers who are tasked to collect evidence, draw conclusions and report back to the sponsor are potentially threatening to participants, particularly the director of the programme. In all sponsored research, therefore, but particularly in evaluation research, it is important to negotiate the rights and responsibilities of all the parties carefully in advance. For example, if the sponsor appoints a Steering Group (or Advisory Group), what will be its remit? And if participants in a project will be recognizable to the sponsors of an evaluation, what control will the researchers give participants over the release of data and negotiation of interpretations and findings contained in reports?

Research contracts

The contract constitutes a legally binding agreement where one party agrees to provide goods or services to another in return for a consideration. In universities or research institutes, the service offered is usually research and the consideration is usually money. In order for it to be legally binding it must specify rights and obligations of both parties although it will still be legally binding even if it is not complete or exhaustive. In some cases, particularly where the legal department of a government department draws up the draft contract, the primary concern may be with the interests of the sponsor. Individual researchers working for an organization such as a university must forward the contract for signing by the organization's authorized signatory. However, before doing so the contract should be closely examined to ensure that it does not bind either the researchers or the organization in any way that is unacceptable. It is always worth negotiating on unacceptable clauses. In practice, sponsors are nearly always agreeable to rewording them in a way that is acceptable to both sides. The organization, or any other party to a contract, should employ a lawyer to scrutinize the contract before signing.

Intellectual property rights

Intellectual property (IP) is governed by a body of law that allows owners to protect their intellectual creations and innovations. IP itself relates to the novel output of any intellectual activity. It has an owner, it can be bought, sold or licensed and should be protected. Therefore IP rights are legally defined rights that enable the owner to exert control over its use and exploitation, normally for commercial gain. Of the various categories of IP, some are automatically granted at the point of expression, e.g. copyright, and others have to be applied for before being granted and registered e.g. patents, trademarks, registered design. Depending on jurisdiction, there are up to six categories of IP:

- *Copyright* is the protection of the physical expression of an idea.
- *Patent* is a property granted by a state authority, which gives the owner the right for up to twenty years to stop others from using or selling their invention without permission.

- *Trade mark* is a sign which is used by a trader to distinguish his/her goods or services from those of another trader.
- *Design*, in the UK, protects the physical appearance of an article.
- *Know-how* is the knowledge or expertise, which does not have to be kept secret and may not always be formally protected.
- *Trade secrets* provide protection for secret formulas or methods of operation of a business.

The one we are mainly concerned with in social science research is copyright. However, detailed information on a range of IP is available from the following websites:

- UK Patent Office: <www.patent.gov.uk>
- UK Copyright Licensing Agency: <www.cla.co.uk>
- UK Institution of Trade marks: <www.itma.org.uk>
- European Patent Office: <www.european-patent-office-org>
- UK government information site on IP: <www.intellectual-property.gov.uk>
- World Intellectual Property Organization: <www.wipo.org>
- United States Patent and Trademark Office: <www.uspto.gov>
- United States Copyright Office: <www.copyright.gov/circs/circ1.html>

Copyright

Copyright protects the physical expression of an idea, *not* the idea itself. It is achieved at the point when an original work of authorship is fixed in a tangible medium of expression, without registration and at no cost. However, it is always advisable to affix the symbol © followed by your name and/or the organization's name and the date of publication to warn others against copying it. In UK and European law it is also advisable to affix the symbol © and the date at the time of first creating the original work, but in the USA it is important that copyright work only has one date – the date of publication. In the USA there are some advantages to registering with the Copyright Office and registration is a prerequisite to bringing a suit and obtaining remedies provided by the USA Copyright Act, but registration is generally more important for works that have commercial value. In all academic writing it is expected that the origin of ideas, as well as quotations from the writing in which they are presented, will be acknowledged with a full citation.

The UK, the USA and many other countries are members of several international conventions with regard to copyright. Under these conventions, material produced in one country will be afforded the same protection as that in member countries of the international conventions. Most countries will belong to at least one of the conventions and this includes all of Western Europe, Australia, Canada and Russia. The length of time copyright protection will last is partly dependent upon the type of work being protected but, in general, it lasts for 70 years plus the life of the author. Alternatively, it could last for 70 years from the first publication of the protected work. In countries that are signatories to international conventions, work that appears on the Internet is protected by copyright law in the same way as other publications. Hence, it is normal practice to mark every page of a website with the © symbol, the copyright owner and the date of publication. However, any legal action would have to be taken in the country in which the material had been illegally used and in practice there is no protection if that country is not a signatory to the conventions.

The work itself does not have to be profound for it to have copyright protection – in fact it can be mundane and still be automatically protected, for example a label on a box of cake mix. Remember, copyright is a right to prevent copying, and truly independent creation of a similar work is a defence to an infringement claim. In practice it is often difficult to bring successful prosecutions for copyright infringement, so it is worth noting these recommended steps that can be taken to help make enforcement of copyright easier:

- In the UK and Europe, at the point of creation of original work, label it with the symbol © followed by your name, and/or the organization's name and the date. In the USA, however, when the work is published, in addition to the creator's name and copyright symbol, affix the date of first publication rather than the date of creation, as attaching a date other than the date of first publication to a work would nullify notice and reduce the copyright owner's rights. Ensure that original work is kept in a safe place.
- Get either a third party to sign the work stating the date on which it was created and that it was

presented as an original work, or send the work 'recorded delivery' to yourself and then leave the envelope unopened and in a safe place on its return. Make sure there is a copy of the work before it is put in the envelope. Some banks or solicitors may accept deposits of your work for a small fee.

- Ensure that a chronological record is kept of any developments or changes made to the work.

If you publish your work in a book or a journal, the publisher may ask you to assign rights to the copyright. Once this has been done, the publisher becomes the owner of the copyright, which means that permission to reproduce the work can only be given by the publisher and any fee accruing for such use will go to the publisher. Most books contain a statement at the front (near the details about date and place of publication) stating that copying any part of the work without permission is illegal. Some copying, however, is permitted for the purposes of research and scholarship and university libraries will normally be able to provide information on the legal requirements (e.g. in the UK individuals are permitted to copy for their own use one article from a single issue of an academic journal).

Human subjects approval

United States law regulates research in order to protect human subjects from harm during the course of research. The regulations specify procedures research institutions and individual researchers must follow in any research, including interviews and surveys, involving human subjects. The regulations apply to any researcher in any organization that receives funding from the United States, and the penalties for non-compliance can include termination of all federal funding to the organization. Organizations must appoint an institutional review board, and the researchers must get approval from that institutional review board before any contact with human subjects.

THINGS TO REMEMBER WHEN CARRYING OUT SPONSORED RESEARCH

- Go for it! Research funded by an external sponsor has many advantages in terms of increasing available funds, raising the

profile and prestige of both yourself and your organization, and making it more likely that your research will have an audience and wider impact.
- Negotiate and clarify in advance the rights and responsibilities of all stakeholders (sponsors, researchers and project participants). In the case of sponsored evaluations it may be useful to produce a written statement that specifies what control participants will have over the release of data and reporting.
- The contract is the legal agreement between the researcher's organization and the sponsor. We suggest that only the authorized signatory in your organization should sign the contract. Clauses that the authorized signatory may not accept before signing include those which:
  - *bind the organization to high financial penalties in the event of a researcher's inability to complete the work* – though in some cases the organization may have taken out an insurance policy that enables the contract to specify financial penalties up to a certain limit;
  - *remove researchers' rights to have their name published on the work and the right to object to derogatory treatment of their work* – this is known as a 'moral waiver' and is commonly practised by some major international organizations such as the OECD;
  - *remove researchers' rights to publish their research* – this is commonly a clause in evaluation contracts but for an organization whose core business lies in publication of research it is normal to ask for rights to publish after a specified time delay or after the sponsor has published the main report and the work is in the public domain in some form;
  - *give ownership of all data to the sponsor* – particularly if the organization is not free to use the data for research and/or teaching purposes. This also implies that researchers will be unable to protect the confidentiality of the informants/ participants.

- Ensure that original work at the point of creation is marked with a © sign, your name and/or the organization's name along with the date of first publication, and, in the case of websites which can be accessed internationally, affix this mark to every page.
- In the USA, before beginning research funded by the government, get approval from your organization's institutional review body.

Building a research career

The job of a full-time researcher is typically insecure and extremely rewarding. At the start of their careers many researchers in universities are employed on short-term contracts which do not provide them with the same terms of employment as colleagues with 'permanent' or 'tenured' contacts. Nevertheless, since significant track records in research experience and publications are the main criteria for full professorships, the long-term career prospects of contract researchers are generally good. Once established in a tenured post, a researcher's time for research is likely to drop significantly, but if research activity and publications are maintained over time this position is likely to change. Research is the main activity for many full professors and a substantial proportion of their teaching is likely to be supervision of graduate students registered for PhD degrees.

From the start, therefore, the work of researchers involves a far wider range of activities than carrying out research itself. Here is where we recommend you read another great novel, David Lodge's *Small World* (1985), as a good way of gaining insights into the process of international networking. This will either put you off completely or get you in the mood to begin to build your track record. First steps might be by getting involved in writing proposals for externally funded research projects and starting to write for publication. As well as raising funds for research and writing for publication, university researchers engage in a number of activities which, although not strictly for the benefit of their own university, have a recognized value in terms of promoting its reputation and status. These include presenting papers at conferences (including, for well-established researchers, invitations to present keynotes), reviewing papers for journals (and for well-established researchers, becoming a journal editor or member of the editorial panel) and presenting papers in local and national gatherings attended by practitioners and government officials (and for well-established researchers, becoming an adviser to governments, at home or abroad, and international organizations).

None of these activities is difficult, but they all require a certain degree of courage and determination. For example, all researchers have had the experience of sending articles to journals and having them rejected in the first instance: this is normal and it's best to see it as an opportunity to use the reviewers' comments to revise and improve the paper for resubmission. For another example, all researchers remember finding their early experiences of presenting papers at conferences stressful, if not intimidating: the way to get over this is to practise in advance (in one of our cases, this still involves presenting the whole paper to the mirror in hotel rooms); another good strategy, especially for your first keynote presentation, is to imagine you are playing the role of a very confident person in a play – just go into role and it is amazing how your confidence quickly rises to turn the play-acting into a reality.

Fifteen years ago, as part of an evaluation of a national research programme sponsored by the UK Economics and Social Research Council, one of us (Stronach) carried out a case study of the researchers employed on three-year contracts by the individual funded projects based in different university departments. What was the job like? What did it take to make a success of the job? How did they see their future?

There are two ways of being in the contract research world. The first centres on doing the job: the second on having a career. People who just do the job sound like this: 'I mean I've never been ambitious. I've only, all I've ever done is enjoyed what I'm doing and just, I work hard. Just do it. And people have always mistaken that, I feel. They say "you're really ambitious".' But the ambition centres on the particular project. These people also have foreshortened horizons: 'What am I going to do when I grow up? I'm beginning to get towards 40 and I still don't think I'm in a career yet.' People who 'have a career' are described in very different terms: 'I mean you meet people who, now you realise that that's what they were doing all along, thinking strategically, acting strategically, making

sure that they got all the right things at the right sort of time ... and they knew that.' Their stories have a more singular and purposeful ring to them. (Stronach and MacDonald, 1991: Appendix 3)

The study showed that a job as a contract researcher on a sponsored project is an excellent way of starting a successful research career, but some people make much more of their opportunities than others. Key ideas to hold onto are the need to: cherish the 'buzz'; know what your own research interests are and keep working on these even if project funding threatens to drag you elsewhere; actively sell yourself through networking; write joint proposals with someone who already has a track record (hitch yourself to a star); and realize how important research reputation is to universities and the role (and hence potential power) of contract researchers in building this. Ten years later, the British Educational Research Association carried out a study of the same issues through a survey of its members and review of the research and policy literatures. The resulting publication included recommendations for UK university Departments of Education (Freedman et al., 2000).

FEATURES OF BUILDING A RESEARCH CAREER

- You need to be prepared to take risks and make the most of opportunities (be flexible and look for ways in which you could 'make something' out of what is on offer).
- Take opportunities to assist in writing research proposals and become named as a co-proposer alongside someone with an established 'track record'.
- Write articles for refereed journals and don't be put off if your first attempts are rejected. It is standard practice for academic reviewers to suggest 'further work' and their comments are always useful in helping you to improve the article.
- Write chapters in edited books, and maybe produced your own edited (or co-edited) book.
- At the end of five years, perhaps as an outcome of your PhD or a major funded

project, plan to write a single- (or co-) authored book.
- Build a national and international network of contacts through presenting papers at conferences; spending time talking to people between sessions, over lunch, in

the bar; and sending follow-up emails. Time spent networking at conferences is just as valuable as attending sessions.
- Develop and maintain a personal website with an up-to-date CV and examples of publications.

References

Black, P. and Wiliam, D. (1998a) 'Assessment and classroom learning', *Assessment in Education*, 5(1): 7–74.

Black, P. and Wiliam, D. (1998b) *Inside the Black Box: Raising Standards Through Classroom Assessment*. London: King's College London Occasional Paper.

Bruner, J. (1986) *Actual Minds, Possible Worlds*. Cambridge, MA and London: Harvard University Press.

Cronbach, L. (1981) *Towards Reform of Program Evaluation*. San Francisco: Jossey-Bass.

Festinger, L., Riecken, H. and Schachter, S. (1956) *When Prophecy Fails. A Social and Psychological Study of a Modern Group that Predicted the Destruction of the World*. New York: Harper & Row.

Freedman, E.S., Patrick, H., Somekh, B., McIntyre, D. and Wikely, F. (2000) *Quality Conditions for Quality Research: Guidance for Good Practice in the Employment of Contract Researchers in Education*. Nottingham: British Educational Research Association.

Lodge, D. (1985) *Small World*. London: Penguin Books.

Lurie, A. (1978) *Imaginary Friends*. London: Penguin Books.

Schön, D.A. (1983) *The Reflective Practitioner*. New York: Basic Books.

Stenhouse, L. (1981) 'What counts as research?', *British Journal of Educational Studies*, 29(2): 103–14.

Stronach, I. and MacDonald, B. (1991) *Faces and Futures: An Inquiry into the Jobs, Lives and Careers of Educational Researchers*, in an ESRC Initiative, Centre for Applied Research in Education, University of East Anglia, Norwich NR4 7TJ.

Wiliam, D. and Black, P. (2002) *Working Inside the Black Box*. London: King's College, University of London.

GLOSSARY

The aim of this glossary is to give an indication of the breadth of meaning attaching to a number of terms in common usage among different groups of social science researchers rather than simply to give dictionary definitions. Where terms have been used only once and glossed at the point of use they are not included in the glossary. Some terms are defined fully in specific chapters; readers are recommended to use the index to locate the actual page(s) where the term is described.

As it has not been possible to go into any real depth, readers are recommended to use a reference book such as the *Fontana Dictionary of Modern Thought* (Bullock and Stallybrass, 2000) in addition to this glossary. Numerous definitions can also be found on the Internet through <www.google.com> by searching on: define: [term].

Agency refers to the capacity of a human being to take action and exercise control in formal or informal social groups. Whether or not individuals have agency is sometimes disputed on the grounds that their actions are determined by the social structures within which they live. This is known as the 'structure and agency debate' (see below).

Anthropological refers to a tradition of research which focuses on human beings (the original meaning of anthropology was 'the study of mankind'). It is used to refer to research methods which give importance to spending long periods of time collecting data 'in the field' (the site of study), often using participant observation and/or interviewing.

Artefacts are constructed objects which may be tools or texts or any products of human beings. In post-Vygotskian theory they have a special significance because tools or cognitive frameworks/procedures mediate all human activity.

Axiology refers to philosophical questions relating to the nature of values.

Belief is a conviction of the truth of something which is based on faith rather than evidence.

Bias means an in-built tendency to see the world – and hence to interpret data – in a particular way. Researchers either need to eradicate bias or understand it through a process of reflexivity and account for it in reporting their work.

Cause and effect (causal, causation) refers to the process of establishing a causal link between a 'treatment' and a research outcome.

Concepts are internal representations of ideas and/or phenomena which are key component parts in human understanding. In quantitative research a concept will need to be operationalized, that is represented by a number of measurable/observable indicators.

Constructivism is the term used to describe a theory of knowledge which stresses the active process involved in building knowledge rather than assuming that knowledge is a set of unchanging propositions which merely need to be understood and memorized.

Correspondence theory of truth is one of the long-established ways of verifying the truth of a proposition, based on the assumption that if the statement to be judged true or false corresponds to the facts it can be said to be true.

Critical is used to describe engagement with assumptions and meanings beneath the surface. It does not have the straighforward negative connotations that it has in common usage. However, it often denotes an oppositional stance to assumptions of authority.

Critical theory started with a group of philosophers in Germany who emphasized the importance of looking beyond the surface of what people say, write, do to analyse the unspoken power relations governing their actions and understandings. It incorporates from the work of Marx the notion of 'false consciousness' to describe how individuals are disempowered by the social structures which shape how they think as well as how they act.

Cultural icons refer to aspects of the culture which have the status of 'sacred images' (the literal meaning of 'icon', holy picture).

Cultural norms refer to the expected social practices, value assumptions and so forth which social groups impose on their members and mutually enforce.

Cultural texts refer to any publication that reflects the interests, values and opinions of a cultural group.

Culture as used in social science research means the whole range of social practices, artefacts, value assumptions and daily routines which are associated with a social group.

Cyberspace is the location of Internet surfing, email interactions, online chat and interactive web-based games. People enter cyberspace when they go online.

Data saturation is used to describe the point in qualitative research when the issues contained in data are repetitive of those contained in data collected previously.

Deductive (deduction) refers to the process of using established theories as a framework to develop hypotheses, in contrast to inductive/induction (see below).

Demographic data are data relating to population, such as age range, socio-economic status, ethnicity.

Dialectics refers to the shaping of ideas through considering oppositional points of view, challenging one with the other and reaching conclusions through a process of recognizing the competing claims made by each.

Dialogic strategies (dialogue) are research methods which involve discussion between participants and genuine sharing of ideas on the basis of equality.

Discovery learning is a teaching method which puts priority on students constructing knowledge through engaging in enquiry.

Discursive practices are the speech and utterances that are socio-culturally produced. Postmodern theory suggests that individuals in a particular social group are likely to conform to them and be constrained by them.

Disrupt is a word used in feminist and poststructuralist theory for the creative agency which disturbs and unsettles assumptions that would otherwise be oppressive.

Distributed cognition – see 'mediate' below.

Empiricism (empirical) describes an approach to research which assumes that all concepts are derived from experience. Empiricism, therefore, gives high priority to the collection of data by observation (using the five senses: sight, hearing, touch, smell and taste).

Epistemological (epistemology) refers to philosophical questions relating to the nature of knowledge and truth.

Ethnomethodology refers to a research approach which adopts the methods of ethnography but may not strictly be classifiable as ethnography. It tends to be used loosely to define research which gives priority to collecting data about people using methods such as interviewing and unstructured observation, and using description and narrative in reporting.

Experimentalism (experiment) is an approach to research such that participants are randomly assigned to conditions (groups) and one or more variables are manipulated to see if this has any different effects.

Factor analysis in quantitative research is a technique that identifies the general dimensions or concepts within a set of responses to questions, bringing together a range of correlated measures into a smaller number of variables which can be interpreted more easily. It is also used in scale development and to reduce data.

Falsifiability is the term used in Popperian philosophy of science to replace verifiability. Popper argued that it would never be possible to prove the truth of any proposition because of the limitations of human experience. It was, therefore, preferable to seek to falsify a proposition, so that if this proved impossible the proposition could be said to have been established as true until such time as evidence was found to disprove it.

Fourth-generation evaluation refers to the latest in a series of approaches to program (sponsored) evaluation presented in books by Egon G. Guba and Yvonna S. Lincoln. It places emphasis on constructivist enquiry as a means of engaging with both policy and practice.

Generalizable (generalization, generalizability, generalizable laws) is the term used to claim that knowledge generated by research in a specific context will also be true in all other contexts or for the population which the sample represents. It is an important concept in natural science research but is regarded as highly problematic by many social science researchers who believe that knowledge is always context-dependent.

Grand narratives is a term used in postmodern and poststructuralist theory for the explanatory stories – or theories – which impose an all-encompassing framework on the complexity of human experience. They distort human understanding as well as constituting manipulative and oppressive control.

Habitus refers to the whole socio-cultural environment in which individuals or groups live and by which their social persona are constructed. Habitus envelops the whole person, incorporating gestures, discourse, clothes, intellectual assets, social class, gender and so forth, all of which are constructed by learned behaviours and interactions within the family group, school and community.

Hegemony is the process by which power is allocated and exercised in social groups.

Heterogeneous is applied to individuals or things which are different from one another.

Heteronormativity refers to the societal assumptions that give authority to heterosexual relations and assume that other sexual orientations are abnormal.

Heuristic refers to the process of discovery or problem-solving that is central to the research process. It involves informed judgement grounded in experience rather than systematic analysis of data. It is the creative, heuristic process that takes researchers beyond the data to deeper insights.

Homogeneous is applied to individuals or things which are similar to one another.

Hypothesis is the term used for a proposition that will be tested in subsequent research. Alternatively, hypotheses emerge during the early stages of data analysis and are tested in later rounds of data collection and analysis. In this case, emerging hypotheses can be seen as the first step in theory development.

Idealism (ideal) is the term for belief in the best possible opportunities, processes and outcomes.

Identity (identity formation) is the socio-culturally constructed sense of self which is centrally important in terms of human agency. Identity either empowers or constrains individuals depending on its social formation.

Ideology is the term for a body of ideas that is shared by a social group, nation or political party and provides the basis for action.

Illuminate (illuminative) is used in qualitative research to mean that light is being shed on things which would otherwise be hidden because they are linked to unquestioned assumptions.

Inductive (induction) refers to the process of constructing theories from empirical data by searching for themes and seeking to make meanings from the evidence, in contrast to deductive/deduction (see above).

Instruments is the term for materials developed by researchers for data collection and analysis. They include interview schedules/protocols, questionnaires, pro-forma for observations, record sheets for coding, and so forth.

Inter-observer (inter-rater) reliability is a technical term for making sure that when several researchers work together and conduct observations in different settings they are, as far as possible, observing the same things and reaching similar judgements.

Interpretivist is the term given to research in the hermeneutic tradition which seeks to uncover meaning and understand the deeper implications revealed in data about people. Interpretivist is a broad category which encompasses a wide range of research approaches including ethnography and case study.

Intervention refers to the process in some research methodologies whereby the researchers invite the participants in a social group to introduce a change. The research then focuses upon the impact of the change and its implications for future development.

Logical positivism was the original form of positivism (see below) which established logic and the principle of verification as essential elements in the search for knowledge and truth.

Marxism refers to the social, economic and political theories developed by Karl Marx through a process of historical analysis; it focuses particularly on the means of production (labour) and the inequalities inherent in capitalism. The ideas of Marx were influential in the development of critical theory.

Mediate is used in post-Vygotskian psychology to refer to the process whereby human activity becomes integrally related to the tools which are being used to achieve it. Human being and tool become as one when a tool is used skilfully.

Meta-discourse (meta-narrative, grand narrative) is used in postmodern theory to mean a set of ideas or theories which have been constructed and imposed on the complexity of human experience and constitute a manipulative and oppressive act of control.

Metaphysical refers to the process of developing ideas, concepts and philosophical positions without any direct reference to human experience. It develops theories from what are called 'first principles' (abstract notions of worth and value) rather than empirical data.

Methodology in its narrowest sense is the collection of methods or rules by which a particular piece of research is undertaken. However, it is generally used in a broader sense to mean the whole system of principles, theories and values that underpin a particular approach to research.

Normalization refers to the hidden processes whereby individuals are socially conditioned to conform to normative standards and practices.

Normative is a term that denotes conformity to an authoritative standard. It implies lack of concern with differences of opinion or individual views.

Objectivity (objectivist, objective) refers to the removal of the persona (emotions, knowledge, experience, values and so forth) of the researcher from the research process. It is seen as central to the quality of research based on epistemological assumptions that truth can be determined as something distinct from particular contexts or participants.

Ontological (ontology, ontologically) refers to philosophical questions relating to the nature of being and purpose of existence (in everyday conversation 'the meaning of life').

Outcomes is used as an alternative to 'findings' or 'results' to describe the knowledge that is generated by research. The choice of the word 'outcome' indicates that epistemologically the research is not concerned with producing measurable, generalizable truths.

Paradigm is a term used to describe an approach to research which provides a unifying framework of understandings of knowledge, truth, value and the nature of being. There are a number of different paradigms (for example interpretivism, positivism).

Phenomenography is a research methodology which seeks to identify and understand how human beings apprehend phenomena. It assumes that human awareness is organized in terms of a central core, surrounding field and outer fringe, and that different individuals will develop different patterns of awareness of phenomena. *Note*: Phenomenography is quite separate from phenomenology.

Phenomenon (plural: phenomena) refers to anything which can be observed or experienced by human beings.

Philosophy is the study of knowledge and wisdom. It has been hugely influential in the development of Western thought, going back to the time of the ancient Greeks in the fourth century BC. Other notable early contributions to Western philosophy came from Arab and Jewish scholars during the Middle Ages.

Population refers to all the people or phenomena under study, from whom a sample will be selected for research.

Positivist (positivism) is used to describe an approach to research based on the assumption that knowledge can be discovered by collecting data through observation and measurement and analysing it to establish truths (see Crook and Garratt, in this volume).

Postcolonialism refers to a social movement – and a research approach – which seeks to oppose the racist and oppressive features which self-perpetuate in societies that were formally colonies of the British Empire or another great power.

Power is an important concept in qualitative research and what exactly constitutes power has been the source of considerable debate. Power is seen to be a factor in all organizations and human groups, and is the means by which some have greater autonomy than others and are able to control others.

Praxis refers to the process of embedding the development of theory in practical action. Theory and practice are seen as reciprocal rather than hierarchical or sequential.

Protocol is the term used for the outline framework which will be used in data collection (see 'instruments' above).

Random sample (random sampling) is a selection from a population in which each item has an equal chance of being selected and the selection of one does not affect the selection of any other. In other words, the selection is made by 'chance', for example by allocating a number to each item and using a random number generator on a computer.

Rationality is the process of establishing concepts and theories by rational means, using logical reasoning.

Realism (real, realist, reality) is based on the epistemological assumption that truth can be determined as something distinct from the processes of mind. It assumes that there is a reality 'out there' which can be investigated and understood on the basis of collecting data and identifying supportive evidence.

Reductionist refers to the process of 'data reduction' by which complex data sets are organized and presented in briefer, more coherent forms, often by means of coding responses. This process is an important step in data analysis, but care needs to be taken not to oversimplify when coding open-ended data since this can lead to superficial analysis.

Reflexivity (reflexive) combines the process of reflection with self-critical analysis. It is highly valued as a means whereby social science researchers are able to explore their own subjectivity, be more aware of the impact they necessarily have on the research data they collect and increase the sensitivity of their analysis and interpretations of data.

Relativism is a philosophical position that holds that truth is not constant but varies in relation to context, time, circumstances and so forth.

Reliability is the term used to mean that the truth of the findings has been established by ensuring that they are supported by sufficient and compelling evidence. In quantitative research, it refers specifically to a measurement repeatedly giving the same result (being consistent).

Representation (1) (representative, representativeness) is used in relation to the selection of a research sample, for example those selected for interview. It may be important to select individuals who, together, are representative of the larger group (for example if there are 30 men and 10 women a sample of 6 men and 2 women might be said to be representative).

Representation (2) is used in semiotics to describe the process whereby human beings make meaning through creating a range of written texts, images and visual designs. Once created, texts require interpretation to understand how they socio-culturally construct meaning.

Representation (3) is used in deconstruction and poststructuralism to describe the way in which concepts like childhood or marriage are constructed and positioned to give them particular cultural meanings which enforce particular kinds of behaviour.

Researcher bias refers to the process whereby data collection and analysis may be strongly influenced by the assumptions and values of the researcher. However, some social science researchers would claim that researchers should clarify their own values and assumptions through a process of reflexivity and be able to account for the way this influences their judgements rather than attempt the impossible task of screening them out.

Responsive evaluation is a term for an approach to program evaluation which puts particular emphasis on interaction with participants and their involvement in the generation of knowledge.

Sample refers to the individuals who are included in data collection, who are selected from the whole population.

Social constructivism refers to the process by which phenomena in the social world are formed and sustained by social structures and interactions rather than being constants that conform to natural laws. Researchers who adopt this approach are likely to use mainly qualitative rather than quantitative methods.

Standpoint is the position adopted by a researcher who recognizes the need to be an advocate for a particular point of view. It embodies the assumption that the researcher is working in a context which is oppressive and in which certain groups are routinely denied social justice.

Structure and agency refers to the degree to which individuals have free will or are constrained by circumstances. Structure refers in particular to the social norms and organizational/administrative structures within which individuals live. See also 'agency' above.

Subjectivity (subjectivist) refers to the human persona (emotions, knowledge, experience, values and so forth). The subjectivity of the researcher – the self as a research instrument – is seen as central to the quality of research based on epistemological assumptions that truth is not something that can be 'found' separately from the particular contexts or participants in the area of study.

Surveys are a form of research which seek information from a large number of people by means of questionnaires. These are often delivered and collected postally, but more recently some surveys are being administered and collected online.

Symbolic interactionism refers to a set of theories concerning the way that individuals form and maintain their identity in relation to others. It is based on the notion that social interaction is made up of patterned (and often habitual) behaviours or utterances which have easily recognizable symbolic meanings which invite responses of similarly patterned behaviours from others.

Systematic evaluation is a term that suggests that in evaluating the program priority will be given to quantitative methods.

Systematic review refers to a particular approach to reviewing research literature in order to establish evidence that should be put into practice (evidence-based practice). It begins by establishing the criteria by which published research will be selected for or excluded from the review. It tends to pay little attention to the contextual differences between research sites (for example the country where it was carried out).

Teleological refers to the process of explaining or evaluating events and phenomena in terms of their outcomes. The concept is often used by social science researchers to indicate a mechanistic process; it is seen as akin to the determinism of social Darwinism.

Temporal means with reference to a specific time.

Theories are explanations or propositions. In the natural sciences they are generally recognized as true, as for example Einstein's theory of relativity. In the social sciences they are more open to challenge, especially if the methodology is grounded in epistemological assumptions that truth and reality are socio-culturally constructed. Social science research normally starts with a theoretical framework and develops new theories (or variations of existing theories) as research outcomes.

Totalitarian is used to describe states of government in which one authority has total control and no opposition is allowed. In postmodernism it is used to describe systems of thought which impose conformity. It can also be used for research methods in which the researcher assumes complete control.

Triangulation is a method whereby data from at least three different perspectives (for example, teacher, students and observer) are collected on the same issue/event so that they can be cross-validated. Alternatively, three or more different kinds of data (for example video, interview and questionnaire) are collected on the same issue/event and used to shed light on each other.

Typology is the term used for a list or table which organizes phenomena into categories and hierarchies. Typologies are often used as an organizing framework in research, or the development of a typology may be an outcome of the research.

Universal theory (universalist) is the term used for an elaborate system of thought that organizes all existing knowledge into one conceptual framework. Postmodern and poststructuralist thinkers consider the whole notion of a universal theory to be both oppressive and unsustainable.

Universal truth – (see 'generalizable' above).

Utilitarian refers to practices, including research practices, which place high priority on the usefulness of outcomes.

Utopian comes from Thomas Moore's book, *Utopia*, written in the sixteenth century, and refers to a place or a set of ideas which verge on perfection and are unobtainable.

Validity is the term used to claim that research results have precisely addressed research questions. With matters of measurement in quantitative research there are many threats to validity. In qualitative research the effort to ensure validity by narrowing the field of study to something which can be measured may have the effect of undermining the extent to which the outcomes can be generalized.

Value literally means 'merit, worth, significance' (see Abma and Schwandt, in this volume) but in social science research the term 'values' ('value systems') has much wider significance, denoting the entire set of beliefs and principles which underpin a set of judgements or a particular endeavour.

Variable(s) is the term that refers to the characteristics which can be counted or measured in quantitative research.

Verification (verificationist) refers to the process of collecting evidence to prove the truth of a proposition. It is the opposite approach to falsificationist (see 'falsifiability' above).

Reference

Bullock, A. and Stallibrass, O. (2000) *New Fontana Dictionary of Modern Thought*. London: HarperCollins.

CONTRIBUTOR BIOGRAPHIES

Tineke Abma's work concentrates on responsive approaches to evaluation and narrative and dialogue in the domain of evaluation.

Dr John Ainley has extensive experience in longitudinal and survey research in different contexts and directed the Literacy Advance Research Project (LARP). See: <http://www.acer.edu.au/about/staffbios/ainleyjohn.html>.

Herbert Altrichter is a Professor of Education and Educational Psychology. His research interests include school improvement, teacher education and research methodology. See: <http://paedpsych.jku.at/>.

Rosaline S. Barbour is a Medical Sociologist who researches professionals' response to change and user perspectives. She has a particular interest in strengthening the rigour of qualitative research. See: <http://www.dundee.ac.uk/nursingmidwifery/research/index.html>.

Sally Barnes teaches Statistics and Quantitative Research Methods. Her area of research is how technology is integrated into teaching and learning. See: <http://www.bris.ac.uk/education/people/academicStaff/edsbb>.

David Benzie both teaches on undergraduate and postgraduate courses and conducts research concerned with IT in education.

Jill Blackmore is a Professor in the School of Education, Deakin University, Australia whose research interests include globalization and localization in educational restructuring, educational reform and organizational change, and feminist issues.

Tony Brown is currently the Professor of Mathematics Education at the University of Waikato in New Zealand.

Erica Burman researches intersections between gender, childhood and subjectivity in therapeutic and educational practices, integrating feminism and psychology. She co-directs the Women's Studies Research Centre and Discourse Unit at MMU.

Diane Burns has research interests in the voluntary sector and community-based organizing, empowerment and participation, equality and diversity issues, family and social policy.

Terry Carson is Professor and Chair of Secondary Education at the University of Alberta where he conducts research in the areas of teacher education, culture, and curriculum studies. See: <http://www.ualberta.ca/~tcarson/>.

Julianne Cheek is a Professor at the University of South Australia in the Division of Health Sciences, Adelaide, South Australia, and Director of Early Career Researcher Development.

Edith J. Cisneros-Cohernour is a Professor of Evaluation and Higher Education, and research coordinator for the University of Yucatan. See: <http://www.ed.uiuc.edu/circe/CIRCE/Edith_Cohernour.html>.

Juliet Corbin, DNSc is an Adjunct Professor at the International Institute of Qualitative Research at the University of Alberta, Canada.

Charles Crook is Reader in Education at Nottingham University. His research takes a cultural psychological perspective on young people's use of new technology. See: <http://devpsy.lboro.ac.uk/psy/ckc/>.

Bronwyn Davies, an Australian Professor of Education, is interested in poststructural discourse analysis, subjectivity/subjectification, gender and body/landscape relations.

Brent Davis is Professor and Canada Research Chair in Mathematics Education and the Ecology of Learning in the Department of Secondary Education at the University of Alberta, Canada.

Sara Delamont is a reader in Sociology at Cardiff University. Her research interests include classroom interaction, school ethnography, higher education and gender. She has published widely on qualitative research and feminism.

Gayle Dillon is a Research Fellow in Psychology. Her research interests include new technologies and their impact on autistic children.

Brian Doig lectures to undergraduates and postgraduates in primary mathematics education, with an emphasis on quality assessment and reporting.

Gloria Filax thinks, writes and teaches in the areas of sexuality and gender within youth studies, feminist studies and cultural studies.

Susanne Gannon lectures in secondary education. She is interested in how poststructural theory opens spaces for writing otherwise in academia. See: <http://www.uws.edu.au/about/acadorg/caess/seecs/staff/susanne_gannon>.

Dean Garratt is a Research Fellow in Education. His interests centre upon the philosophy of qualitative research and issues of citizenship and identity.

Julia Gillen studies the discourse of new users of communication channels, including young children on the telephone and Edwardian postcard writers. See: <http://fels-staff.open.ac.uk/julia-gillen>.

Juliet Goldbart is a psychologist involved in collaborative research on culturally appropriate interventions for families with members with severe disabilites. See: <http://www.psychology.mmu.ac.uk/staff/speech_pathology/dr_juliet_goldbart.htm>.

Noel Gough teaches curriculum enquiry and educational research methodologies/methods. His own research privileges narrative theorizing, poststructuralism, postcolonialism and science fiction. See: <http://cducation.deakin.edu.au/members/show details.asp?Member=428>.

Jennifer C. Greene is a scholar-practitioner of evaluation, committed to advancing evaluation as a vehicle for greater democratization in our societies.

Daniel Heggs is a Lecturer in Psychology, and is interested in varieties of discourse, subjectivity and media representations of risk.

David Heywood is Senior Lecturer and Designated Researcher in Science Education at Manchester Metropolitan University. His research interests are focused on developing teacher subject and pedagogic knowledge as well as language and learning in science.

Dawn Hobson has a PhD in Nursing and is a visiting lecturer at the St Bartholomew School of Nursing and Midwifery.

Mary Louise Holly is the Director of the Faculty Professional Development Center and Professor of Teaching, Leadership and Curriculum Studies, Kent State University, Ohio. Her research interests are adult development and learning.

Nicholas L. Holt has lived and worked in the UK and Canada. He researches psychosocial issues associated with youth and adult sport.

David Hustler, now retired, was Professor of Education and Head of Educational Research at the Manchester Metropolitan University until 2003.

Ingrid Johnston is an Associate Professor in Secondary Education and Associate Dean (Research and Graduate Studies). Her research interests are in postcolonial literary studies, teacher education and curriculum. See: <http://www.ualberta.ca/~ijohnsto>.

Kelvyn Jones is a Professor of Geography with a particular interest in health. He regularly teaches multilevel modelling at the Essex Summer School. See: <http://www.ggy.bris.ac.uk/staff/staff_jones_kelvyn.htm>.

Liz Jones is a Senior Lecturer with a particular interest in early years education and practitioner research.

Holly Kreider, EdD, conducts applied research on family educational involvement. She lives in Cambridge, MA. See: <www.finenetwork.org>.

Gunther Kress is Professor of English at the Institute of Education, London, and researches on literacy, social semiotics, multimodality, discourse analysis and learning theory.

Ines Langemeyer is an Associate Researcher at the Center for Media Research with research interests in cultural studies, critical pedagogy, Brecht and Gramsci. See: <http://www.cmr.fu-berlin.de/faculty/ines/index.html>.

Colin Lankshear researches literacy and social practices mediated by digital technologies, drawing mainly on socio-cultural and philosophical perspectives. See: <www.coatepec.net>.

Hugh Lauder is Professor in the Department of Education, University of Bath and has research interests in the political economy of skill formation and education, educational policy and school effectiveness.

Kevin M. Leander researches youth literacy practices, drawing on socio-cultural theory, critical and human geography, and social practice theories. See: <www.vanderbilt.edu/litspace>.

Cathy Lewin is an educational researcher interested in young peoples' ICT use at school and at home. She teaches quantitative research methods. See: <http://www.ioe.mmu.ac.uk/research/res-ppl/c-lewin.shtml>.

Yaojun Li is a quantitative sociologist with interests in social mobility, social divisions and social capital. See: <http://www.sociology.bham.ac.uk/staff_profiles/yaojun_li.htm>.

Maggie MacLure is interested in deconstruction and poststructuralism, having written *Discourse in Educational and Social Research* (Buckingham: Open University Press, 2003). See: <http://www.ioe.mmu.ac.uk/research/res-ppl/m-maclure.shtml>.

Jyoti Mangat is a doctoral candidate in the departments of Secondary Education and English at the University of Alberta.

Diane Mavers, a Research Fellow at the Centre for ICT, Pedagogy and Learning, Manchester Metropolitan University, works in educational evaluation and research.

Ellen Mayer has an MPhil in sociology and researches family educational involvement, developing research-based materials for practitioners. She lives in Cambridge, MA. See: <www.hfrp.org.>.

Julienne Meyer is both a nurse and teacher whose research focuses on improving care for older people through action research. See: <http://www.city.ac.uk/barts/adultnursing/staff/meyer_j.htm#top>.

Lee Miller is a Lecturer in Drama whose current research is focused on performative challenges to the habitus of non-place. See: <www.dogshelf.com>.

Morten Nissen has studied 'wild' social work projects since 1990, and has edited the journal *Outlines – Critical Social Studies* since 1999. See: <http://www.psy.ku.dk/mnissen/>.

Susan Noffke has written about and practised participatory action research in the field of social studies with a particular interest in anti-racist education.

Máire Nolan joined Lancaster University as Contracts Manager in 2004 having previously worked in technology transfer for Manchester Metropolitan University and the National Health Service.

Nigel Norris is Professor of Education, University of East Anglia. His research interests include the history, theory and practice of evaluation and applied research.

Laurence Parker is an Associate Professor in the Department of Educational Policy Studies, University of Illinois at Urbana-Champaign. His research and teaching interests are in the area of educational policy analysis and critical race theory and equity issues.

Malcolm Payne is Director, Psycho-social and Spiritual Care, St Christopher's Hospice, London and Emeritus Professor at Manchester Metropolitan University. See: <www.stchristophers.org.uk>.

Matthew Pearson is conducting research into the use of information and communications technology in schools in the UK. See: <www.mpearson.co.uk>.

W. J. Pelgrum is a Senior Researcher with interests in international comparative assessments, educational monitoring, indicator development and innovative pedagogies for e-learning.

Alan Petersen researches and teaches in the fields of the sociology of health and illness, and the body and society.

Heather Piper is a researcher with interests spanning violence, touch, gender, ethnicity – in fact anything of anthropological intrigue. See: <http://www.ioe.mmu.ac.uk/research/res-ppl/h-piper.shtml>.

Lorna Roberts is a Research Associate and doctoral student. Her PhD explores trainee teachers' transition to qualified teacher status. Other research interests focus on minority ethnic trainees' experiences of initial teacher training.

John Schostak is a research Professor of Education, interested in qualitative methodologies, postmodernism, poststructuralism and post-theory. See: <http://www.enquirylearning.net/ELU/JScv.html>.

Thomas A. Schwandt is University Distinguished Teacher/Scholar and Professor of Education at the University of Illinois at Urbana-Champaign, USA.

Geoff Shacklock has research interests in the sociology of teachers' work, at-risk youth, cultural studies and narrative methodologies. See: <http://education.deakin.edu.au/members/ShowDetails.asp?Membe r=511&AreaID=3>.

Debra Shogan is a Professor in Cultural Studies of Sport and Leisure in the Faculty of Physical Education and Recreation at the University of Alberta.

Helen Simons is Professor of the School of Education and Evaluation, University of Southampton, and has research interests which include the ethics and politics of research, programme and policy evaluation, and utilizing creative arts in evaluation and professional practice.

Bridget Somekh's research interests are in the process of innovation, particularly relating to ICT, and in developing appropriate research methods. See: <http://www.ioe.mmu.ac.uk/research/res-ppl/b-somekh.shtml>.

Jeffrey E. Stake is Professor specializing in property law at Indiana University. His research applies economics, evolution and psychology to legal questions.

Sheila Stark is a Reader in the Department of Health Care Studies, Manchester Metropolitan University and her research interests include professionalism, action research/action learning, evaluation and multi-professional teamworking.

Ian Stronach is Research Professor at Manchester Metropolitan University, and current Lead Editor of the *British Educational Research Journal.*

Dennis Sumara is Professor of Curriculum Studies and Teacher Education in the Department of Secondary Education at the University of Alberta.

Laurie Thorp's interests lie at the intersection of sustainable food systems, elementary education, and participatory research methodologies. She can be reached at: <ThorpL@msu.edu>.

Richard Thorpe is Professor of Management Development at Leeds University Business School. He is co-author of *Management Research: An Introduction* (Sage) and a member of the ESRC Training and Development Board.

Angie Titchen's work is rooted in her clinical experience as a physiotherapist and she has published extensively on action research methodology and on the development of patient-centred practice

Harry Torrance is Professor of Education and Director of the Education and Social Research Institute, Manchester Metropolitan University. He was formerly Professor of Education at the University of Sussex. See: <http://www.ioe.mmu.ac.uk/research/res-ppl/h-torrance.shtml>.

Jennifer Tupper is completing doctoral studies in Social Studies Education in the Department of Secondary Education at the University of Alberta.

Jean Underwood is a Professor in Psychology. Her research interests include the impact of new technologies on teaching and learning.

Melanie Walker's research interests include social justice, identity formation and student and teacher experiences of education in the UK and South Africa. See: <www.sheffield.ac.uk/education/staff/Walker.shtml>.

Rob Walker is Director of the Centre for Applied Research in Education (CARE), at the University of East Anglia. See: <http://www.uea.ac.uk/care>.

Terry Warburton has a particular interest in 'image based' research and has developed semiological techniques for the analysis of images and political discourse relating to teachers and their practice.

Joanne Whitehouse is a Research Fellow in the Performance Studies Division at University College Northampton whose current research is focused on performative challenges to the habitus of non-place. See: <www.dogshelf.com>.

INDEX

Added to a page number 'f' denotes a figure, 't' denotes a table and 'g' denotes glossary.